W9-CLG-922

Daniel U. Levine

University of Missouri at Kansas City

Robert J. Havighurst

University of Chicago

Society and Education

Theodore Lownik Library
Illinois Benedictine College
Lisle, IL 60532

SEVENTH EDITION

Allyn and Bacon

BOSTON LONDON SYDNEY TORONTO

LC
191.4
.L48
1989

Copyright © 1989, 1984, 1979, 1975, 1967, 1962, 1957 by Allyn and Bacon
A Division of Simon & Schuster
160 Gould Street
Needham Heights, Massachusetts 02194–2310

All rights reserved. No part of the material protected by this copyright notice may be reproduced or utilized in any form or by any means, electronic or mechanical, including photocopying, recording, or by any information storage and retrieval system, without the written permission of the copyright owner.

Chapter-Opening Photo Credits: p. 1, © COMSTOCK, Inc./Tom Grill; p. 44, FourByFive; p. 93, © COMSTOCK, Inc./C. R. Mufsom; p. 113, Tom Rosenthal/FourByFive; p. 151, © COMSTOCK, Inc./Skip Barron; p. 179; Tom Rosenthal/FourByFive; p. 215; © COMSTOCK, Inc./Tom Grill; p. 260, Jeffry Myers/FourByFive; p. 307, © COMSTOCK, Inc./Tom Grill; p. 359, Jeffry Myers/FourByFive; p. 435, Owen Franken/Stock, Boston, Copyright © Stock, Boston, Inc., 1978, All rights reserved; p. 466, Jeffry Myers/FourByFive; p. 493, Courtesy of National Education Association, Joe DiDio.

Series Editor: Sean W. Wakely
Production Administrator: Annette Joseph
Production Coordinator: Susan Freese
Editorial-Production Service: Grace Sheldrick, Wordsworth Associates
Cover Administrator: Linda K. Dickinson
Cover Designer: Design Ad Cetera
Manufacturing Buyer: Bill Alberti

Library of Congress Cataloging-in-Publication Data

Levine, Daniel U., 1935–
Society and education.

Includes bibliographies and index.
1. Educational sociology—United States.
2. Educational equalization—United States.
3. Minorities—Education—United States. 4. Pluralism (Social sciences)—United States. I. Havighurst, Robert James, 1900– . II. Title.
LC191.4.L48 1988 370.19′0973 88–19250
ISBN 0–205–11692–2

Printed in the United States of America

10 9 8 7 6 5 4 3 2 93 92 91 90 89

Brief Contents

Contents

Preface

The seventh edition of *Society and Education* continues the emphasis found in previous editions on delineating and assessing social changes that have major implications for education. Because education has been the object of increasing concern and attention nationally during the 1980s, critical problems in society and the educational system are emphasized throughout the volume, and considerable material has been added on school reform. This edition also has been reorganized to reduce its overall length.

For example, Chapters 12 and 13 have been brought together, updated, and combined with related material as part of Chapter 2. Material on desegregation has been drawn from a number of chapters to constitute Chapter 9 in this seventh edition. Material on cultural pluralism and major minority groups (black Americans, Hispanics, Asians, and Indians), which was spread through several chapters, has been systematically updated and reorganized as Chapter 10.

Two other notable changes in preparing this edition of *Society and Education* are the addition of more tables and figures and the deletion or consolidation of miscellaneous material in order to reduce the book's length despite the concomitant emphasis on updating topics throughout the book.

Among the new topics and themes introduced or greatly expanded in the seventh edition are:

- Generational conflict and poverty (Chapter 1)
- Subgroups within social classes (Chapter 1)
- Proprietary institutions in higher education (Chapter 2)
- Trends in reading and mathematics achievement (Chapter 2)
- Sorting and selecting in the educational system (Chapter 2)
- Equity themes in higher education (Chapter 2)
- Latchkey children and homeless children (Chapter 4)
- Possible negative effects of high school students' employment (Chapter 6)
- National service opportunities and obligations for youth (Chapter 6)
- Resistance theory (as part of the Chapter 7 discussion of critical theory)
- Controlled-choice desegregation plans (Chapter 9)
- Magnet schools (Chapter 9)
- Plight of the inner-city black male (Chapter 10)
- Crisis in the employment of minority teachers (Chapter 10)

- Learning styles and minority students (Chapter 10)
- Sex roles and elementary school peer groups (Chapter 11)
- Rural education (Chapter 12)
- Grouping and tracking (Chapter 13)
- Dropouts and other marginal or at-risk students (Chapter 13)
- Research on the teaching of higher-order skills (Chapter 13)
- National school reform reports (Chapter 13)

Another major change that will be obvious to readers of previous editions of *Society and Education* is the restructuring and introduction of new material in Chapters 1 and 2. Chapter 1 now begins with material on social class and then describes recent socioeconomic trends that affect the schools. Chapter 2 provides a broad overview of the crisis in selecting and sorting students for success through education in postindustrial, metropolitan society in the United States.

Chapter 13, "School Reform and Effectiveness," is largely new. Summarizing recent developments involving national reform and school effectiveness research, this final chapter considers the prospects for solving the crucial problems and challenges identified in preceding chapters.

As in previous editions, much of the emphasis in *Society and Education*, seventh edition, is on the education of disadvantaged students, particularly of minority students in big cities. In accordance with the changes and challenges emerging as the United States moves further into the postindustrial age, improving the performance of the growing proportion of disadvantaged students has become a critical task facing both our schools and our society.

Society and Education, seventh edition, also continues the emphasis on assessment of relevant research in drawing conclusions about the role and functioning of schools in U.S. society and on presentation of a range of perspectives and conclusions based on differing and even contradictory studies, rather than on a single ideological point of view. When we describe our own conclusions and the data or analysis on which they are based, we are conscientious in identifying other views and in providing pertinent sources for further information.

Although the presentation and summaries of research throughout *Society and Education* are nontechnical, we provide enough information to give the reader a sense of the complexities and uncertainties in conducting and interpreting research. Many readers have viewed this effort as a particular strength of previous editions.

We also stress social-systems considerations that affect the functioning of schools and the context in which they operate. Such considerations are, after all, among the major factors that help distinguish educational sociology and study of the social foundations of education from educational psychology or social psychology. Examples of this emphasis include:

- Analysis of threshold forces in the functioning of schools as institutions
- Analysis of student promotion/retention policies in terms of their effects on students as a group, not just on individual students
- Description of the (limited available) research on home environment differences between students in magnet schools and so-called regular schools

- Analysis of the peer group as a reference group inside and outside the schools
- Analysis of desegregation in terms of social-class mixture
- Description of effective-schools research dealing with the importance of schoolwide characteristics
- Identification of the educational implications of major social and economic trends

Related to our efforts to avoid dogmatic positions and instead to encourage the reader to seek further information and opposing points of view, this latest edition of *Society and Education* also continues the practice in previous editions of explicitly avoiding either-or propositions or solutions when considering problems involving the educational system and its place in the larger society. Complex problems in the real world of the schools seldom if ever are amenable to understanding or solution through relatively simple analysis that postulates a dichotomous explanation or response. For example, it is not true that the educational system either functions universally to provide socioeconomic mobility or else does nothing but reinforce inequality, that desegregation plans must be either all mandatory or all voluntary, or that the growth of single-parent families either must cause insurmountable problems for the schools or can have no probable negative consequences. These and other current issues in research and analysis involving education and society are discussed at length in a balanced presentation.

That does not mean, however, that we never take a position. For example, we believe that the education system has entered a period of crisis, involving national and societal requirements to improve the performance of disadvantaged students in big cities and to upgrade the system as a whole with respect to teaching of higher-order skills and understandings. We have endeavored to portray this crisis as clearly and convincingly as possible but without ignoring contrary evidence indicating that genuine progress is being registered in some locations.

As in previous editions, information on references cited in the text and on the list of suggested readings at the end of each chapter is provided in the extensive Bibliography. To assist the reader further, each reference in the Bibliography concludes with the page number(s) (in parentheses) indicating where in the text it is cited.

Acknowledgments

Special thanks in preparing this seventh edition are extended to Bianca Shields of the University of Missouri at Kansas City School of Education; to Sean Wakely, Sue Canavan, Elizabeth Brooks, and Sue Freese of Allyn and Bacon; to Robert B. Brumbaugh, Kutztown University; Shirley M. Clark, University of Minnesota; Russell L. Hamm, Indiana State University; and Charles C. Wilson, University of Wisconsin-Oshkosh, who made valuable suggestions regarding revision; and to Grace Sheldrick, Wordsworth Associates, whose editorial assistance resulted in a variety of improvements and refinements in preparing the text. We also want to express gratitude again to the many persons who assisted in producing previous editions of *Society and Education*.

1

Socioeconomic Trends and the Social Class Structure

The Social Class Hierarchy

A social-class group consists of people who have similar social habits and values. One test of membership in a social class is that of association, actual or potential. In a small community, the members of a particular social class tend to belong to the same social organizations and to entertain one another in their homes. If they live in a big city, their numbers are so large that only a few can actually associate with one another; yet, even in large cities, if members of the same social class meet as strangers they soon recognize a good deal of similarity in their ways of life and recognize each other as social equals.

The various social classes are organized into an overall hierarchical structure. Most persons recognize that they occupy a position on a social scale. They acknowledge that there are other people and other groups that have more or less economic or political power or social prestige than their own group. Within a particular community, people can rank themselves and their neighbors according to power or prestige; that is, they can assign different individuals to particular positions on a social ladder.

All societies, large or small, primitive or modern, show this phenomenon of rank: the leaders and people of high prestige occupy positions at the top; others occupy intermediate positions; and still others are at the bottom of the social scale. This is true regardless of the political form of government. A democracy has rank; so does an absolute monarchy; so also does a communist society such as the Soviet Union. The king and the nobility are at the top in a monarchy; the top people in the Soviet Union are the leaders of the Communist Party and the high government and military officials. In a democracy, the people at the top are those who have earned or inherited economic power or social prestige.

Studying the Social Structure

Various sociologists have chosen to highlight one or another of the dimensions listed above in undertaking studies of social stratification; this text focuses on studies of American communities according to the methods developed by W. Lloyd Warner and his associates (Warner, Meeker, and Eells 1960). These investigators stressed the dynamics of community organization; that is, they focused on prestige and the patterns of social interaction that constitute the social life of a community.

The usual procedure was for the social scientist to move into the community and live there for a time, talking with people and observing the social scene.

He or she discovered the social groups that existed; he or she talked with the members of various social groups and asked about the social structure of the community. The social scientist learned who associated with whom, who were considered the top people, who the bottom, and why. Gradually he or she pieced together a picture of the community as it was viewed by its members. Seldom did any one citizen see the whole structure of the community clearly, but the social scientist combined the views of many people into a single composite picture representing the consensus. This picture showed groups of people arranged in a network, as well as on a social scale from top to bottom in terms of the status assigned them by their fellow citizens.

After the major lines of the social structure had been delineated and the positions of a few key people had been agreed on, it was possible to locate other people in relation to the original persons. Eventually, the majority of the population could be located on the social map in this way.*

This method, of course, worked well only in small communities, where it was possible to meet with, or at least find out about, practically every adult inhabitant. Somewhat different methods had to be devised for use in larger, more urban communities. To conduct larger studies of social status in urban communities, sociologists identified four types of socioeconomic measures that seemed particularly useful in determining the social class of individual respondents: occupational prestige (i.e., occupational status as determined originally by asking people to rank occupations according to their prestige), education (usually in number of years), income, and housing and/or neighborhood prestige (as determined by the value of one's house and/or the prestige of the neighborhood) (Warner, Meeker, and Eells 1960). Men who scored high on all these indices were considered high in status or upper class, and those who ranked low were considered lower class, with many possible social-class or social-status levels in between. Women and children generally were assigned the social-class score of the male head-of-household.

Most research involving social status or social class uses only one or two of the possible measures of social status in categorizing individuals on some scale of status. One of the most frequently used approaches asks respondents to indicate occupation and education using categories devised by August Hollingshead (1957) as part of his Two Factor Index of Social Position; respondents are then placed in social-class categories I (High) to V (Low). Many other studies use only occupational status scores such as the North-Hatt scale (Reiss 1961),

* This method of mapping the social system and of discovering the social class of a particular person is called the "method of evaluated social participation," often abbreviated as E.P. First, by interviewing members of the community, the major lines of social structure were ascertained, and the names obtained of a few people who interviewers agreed occupied given positions in the structure. It was then noted with whom these people associated in social clubs, informal social cliques, service clubs, church associations, and so on. Thus, other people were placed in relation to the original group. Eventually, the majority of the population was placed in this way. Then, if the social scientist wished to know the social status of Mr. X, whose name had not previously been brought into the study, he asked who Mr. X's friends were, what clubs or associations he belonged to, and then found that Mr. X was close to one of the groups already defined on the social map. Mr. X's social participation was thus evaluated in relation to that of others in the community, and his place in the social structure was determined.

which ranks occupations on a scale of 8 (shoe shiner) to 93 (Supreme Court Justice), particularly when other measures of social position are difficult to obtain for a large sample of respondents. In recent years, some studies of children from female-headed families in poverty neighborhoods have had to use education of the mother as the sole measure of social class because other information was unavailable.

Researchers often feel justified in using only one or two measures of social status because occupation, education, income, housing/neighborhood, and other social-status variables generally are highly correlated with one another. Income, for example, is partly a function of occupation, and amount of education helps determine a person's occupation and income. Research by Hope (1982) indicates that occupation prestige scores are based partly on the economic rewards people believe are associated with an occupation and partly on its perceived value to society. Physicians, for example, rank very high on both measures. Thus, it is not surprising that occupational prestige is highly correlated with income.

Treiman (1977) has examined and conducted cross-national studies of occupational prestige and other measures of social status. Among his major findings are the following:

1. Occupations that have high prestige in one country tend to have high prestige in other countries, regardless of differences in political, social, and economic characteristics. For example, rankings of occupations are almost exactly the same in the United States and Chile, in Brazil and West Germany, in Poland and the Ivory Coast, in New Zealand and Spain, and in Yugoslavia and Argentina.
2. Within and across countries, there are high correlations between occupational status and education and between occupational status and income.
3. An International Standard Occupational Scale has high correlations with scores from local occupational scales developed in individual countries.
4. Occupational status is stable over time. Although there have been vast changes in the types of occupations in which people worked at different historical periods—there were many chimney sweeps two hundred years ago and there are many computer operators today—occupations that have continued to exist over long periods of time generally undergo little change in relative status. For example, ruling warriors were the highest caste in Nepal in 1395, just as high military officers are now near the top of the International Standard Occupational Scale. Similarly, saddlers and tanners were ranked near the bottom among guilds in fifteenth-century Florence, just as tanners and leather workers rank near the bottom today on the international scale.
5. The close relationship between occupation and income or wealth also has been very stable over time. For example, income data associated with differing occupations in the United States in 1776 correlate highly with income data associated with London occupations in 1890, with income data on English occupations in 1688, and with wealth data on Florentine guilds in 1427.

It is important to note that measures of occupational status and other status indicators are not exactly the same as measures of social class. Strictly speaking, the term *social class* refers to large groups of persons who have common political and economic goals and interests related to their position in the social structure. Probably the most influential conception of social class has been that of Karl Marx and his followers, who made the following distinctions:

Capitalists: those who controlled large amounts of capital
Bourgeoisie: middle-class persons with significant amounts of property and some control over investment, the means of production, and the labor powers of others
Petitbourgeoisie: lower-middle-class persons with significant control of property, investments, and production but not the labor of others
Proletariat: manual workers with no real control of property or production
Lumpenproletariat: very poor, unskilled workers
Intelligentsia: persons whose influence and wealth derive from working with knowledge rather than material goods

In the early industrial period, the large majority of individuals in most societies were proletarians with little real control over production or their own labor power.

The most fundamental distinction between social classes in most conceptualizations has been that between manual workers, who are relatively unskilled and have relatively little power to influence economic decisions, and nonmanual workers with relatively greater education, occupational status, or knowledge that yields at least some degree of control over the disposition of their labor. If social classes do exist and have some importance in determining—or reflecting—what happens to people, social class should be more closely related to various measures of behavior and outcomes than should single status measures such as occupational prestige. That is, knowing a person's social class—for example, a classification according to manual or nonmanual occupations or a classification of lower class or upper class according to occupation prestige and education—should be more highly related to behaviors and outcomes than a simple score on occupational prestige. Research continues to show that social class is a meaningful concept from this point of view.

The terminology most commonly used to categorize social classes uses the distinction between upper (high status), middle, and lower or working classes. Sociologists frequently distinguish between the lower working class and the upper working class and between the lower-middle and the upper-middle class (see below). In some cases, a distinction also is made between upper-upper and lower-upper class groups.

A New Class? In recent years, a number of observers have argued that a "new class" has emerged that has distinctive political and economic interests and cultural patterns within modern, postindustrial societies. Bruce-Briggs (1979) has reviewed this literature and identified three major overlapping groups that have been identified as the new class. First is the new middle class, consisting of white-collar workers who generally are not highly paid but have gained access to secure and physically nondemanding jobs through education. Second are the managers, who have considerable power and high income but do not own the property of the corporations they work for, as did the capitalists of the industrial era. Third is group X, which Bruce-Briggs describes as earning its living "by the use of learning, especially the ability to use words" (1979, 16).

Bruce-Briggs and other researchers believe that the latter group *(X)* of people who work with symbols is becoming larger and more important in the post-industrial period and may be a pivotal force in contemporary society because it does so much to shape the society's ideas and policies. Sociologist Peter Berger, for example, believes that this new class of intellectually oriented citizens adheres to "secular humanism" in its value structure; that is, this class advocates pluralism in values rather than acceptance of traditional values and attitudes. While this orientation helps the intellectually oriented to learn and adapt flexibly as society changes, it also challenges and antagonizes large segments of society that support traditional values and cultural patterns (Berger 1979).

Other observers, however, dispute the conclusion that there really is a new class defined in terms of a separate part of the population with distinctive political and economic interests. Andrew Hacker has summarized this argument as follows:

> *Do people afflicted with the rationalist attitude constitute a "new class?" . . . The individuals in new occupations entered them because the openings were there. They produce words and numbers and notations because that output is expected of them. If anything, they belong to a very old class: they work for their living, just as most people always have. The color of their collars may have changed. They have larger vocabularies and greater verbal facility. They receive comparatively generous salaries; many live varied and interesting lives. Yet when all is said and done, they remain workers beholden to the organizations employing them . . . and do not constitute a special class by themselves. (Hacker 1979, 167)*

Social Structure in the United States

The results of many community studies have enabled social scientists to draw certain general conclusions about social structure in the United States. In general, there is a basic five-class structure (see Figure 1.1). The proportion of people in each class varies depending on the size, the age, and the economic character of a given community. Thus, in comparison with the country as a whole, a community in a coal-mining or steel-mill area is likely to have a higher proportion of working-class people, whereas a community with a college or university is likely to have a higher proportion of upper-middle-class people. If the economic situation of a community changes drastically, the social structure of that community also is likely to change.

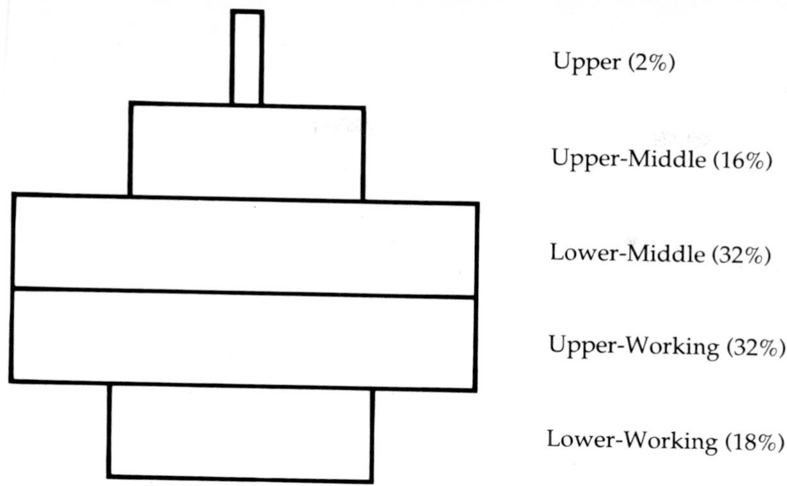

Figure 1.1 ***The Social-Class Structure in the United States*** (*Source:* Authors' estimates based on a variety of national and community studies and data sets.)

Small Communities

It is very common for people, particularly if they live in small, self-contained communities (that is, communities that are not satellites of big cities), to stress equalitarianism and to play down, or deny, the existence of social classes. At the same time, they recognize that there are different types of people in their community. As a respected citizen of Jonesville, a city of 6,000, explained:

> *Almost everyone in this town is rated in some way; people can rate you in just a few minutes by talking to you. It's remarkable how you can size people up in a hurry—suppose I use a rating scale of zero to 100 and rate people on it. You can be sure this is not a hypothetical thing either. Not to the people of Jonesville. People like the Caldwells and Volmers . . . rate 100. The Shaws would be up there, too. People like me, oh, a 70 maybe, and people like John (a janitor) about a 40, no better than that. Remember, this is the social rating. If we rated them financially, some of them would rank differently. (Warner and associates 1949, 22)*

This man did not speak of social classes as such; however, he recognized that his community reflected a social hierarchy.

The Small Rural Community. Studies of extremely small communities, villages ranging from a few hundred in population up to about 1,500, generally showed a three-class structure consisting of an upper-middle class, a lower-middle class, and a few families at the very bottom. Class lines in these communities were relatively indistinct as compared to larger communities, and there was more social intercourse between classes (Havighurst and Morgan 1951; West 1945).

The Small City

Cities with a population from about 5,000 to 15,000 tended to exhibit a five-class structure. A good example is a midwestern community that was described under the names of Jonesville, Elmtown, and Midwest (Warner and associates 1949; Hollingshead 1949; Warner, Meeker, and Eells 1960). This city had a population of about 6,000 and represented the most common type of small city in the north central states—a county seat, with both an industrial and an agricultural population.

In this community, the upper class constituted about 3 percent of the population. Some members of this class were the descendants of a pioneer settler who, a hundred years earlier, had acquired large tracts of farmland that had now become the best real estate in the city. Others were executives of a small factory, or they were the owners of the banks, the largest farms, and the most profitable businesses.

The upper-middle class contained about 10 percent of the population and consisted mainly of professional men, business executives, and owners of businesses and of large farms. The lower-middle class, about 30 percent of the whole, consisted mainly of white-collar workers, owners of small retail businesses, a few foremen and skilled manual workers, and the bulk of the prosperous farmers. These people were said by those in the classes above them to be "nice people" but social "nobodies."

The upper-working class, numerically the largest group (with 35 to 40 percent of the population), were described as "poor but honest" people who worked as skilled and unskilled laborers or as tenant farmers.

The lowest class, about 15 percent, consisted partly of people who were working hard to maintain a respectable kind of poverty and partly of people who seemed to the rest of the community to be generally immoral, lazy, and defiant of the law.

After the Jonesville studies were made, two other midwestern communities, one of 40,000 and one of 100,000, were studied. In these communities essentially the same picture of social structure emerged (Havighurst et al. 1962).

A somewhat more complicated six-class social structure was found, however, in a New England community of about 17,000 called "Yankee City" (Warner and Lunt 1941). In that community, there were two upper-class groups: an upper-upper, consisting of families who traced their lineage back to colonial times and who had had wealth and high social position for several generations; and a lower-upper group, or *nouveaux riches*, families who had moved into the community more recently and whose money had been acquired for the most part in the present generation or in the one just preceding. There was a clear separation between these two groups in terms of their social participation.

The Large City

In a large city, it is impossible for the sociologist to analyze social-class differences on the basis of actual social participation (who associates with whom), for only a handful of people are known to each other and any given pattern of face-to-face interaction can involve only a small number of the total population.

In attempting to study the social structure of the metropolitan area of Kansas City in the late 1950s, however, investigators found that residents made consistent evaluations of various symbols of status (Coleman and Neugarten 1971). Kansas Citians had a highly developed awareness of the status hierarchy in their community; and, although average citizens could name only some of the persons who were at the top and some who were at the bottom of the social ladder, they nevertheless ranked their fellow residents on the basis of such dimensions of status as area of residence, quality of housing, occupation, club membership, ethnic identification, and so on. Thus, for example, Kansas Citians were particularly aware of the prestige ranking of various neighborhoods and tended readily to place persons on the social ladder according to their home addresses.

As anticipated, the heterogeneity and complexity of the large city produced a much more highly differentiated social structure than found in a small town. Thirteen different social strata were visible, each stratum representing a gradation on the social scale. At the same time, the basic five-class system seemed applicable. There were five core groups of people, readily distinguishable on the basic social characteristics mentioned above; with each of the other eight groups forming a variant of one of the basic patterns; and with greater differences appearing between the five larger groups than between the thirteen smaller ones.

Large cities, then, can be described in terms of the basic five-class structure, granted that there will be many subgroups. The proportions of people in the five classes are probably roughly the same as those for small cities. In Kansas City in the 1950s, for instance, the percentages of the population in the five social classes were estimated to be, from upper to lower, 2.5, 11, 32, 40, and 14. In the same way, Hodges (1968), after studying the peninsula area of California (from San Francisco to and including San Jose) and after studying data obtained from almost 2,000 heads of households in the area, summarized the social structure as a five-class structure.

The Occupational Structure

Another way to examine social-class structure is by studying the occupational structure—one of the main components of social class. Table 1.1 shows the development of the U.S. occupational structure between 1910 and 1979. (Changes in Census Bureau reporting categories make it difficult to extend this comparison past 1979.) In 1910, the large majority of the population was in

Table 1.1 ***Occupational Distribution in the United States, 1910–1979***

	Percentage of Men						Percentage of Women					
Occupational Class	*1910*	*1930*	*1950*	*1960*	*1970*	*1979*	*1910*	*1930*	*1950*	*1960*	*1970*	*1979*
Professional and technical	3.1	4.0	6.4	10.7	14.0	15.1	9.2	13.6	10.0	12.2	14.5	16.1
Managers, proprietors, and officials	7.9	9.0	12.9	13.4	14.2	14.0	1.6	2.2	5.7	5.0	4.5	6.4
Clerical	9.2*	12.8*	7.2	7.1	7.1	6.1	13.9*	28.8*	26.2	29.8	34.5	35.0
Sales			5.7	6.1	5.6	6.0			8.3	7.6	7.0	6.9
Craftsmen and foremen	14.5	16.4	17.7	18.7	20.1	21.5	1.2	0.8	1.1	1.0	1.1	1.8
Service workers, including private household workers	2.0	2.7	6.4	6.6	6.7	8.5	24.9	21.6	22.0	24.6	21.6	19.8
Farmers and farm managers	19.9	15.2	9.4	6.4	3.2		3.5	2.5	1.5	0.5	0.3	
Farm laborers	14.0	9.5	5.3	3.5	1.9	3.9‡	16.4	5.4	5.5	3.9	1.5	1.2‡
Operatives (semiskilled)	11.2	14.4	20.8	19.4	19.6	17.5	27.9	23.7	19.1	15.0	14.5	11.5
Nonfarm laborers (unskilled)	18.2	16.1	8.1	8.1	7.3	7.3	1.4	1.5	0.5	0.4	0.5	1.3
No. employed (millions)	29.5	37.9	42.2	44.5	49.0	56.5	7.8	10.7	17.5	22.2	29.7	40.4

* Clerical and Sales are combined

‡ Farmers and farm laborers are combined

Source: U.S. Bureau of the Census; *Statistical Abstract of the United States*, 1981.

working-class occupations involving either farming or blue-collar work in such fields as manufacturing. Throughout the twentieth century, however, the proportion of middle-class occupations has increased. By 1979, 15 percent of men and 16 percent of women were in professional or technical occupations, and the relative percentages of managers and proprietors as well as clerical workers also had increased. The growth of the middle class led some observers to conclude that by 1970 or 1980 the United States had become perhaps the first very large nation in history in which the modal population was middle class. Although there are indications that the United States may have become more bifurcated with a diminishing middle class in the 1980s, the long-range trends historically have been toward growth of the middle-class segments and relative decline of the working class.

Perspectives on Social Class Structure

Not all sociologists agree that the social structure of the United States is fairly represented by the five-class hierarchy shown in Figure 1.1. For one thing, the economic and technological changes occurring in our society are raising standards of living and changing relations among various classes. From certain perspectives, the differences between classes are becoming obliterated. For instance, the lines between the upper class and the upper-middle class seem to be disappearing, with less emphasis given to lineage in all but the oldest and most conservative communities, and with upper-status people taking active leadership roles in community affairs. Blue-collar workers have had greater relative gains in income during the past three decades than have white-collar workers, and patterns of buying and spending have become more similar between these two groups.

From other perspectives, the differences between social classes are becoming sharpened—as, for instance, between the group on public assistance in metropolitan and rural areas and all the other groups in the society.

Some observers describe the social-class structure in the United States as a three-class system in which there is a growing upper-middle class that encompasses the old upper class; then a huge, increasingly undifferentiated "common man" or blue-and-white-collar working class; and an "under class" of unskilled, public-assistance families, sometimes referred to as the "hopeless" class. Mayer (1963), for one, describes the changing social-class outlines of the United States not as a pyramid but as approximating a diamond in which there are small groups of nonmobile people at both the top and the bottom, with all the rest of society in between, and in which gradations in the undifferentiated middle are so numerous and so gradual that class lines are relatively obliterated.

Other sociologists go further. Although they do not deny differences in rank, they feel that class lines cannot be drawn at all in an open society like our own, where there is so much movement or mobility up and down; where networks of informal social interaction overlap friendship, clique, and membership groups to form a series of gentle gradations; and where, accordingly, the concept of social class itself lacks meaning.

Social classes can be thought of, however, as conceptually discrete, even though, in an increasingly urbanized society, the social scientist finds it difficult to establish empirically the boundaries between classes. In this view, social classes can be described in terms of averages; social classes differ, on the average, by income, by occupational level, by attitudes toward education, and by other value systems that we have been describing. People who rank high on one class indicator such as education will tend to rank high on others such as occupation or income; yet there will be many exceptions. Probably everyone has met such exceptions: a successful businessperson who never completed high school; a service station operator who has a college degree; a social worker who lives in the slum neighborhood in which he or she works; a graduate student who is scraping along on a very meager income. There are many people who share socioeconomic characteristics of a given social class but who do not follow its characteristics in all respects. There are also large numbers of persons who will show status discrepancies, or inconsistencies; that is, they will rank higher on some dimensions of status than on others.

However, people whose characteristics are very different from the average on many characteristics of their class will be very possibly in the process of moving into the class immediately above or immediately below their own. As we show later, there is much movement between classes.

Subcultures of the Social Classes

Finding that people can be described as belonging to different classes is only a first step. How do the class groups differ in behavior, in beliefs, in attitudes, and in values? In other words, what is the subculture that characterizes each social-class group?

In describing subcultures, we use the five-class structure found to be useful in studying communities in the United States, even though this structure is an oversimplification, especially of the complex metropolitan area. The following descriptions are based on studies carried out in large cities (such as Kansas City) and in larger geographical areas (such as the San Francisco peninsula) as well as in smaller communities. Even though they are only thumbnail sketches and thus cannot do justice to the variety of patterns found at each class level, they do point out the most salient differences in life-styles as these differences bear on the educational system. A more expansive portrayal of social-class subgroups appears in the Appendix at the end of this chapter. The Appendix presents a useful portrayal by the Claritas Company of twelve major social groups subdivided into forty life-style clusters in the U.S. social structure.

It should be remembered that the classes are in many respects more alike than they are different. People of all classes, for instance, share the modern mass culture of the United States: they read the same newspapers, go to the same movies, listen to the same music, and watch the same television programs and commercials. Riesman et al. (1950), Hodges (1968), and Bronfenbrenner (1977) believe that the mass culture is obliterating class differences, particularly between the lower-middle and the working classes.

The Upper Class

Upper-class people generally have inherited wealth and usually have a family tradition of social prominence that extends back several generations. A few may not be wealthy, but as the respected cousins, nieces, or nephews of upper-class families, they also belong in the upper class. All these people will be listed in the *Social Register* (if the community has one) and will belong to the most exclusive social clubs. They are likely to be well versed in family history.

Upper-class people belong to the boards of directors of art museums, of symphony and opera associations, and/or of Ivy League colleges. They tend to support charitable organizations and chambers of commerce. In older New England communities, their support was often silent ("the power behind the throne") and they left the offices in these organizations to be filled by upper middle-class people. In newer and in larger cities, however, they are likely to be indistinguishable from upper-middles in this respect and are visible as community leaders. Upper-class people usually belong to the Protestant Episcopal, Presbyterian, or Congregational churches in the Midwest, or to the Unitarian or Congregational churches in New England. Relatively few are Catholics or Jews.

Only rarely do upper-class people indulge in conspicuous consumption—showy parties, ostentatious mansions with numerous servants, jewels, and furs. Their houses, gardens, summer places, automobiles, and clothes are more likely to be conservative and inconspicuous (but of good quality).

In the eyes of upper-class people, education is a matter of proper rearing; formal schooling is no more important in this connection than are other aspects of training that children need if they are to fill their adult roles properly. Training for an occupation is not of primary importance, because these children will inherit high status and cannot go any higher by occupational success. Nevertheless, the occupation must be of the right type for the upper class. Young men and women go into business or into one of the higher status professions such as architecture, medicine, law, and (infrequently) the ministry in an upper-status denomination. Children generally attend private schools and the prestigious Ivy League and selective coeducational and women's colleges.

The Upper-Middle Class

Many adult members of this class have climbed to their present status from lower beginnings. Hence this class seems to include many active, ambitious people. The men are business executives and professional men; the women are active in club work, PTA, and civic organizations, and many work as professionals or technicians. The members of this class do not have aristocratic family traditions. Although some are interested in building up such traditions, the typical comment is, "We do not care about our ancestors. It isn't *who* you are, but *what* you are."

The majority of positions of leadership in civic, business, and professional organizations are held by upper middle-class people—organizations such as Rotary and Kiwanis clubs, the League of Women Voters, the Chamber of Commerce, the Medical Society, the Ministerial Association, the Bar Assocation, and the National Association for the Advancement of Colored People.

The upper-middle-class family may be quite wealthy, with money earned in the present generation; more commonly, the income is adequate, enough to pay for a comfortable home, a new automobile every few years, a fair-sized insurance and pension plan, and college education for the children.

Most such families patronize the theater and the symphony concerts, and they read such periodicals as *Harper's Magazine*, the *Atlantic Monthly*, and the *New Yorker*.

Active church leaders come mainly from this class. The most favored churches are Presbyterian, Congregational-Christian, Methodist, Baptist (in the Middle West) and Unitarian (in New England). There are also many Roman Catholic, Lutheran, and Jewish upper-middle-class people. Most members of this class are native born, and most of them have native-born parents and grandparents.

Upper-middle-class people stress harmonious relations with others; they want to be flexible, tolerant, and nondogmatic. In the California suburban area studied by Hodges (1968), the upper-middle parents were found to be less anxious and more easygoing in rearing their children than were lower-middle- and working-class parents.

Education is extremely important to people in this group. Many of them have risen into this class through professional careers, and they feel it is almost essential that their children secure a college degree if they are to maintain upper-middle status in the next generation. The children generally go to public schools and then to the state university or to privately supported liberal arts colleges including Ivy League colleges in the East.

The Lower-Middle Class

This large group is often called the common man group by those above them in the social scale, although they themselves think of the working-class people below them as being the common person.

The lower-middle class consists of white-collar clerical and sales workers. Some are factory foremen or members of the labor aristocracy, such as railroad engineers, conductors, and photoengravers; some are small building, electrical, and plumbing contractors. Most farm owners who operate their own farms are also in this class. These people tend to be at the national average; their income is at about the middle of the national income range, and the magazines, sports, television programs, movie stars, and comic strips they prefer tend also to be the national favorites.

Lower-middle-class people stress thrift and are proud of their economic independence. Their houses are usually comfortably furnished and well-kept but are small to medium in size and located nearer the wrong part of town or in inexpensive suburban tracts.

This group makes up the bulk of members of fraternal organizations such as the American Legion and their corresponding women's auxiliaries. They are fairly active in the PTA, and they furnish much of the membership in the Protestant and Catholic churches. They also furnish the lay leadership of some churches, especially the Baptist, the Lutheran, and in many places the Methodist churches. Many lower-middle-class people are Catholics, and some are Jews. Appreciable numbers of this class are children or grandchildren of immigrants.

Most members of the lower-middle class finished high school, and approximately 75 percent of their children go on to college. Schooling is considered essential for a good job, and the children are expected to be obedient pupils. In the suburbs, lower-middle-class and working-class people often live in the same developments and have many characteristics in common. In time, the two classes may become enough alike to be considered together as the common person group.

The Upper-Working Class

The respectable working people, the skilled and semiskilled blue-collar (as opposed to white-collar) workers, make up the upper-working class.* They are often Catholics, but there are also considerable numbers in the fundamentalist Protestant denominations such as the Assembly of God, the Pentecostal, and Holiness churches. They are also frequently Baptists and Methodists. At the same time, a considerable minority of this group are not church members, and some are hostile to churches.

Working-class people in small towns and cities live across the tracks or on the wrong side of town in small houses that are usually well kept. Particularly in the big cities, the working class has enjoyed a considerable increase in real income in recent decades, which has enabled increasing numbers to buy homes in inexpensive suburban tracts. Working-class people are as fond of labor-saving gadgets as are middle-class people and frequently show concern about keeping

* In earlier studies of social structure undertaken by Warner's methods, the upper-working class was referred to as "upper-lower," and the bottom class as "lower-lower." It is not easy to find substitute terms that are free of implied derogation; we have chosen the terms *working class* and *upper-working class* and *lower-working class* as at least somewhat less biased and as reflecting more accurately the fact that most persons at the lowest social level are also workers. At the same time, to do as certain other sociologists have done and draw no distinctions within the working class is to obliterate some very significant differences between the large group of stable, blue-collar workers at the common man level and the smaller group who in many respects stand apart from all the other levels of society due to poverty and other social and economic deprivations.

up with the Joneses by buying more household equipment and newer and bigger cars and by frequently remodeling their homes.

Working-class men provide much of the membership in veterans' organization and fraternal orders. Their wives join the ladies' auxiliaries and are often members of PTA when the children are small. The men enjoy hunting and fishing; most working-class people, however, spend their leisure time at home, watching television or fixing up around the house. They seldom read more than the local newspaper and one or two magazines.

Typically, working-class adults put little value on learning for learning's sake; but they do recognize that education is the key to a good job, and they want their children to go further in school than they themselves have gone. At present, most of the children from this social class complete high school, and many go on to the local college or junior college.

The Lower-Working Class

Lower-working-class people are easy to stereotype because they live in highly visible and often shockingly poor quarters—big city slums or low-income public housing developments; shacks at the edges of cities; or tenant farmers' cabins. Miller (1964) has distinguished four groups within this class: the stable poor, unskilled workers who have steady jobs and a stable family life; the strained, who have steady jobs but who have major family or personality difficulties; the copers, people who have economic difficulties but strong family relations and who manage to get along most of the time; and the unstable, people who have both financial and familial or personal problems and who may end up on the welfare rolls as multiproblem cases.

Historically, the lower-working class included the newest immigrants who perform the most menial tasks of the society while they are learning the ways of life in the United States. In the past, such people were frequently Irish, German, Swedish, or Polish. Today, they frequently are Hispanic or Asian immigrants or black Americans with recent rural origins.

Lower-working-class people have few occupational skills and frequently have less than a high school education. Many have difficulty finding jobs because of their color. Because they are the last to be hired and the first to be fired, they have difficulty acquiring job seniority. A business recession that has only a slight effect on the other classes will put many lower-working-class people out of work, swelling the welfare rolls. Many people in this class spend a great deal of time seeking work that will provide a decent living for the family. It is not surprising that many believe that diligence and thrift have little to do with getting ahead and that only by luck or connections will they ever better themselves.

Families of this class produce a disproportionate share of problem children in the schools: the slow learners, the truants, the aggressive, and the delinquent. These children draw a good deal of attention from the educational authorities. Identified as needing compensatory education, some get considerable help from remedial reading specialists, counselors, truant officers, and volunteer tutors.

Development of a Big-City Underclass

Our description of social class has used a frequently used classification including five categories ranging from lower-working class to upper class. This classification has been widely followed in analysis and research dealing with the social class structure.

However, in recent years many social scientists have begun to identify and refer to a sixth class of individuals at the very bottom of the class structure: an underclass. As the term implies, this group can be considered as the lowest status and most depressed segment of the lower-working class. The term *underclass* also generally is used to connote a degree of permanency greater than is implied in referring simply to a lower class. People in the underclass are stuck at the bottom of the social structure and perceive themselves as having little chance of ever escaping from a pervasively poverty-ridden environment (Wilson 1987; Alter 1988).

Acknowledgment of the existence of an underclass became more common when *Time* magazine printed a cover story under this title on August 28, 1977, following looting that occurred in New York City during a power failure brought about by a storm in that area. The story tried to help readers understand why such widespread stealing could occur in the largest city in one of the richest countries in the world, even though such events seldom occur in the slums of cities in underdeveloped countries in which the population is objectively much poorer than in the United States.

Time magazine reporters interviewed a number of social scientists and government officials in an effort to define the nature and size of the underclass. They were not able to be very precise in their estimates, concluding that the underclass constituted 10 to 12 million people in the United States. Given its great importance for education, we are concerned with the underclass in several parts of this book, and the term is generally used to refer to low-income families who live in concentrated poverty neighborhoods in the inner core of large cities. Not all members of the underclass live in concentrated poverty neighborhoods in cities, but here the problems posed by the underclass are overtly most acute.

By *concentrated poverty* neighborhoods we mean low-income neighborhoods that are larger in area and population than historically existed in the slums of United States cities, and in which nearly all of the population is either below or only slightly above the poverty level designated by the federal government. The concentrated poverty neighborhoods in which the big-city underclass live are characterized not just by low income but also by a variety of other indicators of disadvantaged status such as the following:

1. Many but not all of their inhabitants are from disadvantaged minority groups (Coughlin 1988). White families who live there and can be considered part of the underclass tend to be problem families in which urban poverty has

been transmitted across a number of generations, or relatively new urban immigrants from economically depressed sections such as Appalachia.

2. There is a very high percentage of female-headed families, so high that in some concentrated poverty neighborhoods as many as 90 percent of the families are classified as female-headed. This high a degree of family disorganization exists in concentrated poverty neighborhoods, for many reasons, including (a) the existence of welfare policies that reduce assistance for families in which the husband remains in the home; (b) many unemployed or underemployed adult males who give up looking for a good job and become part of a street culture whose members drop out of normal family life; and (c) high rates of crime and personal violence that result in the incarceration of a relatively high percentage of the male population (Wilson 1987; Wilson and Aponte 1985).

3. Social institutions such as the family, the school, and the law enforcement system frequently appear to have broken down and no longer function effectively to achieve their traditional social purposes. Parents find it increasingly difficult to control their children, educators are overwhelmed with the problems of teaching a concentrated poverty population, and law enforcement agencies are unable to cope with relatively high rates of juvenile delinquency and adult crime.

The problems of concentrated poverty neighborhoods are discussed in greater depth in Chapters 2, 8, and 10, but at this point it is important to emphasize that the underclass concentrated poverty neighborhood also is characterized by a sense of hopelessness and powerlessness. This attitude appears to be both a result and a cause of the social disorganization that exists in big-city slums. Reasons that this vicious circle of psychological despair and social disorganization has become so pronounced in concentrated poverty neighborhoods in big cities include the following:

1. In some ways, inhabitants of concentrated poverty neighborhoods are more segregated from the larger society than was true in the past, if only because the poverty area is now physically larger and the middle classes are more removed from it due to suburbanization than was true in previous generations (Goldsmith 1982; Hacker 1988). Data illustrating the increase in the number of persons in poverty areas in big cities have been compiled by Winard (1970), who found that the population of poverty areas in a sample of fifty-nine big cities increased by 18 percent between 1960 and 1970, and the percentage of city residents who lived in these areas increased from 32 percent to 39 percent. Wilson and Aponte noted that the number of poor people in central cities increased from approximately 8 million in 1969 to 12.7 million in 1982. They concluded that this increase represented a "remarkable change in the concentration of poor people in the United States in only slightly more than a decade" (1985, 239).

The concentrated poverty neighborhoods of big cities are now more homogeneously low-income than were comparable neighborhoods in the past. As long ago as 1967, a study of these neighborhoods in the Hough section of Cleveland and the Watts section of Los Angeles demonstrated that middle-class and upwardly mobile residents were leaving to escape the physical deterioration and social disorganization that are characteristic of big-city poverty areas:

> *Despite the general improvements in the conditions of life for Negroes nationally, conditions have grown worse in places like Hough and Watts. As Negro families succeed, they tend to move out of these economically and socially depressed areas to better neighborhoods where they and their children have the opportunity to lead a better life. They leave behind increasing problems of deprivation in the heart of our cities. (U.S. Bureau of the Census 1967, xi)*

Since 1967, concentrated poverty neighborhoods in many big cities have continued to become still more homogeneously poor. By 1975, for example, virtually all the children in a number of Cleveland elementary schools were from families receiving public assistance. Even though the overall population of these neighborhoods has declined in some cities, much of this decline has been due to further withdrawal of upwardly mobile families, leaving still fewer models of successful families for children to emulate than had been available in the 1960s.

2. For young people lacking specialized skills and knowledge, it probably is more difficult to become mobile now than it was in earlier periods of United States history. As the number of unskilled and semiskilled jobs has decreased relative to highly skilled jobs, young people entering the economy in a low-level job perceive fewer prospects of advancement than did unskilled workers in the past (Howe 1988).

3. Forty or fifty years ago, inner-city parents striving to persuade their children to work hard to attain long-range goals in schools and society were aided by newspapers, magazines, and other mass media that told the child to save for the future and to view the satisfaction of many impulses as sinful and pagan. Today, the messages communicated to children by the mass media tell them to buy now, pay later, and to regard the satisfaction of worldly desires as the most glorious of human pursuits. These messages also are directed, of course, at children outside of concentrated poverty neighborhoods, but it is the children of the poor who tend to be most victimized because such messages reinforce feelings of isolation in a have-not environment.

4. The high proportion of low-income, female-headed families in many concentrated poverty neighborhoods in itself is both a cause and an indicator of intergenerational poverty in these neighborhoods. Because families in this situation generally are dependent on the income of one typically unskilled adult, it is perhaps inevitable that a very high percentage will be below the poverty level. Because so many husband-wife families escape the problems that exist in these neighborhoods at the first opportunity, a big-city neighborhood with a high proportion of female-headed families tends to become progressively more characterized by the problems associated with concentrated poverty. Thus, it is not surprising to find that female-headed families not part of the labor force

constitute an increasing percentage of the poverty population and a substantial proportion of the underclass in big cities:

> *The low-income population is becoming less and less similar to the population as a whole. . . . Poverty reduction has been more successful for those with a strong attachment to the labor force. In 1959, two-thirds of the heads of poor families had worked at least part of the time; the proportion had fallen to just over half in 1972. . . . Poverty among the aged and among male-headed families was dropping both absolutely and proportionately.*
>
> *The implications of these data for public policy are sobering. Those who remained poor in the early 1970s were increasingly those for whom it has been most difficult to design and implement effective social programs. (Lynn 1977, 98)*

In short, the slums of earlier years have become concentrated poverty neighborhoods characterized by intergenerational transmission of low status. Since World War II, suburbanization has left many of the poor to inhabit the inner core of central cities. Where big-city slums once functioned significantly as staging areas from which children of the poor perceived themselves as having a good chance to fight their way out, today they appear to many of their inhabitants as symbols of an oppression they have little chance to escape. There is still some mobility out of the underclass, but thousands of youngsters who grow up in big-city poverty areas believe there is little real possibility they will escape.

Formation of Street Cultures and a Dual Labor Market

The preceding discussion of how the big-city underclass is locked into the lowest status position in the social structure makes it clear that the causes of the situation are both cultural and structural. The causes are cultural in the sense that they involve the attitudes of a group of people who develop distinctive modes of behaving in a shared environment. They are structural in the sense that they involve the ways in which opportunities and statuses are provided and determined within a large social and economic structure. Social scientists who have been studying big-city working-class and underclass groups have found it useful to view their situation and problems from both points of view. In particular, they have examined two related phenomena that appear to be important in understanding the plight of the underclass—the street culture, within urban society in the United States, and the operation of a dual labor market in the United States economy.

The street culture in low-status sections of United States cities has attracted the attention of many sociologists. One of the best descriptions of the street culture and its effects on underclass blacks in big cities has been provided by Elliott Liebow, who spent months as an observer documenting the day-to-day events in the lives of men whose interaction centered on a street corner in Washington, D.C. In a poignant book named after one of its principal characters,

Tally's Corner (1967), Liebow summarized the major events and beliefs that seemed to characterize the lives of these young men as follows:

> *Making a living takes on an overriding importance at marriage. . . . He wants to . . . support a family and be the head of it, because this is what it is to be a man in our society. . . . Although he wants to get married, he hedges on his commitment from the very beginning because he is afraid, not of marriage itself, but of his own ability to carry out his responsibilities as husband and father. His own father failed and had to "cut out," and the men he knows who have been or are married have also failed or are in the process of doing so. He has no evidence that he will fare better than they and much evidence that he will not. However far he has gone in school, he is illiterate or almost so; however many jobs he has had or how hard he has worked, he is essentially unskilled . . . jobs are only intermittently available . . . [and] are almost always menial. . . . He has little vested interest in such a job and learns to treat it with the same contempt held for it by the employer and society at large. From his point of view, the job is expendable; from the employer's point of view, he is. . . . Sometimes he sits down and cries at the humiliation of it all. . . . Increasingly he turns to the street corner. (pp. 210–214)*

Liebow's description of the major life events of men in a big-city street culture makes it clear that even though statistics on the problem of the underclass center on females as family heads, the underlying difficulty is as much or more a problem involving the situation of males growing up in concentrated poverty neighborhoods. (See Chapter 10.) Statistics on inner-city males are not as frequently collected or scrutinized as those on females, but in general it is known that females are overrepresented compared to males in graduating classes in poverty-area high schools and in employment training programs for the big-city poor, both of which should be improving economic and social opportunities for the underclass. Without the participation of males, it is difficult to see how much progress can be made in alleviating the plight of the underclass.

Economists use the term *dual labor market* to refer to the division of jobs between the primary market, consisting of jobs with relatively high wages and skill requirements, high tenure of employment, and opportunities for promotion to higher-status positions, and a secondary market, in which jobs barely provide a living wage and are characterized by low skill requirements, high absenteeism and turnover, and low opportunity for advancement. Many or most jobs available to big-city poor—particularly the black poor—are in the secondary labor market (Harrison 1972b).

Employment-training programs that the government has sponsored for low-income groups in big cities generally have not succeeded in helping enrollees enter the primary labor market. In general, these programs have been designed to provide unskilled persons with beginning skills required for jobs realistically available to them. In most cases, these jobs pay very little, and for various reasons the trainees who fill them do not stay employed for very long. "Government institutions designed to place low-income workers into 'good' jobs,"

Harrison concluded (1972b), have succeeded only in "recirculating the poor among the very low-paying, unstable jobs which they already held" (p. 123).

The street culture and the secondary labor market are closely interrelated. On the one hand, the irregular economy of the street culture (gambling, narcotics, hustling) is an attractive alternative to low-paid jobs in the secondary labor market for some residents of concentrated poverty neighborhoods (Williams and Kornblum 1985). Conversely, the availability of this alternative helps account for the tendency toward high turnover among some workers in poverty neighborhoods. The interaction between these phenomena was apparent in Glasgow's study of *The Black Underclass* in the Watts section of Los Angeles. Based on inteviews reminiscent of those Liebow conducted in Washington, D.C., Glasgow concluded that

> *the trap in which these youths are caught cannot be fully understood in terms of theories, statistics, or comparison. It must be seen as a way of life. . . . It means having high aspirations but having to find the ways to achieve them outside the mainstream. It involves feeling capable of handling the task if opportunity were available but believing the chances are limited. . . . Still more unfortunate is the man who no longer even hopes for a legitimate opportunity. . . . His struggle for economic survival has shifted to another arena, the world of hustling, thugging, and burglary.*
>
> *Defensive behavior such as limited investment in goal striving, limited aspirations, and assumption of a psychological readiness for failure are some of the devices employed. . . . Hence institutional racism (which involves ghetto residence, inner-city educational institutions, police arrests, limited success models) . . . destroys motivation and, in fact, produces occupationally obsolete young men ready for underclass encapsulation. (Glasgow 1980, 81–84)*

The Underclass in Big-City Poverty Neighborhoods

To avoid misunderstanding and neither to exaggerate nor underestimate the magnitude of the problems faced by the big-city underclass, it is important to be as clear as possible about its composition and also about its situation in the inner core of large metropolitan areas. The underclass includes members of white ethnic groups, but the majority of its members probably are from racial and ethnic minority groups that have been confined and piled up in the older, deteriorating, inner core of big cities (Magnet 1987). In Los Angeles, Houston, New York, and some other cities, a high proportion of the underclass is Hispanic; but in other cities the underclass is predominantly black. Perhaps for this reason most research involving the emergence of an urban underclass has been focused on the black population. Mitchell Sviridoff has pointed out that although most of the poverty population in the United States is not in the underclass, the underclass is "making a disproportionate contribution to violent crime, the decay of inner-city neighborhoods, school failure, family disruption, illegitimate births, [and social welfare] dependency" (quoted in Brotman 1982, 1).

Ken Auletta (1982) has studied a group of underclass youth and adults participating in a work-training program in New York City and has also reviewed the research and analysis dealing with the development of an underclass in big cities in the United States. (Auletta additionally provides a comparison of the urban poor with the rural underclass among whites in Appalachia and blacks in Mississippi.) He cites data indicating that the underclass is about 70 percent nonwhite and that a majority of its members are children under age eighteen. His overall conclusions include the following:

> *If we strip away the rhetoric of the right and left, a surprising consensus emerges. There is broad agreement that America has developed an underclass. . . . Those on the right tend to use words like 'pathology,' 'passivity,' and 'hostility'; those on the left tend to speak of 'despair,' 'hopelessness,' and 'alienation.' . . . For the first time in America's relatively young history, the ghetto has become a permanent home for too many broken families. For some, upward mobility is a lie, and organized society is the enemy; for others, the temporary crutch of welfare has turned into a straitjacket of permanent dependency. Whether you are compassionate or scared, the underclass should command your attention. . . . Pushing aside the pieties, charts, and stereotypes, one sees that a segment of the poor are sometimes victims of their own bad attitudes, and sometimes victims of social and economic forces. Neither the right's desire to blame individuals, nor the left's to blame the system, addresses the stubborn reality of the underclass. (Auletta 1982, 50, 319)*

Auletta's portrayal of the underclass and its distinguishing characteristics agrees with the findings of a study Glaser and Ross (1970) conducted to identify the characteristics of successful men who had been upwardly mobile from seriously disadvantaged backgrounds. Glaser and Ross compared the histories and attitudes of successful and unsuccessful black and Mexican-American men from working-class communities. They found that compared to the unsuccessful group, the successful men had more positive attitudes toward representatives of mainstream society, exhibited relatively more loyalty to their families than to peers or street groups, experienced more stable and satisfying marital relationships, had more specific long-range goals and realistic strategies for achieving these goals, and based their self-esteem more on achievement than on "the good opinion of peers on the streets" (p. 74).

Improving Opportunity for the Underclass

The solutions one proposes for any problem depend, or should depend, on one's diagnosis of its causes. If the causes of the plight of the underclass in big-city poverty neighborhoods are both cultural and structural, it is legitimate to conclude that solutions that do not take both types of phenomena fully into account will not have much chance to succeed. Our argument here and elsewhere in this book is that educators have an important part to play in working to eliminate both the cultural and structural causes of intergenerational poverty in big cities, as in other communities in the United States.

The structural causes of big-city underclass status are relatively easy to enumerate, though extremely difficult to modify with social programs. As we have seen above, interrelated causes include residence in a concentrated poverty neighborhood, isolation from the wider society and from resources such as jobs in the suburbs, lack of access or failure to enter the primary labor market, lack of material resources required to get a start in the economy, and discrimination or other barriers to employment and education.

To a degree, naming the causes implies the direction for a solution. If a primary cause of underclass status is isolation from the larger society and residence in a concentrated poverty neighborhood, then efforts to help the big-city underclass should give some priority to reducing its isolation and deconcentrating big-city poverty. If the structural causes also include failure to enter the primary labor market, then efforts also should be made to change the economy so that better opportunities are available to the poor. Gans (1976) sums up this part of the argument:

> *Since jobs, particularly for the unskilled, are now scarcer than they were during the time that the immigrants escaped poverty, it will be necessary to resort to deliberate job-creation. The jobs to be created should mesh with the needs of the private and especially the public economy, but they must also mesh with the long-range need of the poor: to become part of the primary labor market. In other words, such jobs must provide enough income, security, and opportunity for advancement to enable their holders to feel that they are participants in the economy and the society, so that their children will be able to advance further through education.*
>
> *The historical record suggests that parental establishment in the primary labor market was a prerequisite and a takeoff point for using education to achieve further mobility, but whether history must repeat itself, or whether a different takeoff point can be found is as yet an unanswered question. No one knows where the takeoff point is at which people feel that they are participants in the economy and the society so that their children will feel it is useful to go to school. (Gans 1976, 66–67)*

Along with programs to provide employment and income, education also is a central component in carrying out a comprehensive program to improve conditions for the underclass in big cities. Desegregation of the public schools, for example, should be concerned with reducing the social isolation of the poor. Whether the poor acquire good jobs in the future will depend to an extent on what low-status youth learn in the schools. These issues are discussed at much greater length in subsequent chapters, but at this point it is important to emphasize that education should be seen as one key component in a larger effort to improve the quality of life for the residents of poverty areas in big cities.

The social and cultural causes of underclass status also must be explicitly addressed if progress is to be made in alleviating the problems of big-city poverty. Because these causes involve such phenomena as are exemplified in the street culture, efforts to improve the conditions and status of the underclass must take into account the sense of hopelessness of people in the inner city and the difficulties the family, the schools, the labor market, and other institutions encounter in working with young people attracted to the street culture (Hacker 1988). Our discussion in subsequent chapters of efforts to improve the effectiveness of education for students from disadvantaged backgrounds places considerable emphasis on the social and cultural causes of low performance among students in concentrated poverty neighborhoods.

Economic, Social, and Demographic Changes

Many of the economic, social, and demographic changes occurring in the United States have important implications for the social structure and for education. This section describes and discusses some of the most significant changes. Much of the material in this book is concerned with the past and future effects of these changes on the educational system and with how the schools have responded or might respond most productively in the future. Trends considered involve the occupational structure, the age structure, racial/ethnic minority population, and poverty and female-headed families.

The Occupational Structure

A general name for the new society into which we are moving is the postindustrial society. Daniel Bell (1973) and David Riesman (Riesman et al. 1950) used this term to denote the coming nature of our society, which began two hundred years ago as an agricultural society and changed in the period around 1900 to an industrial society. The personnel and wealth of an industrial society are devoted to transforming raw materials into many forms of material goods and selling or trading a part of these products for the goods and services wanted by the people of an affluent society.

As shown in Table 1.1 and in Figure 1.2, the number of jobs in manufacturing rose slightly between 1959 and 1984 and is expected to hold relatively steady at slightly more than 20 million through 1995. The largest increase has been in service occupations, which increased from less than 10 million jobs in 1954 to about 25 million in 1984; these occupations are expected to constitute more than 30 million jobs by 1995. The service occupations that have increased most rapidly generally involve health, education, commerce, legal services, clerical work, and sales. Jobs in trade and in government also have increased significantly and are expected to increase slightly in the future. The largest declines generally have been in extraction industries, such as agriculture, fishing, forestry, and mining (not shown in Figure 1.2). Because services and government both involve white-

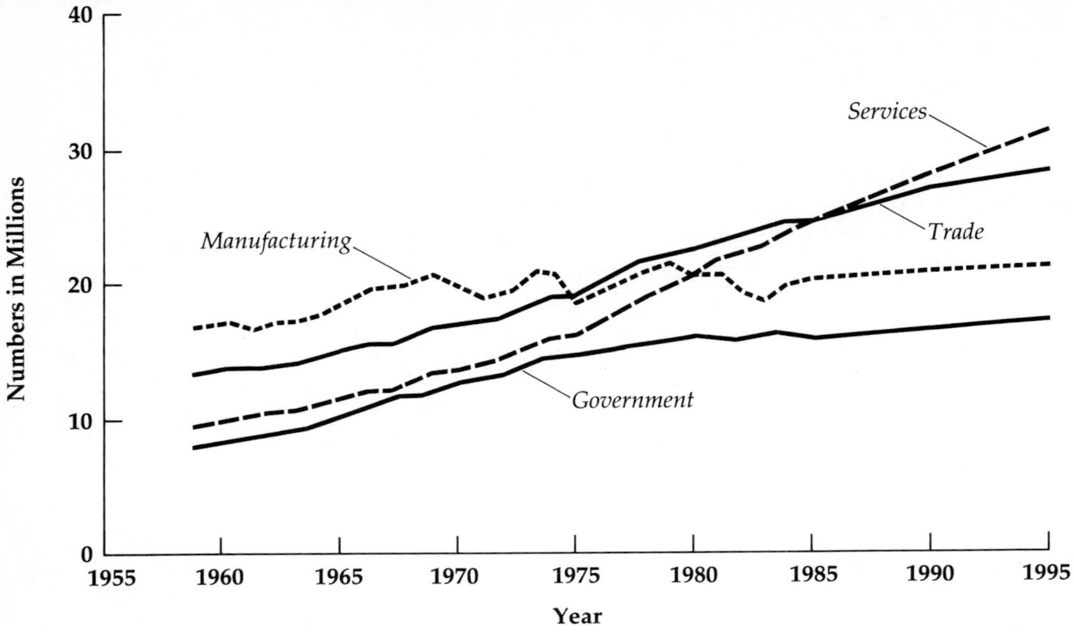

Figure 1.2 ***Total Employment in Selected Major Economic Sectors, 1959–84, and Projected, 1985–95*** (*Source:* Personik, 1985.)

collar occupations, there has been an increase in the ratio of white-collar to blue-collar jobs.

Projections prepared by the U.S. Bureau of Labor Statistics (1982) indicate that by 1990, 51 percent of U.S. workers will be in white-collar fields and only 31 percent will be in blue-collar occupations. Even in the manufacturing sector, which traditionally has consisted largely of blue-collar workers, the proportion of white-collar workers is expected to increase from 33 percent in 1980 to about 50 percent in the first part of the twenty-first century.

Many of the services inherent in postindustrial society involve processing of information, so that some observers view current trends as evolving toward the emergence of an information society. For example, some social scientists have shown (Beniger 1986; Naisbitt 1982) that the percentage of workers in information-processing jobs (teachers, secretaries, accountants, insurance, etc.) grew substantially after 1950. Marc Porat (1977) prepared a U.S. Department of Commerce report that explicitly analyzed the information-processing components within the service segment of the economy. He was unable to say exactly how much the information sector has increased, but he did point out that it has grown by "leaps and bounds" (Naisbitt 1982). Analysis provided by the Education Commission of the States indicated that this trend toward emphasis on information-processing in the economy will require that many workers probably will need "improved skills in the selection and communication of information. . . . Attention given only to the minimum competencies as currently defined shows a lack of foresight and leaves many students without adequate preparation for future learning and employability" (Gisi and Forbes 1982, 1–2). For this reason, editors of the *Economist* have called recent change in the occupational structure a cerebral revolution.

Trends regarding growth in the service economy and information-processing have been accompanied by accelerating emphasis on high technology involving computers, automation and robotics, introduction of new media, and other aspects of work based on advanced scientific knowledge and methods. All of these trends are expected to continue during the next decade (Howe 1988).

The fastest-growing areas of employment will involve information-processing jobs such as computer system analyst, data-processing machine repair, computer programming, and various types of engineering and high technology employment related to recent scientific advances in communications, genetics, and energy (Personik 1985; United States Department of Education and United States Department of Labor 1988).

Analysts concerned with economic and occupational trends differ on such issues as whether most jobs in the future will require higher levels of skills and education than is true today, whether the number of higher-status jobs that are created will be larger or smaller than the number of low-status jobs, whether current arrangements for education and training are likely to produce sufficient numbers of highly skilled workers, and whether or how much improvements in education and training might result in improved economic productivity and prosperity. Spenner (1985) reviewed research bearing on these types of issues and reached the following conclusions:

> *Deciphering the skill impacts of technology change proves extraordinarily elusive. . . . The spectrum of positions ranges from education as a leading institution that anticipates and even modifies skill requirements for jobs, to education as a training institution that has little to do with skills needed for work. . . . For example, some observers suggest mathematics and science education in Japan as the chief causal factor fostering industrial robotics in Japan. . . . The causal link is not proven. . . . Our knowledge of skill transformation is limited. What we know suggests mixtures of upgrading and downgrading, and changes at evolutionary versus revolutionary rates. Policies and programs based on the extremes of change . . . are likely to be in error. (Spenner 1985, 146, 150)*

Economic dislocation associated with the introduction of high technology will pose serious problems but will also help generate exciting possibilities for the educational system. Many large school districts obviously will suffer severe financial crises in locations in which employment and the tax base are most negatively affected. Following one possible scenario, the educational system will significantly decline as financing becomes even more inadequate and as white-collar unemployment reduces young peoples' motivation to stay in high school and go to college. According to an alternate scenario, however, the motivation of youth may increase because they will be in competition for a shrinking number of jobs (Howe. 1988; Sternlieb and Hughes 1988).

In either case, the educational system—elementary schools through higher education—will be challenged to prepare young people for success in a high technology economy and to help in supporting the development of modernized business and industry (Lewis, 1988). This challenge seems to have been met relatively successfully so far in some locations such as high tech regions in California and New England, where the educational system has produced a skilled work force and unemployment rates are much lower than in the United States as a whole.

Technological changes in recent years also suggest that future economic prosperity will depend on comprehensive efforts to retrain many adults for employment in jobs that require new skills. In this regard, an assistant secretary in the U.S. Department of Labor told participants in a 1983 seminar conducted by the National Association of Manufacturers that "our people are going to have to realize that on a regular basis they are going to have to re-educate themselves and retrain themselves . . . [or] they won't have jobs." Since most of the work force in the year 2000 is already on the job, retraining will have to be provided by postsecondary educational institutions, local and state governments, and, particularly, by business. The business sector is already spending more than thirty billion dollars per year on training, but its expenditures in preparing workers for jobs in today's economy undoubtedly will have to be substantially greater if the United States is to be internationally competitive in high technology industry.

Even though there are many disagreements and uncertainties regarding the future of technology and its effects on society and the schools, all or nearly all informed observers would probably accept several conclusions. Among these conclusions are the following:

1. Computerization and other aspects of new technology are "deskilling" some jobs (e.g., bank teller) but increasing the skill requirements in other fields, such as military service (Levin and Rumberger 1985; Burke and Rumberger 1987).

2. Jobs with relatively high pay and status will require higher levels of skill and knowledge. Success in the economy will depend even more than it does now on mastery of increasingly more complex and abstract information and skills (Applebaum 1985; Howe 1988).

3. Accelerated introduction of new technology is bringing about major changes in the occupational structure and the social-class structure. Leontief (1985) studied recent trends and concluded that continuing emphasis on new technologies such as computer-based automation may require 20 million fewer workers in the year 2000 than would maintenance on the old technology, but at the same time the percentage of professionals in the work force would be about 38 percent higher (1985, 39). This would mean that even though millions of persons would have higher status jobs, many millions of others either would be unemployed or would have to be absorbed in new jobs—many of them low in pay and status—in other fields. Similarly, Castells (1985) reviewed developing

trends and concluded that the impact of automation on the occupational structure may result in a "bifurcated labor market, with the upgrading of a minority of workers and rapid growth of professional sectors, while a majority of workers are deskilled and reduced to low-paying jobs, either in labor-intensive services or in down-graded manufacturing" (1985, 21).

4. Both general education and vocational education at the secondary and postsecondary levels should place greater stress on providing students with broad learning and problem-solving skills as contrasted with narrow preparation for specific occupations in order to prepare them for a range of occupational possibilities that will become important in the future (Panel on Secondary School Education for the Changing Workplace 1984; Grubb 1984).

5. The groups most hurt by introduction of high technology will include black and Hispanic males, who now depend on manual-labor jobs that are being eliminated by technology (Carnoy 1987).

In addition to these direct implications for the educational system, developments now impacting the occupational structure point to a multitude of important questions about the functioning of the schools in society. Do students from differing social-class and racial/ethnic backgrounds receive equal or even adequate opportunity to pursue success in our postindustrial economy through the schools? Are women disadvantaged in pursuing equal opportunity through education? How are trends in the family and the home affecting students' opportunities to succeed academically and economically? What problems do youth encounter in striving to become productive adults? What can the schools do in responding to such questions? What should they do? Changes involving the occupational structure provide the background and context for much of the succeeding presentation and discussion of material throughout this book.

Bifurcation in the Social Structure? As indicated, some scholars believe that new technologies are causing a bifurcation such that the high-income, high-status segment of U.S. society is becoming larger at the same time that the low-income, low-status segment also is becoming larger. In other words, the rich are getting richer and relatively more numerous, the poor are getting poorer and relatively more numerous, and the middle segments thereby are shrinking.

Data supporting this point of view include information indicating that:

- The relative difference in income between the highest income groups and the lowest increased by more than 20 percent between 1978 and 1985 (Harrison, Tilley, and Bluestone 1986).
- Forty-four percent of the new jobs created between 1979 and 1985 paid poverty-level wages (Bluestone and Harrison 1987).
- An increasing economic squeeze on the middle class has, among other manifestations, increased the percentage of income young families spend on home mortgages from about 15 percent in 1949 to more than 40 percent in 1984 (Levy and Michel 1986).

- The relative proportion of the median income spent on taxes doubled between 1965 and 1984 (Brophy 1986).
- The percentage of poor and near-poor families served by Medicaid decreased from 65 percent in 1969 to 46 percent in 1985 ("The Split-level Economy" 1986).
- Young adults appear to be having increasing difficulty in obtaining a college education and purchasing a home unless their parents are able (and willing) to provide a large financial contribution (Kuttner 1987).
- The percentage of the population in the middle-income category fell by 8 percentage points between 1978 and 1984. (The percentage in the bottom quarter increased by 5 points, and the top quarter by 3 points.)

Levy and Michel (1985) have pointed out that one group much affected by social and economic changes has been the baby boomers entering adulthood and middle age, and that many persons in this generation believe they will never live as well as their parents and are part of a vanishing middle class. "In summary," Levy and Michel concluded, "the baby boomers . . . see themselves portrayed in television commercials which tell them that they can 'have it all.' But the living standards they saw as children—a single family house, two or three children, provision for retirement, and all this on one salary—seem wildly out of reach" (1985, 40–41).

Other observers disagree with the emphases and implications drawn from data indicating that the social structure may be growing more bifurcated. Levels of consumption, they point out, have continued to rise for most Americans despite the financial difficulties and obligations thereby incurred, the proportion of workers in lower-paying occupations has decreased (McMahon and Tschetter 1986), the U.S. economy has created new jobs at a rate faster than ever before, millions of women have entered the labor force in little more than one generation, and the generations following the baby boom should be in greater demand in the labor market because there will be fewer young adults competing with each other (Kosters and Ross 1988). These observers also argue that discouraging data for the 1980s (such as reported above) have been largely due to a significant economic recession in the first part of the decade and, in any case, represent temporary dislocations and setbacks as the nation adjusts to a new technological age and to increased foreign competition.

Time will allow for determining whether the social structure in the United States has become permanently more bifurcated in recent years and whether an accompanying increase in poverty among children and youth will exacerbate problems in the educational system. Meanwhile, it is difficult to perceive recent trends toward bifurcation as having any positive implications for the schools.

The Age Structure

The population of the United States is becoming older as the baby boomers born after 1945 advance into and through middle age. As shown in Figure 1.3, the

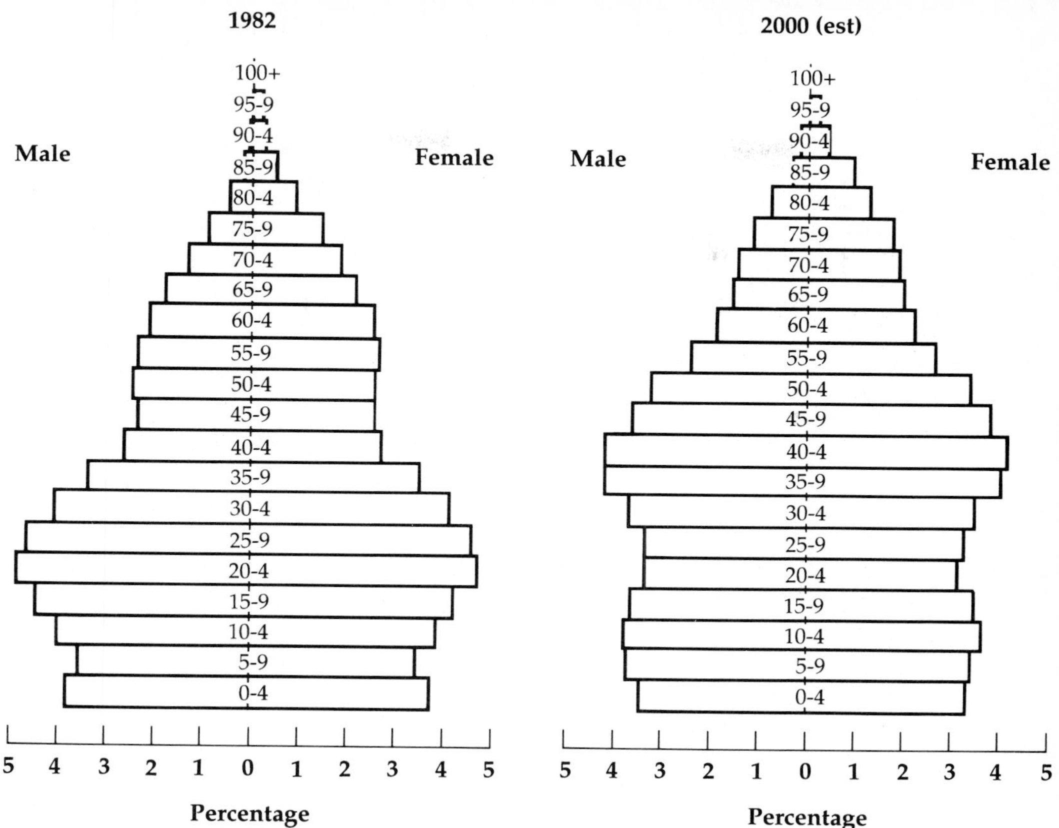

Figure 1.3 ***Estimated and Projected Percent Distribution of the U.S. Population, by Age and Sex, 1982 and 2000 (est)*** (*Source:* U.S. Bureau of the Census, 1984.)

polygon representing age distribution will look less like a pyramid and more like a square (through age fifty-four) as generational progression proceeds during the remainder of this century.

Government projections also underline changes that will occur in the school-age population. As shown in Table 1.2, the size of the cohort under fifteen years of age is expected to increase by 8 percent between 1985 and 2000, as the baby boomers raise their own children. Some demographers studying population change in the early 1980s thought that this echo of the baby boom would become much more pronounced, but it now appears to be a relatively small and transient blip in long-range trends functioning to reduce the relative percentage of children and youth in the United States.

Figure 1.4 provides a graphic representation showing government projections of the size of four cohorts of youth under twenty-four years of age. Con-

Table 1.2 ***Estimates and Projections of the Population of the United States, 1985–2000***

Age Group	Numbers in Millions				
	1985	*1990*	*1995*	*2000*	*Percent Change 1985–2000*
Under 15	52.0	54.6	56.7	55.9	08
15–24	39.5	35.6	34.1	36.1	−09
25–34	42.0	43.5	40.5	36.4	−13
35–44	31.8	37.8	42.0	43.7	37
45–54	22.6	25.4	31.4	37.1	64
55–64	22.3	21.1	20.9	23.8	07
65 and older	28.5	31.7	33.9	34.9	22

Source: U.S. Bureau of the Census, *Current Population Reports,* Series P–25. No. 952, 1984; No. 998, 1986.

clusions and implications that can be drawn from Figures 1.3 and 1.4 and Table 1.2 include the following:

1. Enrollment at the preschool level probably will rise slightly until about 1990 and then decline slightly before levelling off.
2. Enrollment at the elementary level probably will rise until 1995 or 2000 and then decline.
3. Enrollment at the secondary level probably will continue declining until about 1990 and then rise.
4. Enrollment in postsecondary institutions of youth between eighteen and twenty-four years of age probably will decline until about 1995 and then rise.
5. It may be easier to finance education in the year 2000 than it was in 1985 because the percentage of persons under twenty-four will be smaller by one-half percent and the percentage in the most productive working years (ages twenty-five to sixty-four) will be larger by 19 percent.
6. Young adults entering the labor market may have an easier time obtaining employment than has been true in recent decades, because the size of this cohort will not be increasing rapidly as it has in the past twenty years (Howe 1988).

Racial/Ethnic Minority Population

Another major change taking place in the social structure involves the relative increase in the percentage of racial and ethnic minority groups. The largest of these groups include black Americans, Hispanics (Cuban, Mexican American, Puerto Rican, and others of Hispanic background), and Asian Americans (Chinese, Japanese, Vietnamese, and other subgroups). The Hispanic minority

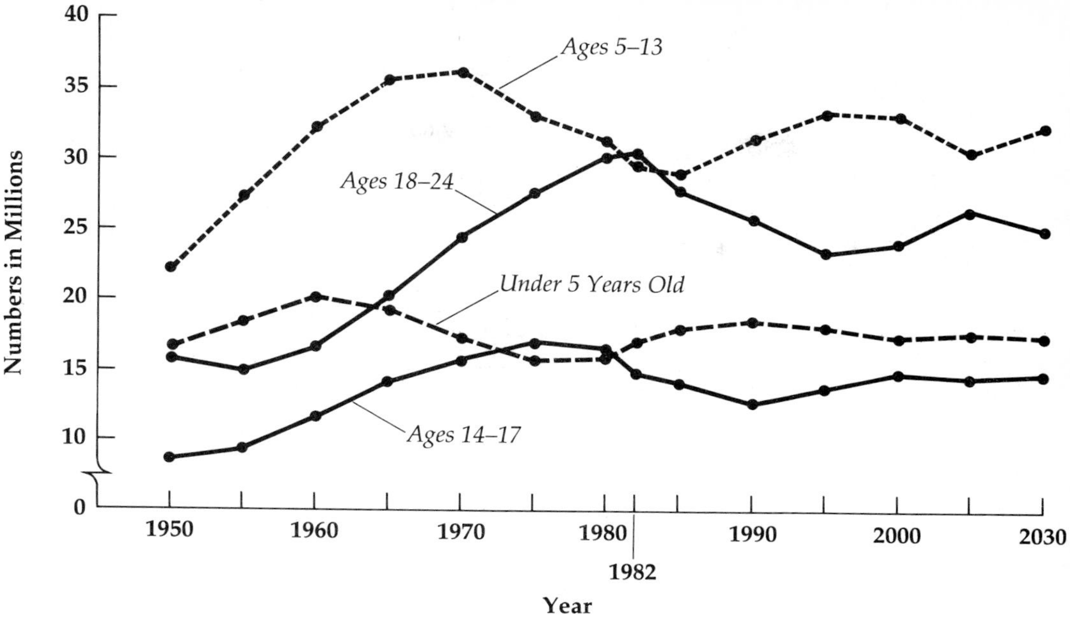

Data for 1950 to 1982 are estimates; data for 1983 to 2030 are midrange projections.

Figure 1.4 ***Estimates and Projections of the Population under Twenty-four Years of Age, 1950 to 2030, by Age Group*** (*Source:* U.S. Bureau of the Census, 1984.)

is growing more rapidly than is the black population and may become the largest U.S. minority group in the twenty-first century (see Chapter 10). The percentage of whites in the United States population is expected to decline from 85 percent in 1982 to 82 percent in 2010 to 77 percent in 2050. (Hispanics constitute an ethnic group whose members sometimes are classified as white or black, depending on their racial background.) The number of U.S. citizens in the "black and other races" classification is expected nearly to double between 1982 and 2030 (U.S. Bureau of the Census 1984).

The increase in the number and proportion of minority population in the United States is due primarily to relatively high fertility in some minority groups—particularly the Hispanic and black subgroups—and to in-migration of Asian, Hispanic, and other groups. Increase occurring due to relatively high fertility and to in-migration of families with young children means that minority students will constitute a rapidly increasing proportion of the school-age population in the future. For example, the percentage of births classified as "black and other race" increased from 14 percent in 1950 to 19 percent in 1982 and is expected to increase to about 25 percent by the year 2010 (U.S. Bureau of the Census 1984). Reflecting this trend, the percentage of non-Hispanic whites in public school enrollment declined from 80 percent in 1968 to 71 percent in 1984 and will decline still more in the future. During this period, the number of Hispanic students in public schools increased by 80 percent, enrollment of Asian students increased by 412 percent, and the number of native American (Indian) students increased by 105 percent (Orfield 1987). Just as the educational system was a main agency for the socioeconomic mobility of European immigrants from 1840 to 1915, it will be challenged to perform a similar function for minority children and youth who will constitute a substantial proportion of the school-age population during the remainder of this century and thereafter.

Poverty and Female-Headed Families

The percentage of U.S. citizens in poverty as defined by federal income guidelines declined substantially from 23 percent in 1959 to 12 percent in 1969, held steady at 12 to 13 percent throughout the 1970s, and then slightly increased during the recession years of the early 1980s to about 14 percent in 1983. The percentage of children and youth between six and seventeen years of age who were in poverty followed the trend of large decline in the 1960s, decreasing from 26 percent in 1959 to 14 percent in 1969 but then rose substantially to 20 percent in 1984—an increase of 43 percent from 1969 to 1984 in the poverty rate for persons in this age group.

As shown in Figure 1.5, the poverty rate for black and Hispanic children and youth has been and remains much higher than the rate for non-Hispanic whites. In 1984, the rate for Hispanics between six and seventeen years of age was more than 2.5 times higher than the rate for non-Hispanic whites, and the rate for blacks in this age group was nearly three times the white rate. However, because the white group is much larger, whites comprise nearly 50 percent of U.S. children and youth whose families live in poverty.

In addition to being disproportionately minority, children and youth in poverty are much more likely to live in female-headed families than are those in higher-income families: the average income of two-parent families is more than 2.5 times higher than that of female-headed families (Congressional Budget Office 1988). Conversely, 55 percent of the children and youth in female-headed families were living in poverty in 1983, as compared with only 13 percent of those in two-parent families.

Much of the increase in the percentage of children and youth in poverty after 1969 was associated with a simultaneous increase in the percentage of children in families headed by females, which almost doubled between 1969 and 1983 (see Figure 4.2). Sixty-nine percent of the increase in the number of children in poverty from 1970 through 1982 occurred in households headed by women (Preston 1984). The percentage of children in female-headed families who live in poverty increased from 6 percent in 1969 to 10 percent in 1983. During this same time period, the percentage of black children who live in female-headed families increased from 33 percent to 51 percent, and the percentage of low-income, minority families headed by females in urban poverty neighborhoods continued to increase. The confluence of all these trends has

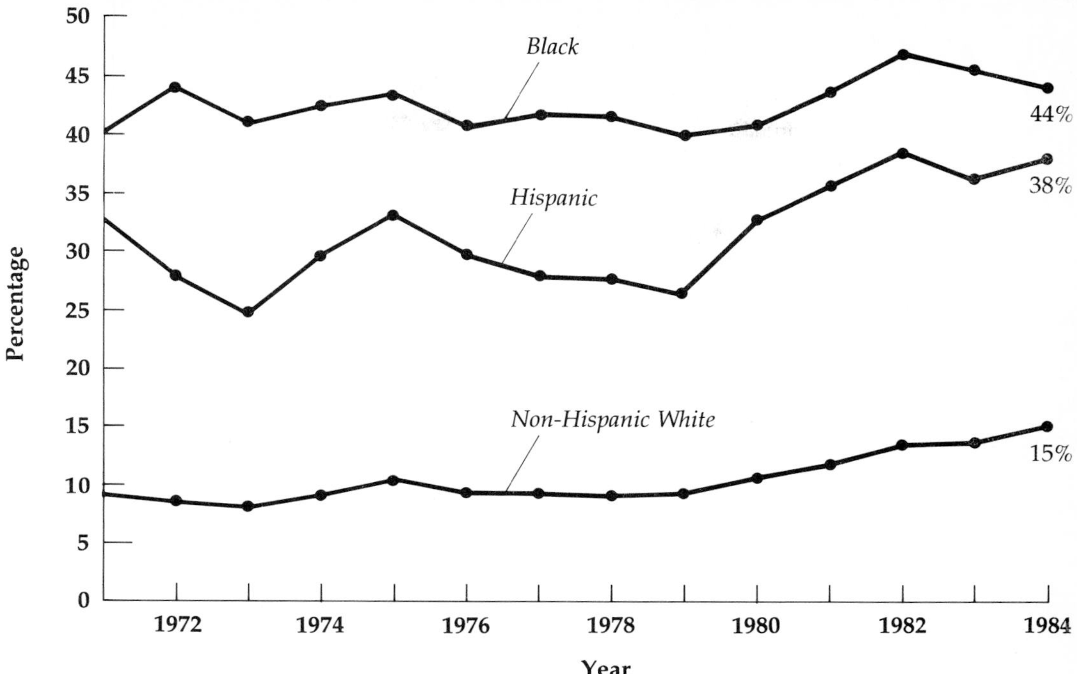

Figure 1.5 ***Percentage of Children and Youth Ages Six to Seventeen in Poverty, by Race and Ethnicity, 1959 to 1983*** (*Sources:* Koretz and Ventresca 1984; Select Committee 1986.)

produced a situation in which poverty among children and youth has become much more concentrated in urban neighborhoods inhabited by low-income, minority families without an adult male in the home.

Interaction of some of the trends described above is illustrated in Figure 1.6, which shows that 69 percent of children and youth under eighteen in female-headed, black families lived in poverty in 1983, as compared with only 12 percent of those in two-parent, white families. The most direct consequence for the public schools has been that the percentages of poverty students, minority students, and students from female-headed families in elementary and secondary enrollments generally have increased substantially. All these trends have been particularly pronounced in big-city school districts. Much of this book discusses the effects and implications of these trends.

Generational Conflict and Poverty? As noted, the percentage of children and youth in poverty increased greatly since 1969, while the percentage of poor persons in the population increased only slightly. One major reason for this discrepancy is that the percentage of the elderly (individuals more than sixty-five years old) who live in poverty decreased almost as rapidly from 1969 to

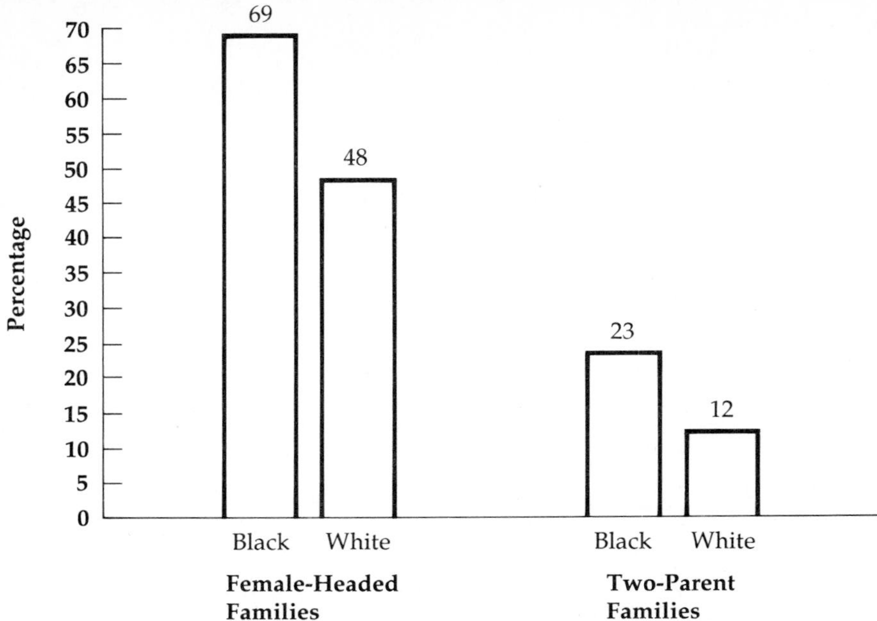

Figure 1.6 ***Percentage of Children under Eighteen Years of Age in Poverty, by Race and Family Type, 1983*** (*Source:* Adapted from Children's Defense Fund 1985.)

1984 as it had from 1959 to 1969. By 1984, only 12 percent of the elderly were living in poverty, compared with 36 percent in 1959 (Congressional Budget Office 1988).

Among the causes of this impressive decline in poverty among the elderly were the expanded functioning of federal Social Security and health-care programs, relaxation of retirement regulations, and general economic prosperity through much of this period. At the same time, state and federal budget deficits led to reductions in various programs for children, including nutrition and day-care services and financial support for low-income parents. By 1975, total per capita expenditures by government on the elderly were more than three times as great as per capita expenditures on children under age seventeen (Longman 1985). Between 1977 and 1983, the average net worth of persons over age sixty-five increased by 58 percent, while the net worth of persons seventeen to twenty-four years of age declined by 34 percent (Carlson 1987).

The coincidence of a large decline in poverty among the elderly and a large increase among children and youth has raised a number of important questions involving the social structure and political arrangements in postindustrial society. Longman (1985) has described shifts that have been occurring in postindustrial patterns involving the needs of differing generations:

> *The middle generation in any given era either must strike a prudent balance between the demands of its parents and the demands of its children or prepare itself*

> *for an unhappy retirement. . . . [If] the government spends so much on the elderly that it must skimp on the education of the young or an investment in economic growth, then . . . [the young later may be unable to provide] enough support. Alternatively, if the government is stingy with the elderly, the young may come to feel . . . free to shirk their responsibilities to the old.* (Longman 1985, 78)

After pointing out that the elderly in pre-industrial society frequently maintained some economic power and security by retaining title to land or other property, Longman pointed out that industrialization changed the balance of power between the generations: "Factory workers could . . . achieve a tolerable standard of living without first inheriting an estate. But, by the same token . . . most could not save enough out of their wages" to provide for their own old age. For this reason, economic arrangements shifted so that each generation could tax its own children through such programs as Social Security and Medicare. As in earlier periods, however, each generation thus "appears simply to appropriate by law some share of the next generation's wealth." However, this arrangement cannot succeed unless each generation also provides the resources to ensure the future economic productivity of its children. "Each generation, in exchange for support in its old age, still must provide its children with a legacy" (Longman 1985, 81).

Preston (1984) also reviewed recent data on poverty differentials between generations and called attention to underlying economic and social forces that function to generate relatively more poverty among the young. The elderly, he pointed out, have increased their relative political influence as the percentage of older persons in the population has increased and as persons under age sixty-five realize that they will benefit later from programs designed to assist the elderly. Children and youth, on the other hand, cannot vote and must depend on the political influence of parents acting on behalf of their progeny. However, Preston also argued, the conjugal family

> *has begun to divest itself of its responsibility for the young, just as it earlier abandoned much of its responsibility for the elderly. Absent fathers are the main factor in this divestiture. . . . It is unrealistic simply to wish away the possibility that there is direct competition between the young and old for society's resources. . . . U.S. society has chosen to place almost exclusive responsibility for the care of children and youth on the nuclear family. Marital instability, however, has much reduced the capacity of the family to care for its own children. Hence insisting that families alone care for the young would seem to be an evasion of collective responsibility.* (Preston 1984, 46, 49)

Preston and other authors (e.g., Hodgkinson 1986) have also pointed out that increase in the proportion of minority groups among children and youth in general and low-income youngsters in particular may reduce the likelihood that the majority white adult population will be willing to assume and discharge its collective responsibility for the welfare of the young. The problem may be particularly acute because, as we point out in many parts of this book, a high and apparently increasing proportion of low-income children and youth are now concentrated in big-city poverty neighborhoods and schools characterized by massive social disorganization and very low academic achievement; and given the continuation of current patterns, many of these youngsters will not be in a position to contribute productively to the welfare of subsequent generations.

In addition, the increasing difficulty young adults experience entering the housing market and attaining a college degree without extensive parental support also has implications for generational equity. Robert Kuttner has summarized these implications:

> *The biggest imperative is the restoration of some measure of economic opportunity to those without family wealth. America has indeed been a land where people from humble origins can find economic success. If it becomes instead a land of patrimony, where the social class of the parents dictates the economic prospects of the children, it will cease to have any special moral claim. (Kuttner 1987, 21)*

Conclusion

After describing the social-class hierarchy and the occupational structure of post-industrial society in the United States, this chapter identified several major trends that have important implications for the educational system. Trends discussed included a growing emphasis on high technology, the increasing average age of the population, increase in the percentage of minority groups in schools and society, and growth in the proportion of children and youth in poverty.

The confluence of these trends is likely to generate enormous problems and challenges for the educational system in the future. At the same time that education is becoming a more decisive factor in determining the success of individuals and social groups (see Chapter 7), an increasing proportion of students are disadvantaged by their socioeconomic and/or racial/ethnic background. Also, commitment to providing children and youth with a good start in life may be declining as the adult population grows older and less similar demographically to subsequent generations. The full extent and nature of these problems and challenges are reviewed and analyzed in the following chapters.

EXERCISES

1. A person's social position as measured by socioeconomic indices (occupation, income, level of education, etc.) does not always coincide with social position as evaluated by the people in the community. (For example: a poor, but upper-class woman; or a wealthy, but lower-class businessman.) Have you

known such a person? What does that case illustrate about the bases of rank in the community?

2. Obtain a map of your community. Interview a few people and ask them to point out the areas that are best, average, and worst neighborhoods. (One of the best persons to interview will be a real estate agent.) How much agreement do you find among your informants? On what kinds of factors are their judgments made?
3. Select an elementary school in your community and make an informal investigation of the community from which it draws its pupils. Walk up and down the streets of the neighborhood, observing the houses, lawns, alleys; look at the names on doorbells; go into the stores and notice what kinds of food, clothing, and other goods are sold; and so on. From what social classes would you say the school draws? How heterogeneous is the neighborhood?
4. Think about the community in which you grew up. (If it was a large city, interpret this to mean your neighborhood.) Write a description of that community in terms of its social-class structure. How many social classes were there? Were class lines clearly drawn? What kinds of people occupied positions of highest and lowest status? Does it make sense to think of your community as a system of social classes? Why or why not?
5. Read *The New Class?* edited by B. Bruce-Briggs, and outline the main points in a debate between an advocate and an opponent of the conclusion that a new class of intellectuals is distinguishable within a modern society.
6. In a school to which you have access, make a list of the children in a given classroom. Estimate their socioeconomic positions. Compare these positions with such things as their school grades, their extracurricular activities, and their vocational goals.

SUGGESTIONS FOR FURTHER READING

1. There are a number of studies of social structure in various United States communities. The first and most elaborate was of a New England community, reported in a series of volumes called the Yankee City Series. Volume I of the series, *The Social Life of a Modern Community,** by W. Lloyd Warner and Paul S. Lunt, is the most appropriate for students of education. A midwestern community is reported in *Democracy in Jonesville,* by W. Lloyd Warner and associates. A small agricultural town in a border state is described in *Plainville, U.S.A.* by James West; the same community studied again is described by Gallaher in *Plainville Fifteen Years Later.* The social structure of the San Francisco peninsula is described in Hodges, *Peninsula People.* For a discussion of the social-class structure in the United States at large (rather than a study of a particular community), read *American Life: Dream and Reality,* by W. Lloyd Warner. The most comprehensive study of the social structure of a large city

* For each of these references, see Bibliography for facts of publication.

(Kansas City) is reported in *Social Status in the City* by Coleman and Neugarten. Chapter 12 in that book summarizes studies of social-class structure in eight different communities.

2. The methods of investigating and measuring social status are described in *Social Class in America*, by W. Lloyd Warner, Marchia Meeker, and Kenneth Eells; *Social Status in the City*, by Richard Coleman and Bernice Neugarten; and Chapters 1 and 2 in Kahl's book, *The American Class Structure*. Also, *Class, Status and Power: A Reader in Social Stratification* edited by Bendix and Lipset is a good reference for the student who wishes to explore further the theoretical issues of social structure, or to study different theories of stratification.
3. A number of books analyze value patterns and life-styles of particular social classes. For example, C. Wright Mills's book, *White Collar*, is a penetrating analysis of the American middle class. Spectorsky's *The Exurbanites* describes the lives of upper-middle-class suburbanites. Chinoy's *Automobile Workers and the American Dream*; Walker and Guest's *The Man on the Assembly Line*; and Rainwater, Coleman, and Handel's *Workingman's Wife* are all interesting studies of the working class, as is *Whitetown* by Binzen. *Blue-Collar World*, edited by Shostak and Gomberg, reports research findings on working-class life prepared by various authors. Baltzell's *Philadelphia Gentlemen* deals with a national upper class. *Social Standing in America*, by Coleman and Rainwater, reports on perceptions of social class in Boston and Kansas City.
4. Religious groups function as subcultures in U.S. society. A book by Lenski comparing Protestants, Catholics, and Jews in Detroit shows that different religious subcultures exist within a given social class. Also, Rossi and Rossi have studied the effects of a parochial school system on the attitudes and beliefs of Catholics. Gordon's *Assimilation in American Life* deals with religious as well as ethnic factors. Greeley's book, *Religion and Career*, is a study of differences between Catholics, Protestants, and Jews in a large sample of college graduates.
5. The heterogeneity of suburban life is described in Dobriner's *Class in Suburbia*. Berger's book, *Working Class Suburb*, describes a relatively homogenous blue-collar suburb. *The Levittowners* by Gans reports on the public schools in a Philadelphia suburb.
6. The effect of the social-class structure on education is treated at length in *Elmtown's Youth* by August B. Hollingshead; in *Children of Brasstown* by Celia B. Stendler; in *Social-Class Influences upon Learning* by Allison Davis; and in *Growing Up in River City* by Robert J. Havighurst and colleagues. For a somewhat different perspective on the role of the school in relation to the social and economic structure of the society, see the book by Kimball and McClellan, *Education and the New America*.
7. Numerous authors have described the street culture in various racial and ethnic groups. *Street-Corner Society* by William F. Whyte describes this culture in an Italian community, and *Down These Mean Streets* by Piri Thomas describes it in a Puerto Rican community. *The Social Order of the Slum* by Suttles contrasts several Chicago communities with respect to the operation of a street culture and other, related manifestations of social behavior in low-

status neighborhoods. *Strategic Styles: Coping in the Inner City,* by Janet Mancini, describes five differing coping styles among inner-city youth.

8. One of the best discussions of the dual labor market can be found in *Internal Labor Markets and Manpower Analysis* by Peter Doeringer and Michael J. Piore. An excellent summary on this and related topics is available in A. Dale Tussing's 1975 article in *Intellect* magazine.

Appendix *Twelve Social Groups Subdivided into Forty Community or Neighborhood Life-Style Subgroups (Claritas Company PRIZM Cluster System for Market Segmentation and Targeting)*

Social Group	Subgroup Nickname	Modal Location*	Modal Education Level**	Modal Employment Classification***	Modal Adult Age Groups****
1. Educated, affluent executives & professionals in elite metro suburbs	1. Blue Blood Estates	Subs	CG	WC	4/3
	2. Money & Brains	Subs	CG	WC	4/5
	3. Furs & Station Wagons	Subs	CG	WC	3/4
2. Pre & postchild families & singles in upscale, white-collar suburbs	1. Pools & Patios	Subs	CG	WC	5/4
	2. Two More Rungs	Subs	CG	WC	6/5
	3. Young Influentials	Subs	CG	WC	1/2
3. Upper-middle, child-raising families in outlying, owner-occupied suburbs	1. Young Suburbia	Subs	CG	WC	3/2
	2. Blue-Chip Blues	Subs	BW	BW	3/2
4. Educated, white-collar singles & couples in upscale, urban areas	1. Urban Gold Coast	City	CG	WC	2/6
	2. Bohemian Mix	City	CG	WC	2/1
	3. Black Enterprise	City	SC	WC	3/4
	4. New Beginnings	City	SC	WC	2/1
5. Educated, young, mobile families in exurban satellites & boom towns	1. God's Country	Town	CG	WC	3/2
	2. New Homesteaders	Town	SC	BW	1/2
	3. Towns & Gowns	Town	CG	WC	1/2
6. Middle-class, postchild families in aging suburbs & retirement areas	1. Levittown, U.S.A.	Subs	HS	WC	5/6
	2. Gray Power	Subs	SC	WC	6/5
	3. Rank & File	Subs	HS	BC	5/6

7. Mid-scale, child-raising, blue-collar families in remote suburbs & towns	1. Blue-Collar Nursery	Town	HS	BC	3/2
	2. Middle America	Town	HS	BC	5/4
	3. Coalburg & Corntown	Town	HS	BC	6/3
8. Mid-scale families, singles & elders in dense, urban row & hi-rise areas	1. New Melting Pot	City	NC	WC	6/5
	2. Old Yankee Rows	City	HS	BW	6/5
	3. Emergent Minorities	City	SH	BS	1/2
	4. Single City Blues	City	SC	BW	1/2
9. Rural towns & villages amidst farms & ranches across agrarian mid-America	1. Shotguns & Pickups	Town	HS	BF	3/4
	2. Agri-Business	Farm	NC	BF	6/5
	3. Grain Belt	Farm	HS	BF	6/5
10. Mixed gentry & blue-collar labor in low-mid rustic, mill & factory towns	1. Golden Ponds	Town	NC	BW	6/5
	2. Mines & Mills	Town	HS	BC	5/4
	3. Norma Rae-Ville	Town	SH	BC	1/4
	4. Smalltown Downtown	Town	HS	BW	6/1
11. Landowners, migrants & rustics in poor rural towns, farms & uplands	1. Back-Country Folks	Town	SH	BC	6/3
	2. Share Croppers	Town	GS	BF	6/5
	3. Tobacco Roads	Town	GS	BF	6/5
	4. Hard Scrabble	Farm	GS	BF	6/5
12. Mixed, unskilled service & labor in aging, urban row & hi-rise areas	1. Heavy Industry	City	SH	BC	6/5
	2. Downtown Dixie-Style	City	SH	BS	1/6
	3. Hispanic Mix	City	GS	BC	1/2
	4. Public Assistance	City	GS	BS	1/6

* City = dense, urban row or high-rise; Subs = suburban or urban-fringe residential; Town = outlying towns or satellite suburbs; Farm = farms, ranches, or other rural.

** CG = college grad and above; SC = some college; HS = high school grad; SH = some high school; GS = grade school; NC = not classified.

*** WC = white collar; BC = blue collar; BW = mixed white and blue collar; BS = blue collar and service; BF = blue collar and farm.

**** 1 = 18–24; 2 = 25–34; 3 = 35–44; 4 = 45–54; 5 = 55–64; 6 = 65+

Source: Adapted from "PRIZM the 40 Cluster System." Reprinted with permission of Claritas, Alexandria, Virginia.

2

Educational Selecting and Sorting in Postindustrial, Metropolitan Society

Since the landing of the Pilgrims in Massachusetts more than 350 years ago, the United States has been perceived as a land of opportunity. During the eighteenth and nineteenth centuries, good land could be obtained at low prices and jobs were available in the expanding economy. New cities were being built and new industries were being established. Since 1900, the areas of economic opportunity have shifted to expanding industry and to the expanding professional, managerial, technical, and service professions. These postindustrial occupations generally require postsecondary education. The professions all require at least a college degree, and executive positions in business and industry are awarded more and more to college graduates.

Sorting and Selecting in the Educational System

Realizing that an avenue of opportunity is provided by the educational system, parents have encouraged their children to continue further and further in school. Since 1910 the proportion of young people attending high school has more than tripled, and the proportion attending college has multiplied by seven. Table 2.1 shows the increase in high school and college attendance since 1910.

Amount of education is a good indicator of socioeconomic status, from lower-working class up through upper-middle class, because education leads to economic opportunity. Young people, through education, secure higher-status jobs than their fathers. With greater incomes, young adults from lower-status families tend to associate with persons of higher status and adopt their ways. It may be concluded, consequently, that education provides a channel not only to better socioeconomic status, but also to social mobility in the broader sense.

These statements are so widely accepted that few people, even those most critical of the educational establishment, disagree with them. Research on amount of schooling in relation to success in adult life (Levin, Guthrie, Kleindorfer, and Stout 1971) affirms the view that amount of education (not school marks) is linked with later success. These authors conclude their report by saying, "The evidence is overwhelming in support of the proposition that the post-school opportunity and performance of a pupil are related directly to his educational attainment" (p. 14). In 1985, for example, the average college graduate earned nearly twice as much as the average high school dropout (Cohany 1986).

The American educational system is expected to provide opportunity for social and economic mobility by selecting and training the most able and industrious youth for higher-status positions in society. Insofar as the school sys-

Table 2.1 *Change in the American Education System As a Selecting Agency*

Educational Level Reached	Number (per thousand)					
	1910	*1938*	*1960*	*1970*	*1980*	*1983*
First year high school (age 14)	310	800	908	959	994	996
Third year high school (age 16)	160	580	746	860	886	900
Graduation from high school (age 18)	93	450	621	750	744	760
Entrance to college or a similar educational institution	67	150	328	461	463	475
Graduation from college (Bachelor's degree)	22	70	170	227	348	356
Master's degree	1.5	9	34	61	90	95
Doctor of Philosophy degree	0.2	1.3	4.7	11	15	16

Sources: U.S. Department of Education 1982, 1985–86; authors' estimates.

tem does this job efficiently and fairly, it equips youth for career opportunities and it contributes to the success of democracy.

The degree of selection can be observed in Table 2.1, which shows the number of students per thousand born in a given year who reach various levels of the educational ladder. It will be seen that the high school is much less selective than it was 40 to 50 years ago; and the college, too, while still selective, is less so than before. This pattern reflects the fact that the focus of selection in the social structure has shifted somewhat from the high school to college. That is, a main prerequisite for obtaining a relatively high-status job used to be possession of a high-school diploma, but many jobs now require completion of two or more years beyond high school.

The process of selection is not carried on in a formal sense by the school alone. Several factors determine how far a student goes in school: the parents' wishes, the individual's aspirations and ability, the financial status of the family, as well as the school's effects in encouraging some students and discouraging others. The end result, however, is selection.

Intellectual Ability

As mentioned, one goal of the educational system is to select and carry along the most able young people. The extent to which the system succeeds in this regard can be assessed in part by examining data on relationships between students' performance and their continuing participation in the system. Data of this kind are provided in Table 2.2, which indicates that high school seniors high in test performance are much more likely to attend college than are those low in test performance. (Test performance is an indirect, though, of course,

Table 2.2 ***Percentages of 1972 High School Graduates Who Entered and Graduated from College, by Socioeconomic Status (SES) and Test Performance***

Socioeconomic Status (SES) Level	Percentage Entered in College Test Performance				Percentage Graduated from College in 1976 Test Performance			
	Lowest 25%	*Middle 50%*	*Highest 25%*	*Total*	*Lowest 25%*	*Middle 50%*	*Highest 25%*	*Total*
Lowest 25%	21	33	63	30	02	05	20	05
Middle 50%	23	47	73	47	02	10	27	12
Highest 25%	46	76	93	82	03	18	47	31
Total	24	50	81	51	02	10	35	15

Percentage of lowest socioeconomic group in highest test performance level	11
Percentage of middle socioeconomic group in highest test performance level	25
Percentage of highest socioeconomic group in highest test performance level	50

Note: College attendance refers to entry in an academic program in 1972. College graduation refers to acquisition of a bachelor's degree four years later. Test performance is measured by a composite reading and mathematics score. Socioeconomic status scores are a composite of father's and mother's education, father's occupation, parental income, and types of items in the home. Data were collected as part of the National Longitudinal Study of the High School Class of 1972.

Source: Computed and adapted from Bruce E. Eckland, Louis B. Henderson, and Andrew J. Kolstad 1981.

imperfect measure of intellectual ability.) Only 19 percent of students in the highest quartile on test performance did not attend college.

However, data on college completion indicate that many students high in test performance do not complete college. As shown in Table 2.2, only 35 percent of 1972 seniors in the highest quartile on test performance graduated from college four years later. Although this figure should be interpreted cautiously because many college students graduate after the fourth year and because college graduation rates have improved in the 1980s, many high-achieving students undoubtedly do not graduate due to lack of financial support, poor motivation, personal problems, or other causes. Dropout from college is particularly a problem for high-achieving students in the bottom quarter on social class, of whom only 20 percent graduated in four years. Thus, it appears that the educational system has substantial room for improvement in facilitating the progress of high-achieving students.

As one might expect, available data show that high-achieving high school students are much more likely to participate in college preparatory programs than are low-achieving students. Thus, the federal government's national study of high-school sophomores in 1980 showed that students in the academic track had an average score of 9.32 on a test of reading achievement, compared with 6.05 for students in the general track and 5.14 for students in vocational programs (National Center for Education Statistics 1985, 56).

Ability Grouping and Tracking

Sorting and selecting for further success in the educational system take place in part through ability grouping and tracking. At both the elementary and secondary levels, many schools use ability grouping (or homogeneous grouping) in attempting to facilitate teaching and learning (Passow 1988). Students with high academic performance are placed in a class of high achievers or in a subgroup of high achievers within the classroom; those with low performance are placed in low-achieving classes or subgroups; and those in between are placed in average groups. In many schools, the high, average, and low levels are further subdivided according to previous achievement.

Tracking refers to the practice in high schools of enrolling students in college preparatory classes (usually high-achieving students), or general, business, or vocational tracks for lower achievers or students not intending to go to college or preferring to pursue less academic subjects. (The general curriculum usually includes little mathematics and no advanced science or foreign language courses.)

Ability grouping or tracking in schools enrolling a socially diverse population tends to be correlated with social class and racial/ethnic status. Partly because economically and socially disadvantaged students have lower average achievement scores than do middle-class students and nonminority students (documented later in this chapter), they are found disproportionately in low-achieving classes and nonacademic tracks, while middle-class students are disproportionately represented in higher-achieving classes and college preparatory courses and tracks. In addition, social class has an independent effect on track placement beyond its association with achievement. In 1982, 80 percent of high-achieving seniors high in socioeconomic status were in an academic track, compared with only 52 percent of seniors who were high in achievement but low in status (Vanfossen, Jones, and Spade 1987).

The pattern of grouping varies from community to community and school to school. In some schools, ability groups are formed only in particular subject-matter areas, as when those children in a grade who are poor in reading, or those who are particularly good in science, are given special instruction as a group. In such schools, the child may spend only one period a day with a special group; the rest of the time, with his or her regular group. This modification of homogeneous grouping tends to counteract the possible social-class biases that may otherwise operate.

To take another example, schools in homogeneous parts of a large city, where the school population is drawn from one or two social classes, may use a scheme of sectioning by ability that brings together those children with the most motivation for education. The children who consistently work hard often seem to teachers to be the abler ones and will tend to be grouped together.

Ability grouping has been severely criticized since about 1965 on the basis of the double-barrelled argument that (1) the ability tests as they now exist tend to favor middle-class children and (2) the tests now in use tend to segregate students by social class and by race. In some places, ability grouping has been ruled illegal by the courts, and school boards in some of the larger cities have abandoned or reduced the extent of ability grouping. This trend became widespread after the Supreme Court's 1967 ruling in *Hobson* v. *Hansen*, which stated that separation of Washington, D.C., students into fast and slow tracks resulted in unconstitutional segregation of minority and nonminority students. After 1967, the courts and the federal government frequently required desegragating school districts to reduce or eliminate grouping of students based on ability test scores, previous achievement, or other measures that might reflect a student's disadvantaged background rather than his or her true academic potential.

Although ability grouping usually has been introduced in order to facilitate teaching and learning, much research indicates that it generally has not improved student achievement. Reviews of research on this topic have most often concluded that ability grouping has little or no consistent effect (Good and Marshall 1984). Some studies, however, indicate that homogeneous grouping promotes better performance among high achievers (Kulik and Kulik 1987) and/or further depresses the performance of low achieving students (Dar and Resh 1986; Sørensen and Hallinan 1986). Instances in which ability grouping appears to be harmful to the performance of low achievers are thought to occur because teachers have low expectations for students and thus pace instruction at a very slow rate (Gamoran 1986a), because students are stigmatized and thus not motivated by being placed in slow classes or groups, and also because low achievers frequently reinforce each other's negative attitudes and behaviors.

Detrimental phenomena associated with ability grouping and tracking have been documented by Jeannie Oakes in a study of the school experiences of students in more than 1,000 classrooms. Using data collected as part of A Study of Schooling in thirty-eight nationally representative districts including both elementary and secondary schools, Oakes found that students in high-ability classes generally had more challenging instruction than did those in low-ability classes, which tended to emphasize "simple memory tasks" and literal comprehension. Oakes concluded that the rudimentary curriculum content in low-ability classes "was such that it would be likely to lock students into that track level . . . [by omitting topics] that constitute prerequisite knowledge and skills for access to classes in . . . higher track levels" (Oakes 1985, 77–78).

Oakes also found that students in high-ability classes were significantly more "involved" in their learning than were those in low-ability classes. The latter students, she concluded, "reported that they were far less concerned about completing classroom tasks . . . [and] also reported far greater degrees of apathy—not caring about what goes on in class or even concerned about failing" (Oakes 1985, 130). One of her overall conclusions was that given the correlation between economically and socially disadvantaged background on the one hand and low-track placement on the other, ability grouping and tracking frequently constitute "in-school barriers to upward mobility for capable poor and minority students. . . . [Once placed in low-level classes, their] achievement seems to be further inhibited by the type of knowledge they are exposed to and the quality of learning opportunities they are afforded" (Oakes 1985, 134).

Ability grouping and tracking thus frequently seem to reinforce the low performance of disadvantaged students as part of the educational system's general arrangements for sorting and selecting meritorious students who are likely to be successful at the next level. Tracking at the high-school level also operates to depress further low-status students' self-esteem, contact with highly motivated peers, participation in extracurricular activities, and subsequent enrollment in postsecondary education (Vanfossen, Jones, and Spade 1987). Therefore, what begins as an attempt to ensure that instruction is appropriate for students given their previous performance (Nevi 1987) may be harmful for low achievers who might achieve more in heterogeneous classes with more challenging instruction.

This problem in the sorting and selecting process raises a number of complicated and difficult questions for which there are no simple answers. For example, how can the pace of instruction in heterogeneous classes be maintained at a level that challenges high achievers without frustrating low achievers? How might instruction in low-ability classes be improved to avoid the detrimental effects frequently associated with homogeneous grouping of low achievers? How can high expectations be maintained in low-level classes so that grouping and tracking function to provide remediation and special assistance for selected students rather than increasing the gap between high and low achievers? We return to these types of questions elsewhere in this book, particularly in Chapters 8 and 13.

Reading Achievement

Because reading is important to success in most academic fields, reading achievement probably is the best single measure of academic achievement in general. Data on the reading performance of students nine, thirteen, and seventeen years of age have been collected periodically since 1971 by the National Assessment of Education Progress (NAEP). The NAEP uses a sophisticated sampling design and advanced technical methods to obtain estimates of reading proficiency that allow comparison of performance over time and among subgroups in the national population. Reading proficiency is categorized according to the following scores and definitions (NAEP 1985):

150: *Rudimentary.* Readers can follow brief written directions. They can also select words, phrases, or sentences to describe a simple picture and can interpret simple written clues to identify a common object.

200: *Basic.* Readers can locate and identify facts from simple informational paragraphs, stories, and news articles and can combine ideas and make inferences based on short, uncomplicated passages.

250: *Intermediate.* Readers can search for, locate, and organize information in relatively lengthy passages and can recognize paraphrases of what they have read.

300: *Adept.* Readers can understand complicated literary and informational passages and can analyze and integrate less familiar material.

350: *Advanced.* Readers can extend and restructure the ideas presented in specialized and complex texts.

The NAEP data in Figure 2.1 portray large differences in the reading proficiency of students according to their level of socioeconomic status. (Most NAEP reports have used parental education to represent social class background.) At nine years of age, students whose parent(s) did not complete high school have an average proficiency score of 197 (basic level), compared with an average of 224 (halfway between basic and intermediate) for nine-year-olds whose parent(s) had postsecondary education. Similar differences in reading proficiency by socioeconomic status (SES) are apparent for thirteen-year-olds and seventeen-year-olds. The average reading proficiency of seventeen-year-olds whose parent(s) did not complete high school is only 270 (between intermediate and adept), which places them at about the same level as high SES thirteen-year-olds. Because 270 is far below the 300 level at which readers are described as being able to "understand complicated literary and informational passages," average seventeen-year-olds from low SES families presumably would experience many problems if they sought to obtain additional education after high school.

However, the patterns shown in Figure 2.1 underestimate differences in reading performance by SES because the parental education categories are crude indicators of social class that do not consider such factors as occupational status and income, neighborhood location, correlations between social class and race-ethnicity, and disadvantages associated with underclass status. To obtain a more refined understanding of differences related to social class and other variables, NAEP data can be analyzed in more detail, taking more account of the characteristics of students and schools included in the national sample. The results of such an analysis are shown in Table 2.3, which presents data on the 1984 reading proficiency scores of thirteen-year-old students in public schools.

As shown in Table 2.3, the average reading proficiency score of students who attend schools with more than 60 percent poverty and minority enrollment in so-called disadvantaged urban areas (defined by the NAEP as having a population greater than 200,000 and a high proportion of residents on welfare or unemployed) and whose parent(s) did not continue with education beyond high school is 229. (*Poverty* is defined in this analysis as eligibility for federal lunch subsidy.) Students who live in the same type of community and whose parents have the same education level but who attend schools with enrollment less heavily poverty and minority have an average of 260. Students whose parent(s) attended college and who live in advantaged urban communities (more than 200,000 people but low on welfare and unemployment) have an average score of 233 if they attend heavily poverty/minority schools and an average of 278 if their schools are relatively low in poverty/minority enrollment.

It should be noted that the average reading proficiency scores of thirteen-year-olds in public schools with enrollment more than 60 percent poverty and minority (scores of 229 and 233 in disadvantaged and advantaged urban areas, respectively) are only slightly higher than the 224 average the NAEP reported for all nine-year-olds whose parents had acquired some education beyond high

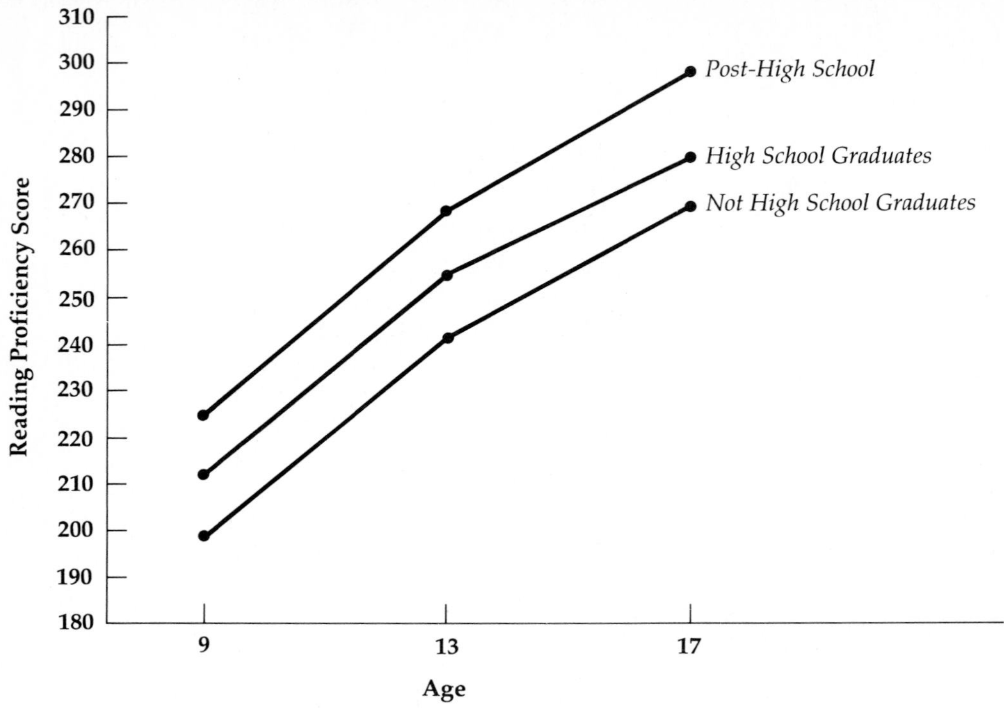

Figure 2.1 ***Reading Proficiency Scores of Nine-, Thirteen-, and Seventeen-Year-Olds, by Parental Level of Education, 1984*** (*Source:* National Assessment of Educational Progress [NAEP] 1985.)

Table 2.3 ***Reading Proficiency Scores for Public School 13-Year-Olds, by Type of Community, Parent Education, and School Percentage of Poverty/Minority Students, 1984***

Disadvantaged Urban Community		Advantaged Urban Community	
Parent(s) Graduated from High School or Less		Parent(s) Some College or More	
School Percentage Poverty/Minority		School Percentage Poverty/Minority	
More than 60	229	More than 60	233
Less than 60	260	Less than 60	278

Note: Disadvantaged urban refers to communities with a population greater than 200,000 and a relatively high proportion of residents on welfare or unemployed. *Advantaged urban* refers to communities above 200,000 with lower percentages of residents on welfare or unemployed. *Poverty* is defined as eligibility for federal lunch subsidy. Minority students in this analysis are black or Hispanic.

Source: Analysis using data tape available from the National Assessment of Educational Progress.

school (National Assessment of Educational Progress 1985). Conversely, the 278 registered by thirteen-year-olds whose parents had at least some college education and who attended schools relatively low in poverty/minority enrollment in advantaged urban communities is approximately the same as that for seventeen-year-olds whose parents did not attend college.

In addition, the scores for the thirteen-year-olds in heavily poverty/minority schools are considerably below the "intermediate" level of 250, which the NAEP defines as characterizing readers who can "search for, locate, and organize the information they find in relatively lengthy passages." The standard deviation of NAEP reading scores is approximately 35. This means that only about 10 percent of urban thirteen-year-olds attending disadvantaged urban schools with heavily poverty/minority enrollment have scores as high as the average student in advantaged urban schools with lower minority/poverty enrollment, and only about 10 percent of thirteen-year-olds in advantaged urban schools relatively low in poverty/minority enrollment have scores below the average student in disadvantaged urban schools with high poverty/minority enrollment. There thus is little overlap between the two groups, and a large proportion of urban students attending public schools high in poverty/minority enrollment are not acquiring reading skills adequate to learn well in high school.

Researchers at the NAEP also have carried out analyses comparing the performance of students at different time periods and on various background measures other than SES and race/ethnicity. Among the important conclusions from these studies have been the following:

1. Reading proficiency scores for nine- and thirteen-year-olds improved between 1971 and 1980, and scores for seventeen-year-olds improved between 1980 and 1984. Although reading performance is not deteriorating, the upward trends for earlier cohorts of students have not continued in the 1980s.
2. Nine-year-olds whose parents did not finish high school gained relative to other students between 1971 and 1984, but for thirteen- and seventeen-year-olds in this SES group, reading scores were about as far below other students in 1984 as they had been in 1971.

Given that students in schools high in poverty/minority enrollment constitute an appreciable proportion of the high school population, it is not surprising to learn that average reading performance levels of high-school seniors are cause for concern regarding national needs for an increasingly better educated and more highly skilled citizenry. Archie Lapointe, director of the NAEP, called attention to this problem when he reported that only about 40 percent of high school seniors are "comfortable" with academic track textbooks and "relatively sophisticated magazines," that the "bulk of our population seems stuck at the three lowest levels of reading skill achievement," and that the majority of students do not write "adequate responses to the informative, persuasive, or imaginative tasks included in the assessment" (Lapointe 1987, 76–77).

Other data collected by the NAEP have examined literacy and other skills among young adults age twenty-one to twenty-five years. Among the findings are that less than half of young adults whose parents did not graduate from high school and only 53 percent of black young adults had reading proficiency scores above the national average for eighth graders in 1985 (Kirsch and Jungeblüt 1986). Richard Venezky, Carl Kaestle, and Andres Sum (1987) reviewed these data for the Educational Testing Service and concluded not only that the "literacy skill levels found in the NAEP survey are not adequate, on average, for maintaining world leadership in a changing, technological society," but also that the poor performance of many black and Hispanic high school graduates who did not go to college should be viewed as a "major national concern by educators and economic policymakers" (pp. 7, 35). These authors also extracted NAEP data demonstrating that among young adults who did not attend postsecondary schools, those with high literacy scores had much higher income and much lower unemployment than did those with low literacy scores.

It also should be noted that NAEP data agree with other sources of information. Data collected by the College Board using the Degrees of Reading Power (DRP) Test indicate that less than 33 percent of high school seniors can fully comprehend front-page and editorial material in newspapers (Burrill 1987), and that students disadvantaged by poverty or race/ethnicity have much lower performance levels on the DRP than do more advantaged students (Cooper 1986).

Mathematics Achievement

The situation with respect to mathematics achievement in U.S. schools is similar to that for reading achievement. As portrayed and reported in the second international study of mathematics (Crosswhite et al. 1985; McKnight et al. 1987), students in the United States perform at an acceptable level as long as the curriculum narrowly emphasizes arithmetic and relatively mechanical skills through the eighth grade, but compared to students in other industrial countries, they perform poorly with respect to higher-order mathematics skills at the senior-high level. Analyses of the data for U.S. students (McKnight et al. 1987) indicated that reasons for this low performance included a "fragmented" curriculum combined with slow-paced, "low intensity" instruction, and that the United States had become a "nation of underachievers" as regards achievement in mathematics (Rothman 1987a).

As in the case of reading achievement, math achievement is highly correlated with socioeconomic status and racial-ethnic group membership. For example, NAEP data collected in 1981 showed that the average seventeen-year-old in disadvantaged urban areas correctly answered only 48 percent of the items on the mathematics test, compared with an average score of 60 percent for the average seventeen-year-old in the nation as a whole (Congressional Budget Office 1986).

As regards race/ethnicity, black students correctly answered only 24 percent of the math basic-skills items administered in 1982 to graduating seniors in the High School and Beyond Study, and Hispanic students responded correctly on only 25 percent, compared with a score of 50 percent for non-Hispanic whites

(Plisko and Stern 1985). The discrepancy with respect to higher-order skills in math problem solving was even greater: non-Hispanic whites scored 35 percent, blacks scored 16 percent, and Hispanic students scored 18 percent.* (Also see Table 10.4 for NAEP math data by race/ethnicity.)

In addition, fewer female students than male students score very high in mathematics achievement in the United States. (See Chapter 11.) After reviewing this discrepancy as well as the data indicating that Japanese and Chinese high-school students perform much higher in mathematics than do U.S. students, Steen (1987) concluded that, except for Asian students, advanced mathematics achievement in the United States is "primarily part of white, middle-class male culture, readily available only to those who have the nourishment, solitude, and luxury to spend time in concentrated thought." Steen also concluded that the "practice of tracking students . . . introduces substantial variation in their opportunity to learn and magnifies the range of achievement from grade to grade," and that overcoming our international competitive disadvantage in mathematics education will require an "extraordinary redirection of energy by the American political and economic systems" (pp. 251–252).

Dropout from High School

Due in part to their relatively low achievement levels, students low in socioeconomic status and racial/ethnic minority students (except Asians) are much more likely to drop out of high school than are high SES students and nonminority students. Based on data collected from 1980 high-school sophomores in the High School and Beyond Study and follow-up information collected in 1982, this pattern is shown in Figure 2.2. Twenty-two percent of the sophomores in the bottom SES quartile dropped out of school between 1980 and 1982, as compared with only 7 percent of those in the highest quartile. As regards race and ethnicity, 19 percent of Hispanic students dropped out, compared with 17 percent of black students and 13 percent of non-Hispanic whites.

However, it should be noted that the dropout rate among black students has been declining steadily in recent decades. Whereas the rate among whites between 16 and 24 years of age dropped by only 1 percentage point (from 14 to 13 percent) between 1974 and 1984, the rate for black youth in this age group declined from 21 percent to 16 percent (United States General Accounting Office 1986). In addition, a 1984 follow-up component in the High School and Beyond Study indicated that approximately 30 percent of the black and Hispanic students who dropped out subsequently returned to and completed high school or obtained an equivalency diploma (Kolstad and Owings 1986).

On the other hand, 1985 data on employment rates among youth between sixteen and twenty-four years of age indicate that high-school graduation is not

* It should be noted that math problem-solving tests depend even more on reading than do most other subject-area tests; therefore, the low performance of disadvantaged students in part reflects reading deficits.

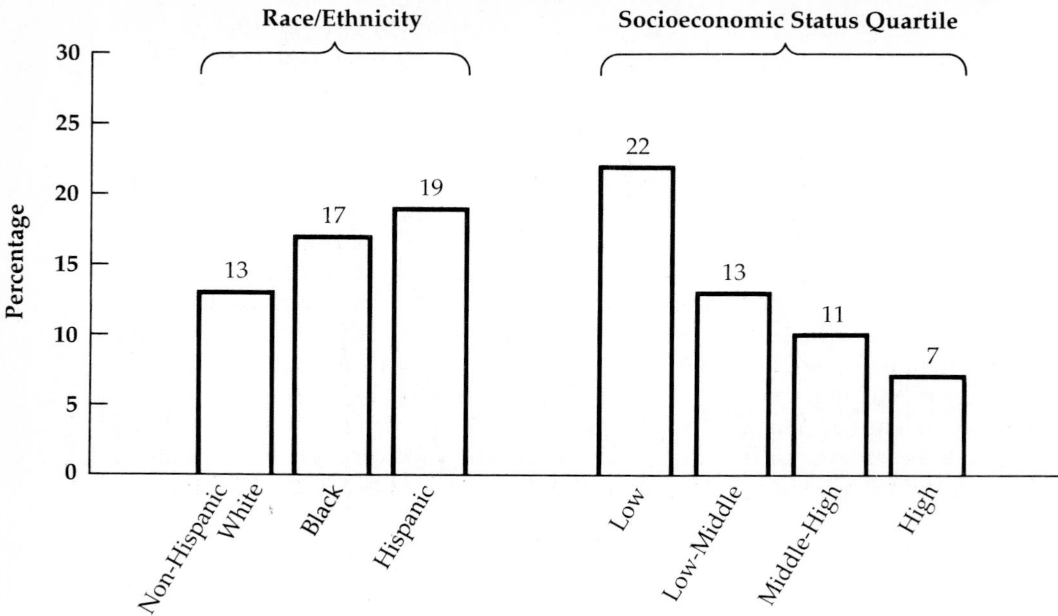

Socioeconomic status scores are a composite of father's and mother's education, father's occupation, parental income, and types of items in the home.

Figure 2.2 ***Percentage of Students who Drop Out of High School, by Race/Ethnicity and Socioeconomic Status*** (*Source:* National Center for Education Statistics 1985.)

closely related to employment among black youth, as it is among whites. As shown in Figure 2.3, white youth (not enrolled in college) in this age group were much more likely to be employed if they were high school graduates, but there is almost no difference between black graduates and nongraduates. In addition, black youth who are high-school graduates are less likely to be employed than are white dropouts.

Although employment rates do not differ between black students who drop out of high school and those who obtain their diplomas but do not go to college, attainment of some college education is associated with greater economic success among black Americans. The meaning of this pattern is discussed in Chapter 7.

Although appropriate data for a comparison apparently are not available, the pattern in Figure 2.3 for black youth probably also holds for Hispanic students, particularly in urban areas. Lack of a strong association between high-school graduation and employment among minority students is related to patterns of metropolitan stratification and segregation that have created a poverty underclass in big cities and that overwhelms the traditional processes of educational- and occupational-status attainment in the United States. The devel-

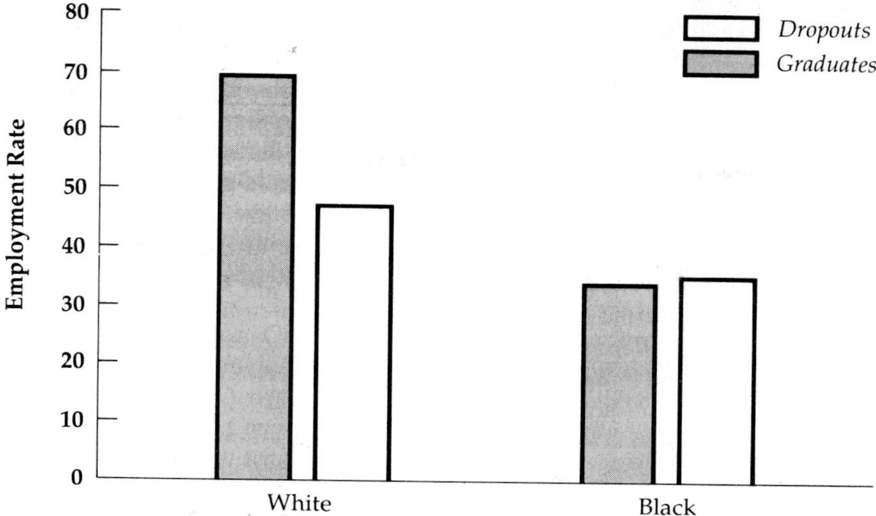

Figure 2.3 ***Percentage Employed among White and Black Youth Sixteen to Twenty-four Years of Age (not enrolled in college), by High-School Graduation Status, 1985*** (*Source:* United States General Accounting Office 1986.)

opment and implications of these patterns are discussed elsewhere in this chapter and throughout this book.

The challenge involved in reducing dropout rates and providing productive secondary education for low-income minority students in big cities is likely to prove enormous. The sons and daughters of low-income immigrant families who preceded them fifty to one hundred years ago did not have high secondary-school completion rates at a time when high schools were still relatively elite institutions and unskilled jobs were available and accessible for most working-class youth. Unfortunately, today's emerging postindustrial economy provides relatively limited opportunities for unskilled high-school dropouts, and the educational system thereby has been given the responsibility vastly to upgrade the education and skills of inner-city students in an historically telescoped period of time. Fernandez and Vellez reviewed past and current trends bearing on this challenge and reached the following general conclusion:

> *The dropout problem has existed for a long time and is likely to continue to plague major urban school systems in the years to come. Second, . . . most of the studies about dropouts have a very short longitudinal range, usually four years, when it is clear that the problem needs to be studied across generations. Is it possible for a socializing agency such as the school to do for newcomers and for racial and language minorities in general what it failed to do for earlier generations of immigrants? (Fernandez and Vellez 1985, 138)*

Table 2.4 *Percentages of 1980 Seniors Who Had Entered Postsecondary Education, by Selected Student Characteristics, 1982.*

Characteristics	Four-Year College	Two-Year College	Total, Two-Year and Four-Year Colleges
Test performance			
High quartile	69	21	90
Middle quartiles	33	30	63
Low quartile	11	20	31
Socioeconomic status			
High quartile	61	27	88
Middle quartile	32	27	59
Low quartiles	19	20	39
High School program			
Academic	64	24	88
General	24	27	51
Voc./tech.	11	25	36
Race/ethnicity			
Hispanic	20	28	48
black	33	20	53
non-Hispanic White	37	25	62
Asian	51	37	88
American Indian	20	22	42

Note: Socioeconomic status scores are a composite of father's and mother's education, father's occupation, parental income, and types of items in the home. Test performance is measured by a composite of reading and math scores.

Source: Adapted from National Center for Education Statistics 1984.

Postsecondary Education

Social background also is correlated with enrollment in postsecondary education. This pattern is shown in Table 2.2 earlier in this chapter and in Table 2.4, which provides data on the percentage of 1980 high-school seniors who had entered postsecondary institutions by February 1982. This information from the High School and Beyond data set collected by the National Center for Education Statistics indicates that postsecondary participation rates vary greatly by socioeconomic status, test performance, race/ethnicity, and type of high-school program. Note also that the percentage of high-school graduates entering college increased from 52 percent in 1982 to 58 percent in 1985, after fluctuating in the 50 percent range throughout the 1970s (Cohany 1986; Office of Educational Research 1988).

As shown in Tables 2.2 and 2.4, high-school seniors in the highest quartile on socioeconomic status are much more likely to attend postsecondary institutions than are those in the bottom quartile. Enrollment in the academic, general, and vocational/technical tracks in high school is also related to enrollment in college. Hispanic and American Indian seniors are least likely to enroll in college, and Asian students and non-Hispanic whites are the most likely.

Recent data indicate a sizable decline in college enrollment of lower status students in the 1980s. For example, one 1986 study found that only 32 percent of 1985 college freshmen were from families below the national median on income, compared with 45 percent in 1979 (Rothman 1986). Much of this decline probably was due to changing patterns of federal aid (discussed later in this chapter).

Table 2.2 also provides data on college graduation as well as on enrollment, when SES and test performances are taken into account simultaneously. Data are for high school seniors who graduated in 1972. (College enrollment rates for the 1980 seniors shown in Table 2.4 were generally similar to those for 1972 seniors.) As indicated in Table 2.2, students in the top quartile on SES were much more likely to attend college than were those in the bottom quartile, even after taking account of test performance. For example, 93 percent of high SES students who also were high in test performance enrolled in college, compared with only 63 percent for students high in test performance but low in SES. Only 30 percent of students in the lower quartile on SES enrolled in college, compared with 82 percent in the high quartile. A somewhat similar analysis for seniors graduating in 1980 showed that only 27 percent of students in the low third on both test performance and family income subsequently enrolled in college, as compared with 45 percent of those low in test performance but in the high third on family income. This analysis also showed that, as has been true for decades, black students are more likely to attend college than are white students, after considering SES and ability level (Chaikind 1986).

The patterns are even more pronounced for college graduation. Only 20 percent of 1972 students high in test performance but low in SES graduated from college four years later, compared with 47 percent of those high on both measures, and only 5 percent of students in the low quartile on SES graduated in 1976. It should be noted, however, that many students took more than four years to complete their degrees. By 1982, 60 percent of the 1972 graduates in the top quartile on SES had obtained a bachelor's degree, compared with 9 percent of those in the lowest quartile (derived from Hill and Owings 1986).

Sorting and Selectivity by Types of College

As delineated, students who are high in SES and test performance, are non-Hispanic white or Asian, and/or are enrolled in the academic track or, to a lesser extent, the general track in high school are the most likely to attend college and, in so doing, enroll in four-year colleges. It thus is not surprising to find that students in four-year colleges are higher in test performance and SES than are those at two-year colleges. These patterns are shown in the information presented in Tables 2.5 and 2.6.

As shown in Table 2.5, 18 percent of public four-year colleges and 27 percent of private four-year colleges have student bodies with an average combined SAT

Table 2.5 *Average SAT Score by College Type*

College Type	Average Combined SAT Scores (percentage of colleges by type)			
	1150 or above	*1000–1149*	*850–999*	*Less than 850*
Public 4-year (N = 496)	02	16	50	33
Private 4-year (N = 1033)	07	20	53	19
Public or private 2-year (N = 1161)	00	01	16	84

Note: Percentages do not add to 100 due to rounding.
Source: Adapted from Astin 1985.

score of 1,000 or above, but only 1 percent of two-year colleges (public or private) have enrollment with this level of SAT performance. Conversely, 84 percent of two-year colleges, as compared with 33 percent of public four-year colleges and 19 percent of private four-year colleges, have student bodies with average SAT scores below 850. Public four-year colleges are thus much more likely to enroll students with SAT scores below 1,000 than are private four-year colleges.

As indicated in Table 2.6, colleges at which the average combined SAT score is 1,150 or higher have student bodies in which 40 percent of students are from families with annual income of $50,000 or more (in the early 1980s), as compared

Table 2.6 *Percentage of Students at Three Annual Family-Income Levels, Percentage of Students with A or A− High-School GPA, and Average per Pupil Expenditure for Instruction at Colleges, Classified by Average SAT Score*

Colleges Classified by Average Level of SAT Scores	Percentage of Students by Annual Family Income Level			Average Annual per Pupil Expenditure on Instruction	Percent of Students with A or A− High School GPA
	Over $50,000	*$15–50,000*	*Under $15,000*		
1150 or above (*N* = 81)	40	53	07	$9,395	66
1000–1149 (*N* = 293)	23	64	13	$5,236	35
850–999 (*N* = 983)	13	66	21	$3,932	16
849 or below (*N* = 1333)	10	62	28	$3,500	12

Note: Expenditures for instruction include those classified as *instruction, academic support,* and *student services* and exclude those classified as *administration, physical plant,* and *research.*
Source: Adapted from Astin 1985.

with 23 percent at colleges in which the average SAT score is between 1,000 and 1,149, and 10 percent at colleges with average SAT scores below 1,000. Conversely, 28 percent of students at colleges with low SAT average scores were from families with annual income below $15,000, compared with 7 percent at colleges with high SAT averages. Similarly, 66 percent of students at high SAT colleges had a high-school grade-point average of A or A−, compared with 12 percent at low SAT schools.

In addition, annual per pupil expenditures related to instruction were $9,395 at the highly selective colleges (i.e., those with high average SAT scores), as compared with $5,326 at colleges with intermediate selectivity, and $3,688 at nonselective colleges. It is unlikely that these patterns have changed since the early 1980s.

Other statistics that can be calculated from the data presented in Tables 2.5 and 2.6 include the following:

1. Eighty-six percent of the colleges included in the data set have average SAT scores below 1,000. Of the 14 percent with average SAT scores above this level, 75 percent are private four-year colleges, even though this group constitutes only 38 percent of the colleges in the study.
2. Seventy-three percent of the colleges with average SAT scores below 1,000 are two-year colleges, even though this group constitutes only 43 percent of the colleges in the study.
3. Colleges with average SAT scores above 1,000 have an average annual per pupil expenditure of $6,137 for instruction, whereas those with average SAT scores below 1,000 have an average expenditure of $3,683.

The overall pattern that emerges from the preceding information on sorting and selectivity in postsecondary education is one in which students low in social status are much less likely to enter and graduate from college than are high-status students with the same test performance level. In addition, low-status students tend to be concentrated in two-year colleges with low expenditure levels, whereas high-status students are relatively concentrated in four-year colleges—frequently in elite private colleges—with much higher average expenditures and student bodies much higher in academic performance. Research indicates that baccalaureate aspirants entering community colleges subsequently have lower educational and economic attainment than do comparable students who attend four-year colleges, probably because this aspect of tracking contributes to attrition and later difficulty in transferring to four-year colleges (Dougherty 1987).

Furthermore, available research also indicates that social-class advantages and disadvantages in type of college attended are transmitted thereafter into graduate school patterns. Stated differently, and despite numerous exceptions, social class and the prestige of college attended are the best predictors of the prestige of graduate schools in which students eventually enroll after college (Lang 1987).

Bear in mind that as demonstrated in the first part of this chapter and discussed extensively elsewhere in this book, low-status students on the average have much lower achievement levels by the time they reach high school than do high-status students. Following high-school graduation, the higher education system reinforces the disadvantages experienced by low-status students throughout their school careers by generally selecting the most successful students to attend highly rated colleges with high expenditure levels and selecting the least successful to attend colleges with low expenditures, low achievement levels, low prestige, and concomitantly severe difficulties in trying to establish and maintain high standards for student performance.

Additional Topics Involving Sorting and Selecting

The preceding sections of this chapter describe the results of sorting and selecting in the educational system with respect to reading achievement, dropout from school, and participation in higher education. This section briefly discusses four important topics that involve the process of sorting and selecting in the U.S. educational system: vocational education, financing of students in higher education, proprietary schools in postsecondary education, and intelligence in relation to social class and race.

Vocational Education

As of 1987, nearly ten million students 18 years of age or younger were enrolled in vocational education courses. The vast majority of these students either participated in vocational education courses in comprehensive high schools or attended vocational and/or technical high schools. Students in vocational education participate either in general programs (e.g., consumer/homemaking; prevocational studies in industrial arts, agriculture, or other subjects; basic skills coordinated with vocational exploration; employability skills such as communications) or in occupationally specific programs emphasizing preparation for a specific job. Recent research indicates that the most effective vocational education provides for a carefully balanced mix of classroom experience coordinated with supervised on-the-job experience (Bottoms and Copa 1983).

Vocational educators and researchers have been trying to determine whether students in vocational education do better when they enter the job market than do students with comparable background and ability who do not participate. Conversely, educators also are concerned whether vocational education for high-school students may provide overly narrow learning opportunities that inhibit later participation in postsecondary education and direct students into dead-end employment. Research indicates that vocational education does help keep some potential dropouts in school and also is associated with better employment and higher earnings for some participants, particularly female graduates of business and office programs (Weisberg 1983). It also appears that most students in vocational education participate in some form of postsecondary education later (Campbell, Gardner, and Seitz 1982).

However, employment effects of vocational education generally are not very strong, partly because many or most vocational programs do not provide intensive training using modern equipment to prepare students for jobs currently or potentially in high demand. Campbell, Gardner, and Seitz have studied data on the postsecondary experience of 1972 high-school seniors and found that vocational education appears to be least helpful to minority youth, who tend to live in central cities with relatively limited job opportunities and frequently do not receive adequate preparation to gain and hold a job. Their discussion of policy implications concludes that improvements in the long-range effectiveness of vocational education depend on clear recognition of the goals that are postulated for it:

> *If . . . immediate employment is the desired outcome, youth should receive sufficient training at the secondary level to accomplish this goal. If meeting this end is not possible in the high school, however, students should be encouraged to pursue postsecondary education and be provided the necessary skills to do so. On the other hand, if higher education for most vocational students is considered to be an appropriate outcome, policy should be directed toward improving articulation between secondary and postsecondary schooling. (Campbell, Gardner, and Seitz 1982, x)*

Alan Weisberg also examined the policy implications of research on vocational education, with emphasis on programming in comprehensive high schools. The research strongly suggests, he concluded, that comprehensive high schools "ought to stop teaching specific occupational skills" because they are unable to "stay current with the equipment and training requirements of business and industry." Thus, he supports developments since 1950 according to which "many school systems . . . are moving toward regional occupational programs, separate vocational-technical schools, shared-time skills centers, and cooperative arrangements with postsecondary vocational education institutions" (1983, 358).

Vocational education's role in sorting and selecting for success in schools and later life can be positive to the extent that it provides improved economic opportunities for students who want to prepare for an occupation during high school or probably would not be motivated or successful in the general or college-preparatory tracks. But to the extent that vocational education does not provide adequate preparation for employment or serves as a dumping ground for unsuccessful students who have inadequate basic academic skills to succeed later, it may have a negative effect by sorting students into low-level learning environments in accordance with their social background and other factors. The National Commission on Secondary Vocational Education studied the problems involved in making vocational education more beneficial for high school students. Its 1984 report, *The Unfinished Agenda*, offered numerous recommendations for improving equity, course content, articulation with business and industry, and other aspects of current programs. Linda Lotto (1985) summarized the report's general conclusion:

> *The commissioners feel that vocational education has for far too long been relegated to the periphery of the high school curriculum. . . . [They] are convinced that vocational education can, and frequently does, offer much more. They see vocational education as capable of functioning coequally with academic education to serve the needs and interests of all high school students.* (Lotto 1985, 568–569)

It should be noted that some traditional proponents of vocational education at the high-school level have begun to question its utility in a postindustrial society. In particular, some leading business groups that historically were key actors in introducing and expanding secondary vocational education have now concluded that it has largely outlived its usefulness. Elizabeth Useem has summarized this development in *Low Tech Education in a High Tech World*, a book she prepared for the American Association for the Advancement of Science:

> *Corporate insistence on vocational education in high schools has now been dropped in favor of a broad-based academic education, with vocational programs now being emphasized at the community college and four-year college level instead. The push for secondary students to learn communication, science, and mathematics skills along with problem-solving abilities and an aptitude for "learning how to learn," has replaced earlier corporate concerns with narrow vocational skills training, which is now inappropriate in such a rapidly changing work environment.* (Useem 1986, 226)

Financing of Students in Higher Education

The first chapter pointed out that success in the occupational structure and the economy increasingly requires acquisition of advanced knowledge and skills through postsecondary education. In Chapter 7 we summarize research supporting this conclusion, particularly for black students. Because higher education has become so important for later success, financing higher education for students from economically or socially disadvantaged families has become an increasingly central issue in determining whether equity is present in the process of sorting and selecting within the educational system.

Problems involving participation in higher education have become prominent in part because the costs of going to college have escalated rapidly while federal budget deficits have led to changes in policies and practices for helping students participate in higher education. Between 1978 and 1985 average tuition and fees increased from 21 to 26 percent of the median family income (O'Keefe 1986). During this same period, federal grants and scholarships declined by nearly 60 percent, loans replaced grants as the most common form of federal suppport for college students, and the number of students receiving federal loans for postsecondary education nearly tripled (Fiske 1987). By 1986, the average indebtedness of students graduating from four-year colleges was more than $7,000 (Evangelauf 1987). Considerations such as these led the Congressional Joint Economic Committee to commission a 1986 report that reached the following conclusion regarding borrowing for higher education:

> *Growing student indebtedness has raised questions about the implications of the debt burdens for the national economy, for the economic well-being of borrowers, for equality of access to higher education and even for the educational process itself. . . . The federal strategy for fostering equality of opportunity in higher education, which initially focussed on a balanced array of grants, loans, and work opportunities for the disadvantaged, has been transformed, with uncertain and largely unexamined implications for the groups who were the original focus of federal concern. (quoted in Evangelauf 1987, 1, 18)*

Escalation of both costs and borrowing for higher education also raises even broader questions regarding general societal arrangements for preparing youth for the future in a postindustrial society. For example, D. A. Hansen (1986) studied recent trends and concluded that growing indebtedness may discourage college students from entering socially important but relatively low-paid fields such as teaching and social work. After examining data on recent trends, economist Michael McPherson pointed out that large debts being incurred to participate in higher education probably will make it more difficult for graduates to save for their own children's higher education in future generations, and that the issues thereby raised "go beyond the merely financial." A parental savings strategy, he further concluded, "might strengthen generational bonds, but it could also sour familial relationships by making parents feel too burdened and children too dependent. Also, parents and students may have different ideas about which educational investments to make; who's paying for the education may affect the balance of power between them" (McPherson 1986, 9).

Major equity issues involved in the escalation of college costs include the question of whether low-income students are being increasingly foreclosed of the opportunity to attend relatively prestigious and well-funded colleges, and whether low-income citizens thus are receiving a fair return for their investment in taxes for higher education. On the first question, we have noted that working-class students are disproportionately represented at two-year colleges, which generally have smaller expenditures per pupil and enroll lower-performing students than do four-year colleges; declining availability of grants for low-income students in the 1980s may have significantly exacerbated tendencies toward development of a two-tiered system in higher education. Regarding this possibility, the president of the Consortium for the Advancement of Private Higher Education reviewed recent trends and concluded that

> *cutbacks in federal student aid combined with greater than inflationary increases in tuitions are pushing more and more colleges beyond the reach of low-income students. . . . [Private college's ability to maintain access] unaided is limited. For*

this reason, we must be unflagging in our efforts to convince state and federal governments that society, and not just students and their families, must pay the price of accomplishing that goal. (O'Keefe 1986, 8)

In addition, the switch from grants to loans has played an important part in reducing the percentage of black students in higher education in the 1980s. (See Chapter 10.) Particularly affected have been students at predominantly black colleges. In these schools, the percentage of students receiving grants greatly declined and the percentage receiving loans increased from 4 percent in 1979 to 46 percent in 1985, thus leading the president of the National Institute of Independent Colleges to observe that the "truly neediest are being hurt by a federal policy" asking them to take on loans larger than their families' income (Associated Press 1987).

Proprietary Schools in Postsecondary Education

Many students receive some or all of their postsecondary education at tuition-charging proprietary schools. Wilms (1987) estimated that there were more than 6,000 proprietary institutions (other than correspondence) schools in the United States in 1986. His extensive analysis of these institutions included the following four observations and conclusions:

1. Proprietary schools are the largest provider of postsecondary vocational education. Although they offer instruction in many subjects from accounting to zookeeping, the bulk of the programs fall in the four major categories of trades (e.g., aviation, allied health), business and secretarial, cosmetology, and barbering.
2. Enrollment is directly related to prevailing wage rates and unemployment rates.
3. Most proprietary schools enroll fewer than 200 students and operate on very small profit margins. Their main competition is from public two-year community colleges. This competition has become more intense as the number of eighteen- to twenty-one-year-olds has declined.
4. Enrollment at proprietary schools is disproportionately low-income and minority. Dropout rates frequently exceed 50 percent. However, dropout rates for similar students at public two-year colleges probably are even higher.

Major controversies involving proprietary schools have centered on whether they should receive governmental support in the form of grants and loans for their students. Some observers believe they make an important contribution in providing opportunities for students who otherwise would not have the financial capacity or motivation to continue their education. Others believe that proprietary schools place too much emphasis on vocational training to the exclusion of other educational goals, fail to provide many of their students with usable skills, and are providing undesirable competition for nonprofit colleges.

Intelligence in Relation to Social Class and Race

The school system could sort and select more or less mechanically if there were a close relationship between intellectual ability and social status, or between intellectual ability and ethnicity or race. In the absence of such relationships, sorting and selecting that eliminate economically or socially disadvantaged students may reflect serious inequity in the educational system and in society as a whole.

Until the middle of the twentieth century, it was widely believed that there was an inborn intellectual inferiority in people of lower-class status and in people of nonwhite skin color. Many white people believed that whites had the highest innate intelligence and that the intelligence of other races descended in order of their departure from this color, with the darkest-skinned blacks lowest on the intelligence scale. This idea was supported by some early intelligence-test studies, in which it was found that black children scored lower than white children, with children of mixed white and black parentage scoring in between.

However, critical studies of intelligence testing (Eells et al. 1951) have shown that the ordinary intelligence tests favor children whose parents are of middle- or upper-class status. The problems in the tests are ones for which life in an upper-class or middle-class home give superior preparation.

For example, in the following test item,

A symphony is to a composer as a book is to what?
( ) paper ( ) sculptor ( ) author
( ) musician ( ) man

the problem is probably easier for middle-class children. They are more likely to have heard their parents talking about symphonies than are working-class children.

On the other hand, the following item is probably as difficult for high-status as for low-status children:

A baker goes with bread the same way as a carpenter goes with what?
( ) a saw ( ) a house ( ) a spoon
( ) a nail ( ) a man

The ordinary intelligence test contains many items of the first type. As a consequence, the test, by bringing in words that are less familiar to them, tends to penalize children of low socioeconomic status.

Furthermore, children of upper- and middle-class families are more often pushed by their families to do good work in school. School training itself helps one to do well in most intelligence tests. Therefore, many social scientists now believe that the differences in intelligence test performance between black and white children are mainly due to the fact that more black children are working-class. When middle-class black children are given intelligence tests, they do about as well as middle-class white children. Innate differences exist between individuals within these groups, but the average innate intelligence of the groups is the same, it is thought, if the groups have equal opportunity and similar training in solving the ordinary problems of life.

The Theory of Innate Group Differences

The possibility of racial group differences in intelligence has not been ruled out by all scientists. A vigorous controversy developed in 1968–69 over the publication by Professor Arthur R. Jensen, a distinguished educational psychologist, of his conclusions from his own and other research on intelligence in relation to heredity, social class, and race (Jensen 1968; 1969). Jensen believes that intelligence is inherited to a considerably larger degree than most other psychologists believe. He also believes that certain research studies demonstrate a genetic difference between whites and blacks in the quality of abstract intelligence.

Peggy R. Sanday (1972) takes issue with Jensen by supporting the following three propositions:

1. The magnitude of the genetic contribution to a given trait cannot be measured with present methods if the trait is determined by more than one gene, as is true for intelligence.
2. The methods used to measure intelligence (the ordinary tests) are not equally valid for various socioeconomic groups.
3. When the sociocultural factors for different socioeconomic and racial groups are equated, the measured intelligence does not differ reliably, or differs very little.

This last proposition is disputed because a variety of published researches give a variety of results. However, the most recent studies, on which black and Chicano children of middle-class status have been studied in sufficient numbers to give stable results, appear to support this proposition. For example, in a study of school-age children in Riverside, California, Mercer (1973) found that when the sociocultural factors (such as home background and education of mother) were kept equal, there was no difference between the intelligence of Hispanic, black, and white elementary school children. But Jensen's response to Mercer is that sociocultural factors are themselves determined at least partly by the innate intelligence of the parents. That is, parents who are more intelligent create a favorable sociocultural environment for their children; but it is their own innate intelligence passed on to their children that gives the children high intelligence test scores.

Most social scientists agree with Jensen that the quality measured by intelligence tests is partially determined by heredity. The difference between Jensen and other scientists is over the degree to which this quality is determined by heredity and the degree to which it is determined by the person's experience or environment. In technical terms, what proportion of the variance on an intelligence test is to be attributed to heredity, and what proportion to environmental influence? Jensen and his supporters designate the percentage of variance in intelligence test scores accounted for by heredity at about 80 percent (Herrnstein 1982); their opponents frequently place this percentage at 50 to 60 percent or less (Jencks 1987). Jensen (1980) also argues that intelligence tests provide valid data on respondents' innate intellectual capabilities, but his opponents believe that the tests are susceptible to environmental bias associated with race, social class, and other considerations.

Critics of the hereditarian position generally argue that environmental influences on mental development are not fully taken into account in most research comparing the effects of heredity and environment on IQ. Flynn (1980; 1987), for example, has reviewed much of the research on each side of the issue and concluded that such factors as relatively poor nutrition and relatively poorer quality parent-infant interaction among blacks as compared to whites of the same socioeconomic status may account for much of the fifteen-point differential. "Not one piece of evidence" on either the environmentalist or the hereditarian side, he further states, is "so firm that it is proof" against exacting criticism (p. 214). Similarly, Scarr (1981a; 1981b) has summarized the thrust of this viewpoint:

> *A growing literature on black socialization indicates that there are important differences from the socialization of white families that affect the intellectual development of children as measured by tests. . . . Black families emphasize affect, nonverbal communication, motor activity, willfulness, and tolerance for high levels of sensory stimulation for their children. By contrast, white families stress object orientation, verbal communication, low motor activity, obedience, and tolerance for low levels of sensory output, such as working quietly alone in a classroom. . . . Intelligence tests sample predominantly from the object-oriented, abstract world of the white child, rather than the interpersonal, affective world of the black child. (Scarr 1981a, 335–336)*

Those who support the environmentalist position also point to changes that have occurred in IQ scores nationally and in average IQ scores for various racial and ethnic groups. Gould (1980; 1981), for example, reports that United States IQ scores averaged 100 in 1937 but 106 in 1972 and concludes that

> *this general gain can hardly be ascribed to genetic causes; it reflects whatever improved literacy, earlier access to information through radio and television, better nutrition, and so forth have wrought in just thirty-five years. When we recognize that the average black-white difference is 15 points, and that gains of up to two-thirds this amount have occurred in certain age groups as a result of general changes in environment not specifically directed toward this end, then why should we be ready to conclude that group differences are ineluctable? (Gould 1980, 43)*

Similarly, Sowell (1978) has studied data on changes in the average IQ scores of various racial and ethnic groups. He reports that between 1920 and 1970, average IQ scores for Italian Americans increased from 92 to 100, and scores for Polish Americans increased from 91 to 109, but scores for Mexican Americans and Puerto Ricans remained in the 80s. The absence of a significant increase among the latter groups can be explained, according to Sowell, by (a) genetic differences; (b) relatively static socioeconomic position; (c) enduring prevalence of Spanish as the language spoken in the home; or (d) the high incidence of return migration. He rejects the genetic explanation and cites 1958 data from the New York City Board of Education showing that average IQ was 93 among Puerto Rican students with 9 or 10 years in mainland schools, but the average was only 72 among students with only 1 or 2 years of mainland schooling.

The related argument concerning the validity of IQ tests has become a raging controversy in the 1980s. Jensen's books *Bias in Mental Testing* (1980) and *Straight Talk about Mental Tests* (1981) provided many arguments indicating that the tests do measure general intellectual ability, but critics have not been convinced and have offered a variety of rebuttals and counterevidence. Hafner and White (1981), for example, criticized Jensen's data and conclusions as follows: "By ignoring the evidence that tests are biased, educators who measure student progress with test scores do their students a disservice, especially if these tests are better at discriminating subgroups than in reflecting educational attainment or predicting accomplishment" (p. 585). Similarly, a four-year study conducted by the Committee on Ability Testing (1982) of the National Academy of Sciences concluded that standardized ability tests do not measure the "inborn, predetermined capacity" or "potential" of an individual, but rather reflect his or her previous learning and achievement. The Committee also concluded that such tests are not inherently or intentionally biased against minority groups, but instead reflect the general socioeconomic disadvantages that minorities and the poor suffer in United States society as a whole. The Committee cautioned against indiscriminate use of such tests to make educational or employment decisions about individuals based solely on test scores.

Evidence against the validity of ability tests also was presented in a 1980 study by Allan Nairn et al. titled *The Reign of ETS: The Corporation That Makes Up Minds* and a 1982 study of the Scholastic Ability Test by Christopher Jencks and James Crouse (1982; Crouse 1985), but supporters of the validity of commonly used tests responded with rebuttal data of their own (Bond 1982; Educational Testing Service 1980).

Sternberg (1984) recommended that ability tests should be used carefully, based on such considerations as the following:

> *When criterion information is unavailable or scanty, test scores can serve a useful function; people who might otherwise be denied admission to programs on the basis of inadequate evidence may be admitted because their test scores show them capable of high-level performance. But when criterion information is available, the tests may be superfluous or even counterproductive. (Sternberg 1984, 14)*

The Crisis in Sorting and Selecting

The confluence of several trends has led to a crisis in the functioning of the educational system in the United States. Education is becoming more important for later success as the postindustrial economy introduces high technology and reduces blue-collar employment. (See Chapters 1 and 7 for additional information on these topics.) At the same time, strong associations persist between social-class background and racial-ethnic status on the one hand and educational achievement and attainment on the other. The combination of these factors is making it relatively more difficult for many low-status citizens to take advantage of economic opportunity, and meanwhile the percentages of poverty students and minority students in the public schools are increasing steadily and will continue to increase in the future.

In addition, education has become increasingly central in determining whether the United States will be successful economically, particularly with respect to international competition. Growing emphasis on services in the economy and the introduction of new technology have created needs for a better educated work force in general and for additional highly educated personnel in many occupations involving delivery of services or use of science and technology. Thus, some recent research indicates that substantial proportions of workers do not now possess the intellectual skills required for adequate performance in many occupations (e.g., fire fighter, police officer) that have become increasingly complex (Gottfredson 1984). Also, the National Assessment of Educational Progress has reported that although the "overwhelming majority of young adults [twenty-one to twenty-five years of age] adequately perform tasks at the lower level [of literacy] . . . sizable numbers appear unable to do well on tasks of moderate complexity" (Kirsch and Jungeblut 1986, 4). Information on these trends and problems has led influential business groups, such as the Committee on Economic Development, to demand and support major reforms in the educational system, with particular emphasis on strengthening academic preparation to ensure acquisition of abstract thinking and independent learning skills:

> *For most students, employers would prefer a curriculum that stresses literacy, mathematical skills, and problem-solving skills: one that emphasizes learning how to learn and adapting to change. The schools should also teach and reward self-discipline, self-reliance, teamwork, acceptance of responsibility, and respect for others. (Committee for Economic Development 1985, 15)*

Political leaders also have become increasingly concerned with making the educational system more effective for a larger proportion of children and youth. For example, President Reagan made international competiveness the major theme of his 1987 State of the Union address, emphasizing the importance of education in improving the nations' ability to compete. Presidential aspirant Gary Hart (1987) also emphasized education in his campaign platform. He released a paper entitled "Education: The Key to the Third Century" in which he stated that "fate and circumstance have now seen fit to bind that future to our willingness to inform the minds of our citizens" and to reverse "the emerging colonialism of ignorance and economic domination" (pp. S1527–S1528).

As documented earlier in this chapter, much of the problem of low performance in the educational system centers on and reflects the disadvantaged status of students from low-income families and social/ethnic minority groups, particularly in concentrated urban poverty areas. This outcome of the sorting and selecting process not only detracts from the nation's capacity to prepare a highly skilled work force capable of improving our competitive position internationally, but it also raises the prospect that the United States will become even more divided into a prosperous, largely nonminority segment on the one hand and an embittered segment of low-status citizens with mostly working-class and substantially minority family background on the other. Arkansas Governor Bill Clinton was concerned with this and other trends documented in Chapter 1 when he told members of the American Association of Colleges for Teacher Education in 1987 that "we don't have as much time as most people think" to improve the schools; if recent trends continue, "40 percent of the U.S. population will be worse off economically in the year 2000, while 20 percent will hold their own and 40 percent will better their lot" (quoted in Teske 1987, p. 4).

Metropolitan Evolution and the Crisis in Sorting and Selecting

Urbanization is the most characteristic aspect of modern society. Urbanization is the process of making people into city-dwellers. Until 1800, the people of even the most powerful societies were mainly engaged in getting food and fuel from the land—some 80 percent of the working population were tillers of the soil, or sheep and cattle tenders, or fishermen, or foresters. Then the growing technification of society enabled fewer and fewer people to raise more and more food, until, today, less than 10 percent of the working force in the United States produces enough fuel and food to provide a high standard of living for all the population.

The farm, the home, the office, as well as the workshop, have all been technified, and with this process has come increasing urbanization. Larger and larger proportions of the population have come to live in cities and suburbs. Together, the city and the suburbs comprise the metropolitan area, defined as a central city of 50,000 or more people plus the surrounding county or counties in which the population has significant economic, social, and cultural contact and interchange with the city.

As shown in Table 2.7, the population of the United States became steadily more concentrated in metropolitan areas between 1910 and 1984. However, after 1960 population growth was greatest in suburban areas and smaller cities, and the percentage of the population in cities of more than 100,000 declined. By 1984, 76 percent of the U.S. population was located in 280 metropolitan areas. Twenty-three of these metropolitan areas were Consolidated Metropolitan Statistical Areas with more than one million people each. The United States had become a predominantly metropolitan society.

Population shifts underlying these changes constituted an important development in the United States in the 1970s and 1980s. For the first time in United States history, some older and larger metropolitan areas—including their

Table 2.7 ***Growth of Urban Population in the United States***

	Distribution of Total Population (by percentage)			
Year	*Rural (under 2,500)*	*Total Urban (2,500 and over)*	*Cities over 100,000*	*Metropolitan Areas*
1790	95	5	–	–
1810	93	7	–	–
1830	91	9	2	–
1850	85	15	5	–
1870	74	26	11	–
1890	65	35	15	–
1910	54	46	22	46
1930	44	56	30	54
1950	36	64*	29	59
1960	30	70*	29	63
1970	37	73*	28	69
1980	26	74*	25	75
1984	NA	NA	25	76

* Current U.S. Census definition of *urban* adds about 5 percent to numbers based on pre-1950 definition.

Note: NA = not available

Sources: U.S. Bureau of the Census, 1970; *Statistical Abstract of the United States* 1986.

suburbs—lost population, and for the first time in this century nonmetropolitan counties gained rather than lost population. These trends in turn reflected at least three major developments: (1) a lower birthrate; (2) out-migration from central cities and, in some cases, suburbs in older and larger metropolitan areas, particularly in the East and Middle West; and (3) general movement of population from economically depressed regions in the snowbelt to economically vigorous or otherwise attractive regions in the sunbelt.

As a result of these changes, approximately one of every three United States citizens resides in a metropolitan area that declined or registered virtually no population growth since 1970. This unprecedented situation in United States history both reflected and caused serious problems in metropolitan schools and society, particularly in the central cities. However, population decline in many metropolitan areas also opens up possibilities for urban renewal and revitalization of deteriorating SMSAs.

Movement to the Suburbs and Deterioration of the Central City

By 1920, a number of United States cities were developing into complex metropolitan areas. Choice residential suburbs were being established outside many central cities, at first strung out along the railway lines that led into the city. These suburbs were exclusive residential areas, expensive to live in, with more living space and with superior schools provided at no greater cost to the taxpayer than in the central city. These suburbs were heavily upper-middle class, with fringes of upper-class and of lower-middle-class residents. Their schools, elementary and secondary, were relatively homogeneous along socioeconomic, racial, and ethnic lines.

Because the suburb is a part of the metropolitan complex, the fact that some suburbs draw mainly middle- and upper-class people results in an increase in the proportion of working-class population who live in the central city. As the population expands, and as more persons move into metropolitan areas, the working-class areas of the central city expand, creating obsolescence and reduced monetary values in former middle-class residential areas. Slum areas expand. The area of solid middle-class residences becomes smaller and is often cut up into small islands contiguous to lower-class areas.

The slum areas of the central city expand during this stage of metropolitan development because the dynamics of the housing market lead to deterioration of entire neighborhoods where there is substantial segregation of low income groups in separate communities (i.e., socioeconomic stratification). Abandoned housing has become a key factor in the spiral of deterioration that has been occurring in many big cities in the United States. Sternlieb and Burchell (1973) have studied the process of residential abandonment in big cities and concluded that the root cause is the lack of buyers for housing units that become vacant or in tax arrears, particularly in homogeneous lower-working-class neighborhoods. Sternlieb and Burchell also addressed the next logical question, "Why are there so few buyers for vacant housing in these neighborhoods?" and concluded, "The environment of abandonment is the key here. This is illustrated by both growing fiscal incapacity of the city and by a fear on the part of remaining residents that they will be victimized by either crime or fire" (p. xxix).

Socioeconomic Stratification Intensified by Racial Segregation

Because many of the families migrating to the cities were from racial or ethnic minority groups that were confined to segregated neighborhoods, racial and ethnic segregation also increased during the period of rapid suburban growth after World War II, with minority families concentrated in the central cities. At the same time, families moving from the central city were predominantly white. Thus, the metropolitan area as a whole became increasingly both stratified and segregated, with working-class families and minority families concentrated in the central city, and middle-class white families predominating in the suburbs. The intensification of racial segregation on a metropolitan basis is shown in Table 2.8 which portrays an eighty-year trend toward racial differentiation between the central city and the suburbs. As of 1980, blacks constituted 70 percent of the central city population in Washington, D.C., 67 percent in Atlanta, and 63 percent in Detroit, but they constituted only 17 percent, 14 percent, and 5 percent of the respective suburban populations in these metropolitan areas.

Stratification of the metropolitan area has been compounded by racial seg-

Table 2.8 *Proportion of Population in Metropolitan Areas That Is Nonwhite, 1900–1980**

Year	Percentage in Metropolitan Area: Nonwhite	Percentage in Central City: Nonwhite	Percentage Outside Central City: Nonwhite
1900	7.8	6.8	9.4
1910	7.3	6.9	8.1
1920	7.2	7.3	7.0
1930	8.1	9.0	6.4
1940	8.6	10.1	6.0
1950	10.0	13.1	5.7
1960	11.7	17.8	5.2
1970	12.8	21.4	4.9
1980	16.4	29.4	8.8

* Hispanics may be either white or nonwhite.

Sources: U.S. Bureau of the Census, U.S. Census of Population; 1960, *Final Report*; 1970 data from *Final Report* PC (IA); 1980 data from *Statistical Abstract of the United States*, 1982.

regation. As the population of working-class minority communities increased, pressure built up to open additional housing opportunities in surrounding neighborhoods. A few racial minority families would begin to move into these neighborhoods, realtors would steer even more minority families toward them, and before long these neighborhoods were undergoing racial transition and soon became predominantly minority. A variety of real estate and housing practices including "blockbusting" tactics designed to scare whites into leaving changing neighborhoods, discriminatory covenants that prevented minorities from purchasing property in white neighborhoods further away, and refusal of banks and federal agencies to support loans to minority families seeking to move into predominantly white neighborhoods combined to cause increasingly rapid turnover.

However, it is important to emphasize that the socioeconomic stratification of metropolitan areas in the United States was exacerbated but not created by racial segregation. According to urban analysts such as George Sternlieb, stratification and its accompanying "defunctioning" of the central city "would have occurred even if there had not been a problem of race" (1974, 225). On the other hand, racial segregation not only speeded up socioeconomic stratification but also helped obscure the real nature of what is going on in the central city, that is, the effects of concentrating poverty so heavily in one part of the metropolitan area.

Stratification and segregation combined with suburbanization have continued to concentrate low-status minority groups in the central cities in the 1970s and 1980s and thus to generate an increasingly high proportion of economically disadvantaged minority students in central city school districts. In the fifty largest U.S. cities, for example, the overall population declined between 1970 and

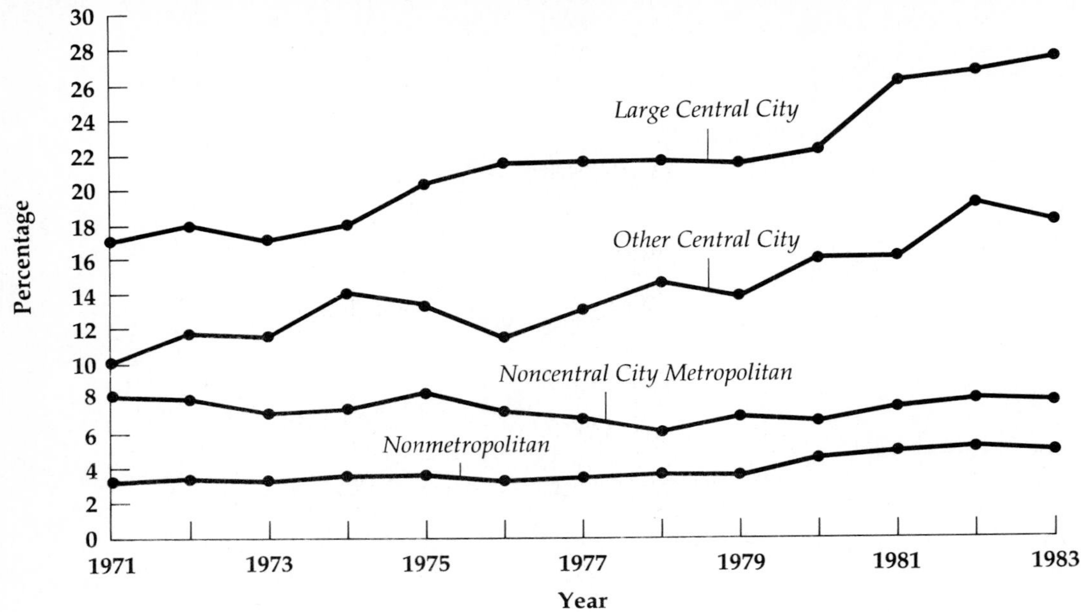

Figure 2.4 ***Percentages of Children and Youth between the Ages of Six and Seventeen Both Poor and Minority, by Community Type 1971 to 1983*** (*Source:* Koretz and Vantresca 1984.)

1980, but the number of low-income black Americans living in poverty areas increased by 23 percent (Herbers 1987). In 1987, 84 percent of the students in the Detroit public schools were from poverty families, and 90 percent were minority students (Viadero 1987b).

As shown in Figure 2.4, 28 percent of the children and youth between the ages of 6 and 17 living in large central cities were both poor and minority in 1983, as compared with only 17 percent in 1971. Similarly, the comparable percentages in other (i.e., smaller) central cities increased from 10 percent in 1971 to 18 percent in 1983. Meanwhile, the percentage of poor and minority children and youth in metropolitan communities outside the central city remained at a relatively low 6 to 8 percent throughout the 1971 to 1983 period, while the comparable percentages in nonmetropolitan communities increased from a very low 3 percent to only 5 percent.

The Stratified and Segregated Metropolitan Complex

The movement of population to the suburbs has continued through the 1970s and 1980s. In the 1950s and 1960s a new and more complicated pattern appeared wherein working-class migration to the suburbs also became significant. Most of these working-class families were white, and many settled in areas that became predominantly working-class suburbs, but in many metropolitan areas one or more centers of black working-class residence also existed or began to form in the suburbs. Thus, even though most of the suburbs do not include the lowest socioeconomic group found in the central city, many suburbs have become differentiated into communities that are either predominantly upper-middle class, lower-middle class, or working class. The overall results of this stage of metropolitan evolution are that within the larger pattern of metropolitan stratification, working-class residents constitute a major part of the central city population, and the suburbs also have become increasingly stratified according to social class.

Another complicating factor in metropolitan evolution emerged in the 1970s, when middle-class black families began to move out of the central city in sizable numbers. Commenting on this trend, Detroit Urban League Director Francis Kornegay noted, "It's a human urge as a person climbs the economic ladder to spend and get the best for his family. And where is the best now? In the suburbs" (quoted in Wolman 1976, 27). While the white population increased more rapidly between 1970 and 1980 in outlying suburbs (exurbia) and nonmetropolitan areas than in metropolitan areas, black population increased by 49 percent in the suburbs and by 12 percent in the central cities.

An analysis of black suburbanization indicates that in some metropolitan areas, black population—particularly the middle class—is dispersing to some degree throughout the suburbs, but in other metropolitan areas black movement appears to be mostly spillover of central city population into first-ring and adjacent suburbs. This latter pattern appears to be particularly the case in the largest metropolitan areas, which have the largest black populations and have had the greatest black migration to the suburbs. It is clear that first middle-class and then working-class black families in Atlanta, Chicago, Cleveland, St. Louis, and other big cities have been moving to the inner tier of suburbs adjoining the central city ghetto, and that some of these inner suburbs now are becoming heavily black (Rose 1982). What has been happening, in other words, is that middle-class and upwardly mobile black families have been escaping from the inner-city ghetto, but the same pattern of socioeconomic and racial segregation that had marked the decline of the central city is appearing in the suburbs (Lake 1981).

Looked at in a slightly different way, the deteriorated inner core of the metropolitan area has expanded into the suburbs just as it previously had grown to consume large parts of the central city. If these trends continue, black and white middle-class families who now live in inner suburbs will move farther out as working-class families begin to move in, and the overall stratification of the metropolitan area will be further reinforced.

The pattern of metropolitan development described here is typical of older and larger United States metropolitan areas that have evolved toward a high degree of socioeconomic stratification and racial segregation. However, it should not be assumed that all metropolitan areas in the United States have followed the same pattern of development or necessarily will evolve in the same direction as those that best illustrate the pattern. Metropolitan areas differ considerably in accordance with their age, size, region, unique history, and other characteristics. For example, small metropolitan areas tend to be less stratified than larger ones and may not necessarily become highly stratified in the future if steps are taken to prevent this from happening. Metropolitan areas in the south historically exemplified an opposite pattern from those in the north, with high status population tending to be concentrated in the central city and very low status population residing in the periphery. However, larger metropolitan areas in the south have begun to follow the northern pattern.

Stratification, Segregation, and the Underclass in Large Metropolitan Areas

One of the most important facts about racial segregation in larger and older metropolitan areas is that it appears to have become self-perpetuating despite attempts made to ensure that racial and ethnic minorities have equal access to housing throughout the city and the suburbs. Federal, state, and local open housing laws were passed in the 1960s, and government programs in housing and other activities since then have included an emphasis on reduction of racial segregation. As noted, substantial numbers of black families have begun to move to the suburbs. Nevertheless, racial segregation in housing appears to have increased, thereby bringing about a slight decline in residential segregation on a national basis (McKinney and Schnare 1987).

However, the movement of middle-class minority families out of segregated city ghettoes has *increased* concentration of poverty in the inner city. As noted earlier in this chapter and elsewhere in this book, socioeconomic stratification and racial segregation thus have placed many minority citizens into underclass communities in big-city poverty neighborhoods. By definition, the underclass consists of individuals locked into an integral cycle of poverty, welfare dependency, and social despair. But the negative effects of having a large underclass in the heart of our metropolitan areas damage not just the individuals directly involved but also the larger communities in which they live. In a paper titled "The Black Community: Is There a Future?" Orlando Patterson has examined the broader consequences of this demographic pattern and reached the following conclusions:

> *On the whole . . . the range and variety of black ghetto styles are rapidly declining. . . . The "achievers" have almost all left or are scrambling to leave. The activists and revolutionaries of the sixties are now almost nonexistent. . . . What remains . . . are the "defeated," the 'rebels without causes' or criminal elements, and, most pervasive of all, the 'street people.' . . . For the mass of the black poor, and for the poor generally, this . . . must seem like a social nightmare. . . . What in the world will the post-industrial world do with them? (Patterson 1979, 274, 278)*

Effects on the city and the metropolitan area as a whole have been similarly dysfunctional and foreboding. In 1982, the staff of the Joint Economic Committee of the U.S. Congress analyzed the fiscal condition of the big cities and concluded that patterns of stratification and segregation had combined with economic decline to produce grave problems for much of urban America:

> *The outlook for the cities is bleak. In the declining cities where capital deferrals are accompanied by reductions in service levels and large tax increases, it appears that crises cannot long be avoided. . . . This will not only leave these cities in a deepening state of distress, but will render these cities home for the most dependent segments of society—the undereducated, the unemployed, the aged, and the minorities. These individuals have neither the means to leave nor the skills to improve their plight if they did. This scenario makes it difficult to imagine that the private sector in these cities—even those firms that remain—will make a dent in training or employing the unemployed or in significantly enhancing the local tax base. (Galbraith 1982, xiii–xiv)*

Recommendations and opinions concerning possible responses to the problem of stratification and segregation in United States metropolitan areas differ greatly in accordance with each observer's social, political, and economic philosophy. Patterson's (1979) analysis concluded that long-range improvements in opportunities for twenty million blacks in urban ghettoes will require a much greater emphasis on full employment policies at the federal and state levels, even if this reinforces inflationary tendencies in the economy, and a much greater government effort to combat discrimination and ensure economic growth in the cities. President Jimmy Carter's Commission for a National Agenda for the Eighties first noted that "a sizeable portion of the urban underclass" has become "relatively permanent," and then offered a number of recommendations including emphasis on "a guaranteed job program for those who can work and a guaranteed cash assistance plan for both the 'working poor' and those who cannot work" (Panel on Policies and Prospects 1980, 15, 102).

In further recommending that "federal urban policy efforts should not necessarily be used to discourage the deconcentration and dispersal of industry and households from central urban locations" and that "relocation of population and economic vitality to nonmetropolitan and previously rural areas also should not be discouraged" (p. 104), the commission set off a storm of controversy pitting those who would concentrate on developing or redeveloping deteriorated cities in the North and Middle West against those who would encourage migration of population to more prosperous metropolitan areas in the South and West. President Ronald Reagan proposed to establish big-city "Enterprise Zones" in which businesses would receive tax reductions and other government benefits and also expressed support for the philosophy that the poor should migrate from declining communities to seek opportunity in growing cities and regions. Many political leaders—particularly big-city mayors—expressed disagreement with this latter policy and argued that deteriorating older cities are too large and important a part of the United States thereby to "abandon" or "neglect." Probably the only policy direction on which there is now widespread agreement is that revitalization of the United States economy as a whole is badly

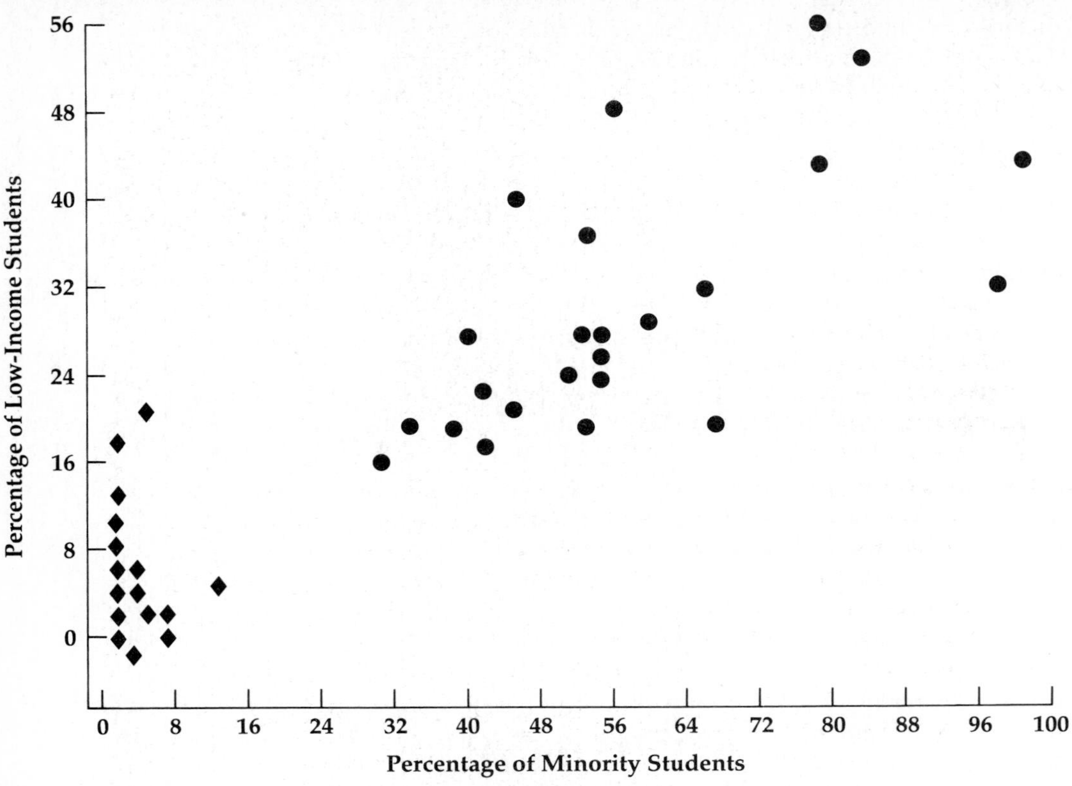

Figure 2.5 *Percentage of Low-Income Students Plotted against Percentage of Minority Students, Milwaukee Metropolitan Area Elementary Schools, 1983–84* (*Source:* Analysis of data available from the Study Commission on the Quality of Education in the Metropolitan Milwaukee Public Schools.)

needed if progress is to be made in overcoming patterns of decay and decline in many of our metropolitan areas.

Big-City Schools Reflect Stratification and Segregation

Due to concentration of working-class/underclass and minority populations in central cities, public school districts in the central cities generally have much higher proportions of low-status students and minority students than do surrounding suburban districts. An example illustrating this pattern is provided in Figure 2.5, which provides data on the Milwaukee Metropolitan Area. (Milwaukee is a medium-sized metropolitan that in many ways is typical of others in the United States.) Data for 1983–84 were available for 141 city and suburban elementary schools from which the Study Commission on the Quality of Education in the Metropolitan Milwaukee Public Schools was able to collect appropriate information.

Figure 2.5 arranges the percentage of low-income students against the percentage of minority students for a random sample of one-third of the schools in the data set. As shown in Figure 2.5, only two of the sixteen suburban schools have a percentage of low-income students as low as the city schools that scored lowest on this variable,* and none of the suburban schools had a percentage of minority students even half as high as the lowest city school. The average percentage of low-income students among the thirty-one city schools was 30 percent, as compared with 6 percent for the sixteen suburban schools. The average percentage of minority students for the city schools was 57 percent, while the average for the suburban schools was 4 percent.

Consequences for the educational system are illustrated in Figure 2.6, which shows the percentage of low-income students plus the percentage of minority students at high schools in the Milwaukee Metropolitan Area against average tenth-grade achievement scores at high schools for which the Study Commission was able to collect appropriate information. Achievement scores are composites showing the percentage of students in the top half nationally in reading and math. The percentage of low-income/minority students in the suburban schools is slightly exaggerated and the percentage of high achieving students there is slightly deflated because some suburban schools receive transfer students from the city. The data for the city are averages across city high schools.

As shown in Figure 2.6, the average percentage of low-income students plus percentage of minority students in city high schools is more than four times higher than that at the suburban high school with the highest score on this variable. Conversely, the achievement score at the lowest suburban high school is much higher than the city average of 38 percent. All of the suburban high schools have achievement far above the national average, whereas the city is far below. The fact that more than half the city tenth-graders are in the bottom 38 percent nationally also means that a larger proportion of city students are reading below grade level, and that many students are not learning much in high-school courses that require students to learn through reading.

Another major consequence for central-city school districts involves the high concentrations of high-school dropouts. As shown in Figure 2.7, the average dropout rate at city high schools during the 1983–84 school year was approximately five times as high as those at suburban high schools in the Milwaukee Metropolitan Area. (The low-income/minority percentage and the dropout percentage are slightly exaggerated at suburban schools due to the fact that some enroll low-income, minority students as part of a city-to-suburban transfer program.) Because some students leave school at each high-school grade each year, the percentages of students who drop out before graduation is much higher

* Most big cities have a number of elementary schools with enrollment virtually all poverty and minority, but Milwaukee's desegregation plan has nearly eliminated this type of school.

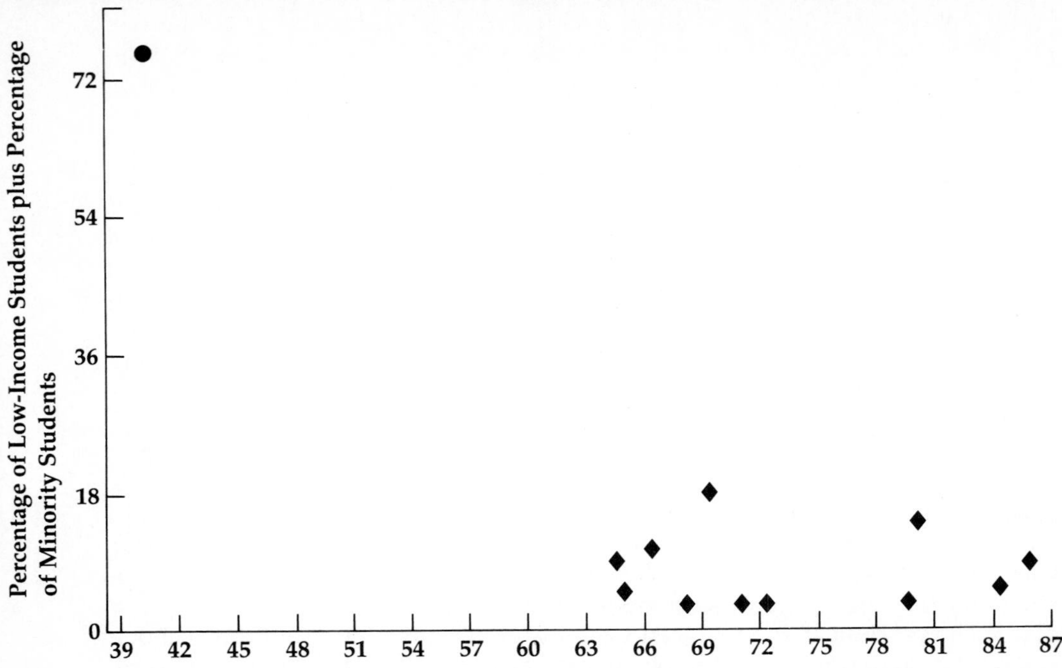

● = City; ◆ = Suburban. Each symbol represents the location of one school on each axis.

Figure 2.6 ***Percentage of Low-Income/Minority Students Plotted against Average Reading and Math Achievement, Milwaukee Metropolitan Area High Schools, 1983–84*** (*Source:* Analysis of data available from the Study Commission on the Quality of Education in the Metropolitan Milwaukee Public Schools.)

than the one-year percentage. At some individual city schools with mostly poverty/minority students, the percentage of students who leave before graduation is higher still—in the range of 40 to 60 percent.

These data for the city of Milwaukee are in line with those from other big cities. For example, data from Chicago indicate that nearly 45 percent of high-school students citywide do not graduate from high school, and some Chicago high schools have dropout rates above 60 percent (Hess and Lauber 1985). The dropout rate in New York has been estimated at more than 50 percent (Snider 1987b), and a few high schools in that city may have a rate above 80 percent.

National data on the percentage of students who are members of minority groups indicate that most big-city school districts now enroll a preponderance of minority students. (The official federal definition of *minority* students includes those designated as American Indian, Asian, black, and Hispanic, as well as

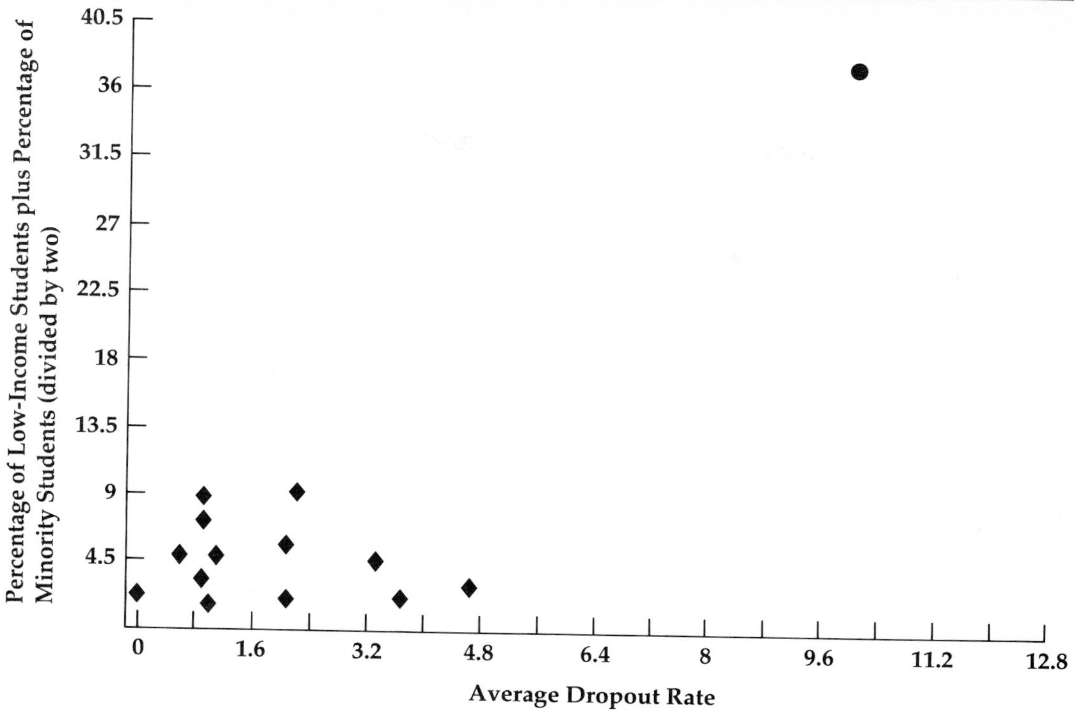

● = City; ◆ = Suburban. Each symbol represents the location of one school on each axis.

Figure 2.7 ***Percentage of Low-Income/Minority Students Plotted against Average Dropout Rate, Milwaukee Metropolitan Area High Schools, 1983–84*** (*Source:* Analysis of data available from the Study Commission of the Quality of Education in the Metropolitan Milwaukee Public Schools.)

several much smaller groups.) As shown in Table 2.9, 23 of the 26 largest urban school districts had at least 50 percent minority students in 1983–84, and two of the remaining three had more than 40 percent minority students. Nine of these 26 districts enrolled 80 percent or more minority students. The Council of Great City Schools (1987) further reports that 80 percent of the students enrolled in 44 of the nation's largest school districts are from low-income families eligible for federal lunch subsidies.

Note that the metropolitan educational structure as portrayed in this section is compatible with the view (described in Chapter 1) that the United States recently has become increasingly bifurcated, with an increasing proportion of low- and high-income persons and a decreasing proportion of middle-income persons. In any case, regardless of whether bifurcation is increasing or decreasing in society as a whole, increasing stratification and segregation by socioeconomic status and race/ethnicity do appear to be defining characteristics of metropolitan evolution in the past four or five decades.

Table 2.9 *Percentage of Minority Students, 1984, and Minority Distribution, 1980, in Twenty-Six Large Urban School Districts*

	Total Enrollment in Thousands, 1984	Percentage Minority 1984	Percentage Major Minority Groups, 1980		
			Black	*Hispanic*	*Asian*
1 New York	924	74	39	31	4
2 Los Angeles	544	78	23	45	7
3 Chicago	436	84	60	19	2
4 Dade County (Miami)	222	71	30	38	1
5 Philadelphia	208	73	63	7	1
6 Detroit	203	89	86	2	—
7 Houston	189	77	45	28	2
8 Dallas	128	74	49	19	1
9 Baltimore	120	80	78	—	—
10 San Diego	110	51	15	18	11
11 Memphis	105	77	75	—	—
12 Washington	92	97	93	2	1
13 Milwaukee	86	58	46	6	1
14 New Orleans	81	90	84	1	3
15 Columbus	69	36	39	—	1
16 Albuquerque	73	47	3	39	1
17 Atlanta	68	93	91	—	—
18 Fort Worth	65	57	37	18	1
19 Denver	63	61	23	32	3
20 San Francisco	60	83	26	16	31
21 El Paso	60	74	4	67	1
22 San Antonio	60	90	15	74	—
23 Long Beach	56	53	NA	NA	NA
24 St. Louis	56	80	79	—	—
25 Austin	56	48	19	27	1
26 Boston	56	70	46	14	5
Total	4,190	75	45	25	3

Source: Council of the Great City Schools.

Urban Renewal

During the 1950s, civic ills accompanying metropolitan growth led to social action called urban renewal. The emphasis of urban renewal in this early period was on tearing down the worst of the slums and building large blocks of public housing for low-income families. For example, much of Boston's oldest housing was torn out to make room for expressways. Hundreds of acres of tenement houses were torn down on Chicago's South Side, on New York's Lower East Side, and in the area in Washington south of the Capitol. Los Angeles cleared the area on which the new Civic Center was built. The Golden Triangle of Pittsburgh was modernized with new office buildings, hotels, and expressways.

Not only were slums cleared, but a good deal also was done to arrest and reverse the process of decay of the downtown business district. This meant building a second generation of ultramodern skyscrapers to replace those erected in the early 1900s. It also meant building expressways to provide easy automobile transportation for commuters who do not use old-fashioned public transit services. In addition, new and attractive apartment housing was built within walking or taxi distance of the downtown offices and stores for those people who have the money and the inclination to live in upper- or middle-class style without going out to the suburbs or the city fringes.

In the 1960s, 1970s, and 1980s, the federal government continued to award significant sums of money to what is now called Housing and Urban Development. An Act of 1965 provided a variety of aids for housing, including substantial numbers of new low-rent public housing units, rent supplements to aid low-income families to secure better private housing, and subsidized low interest rates for housing for people of moderate income. Community development legislation was updated in the 1970s to place a greater emphasis on *conservation* of neighborhoods that might otherwise become slums, and on *redevelopment* of deteriorated or unused land as part of a long-range plan for the improvement of the central city and the entire metropolitan area. The federal government also began to place some stress on reducing metropolitan stratification and segregation, for example, by refusing to approve some applications for housing projects that would concentrate more low-status population in the central city and by requiring suburbs to consider low-cost housing in their plans for future development. These emphases were foreshadowed in the 1960s by Robert C. Weaver, who served in President Lyndon Johnson's Cabinet:

> *I am convinced that the recent decline in the population of central cities has been due, in large part, to the concentration of new construction in the suburbs and the scarcity of competing living facilities in the central cities.*
>
> *The city today is, or should be in my opinion, the heart, and in a sense the soul, of a metropolitan area. The suburbs around it, to a large degree, draw their life and their spirit from the city's economy and culture. The city should be revitalized as the anchor holding together our metropolitan areas. It does not perform this function effectively today. (Weaver 1964, 6)*

However, urban renewal activities through the 1970s and 1980s generally have not yet succeeded in reversing the process of segregation and decay in large metropolitan areas. Part of the reason is that most housing built for or made available to low-status families has been in or next to low-status neighborhoods and has compounded as much as it has alleviated the problems generated by stratification and segregation. Slums were cleared in many cities, but in the absence of long-range plans for metropolitan development there was no place for evicted families to move except to nearby low-status neighborhoods, which then experienced accelerated deterioration. Most public housing built in the 1950s was in the form of high-rise apartments, which magnified the problem of concentrated urban poverty. Housing programs since that time have not contributed as blatantly to additional stratification and segregation, but neither have they succeeded in greatly reducing the concentration of low-status families in the central city and in some of the suburbs.

Redevelopment of Deteriorated Neighborhoods in the Central City

Several forces favor the redevelopment of large sections of the central city as stable neighborhoods with a substantial middle-status population base. Redevelopment of this sort can take place either through renovation of older housing in which middle-class families are willing to invest large sums of time and money or through the construction of new housing on land previously nonresidential or cleared of slums by government action. Most big cities already have some housing that fits this description, where a neighborhood with old mansions has become a prestige address for young couples interested in renovation or middle-class apartments and townhouses have been built in or near the downtown. These clusters of redevelopment generally could serve as nuclei for much larger renewal efforts, provided that potential residents have confidence in the future viability of neighborhoods in the central city.

An example of redevelopment of a well-situated but deteriorated central city area is the project for twenty-first century renewal by the Chicago 21 Corporation. Favored by city government, this organization with private financing is in the process of buying and developing vacant areas close to the downtown business district of Chicago. There are about four square miles of mainly vacant land to the south and west of the Chicago Loop.

The first phase of the plan has been carried through by the Dearborn Park Corporation. This corporation bought a 51.5 acre site, including the old Dearborn Station and unused railroad tracks. The Corporation has built several hundred town houses and two high-rise apartment buildings, with a total of 3,000 residential units, which have been rented or sold either to young married couples or to older families who are employed in the central business district.

The Problem of a Viable Economic Mixture in the Central City and in Its Schools

The confluence of trends such as those described means that it now may be possible to redevelop deteriorated central city neighborhoods into attractive communities for people of varied racial and ethnic background and socioeconomic status. Paul R. Porter, formerly administrator of the Marshall Plan for the redevelopment of Europe after World War II, has examined some of these trends and written a book on *The Recovery of American Cities*, which concluded that they represent *a superb opportunity for cities . . . as long as low-income housing was in acute short supply, and as long as there was a strong stream of migration from the countryside, renewal policy (with some exceptions) has been to preserve this land for low-income residents. The policy, like most buildings on the land, is obsolete. The proper goal should be to transform the decaying districts into new neighborhoods attractive enough to* compete with suburbs *as a place of residence for people who work in the central business district. (Porter 1976, 14)*

It is clear that the restoration of middle-income housing contiguous to the downtown core of the big city is a part of the larger problem of maintaining a viable mixture of social classes within the central city of the metropolitan area. The problem is partly one of racial and ethnic residential integration, and of desegregation of public schools, considered at length in Chapter 9. In general, the position of the public schools is likely to become more and more strategic. William G. Colman, an authority on the structure of the metropolitan area, has written:

Until central city schools become as good as, or somewhat better than, suburban schools, few middle and higher income families with school-age children will remain in the city, particularly if the public school servicing their neighborhood is attended by children who are all or mostly from low income families. . . . Undoubtedly the public school is a major, if not the dominant factor, in restoring a socioeconomic balance in central cities. (1977, 34)

To a significant degree, the problems of city and metropolitan revitalization are centered in the older and larger metropolitan areas in the northern, eastern, and middlewestern parts of the United States. Constructive revitalization will be difficult to bring about, but scholars studying urban development in the United States are not entirely pessimistic. For example, Richard Knight has examined recent developments and has tried to identify the major actions and policies required to rebuild United States cities for the twenty-first century. His overall conclusions are as follows:

Industrial cities are easily misread. If one thinks of them in terms of plant and equipment, all one sees is abandoned plants and neighborhoods in the center of the city, and thus their image of inevitable decline is reinforced. . . . [But, viewed] in perspective, the worst is over. Most of the production jobs that will be lost have already . . . [been lost]. The challenge they now face is one that all cities have faced in history: to rebuild. This requires a clear vision of how their role has changed so that they can be redesigned in ways that are supportive of their expanding functions.

The real success of any city in the future, as in the past, will depend on its ability to pass on its knowledge base from one generation to another, to retain its young once they have been educated . . . to recruit talent to apply and advance the wide range of technology that is required. . . . [Thus] development strategy for cities in the future will have to be oriented toward rebuilding a city that is

> *. . . attractive to the middle class. Although this may seem like the obvious direction, it would require a major shift in values, behavior, and policies. (Knight 1982, 64)*

Conclusion: The Crisis in Sorting and Selecting in Metropolitan Schools and Society

This chapter has documented that much of the crisis in educational sorting and selecting in the United States involves and reflects recent trends that have concentrated working-class and under-class students, many of whom are disadvantaged minority students, in the inner-city portion of a postindustrial, metropolitan society. Scott Miller of the Exxon Education Foundation has surveyed developments regarding the differential development of inner-city schools and communities and has summarized them in the trenchant observation that "several of our inner cities have effectively become the planet's first truly international multicultural, multilingual 'developing countries.' . . . The nation-building agenda concerning nonwhites [in the inner city] has been transformed in recent years into a much larger, more complex challenge . . . [and] has become a matter of even more pressing concern for the overall moral, political, and economic health of the nation " (Miller 1986, 52).

Miguel Castells also has examined recent patterns of metropolitan development in relation to larger economic and social trends and noted that "we are witnessing the rise of urban schizophrenia . . . [involving] the contradictory coexistence of different social, cultural, and economic logics within the same spatial structure . . . [thereby inducing] a *new territorial division of labor*, based on *polarized growth* and *selective development*, which reflects itself in the interregional cleavages, intrametropolitan dualism, and *simultaneous* life and death of our great cities" [italics in original]. He further pointed out that much of the problem involving schools and society in inner-city poverty neighborhoods has its origins in the "upgrading of professional and technical jobs in advanced service and high technology manufacturing . . . [which require] a fundamental retraining of labor, something the educational system is hardly able to assure, particularly in the secondary public school" (Castells 1985, 22, 24, 32, 33).

Concerned with both the international economic challenge faced by the society as a whole and the equity issues raised by the inadequate performance of many disadvantaged students, educators also are reviewing the trends that have produced the crisis in educational sorting and selecting. One of the most useful analyses of the general problem in education has been provided by Daniel and Lauren Resnick. They have reached the conclusion that traditional arrangements for sorting and selecting are no longer functional for the United States. The Resnicks first recognize that our historic efforts to provide equal educational opportunity and to stimulate national growth involved the movement to make high-school education not just available but compulsory for all students. With the exception of contemporary Japan, no other large nation has established a system of comprehensive high schools providing some common academic emphasis for nearly all its youth.

The Resnicks also point out, however, that traditional efforts to provide a common curriculum for all secondary students were possible only because ability grouping and tracking allowed the schools to differentiate within the comprehensive public-school system. "Where do American schools stand," they ask, "with respect to curriculum and tracking?" After reviewing the history of the comprehensive high school in the twentieth century, their answer is that

> *we have compromised. Our rhetoric and our provision in most school systems of an undifferentiated high school diploma all suggest a decision against tracking. However, in reality we have considerable tracking . . . even if it is not always formally so labeled. Comprehensive high schools usually house several quite different sets of courses in which expectations and standards vary considerably. (Resnick and Resnick 1985, 10)*

According to the Resnicks and many other observers, the most destructive consequence of the compromise educators reached in trying to provide opportunity for all while maintaining high standards for only a few has been that the great majority of students have not been challenged and helped to attain a high level of academic performance. Some students in the top track become advanced, independent learners, while the vast bulk of students receive relatively low-level instruction emphasizing passive learning, memorization and regurgitation of factual material, and mastery of only very minimal standards (Goodlad 1984; Wise 1988). This basic pattern has been significantly reinforced during the past fifteen years by introduction of minimum competency testing, continuing and probably growing reliance on simplified textbooks, and mandated reforms that require or at least encourage teachers to emphasize such low-level skills as computation in math and the mechanics of language (Madaus 1988). To do otherwise would have required truly fundamental system reforms involving introduction of active learning methods, reduction of class size in many schools, continuous and expensive teacher-retraining, provision of much more administrative support, and many other costly and difficult interventions.

In addition, the traditional pattern appeared to be producing relatively acceptable results for most students, until the emergence of postindustrial society and escalation of international competition substantially magnified the need to attain a higher level of performance on a more equitable basis that ensures improved achievement on the part of economically and socially disadvantaged students. After reviewing the current status of curriculum and instruction in elementary and secondary schools as well as of recent national and state efforts to improve instruction, the Resnicks conclude that an important first step in raising educational standards is to improve the level of instruction through a nontracked curriculum that sets strong intellectual requirements for all students. "Nobody knows," they argue, "whether a strong intellectual program" for all students could work—whether most students would remain in school and perform successfully. The idea of a high-level, academically oriented common curriculum'' is radical because it ''takes seriously the goal of a fully educated citizenry'' (Resnick and Resnick 1985, 18).

Later chapters describe efforts to provide compensatory education to improve the performance of low-status students (Chapter 8), the role of desegregation in improving educational opportunity for minority students (Chapter 9), problems and obstacles that make it difficult for educators to overcome disadvantages in students' home environment (Chapters 3 and 4), and other topics bearing on improvement of students' performance. The entire final chapter is devoted to an examination of recent educational reforms and of promising approaches for improving achievement. Indeed, much of the remainder of this book constitutes in effect an extended meditation and commentary on the causes and consequences of the crisis in sorting and selecting that is occurring in postindustrial, metropolitan society, and the actions that can or should be taken to deal with this crisis.

EXERCISES

1. Describe the steps being taken for urban renewal in a metropolitan area, and discuss the relations you think the schools should have to urban renewal in this area.
2. If you live in a city of fewer than 50,000, study it and its county as an example of tension between urban and rural styles of life. How do the schools fit in? Do they tend to work toward urbanization?
3. After reading Paul R. Porter's book on *The Recovery of American Cities*, describe ways in which education might affect the success of comprehensive plans to bring about systematic renewal in the metropolitan area.
4. Select a college you know. Analyze the student body in terms of socioeconomic backgrounds. What is the relation of socioeconomic background to fraternity membership, participation in athletics scholarship awards, participation in religious organizations, and enrollment in various curricula or courses of study?
5. Interview several high-school students of different social backgrounds to find out what their attitudes are toward the school and its various curricula.

SUGGESTIONS FOR FURTHER READING

1. A number of classic books deal with the growth of metropolitanism and the problems of the city. The book by Bollens and Schmandt, *The Metropolis*, is particularly relevant, as is also *Anatomy of a Metropolis* by Hoover and Vernon, and *The City Is the Frontier*, by C. Abrams. The book *Metropolis, 1985* by Raymond Vernon is one of a series describing the New York Metropolitan

Region Study. Jean Gottmann's *Megalopolis* gives a striking account of metropolitan development in the chain of urban areas that stretches from Boston to Washington, D.C.

2. For a general consideration of metropolitan aspects of educational systems, see the two volumes edited by Troy V. McKelvey, entitled *Metropolitan School Organization*. These volumes and the Yearbook of the National Society for the Study of Education entitled *Metropolitanism: Its Challenge to Education* (Havighurst 1968) argue for the establishment of a single educational authority for a metropolitan area.
3. The American metropolis is rather different in its history and structure from the great cities of other parts of the world. To see the range in types of cities, the following books are useful: *The Urban Community: A World Perspective* by Nels Anderson; *The City* by Rose Hum Lee; *Images of the City* by Anselm L. Strauss; and *The City in History* by Lewis Mumford.
4. Patterns of resegregation in suburban areas are among the topics documented and discussed in *The New Suburbanites* by Robert Lake.
5. Many key aspects of urban evolution and policy are discussed in *Cities in the 21st Century* edited by Gary Gappert and Richard V. Knight. Chapters dealing with "The Evolving Dynamics of Urban Development," "The Hispanic-American Urban Order," "The Future of Black Ghettos," "New Technologies and Their Urban Impact," "Toward the Androgynous City," and "Changes in the Provision of Public Services" are particularly useful to educators.
6. *Making Inequality* by James E. Rosenbaum is a case study of a white, working-class school in which the academic track into which students were assigned had substantial independent effects on their subsequent careers. Rosenbaum shows how tracking is used to select and sort secondary students and discusses implications for public policy. He concludes that tracking sets up a tournament mobility system that successively eliminates students on meritocratic grounds such as ability and effort but also on other grounds such as efficiency and convenience in organizing the public schools.
7. A critical analysis of the community colleges and their role in higher education was published in the *Harvard Educational Review* by Fred L. Pincus in 1980 under the title "The False Promises of Community Colleges: Class Conflict and Vocational Education." A somewhat more balanced report on Community Colleges was presented by Virginia Robinson: "Community Colleges: Education's Biggest Growth Industry Has an Uncertain Mission," *Education Times*, Nov. 23, 1981.
8. A good summary of the issues and of the research program that attempted to create culture-fair tests of intelligence (tests that would not penalize children from lower socioeconomic level) is given in "Social Class and Intelligence Tests" by W. W. Charters, Jr., and N. L. Gage, in *Readings in the Social Psychology of Education*.
9. The important questions about relative influence of heredity and of environment in the production of intelligence cannot be answered in simple terms. There is always an interaction of heredity and environment. In the

United States, the practical question concerns the relation of IQ to race and to social class. But no two racial groups have the same social-class or social environmental experience. Therefore, information about racial status is mixed up with information about the social environment. A student who is reasonably knowledgeable about statistics and about socioeconomic status could usefully study the recent publications of Jensen and of those who disagree with him. See Sanday, Scarr-Salapatek, Mercer, and Herrnstein.

10. Read and compare *The Paideia Proposal* by Mortimer Adler and *The American High School Today* by James Conant. What are the similarities in the authors' proposals for curriculum and instruction in high schools in the United States? What are the differences? How does each author propose to deal with tracking? In what ways was each book a response to the social problems of the particular time period in which it was written?
11. *The New Heartland* by John Herbers describes recent changes in urbanization and metropolitan evolution in the United States. Topics dealt with include the growth of exurbs, deindustrialization in the East and North, long-range commuting, and movement to small towns and cities.

3

Problems of Children and Youth in Differing Social Class Environments

This chapter describes some of the most important problems children tend to encounter in three differing types of environments categorized by social class: working class, underclass, and middle class. Describing and discussing environments in this way necessarily oversimplifies reality. For example, implying that there are no major differences between differing working-class communities and suggesting that all families in a given working-class neighborhood behave and react the same way obviously is incorrect. The reader should keep in mind the fact that we are trying to portray general tendencies rather than implying that communities and families can be universally categorized according to social class.

Evolution of the Child-Nurturing, Modern Family

Before describing the problems that children and youth encounter in differing types of communities categorized by social class, it is important to review how the family has evolved toward greater emphasis on nurturing children for success in the educational system and later in life. This evolution is connected with larger patterns of change that have occurred in family structure and in the relationship between the family and other social institutions.

We begin by noting that the family was much more of an economic unit in earlier times than it is now. Before industrialization, most families lived on the land, and children grew up in close contact with their parents and other adults. All members of the family contributed to production, and education for most children consisted largely of learning how to function as a member of the family and the community in which they lived. Thus, the family together with the larger community was the major educational influence in the life of the child and worked in conjunction with other community institutions such as the church and the apprenticeship system in preparing young people for their roles as adults.

The family as a social institution has undergone marked changes, particularly in the past 100 years. In contrast to the rural or frontier family, the modern urban family remains the unit of economic consumption but is no longer the unit of economic production. Formal education, as well as many types of informal education, have been taken over by the school, the mass media, and other agencies. Even the function of character building has been taken on more and more by such nonfamily agencies as the church, the school, and such special youth-serving organizations as the Boy Scouts and Girl Scouts, the 4-H clubs, Future Farmers of America, and the YMCA and YWCA. In this sense, the family can be thought of as a less important educational institution today than it was in traditional society.

In other respects, however, the educational role of the family has become even more important today than it was in the past. Change in this direction has been associated with changes in the role the family plays in society as a whole. These latter changes involve the historical evolution of the family in the direction of (1) setting itself apart from the life of the larger community and (2) specializing to a greater extent than it did in satisfying the emotional needs of its members.

A number of historians have been struck by the degree to which the family and the community in traditional and early industrial society were more closely intertwined than they tend to be in Western society today. On the one hand, people participated in communal activities and events such as festivals and open-air marketing to a greater extent than most adults do now. People lived their lives more in the immediate local community than is true today, in the company of others from their community at work, at church, and in other settings in which children became a part of the adult world at an early age. In addition, in many parts of the Western world the home was penetrated much more frequently by outsiders—particularly boarders, guests, and apprenticed youth—than is true today. In early industrial England, for example, families frequently sent their children to work for other people at an early age and accepted the children of others as servants or apprentices in their own homes. Phillipe Ariès has summarized the preindustrial community as follows:

> *The historian who studies iconographic documents . . . promptly makes the acquaintance of . . . the crowd—not the massive, anonymous crowd of our overpopulated cities, but the assembly of neighbors, women and children, numerous but not unknown to one another. . . . It is as if everyone had come out instead of staying at home: there are scenes depicting streets and markets, games and crafts, soldiers and courtiers, churches and tortures. . . .*
>
> *Life in the past, until the seventeenth century, was lived in public. We have a good many examples of the ascendancy of society. The traditional ceremonies which accompanied marriage and which were regarded as more important than the religious ceremonies . . . the visit paid by the guests to the newly-married pair when they were already in bed . . . afford further proof of society's rights over the privacy of the couple. What objection could there be when in fact privacy scarcely ever existed, when people lived on top of one another, masters and servants, children and adults, in houses open at all hours to the indiscretion of callers? (Ariès 1965, 405)*

Closely related to the tendency for premodern families to "live life in public" as compared with families today was the relative overcrowding in housing which was typical of traditional and early industrial families. Shorter (1975) and other historians have examined data on housing in several countries and have concluded that both in traditional rural areas and in early industrial communities, family members generally lived and slept in much more confined quarters than do families today.

In addition, families in traditional society were in much closer contact with relatives; partly as a consequence, much more emphasis was placed on family heritage and honor than is true of most families in today's geographically and socially mobile society. Shorter has summarized this aspect of traditional society and the change that has occurred during the past 400 years as follows:

> *People in traditional families are willing to renounce a number of personal ambitions. They're ready to postpone marriage until late in life, or indeed forego it entirely so that the farm may prosper under the eldest; they're willing to overcome whatever strivings towards privacy slumber in their breasts, and go to the communal bonfire on St. John's Day. . . . [in the] Old Days—let us say the sixteenth and seventeenth centuries—the family . . . was held firmly in the matrix of a larger social order. One set of ties bound it to the surrounding kin, the network of aunts and uncles, cousins and nieces who dotted the old regime's social landscape. Another set fastened it to the wider community, and gaping holes in the shield of privacy permitted others to enter the household freely and, if necessary, preserve order. A final set of ties held the elementary family to generations past and future. . . . In its journey into the modern world the family has broken all these ties. (From* The Making of the Modern Family, *by Edward Shorter, © 1975 by Basic Books, Inc., Publishers, New York, pp. 3, 18. Reprinted by permission.)*

Along with this change from looking outward to looking inward, the modern family became more child-centered than had been true before. In addition, middle-class families began to place some stress on raising children to think independently, as contrasted with traditional emphasis on obedience and authority. Whereas in the traditional and early industrial periods the family had been oriented to the larger community, the modern family appears to be relatively oriented more toward interactions among its members, and much of this interaction centers on the welfare of the children. Children probably receive at least as much individual attention from parents in the modern family as was true in earlier periods, even though parents in modern society are at work, away from children a high percentage of the time.

What has been responsible for the change from the community- and heritage-oriented family of the preindustrial and early industrial periods to the conjugal family more typical of modern times in which husband, wife, and children are largely set apart from the outside world? Historians disagree on which causes are the most important (Pollock 1983), but most would list a number of developments that helped either bring about or make possible this change. Among these are:

1. Industrialization and urbanization, which had the effect of detaching people from the communities in which their families previously had been rooted.
2. Economic progress, which made it possible for many families to have larger housing units with more private accommodations.
3. Loss of economic and other family functions to other institutions, which freed

the family to specialize more in meeting the psychological needs of its members. "The modern family," according to Frank Musgrove, "specializes in affection. It can do this job precisely because it need do little else" (Musgrove 1966, 37).

4. Reduced family size, which made it possible for parents to devote more resources and individual attention to children than could be done in large households.
5. Reduced child mortality, which made it more rewarding to lavish attention and resources on children than was the tendency when a high percentage of children died at an early age.
6. Spread of the idea of "romantic love," which Shorter describes as unseating "material considerations in bringing the couple together. Property and lineage . . . [gave] way to personal happiness and individual self-development as criteria for choosing a marriage partner. . . . Domesticity, beyond that, sealed off the family as a whole from its traditional interaction with the surrounding world" (Shorter 1975, 5, 228).

Whatever the relative importance of these and other interrelated causes, it seems safe to conclude that the emergence of the inward-looking, child-nurturing, conjugal family was a development that spanned several centuries and proceeded at a different rate among various social groups in Western societies. It also is apparent that this development was at first substantially a middle-class phenomenon and indeed was simultaneous if not actually synonymous with the rise of the middle class. In this regard, Young and Willmott (1973) have described how "domesticity" and separation from the larger community did not become characteristic of the English working class until the late nineteenth or early twentieth centuries, and Stone (1974) has explained that it was the propertied and bourgeois families that first turned inward because these were the "families which were not so grand as to be able to maintain a small army of nursery staff to take care of the children for them, but rich enough to indulge in the luxury of sentiment" (p. 31).

The analysis to this point has described the evolution of the family in the direction of modern emphases on privacy, child nurturance, and sentiment. It also has linked this evolution to the emergence of the middle class, as part of a long-term change in society toward the creation of contemporary social classes that to a significant extent pass the advantage of wealth and the disadvantages of poverty on to following generations. When one views these developments as part of a single, larger pattern, it appears as if the middle-class family historically acted to shelter its children from the outside world and to provide relatively permissive nurturance of a kind that would give the child good preparation for succeeding in school and later in life. "Family and school together," Ariès has observed, "removed the child from adult society" (p. 413). The working-class family, by way of contrast, was not as quickly able and willing to shut out external influences that might be deleterious in terms of preparing children to function independently in the classroom and the economy; instead, it continues to this day to stress obedience and authority—values that parents apparently perceive as more functional in a difficult and often threatening low-income environment.

The reader should not conclude that stress on authority and obedience in child raising is necessarily inimical to the development of skills that will help children succeed in society. Stone (1974) has described how the "nuclear child-centered" family was relatively authoritarian in the sixteenth and seventeenth centuries, more "permissive and affectionate" in the eighteenth century, and again relatively more authoritarian in the nineteenth century, thus indicating that emphasis on child nurturance for success in school and society is not strictly a function of permissive versus authoritarian family relations. Stress on obedience probably does not damage a child's cognitive development unless this stress is so insistent and pervasive as to inhibit exploration of the social, intellectual, or physical environments in which the child grows up. The following chapter summarizes what is known about home environments that contribute to achievement in the educational system. Before turning to this topic, more should be said about the efforts of contemporary families to isolate their children from external influences that might have a negative effect on their performance in school.

The ability to achieve this latter goal probably is more directly linked with social class than are variations in the actual learning environment provided in the home, because social class plays such an important part in determining how a family relates to the surrounding community and whether it is able to shield children from negative external influences (Cohen 1981). Middle-class families typically are more successful in this regard than are working-class families, because their economic level and their emphasis on sentiment and nurturance have enabled them to attain a relatively high level of separation (privacy) from the outside world. However, middle-class families appear to be having more difficulty protecting their children from external influences now than they did in the past few generations before television invaded their homes, and before automobiles and drugs became more important parts of the subculture of teenagers. Like the family, the school confronts similar difficulties in a modern urban environment (Gabarino and Plantz 1980).

Is it better to shelter the child from the adult environment than to have the child learn how to get along in it at an early age? Is it desirable to separate the family from the community in order to nurture the cognitive growth of children and make the family a more self-sufficient unit emotionally? The answers to these types of questions depend on many considerations, including the goals established for children and other family members and the nature of the environment in which the family functions. Examining such questions from the viewpoint of social-class differences among families and communities can help us understand the problems children encounter growing up and going to school.

Working-Class Environments

The upper working-class family frequently is still a traditional family in many respects. Although in some ways it is gradually becoming more similar to "modern" middle-class families (Young and Wilmott 1973; Rubin 1976), particularly when it is located in suburban parts of the metropolitan area (Tallman and Morgner 1970), it still emphasizes close ties with kin and segmentation of family roles by age and sex. These patterns have been described by Gans (1962) in his study of a working-class Italian community in the West End of Boston:

> *The* working-class subculture *is distinguished by the dominant role of the family circle. Its way of life is based on social relationships amidst relatives. The working class views the world from the family circle, and considers everything outside it as either a means to its maintenance or to its destruction. (Gans 1962, 244)*

There are definite advantages for child rearing in the upper working-class style described above. (Gans uses the term *lower class* to describe the lower-working class.) Children receive much support from a variety of adults, and many parents do succeed in protecting their children from negative influences in the environment. However, one might almost say they do so by shutting out the world beyond the family and neighborhood as long as possible. This type of childhood tends to result in limited preparation and aspirations for education, and it does not help children learn to function independently in institutions like the modern school.

In addition, working-class children in an urban setting tend to be drawn into the lower working-class street culture that has the effect, among other things, of reducing the likelihood that they will succeed in the school. This is particularly a problem for young males, and for children from those working-class families that exemplify considerable marital instability and detachment from the primary labor market (i.e., which may be part of a culture of poverty). Gans calls these the "action-seeking" families and youth and reports that

> *mothers do attempt to teach their departing children rules of proper behavior, namely the rules of the adult-centered and routine-seeking home. . . . During this time, however, the child is also learning what are called the rules of the street, that is those of the peer group. Thus, for some years, parents fight the ascendancy of street rules over home rules. . . .*
>
> *Interestingly enough, the home-rules that are preached to the child differ little from those held by the middle class. . . . The extent to which these rules are enforced, however, varies between action-seeking and routine-seeking or mobile families. The former, for instance, seem to surrender earlier, with less resistance to the child's inevitable adoption of the rules of the street. Moreover, the child himself reacts differently to the enforcement of these ideals. The child of a routine-seeking family, discovering that there are home rules and street rules, soon learns therefore to act accordingly in both places. In an action-seeking family, however, the child learns that the rules which the parents preach and those which they themselves practice diverge sharply. (Gans 1962, 58–59)*

Underclass Environments

Problems parents experience in trying to protect children from the environment in which the big-city underclass live represent a different order of magnitude. Poverty is more concentrated in these inner-city neighborhoods, social disorganization is more widespread, and families find it even more difficult to protect their children from negative forces in the environment than do upper working-class families that have built a compact family circle around the child. Rainwater (1970) has studied an underclass housing project in St. Louis and has shown that the environment for children in this setting is highly stimulating and anxiety producing, particularly with regard to frequency of violent behavior and exposure to adult sexual activities. Rainwater found that early sophistication thus acquired by the children bothered their mothers, who then tried to

> *keep their children within the apartment as much as possible. . . . One often gets the impression that mothers try to hold them virtual prisoners within the house, so great is their fear for their physical and moral safety outside.*
>
> *However, mothers know they cannot succeed with this strategy as the children grow up. Children get a taste of freedom as they walk to and from school and they increasingly demand the right to come and go as their peers do. . . . Only parents who remain energetically vigilant can isolate their children through adolescence. Teenage girls, for example, may not be allowed to spend time outside the home (except for school) unless they are accompanied by a responsible adult. But few mothers can maintain sufficient authority to carry out such strict discipline more than intermittently. . . . The parents try to teach the child what life is supposed to be like and how he is supposed to live it. In doing so they communicate an image of conventional American family and community life, but always in the context of the quite different life actually experienced by both parents and child. . . . Parents communicate to the child that only if he does right he may be safe, but in fact, he discovers that when he does right he is* not *safe, and very often he does not want to do right because the things that are wrong are more interesting and stimulating. (Rainwater 1970, 223, 225, 226)*

As Rainwater's account makes clear, the socialization of underclass children in concentrated poverty neighborhoods generally is not conducive to success in the school and the economy. It seems almost as though the inner-city environment reproduces some of the most important social characteristics of premodern communities that offered children little protection from the dangers as well as rewards of adult society, before the modern family came into prominence partly to provide refuge for its members and develop resources required for success in a modern economy. The difficulty of raising children in the inner city is underlined when it is recognized that the brightest and most talented youngsters frequently tend to be the ones who are most quickly destroyed, perhaps because they may be most likely to become leaders among their peers and are quickest to perceive the hopelessness of their situation. It is no accident that the most common refrain among parents of teenagers in the inner city is, "I can't control my children anymore," or that children asked to write essays in the inner-city classroom frequently respond like the teenager who titled his story "In Hell," or another who ended her story with the comment, "Earth is Hell to live on. I wonder if we could live on the moon."

Some social scientists familiar with the big-city underclass believe that children and youth in the inner city will never have an adequate opportunity to succeed unless they are removed from their families and neighborhoods and placed in an entirely new environment somewhat as many middle-class children historically were placed in boarding school to give them special preparation for education and careers (Coleman and Hoffer 1987). Even today, governments in many countries take the brightest teenagers from their homes and send them to schools in communities distant from their families and neighborhoods (Joyce and Showers 1987). However, there obviously are disadvantages in removing children from their families even if this is thought to be legally and morally acceptable, and there are other alternatives for improving the home environment of children in the inner city. Some of these alternatives are discussed elsewhere in this book, particularly in the sections in Chapters 4, 8, and 9 dealing with home environments and the schools and with deconcentrating the poverty population in big-city schools.

Middle-Class Environments

The dangers to children growing up in a middle-class environment are quite different than those faced by children in working-class or underclass environments. Whereas underclass environments pose clear threats to physical, cognitive, and emotional growth, and working-class environments tend to limit the child's range of experience and opportunities to become well prepared to participate in the school, many youngsters in predominantly middle-class neighborhoods now face an excess of opportunities that make it difficult to attain a stable and authentic sense of identity.

In general, middle-class children are well prepared to enter and succeed in school, and they tend to acquire much information about the world beyond their immediate neighborhood. However, their families tend to have few real roots in the communities in which they live. Their parents attempt to develop self-direction but frequently are unable to provide very much actual direction for the future, and the knowledge that they acquire is difficult to integrate into a coherent set of values to guide growth and development. Orr and Nichelson (1970) have described some of the characteristics of this type of environment, which they call the *radical suburb*, in terms of its emphases on openness to new experience and on empirical testing of reality as contrasted with acceptance of traditional opinion:

> *It is a very short step from the empirical notion that truth is what is verifiable by experience to the expansive belief that experience itself is valuable. . . . From*

there it is but another short step to the notion that the richest life is one that includes the most varied kinds of experiences. The style of the suburban radical is not as it appears—a backlash against the stainless-steel grayness of a scientific atmosphere—but instead is the predictable spin-off from a culture that is infatuated with scientific experimentation. (Orr and Nichelson 1970, 50)

As Orr and Nichelson suggest, emphasis on new experience may lead to a lack of regard for the quality and effects of experience, to the feeling that "a bad trip may be better than no trip at all" (p. 62). It may provide children with a large amount of information about the world, but this knowledge, as Ortega y Gasset has pointed out, may be "in a form so intricate, so overloaded with distinctions, classifications, arguments, that . . . [there is] no way in so overgrown a forest to discover the repertoire of clear and simple ideas which truly orient man in his experience" (Ortega y Gasset 1958, 100).

The very fact that abundant opportunities for personal and career growth are available to the middle-class child presents problems of its own. When "anybody can be anybody," Klapp has observed, it may be that "nobody can be somebody" (Klapp 1969, 122). Young people in this type of environment have an opportunity to develop a multitude of identities, but too much impermanence in self-definition can destroy the sense of self that is to be fulfilled. The environment in which a person with shifting or unfinished identity functions also is likely to seem abstract and unreal, thus generating a ceaseless search for a more satisfying definition of self.

Emphasis on new experience and opportunity to experiment with a variety of identities can also lead to feelings of satiation and boredom with the world. Young people who are satiated with the everyday world and perceive their environment as unreal or plastic, who lack a stable sense of identity and the simple ideas which truly orient man in his existence, are likely to have problems in working to attain long-range goals in the school and the economy. As Klapp has summarized the situation

identity is a delicate psychosocial equilibrium requiring various kinds of support for its maintenance. But in the very society that proclaims abundance for everybody, we see interactional and symbolic deficiencies: . . . the wiping away of traditions and places; shallow, inconsistent relationships. . . . an inability of people to get through facades and roles to each other. . . .

A person whose interactions lack psychological payoffs will find life unutterably boring. The success symbols, though he has them, will seem empty. . . . He will, therefore, have a tendency to become a dropout or a deviant, turning to escapes or kicks for compensation. (Klapp 1969, 318–319)

In a sense, the dangers to youth most characteristic of a contemporary, middle-class environment tend to be manifested in ways similar to those in an underclass environment. In both situations, though for different reasons, the problems young people experience growing up tend to result in the formation of peer subcultures emphasizing drugs and escape from institutions in the local community. This is why alienation from school has been particularly evident and problematical in inner-city, poverty schools on the one hand and in homogeneous middle-class schools on the other. Middle-class youngsters tend to do well in the elementary school, but many are experiencing problems connected with alienation at the secondary level. To some extent, of course, the problems of youth subcultures are similar across social-class groups and present challenges to educators in any secondary school, because they represent age-based problems in growing up in a modern society. Brake (1980) has summarized this relatively universal aspect of youth development:

> *Youth culture also offers a collective identity, a reference group, from which to develop an individual identity, 'magically' freed from the ascribed roles of home, school and work. . . . Once they have made this separation, which makes a dramaturgical statement about their difference from those expectations imposed upon them by others, they feel free to explore and develop what they are. They will create an image, often of a quasidelinquent, or rebellious style, which marks them apart from the expectations in particular of their family and other adults. (p. 166)*

It is interesting to consider in the context of this discussion some possible ways in which middle-class families with their emphasis on privacy sometimes may overprotect their children from the world outside the home. Sennett (1973) has identified this type of situation in his study of late nineteenth-century families in Chicago, at a time when industrial growth was rapid and many opportunities were available for upward mobility. Based on his study of family records, Sennett found that sons who grew up in large middle-class homes including relatives of the husband and wife generally equalled or exceeded their fathers in social status, whereas sons who grew up in small, nuclear families showed less upward mobility and frequently experienced downward mobility. Sennett's conclusion was that sons in the latter families had been given security at the cost of opportunity: "the intensive family . . . became a shelter from the work pressures of the industrial city, a place where men tried to institute some control and establish some comforting intimacies in the shape of their lives, while withdrawing to the sidelines as the new opportunities of the city industries opened up" (Sennett 1973, 127–128).

Implications for Education

Dangers or deficiencies in differing social-class environments have implications for the types of approaches to curriculum and instruction that should be emphasized in the schools. Some of these implications are considered with reference to the three types of environments described in the preceding pages.

Inner-City Schools

Implications for inner-city schools attended by underclass students in concentrated poverty neighborhoods follow primarily from the fact that the inner-city environment is an unstable and damaging one for many children. Children who grow up in this environment frequently are unable to function effectively either in a traditional school setting or in an educational environment in which they are expected to work autonomously before being given preparation to work in this way. They need a good deal of close guidance from supportive adults, in an environment that provides both structure and consistency. In addition, action must be taken to help inner-city students and parents gain greater control of the forces that operate both inside and outside the inner-city school.

Structure and Consistency in the Educational Environment. One reason structure and consistency are necessary in inner-city schools involves the fact that a large proportion of students in these schools have failed to master basic academic skills; they require close guidance and support in overcoming gaps in their education. Another reason involves the fact that the inner-city environment tends to be chaotic for children. Chaos in daily life is a direct effect of poverty. For example, the world, and the future, obviously will seem disorderly and unpredictable to the members of families constantly on the verge of being evicted from their living quarters for inability to pay rent.

It is difficult to see how very much learning can take place in an inner-city school that recapitulates the chaos of the world outside. Herndon has described some of the effects such an external environment has on an inner-city elementary school:

> *Why would a kid, or a whole row of kids, become frantic because they weren't getting any pencils? Why was it no one could pass out paper for a routine assignment without all the kids in the back pushing up to the front, grabbing at the paper, crumpling it, and spilling it out onto the floor out of fear they wouldn't get any? They always did, every day, every period, all year long.*
>
> *[One reason for this behavior was their] concern to get their fair share of whatever was being passed out. . . . What was being passed out today, what probably would be passed out tomorrow, but on the other hand just might not be. (Herndon 1968, 62–65)*

Few teachers in the inner city would disagree that structure is a prerequisite for productive learning there, but it is difficult to define just what structure means, or should mean, for the conduct of instruction in the classroom. Doll and Levine (1972) have tried to work out a definition of structure for application in the classroom and have identified some of the key elements of structure as involving

> *the choice and sequencing of instructional experiences and materials in accordance with the particular learning problems and characteristics of disadvantaged students. . . .*

> *The initiation of procedures and arrangements to obtain order, so that teaching and learning can begin to take place. . . .*
>
> *The use of requirements and ground rules in such a way as to (a) clearly define what students are expected to do; (b) require initial participation on the part of the students; (c) provide for increasing student participation in setting subsequent ground rules; and (d) ensure that students understand . . . the rationale underlying the instruction. (Doll and Levine 1972, 152–154)*

It also is important to emphasize what structure is not. It is not repression of pupils, exclusion of pupils from decision making in the classroom, or simple provision of busywork to keep pupils occupied. Nor should it be defined as preventing a teacher from building on or encouraging the expression of students' spontaneous interests. Structure does not in any way obviate the need for inner-city teachers to be flexible in working with their students and to treat each student as a worthwhile human being.

One danger in emphasizing the importance of structure for inner-city students is that teachers will equate structure with order and will fail to move beyond the attainment of order to provide suitable activities to achieve the goal of improved learning. Another danger is that structure and guidance will not be provided consistently from one teacher or classroom to another. Levine (1968) has pointed out that consistency is particularly needed in inner-city schools because of the unusually large gap that exists between the students' competence and motivation to fulfill the role of student and the need to hold students to high standards of performance in order to overcome their relative lack of preparation for learning in the classroom:

> *Ambivalence in the child's orientation is reflected in the way he fulfills the role of student. . . . On the one hand he tends to accept the demands and expectations of the teacher as legitimate, at least to the extent that in general he outwardly acquiesces when instructed in what he should do and even when berated for not doing it. Though he often fails in trying to carry out his intentions, he does aspire to do well in his work and often he almost pitifully resolves to do better even after an unbroken record of years of failure to act on this resolution. Unfortunately, however, he has developed only fragments of the intellectual skills and the [academic self-discipline necessary to succeed]. . . .*
>
> *Students make more or less superficial attempts to live up to expectations, but fall far short. The exasperated teacher may either lower the level of expectations set for students and/or admonish them to overcome the personal 'defects' responsible for their failure. To protect their egos from further attack, students withdraw psychologically or become ever more resistant to the demands of teachers. They learn to play off the behavior of one teacher against that of another, by protesting against the threat in one classroom of requirements which "other teachers don't make us do" or which are unfairly "forced on us only because we are poor." (Levine 1968, 208–210)*

Before a person is able to perform satisfactorily in any role, he or she must know what is expected, must be able to meet the role requirements, and must practice the behavior appropriate to the role. The inner-city school in which teacher behaviors and expectations differ from one classroom to another fails on all three counts to provide a social situation in which the child can learn to perform well in the role of student. Less certain of what is expected, less proficient in carrying out the tasks that define the role, and less committed to devoting serious effort to reach distant academic goals than is the middle-class pupil, the inner-city child needs to be continually reinforced in mastering clearly defined aspects of the role of student. Thus, one major problem faced by the teacher is "not to overcome a hostile set of values, but to help pupils whose values [related to the role of student] are confused and underdeveloped to clarify their values and to work effectively toward the realization of them" (Havighurst 1966, 56).

Control of the Inner-City Environment. In using this phrase we have in mind the need to help inner-city parents and students gain control over the forces that presently reduce the effectiveness of educational programs inside the school and are part of the out-of-school conditions—that is, the street culture—that are detrimental to the development of children and youth. As indicated above, much can be done to design a school environment suitable to the needs of inner-city students, but in the end such efforts are not likely to be successful unless inner-city parents and students acquire and act on a belief that they can control their general environment and can work with the school to make learning more productive there.

It may be thought naïve to advocate action based on the belief that inner-city residents can gain more control over their future inside and outside the school, given the fact that for various reasons individuals in the inner city presently exercise very little power over the development of their neighborhood and its institutions. Indeed, a defining characteristic of the inner city is the sense of powerlessness people develop in adapting to the reality they see around them. But even though this is a defensible sociological explanation, which accounts in part for the situation in the inner city, it is not a sound ideology to govern the behavior of individuals and groups. Unless and until individuals in any community take responsibility for what happens to them and begin to perceive a possibility that they can improve their environment, it is hard to see how they can make good use of opportunities that may be available now or can be gained in the future.

Some organizations in inner-city neighborhoods thus are arguing that reform must come partly from within, through exercising greater control over what happens in families, schools, and other institutions in the inner city. In the 1970s and 1980s, the foremost of these groups has been the People United to Save Humanity organization, founded by the Reverend Jesse L. Jackson. Jackson and PUSH have worked in a number of big cities to reform schools and other community institutions, particularly in the inner city (Eubanks and Levine 1977). The PUSH Program for Excellence in Education has been described as aiming at "total involvement" to improve the conditions of teaching and learning in the inner city. Information about the PUSH program is provided in Chapter 6.

Working-Class Schools

At the outset, we should emphasize that in many respects the problems students and teachers face in working-class environments are similar to those in underclass neighborhoods. (By our definition, the underclass is the lowest-status segment of the working class.) Working-class neighborhoods are those in which there is a preponderance of upper and lower working-class residents, with some underclass families whose children are most in danger of being drawn into the street culture. Because children in working-class neighborhoods come to school poorly prepared as compared with middle-class youngsters, and because lack of economic resources and other environmental influences in these communities impede the scholastic performance of children growing up there, we view structure and consistency in the educational environment and control over the child's socializing environment as desirable developments not just in inner-city schools but in other working-class schools as well.

If students in working-class schools are to have a greater opportunity to succeed academically and, if so desired, go to college and become professional or white-collar workers, then schools in working-class neighborhoods must do a better job of teaching basic skills, enlarging pupils' horizons to understand the opportunities that later could be available to them, and guiding students toward careers that will provide them with security and with opportunity for mobility in the future. At the present time, academic performance in working-class schools tends to be very low, frequently as low as in inner-city schools, and a high percentage of students in working-class high schools drop out or graduate with minimal skills needed for success in the future.

Part of the reason this happens is that parents in working-class schools tend to press local school officials to provide an environment with considerable stress on obedience to authority and continuation of tradition. There is nothing inherently wrong with these goals, but in the school they frequently are translated into rote learning of traditional curricula and minimal expectations for achievement on the part of children. Like underclass students and, indeed, any group of students, working-class students can benefit from a certain amount of drill and an emphasis on mastery of traditional material, but continuing success in a modern education system requires more than this. It also requires some mastery of the skills involved in self-directed learning and understanding of many types of subject-matter that are not included in the traditional curriculum.

To the extent that parents in working-class neighborhoods tend to resist potentially more effective approaches to curriculum and instruction, educators in these neighborhoods face the same types of obstacles as do other public-service workers who endeavor to introduce "modern" institutional patterns and technologies into traditional communities. Many working-class parents can be viewed as wishing to preserve the traditions of the past while at the same time gaining access to the benefits of modern technology. This is a praiseworthy goal, but it also is true that modernization of local institutions cannot be achieved without changing them to some extent. Failure to institute an appropriate degree of change in local institutions can make them ineffective in carrying out their goals in a modern society, thereby depriving their clients of an opportunity to make good use of institutional resources. Peter Binzen, who has sympathetically studied working-class schools and communities in a number of large cities, has summarized this situation as follows (Binzen refers to these neighborhoods as "Whitetown," but he does make it clear that they include many upper and lower working-class minority families):

> *In this period of sexual permissiveness, God-is-dead theology, student revolts, . . . their [Whitetowners'] old-fashioned patriotism, religious fundamentalism, and family togetherness has gone out of style. . . .*
>
> *Whitetown was not ready for the technological revolution, either, having traditionally valued brawn over brains. . . .*
>
> *[Whitetown] appears to be on the skids. Its housing is deteriorating. It is losing population. . . .*
>
> *Any attempt to help the "stepchildren" of Whitetown should start with their schools. For in our . . . society education is the passport to progress. . . .*
>
> *[But in] changing times, the Whitetowners oppose change. . . . They tend to reflect . . . the "Little Red Schoolhouse Ideal" [and] look back to a "past golden age which has been lost. . . . What was good enough for me is good enough for my children." And at a school meeting one night I heard a hard-core Whitetowner utter those very words. (Binzen 1970, 27–28, 36–37)*

From this point of view, what appears to be most important in working-class schools is for administrators and teachers to take the lead in helping parents and students understand that educational approaches designed to help each student become a more independent learner and to acquire broader horizons do not completely conflict with community emphasis on authority and traditions. Parents also must be helped to understand that modern instructional approaches that aim at diagnosing and solving each student's learning problems can, if properly implemented, result in more rather than less success in mastering basic skills and attaining other traditional goals of the school. It is true that there is likely to be some degree of tension between a community that emphasizes tradition and an educational approach that may be thought of as "innovative," but appropriate explanation of the purpose and potential benefits of new approaches can help to minimize this tension.

Another major problem typically found in working-class schools is more straightforward: many working-class schools have too few resources to introduce and operate an outstanding instructional program effectively. This is partly because working-class schools tend to be located in big-city school districts with an inadequate financial base for public education. Financial pressures in big-city schools have become very severe in the 1970s and 1980s; working-class schools, which generally have students who need a large amount of extra help but do not have enough below-poverty-level pupils to qualify for special government assistance, have borne much of the brunt of these budget problems. In addition, school buildings in working-class neighborhoods are among the oldest in the cities, and their teachers tend to have been trained in out-dated methods.

Middle-Class Schools

Many students in a predominantly middle-class neighborhood tend to have difficulty in school if placed in a classroom in which social control and instruction are highly structured or are externally imposed in a teacher-centered curriculum. Because middle-class home environments tend to stress egalitarianism and development of self-direction, a highly structured, teacher-centered classroom can be not only discrepant for middle-class students but also can cause them to lose interest and motivation in learning. However, classrooms in middle-class elementary schools tend not to be highly structured, because parents and school administrators there tend increasingly to push for the development of instructional programs stressing student-centered learning and self-direction.

At the secondary level, however, school tends to become more problematical for students from a middle-class environment. Secondary schools tend to be large and impersonal, maintaining rules and traditions designed to provide external coordination of the activities of a thousand or more people; and because the problems of middle-class youth tend to become manifested most clearly during adolescence, alienation in middle-class secondary schools has become widespread. Levine (1972) has analyzed the middle-class environment in the modern metropolis and concluded that the following guidelines should be considered in designing educational programs—particularly secondary programs—for students growing up in this environment:

> *Every young person [should be provided] with opportunities to test and define himself against difficult challenges in the physical and social environment. . . .*
>
> *Students' educational experiences should be provided in a setting which brings them into close and continuing contact with others of differing social, racial, ethnic, and religious backgrounds. It is all very well to teach students about other people who reflect or embody the diverse character of the metropolis, but learning about them is too abstract an activity to counteract perceptions of isolation from metropolitan reality. . . .*
>
> *Much of the curriculum . . . should be explicitly concerned with the study of urban and metropolitan affairs.*
>
> *[Much more should be done] to provide adolescents and young people with opportunities to perform socially important and personally meaningful work in the metropolis. . . .*
>
> *Students should have more scope in choosing what to learn and in deciding how to learn it. (Levine 1972, 41–44)*

Social Class Environments and the Ideology of Social Control in the School

Chapter 7 indicates that there is a tendency for schools with many lower-status students to place more stress on rote learning and discipline than do middle-class schools, which put relatively more emphasis on creative and independent learning. The material in this chapter helps in understanding why this difference between working- and middle-class schools gets built into the educational system. Teachers frequently emphasize discipline and authority in working-class schools partly because students are accustomed to this type of emphasis, and their parents also tend to demand it. Thus, some research indicates that children from homes with coercive interactions perform better in coercive classrooms than in classrooms based on cohesive or laissez-faire interactions (Hansen 1986). Schools in middle-class communities, by way of contrast, frequently emphasize the development of self-directed learning, in response to the perceived needs of and preferences of students and parents. Bernstein (1975) describes this difference as involving a lack of distinction between work and play in middle-class schools, in line with the intermingling of work and play that characterizes the culture of the middle class.

From our point of view, the issue is not so much whether these differences tend to exist in differing types of schools but what if anything should be done to improve the effectiveness of education for students from differing backgrounds. In recent years, attempts have been made in some working-class and inner-city schools to introduce instructional programs emphasizing independent, self-directed learning. Most such attempts at innovation have not succeeded; conditions in these schools have been extremely chaotic, and both students and teachers have ended up feeling frustrated and defeated. Typically, however, neither teachers nor students in these innovative projects have been well prepared to participate in them. Without a substantial amount of special training, continuous staff development, and appropriate supporting resources, teachers cannot be expected to implement them successfully. Without careful and substantial preparation, students who are not used to working independently cannot be expected to function successfully as self-directed learners.

In a few instances, such programs do appear to have worked well for working-class and underclass students when they have been carefully planned and expertly implemented based on the premise that appropriate learning arrangements can provide internal structure in an "open" environment. Some elementary-school programs for economically disadvantaged students seem to have been most successful when emphasizing direct instruction (see Chapter 8), but this type of instruction can be provided within a program that also emphasizes the development of self-directed learning skills. Thus, it would seem desirable to work toward the goal of helping students in low-status schools become more self-directed, beginning with carefully structured instructional experiences and shifting later, when students are ready, to less structured learning environments.

However, relatively few attempts seem to have been made to work in stages toward the development of self-directed learning skills in low-status schools. Instead, programs emphasizing self-direction and creativity frequently have been initiated by sponsors imbued with an ideology of freeing the low-status child from the oppression of the school. Such projects have seldom involved careful longitudinal planning and goals; as a result, most have failed abjectly.

The problem behind simpleminded attempts to move instantly from structured to unstructured school environments sometimes can be traced back to confusion about concepts such as *structure*, *oppression*, and *freedom*. Proponents of unstructured schooling who equate structure with oppression and lack of structure with freedom fail to recognize that structure can be as liberating if properly provided as it is restricting in other circumstances. To the extent that ideologues who confuse structure with oppression have organized structureless free schools that quickly failed, ideology has discredited what might have been a productive movement to modify and reduce structure gradually as pupils are helped to become more self-directive.

Other ideological positions that may serve to block serious attempts to help low-status students develop more competence in self-directed learning are represented by people who believe either that those students are inherently incapable of developing such skills or that improved instructional programs for low-status students will not help them much in the absence of a political and social revolution to correct underlying inequalities in society. The first position may be true for some low-status students, but it clearly is not legitimate to conclude that most cannot become autonomous learners when few systematic, longitudinal attempts have been made to achieve this goal. The second position is equally narrow in not recognizing that millions of low-status people have achieved mobility through education, and many more can be helped to do so in the future if the schools can succeed in developing their skills and competence to function more successfully in the educational system. How the schools can help to do this is discussed in Chapters 8, 13, and elsewhere in this book.

EXERCISES

1. Read Oscar Lewis's account of slum communities in Puerto Rico and Mexico, respectively (*La Vida* and *Children of Sanchez*), and Lee Rainwater's account of a predominantly black inner-city housing project in the United States, *Behind Ghetto Walls: Black Families in a Federal Slum*. Compare and contrast these manifestations of the culture of poverty.
2. What are some of the causes of alienation toward society among children and youth from: (1) lower working-class communities and (2) upper middle-class communities? In what ways are the causes and consequences of alienation among these groups different? In what ways are they similar?
3. Read James Herndon's *The Way It Spozed to Be* and prepare a list of the ways in which environmental conditions in the lives of the children described in it affect their behavior in schools.

4. Why do underclass parents encounter so many problems in trying to raise their children to be good children? What do you think can or should be done to give their children a better chance to succeed in United States schools and society?
5. Frank Reissman's *The Culturally Deprived Child* argues that as compared with middle-class students, disadvantaged students frequently have learning styles that are physical or visual rather than aural, content-centered rather than form-centered, and problem-centered rather than abstract-centered. He sees these and other aspects of their "mental style" as qualities that teachers should consider in designing effective instruction. Read Reissman's analysis and discuss the merits and demerits of his proposals.
6. Read *To Kill a Mockingbird* by Harper Lee, and describe how the classroom lesson portrayed in Chapter 26 created special problems for disadvantaged children.

SUGGESTIONS FOR FURTHER READING

1. *White Ethnics: Their Life in Working-Class America,* edited by Joseph A. Ryan, includes chapters describing the social environment of Italian-American and Polish-American working-class families, as well as analyses of religion, employment, and school conditions in white working-class neighborhoods.
2. Descriptions of the environment for youth in underclass neighborhoods can be found in Claude Brown, *Manchild in the Promised Land,* and Roger D. Abrahams, *Deep Down in the Jungle . . . Negro Narrative Folklore from the Streets of Philadelphia. The Autobiography of Malcolm X* provides an excellent account of the problems such an environment creates for children and youth, and the unusually difficult time a youngster encounters in surmounting them.
3. Lillian Rubin's *Worlds of Pain: Life in the Working-Class Family* reports the results of interviews with a sample of working-class adults, and the author's thoughtful comments and evaluations of the interview information.
4. *The Children of the Counterculture* by John Rothchild and Susan Berns Wolf provides a fascinating account of the social environment of children growing up in a variety of countercultural settings. The problems involved in trying to create a new kind of social environment are vividly portrayed, and considerable attention is given to the issue of educating the young in circumstances that markedly differ from those characteristic of normal working-class and middle-class environments.
5. Oscar Handlin's books on *The Newcomers* and *The Uprooted* and Bernard Bailyn's *Voyagers to the West* describe how migration to the United States modified people's sense of community and identity. *The Hunger of Memory* by Richard Rodriguez provides a vivid account of this process from the viewpoint of an Hispanic American.
6. *Past, Present, and Personal* consists of essays by John Demos on the history of the family, with particular emphasis on the United States.
7. *Children of the City* by David Nasaw (1985) describes the environment experienced by working-class children in New York City between 1900 and 1920.

4

Home Environment and Cognitive Development

The relationship between social-class background and achievement has been emphasized in preceding chapters. Working-class children are less prepared for school and less successfully sheltered from influences detrimental to school achievement than are middle-class children. An average working-class child performs less well academically than does the average middle-class child, and the educational system helps to sort children of differing backgrounds into higher- or lower-status careers in accordance with their performance in school. Hess and Shipman (1965) have summed up the results of many studies documenting these kinds of differences:

> *Children from deprived backgrounds score well below middle-class children on standard individual and group measures of intelligence (a gap that increases with age); they come to school without the skill necessary for coping with first grade curricula; their language development, both written and spoken, is relatively poor; auditory and visual discrimination skills are not well developed; in scholastic achievement they are retarded an average of two years by grade six and almost three years by grade eight; they are more likely to drop out of school before completing a secondary education; and even when they have adequate ability, are less likely to go to college. (Hess and Shipman 1965, 869)*

Thus, it has long been observed that children from lower socioeconomic groups provide by far the greater share of a school's academic failures and dropouts. These phenomena were explained away in earlier periods as due, first, to lower native intelligence of these children; and second, to lack of concern on the part of their parents. Today, it is known that neither explanation is adequate. The likely explanation is that although parents of all classes realize the importance of education and prize good schooling for their children, different families create environments that influence children's intellectual growth and educational motivation in different ways. When one parent ignores the child's questions but another parent makes a point of reading to the child every day, two different environments are created. The first parent has created an environment that operates against learning; the second, one that promotes learning. Because the social classes tend to provide differing home environments, their children tend to be more or less prepared for or helped to do well in school (Holmes 1988).

Conversely, even though family socioeconomic status is statistically correlated overall with children's school achievement, there are many exceptions. The exceptions show that the causes of the relatively low achievement of lower-class children are characteristics of individual families and are not universally connected with low socioeconomic status. This was demonstrated in a study of children from a working-class population in New York City's Harlem, where high-achieving and low-achieving fifth-grade pupils were compared (Davidson and Greenberg 1969). Eighty boys and eighty girls were selected from twelve elementary schools; all children met the following criteria:

- Parents were of low socioeconomic status according to occupation, educational level, and type of dwelling unit.
- Parents were all born in this country.
- Child attended school in a northern city since first grade.
- IQ between 75 and 125.
- Age between 9 years, 11 months and 11 years, 4 months.

The forty boys and forty girls who were high achievers averaged at the 6.45 level in reading and the 5.4 level in arithmetic. The forty boys and forty girls who were low achievers averaged 2.85 in reading and 3.35 in arithmetic.

The two groups—the high achievers and the low achievers—were compared on a variety of psychological and social characteristics. High achievers were superior to low achievers on a number of psychological characteristics, as would be expected. But the striking thing was the relationship of certain home or family characteristics within this working-class group to school achievement. An experienced interviewer visited in the homes and talked with the mother about the child and about the mother's behavior. He was not informed as to the achievement level of the children. The families of high achievers were rated as substantially superior to that of low achievers in "Concern for the Children's Education," "Thinking and Planning for the Child as an Individual," "General Social-Civic Awareness and Concern of the Parent," and "Structure and Orderliness of the Home." Thus, within the black lower-class group some children score above the national norms on educational achievement, and they tend to come from homes that prepare them well for school achievement.

Home environment and other family characteristics constitute one of the four most important factors that influence a child's level of achievement in school. Another is the inborn ability of the child. A third is the quality of the schooling the child receives. The fourth is the child's self-concept or aspiration level, which grows out of family and school experiences. After several years of school experience, the child determines how hard he or she shall work in school and toward what goals.

Inborn or biological differences of intelligence exist, but between individuals, not between large social or racial groups. Inborn differences in intelligence exist among children in a single family; and every school class of thirty children includes thirty different levels of intellectual potential.

Once a child is born, a home environment that promotes learning can operate so that a child with only average inborn ability does well in school. A very good school can operate so that a child with only average innate ability does well; and it can operate also to compensate a child for a poor home environment.

Importance of Early Environment

Research on the cognitive development of children summarized by Bloom (1964) and Hunt (1979) points to the family as the major influence and to the preschool years as the crucial ones for mental development. A dramatic illustration of the importance of early environment on later cognitive and social development has been provided by a follow-up study of a group of children first studied in the 1930s by Skeels and Dye (1939). The children were described in the original study as follows:

> Thirteen infants ranging in age from 7 to 30 months who were considered unfit for adoption because of mental retardation (mean IQ, 64.3) were removed from an orphanage and placed in an institution for the feebleminded. Another group of twelve children who came from comparable family backgrounds but who seemed of better intellectual endowment (mean IQ, 90.0) remained in the orphanage where they were periodically observed and tested.
>
> The orphanage nursery, as it was being operated prior to the study, was limited to a rather small playroom with additional dormitory rooms. . . . The children were cared for by two nurses assisted by two young girls. . . . Contacts with adults were largely limited to feeding, bathing, dressing, and toilet details. . . . The girls who assisted the nurses accepted the work as a necessary evil and took little personal interest in the children as individuals. Few play materials were available. The children were seldom out of the nursery room except for short walks for fresh air.
>
> At age two the children moved on to "cottages," where 30 to 35 children of the same sex under age six lived in the charge of one matron and three or four untrained girls aged thirteen to fifteen. Their waking hours were spent (except during meal times and a little time outdoors) in an average sized room, a sun porch, and a cloak room. . . .
>
> The duties falling to the matron were not only those involved in the care of the children but also those related to clothing and cottage maintenance, cleaning, mending, and so forth. . . . The result was a necessary regimentation. The children sat down, stood up, and did many things in rows and in unison. They spent considerable time just sitting on chairs for there was inadequate equipment. . . .
>
> The experimental situation in the school for the feebleminded provided quite a different environment. Generally one, and no more than two, of the experimental children were placed in wards that contained only older, brighter girls. The attendants and the older girls became very fond of the child placed in their ward and took great pride in the child's achievement. There was considerable competition between wards to see which one would have "their baby" walking or talking first.The girls would spend a great deal of time with the children, teaching them to walk, talk, play with toys. . . . They spent their small allowances to buy

them special foods, toys, picture books, and material for clothing.

Similarly, attendants frequently took the children on excursions, car rides, and trips. In addition, it was the policy of the matron in charge to single out certain of these children whom she felt were in need of individualization, and permit them to spend a portion of time each day visiting her office. This furnished new experiences, including special attention and affection, new play materials, additional language stimulation, and contacts with other office callers. . . .

The children were sent to the school kindergarten as soon as they could walk. . . . As part of the school program, the children each morning attended chapel exercises, including group singing and music by the orchestra. The children also attended the dances, school programs, moving pictures. (Adapted from Skeels and Dye 1939)

Results of the follow-up study (Skeels 1966) were reported as follows:

Findings

The results of this experiment were unexpected. All experimental children (who had been considered mentally retarded by the trained members of the orphanage staff as well as by a psychiatrist) achieved the normal range of intelligence within 6 to 52 months. The average gain in IQ was 27.5 points, with three children gaining 45 points or more. A year after the experiment ended, two of these children were above average in intelligence and only one had an IQ below 80.

The children who remained in the orphanage, on the other hand, fell increasingly behind in intellectual development. Except for one child, all suffered losses ranging from 8 to 45 IQ points.

The radical improvement in the experimental children cannot be attributed solely to environmental enrichment. Nine children who became greatly attached to one or two adults gained an average of 34 IQ points, while the four children who did not develop close personal attachments to an adult made an average gain of only 14 points. A parent surrogate whom the child learns to love and imitate is apparently an important factor in optimum development.

When these results became known, the orphanage staff made heroic efforts to improve conditions by adding more personnel to the staff, cutting down the numbers of children in the cottages, and initiating a preschool program in the nursery. Nevertheless, the damage to the orphanage group could not be undone; and the differences persisted between the children who had received special attention in infancy and the children who had not.

Follow-Up

Twenty-one years later all the children were located and restudied (Skeels 1966). Every one of the thirteen children of the experimental group had eventually been placed in a family and was now found to be living a nor-

> mal life. They had completed, on the average, twelfth grade; four had entered college, and one had received a B.A. Eleven had married, and nine of these had children.
>
> In contrast, of the orphanage group (originally the better endowed), one had died in adolescence after prolonged institutionalization for mental retardation, and three others were still inmates of such institutions. One was in a mental hospital. Of the two who had married, one was divorced. In conformity with state law, three girls, classified as retarded, had been sterilized before they had been permitted to leave the institution. On the average, this group had completed less than third grade in school. Half were unemployed; and of those who were working, all but one held the lowest of menial jobs.

Even though the Skeels findings are dramatic, they should be interpreted cautiously because they do not themselves prove that the effects of early enrichment are pervasive or permanent. The two groups studied by these investigators were not only different in early childhood experiences, but they were also different with regard to the experiences that intervened between early childhood and the time of follow-up some twenty years later (Spitz 1986). In addition, the story dealt with the effects of severe environmental deprivation, and one cannot conclude that mild retardation is necessarily due mostly to environment or that mild environmental deprivation is responsible for most low intellectual performance.

Home Environment Conditions, Cognitive Development, and Scholastic Achievement

During the past fifteen years, sociologists and psychologists have tried to identify home environment characteristics that are directly related to cognitive development and to achievement in schools. Skeels and others had shown that the amount and quality of stimulation provided for infants was associated with their intellectual development, but beyond that little was known about how home process variables are related to children's intellectual and scholastic performance. Thus, researchers began to examine a whole set of additional variables in order to identify home and parent characteristics that are consistently related to intellectual development. Dave (1963) and Wolf (1964) devised interview protocols that could be used to categorize the home environment on a number of characteristics likely to be related to performance on tests of ability and school achievement. Data they collected on fifth graders showed that information on the following six home environment characteristics accounted for nearly two-thirds of the variation in scores on the Metropolitan Achievement Battery:

1. Achievement pressure: (a) parental aspirations for the education of the child; (b) parents' own aspirations; (c) parents' interest in academic activities; (d)

knowledge of the educational progress of the child; (e) preparation and planning for the attainment of educational goals.

2. Language models: (a) quality of language usage of the parents; (b) opportunities for the enlargement and use of vocabulary and sentence patterns; (c) keenness of the parents for correct and effective language usage.
3. Academic guidance: (a) availability of guidance on matters relating to schoolwork; (b) quality of guidance on matters relating to schoolwork; (c) availability and use of materials and facilities related to school learning.
4. Activeness of the family: (a) extent and content of the indoor and outdoor activities of the family; (b) use of television and other such media; (c) use of books, library, and other such facilities.
5. Intellectuality in the home; (a) nature and quality of toys, games, and hobbies made available to the child; (b) opportunities for thinking and imagination in daily activites.
6. Work habits of the family: (a) degree of structure and routine in home management; (b) preferences for educational activities over other pleasurable pastimes.

In several studies examining relationships between students' social background and academic achievement, the single best predictor of achievement has been the amount of reading materials in the home. (The reader should keep in mind that social class, level of education, occupation, income, and other indicators of social status are highly correlated with reading materials in the home and with other measures of home environment.) The extent of this relationship is shown in Figure 4.1, which uses 1984 data on nine-, thirteen-, and seventeen-year-olds sampled by the National Assessment of Educational Progress (NAEP). As shown in Figure 4.1, students in each age group who reported that there were "many" reading materials in their home scored higher than those who responded "some," who in turn scored higher than those reporting "few" reading materials in their home. In addition, the standard deviation for NAEP reading data is relatively small in relation to the mean (National Assessment of Educational Progress 1985), which indicates that few students who report there are many reading materials at home have low reading scores, and most students who have few reading materials have very low scores.

Note that this relationship between reading materials in the home and students' reading proficiency is strong even after taking account of parental level of education. For example, students who report having a dictionary, more than twenty-five books, and numerous magazines in their homes have an average reading proficiency score approximately fifteen points higher than those whose parents have the same educational level but report fewer reading materials at home (analysis by the authors).

Home environments supportive of cognitive growth provide not just reading materials, but also a variety of opportunities and encouragements to develop and use oral and written language skills. Some of the language-learning opportunities available to children in families that promote cognitive and academic growth have been illustrated as follows by Heath and McLaughlin:

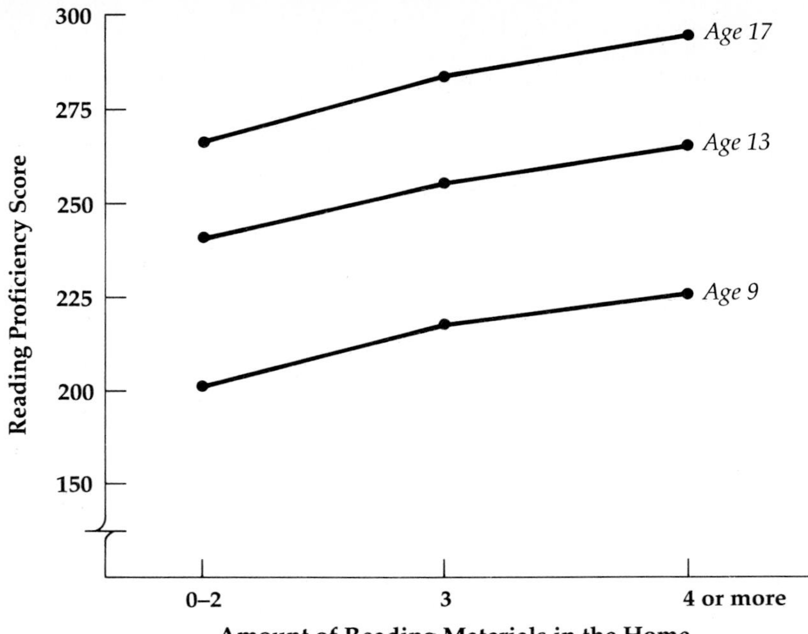

Reading materials = Newspapers, magazines, encyclopedia, more than 25 books.

Figure 4.1 ***Reading Proficiency Scores of Nine- Thirteen-, and Seventeen-Year-Olds, by Amount of Reading Materials in the Home, 1984*** (*Source*: Adapted from National Assessment of Educational Progress [NAEP] 1985.)

> *[Such children] have extensive experience in learning by listening to others tell how to do something, they themselves know how to talk about what they are doing as they do it, and they know how to lay out plans for the future in verbal form. On command, they know how to display in oral or written formats the bits and pieces of knowledge that the school assumes represent academic achievement. (Heath and McLaughlin 1987, 578)*

Research on the relationship between parental behavior and children's cognitive development and achievement has been summarized by Rollins and Thomas (1979), who carefully reviewed and assessed studies carried out during the previous three decades. Among the generalizations for which they found solid research support were the following:

- Greater parental support is associated with higher cognitive development of children.
- Greater parental coercion is associated with lower cognitive development.

- Greater parental support is associated with higher instrumental and social competence of children.
- Greater parental coercion is associated with lower instrumental and social competence.
- For girls, high parental support and frequent parental control attempts are associated with low academic achievement.
- For boys, high parental support is associated with high academic achievement when parental control also is high, and high parental control is associated with low achievement when parental support is low.
- In general, conclusions regarding the relationship between parental behavior and development of the child are stronger for boys than for girls.

Additional evidence regarding the influence of parental control techniques on children's cognitive and academic performance has been provided in a longitudinal study conducted by Hess and McDevitt (1984). After collecting and examining appropriate data on mothers' behaviors and their children's "school-related abilities" at ages four, five/six, and twelve, Hess and McDevitt reported that "in both teaching and disciplinary situations, direct control tactics were negatively correlated with children's school-relevant performance" (1984, 2017). They also found that children of mothers who used a high proportion of direct control techniques performed more poorly than did children whose mothers used a combination of direct and indirect interventions, and that boys seemed to be less affected than did girls by their mothers' control techniques.

Note that parental child-raising techniques appear to interact with social class, environmental setting, gender of the child, and, perhaps, with race and other variables in affecting children's cognitive development and school performance (Holmes 1988). For example, Rollins and Thomas (1979) reviewed the literature and concluded that high parental support in combination with high control internalized by the child function to encourage academic achievement for boys but not for girls. Clark (1983) hypothesized that girls in inner-city communities benefit as much as boys from the combination of high support and control in a threatening environment. He then collected data that provided support for the hypothesis.

In recent years, much has been learned about how differing home environment conditions are related to intellectual development at different ages, though much more remains to be discovered about the interactions between parent behavior, cognitive growth, and school achievement as the child grows older. For example, Wachs, Uzgiris, and Hunt (1971) reported that although intensity and variety of stimulation in the home and opportunity to hear vocal labels for objects, actions, and relationships were significantly correlated with cognitive development in the first two years of life, there also was a tendency for overstimulation to have harmful effects. Four years later, Elardo, Bradley, and Caldwell (1975) reported that stimulation in the physical environment is strongly related to mental test performance in the first year of life but after that time maternal involvement with the child becomes a stronger indicator of cognitive development. This finding suggests that differing aspects of the home environment affect mental capabilities in a complex fashion.

Recent research has focused on further identifying longitudinal relationships between home environment variables, particularly maternal behavior, and specific cognitive abilities. For example, Shipman and her colleagues (1976) have been studying the home environments and development of disadvantaged youngsters in the preschool and elementary grades and have concluded that the mother's level of aspiration for the child may be

> *directly tied to the child's* early *signs of intellectual alertness. If so, the implication is that early cognitive stimulation from within or outside of the home is important for the mother* subsequently *to provide a continuously stimulating climate. . . . The present findings suggest that as the mother interacts more, she feels less powerless, more optimistic and is less likely to resort to status and authoritarian appeals for controlling her child. Thus, programs reducing alienation may in turn increase the child's educability. (Shipman et al. 1976, 173–174)*

Several investigators have been carefully examining the parental behaviors that appear to be related to cognitive and emotional development in young children. They are finding that the ways in which children explore their environment and use objects and concepts are related to the actions of adults who arrange and structure the environment. Conducted through intensive observation of parents or other adults and young children, these types of studies generally take years to carry out and analyze. One of the most important series of investigations along these lines was carried out by Jean V. Carew of Harvard University. After studying a socioeconomically heterogeneous group of twenty-three white children between the ages of one and three in Boston, Carew concluded that there are four types of activities or experiences involving (1) language skills, (2) spatial skills, (3) practical reasoning, and (4) expressive skills that seem to be "intellectually valuable" for the child; children's activities in these areas correlated with IQ and were distinguished from other activities involving simple play-exploration, routine talk, basic care, and gross motor functioning, which did not correlate with IQ.

Carew was further interested in determining whether it matters if the child constructs the intellectually valuable experiences for himself or herself, or whether they are received from the environment. Based on theories of Piaget, it was hypothesized that "the child's active construction of his own experiences is central to his intellectual development," but other learning theories indicated that "structure and appropriateness" of the environment might be more important than the child's active exploration. The results of this study were described as giving "some support to both camps, full comfort to neither":

> *Briefly we found that it does matter a great deal how the child's intellectual experiences are derived but different sources of intellectually valuable experiences become important at different periods in the child's life. The earliest forms of intellectual experiences that were correlated with . . . [both tested and observed*

> *intellectual competence] at age three (and earlier) were experiences in which the* child interacts with another person. *These intellectual experiences included reciprocal interaction in which the child and the interactor contributed jointly to the child's intellectual experience, but most important were encounters in which the interactor was the primary source of the intellectual experience and the child the attentive but basically non-contributing partner. It is not until age two and a half that the intellectual experiences that* the child fashioned through his own activity *began to be significantly correlated with his tested intellectual competence . . . it was the role played by the* interactor *in creating intellectual experiences for the child or reciprocally sharing them with him that was first and most highly related to the child's later intellectual competence. (Carew 1976, 9–11)*

Carew emphasized that understanding the role of the interactor in providing intellectually valuable experiences for the child requires a knowledge of how this role was specifically defined in the study:

> *An interactor is considered to be the primary or joint source of the child's intellectual experiences only when he uses a participatory technique of interaction. The specific techniques defined as* participatory *include teaching, helping, entertaining, conversing and sharing in the intellectual activity like a playmate. The common feature of these techniques is that the interactor plays a direct, active, and integral role in creating, guiding and expanding the child's intellectual experience. . . . His behavior is not merely facilitative (in the sense, say, of praise or approval), or incidental to the intellectual experience. Rather, the interactor's behavior literally creates or helps to create its intellectual content. This content is often judiciously chosen, well structured and attractively presented. But the same or better can be said of certain children's television programs, which we found related not at all to intellectual development in these young children. What seems to distinguish these two types of environmental inputs are two features that are highly salient in the interactor's behavior and seldom present in television programs. These are the* individualized and responsive *quality of the interactor's behavior and its* affective *subtext.*
>
> *When an interactor engages in an intellectual activity with a child he typically tailors his input to the individual child's needs. He tries to match its content and style to what he knows of the child's capabilities and interests. He is responsive to questions, problems, inadequacies in the child's understanding.*
>
> *This point brings us to the affective aspect of interactive experiences. By the very fact of sharing in intellectual experiences with the child the interactor conveys that such experiences are valued and pleasing. It is not necessary that the interactor express approval or affection overtly. The essential message is already transmitted by the sheer fact that the interactor participates positively in the experiences. When the interactor is a parent, a sibling or a friend to whom the child is emotionally attached, it seems very likely that the child will come to value and engage in such activities for the simple reason that these are the ones that people he likes prefer. (Carew 1976, 11–12)*

The importance of home learning environment also has been underlined in a 1979 review of research on home-based reinforcement of school behavior and in a 1982 meta-analysis of research on the effects of school programs that have attempted to improve students' home and family learning environments. (*Meta-analysis* is a method that reviews available quantitative studies on a given topic, screens out those that have inadequate designs or do not report sufficient data to draw a conclusion, and re-examines those that do meet these criteria in order to estimate the effects of the approach being reviewed.) Richard Barth's (1979) review of twenty-four studies dealing with home-based reinforcement showed that many kinds of behavioral and academic problems have been successfully reduced by helping parents learn to deal with the problems at home. In the meta-analysis of home and family intervention programs, Graue, Weinstein, and Walberg (1982) reviewed twenty-nine studies of projects that worked with parents to encourage and reinforce targeted child behaviors. Projects examined worked with parents at various grade levels from kindergarten through grade six and assessed a number of subjects and skills, particularly reading and math. The authors report that the average effect size across projects was 0.76, which means that the average experimental student scored at the 76th percentile compared with an average at the 50th percentile for control group children. The authors pointed out that effects so large and consistent are very seldom encountered in connection with educational treatments.

Recent Trends in the Family and Youth Development

Trends occurring in family structure and family relations in the United States have implications for the development of children and their treatment in the educational system and other modern socializing institutions. Six of the most important of these trends are described below.

1. *Increase in single-parent families.* The percentage of U.S. families that include a married couple declined from 74 percent of all families in 1960 to 58 percent in 1985. A large majority of the families with only one parent are female-headed households. As shown in Figure 4.2, the rise in the percentage of single-parent families was accompanied by a steady increase in the percentage of children and youth growing up in female-headed families.

The increase in single-parent families reflects increases in the divorce rate and in the proportion of illegitimate births (Christensen 1988). Divorce rates rose each year during the 1960s and 1970s, setting a new record in 1981 of 109 per 1,000 married women—up from 47 in 1970. Divorce rates dropped slightly from 1982 thru 1984 but rose again in 1985 to nearly the 1981 rate. Most demographers now predict that half of newly married couples eventually will be divorced and that one-third or more of all children under eighteen will live with a divorced parent at some point in their lives (Weed 1982). Between 1950 and 1984, the number of out-of-wedlock births per 1,000 babies born increased from approx-

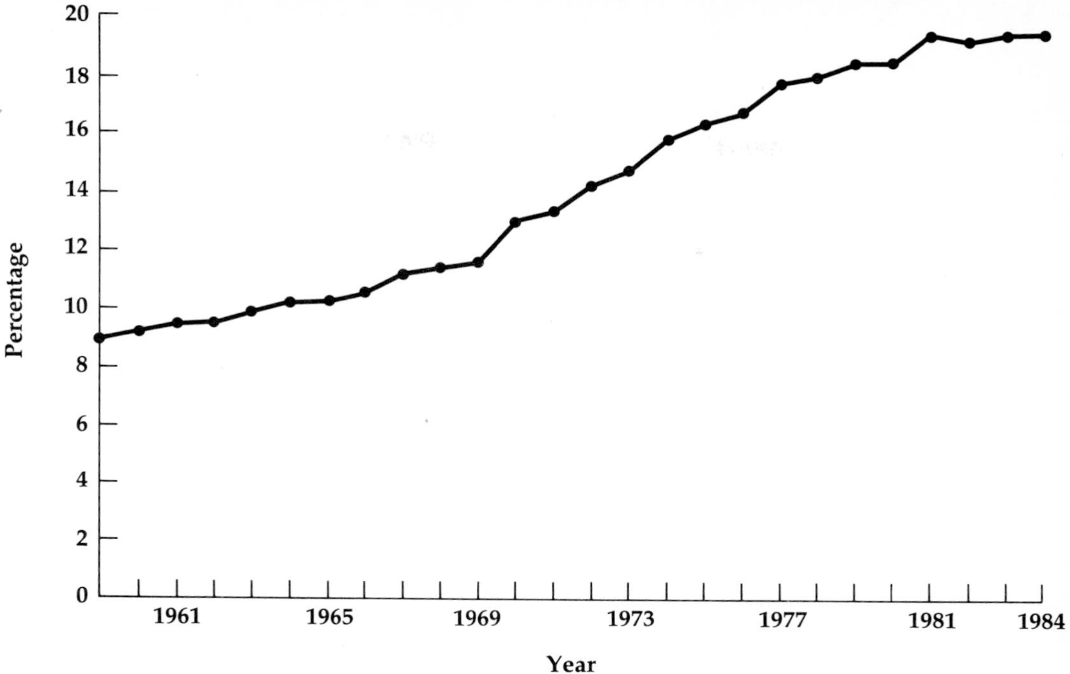

Figure 4.2 ***Percentage of Children and Youth under Eighteen Years of Age in Female-Headed Households, 1959 to 1984*** (*Source*: Koretz and Ventresca 1984.)

imately 40 to 200. Because many of the mothers of illegitimate children did not subsequently marry, the percentage of female-headed families showed a concomitant increase. Some of the effects of divorce on children have been reviewed and summarized by Bianchi and Spain (1986):

> *In sum, an increasing number of children are growing up in situations other than the "typical" two-parent nuclear family. . . . Kramer and Kramer aside, most children still end up in their mother's custody when a marital break-up occurs and a sizable portion will have little or no contact with their father from that time on. In addition, family income in these mother-only households is low. And there is evidence of school problems and poorer health among children who are separated from one of their parents. (Bianchi and Spain 1986, 47)*

It also should be noted that the proportions of children living with both biological parents vary substantially by race and ethnicity. According to federal surveys, only 38 percent of non-Hispanic black children and youth under the age of 18 lived with both biological parents in 1981, compared with 67 percent of Hispanic and 73 percent of non-Hispanic white children and youth (Bianchi and Spain 1986). The percentage of black children living in female-headed fam-

Table 4.1 ***Estimated Total Fertility Rates in the United States, 1800 to 1982***

Year	Rate	Year	Rate
1800	704	1950	304
1840	614	1960	365
1880	424	1970	248
1920	317	1975	177
1940	230	1980	184
		1982	183

Note: Rates represent live births per 1,000 women of child-bearing age.

Sources: Rates through 1920 are estimated in Coale and Zelnik (1963). Rates from 1940 are based on estimates in U.S. Bureau of the Census, *Social Indicators 1976* and on recent census bureau reports.

ilies increased from 24 percent in 1960 to 51 percent in 1984, while the percentage of white children in female-headed families increased from 7 percent to 14 percent (Children's Defense Fund 1985).

2. *Increase in the percentage of working mothers.* The percentage of working women with children under 18 has been increasing fairly steadily since at least 1950, for reasons including the breakup of husband-wife families, improved opportunities in the labor market for women, financial pressures requiring the mother to work, and changes in cultural and social patterns that formerly dictated that many women remain in the home. Fifty percent of mothers with children under three years of age were in the labor force in 1986, as compared with 17 percent in 1959. Along with this change, there was a major shift in child-care arrangements for the children of working mothers. In 1958, 57 percent of the young children of employed mothers were cared for in their own homes. By 1977, this responsibility had shifted to outside caregivers, and only 29 percent of such children were cared for in their homes. However, only about 25 percent of the young children of working mothers are in licensed day-care centers (National Black Child Development Institute 1985).

3. *Smaller family size.* The birthrate in the United States and other Western societies generally has been falling for many decades, interrupted only temporarily by increases such as the one following World War II. As shown in Table 4.1, the total fertility rate fell from 704 in 1800 to 248 in 1970, and after 1972 dropped below and remained below the population replacement rate of 211. Due to the availability of contraceptives, changing attitudes toward marriage, delayed childbearing, and other causes, this decline in the fertility rate means that women are giving birth to fewer children spread over the whole of their childbearing years; as a result, the average number of children per family also has decreased markedly since 1800. Some demographers now predict that as many as 30 percent of women born since 1954 may never have children (Pebley and Bloom 1982). Others predict that birthrates will rise during the late 1980s

and 1990s as youth in the relatively small baby bust group now proceeding through the schools perceive enlarged opportunities for themselves and their children (Easterlin 1980). Most observers, however, believe that the long-range decline in fertility rates reflects a fundamental change in social attitudes and technology and hence is not likely to be reversed (e.g., Westoff 1981).

4. *Increased prominence of peer cultures among youth.* Although peer cultures have constituted an important phenomenon in nearly every society, there is reason to believe that they have become more prominent and influential among youth in the United States in the past generation (Boocock 1976). This development is discussed more fully in Chapter 5, but at this point we should emphasize that the prominence of peer cultures today probably is related to increases that have occurred in the percentages of female-headed families and of working mothers, if only because all these developments reflect an apparent decline in the ability and desire of family members to maintain a conjugal family as a refuge from the outside world.

5. *Increased influence of television and other media.* Another important historical change affecting family relations and the socialization of children involves the increased importance of the mass media—particularly television, comic books, radio, and movies. In 1960, Schramm, Lyle, and Parker studied a sample of children in the United States and Canada and reported that the average child spent as much time watching television as attending school. Siegal (1975) estimated that the average child had spent 15,000 hours watching television by age sixteen.

An activity that consumes this amount of time clearly can play an important part in changing children's attitudes and behaviors, if only because much of this time probably would have been spent interacting with parents and other family members in earlier generations. Comic books also have an important influence in the lives of many children, and radio as well as movies are very effective in influencing the attitudes and interests of teenagers and their peer groups. In recent years, videotapes and games have become a time- and money-consuming activity for many children and youth, and many adults are concerned that the effects may be damaging to development.

Another recent media trend that may have major effects on the family involves the development of teletext and videotext technology. As defined in a report from the Institute for the Future prepared for the National Science Foundation (1982), teletext provides one-way communications services, and videotext is the provision of two-way communications services that deliver information to the home. Presently exemplified by personal computers that instantly draw on sources of knowledge and entertainment anywhere in the world, this developing technology has been described as beginning to change many aspects of daily life as well as the relationship between the home and other institutions. The electronic home of 1998, the report concluded, may give the family much greater capacity than it has now to influence the education of children and the careers of youth and adults. Schools, too, will feel the impact, because information technology at school and at home will facilitate rote learning and free teachers to concentrate on development of creative problem-solving skills, and parents will be responsible for helping their children become generalists who can work with a fantastic variety of information tools.

6. *Increase of violent crimes among youth.* Criminologists are quick to point out that rising crime rates in the United States reflected an increase in the number of teenagers and young adults during the 1960s and 1970s. Delinquency and crime rates have long been substantial in these groups, which account for a substantial proportion of all crimes. Within this pattern, probably the most important development involving crime rates among youth is the increase in the number and proportion of violent crimes (aggravated assault, armed robbery, forcible rape, and murder). Approximately 30 percent of all serious crimes committed in the United States are committed by youths under nineteen years of age (Hindelang 1981). Much of this increase has taken place in big cities, particularly among underclass youth in concentrated poverty neighborhoods. In New York City, for example, arrests of children under sixteen years of age increased from 3,424 in 1950 to 26,153 in 1975. More than 2,500 of these cases in 1975 involved youngsters age ten and under who had been arrested for murder, manslaughter, assault, robbery, burglary, rape, and grand larceny (Pileggi 1977). Nationally, violent crimes accounted for 3.3 percent of juvenile arrests in 1975, an increase of 200 percent from 1964 (Advisory Committee on Child Development 1976).

Changes in the structure of the family and other phenomena clearly are interrelated. For example, the increase in the proportion of working mothers is related to higher rates of divorce and the formation of female-headed families: mothers who must support their children alone are more likely to work, other things being equal, than are those who have a husband working. The increase in youth crime appears to be related to the growing prominence of peer cultures, increase in drug use, and the influence of television and other media, particularly in concentrated poverty neighborhoods in which these influences are related to the functioning of a destructive street culture among children and youth. Hubert Williams, director of the Newark Police Department, has summarized some of the interrelated effects on inner-city children and youth:

> *Although crime may have been lower in the 1950s, seeds were being planted in our cities that would grow and flourish. . . . Narcotics . . . is the most obvious one. . . . But the drug problem points to deeper changes . . . which together constitute an enormous shift in the values and norms that determine how people behave. During the 1950s people in the inner city still generally believed that by working hard they could improve their lives—jobs were available; unemployment was much lower . . . and television . . . was not so influential then. Today, inner-city kids are well aware of the symbols of success—the fancy cars and clothes. . . . [In addition] in the inner cities kids were growing up without the guidance they'd had in the past . . . [as] the number of single-parent households increased tremendously. (quoted in "Images of Fear" 1985, 41)*

Evolution of the Family

In some ways, these trends probably represent a culmination of earlier developments in the evolution of the family. The modern nuclear family as described by Stone (1974) and others is based on a shift from predominantly economic to predominantly emotional bonding, but the emphasis on emotional bonding seems to be evolving toward a greater emphasis on emotional satisfaction as compared with an emphasis on privacy and child nurturance in earlier periods. As described by Shorter, who sees in this the emergence of a "post-modern" family, recent developments are particularly characterized by

> *a growing instability of the couple. Since the mid-1960s, divorce rates have accelerated dramatically in every country in Western society. To be sure, ever since the mid-nineteenth century when divorce first started to be eased, the rates have been inching upwards. But that long, gradual climb (interrupted in the 1950s by a plateau in most places) gave way in the 1960s to an unprecedented explosion. . . . Behind these dry statistics lies a major upheaval in the life of the couple. . . . The conventional explanations for increases in the divorce rate are all inadequate. The upthrust has simply been too powerful and universal to be dismissed as a result of more liberal divorce laws. . . . We may also reject the hysterical proposition that 'the family' is breaking up, for the fact is that all these divorcing people turn right around and marry again. . . .*
>
> *Two developments in the 1960s and 1970s have weakened the force of the permanent union. . . . First, the intensification of the couple's erotic life . . . has injected a huge chunk of high explosive into their relationship. . . . To the extent that erotic gratification is becoming a major element in the couple's collective existence, the risk of marital dissolution increases. . . .*
>
> *Second, women are becoming more independent economically, and can afford to extract themselves from undesired unions. (Shorter 1975, 277–278)*

In other respects, however, current trends in family structure represent a reversal of earlier developments in the history of the family in Western societies (Day 1988). The modern family emerged as a result of centuries of evolution directed partly toward protecting children from external influences in the environment and nurturing them for success in the school and the economy. But it also generated new problems in social relationships and socialization. In some ways, it cut children off too drastically from the life of the larger community, and it has been described as constituting a kind of emotional "hot-house" in which its members became too dependent on each other for affection and support.

It frequently did succeed, on the other hand, in ensuring that children received the type of protection, guidance, and stimulation they needed to succeed in the larger society in which it functioned. Some authorities, such as Ryder (1974), see both the earlier evolution toward the modern family and recent trends toward its restructuring or dissolution as inevitable within the overall context of the history of Western society:

> *The conjugal family serves as an oasis for the replenishment of the person, providing the individual with stable, diffuse and largely unquestioning support, assuaging the bruises of defeat and otherwise repairing whatever damage may have been done in the achievement-oriented struggles of the outside world. . . . The conjugal family is a relatively efficient design for supplying the kind of labor force a productive society needs and for providing comfort to the individual exposed to the consequences of participation in that system. . . . Yet any attempt at further attenuation of family ties, in the interest of optimal allocation of human resources, would probably be self-defeating because of the high psychological cost to the individual. The family is an essentially authoritarian system persisting within an egalitarian environment. The growth of industrialism has been closely linked to the development of the ideology of individual liberty. Family political structure—the authority of male over female and of parent over child—has no immunity to the implications of this ideological change. Grave internal difficulties may therefore be expected. (Ryder 1974, 128)*

Regardless of whether changes now occurring in the family are seen as continuations or reversals of earlier trends, it is important not to exaggerate their impact. Bane (1976), for example, has pointed out that children in earlier periods were involved in marital disruption due to the death of a parent and other disrupting events during the course of their childhoods as frequently as are children today, and that working mothers apparently spend about as much time with their children as do nonworking mothers.

Nevertheless, general indicators of family structure and juvenile behavior have changed substantially, and one can speculate on the implications of these changes for the schools. On the one hand, decreasing family size may signify or result in improvements in the cognitive develpment of children and their preparation for school, since children thus may be receiving more undivided parental attention than was true in the past (Zill 1982; Stafford 1987). In addition, the average parent today has more education than in earlier decades. On the other hand, there is reason to be concerned about the possible effects on children and youth of increases in the percentage of female-headed families, particularly in working-class and concentrated poverty neighborhoods. It is possible that recent increases in the incidence of divorce and female-headed families among middle-class populations are only now beginning to reach a level high enough to detect a consistent and noticeable impact on the development of their children.

Along these lines, Mahoney (1976) views such recent trends as part of a larger pattern and has concluded that their effects are most likely to be detrimental:

> *We have seen that families are much smaller than they once were; that there are fewer adults in the household with whom children can interact; and that even those adults who remain are absent much of the time, working in full-time jobs.*

> *What do these long- and short-term changes mean for the education of the nation's children? All of these changes combine to produce one important result: the isolation of children from adults. . . . The schools cannot possibly bear the full responsibility for the education of children. Cultural values cannot be transmitted* en masse *to a classroom of thirty. The enterprise takes the commitment of one human to another over a lifetime. . . . But because adults have less and less time and support for their roles as parents, what children experience now is a cultural void that is filled, even created, more by television and peers, than by parents or teachers. (Mahoney 1976, 10)*

Efforts to counteract or respond to problems involving change in the family took a conservative direction with the election of a more conservative federal government in 1980 and 1984 and a proposal in Congress for passage of the Family Protection Act in 1981. Major sections of the proposed legislation would (1) provide that no program may receive federal funds to provide a contraceptive device, abortion counseling, or an abortion to an unmarried minor without prior notification of the parents or guardian; (2) prevent application of the Civil Rights Act or other federal laws to enforce nondiscrimination in employment practices affecting homosexuals; (3) strengthen the entitlement of nonprofit, private schools to tax-exempt status; and (4) remove federal court jurisdiction over cases involving voluntary prayer in public schools and other public buildings (Rice 1981). If enacted into law, this legislation obviously would have important implications for teachers and other professionals who work with children and youth.

The central role of poverty environments in damaging the development of young people and the difficulties families in general are experiencing in raising children in our complex postindustrial society have been described by the Carnegie Council on Children in a major report published in 1977. Established by the Carnegie Corporation, the Council spent four years studying the problems of contemporary family life and preparing a set of recommendations that its members believed could be implemented by the end of the 1980s. The Council stressed that at least one-quarter of the children in the United States are growing up in poverty environments that severely limit their opportunities to succeed later in life. In a section titled "The Theft of the Future," the Council pointed out that

> *poor children live in a particularly dangerous world of broken stair railings, of busy streets serving as playgrounds, of lead paints, rats and rat poisons, or a rural world where families do not enjoy the minimal levels of public health. . . . it is frequently a world of intense social dangers, where many adults, driven by poverty and desperation, seem untrustworthy and unpredictable. Children who learn the skills for survival in that world, suppressing curiosity and cultivating a defensive guardedness toward novelty . . . may not be able to acquire the basic skills and values that are needed, for better or worse, to thrive in mainstream society. (Keniston et al. 1977, 33)*

But it is not just poverty families and children who experience severe problems in contemporary society; many others also are having trouble in an environment that has made child raising "demanding and complex." As schools, television, the peer group, and other institutions have become more important in socialization, parents have had to take on something like an "executive function . . . choosing communities, schools, doctors, and special programs that will leave their children in the best possible hands" (p. 12). It is not so much that parents are abdicating, the Council points out; instead they are being "dethroned, by forces they cannot influence, much less control" (pp. 22–23).

Based on this analysis, the Council's major recommendations included proposals stressing the following four goals for family policy:

1. Elimination of discriminatory employment practices and a national full-employment strategy combined with arrangements of family income supports designed to provide nearly all families with children a minimum income of at least half the current median in any given year;
2. A major national push for flexible and "family-conscious" work arrangements including flexible scheduling of working hours, more and better part-time employment opportunities, and time off for child rearing;
3. An improved range of comprehensive and universally accessible public services—especially in health care—to support and strengthen rather than replace the child-raising efforts of parents; and
4. Introduction and implementation of a variety of legal protections to assist troubled families.

In 221 pages of closely reasoned text, the Council set forth a persuasive list of specific proposals to accomplish these goals. The focus of these recommendations was primarily on the structural rather than the cultural causes of poverty and other family problems associated with poor performance in the school and the economy. The Council explained its reason for emphasizing structural forces affecting the development of children and youth:

> *Schools, the institutions traditionally called upon to correct social inequality, are unsuited to the task; without economic opportunity to follow educational opportunity, the myth of equality can never become real. . . . It is on questions of income, health, and family supports that much of a child's early development and later success will turn. (pp. 47, 80)*

Council Chairman Kenneth Keniston has stated that this emphasis on structural solutions to problems of family and child development was deliberate. In an interview published in the *Carnegie Quarterly,* Keniston stated:

> *Money, we would grant, is no guarantor of a decent life—other things, having to do with the human qualities of parents or with the neighborhood in which one grows up may be more important—but if one thinks what a* society *can do to support children, the promise of work and a modest income would empower fami-*

lies with at least the minimum authority to control their lives. (Carnegie Corporation 1977, 11)

Actions of the kind recommended by the Carnegie Council on Children are indispensable in overcoming the structural forces that hamper the cognitive and social development of children and youth, particularly among underclass groups in big cities. However, for reasons explained in the preceding chapters, the cultural aspects of poverty and poor performance in the school and the economy also must be taken into account in working to improve educational and economic opportunities for low-status students. Educators in particular must formulate policy and practice for improving opportunity in terms of all the major causes that limit the mobility of underclass and other working-class students. Taking account of cultural aspects of poverty will require attention to issues involving desegregation as well as major efforts to change the schools and their programs so that low-status students will be more successful than they are now.

Issues Involving Home Environment and Intellectual Development

Researchers are making progress in identifying the specific home environment variables that affect cognitive and scholastic performance and the ways in which home environment is related to performance at differing stages of development. Research in this area has particular relevance for the design of preschool and elementary school programs to improve educational opportunity for economically disadvantaged children. Such programs are discussed in Chapter 8, but at this point it is relevant to mention several major unresolved issues involving the relationship between home environment and intellectual development.

Father Absence and Achievement

Partly because the percentage of children raised in female-headed families has been increasing, there is considerable interest in the issue of whether other things being equal, children from homes with a father present perform better in school than do children without a father in the home. Presumptively it can be argued that a single parent tends to have less time, energy, and material resources to devote to a child than does a husband-wife family. A large number of studies have been conducted examining this issue, with somewhat inconclusive results. That is, some researchers have found that children without a father in the home do not show lower achievement or other indications of impaired development than do children with a father (e.g., Svanum, Ringle, and McLaughlin 1982; Salzman 1988), but other researchers have reached opposite conclusions (e.g., Guidubaldi 1984; Milne, Myers, Rosenthal, and Ginsburg 1986; Myers, Milne, Baker, and Ginsburg 1987).

Marino and McCowan (1976) have usefully defined the issue in larger terms by asking whether parent absence rather than just father absence has effects on the development of children and have reviewed the large body of research bearing on this issue. They pointed out that conclusions on parent absence are very difficult to reach because one should take into account the duration and cause of separation, the age and sex of the child, the quality and quantity of interaction with remaining adults, the context in which separation occurs, and other factors that may influence the child's reactions. They concluded that "parent absence may be a major contributing factor to low achievement . . . [and] personal maladjustment, but clearly not the only factor" (Marino and McCowan 1976, 177).

Clarke-Stewart (1977) also reviewed the research on parent absence and child development. She concluded that one-parent families are not necessarily harmful to the child's development, but she also found evidence to support the conclusion that husband-wife families may be more effective because both parents have an opportunity to exert a positive influence. Shepherd-Look (1982) reviewed the research dealing specifically with the effects of father absence and concluded that "separation of the father from the home environment, either temporarily or permanently, has definite negative effects upon male children. . . . Boys who were separated from their fathers early in life show a sex-role disruption pattern characterized by high verbal aggression, low physical aggression, more dependent behaviors, and a more feminine self-concept" (p. 423). She also concluded that this pattern occurs partly because many mothers who are single parents tend to treat their preadolescent sons in an overprotective manner; when single mothers do not discourage adventurous behavior, problems in sex-role development are minimal.

Complicated methodological problems have made research on father absence difficult to conduct and intepret. Because low social class is associated with both father absence and low scores on achievement or other outcomes, research should control for the effects of social class in estimating the relationship between family structure or disruption and student outcomes (Blechman 1982). However, father absence probably lowers the social class of many female-headed families; in this case, controlling for social class may incorrectly eliminate a true relationship. Similarly, divorce generally reduces the economic resources of families that become single-parent, but controlling for income in research on educational effects will tend to reduce or eliminate (true) relationships between family types and educational performance.

In addition, the growing incidence of father absence in United States society may mean that family disruption is having a much more widespread effect on child development, but it may also mean that effects are lessened when disruption is perceived or experienced as more nearly a normal phenomenon. Svanum, Ringle, and McLaughlin (1982) have pointed out that these and other opposing or contrasting patterns may all be having differential effects on subgroups within a sample of children for whom data are collected, and that in any case most research uses only "crude indexing of familial processes" (e.g., measures of family structure to represent child-parent interaction) that perhaps should not be expected to disclose strong effects of father absence on child outcomes (p. 142).

Although research on parent absence in general and on father absence in particular has not conclusively established the generalization that children in female-headed families perform less well in school than do children in husband-wife families, one tentative conclusion can be drawn from the data. A high percentage of children in concentrated poverty neighborhoods grow up in female-headed families, many of which do not have a male adult permanently in the home; but several studies (e.g., Wasserman 1972) have not found a relationship between family structure and school achievement in these types of neighborhoods. We believe this is because low school achievement in such neighborhoods represents not so much a deficiency of female-headed compared to husband-wife families as it does a concentration of underclass families whose children tend to perform poorly in school regardless of family structure.

Faced with a rapid increase in the percentage of children from single-parent families, educators have been attempting to identify and take account of implications for elementary and secondary schools. As part of their Study of School Needs of Children from One-Parent Families, the National Association of Elementary School Principals and the Kettering Foundation made recommendations such as the following for change in the schools: (1) Schools should review and update student records to identify children from one-parent homes so that guidance counselors and teachers can become more sensitive to their needs; (2) Schools should revise their calendars to provide easier after-hours access for working single parents; and (3) School systems should assume a major leadership role in conducting more effective parenting programs (Brown 1980). Similarly, the National Committee for Citizens in Education (Clay 1981) surveyed 1,237 single parents in 47 states and offered recommendations including the following:

- Copies of report cards and school activities notices should be sent to the noncustody parent.
- Single-parent families should be represented in textbooks and curriculum materials.
- School libraries should include materials that show varied life-styles and should help children deal with death and divorce.
- Schools should cooperate with other agencies in providing child care arrangements before and after school.
- In-service workshops should help teachers become aware of negative expectations they may have for children from single-parent families.

Family Size, Birth Order, and Cognitive Development

Research on home environment and cognitive development also has been concerned with such variables as size of the family, number of siblings, and order of birth of children within the family. Some studies such as those by Walberg and Marjoribanks (1976) and Steelman and Doby (1983) have found that after controlling for socioeconomic status, children in small families with few brothers and sisters are superior in cognitive development to children with more siblings. In addition, Walberg and Marjoribanks found that measures of home support and stimulation for learning were correlated both with cognitive development and number of siblings, after controlling for social status. In other words, it appears that other things being equal, parents with few children seem able to provide a more intellectually stimulating environment than do parents with many children, perhaps because parents' time, attention, and resources are spread much thinner in large families.

Zajonc (1976; 1986) has been studying these types of variables using several large cross-national samples. He has found that the brightest children generally are those born early in the smallest families, perhaps because they have a large amount of undivided adult attention in their early years. Birth spacing also appears to make a difference, because longer spacing between children makes it possible to give each child more attention in the early years of life. And, in some samples, children with no brothers or sisters have IQs slightly below those of children with one brother or sister, perhaps because the second child in a two-child family with adequate spacing has the advantage of having an older brother or sister as an additional teacher in the home.

The Zajonc research findings have been challenged by other researchers who have reported opposite or conflicting results (Stafford 1987). For example, Page and Grandon (1979) analyzed data from a large national sample and concluded that if one takes account of social class and ethnicity, the independent effects of birth order and family size on ability are trivial, and that children are not necessarily "dumber by the dozen." In addition, some of the data collected by the National Assessment of Educational Progress do not show a decline in performance among later-born children as is predicted by Zajonc's hypothesis and other earlier studies, and a study reported by Steelman and Mercy in 1980 concluded that number of siblings has a significant negative relationship with IQ but that birth order and intelligence are not related. Steelman (1985) reviewed the research on this topic and concluded that in general it tends to refute the conclusion that birth order has an independent effect on cognitive or academic outcomes.

Thus, at this time, it is not entirely clear how family characteristics such as family size and birth order are related to specific home environment variables such as degree of intellectual or verbal stimulation provided by the parents or parental aspirations for the child, other than that the two types of variables appear to be connected. Also, much remains to be learned concerning their interactions with school achievement and with other environmental characteristics such as type of neighborhood in which a child grows up and how well the child does in school. The complexity of these issues is suggested by a 1976 study (Nuttall et al.) of teenagers in four suburban communities near Boston, which found "sex-specific patterns" indicating that after controlling for IQ, small family size was related to school grades for boys but not for girls, and firstborn status was related to academic achievement among girls but not among boys.

Race or Ethnicity, Home Environment, and Intellectual Development

Chapter 2 discusses the issue of whether reported racial differences in intelligence are due to heredity or environment and concludes that innate differences if they exist are small and should not determine educational policy. However, even granted this conclusion, it still is important to learn more about the relationships between race or ethnicity, home environment, and intellectual development, in order to identify and understand the effects of home environment on achievement.

Because families of differing racial and ethnic groups differ in both social class and home environment, it is difficult to determine whether differences found in cognitive development and school achievement among their children are independently related to race or ethnicity or are artifacts of the social-class and home environment differences. We already have mentioned that a number of studies (e.g., Mercer 1973) have shown that most of the IQ and achievement differences among groups of students classified by race or ethnicity can be accounted for by differences in social status and home or neighborhood environment. However, other researchers have found that racial and ethnic differences in ability or achievement persisted after controlling for differences in social status or family environment. For example, Epstein (1972) found that ethnic group membership was a better overall predictor of academic performance than was social-class status among a sample of fifth-grade children in Peru, and Marjoribanks (1972) studied mental ability scores among children from five Canadian ethnic groups after controlling for home environment and found that significant ethnic group differences persisted in verbal, number, and reasoning ability scores.

The problem of interpreting these findings is compounded not only by the fact that ethnic groups differ in social class and home environment but also by the possibility that various social-class and home-environment characteristics may have differing meaning or effects in differing groups. Even if it is assumed that social class and home environment are correctly and comprehensively measured for the purpose of understanding or explaining differences in intellectual development (which obviously is very difficult to do), differences in the saliency of a characteristic for a given group and interactions between all these variables may make it almost impossible to disentangle their separate or unique effects.

For example, parental education may result in high achievement only in families in which there is high verbal interaction with children, and income and high achievement may go together only when parents spend money on intellectually stimulating materials. Peterson and DeBord (1966) found that home and family variables predictive of achievement were different for black and white eleven-year-old males, and Carter and Levine (1977) found that home environment characteristics such as reading to the child appeared to have differential effects on achievement among Anglo, black, and Chicano third- and sixth-graders in a large midwestern city.

In addition, some studies (e.g., Laosa 1977) suggest that social-class measures such as parental education or occupation have different meaning for differing ethnic groups, and that these differences may be related to children's performance on tests of ability or achievement. For example, a position as postal supervisor may be indicative of relatively high status for a black male in a big city but not for a white male in the suburbs, and children's performance may reflect more the status achieved by parents in the local community than the ranking of an occupation on a national index of occupational status. Furthermore, parental action to provide a more positive home environment probably has differential effects depending on the social class of the home as well as on the influence of neighbors and peers and other factors. Thus, Benson (1979) studied family background and other variables in a large black ghetto and found that home environment was not closely associated with student achievement among students relatively high in social class (other considerations overrode the effects of negative home environment) or relatively low in social class (positive home influence was overwhelmed by other factors), but that home environment did appear to influence achievement significantly among students in the middle social-class group.

In view of all these difficulties, it does not now appear possible to make definitive statements about relationships between race or ethnicity, social class, home environment, and intellectual development, but it is possible to conclude that both home environment and social class are closely related to the cognitive and scholastic performance of children within most if not all ethnic groups. Research to date also suggests that race and ethnicity may be more closely related to achievement among working-class than among middle-class students, perhaps because individuals from a given ethnic group who attain middle-class status resemble individuals from other groups who have been upwardly mobile. In the process of upward mobility, people who formerly were working class have acquired a middle-class style while losing some of their ethnic characteristics (Havighurst 1976).

Home Environment, Brain Damage, and the Reversibility of Cognitive Retardation

Another aspect of home environment known to be related to cognitive development involves malnutrition and other indicators of poor health conditions such as low birth weight, high incidence of birth complications, inadequate medical care during pregnancy, and high rate of physiological disability among infants. Malnutrition and related indicators of health problems also are associated with poverty. Malnourished children are most frequently from low-income families, particularly one-parent households. Havighurst (1971b) surveyed the research on malnutrition and child development and concluded that severe, early malnutrition does have an effect on development of the brain. Serious impairment of normal cognitive and psychological development is most likely to occur to the extent that malnutrition is severe up to about six months of age. Malnutrition after this time also affects the child's learning development by causing irritability and inattentiveness, but it seems to result in little or no permanent brain damage (Bejar 1981).

However, very few children in the United States and other industrialized countries suffer from severe malnutrition. A number of low-status children probably do experience less severe malnutrition—particularly iron deficiency (anemia)—which affects their performance in school (Read 1976), but a more debilitating cause of impaired cognitive development is lack of adequate or appropriate environmental stimulation during the early years of life. Lack of appropriate intellectual and social stimulation is associated with deficiences in cognitive growth substances in the brain. Thus, infants who do not receive adequate environmental stimulation may be impaired in mental functioning when they grow older. A 1977 report to Congress by the Comptroller General concluded that 75 percent of the 100,000 new cases of mental retardation diagnosed each year are due to this type of sociocultural impairment.

These findings suggest that there probably is considerable sociocultural retardation (as opposed to inherent biological retardation) among low-status children in homes that do not provide appropriate stimulation during the early years or in which nutritional or other related health problems result in inattentiveness or irritability. These conditions in turn cause children to fall behind in acquiring basic learning skills and to develop a poor self-concept as a learner. Such conclusions also suggest, however, that cognitive retardation among low-status students can be avoided by working with parents to (1) improve nutrition and other indicators of physical well-being, and (2) provide appropriate environmental stimulation during the early years of life.

These conclusions further suggest that much of the learning deficit among low-status students in countries like the United States can be overcome or reversed, particularly if action is taken to provide appropriate home environment conditions during the early years (Hunt 1979). Scientists who believe that much of the intellectual retardation evident among many low-status students is reversible cite studies that indicate that brain damage may not be as widely prevalent or as long-lasting in its effect as some scholars previously believed. Read (1976), for example, believes that much retardation is substantially reversible. In support of this conclusion, he cites studies of Korean children who were severely malnourished early in life and after adoption by families in the United States were "normal in intellectual performance by American standards" and of Colombian children who were chronically undernourished but "improved their performance markedly on various behavioral indices" (pp. 30–31) following nutritional supplementation and educational stimulation beginning about age three. We already have cited Skeels's (1966) findings concerning the improvements in cognitive functioning made by children removed from a nonstimulating institutional environment at an early age.

Kagan and Klein (1973) also cite studies including their own research in Guatemala indicating that children who perform poorly on various cognitive tests during early childhood show marked gains after participating in an environment that provides stimulation and experience of the kind they previously lacked and is required for high performance on the tests. They concluded that children who are not too severely retarded have the capacity to overcome most of their learning handicaps when placed in an appropriate environment.

Taken together, these studies all suggest that much can be done to overcome intellectual retardation not just among low-status students but also among any large group of students with impaired cognitive development or low scholastic achievement. It may be true that a significant number of cognitively retarded pupils have brain damage that is basically irreversible and it may even be true that a substantial proportion of youngsters who grow up in physically unhealthy and intellectually nonstimulating environments will never achieve their full cognitive or scholastic potential. On the other hand, there is little or no solid evidence to contradict the conclusion that most such children can learn enough to meet standards of academic performance that would allow them to succeed in the school and in a modern economy.

Classification of Minority Students as Mentally Retarded

Many school districts try to provide special classes for students with an IQ below 70 (the American Association of Mental Deficiency defines the 55 to 69 range as "educable mentally retarded"), and some try to provide such classes for children below 80 in IQ. In some cases, students are placed in special classes for pupils with learning disorders if they have a relatively low IQ and also are diagnosed as emotionally disturbed, since emotional disorders are known to be associated with mental retardation. The number and percentage of students classified as mentally retarded increased regularly for about three decades after World War II and then began declining slowly in the mid-1970s.

Minority students are much more likely than nonminority students to be placed in several special-education categories such as "educable mentally retarded" and "seriously emotionally disturbed" (Ogbu 1982; Gelb and Mizokawa 1986; Lytle 1988). In addition, research indicates that black students and Hispanic students but not nonminority students are much more likely to be in classes for the mentally retarded if they live in states that are high on poverty and other indicators of low socioeconomic status (Gelb and Mizokawa 1986). This pattern points to the possibility that minority students are being disproportionately classified as mentally retarded due to educational disadvantages associated with their social-class background.

However, controversy exists over whether children classified as mentally retarded have been correctly diagnosed and the types of arrangements that should be made for their education. Some observers point out that intelligence tests have been constructed for use particularly with middle-class white populations and that as a consequence minority and low-status children may be diagnosed as retarded partly or largely because they are unfamiliar with the terminology and procedures of the tests (Quantz 1981–82). Some support for this conclusion has been provided by Garrison and Hammil (1971), who found that at least 25 percent and as many as 68 percent of the children—many of them minority—who had been assigned to educable mentally retarded classes in a five-county area in Philadelphia had been misassigned. The federal government Office of Civil Rights investigated 148 school districts between 1975 and 1979 and concluded that the special education placement of minority students frequently could not be justified educationally (Education Advocates Coalition 1980). This outcome can be damaging because children misclassified as retarded may be treated as such and expected to perform at a low level by teachers, parents, and classmates, thus generating a self-fulfilling prophecy wherein children work below their capacity in accordance with their own or other people's expectations (National Academy of Sciences 1982b). If this happens, then classification as retarded is racially discriminatory to the extent that minority students may be misclassified relatively more frequently than majority-white students.

Various groups concerned with the rights and welfare of minority students have raised this issue. Following a study of special education placement in five southern states, for example, the Children's Defense Fund issued a report saying that

> *we do not want to state that, based on these facts above, there were over 32,000 black students in these five states who have been misclassified and misplaced in educable mentally retarded classes. In order to make such a statement we would have to know the proportion of black and white students who should be in EMR [educable mentally retarded] classes in each of these districts, a figure which has not yet been derived even on the national level. . . . Such facts clearly warrant immediate further examination and investigation by local school officials and federal OCR [Office of Civil Rights] compliance officials. (quoted in Klein 1977, 13)*

Some courts have been sympathetic to this type of criticism and have acted to reduce the possibility that students will be misassigned to special education classes. In a 1970 case (*Diana* v. *Board of Education*), for example, a California court examined the claim of nine Mexican-American children who felt they had been improperly classified as mentally retarded on the basis of an IQ test on which their scores ranged from 52 to 68. When tested by a bilingual psychologist and allowed to respond in Spanish or English, their IQs increased by an average of 15 points. The court ruled that (1) all children whose primary language is other than English must be tested in both their primary language and English; (2) the tests must not depend solely on vocabulary, general information, or other experience-based content; and (3) school districts that have a disparity between the percentage of Mexican-American students in regular classes and in classes for the retarded must submit an explanation. In another case (*Larry P.* v. *Riles*) in 1972, a California court ruled that black students could not be placed in EMR classes on the basis of IQ tests "as currently administered," after hearing evidence that the family environment and dialect of many black students caused them to have misleadingly low scores on the tests.

The federal government also has acted to avoid misclassification and misplacement of mentally retarded and other handicapped students, through sections of Public Law 94–142 (the Education of Handicapped Children Act). This law not only mandates and furnishes assistance to the states to provide a free appropriate public education for handicapped children but also establishes due process procedural protections regarding the classification of students. Educators gradually are being placed in the position of having either to prove that approaches that classify or segregate children as mentally retarded really provide the most effective means to overcome deficits in cognitive development or try other approaches for improving the performance of children who previously would have been placed in special classes.

Effects of Television

There has been grave and growing concern with the question of whether the media—particularly television—may be encouraging violence and other antisocial behavior among children and youth. The Surgeon General of the United States appointed an advisory committee on television and social behavior that studied the matter from 1969 to 1971. They reported that the scientific data were not conclusive on the question whether television violence causes aggression in most children, although they went on to say that there was good evidence to indicate a relation between violence on television and aggressive behavior among children who already had a tendency toward aggressive behavior (U.S. Public Health Service 1972).

Later reviews of research (Comstock 1977; Dorr 1986) on this issue indicated that effects are largely dependent on situational factors such as "frustration or anger; similarities between the available target and the target in the portrayal; expected consequences such as success, failure, pain, or punishment; and opportunity to perform" the act of violence (Comstock 1977, 195). Ten years after the Surgeon General's 1972 report, a committee of behavioral scientists reviewed subsequent research for the National Institute of Mental Health and concluded that a relationship between viewing of violence on television and aggressive behavior in children was not well established. The committee further concluded that "television violence is as strongly correlated with aggressive behavior as any other behavioral variable that has been measured," that the percentage of programs containing violence has been stable since 1967 but the number of violent acts per program has increased, and that children "learn to behave aggressively from the violence they see on television in the same way they learn cognitive and social skills from watching their parents, siblings, peers, teachers, and others" (U.S. Department of Health and Human Services 1982, 6, 38, 39).

That television can be an important force for positive socialization also is apparent and has been supported by research indicating that "Sesame Street" has been helpful both for middle- and lower-status children (Leifer, Gordon and Graves 1975; Almeida 1977), and that children can become more cooperative and nurturant after viewing programs emphasizing these behaviors (Poulos, Rubenstein, and Liebert 1975). Recognizing the promises as well as the potentially damaging effects of television on children and youth, critics have been organizing and pushing for changes in commercial programming in the United

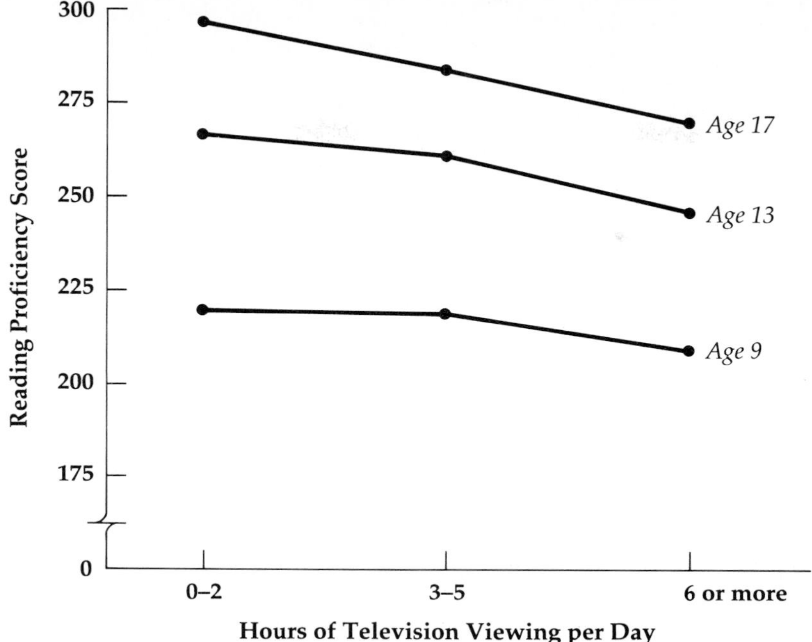

Figure 4.3 ***Reading Proficiency Scores of Nine-, Thirteen-, and Seventeen-Year-Olds, by Hours of Television Viewing, 1984*** (*Source*: Adapted from National Assessment of Educational Progress [NAEP] 1985.)

States. The Parent Teachers Association has made reform in television one of its principal national demands, and groups such as the National Citizens Committee for Broadcasting have been organized to collect data and lobby for change. Critics of television have blamed it for a variety of social ills including the promotion of unintelligent consumerism, declining performance on academic tests in the schools, and the promulgation of stereotypes regarding low-status minorities (Pierce, Carew, and Willis 1977) and women. Winn (1977), Willis, Thomas, and Hoppe (1985), and others present some evidence and strong arguments suggesting that television may be making children physically and intellectually passive, with detrimental effects on their cognitive and academic development.

Research on television viewing and school achievement indicates that there is a relationship, but causes of the relationship are somewhat unclear. The overall relationship between television viewing and reading is shown in Figure 4.3, which presents 1984 data collected by the National Assessment of Educational Progress (NAEP) for nine-, thirteen-, and seventeen-year-olds. As shown in Figure 4.3, students either nine or thirteen years of age who watch television six or more hours per day have lower reading proficiency than their peers who report less viewing. For seventeen-year-olds, this trend also is present, and those who watch three to five hours per day have clearly lower reading scores than those who view television two hours or less per day.

However, the NAEP study and other research (e.g., Hormik 1981) reporting that low reading scores are associated with excessive viewing are correlational studies that have not been able to disentangle cause and effect. In general, children and youth who are doing poorly in school may retreat to television and other nonacademic activities, or television viewing may be a manifestation of family and home environment variables that also affect school achievement.

Recent research indicates that relationships between achievement, television viewing, age of the student, home environment, and other variables are complex and multidimensional. For example, a 1981 study of television viewing among more than 12,000 sixth graders in California indicated that heavy viewing was associated with lower achievement in reading, mathematics, and writing, lower social class, and preference for light entertainment. Viewing in excess of five to six hours per day was associated with low achievement for all social-class groups, but for students of lower social class, watching television up to three to four hours per day was associated with higher achievement (California Assessment Program 1982). (One can speculate that the television environment is more productive of achievement than are working-class home and neighborhood environments.) Findings from a 1981 survey of 580 students in Northern California further indicate that social class is more strongly related to reading achievement among third than sixth graders, and effects of viewing on achievement depend on such considerations as reasons for viewing (e.g., to learn or to escape from other activities), reasons for reading, and degree and type of involvement in reading and television viewing. The investigators concluded that "amount of viewing and amount of reading, although important variables in their own right, are but parts of a larger complex of related television or viewing constructs" (Bachen, Hornby, Roberts, and Hernandez-Ramos 1982, 31).

High amount of television viewing also is associated with relatively poor social skills and peer relations. On the average, children and youth who are less popular and spend less time with peers devote more time to watching television. Dorr (1986) examined this relationship and reported that as in the case of television and achievement, cause and effect are difficult to delineate:

> *Children with less satisfactory relationships may watch television simply because other children avoid them. . . . Or they may watch so much television that they do not leave enough time to learn to get along with peers. Or they may be less satisfactory companions because they spend more time watching television's bad examples. . . . Or all three things may account for the association. Or another as yet unidentified variable may cause both amount of viewing and quality of peer relationships. (Dorr 1986, 105)*

The television industry has not been completely unresponsive to criticism. Between 1975 and 1983, there was a slight reduction in violence and other adult themes during prime viewing hours, and efforts were being made to portray the antisocial nature of violence more meaningfully. The major networks also slightly reduced the number of commericals on Saturday morning programs for children. A study conducted by CBS in 1977 showed that nine out of ten children received at least one positive message from programs such as "Fat Albert and the Cosby Kids," "Shazam," and "Isis." However, Turow (1981) reviewed three decades of network television programming for children and reported that criticism of the television industry has been ineffective at changing basic programming criteria, though it has "eked out" some concessions involving "slightly fewer action-adventure series, a few more live-action shows, a few more realistic dramas about children, [and] more children of both sexes in the programs" (p. 12). He also concluded that cable television is beginning to show some of the same deficiencies in programming for children as did network television in its early days. All things considered, the effects of television on children and the family still pose an important national problem, though little could be said conclusively beyond the truism that television promises extraordinary benefits for education but also sometimes undermines family interaction and other forms of learning, such as play and reading.

Effects of Maternal Employment

Growth in the percentage of women working outside the home has generated concern that maternal employment may be harmful to the development of their children. Partly because the proportion of employed mothers with young children was small until recent decades, relatively little research has been conducted on this topic. Rollings and Nye (1979) reviewed the research on effects of maternal employment and concluded that there is "little evidence of appreciable effects, positive or negative" (p. 217). A panel of the National Academy of Sciences (1982a) reviewed available research on maternal employment and children's school achievement and reached the same conclusion: with some exceptions, most studies show little or no difference in the achievement of children of employed and nonworking mothers.

As maternal employment has increased, the percentage of latchkey children who return to empty homes or apartments also has increased. Some national data indicate that there may be more than ten million such children between the ages of five and thirteen (Rosenberger 1985). However, other data indicate that the number may be much lower—perhaps not many more than two million (U.S. Bureau of the Census 1987).

Considerable attention to the potential problems of latchkey children was generated at 1985 Congressional hearings at which psychologist David Elkind testified that adults should "not kid ourselves that this is a beneficial experience" that builds independence (quoted in Bridgman 1984). Several researchers reported that latchkey children have abnormally high levels of fear and some even lock themselves in closets, but other researchers reported there were no significant differences in personality or behavior between supervised children and latchkey children (Bridgman 1984). Those who favor expanded government services for latchkey children argued that millions of children would benefit, but opponents maintained that too little is known about effective organization and delivery of such services.

Strother (1984) reviewed the literature related to the school's role in providing assistance to latchkey children. After delineating the pros and cons "regarding the involvement of public schools in child care" (1984, 290), Strother pointed out that schools engaging in provision of before- or after-school child care will have to deal with legal and policy issues involving such matters as licensing and liability. She then described a number of programs and practices that might be undertaken, including provision of space and other resources for other nonprofit agencies, direct sponsorship of before- and after-school supervision, busing of children to after-school programs elsewhere, conduct of seminars for parents, encouragement of home-based support services and telephone hotlines, training for children in coping skills, and cooperation with youth-serving organizations such as Camp Fire. Strother concluded her review with the following four specific recommendations for educators:

> *First, they should concentrate on structuring homework carefully . . . [and should] consider starting telephone hotlines for homework, staffed by teachers or by parent volunteers.*
>
> *Second, educators should allow time during the school day for children to discuss personal concerns.*
>
> *Third, school officials should establish better procedures for contacting working parents in an emergency.*
>
> *Fourth, educators should develop extended day-care programs for children. (Strother 1984, 293)*

Homeless Children

Along with economic recession in the early 1980s, a nationwide increase apparently occurred in the number of homeless persons in the United States. At the end of the recession, the homeless population seemed to have remained relatively high and may have increased even more. Whatever the numbers and causes, the homeless population appears to be more diverse than in earlier decades, when it generally was portrayed as consisting primarily of unattached, older adults. Richard Ropers (1985) has described the general situation of the homeless population:

> *The homeless seem to be everywhere. Some are obviously homeless, like the bag-ladies, the shopping-cart people, the disheveled who huddle in doorways, and others who seem to wander aimlessly in streets and alleys. Those whose homelessness is apparent, however, and who look as though they fit the long-held stereotypes of bums, derelicts, winos, or the insane, are only the tip of the iceberg. There are also the invisible ones, many of whom are indistinguishable from the rest of us, and who "pass" during the day, roaming shopping malls or university hallways.*

At night they try to rest in rat- and roach-infested movie theaters, in lonely schoolyards, in their cars, on subways, or in the cold restrooms of public buildings. Most of the contemporary homeless are in fact difficult to detect because of their diversity and "invisibility." (Ropers 1985, 1)

Data collected in the latter part of the 1980s show that there are many families and children among the contemporary homeless population, although estimates of the number of children vary from 250,000 to three million (Pavuk 1987). Studies examining the problems of homeless children indicate that as a group they suffer from relatively high rates of child abuse and low rates of school enrollment and attendance, low achievement, and high incidence of poor health and learning disabilities (Goldberg 1987; Pavuk 1987). One study conducted in eight big cities found that 43 percent of homeless children were not attending school regularly and that shelter space was much too limited to accommodate the local population of homeless families (Goldberg 1987). Local governments frequently have been unable or unwilling to deal effectively with the problems of homeless families and children, and the federal government in the face of a large budget deficit also has provided only limited assistance to address this important national problem (Ropers 1985).

Conclusion

Home influences on intellectual development have been examined in this chapter and we have concluded that home-environment differences that underlie social-class differences are related to cognitive and scholastic performance. In conjunction with the previous chapter, the material in this chapter suggests that families influence the intellectual development of their children particularly through the adequacy of their efforts to protect the child, if necessary, from detrimental external influences, and the kinds of verbal and intellectual stimulation and encouragement they provide inside the home.

Several important issues involving relationships between home environment and intellectual development also were examined. The conclusions reached in this section can be partly summarized by saying that large family size, malnutrition and other indicators of physical health problems, and, possibly, father absence (i.e., female-headed family structure), seem to be implicated to some degree as causes of the below-average intellectual development and performance of students from working-class backgrounds. However, family structure measures such as father-absence and large size do not directly hamper cognitive development but exert their influence through effects on home environment or are themselves indicators of environmental conditions that hamper learning. In addition, malnutrition and related health indicators do not appear to result in permanent brain damage for a very high percentage of children in the United States, thus suggesting that efforts to make home environments more conducive to cognitive development would not be likely to fail for this reason alone.

Our discussion of home environment and cognitive development included an analysis of trends in family relations because these trends have great importance for the future development of children and youth. Developments regarding home environment and learning are inseparable from larger trends in society affecting the evolution of families and social classes. From this point of view, it is very important that society develop national policies and programs to ensure that families are able to provide their children with an environment conducive to success in later life. No one can draw up a master plan that ensures that this will happen for all children or that takes full account of pluralistic values concerning the development of children and youth, but policies can be worked out to provide the resources and nurturance young people need to function effectively in a modern society. It is this possibility that former U.S. Commissioner of Education Terrel H. Bell had in mind when he recommended that proposals for government or private action in United States communities should include a "family impact" statement to go along with required "environmental impact" statements that Congress wrestles with in deciding what types of day-care arrangements to finance in the United States.

From the viewpoint of the educational system, the most important national policies dealing with families and children will include those that affect working-class populations, particularly underclass residents of concentrated poverty neighborhoods in big cities. Our analysis of social mobility and education (see Chapter 7) indicates that the schools need to become more effective in providing opportunities for working-class children in general and underclass children in particular. Our analysis of social-class environments and home environments in relation to intellectual development indicates that steps should be taken to improve home, neighborhood, and school learning environments for working-class children and others who are poorly prepared to function in school, if such children are to have a reasonable chance to succeed later in school and society. Much will depend on what other institutions such as the federal, state, and local governments do to solve problems of poverty, segregation, and big-city deterioration that are connected with the educational problems of working-class children. Much also will depend on what schools do to provide more effective learning opportunities for low-status students. This latter topic is addressed in Chapters 8 and 13.

EXERCISES

1. The Dave-Wolf home environment scale described in this chapter has been widely used in research relating home environment to performance in school. It is administered by interviewing a child's mother and giving a score on each dimension from high to low. A copy of a similar instrument incorporating additional items on home environment is available in a paper by Carter and

Levine (1977). The reader may write for a copy and use it to measure home environment in nearby communities. (Write to Daniel Levine, University of Missouri—Kansas City, 5100 Rockhill Road, Kansas City, Missouri, 64110.)

2. What procedures are being used in nearby school districts to classify students as mentally retarded? What safeguards are being used to avoid misclassification? To what degree are minority and/or low-status students overrepresented in classes for the mentally retarded in comparison to their proportion in local schools?
3. If you were asked to advise friends on how they can provide an intellectually stimulating environment for their young children, how would you respond? What specific suggestions would you give to encourage optimal cognitive development?
4. What are the main arguments suggesting that children from female-headed families are not likely to do as well in school as those from husband-wife families? What are some of the major counter-arguments? Why do researchers have a difficult time determining the answer to this question?
5. After reading *The Nature of the Child* by Jerome Kagan, list things you believe that parents should and should not do to promote their children's development.

SUGGESTIONS FOR FURTHER READING

1. *The American Family in Social-Historical Perspective* edited by Michael Young includes a number of essays that describe historical trends involving the family in the United States and discusses their implications for the present and the future.
2. Many Jo Bane's *Here to Stay: American Families in the Twentieth Century* and *Haven in a Heartless World: The Family Besieged* by Christopher Lasch provide background data and thoughtful discussion dealing with the status of the family in the United States.
3. For an account of how the family acts to produce differences in personality between children of different social classes, read *Father of the Man* by Allison Davis and Robert J. Havighurst.
4. *The Changing American Parent* by Daniel R. Miller and Guy E. Swanson and *Patterns of Child Rearing* by Robert E. Sears, Eleanor E. Maccoby, and Harry Levin are reports of two large-scale studies of child-rearing practices. For an account of how methods of child rearing have changed in America in the past 100 years, read Chapters 9 and 10 in *Childhood in Contemporary Cultures*, edited by Margaret Mead and Martha Wolfenstein. See also the article by Urie Bronfenbrenner, "Socialization and Social Class through Time and Space," in *Readings in Social Psychology* by Eleanor E. Maccoby.
5. There are a number of good textbooks on the family as a social institution. A useful survey of recent research on the family as an agent of socialization has been prepared by Clausen (1966). A book of readings on the *Family in*

Transition (Skolnick and Skolnick) deals with the changing family in the 1970s. *Family Studies Review Yearbook* edited by Olson and Miller (1983) reports many aspects of recent research on the family.

6. Research on the family's role in child development is reviewed and summarized in Alison Clarke-Stewart's 1977 monograph on *Child Care in the Family*.
7. For a comprehensive survey of research on the socialization process, see the review by Edward Zigler (1970) entitled "Social Class and the Socialization Process." See also the chapter "Sociological Correlates of Child Behavior" by Clausen and Williams in the NSSE Yearbook, *Child Psychology*. The political socialization of children and adolescents is described in the book by Hess and Torney.
8. Television, comic books, radio, and movies are important aspects of the culture that operate on the child. The chapter by Eleanor Maccoby, "Effects of the Mass Media," in Hoffman and Hoffman's *Review of Child Development Research* is a good overview of this topic.
9. *Education and the Brain* edited by Jeanne Chall and Allan Mirsky, the 1978 yearbook of the National Society for the Study of Education, includes a large amount of material dealing with the cognitive development of children.
10. The entire November 1977 issue of *Education and Urban Society* is devoted to television and education. Authors explore a number of important issues on this topic.
11. *Contemporary Theories about the Family*, edited by Wesley R. Burr and others, provides a wealth of information on family dynamics and processes.
12. *The War over the Family: Capturing the Middle Ground*, by Brigitte Berger and Peter Berger, argues that the nuclear, middle-class family has been a major force in modernizing and developing a stable, productive society. The authors take a middle ground between liberals and conservatives on family policy issues involving public and private rights and responsibilities.
13. Nearly all of the July 1986 issue of *Sociology of Education* is devoted to research on effects on children and youth of single-parent families and maternal employment.
14. Aimée Dorr's *Television and Children* (1986) is a short but comprehensive and succinct review of the many ways television affects children and their implications for schools, families, and society as a whole.
15. *Family Life and School Achievement* by Reginald Clark identifies and analyzes differences between the families of high- and low-achieving urban black students.

5

The Peer Group

The importance of the peer group in elementary and secondary schools was underlined in data John Goodlad and his colleagues collected in the early 1980s as part of their national research project titled "A Study of Schooling." Information was collected from 17,163 students and 1,350 teachers at 38 representative public schools (Goodlad 1984). In response to the question, "What is the *one* best thing about this school?" students in junior and senior high schools were much more likely to cite "My friends" than anything else about their schools. As shown in Table 5.1, 35 percent selected the response dealing with peers; no other aspect of their schools was selected by more than 13 percent of the students responding. It may be noteworthy that only 11 percent selected either "Classes I'm taking" or "Teachers."

The Nature and Importance of the Peer Group

A child grows up in two social worlds. One is the world of adults: parents, relatives, teachers, club leaders, store clerks, and friends of the family. The other is the world of peers or age-mates: friends, play groups, clubs and gangs, and school groups. For any child, of course, "the" peer group means a succession of specific groups of children with whom he or she interacts, just as "the" family is, for a child, one particular family. Peer groups are of many different kinds—from the informal play group to the organized Scout troop or organized gang, from the clique of three or four members to the wide school group—and the average child will interact with a variety of particular peer groups as he or she grows up. Each group has its own rules, implicit or explicit; its own social organization; and its own expectations for group members.

Even though there is great variation from one group to another, the peer group can be considered in general terms. From a broad point of view, the peer group of the child and the adolescent constitutes a world of its own with its customs, traditions, manners, and even, at times, its own language (Corsaro 1988).

The adult is always, to greater or lesser degree, excluded from the peer group of the child and adolescent. At the one extreme, a peer group may be in open conflict with adults, as in a delinquent gang in a slum neighborhood whose activities may be in express defiance of community standards of law and order; or as in groups of adolescents whose standards of dress, speech, and behavior while by no means delinquent, nevertheless conflict with expectations set by parents. The situation in which a teenager argues with his or her parents that, "The other kids stay out until midnight, why can't I?" has countless variations.

Table 5.1 *High School Students' Response to the Question, "What Is the One Best Thing about This School?"*

Response	Percentage
My friends	35
Sports	13
Good student attitudes	11
Nothing	8
Classes I'm taking	7
Teachers	4
Other	22

Source: Compiled and adapted from Goodlad 1984, 76–77.

Yet the variations are on the same theme, that of reconciling two sets of expectations: one set from the peer world, the other from the adult world.

The other extreme is the situation in which the peer-group expectations are in full accord with adult expectations and are even a direct outcome of adult planning, as in a neighborhood play group formed under the watchful eyes of mothers; or a Boys Club organized through a settlement house, or an urban renewal project; or a high school Hi-Y group meeting under the leadership of a respected teacher. Even in such situations, the adult is to some measure excluded, with youngsters reserving certain areas of communication and interaction to themselves. The child or the adolescent feels comfortable with age-mates in a way that he or she is not comfortable with the adult, however acceptant and understanding the adult may be. There are always certain thoughts, values, and behaviors that youngsters share only with other youngsters.

That the peer group constitutes a social world of its own is well known and accepted by most parents and teachers. Yet the importance of the peer group as a socializing agency is less often recognized. Unlike the family and the school, the peer group is not a formalized, institutionalized agent of society. It has no legal definitions, no formally ascribed functions or duties. Yet it pervades the life of the child to a greater extent as he or she grows older, and it performs increasingly important functions in teaching the ways of society.

Importance of Peer Acceptance and Rejection

Research indicates that acceptance by peers is an important consideration in predicting whether children and youth will experience adjustment problems later in life. Parker and Asher (1986) have examined the literature on this topic and concluded that acceptance/rejection by peers is strongly associated with later at-risk outcomes such as dropping out of school and criminality. One general conclusion of their review of research is that

> *children with poor peer adjustment are at risk. . . . Some idea of the incidence of later maladjustment among children with peer relations problems can be gained by considering the dropout area. The most consistent predictor in this area was low acceptance per se. In study after study, children identified as having low peer acceptance dropped out at rates 2, 3, and even 8 times as high as other children. (Parker and Asher 1986, 7–8)*

Aggressive Children Rejected

Available data also indicate that the children most likely to be rejected by their peers are those who are high in aggressiveness and low in cooperative behavior (Coie and Kupersmidt 1983). Research by Coie and Whidby (1986) found that this generalization was true in a study of predominantly black and low-income third-graders, just as had been the case in a number of previous studies of white and middle-class elementary students. The authors also found that the results were more pronounced for boys than for girls, perhaps because there were relatively few highly aggressive girls. The dynamics of gender in the operation of elementary peer groups are discussed in Chapter 11 dealing with women and education.

Functions of the Peer Group

As a socializing agency, the peer group serves the child in a number of ways (Schunk 1987). Adults generally expect the peer group to teach a child how to get along with others, as witnessed by the distress of parents and teachers over a child who is not accepted by other children and who is therefore denied many opportunities for social learning.

Teaching the Culture

Even though a peer group may be said to have a subculture that is particularly its own, it nevertheless reflects the adult society and reinforces most of the values held by the adult society.* A child learns through peers the prevailing standards of adult morality—competition, cooperation, honesty, responsibility—which, while they may at first be childlike versions, become adultlike with increasing

*The distinction should be made between an organized gang and other types of peer groups. The gang may be defined as an organization of preadolescents or adolescents that does not relate itself positively to adult leadership. A gang may or may not engage in delinquent behavior, but in the eyes of most adults, gangs are undesirable because they are at least potentially antisocial, if not actually so. The efforts of most social agencies in dealing with gangs are directed toward the transformation of gangs into groups by providing adult leadership and thus to guide their activities into socially acceptable channels.

age. Recent research indicates that the peer group becomes increasingly important in the development of moral reasoning as children grow older (Lerner and Shea 1982). For example, Gerson and Damon (1978) studied children who took part with peers in a discussion of how to distribute candy and found that older children (eight- to ten-year-olds) were more likely to distribute it equally.

The peer group teaches children their sex roles, building on but changing and elaborating the earlier teaching of the family. A child learns from peers what behavior is acceptable and admired in a boy and what is accepted and admired in a girl. Thus, the peer group is a powerful agency in molding behavior in accordance with current versions of manhood and womanhood (Eder and Parker 1987).

The peer group is also an important source of information in areas other than social relations. Our modern sophisticate, aged ten, has obtained much up-to-the-minute knowledge of outer space and satellites from television, it is true; but it is after discussion with age-mates that the information takes on value and becomes part of the child's intellectual equipment. It is the peer group that often decides what knowledge is important, and what is not.

Certain areas of teaching and information giving have become the special province of the peer group: for instance, to teach a child by actual experience how rules are made, how they can be changed and, along with this, an understanding of the individual's responsibility in a group situation. The peer group also is important in imparting sex education to the child.

The Peer Group as a Learning Situation

In the adult world, the child is always in a position of subordinate status. In the peer world, the child has equal status with others and learns from persons who are not removed from him or her by wide differences in age, maturity, or prestige. Deference and respect for authority are largely irrelevant issues. Among peers, the child is relatively free to express his or her own attitudes, judgments, and critical faculties, and to explore personal relationships.

One special characteristic of the peer group is the transitory quality of relationships. These relationships may be intense, but not necessarily long lasting. An eight-year-old, for example, may suddenly switch allegiance from one child to another and report to his family that it is now Richy, rather than Don, who is the paragon of all virtues. A twelve-year-old girl said, in similar vein, "I used to think Ellen and Nancy and I would always be friends. We spent a lot of time together, and did our homework together, and all. But now Ellen seems kind of silly, and we get into a lot of arguments. So I've become friendly with Kathy and Jill, and I like them lots better. They're my best friends now."

There are, of course, long-enduring friendships formed in childhood. Still, except in a relatively isolated setting where there are few age-mates, most children form new relationships and break old ones as their level of social and emotional maturity shifts in relation to others, as interests change, and as needs for new social experiences change.

A third differentiating characteristic of the peer group as a socializing agency is that its influence tends to become more rather than less important with the advancing age of the child (Thornburg 1980). Unlike the family, whose influence becomes less monopolistic with time, the peer group becomes more influential. The eight- or ten-year-old wants to do things "like the other kids do." By the age of sixteen, this desire may become an obsession. In adolescence, the peer group takes a certain precedence in many ways over any other group that influences the individual.

Peer Group Serving as Reference Group

Every person wants to look good in the eyes of certain other people and does not care what impression he or she makes on still other groups for which there is no respect or interest. The groups to which he or she wants to be favorably known and seen are called *reference groups*. She sees herself through their eyes; he judges himself as they would judge him; she learns from them her attitudes and aspirations.

Most people have several reference groups. Their family is generally the first, and most important when they are quite young. Then come their friends, their teachers, their peers, their neighbors, and their fellow citizens. Their peer group is generally quite important to them by the age of seven or eight, and it becomes more important as they move into adolescence, reaching its greatest effectiveness as a reference group when they are fifteen to twenty years old.

Still, the parents remain an effective reference group for some purposes. Brittain (1963) studied the relative importance of friends and of parents on various issues. He found that peers are more influential in deciding some things, like what course to take in school; but parents are more influential when, for instance, a girl decides which of two boys to date.

The peer group helps the adolescent become independent of adults—especially of parents. It appears that the adolescent peer group acts as a kind of shock absorber in the relations between adolescents and adults. It defends youth from too stringent demands for scholarly behavior or for adultlike behavior, but it also presses youth to become more mature in their behavior. The research evidence is mixed on this matter. The so-called adolescent society is not simply a group that glorifies athletic skills, social skills, and student leadership.

The peer group also reflects the social-status structure of the wider society. Social-class differences not only operate in the adult society but operate also in the society of children and adolescents.

The first study of social-class differences in the child's society was made in Jonesville. There, Neugarten found that fifth- and sixth-grade children (all of whom were together in the same school), when asked who were their best friends, most often named children above them in social class, then, second, children from their own social class. Few choices were made downward in the social scale, with the result that most working-class children were chosen only by others of their own social status. Similarly, as regarded reputation, children ascribed unfavorable personality traits to children from lower social classes. There was a consistent relationship between social class and reputation: as one moved up the social scale, from lower-working to upper-middle class, children received consistently higher proportions of mentions on favorable characteristics and consistently lower proportions on unfavorable ones.

Among tenth and eleventh graders in Jonesville, social-class differences were also clearly operative, but in somewhat more complex ways. Here, where a large proportion of working-class children had already dropped out of school, adolescents also chose upward or horizontally on the social scale, but seldom downward, in selecting their friends. Adolescents of upper social status, while less uniformly regarded by their classmates in favorable terms, were nevertheless in the limelight so far as social visibility is concerned. Working-class adolescents were rarely mentioned, either positively or negatively (Neugarten 1949).

Research also suggests that middle-status youngsters generally have been more likely than working-class children to designate parents rather than peers as their primary reference group. In line with earlier studies, Curtis (1975) reported this result in a study of nearly 10,000 junior and senior high school students in North Carolina and Ohio. We already have seen (in Chapter 3) that one problem of growing up in a working-class environment is the temptation to participate in antisocial peer groups identified with the culture of poverty. It is probable that middle-class adolescents in some subcultures (e.g., homogeneous middle-class suburbs) are becoming as oriented to peers as are working-class youth, but little systematic research has been carried out to document such convergence if it is taking place.

The Adolescent Peer Group and Problem Behavior

The problem behavior that becomes relatively frequent during adolescence is generally supported by some members of the peer group who thus serve to help adolescents break away from behavior standards set by their parents (Elliott, Huizinga, and Ageton, 1985). A major research paper by Jessor and Jessor studied high school students of a Colorado city, starting with grades 7, 8, and 9, in 1969 and following them to grades 10, 11, and 12 in 1972. They secured confidential reports of problem behavior from the students, including drinking, marijuana, and sexual intercourse. They found the frequency of these behaviors to be closely related to concern for approval by friends as opposed to approval by parents. They report, "adolescents who are likely to engage in problem behavior perceive less compatibility between the expectations that their parents and their friends hold for them, they acknowledge greater influence of friends relative to parents, they perceive greater support for problem behavior among their friends, and they have more friends who provide models for engaging in problem behavior" (1977, 12–13). These results later were replicated with data from a national sample of 10,405 adolescents (Jessor, Chase, and Donovan 1980).

Research indicates that influence of the peer group as compared with parental influence depends on the type of problem behavior and influence being investigated. Biddle, Bank, and Marlin (1980) studied a diverse group of twelve-, fifteen-, and eighteen-year-olds in a large metropolitan area and found that peer behavior was relatively more important than parental behavior in predicting adolescents' preference for and use of alcohol, but parental norms were more important than peer norms in predicting attitudes involving achievement in school. They also concluded that adolescents' own preferences are more important in their decision making than usually has been taken into account in previous research.

The Growing Influence of the Peer Group

Even though the peer group operates informally, as we have said, in the United States its influence has grown more important over the last 100 years. Data collected by Boocock (1976) on the daily lives of children in a variety of communities showed that when not in school, most children spend most of their time with friends or alone, watching television or "fooling around." Boocock concluded that in contrast to earlier times, "relatively few children of the 1970s seem to have strong linkages with the larger society" (p. 10). There are a number of factors involved. More and more children and adolescents live in urban rather than rural settings today, the number of youth organizations of all types has grown, and adolescents spend increasingly more years in school rather than at work—children and adolescents thus are thrown together in groups of agemates to an ever increasing extent.

In our society, adolescents as an age group play a relatively insignificant part. Their labor is not required in economic production, and they remain in positions of economic dependence on the family for longer and longer periods. As adolescence tends to be prolonged, and as youth are excluded from participation in the adult society, young people turn more and more to the peer group for recognition. In return, the peer group takes on an increasingly larger role in the socialization process.

The Peer Group in Other Societies

The peer group can be understood better when its characteristics are examined in contrasting societies. Some interesting studies made in the Scandinavian countries aimed at testing some of the conclusions drawn from studies in the United States. Bengt-Erik Andersson studied a sample of fourteen- to sixteen-year-olds in Gotesborg, Sweden, in 1963 and 1965. He found the attitudes and educational aspirations of this sample to be related to four social environments: the home and family; the school; the local community; and the peer group. There was no one dominant environmental force. Some youth were more oriented toward peers; others were more dependent on their families. Youth could not be considered as one homogeneous group controlled by peer-group norms (Andersson 1973).

Another source of information about peer group influence comes from the study in the Soviet Union reported by Professor Urie Bronfenbrenner of Cornell University. The natural tendency of an age group of children to work together has enabled the Soviet schools to treat the school class as a collective that takes on certain responsibilities as a group. For example, these included the responsibility to get to school on time, or to do a certain amount of homework, or to assist a class of younger pupils. Also, a school class may be divided into two or more subgroups that then compete with each other on tests, on punctuality, or on service to the school community (Bronfenbrenner 1970). Thus, the energy of the individual pupil is turned toward cooperation with a group of peers rather than striving for individual achievement and recognition.

The Peer Group and the Family

Trends toward increasing influence of the peer group are due in part to larger changes taking place in the structure and condition of the family in the United States. Chapter 4 notes that trends in the family include an increase in the proportion of female-headed families and working mothers as well as other changes that appear to be reducing interaction between parents and their children. As a result, parents exercise less influence over their children and the peer group becomes concomitantly more important.

Some support for this point of view can be found in data that Condry and Siman (1974) collected on 766 sixth graders in and around Syracuse, New York. The authors administered questionnaires designed to determine the degree to which children were oriented toward peers and adults, and the types of activities engaged in by respondents with differing orientations. They found that peer-oriented children were more likely than adult-oriented children to say they sometimes were truant from school, smoked and used foul language, and engaged in other activities disapproved by adults, whereas adult-oriented children were more likely to engage in adult-sanctioned activities such as "helping someone" and "making or building something."

Further exploration of their data suggested that peer-oriented children interacted less with their parents and received less adult supervision than did adult-oriented children. Particularly for boys, Condry and Siman also found evidence suggesting that some children were turning to their peers because they were neglected by their parents, or their parents were unwilling or unable to control them.

Data such as Condry and Siman's, which were collected with paper-and-pencil instruments administered to students at one time, must be interpreted cautiously. They cannot conclusively demonstrate that lack of effective parental supervision is a main cause of peer orientation or that young people thereby are pushed rather than pulled into peer-group activities for this or other reasons.

Nevertheless, they do help advance understanding of the problems and dangers inherent in a society in which parental supervision over and interaction with children may be undergoing a long-range decline. During the past century, the family has lost much of its control over socialization to other institutions. Responsibilities for children's learning have been transferred largely to the school, and parents' rights to raise their children as they see fit are now at least partially superseded by educators, child-care specialists, truant officers, and other professionals concerned with the welfare of children. Many of these changes are desirable or even necessary responses to the problem of socializing children in a complex, modern society. However, to the extent that they indicate a long-term decline in the family's capacity to control the socialization of children, they suggest that the peer group will continue to become more important in the socialization process in the future.

The Peer Group and the School

The school is expected to help the child bridge the gap between the child's world and the adult world. This is, in one sense, the expressed function of the school as a socializing agency. Even though this is also a function of the family, the important difference between school and family in this respect is that the school deals with children and moves them along toward adulthood, not as individuals, but as groups. Consequently, the influence of the school on the individual child is always mediated in the setting of the peer group. It is from this point of view that the school and the peer group are inextricably bound together in their influences on the child.

Because peer groups are important in the development of children and youth, and because peer relations affect the child's educational development, educators should give explicit attention to helping youngsters establish positive peer relationships (Webb 1987). After pointing out that poor peer relations in elementary school predict psychological disturbance and delinquency in high school, and that poor peer relationships in high school predict adult pathology and dysfunctioning, Johnson and Johnson (1981) cited sixteen steps that educators and adults should take to promote effective socialization through peer relationships:

1. Ensure physical proximity between children and their peers.
2. Structure cooperative interdependence, and encourage activities that stimulate working or playing together.
3. Emphasize joint rather than individual products whenever possible.
4. Directly teach interpersonal and small-group skills.
5. Give children meaningful responsibility for the well-being of their peers.
6. Encourage feelings of support, acceptance, concern, and commitment.
7. Hold children accountable for discharging their responsibilities to their collaborators.

8. Ensure experiences of success in a cooperative setting.
9. Promote the appropriate exchange of personal information.
10. Occasionally structure appropriate interpersonal and intergroup competition.
11. Occasionally structure appropriate individualistic activities.
12. Encourage perspective-taking dialogues with peers.
13. Provide opportunities for prosocial action.
14. Provide opportunities for participation in decision making appropriate to the child's age.
15. Suppress peer pressure for antisocial behavior.
16. Provide opportunities for older children to interact with and supervise younger ones.

Schools and the Transition to Adolescence

Many young people who are entering adolescence experience particular problems related to variations in their physical development and how these variations affect their peer relationships. Adolescents generally are very concerned with their standing and interactions with their peers, and negative attitudes or self-concepts trouble many of them during the middle school years, when there is most variation in physical maturation and development. Nottelmann (1982) has reviewed the research on this topic and also reported results of a recent study of adolescents' transition to the sixth and seventh grades. She concluded that being "off time" (early or late in physical maturation) at early adolescence damages children's social competence (relationships with peers), particularly among "less mature" boys and "more mature" girls. Given that "we cannot synchronize children's biological clocks," she further concluded, it appears that "we might be able to soften the impact of puberty and the negative social comparison effects on the self-perceptions of children who are 'off time' by helping all children to understand (a) that the process of physical maturation during adolescence is idiosyncratic in onset and rate of progression . . . and (b) that eventually in later adolescence, individual differences in physical maturity will disappear" (Nottelmann 1982, 12).

Thornburg (1979, 1980) has offered specific recommendations for educators working with preteens and teens during the middle school years. First, he identified four important developmental requirements and characteristics of early adolescence: develop friendships with others; become aware of increased physical changes; show interest in planning one's own educational experiences; and begin to develop a system of values. Based on these characteristics, he recommended that teachers in middle schools should emphasize making learning functional to the student, provide learning experiences that develop social contact and responsibility, and include material on environmentally relevant issues in the classroom.

Peer Groups in Secondary Schools

In secondary schools, one can usually find diverse peer groups such as the "leading crowd," the "brains," and the "wild ones." Among these groups an informal hierarchy will exist so that everyone will know which group has the greatest prestige and which the least. The group, with its common values, gives the individual an identity and a sense of belonging.

Not all students, of course, are members of groups; some never become identified with any particular clique, but remain on the fringe, perhaps with one or two friends, perhaps not. These are the "Outs," and their marginal positions may have deleterious effects. Some of these individuals may have no need for group association; but for others, this lack of group identity will affect self-confidence and may retard the normal process of social and emotional development.

Part of the importance the peer group assumes for the adolescent has been documented by James Coleman (1961) in a study of student bodies in eleven different high schools. Even though the schools were carefully picked to reflect a wide range of differences in terms of the size of the community and the social-class backgrounds of the students, there was considerable agreement on major values from one adolescent group to the next as expressed in responses to questionnaires. Thus, for boys, the importance of being a "brilliant scholar" was secondary to being a "star athlete" in all schools in the study; and, for girls, it was less important than being an "activities leader." For both sexes, it was better to be popular than to be intellectually outstanding.

Coleman summarized his data, at one point, in the following terms: "Despite wide differences in parental background, type of community, and type of school, there was little difference in the standards of prestige, the activities which confer status, and the values which focus attention and interest. In particular, good grades and academic achievement had relatively low status in all schools" (Coleman 1959, 338).

Coleman's conclusion regarding widespread peer de-emphasis on academics at secondary schools in the United States has been supported in a number of later studies, including research conducted by Cusick (1983) and by Clasen and Brown (1986). The latter researchers studied a suburban junior high school and identified the major types of peer groups or crowds as consisting of "Brains," "Dirtballs/toughs," "Jocks," "Populars," "Unpopulars," and "Unknowns." Their overall conclusion was that

> *crowd pressure needs to be considered in regard to school performance. Brains, who do best in school, reported receiving significantly more pressure from peers toward school involvement than did dirtballs and unpopulars. . . . Pressures regarding misconduct also seem to play an important role in school performance. Both jocks and dirtballs reported perceiving significantly more pressure to be involved in misconduct activities, such as drinking, smoking, sex, and vandalism, than did brains. Conversely, brains perceived significantly more pressure* against

Table 5.2 ***Junior High Students' Responses When Asked to Identify the Most Popular Students in Their Schools***

Response	Percentage
Good looking students	37
Athletes	23
Gang members	15
Smart students	14
Members of student government	08
Wealthy students	03

Source: Adapted from Tye 1985.

misconduct. . . . There does not seem to be a commitment to outstanding school performance on the part of the student body as a whole. If academic performance is to improve for all, educators must attend to this inertia. (Clasen and Brown 1986, 11–12)

Coleman's general conclusions regarding the sources of popularity in secondary schools also were supported in the national data collected as part of the Study of Schooling mentioned earlier in this chapter. Kenneth Tye (1985) has analyzed the responses junior high students included in the study provided when asked to identify the most popular types of students in their schools. As shown in Table 5.2, 37 percent said "good-looking students," 23 percent pointed to "athletes," 15 percent specified "gang members," and only 14 percent selected "smart students." However, the distribution of responses varied considerably from school to school and community to community.

The School as a Reference Group

Among people who interact again and again, certain norms develop and tend to influence the behavior of these people. This is the *reference-group postulate*, and it can be seen to operate especially in secondary schools. This postulate leads to the hypothesis that a school from which most of the pupils will graduate and go to college would influence its pupils to adopt this pattern of behavior, whereas a school whose pupils drop out early would influence pupils to drop out.

Where an entire school is seen as a reference group, it must be assumed that students and teachers have a general consensus about the desirable forms and outcomes of the school program. There may be subgroups of students who do not share this consensus, but they have little prestige and little power. The average student feels a pressure from the school as a whole to adopt certain attitudes about education, or clothing, or career, or political activities. Examples are a school with a strong tradition of musical and dramatic performance that will lead its students to value music and dramatics and a school with a strong athletic record that will lead its students to value sports, both as participants and spectators.

However, the majority of schools probably are too heterogeneous to view as reflecting the presence of a single, predominant reference group. Instead, there are multiple reference groups within the school, and an individual student will tend to be influenced by the one with which he or she identifies and interacts most strongly. Some students may be influenced by a group of peers who reinforce antiacademic aspirations or values; others may be influenced primarily by friends who stress academics or extracurricular activities.

Reference-Group Influence on College Attendance. Because high school graduation and college attendance are becoming more and more frequent, especially for middle-class students, it might be expected that high schools with a substantial middle-class population would exert a reference-group effect on their students to cause them to graduate from high school and go to college. A study of high school seniors in the Kansas City metropolitan area was designed to test this hypothesis.

The high school seniors in nearly all of the high schools of the Kansas City area were asked by Levine, Mitchell, and Havighurst (1970) to answer a questionnaire in the spring of their senior year, telling about their home backgrounds and telling whether they expected to enter college the next autumn. The fifty-five high schools in the study were categorized as described in Table 7.4.

The college expectations of those high school seniors were related to the socioeconomic composition of their school, as well as to the socioeconomic status of their families. For example, students from middle-class families who attend various types of high schools show decreasing percentages planning to enter college as we go down from "middle-class" to "socially comprehensive" to "working-class" type schools, and the same rule applies to students from lower middle-class families. This is true for both sexes.

Very similar finding were reported by Alan Wilson (1959) from his study of college aspirations of boys in eight public schools in Oakland, California. More recently, Alexander and McDill (1976) confirmed the importance of peer influences in affecting the college aspirations and orientations of high school students. Analyzing 1964 and 1965 data on both male and female students at twenty high schools, Alexander and McDill found that peer relations along with a student's previous academic performance have "considerable unique importance . . . in the determination of subjective orientations to school and schooling" (p. 976). Successful academic performance and "acquiring friends who evidence college plans" appeared to "reinforce or induce commitment to scholarship, a sense of competence and high educational goals" (p. 976). In follow-up research designed to extend Alexander and McDill's study, Alexander, Cook, and McDill (1977) showed that peer relations in the junior high school played a large part in determining whether students later enrolled in college-preparatory curricula and reported friendships leading subsequently to high aspirations, high achievement, and enrollment in college. Thus, available data continue to suggest that association with middle-status peers can help improve the college aspirations and plans of low-status students.

In addition, there also is reason to believe that peer influence on the college plans and aspirations of high school students frequently operates through an intervening mechanism, namely the curriculum placement or type of curriculum in which a student is enrolled. According to this theory, students enrolled in a college-preparatory curriculum come into contact with highly motivated peers who reinforce their own motivation to succeed in high school and go to college. Students in noncollege tracks associate mostly with less motivated peers and are not reinforced in their academic aspirations. Stress on curriculum placement as a factor influencing subsequent academic plans is compatible with data showing that peers play an important part in determining college plans and expectations.

Because middle-status students are more likely than low-status students to enroll in college-preparatory programs, it frequently is argued that discriminatory placement is one means by which the middle class maintains its advantage over the working class. That is, it is argued that school counselors and other decision makers in the educational selection system place middle-status students of a given ability level in college tracks more frequently than low-status students with the same academic ability and history. Critics of the educational system argue that this gives middle-status students the benefit of more highly motivated peers and thereby functions to perpetuate the social structure (Vanfossen, Jones, and Spade 1987). Other observers disagree and argue that curriculum placement gives little or no advantage to middle-status students after taking account of background, ability, and previous academic performance (Gamoran 1986b).

The evidence on this issue is somewhat mixed. Rehberg and Rosenthal (1975) reviewed the results of four major studies and concluded that most showed the high school to be basically meritocratic (i.e., curriculum placement depended on ability rather than social background). They also concluded that high schools probably were more meritocratic in this regard in the 1960s and 1970s than was true in earlier periods. On the other hand, these results were not consistent across all studies, and Alexander and McDill's (1976) study indicated that socioeconomic background was more important than academic ability in predicting curriculum placement. Alexander and McDill concluded that "curriculum differentiation may indeed serve as an important mechanism for maintaining status advantages through the educational system" (p. 973), in part by giving middle-status students more access than low-status students to highly motivated peers. The contradictory nature of research on this issue in turn suggests that counselors and other school faculty should be careful not to help steer working-class students away from college-preparatory courses without very good reasons for doing so.

Participation in Extracurricular Activities. It has been difficult to determine whether participation in extracurricular activities benefits students in other aspects of their development. The main reason for this difficulty involves uncer-

Table 5.3 *Percentages of 1982 High-School Seniors Participating in Extracurricular Activities by Grade Point Average and Socioeconomic Status*

Activity	Socioeconomic Status			G.P.A.				
	High Quartile	*Middle Quartile*	*Low Quartile*	*2.00 or Less*	*2.01–2.50*	*2.51–3.00*	*3.01–3.50*	*3.50–4.00*
Any activity	85	79	75	68	76	81	88	96
Varsity athletics	44	35	29	30	34	35	40	42
Cheerleaders, pep clubs, majorettes	14	15	12	9	12	13	18	21
Debate or drama	19	12	9	9	11	13	18	19
Band or orchestra	16	15	10	9	11	14	19	23
Chorus or dance	22	19	18	18	19	19	21	24
Hobby clubs	21	21	18	21	20	20	16	16
Honorary clubs	25	14	9	3	3	7	32	75
Newspaper, magazine, or yearbook	25	17	15	9	14	20	24	33
Subject-matter clubs	22	20	20	16	17	18	26	37
Student council, government, political clubs	23	15	12	8	12	16	23	31
Vocational education clubs	14	22	39	23	27	24	22	20

Source: Sweet 1986.

tainty regarding cause and effect. Research has shown, for example, that students with a high participation level have higher grades than do nonparticipating students (see Table 5.3). However, students who have high grades are more likely to participate than are students with low grades (Holland and Andre 1988). Thus, research must consider whether participation leads to or reflects high grades, or whether there may be a reciprocal relationship between the two variables.

In addition, students high in socioeconomic status are more likely to participate in extracurricular activities than are those low on this variable. As shown in Table 5.3, this pattern held among 1982 high school seniors for ten of eleven activities for which participation rates were surveyed; the only activity in which socioeconomic status and participation were inversely correlated was "Vocational Education Clubs." However, it is difficult to determine whether high status has a causal, independent effect on extracurricular participation, because status also is related to grades in school.

A considerable amount of research on the effects of participation in extracurricular activities has been conducted in the past twenty years. For example, Braddock (1981) studied data from the National Longitudinal Survey of high school students moving into adulthood and concluded that for both white and black males, participation in high-school athletics is positively associated (controlling for ability and social-class background) with grades, academic self-esteem, educational plans, college enrollment, and college attainment. Using the same data set, Hanks (1979) found that participation in athletics had a much smaller effect on the college enrollment of females than males, and that the influence of athletic participation on college enrollment is mediated by the influence of college-oriented peers. Otto (1982) has reviewed the research in this area and reached the following conclusions:

> *Participation in extracurricular activities contributes to a number of important social and behavioral outcomes measured as late as fifteen years after high school. Though the magnitude of the effect is modest, the breadth of effect on later life outcomes is remarkable. No consistent evidence indicates that participation . . . has negative effects on the variables measured.*
>
> *. . . Several explanations have been offered. One is that useful content is learned—"attitudes," "capacities," . . . or "interpersonal skills." . . . A second is that participation gives a young person visibility and important future "contacts." . . . A third explanation is that participation in extracurricular activities, especially athletics, elevates a student's peer status. . . . A fourth explanation is that some individuals are born achievers. . . . None of these explanations, however, has been supported by research. . . . [A fifth explanation that does have research support is that] students assess their achievement potential, set their own goals, and significant others provide encouragement to them on the basis of the youth's past performance in extracurricular activities as well as performance in the formal academic curriculum. (Otto 1982, 224–225)*

Such conclusions have great importance for educators because participation in extracurricular activities frequently is more manipulable than many other variables related to educational outcomes. For example, we have pointed out that home environment is related to student aspirations, but influencing or changing home environment is difficult and expensive. Facilitating participation in extracurricular activities may be one of the most feasible steps educators can take to improve students' aspirations and attainments (Holland and Andre 1988).

The Peer Group and the Community

The discussion in this chapter has indicated that the peer group is one of the major forces in the socialization of children and youth. In conjunction with the family, the school, and other institutions, it helps prepare the young for the society in which they will live. Relationships between the peer group and other social institutions change over time. Understanding of the nature and implications of these changes is important in developing policies to prepare children and youth for adulthood.

Many sociologists believe that the most important of these changes is that the community of traditional small towns and villages became the society of the industrial and postindustrial periods. Population multiplied and became urbanized, contacts between people became impersonal, young people as well as adults found it easier to travel outside one's immediately vicinity, and large organizations replaced the network of families and small units that were responsible for the conduct of economic activity within the relatively narrow boundaries of the traditional community. As noted in Chapter 3, the family and the community were much more intertwined in traditional settings than generally is true today. Most social activity involved interaction with nearby kin and neighbors, and the community was knit together through churches and interdependent economic enterprises. The family and the community in this setting were hardly separable.

Another characteristic of many traditional communities was that the school functioned directly under the influence of the community and, frequently, the church. In many such communities, only a few years of schooling were provided for most youngsters, through church schools organized to propagate local religious beliefs. Even where the schools were formally independent of the church, they frequently taught religious doctrine that was most prominent in the surrounding community.

The peer group in traditional settings clearly functioned as one of the community's institutions for socializing the young. Peer associations frequently were formed through the church and the school, and many youth activities were organized through the church, but peer groups independent of the church and the school also functioned to socialize youth in the traditions of the community. Peer groups played an important part, as they do today, in governing courtship and sexual relationships among youth, but the morality they developed and transmitted was more clearly attuned to local community standards than is true today (Shorter 1975).

The network in which the peer group functions is now very different from what it was in traditional society. Where formerly the peer group, the family, the church, and the school tended to operate in a complementary and reinforcing manner to prepare youth for roles in a specific community, today the major socializing institutions transmit much more divergent influences reflecting their specialized roles within the wider society. The family still is responsible for preparing children to participate in society, but much of its former educational function has been taken over by the school. The church has become much less important in socialization than it used to be, though it still is a major influence in the lives of many youth (Cremin 1977).

More youngsters of a given age group live near one another in an urbanized than a rural setting, leading to an expansion in the size of peer societies and with this expansion greater autonomy from local adult institutions. Most important, mass media such as television, radio, and films have become key factors in disseminating cultural understandings among young people, but attitudes and values developed through these channels do not necessarily reflect those of the family, the church, the school, or other institutions in the local community. Instead, they frequently constitute the core of a distinctive youth culture that has become a relatively autonomous segment of the larger society. Historian

Lawrence A. Cremin has summarized much of this transformation in discussing changes that have occurred in the "relationships among educative institutions":

> *As the household declined in size and influence, the school increased in holding power and effect. And the school's new potency was both direct and indirect. On the one hand, children spent more time with their teachers and were doubtless more profoundly influenced by them. . . . On the other hand, children, and particularly adolescents, also spent more time with one another, creating a newly powerful element in their education, namely, the peer group. Children had always had friends, to be sure; but now there was a discernible age-structured group that gathered daily in a particular institution, the school. Moreover, that group became the target of special films, special radio programs, and special advertising campaigns for special products; put otherwise, that group became a special market clientele, which was systematically taught styles of dress, entertainment, and . . . consumption. The household mediated this educative influence to some extent, but the influence was powerful nonetheless and in many ways competed with the purposeful efforts of parents, pastors, and school teachers. (Cremin 1977, 111)*

These generalizations are, of course, enormously oversimplified. Relationships between socializing institutions varied from one community and one time period to another. At some times and locations, such as the early industrial period in England, the apprenticeship system played a major part in the socialization of youth. Libraries, museums, and other cultural institutions have been and remain an important factor in socialization. Arrangements varied among religious groups, social classes, and ethnic segments within a given community. Some families still exercise predominant influence over all aspects of socialization through adolescence, and some families in traditional communities exercised so little influence that laws had to be passed requiring them to supervise their children (Cremin 1977). The organization and role of the peer group vary greatly according to whether it is sponsored or facilitated by another institution and the degree to which its members are free to come in contact with other young people. Nevertheless, a fundamental change has occurred in industrial and postindustrial society, wherein the peer group has tended to become a more important influence, and the family, the church, and the community have lost some of their control over socialization. Some implications of this change are explored further in the following chapter.

Inner-City Peer Groups

In recent years, it has become apparent that the peer group among underclass youth in the inner city is a critical component in socialization processes that frequently lead to the formation of an antisocial street culture and hamper efforts to improve education for young people in concentrated poverty areas. Chapters 2, 6, 7, and 8 describe the difficulties that parents and other socializing institutions confront in working to provide a constructive environment for growing up in these neighborhoods and present some of the data indicating that delinquent gangs constitute a major problem for parents and teachers in the inner city. The role of delinquent peer groups has been described in Williams and Kornblum's study of children and youth in four inner-city communities:

> *The child who is afraid to fight faces endless threats: money is extorted; bicycles are taken away. . . . Under these conditions, parents naturally seek to protect their children, most often by keeping them home, calling them from work, and begging them to stay off the streets. But this is a losing proposition as the kids reach adolescence and turn to the peer group for protection and identity. . . . In some situations a peer group may develop into what youth call a crew, the contemporary descendant of the adolescent fighting gangs of the 1950s and 1960s. . . . The root cause of the formation of a crew is a pressing need of some sort: money, protection, recognition, success. For poor teens, all of these things are hard to come by. (Williams and Kornblum 1985, 74–75)*

Recognizing the importance and the destructiveness of much peer-group behavior among underclass youth in the big cities, many community leaders and educators are trying to bring about improvements in the environment in which inner-city children and youth grow up and go to school. The best known effort in this direction has been initiated by Reverend Jesse L. Jackson and the People United to Save Humanity (PUSH) organization he founded in December 1971. By 1978, PUSH had outlined a program for improvement in education that was being initiated in parts of Chicago, Detroit, Hartford, Kansas City, Los Angeles, New Orleans, Washington, and other big cities. Although not necessarily limited to minority or inner-city neighborhoods, the PUSH Program for Excellence is aimed particularly at improving the socializing and educative environments and institutions for minority youth in concentrated poverty neighborhoods.

Efforts of PUSH and some other organizations trying to improve the environment for inner-city youngsters are promising because they are based on an explicit identification of the harmful influences that destroy so many children and youth in concentrated poverty neighborhoods. Jackson has repeatedly pointed out that improvements in academic performance among youth in the inner city depend on a concerted effort of all major socializing agents.

Parents, he insists, must exercise more control over their children, for example by turning off the television at least two hours each night while children study. Recognizing the traditional importance of the church among black families in the United States, he argues that ministers must play a central part in working with parents and teachers to improve the environment for growing up in the inner city. Peer-group influence must become positive rather than negative, with "Peace Brothers and Sisters" organized as monitors and supervisors of behavior in inner-city schools, and "teams of students" functioning to instill pride and achievement in academics in the same way that peer groups now emphasize nonacademic values such as excellence in athletics or antiacademic behavior such as truancy or delinquency. Teachers and administrators must join with the community to improve the effectiveness of instruction and overcome negative influences in the environment. Nor are the mass media neglected: local disc jockeys and other persons exercising influence over inner-city youth through the media also must be involved in establishing a constructive environment for growing up (Eubanks and Levine 1977).

The most striking thing about the PUSH Program for Excellence is its recognition that inner-city youth suffer so severely from fragmentation among the major socializing institutions in modern society. Parents and teachers generally try to provide a positive environment, but the peer group, the mass media, and other influences in the inner-city setting have defeated their efforts to socialize children for mobility in a modern society. Inner-city youth have been particularly victimized by socialization forces that work at cross-purposes: the school versus the streets; parents versus peers. Jesse Jackson perceives the problem in these terms and wants to enclose the inner-city child in a "love triangle" bounded by the home, the school, and the church.

It is not at all clear whether the PUSH Program for Excellence or other comparable efforts will or even can succeed in greatly improving the socialization of youth in the inner city. It is possible that no solution short of large-scale deconcentration of the population in big-city poverty neighborhoods will succeed in making the inner city a constructive environment in which to grow up for most children who now live there. Newspaper columnist William Raspberry summarized both the promise and the inherent difficulty of PUSH-type efforts when he wrote that

> *that sense of entrapment in love may have been a good deal easier to achieve in tiny Greenville, N.C. (pop: about 12,000 when Mr. Jackson was born there in 1941) than in the teeming cities where uprootedness and unconnectedness combine to produce the very anomie Mr. Jackson is trying to attack.*
>
> *To a significant degree, what he is proposing is the establishment of small towns in the city, a series of caring communities in which every adult is parent to every child.*
>
> *Jesse Jackson is, in short, proposing a miracle. And yet, with a little luck and a lot of focused commitment, it could take hold. Not that thugs would suddenly become young gentlemen and hallrovers instant scholars.*
>
> *But it just may be possible to reestablish in the classrooms a situation where serious scholarship, mutual respect and discipline are the norm, and where peer pressure serves to reinforce that norm.*
>
> *It certainly is worth trying.**

Youth-Serving Agencies

The peer group is so important to children and youth that adult society attempts to work through it whenever the opportunity appears. This is especially noteworthy in the case of churches and of youth-serving organizations.

---

* William Raspberry, "The discipline revival," *Washington Post*, February 2, 1976. Used with permission of the *Washington Post*.

Religion-Oriented Agencies. Besides the youth organizations of individual churches, several large-scale organizations have a religious orientation and have had broad support from religious groups. Chief among these are the Young Men's Christian Association (YMCA), Young Women's Christian Association (YWCA), and the Jewish Community Centers. These organizations all provide settings for the social and physical development of boys and girls, settings in which the aim is to promote character development. Usually such an organization will have a building with gymnasium, swimming pool, indoor recreational facilities, and, often, dormitory quarters for older youth.

Originally these agencies were widely separated from the school. They offered programs on Saturdays and on weekdays in after-school hours. Then, about 1915, the YMCA began experimenting with clubs of in-school youth at the secondary school level. Many of the club leaders were high-school teachers. The Hi-Y Clubs thus formed were often closely associated with the school program, even though their meetings were generally held in YMCA buildings or in members' homes. A boy did not usually need to be a member of the YMCA to belong to a Hi-Y Club. In communities that did not have a YWCA, the YMCA launched into work with girls. There, Tri-Hi-Y clubs for both boys and girls were started. Later, a type of boys' club at the grade school level was formed, under the name of Gra-Y. Often these clubs met in the school building after school hours.

The YMCA has grown into a huge organization, with programs and buildings around the world to serve men and boys of various ages. The other organizations have also grown tremendously, and all have strong programs for the social and physical development of youth. The specific religious emphasis of earlier programs has tended to decrease, concomitant with the growing secularization in the middle class.

Since 1940, a new group of religion-oriented youth organizations has emerged. These are nonsectarian, with a Protestant Fundamentalist theology. They encourage their young people to carry the Bible with them to meetings and to rely on it entirely for religious guidance, without using other books that might favor one interpretation of Christian theology over another. Organizations of this type include Youth for Christ, Young Life, and Campus Crusade for Christ. Meetings are held on Sundays and weekdays; there is a social as well as a religious fellowship; and summer camps provide an important part of the program. Possibly, these new organizations perform somewhat the same functions that were performed by the YMCA and YWCA in earlier years, before the latter organizations became more secular in orientation.

Other Youth-Serving Agencies. An important group of youth-serving agencies has less specifically religious motivation. These agencies are primarily interested in bringing adults into active and supportive relations with youth peer groups. There are, for example, the Boy Scouts, Girl Scouts, Camp Fire, Girl Reserves, Junior Achievement, Junior Optimist, Key Club (sponsored by Kiwanis), and DeMolay (sponsored by the Masonic Order). Somewhat similar to these are such organizations as the 4-H Clubs, Future Farmers of America, Future Homemakers of America, and Junior Grange. In general, these organizations do not have buildings of their own but form small units under local leaders and meet in churches, community centers, schools, and homes.

In the big cities, a number of youth-serving organizations have been established in underprivileged areas. For example, settlement houses, in addition to providing recreational facilities for boys and girls whether they are club members or not, usually organize clubs for children and adolescents. Boys' Clubs and Girls' Clubs have been established in slum neighborhoods, independent of settlement houses. The sponsors and financial supporters of these agencies are usually people of middle-class or upper-class status who give time and money to provide better opportunities for underprivileged youth and to reduce juvenile delinquency. These organizations seldom have any connection with the schools, and they serve children from both public and parochial schools.

The earliest youth-serving agencies were designed for boys and girls aged about twelve to sixteen. It was expected that boys and girls of these ages wanted to associate with each other outside of the family circle and under the leadership of adults who were neither parents nor teachers. In most of these agencies, boys and girls were organized into separate groups.

On this basis, there was a tremendous growth of youth-serving organizations with the bulk of the membership aged twelve to fifteen. By age fifteen there was a tendency for boys and girls to drop out of these organizations, in spite of vigorous efforts by leaders to keep them as members (Macleod 1983). Programs were developed for older youth, such as the Explorers (Boy Scouts). Some of these groups kept the sexes separated; others included both sexes. With more and more young people staying in school through the twelfth grade, and with many having no after-school employment, there is clearly a large pool of youth aged fifteen to eighteen or twenty who have a good deal of spare time, yet who do not take part in youth organizations. It has become a major source of concern to the leaders of youth-serving organizations to do a better job of holding youth in the middle and late teens.

At the same time, there has been a downward reach of youth-serving agencies into the age range from age seven or eight to twelve, and some, such as Camp Fire, include infants and young children. This is accomplished partly by lowering the entrance age in some organizations. Responding to rapid increase in the employment of mothers with young children, the Girl Scouts changed its rules to allow for entry of five-year-olds (Neugarten and Neugarten 1987).

More generally, however, this is done by organizing services for younger children in conjunction with the child's family. The Boy Scouts, for instance, organized the Cub Scouts, with a Den Mother in charge of a group of six- to ten-year-old boys, a woman who generally has her own son in the group. The Girl Scouts organized the Brownies on a similar basis. The YMCA not only has organized classes for boys and girls as young as nine to ten, but it has also started the Indian Guide and Indian Princess units for younger children, with fathers and mothers leading the groups that meet in their homes.

This downward reach of youth-serving agencies into middle childhood probably reflects two attitudes on the part of parents; first, the realization that the peer group, if left unaided and unwatched by adults, either would not develop adequately or would move in directions opposed to adult norms. Second, it reflects the intense desire of middle-class parents that their children become socially well adjusted during the elementary school period (Macleod 1983).

Changes in Youth-Serving Organizations

Most youth-serving organizations increased in membership during the 1950s and 1960s as the number of young people in the United States rose dramatically and then declined in the 1970s as the baby boom generation moved into adulthood. The Boy Scouts, for example, reached a high of 6.4 million members in 1973 but then dropped to 4.3 million in 1979. However, youth-serving organizations generally have stabilized their membership in the 1980s, and some have registered small gains. Key factors in reversing the membership decline apparently include a greater willingness among children and youth to participate in adult-sponsored activities, reduced antagonism toward authority figures, and an increased organizational effort to provide appropriate service for contemporary youth. Along these lines, the 4-H Clubs have reached out to disadvantaged students in urban areas (only 20 percent of 4-H members now live on farms), and the Girl Scouts teach urban survival skills such as shopping at the supermarket.

Some of these trends have been apparent in the recent history of the Boy Scouts. In 1968, the Boy Scouts organization asked a research-survey organization (Daniel Yankelovich, Inc.) to interview a national sample of 2,800 boys, aged eight through eighteen. It was found that one of every two boys in the sample belonged to an organized group or club. At the time of this interview, 23 percent of the boys were Boy Scouts, and 33 percent had formerly been Boy Scouts. During the early 1970s, the Boy Scouts attempted to enhance their appeal and service to urban youth by reducing emphasis on outdoor skills that had exemplified scouting since the organization was founded in 1907. However, this change in direction seemed to reduce the organization's attractiveness and membership. Participation in scouting has been increasing since the original emphasis on outdoor skills was restored in 1979. Now, many Boy Scout units emphasize urban topics such as analysis of traffic and reporting of crime, along with traditional outdoor skills. Membership grew to 4.7 million in 1985.

Similar trends and difficulties have been reported for other youth-serving organizations. Konopka (1977) studied a group of adolescent girls and found that 83 percent had belonged at one time to a youth organization but had disaffiliated. The primary reasons given for dropping out were that activities were childish or boring, adult leaders were domineering, or groups were too large for close personal contact. In a report prepared for the Ford Foundation, Lipsitz (1977) reviewed these and other data and concluded that adult-supervised youth organizations "have been unsuccessful in adjusting to the social dilemmas of our urban and ethnic post-industrial society" (p. 173).

Although this interpretation may be somewhat exaggerated and premature, it underlines the need for youth-serving agencies to modify existing programs and services. One unanswered question is whether traditional youth organizations can be helpful to young people who historically have had relatively low participation rates, such as working-class, minority youth in big cities. Related to this question is the issue of whether public funds or money collected through united-charity solicitations should be diverted to new organizations established to help young people not currently served. If the traditional organizations are not successful in revising their approach to reflect change in society, then other institutions may have to be established to help in the socialization of youth, especially beginning in the teenage years when many young people are now disaffiliating in favor of informal peer groups. Both Konopka and Lipsitz offered the following six recommendations to improve the effectiveness of existing organizations:

1. Allowing adolescents to participate actively in planning and executing youth projects;
2. Furnishing opportunities for adolescents to discuss their problems;
3. Establishing coed activities;
4. Reducing organizational structure to leave groups small, informal, and fairly autonomous;
5. Active recruiting of "youth in trouble"; and particularly,
6. Encouraging significant participation in the public life of the community. (Lipsitz 1977, 181)

Phelps (1980) pointed out that many youth-serving agencies have begun to make changes in directions specified above. For example, the Boy Scouts began admitting girls to full membership in its Explorer division in 1971, and both Future Homemakers and Camp Fire have become coeducational. In addition, women are now allowed to serve as leaders of Boy Scout troops (Kimmel 1988). Many organizations such as Future Homemakers, Camp Fire, and the YWCA also have begun asking youth members to serve on their major decision-making bodies, at both the local and the national levels. Some local chapters of national organizations have initiated peer counseling programs, and the Girl Scouts, Camp Fire, and other organizations are doing more than they previously did to reach youth who are delinquent or self-destructive. Phelps concluded that "in recent years, through profound reexamination of purpose, through restructuring organizations and programs, and sometimes through sheer will and determination, the major youth organizations have begun to reach larger numbers and more diverse groups of young people" (p. 113).

After-School Services for Adolescents

Private and public youth-serving agencies historically have offered a variety of services and programs for children and youth. Activities conducted at community centers and neighborhood facilities typically have ranged from athletics and arts to leadership training and scholarly hobbies. After-school and weekend programs have played an important role in providing older children and adolescents with opportunities for learning to function away from the familiar settings of the home and the school, usually in conjunction with other young people in their community. Participation is voluntary, and participants typically engage in activities that teach both cooperation and self-discipline. As pointed out by Kerewsky and Lefstein (1982), these opportunities have become more important as the proportion of working mothers has increased, thus helping generate more of a void in supervision of adolescents in the after-school hours before parents return home.

Elliott Medrich and his colleagues conducted a study to determine how sixth-grade children in Oakland, California, spend their time after school. They found that the average distribution of time was as follows: television viewing—three to four hours a day; activities "on their own" (alone or unsupervised with friends)—two to three hours a day; activities with parents—less than 1½ hours per day; chores and responsibilities—less than one hour a day; and participation in organized recreational and cultural activities supervised by adults—four to five hours a week. They also found that about 20 percent of the children did not participate in organized activities, a few were very heavily involved in a number of activities, and nearly 80 percent participated in at least one organized activity during the school year. Level of participation was not much related to social class, but upper-status children tended to participate in activities that required significant fees and parent involvement (particularly regarding transportation), whereas lower-income children depended more on free activities at nearby locations. Medrich has summarized some of the fundamental conclusions and implications of the study:

> *Over several generations community services for children have developed very successful ways of meeting a wide variety of needs for a large proportion of the young adolescent population. In our survey, almost 80 percent took advantage of community-sponsored organized activities on a regular basis; well over 60 percent used parks and schoolyards for unstructured activities; and 43 percent used neighborhood public libraries on their own. . . .*
>
> *Despite the obvious importance of community facilities for the young, there is reason to believe that children's interests and activity patterns are being compromised as communities respond to economic austerity . . . and the needs of children, the kinds of after-school programs described here are in great jeopardy. Ironically . . . [retrenchment comes] at a time when more and more families have a greater need for the services. . . .*
>
> *Reductions will not affect all children to the same degree. Those from lower-income homes who can least afford private or fee-paying alternatives will be left with the fewest opportunities.* (Medrich 1982, 33, 36, 37)

Conclusion

Peer groups play an important part in the socialization of children and youth in school and elsewhere in society. Among the functions served by the peer group are its roles with respect to teaching the culture, helping children learn to live in society, and providing a reference group that affects attitudes and aspirations. Some research indicates that the peer group has become a more important socializing agent today than was true in earlier periods, but research also indicates that the influence of peers as compared with other reference groups depends on a variety of considerations and circumstances.

Recognizing the importance and centrality of peer groups and peer influences in the school, educators have a responsibility to help students establish positive relationships and to benefit from extracurricular activities and opportunities. Other agencies in the community that can help young people and their peer groups develop in positive directions include such traditional youth-serving organizations as the Boy Scouts and the YMCA. In inner-city communities, groups that provide constructive adult influence may help counteract negative forces in the socializing environment of children and youth.

EXERCISES

1. Are there any learning experiences offered by the peer group that could *not* be offered by other socializing agencies? Explain.
2. Give an example, from your own experience, in which the peer group's standards of behavior for a child (or adolescent) were at variance with adult standards. What did the child do to resolve the conflict?
3. Thinking back over your own experience as a schoolchild, were children in your elementary school more or less democratic as regards social-class differentiations than your high school group? Cite examples.
4. Describe briefly a case in which a boy or girl dropped out of school before graduating. How did the attitudes of classmates toward the child affect his or her decision to leave school? Was there anything the school might have done to change the situation for that child?
5. Have you been in a school that had conflicting peer groups? If so, what were the differences among the groups, and how did the various groups relate to the authority of the school or the teacher?
6. Locate a youth-serving agency in your community and find out how it serves children and youth of different ages, sex, and social class.
7. Select a minority peer group that you know something about and compare the formal and informal teaching within this group to the formal and informal teaching of the school.
8. Many books on classroom management provide instructions for constructing sociograms that show the friendship patterns among students in a class. How might the teacher use a sociogram to identify peer groups in his or her class, and how might this be useful? If you have access to an elementary or junior-high class, construct a sociogram showing the friendship patterns among students and discuss their possible implications for working with particular students.

SUGGESTIONS FOR FURTHER READING

1. Jean Piaget, in *The Moral Judgment of the Child*, describes how children learn through games (and thus through the agency of the peer group) how rules are made and changed, and how children move through various stages of maturity in the development of moral judgment. See especially Chapter 1. Also, Kohlberg (1966) summarizes his theory of moral development as it is affected by the school.
2. A very useful book of readings edited by Muuss (1971) contains articles on the influence of the peer group in adolescence, especially articles by Brittain, Gronlund, Bronfenbrenner, Costanzo and Shaw, Coleman, and Himes.
3. Edgar Friedenberg in his interestingly written little book, *The Vanishing Adolescent*, sounds a note of caution for those who would like to increase adult control over adolescents. Friedenberg views adolescent conflict with adult society as necessary if the adolescent is to mature and become independent.
4. *The Adolescent Society* by James S. Coleman describes in nontechnical language a study of the students in ten different high schools and the implications for education of the differences between adult and adolescent values.
5. For a review of research on peer socialization in elementary schools, see the article by John C. Glidewell, Mildred B. Kantor, Louis M. Smith, and Lorene H. Stringer, "Socialization and Social Structure in the Classroom."
6. Read C. Wayne Gordon's *The Social System of the High School* for more details of the social organization that exists within a socially comprehensive high school.
7. *Growing Up Forgotten* by Joan Lipsitz (1977) includes several chapters dealing partly with research on peer group influences among children and youth.
8. *Rites of Passage* by Joseph F. Kett includes a systematic description of the influence of the peer group, youth-serving agencies, and other institutions affecting the development of adolescents in the United States from colonial days to the 1970s.
9. *Learning to Labour* by Paul Willis describes how peer influence among working-class youth counteracts the efforts of teachers who attempt to raise their educational achievement.
10. David Macleod's outstanding history of the Boy Scouts and other youth-serving organizations draws explicit implications for contemporary practice. Titled *Building Character in the American Boy*, Macleod's book focuses on the period from 1870 to 1920.

6

The Transition from Adolescence to Adulthood

The educational system in the United States has come to dominate the lives of most young people. Of the fourteen to seventeen age group, 95 percent were enrolled in school in 1988. Approximately 76 percent of both sexes complete a high school course, and 48 percent enter college. This situation contrasts with the beginning of the century, when only 11 percent of the fourteen to seventeen age group were in school, and only about 3 percent entered college.

Thus, most young people spend much more time in school than did their grandparents, and substantially more than their parents did. This means less time in employment, less time associating with a variety of adults, and more time in what might be called preparing for adult living. A federal government Panel on Youth, reporting to the country in 1973, starts as follows:

> *As the labor of children has become unnecessary to society, school has been extended for them. With every decade, the length of schooling has increased, until a thoughtful person must ask whether society can conceive of no other way for youth to come into adulthood. If schooling were a complete environment, the answer would properly be that no amount of school is too much, and increased schooling for the young is the best way for young to spend their increased leisure, and society its increased wealth.*
>
> *But schooling, as we know it, is not a complete environment giving all the necessary opportunities for becoming adult. School is a certain kind of environment: individualistic, oriented toward cognitive achievement, imposing dependency on and withholding authority and responsibility from those in the role of students. So long as school was short, and merely a supplement to the main activities of growing up, this mattered little. But school has expanded to fill the time that other activities once occupied, without substituting for them. These activities of young persons included the opportunities for responsible action, situations in which a youth came to have authority over matters that affected other persons, occasions in which he experienced the consequences of his own actions, and was strengthened by facing them—in short, all that is implied by "becoming adult" in matters other than gaining cognitive skills. (Coleman et al. 1974, 5)*

Many of the problems youth face in becoming adults are associated with the long transition to work and the rapid changes characteristic of contemporary society. Before describing some of these key problems, background information is provided on youth as a stage of life in modern society and on the size of the youth group. Succeeding sections of this chapter discuss changes in the attitudes and values of youth, major problems many young people encounter in the transition to adulthood, and a constructive role for the schools in helping youth make a successful transition.

Youth as a Separate Stage of Life: Ages Fifteen to Twenty-Four

As indicated in the next few pages, it is useful to think of the age period from 15 through 24 as a stage of life that is a transition between early adolescence and adulthood. This period is different from what is ordinarily called adolescence, for the latter has usually a biological meaning, referring to puberty and the immediate postpubescent years up to about age 18. For the period of youth, we are dealing with a psychosocial period of transition.

The proposal to designate this as a separate stage of life was made in 1972 by Keniston, in his book entitled *Youth and Dissent*. In the prologue to this book, Keniston says:

> *Millions of young people today are neither psychological adolescents nor sociological adults; they fall into a psychological no man's land, a stage of life that lacks any clear definition. . . .*
>
> *The very fact that so many millions of young people are in a stage of life that lacks even a name seems to me one of the most important psychohistorical facts about modern societies. In this essay I argue that the unprecedented prolongation of education has opened up opportunities for an extension of psychological development, which in turn is creating a "new" stage of life. . . .*
>
> *The opening up of youth as a stage of life to millions of young people seems to me a human advance, whatever its perils and dangers. A prolonged development can make possible a more autonomous, more individuated position vis-à-vis the existing society and can permit the individual to achieve a degree of inner complexity, differentiation, and integration not vouchsafed those whose development is foreshortened or foreclosed. Furthermore, the extension of human development means that we are creating—on a mass scale—a "new" breed of people whose psychological development not only inclines them to be critics of our own society, but might even make them potential members or architects of a better one than ours.*

This transition period, according to Keniston, is one of tension between the selfhood of the young person and the existing social order. The resolution of this tension leads to adult status. During this transition period, which for individual persons may be as short as five years or as long as fifteen, a youth settles a set of questions for himself or herself and thereby becomes an adult: questions of his or her relation to the existing society, of vocation, of life-style and characteristic social roles.

Size of the Youth Group

Fluctuations in the absolute and relative size of the youth group are a striking feature of the population in the United States during the twentieth century. The

Table 6.1 ***Population Aged Fifteen to Twenty-Four, 1890 to 2000***

Year	Number (Millions)	Percent of Total	Percentage Change in Preceding Decade	Ratio, 15–24/ 25–64
1890	12.8	20.4	–	.51
1900	14.9	19.5	+16	.47
1910	18.2	19.5	+22	.45
1920	18.8	17.6	+ 3	.39
1930	22.5	17.0	+20	.39
1940	24.0	18.2	+ 7	.36
1950	22.2	14.6	− 8	.29
1960	24.1	13.3	+ 9	.29
1970	36.5	17.8	+51	.41
1980	42.5	18.7	+16	.40
1990 (est.)	35.6	14.3	−16	.28
2000 (est.)	36.1	13.4	+01	.26

Sources: U.S. Bureau of the Census: 1960 *Final Report* PC1-1B, 1961; *Current Population Reports* Series P–25, No. 601, 1975; No. 998, 1986.

birthrate was very high (above 30 per 1,000 population) from 1900 to 1910 and then dropped steadily (to about 18 per 1,000) in 1933, influenced partly by the economic depression of that decade. The birthrate remained at the relatively low level of fewer than 20 per 1,000 until 1945, when it shot up to 25 per 1,000 by 1955, remaining at about that level for about eight years. Then it dropped again in 1968 to a level below the 1933 depression figure, where it has remained into the 1980s. During this time, the death rate decreased steadily from 17 per 1,000 in 1900 to 9 per 1,000 in 1955, where it has remained to the present.

The result of these phenomena is indicated in Table 6.1, where the absolute numbers of the 15–24 group are shown as well as the ratio of the 15–24 group to the 25–64 group. This ratio clearly presents the problem for the 1980s and 1990s. The 15–24 group is ready to move into the productive labor force, to do the work of the society. But society has changed since World War II; it now needs relatively fewer workers to do the necessary work. Even though the society has increased its gross production, especially in the 1950–70 period, the vast increase in size of the 15–24 group from 1960 to 1970 was more than the labor force could easily absorb. As Table 6.1 shows, the ratio of 15 to 24 to 25 to 64 jumped from .29 in 1960 to .41 in 1970 and stayed at that level through the 1970s and early 1980s. This development has created serious problems for youth, and for society as a whole.

The Values and Attitudes of Youth

With the changes in the lives of young people that we have described, and with the pervasive changes in the society as it has moved into the present postindustrial phase, we might expect the values, aspirations, and expectations of young people to change. There has been a large amount of research on the changing values of youth in the United States over the past half-century. The so-called counterculture that appeared strongly on college campuses in the mid-1960s has made it useful to look searchingly at the values of youth in the 1970s and 1980s. For this, we turn to the work of Daniel Yankelovich, a psychologist who has been making surveys of youth since about 1968.

In October 1968, a sample of 718 young men and women, aged eighteen to twenty-four, were asked to say whether they agreed or disagreed with a number of value-statements. About half of this sample were college students, and the others had not attended college. The college students were asked to select one or the other of the following statements as representing their views about college education.

1. For me, college is mainly a practical matter. With a college education I can earn more money, have a more interesting career, and enjoy a better position in society.
2. I'm not really concerned with the practical benefits of college. I suppose I take them for granted. College for me means something more intangible, perhaps the opportunity to change things rather than make out well within the present system.

Those who chose the first statement were called practical minded. Those who chose the second were called forerunners. After studying his survey data, Yankelovich summed it up by concluding that the forerunners have acquired a system of beliefs and behavior that attempts to place nature and the natural at the center of existence. To be natural means:

- To place sensory experience ahead of conceptual knowledge. To de-emphasize aspects of nature illuminated by science; instead to celebrate all the unknown, the mystical, and the mysterious elements of nature.
- To stress cooperation rather than competition.
- To devalue detachment, objectivity, and noninvolvement as methods for finding truth, to arrive at truth, instead, by direct experience, participation, and involvement. (Yankelovich 1972, 35)

In addition to the practical-minded and the forerunners Yankelovich identified a third group consisting of left-outs, who must be assisted toward a more individually and socially satisfactory youth if our society is to maintain even a fairly healthy condition.

University of Chicago Professor Jacob W. Getzels (1978) reviewed the Yankelovich findings as well as his own and other studies and also reached the conclusion that during the past fifty or sixty years, youth values have evolved toward an emphasis on greater personal and social responsibility. Traditional values changed during a transitional period in the late 1940s and mid-1950s and then were further modified in the 1960s. However, Getzels also concluded that emergent values did not continue to grow more prominent in the late 1970s (i.e., the forerunner group did not continue to grow larger) and that it is difficult to characterize the mixture of traditional, transitional, and emergent values that prevailed among youth in the late 1970s.

Data collected in the late 1970s and 1980s indicate that there has been some shift back to the practical-minded emphasis in the values and attitudes of youth. For example, surveys of high school seniors in the National Longitudinal Study of 1972 and the High School and Beyond Study of 1980 show that the percentage of respondents saying that it is a "very important life value" to help correct social inequalities declined from 27 percent in 1972 to 13 percent in 1980, while the percentage who stressed "having lots of money" increased from 18 percent to 31 percent (Wagenaar 1981). Similarly, surveys of college freshmen conducted for the American Council on Education show that the percentage of respondents saying that "being well-off financially" was one of their most important goals increased from 39 percent in 1970 to 73 percent in 1986 (Greene 1986). In addition, adults under forty-five years of age report that they are more family-oriented and more concerned with their careers than they thought would be true when they were younger (Greider 1988). These changes probably were due in part to the frequent recessions and the growing economic problems in the United States in the 1970s and early 1980s.

In some respects, the values and attitudes of youth appear to have remained mostly constant over the past few decades. The 1960s and 1970s brought a shift away from and then back to practical mindedness, but overall, most youth throughout this period were primarily oriented toward success in the economic system and toward traditional values. Data collected in the surveys cited plus other studies all indicate that marriage and parenthood continue to be designated as very important life goals by a large majority of young people, though changes are occurring in attitudes toward sex roles in marriage, work, and other areas. General stability in the values and attitudes of Americans (including youth) was the most fundamental finding in Veroff, Douvan, and Kulka's (1981) analysis of the University of Michigan Survey Research Center surveys of national attitudes in 1957 and 1976. The authors concluded that on the whole there was "remarkable stability" (pp. 528, 542) in values and attitudes during this twenty-year period.

Within this pattern of general stability, what changes have occurred in the values and attitudes of young people? In addition to several described in the preceding pages, Veroff, Depner, Douvan, and Kulka (1980, 1981) have identified the following six "generational shifts" large enough to have important implications for United States society:

- Increased concern about an uncertain future.
- Movement from social to personal sources of well-being, including an increased focus on self-expression and a shift in concern from relationships in social organizations to relationships involving interpersonal matters.

- A shift away from perceiving marriage and parenthood as critical prerequisites for personal success and a lessened tendency to view fulfillment of societal expectations as necessary for personal happiness.
- For women, increased importance attached to meeting standards of excellence in performing activities in competition with others or with the self.
- For men, decreased importance attached to affiliation, that is, to maintaining or regaining emotional connections to people similar to the self.
- For both men and women, increased fear of being controlled by others.

Conclusions cited in the preceding pages are reminiscent and supportive of Daniel Bell's analyses of emerging problems in contemporary United States society. Following his influential *The Coming of Post-Industrial Society* (1973), Bell published a book titled *The Cultural Contradictions of Capitalism* (1976), in which he called attention to fundamental problems inherent within the nature of modern capitalistic societies. Among the most general of these problems is the contradiction between an economic system organized to stimulate, direct, and reward hard work, and economic-cultural forces that generate demand for material goods:

> *On the one hand the business corporation wants an individual to work hard, pursue a career, accept delayed gratification—to be, in the crude sense, an organization man. And yet, in its products and its advertisements, the corporation promotes pleasure, instant joy, relaxing and letting go. One is to be 'straight' by day and a 'swinger' by night. This is self-fulfillment and self-realization! . . . One can discern the structural sources of tension . . . between a social structure . . . that is organized fundamentally in terms of roles and specialization, and a culture which is concerned with the enhancement and fulfillment of the self and the "whole" person. (pp. 71–72, 14)*

Bell's analysis portrays many of the interactions and the reciprocal influences among the major systems and strands (economic, cultural, political, social, educational, etc.) in modern capitalist society. Emphasis on science and rationality has reduced the influence of the church and the family, thus stimulating a growing orientation toward personal satisfaction. Mass consumption and mass media undermined traditional cultural standards that gave common direction in raising children and youth, geographic mobility required by the economic system cut people off from traditional influence, and economic prosperity further reinforced stress on individual happiness and self-fulfillment. In Bell's words, mass consumption "meant the acceptance, in the crucial area of life-style, of the idea of social change and personal transformation, and it gave legitimacy to those who would innovate . . . in culture" (p. 66). In addition, discretionary income "allowed individuals to choose many varied items to exemplify different consumption styles" (p. 38). Mass education also was required to provide skills for the economy and to maintain a political consensus in a democratic framework, but more education also widened the scope of "discretionary social behavior

. . . [so that] more and more individuals want to be identified . . . by their cultural tastes and life-styles" (p. 38).

Like other citizens, social scientists disagree on the meaning and implications of changes in the values and attitudes of youth. For example, Yankelovich (1981) finds evidence that the search for self-fulfillment and personal satisfaction is giving way to a new "ethic" of social commitment; a "me-first" mentality is beginning to be replaced by a new morality—exemplified by the forerunners—as the "inner journey" turns outward and economic reality forces recognition that the self cannot be "wholly autonomous, solitary, contained, and 'self-created.'"

However, other observers such as Christopher Lasch are not at all optimistic. In two books providing an extended analysis of twentieth-century changes in values and attitudes (*The Culture of Narcissism*, 1978; *Haven in a Heartless World: The Family Besieged*, 1977), Lasch argues that the emphases on personal satisfaction and individual gain are creating disastrous consequences for individuals and society. Parents are abdicating child-raising responsibility to outside specialists, and withdrawal of the father to the world of work has interfered with the development of children's superego and thereby further stimulated emphasis on fulfillment of individual desires and impulses. The likely outcome of additional movement toward emphasis on personal satisfaction, he finally concludes, is the development of totalitarian government: "The only alternative to the superego, it has been said, is the superstate" (1977, 189).

If there is little agreement on the extent and meaning of changes taking place in values and attitudes, there is even less agreement on what to do about them. Some citizens believe that the family should be strengthened by recreating traditional environments, but others believe that government should intervene to provide economic support or professional assistance. Some believe that the school should take the lead in helping students understand and assess moral philosophies and social change, but others believe that teachers either should indoctrinate students in traditional values or should leave these tasks entirely to the family and the church. Some believe that the curriculum should help students self-consciously learn to pursue goals involving personal happiness and satisfaction, but others believe that the school has no business emphasizing anything but traditional academic goals.

The preceding discussion has barely scratched the surface of a large volume of material that describes or interprets changes in the values and attitudes of youth. Because there has been little research designed to identify the appropriate function of the school, the family, and other institutions in helping youth respond to the perplexing problems of modern society, it is not possible to provide definitive guidelines concerning the role of differing institutions. Elsewhere in this chapter and this book some implications have been drawn for the school and other agencies, but it also must be recognized that insufficient knowledge is available to justify conclusive statements about many aspects of the overall problem that society faces in helping youth make a constructive transition to adulthood.

Work Satisfaction

There has been a great deal of interest in the attitudes of American workers toward their work, instigated by the general perception that the postindustrial society carries with it some changes in work attitudes compared with the industrial society. It is fairly clear that the great majority of our youth want to work and expect to enjoy their work. This is one conclusion from the national surveys of high school seniors, which were conducted in 1972 and 1980. In the 1972 survey, titled the National Longitudinal Study, 84 percent of the seniors said that "Being successful in work" was a "very important life value," and 88 percent of the seniors surveyed in 1980 (The High School and Beyond Study) gave this response (Wagenaar 1981).

Regarding older youth, Veroff, Douvan, and Kulka (1981) examined data from two large national studies conducted in 1957 and 1976 respectively and reported that only about 30 percent of the younger male workers (ages twenty-one to thirty-four) said they were not satisfied with their jobs. However, the percentage of female workers who were dissatisfied with their jobs increased from 18 percent in 1957 to 35 percent in 1976. The investigators attributed this change among younger women to increased entry of women into the labor force. In addition, the data suggested that highly educated workers are relatively more insistent that work will fulfill inner desires for interesting and exciting experiences. These patterns led Veroff, Douvan, and Kulka to question whether college-educated persons are coming to expect too much satisfaction (i.e., to have unrealistically high expectations) from their work roles. A recent national survey of adults between the ages of eighteen and forty-four also indicated that many college-educated persons are dissatisfied with their work (Sheff 1988).

Thus, the evidence suggests some cause for concern that youth in the United States—particularly women and the college educated—may be growing somewhat more dissatisfied with work roles and opportunities. The data do not, however, support the proposition that most young people in the United States are *alienated* from work. They are *dissatisfied* with some things about the society, especially with the high level of unemployment among youth. But most do not appear to be resentful about their jobs or seriously unhappy at work.

Suicide

Suicide rates among youth in the United States have risen sharply since 1955, particularly during the 1970s among white males (Wynne and Hess 1986). More than 49,000 youth and young adults between the ages of fifteen and twenty-four took their own lives during the 1970s.

The suicide rate in a country or a society was thought by the French sociologist Emile Durkheim (1956) to be related to the amount of social solidarity in a society. He thought a high suicide rate was indicative of people's uncertainty about the future and a lack of external social rules and expectations on which people could depend. He spoke of a high suicide rate's going together with a high degree of loneliness and a low degree of social interaction. Some social scientists thus believe that suicide among youth is partly a result of anonymity and impersonality in modern, postindustrial societies. Data on suicide rates in various countries suggest that Durkheim's theory has some support. For example, suicide rates of males aged fifteen to twenty-four about the year 1970 were high in developed countries such as Austria, Sweden, Canada, and Japan, and much lower in Mexico and Colombia.

Hobinger and Offer (1982) have examined data on increase in the suicide rate among adolescents in the United States and found that it is highly correlated with changes since 1933 in the number and percent of youth within the general population: as the number and percent of youth aged fifteen to nineteen rose or fell, the suicide rate among this group rose or fell. They speculate that this relationship may be due to at least two psychodynamic explanations:

> *The first involves issues of competition and failure. As the number of adolescents initially increases, there are more competitors for the same number of positions: jobs, positions on varsity sports teams, places in the freshman class of good colleges, access to various social services (e.g., school counselors . . . probation officers, vocational counselors). . . . With an increased adolescent population relatively more adolescents will fail to achieve their goals, will see themselves as failures, will be unable to reestablish a balance in this self-esteem equilibrium, and will begin the downhill slide. . . . Second . . . it may be more difficult for an adolescent to gain a sense of self-worth and to find friends in the large impersonal high schools of today. . . . The lonely, emotionally depleted, depressed adolescent may see most of his peers as functioning relatively well, sharpening his awareness of his personal problems and increasing his loneliness and isolation. (Hobinger and Offer 1982, 306)*

Information on trends among youth in the United States tends to support the argument that increase in the suicide rate during the past few decades may have been due at least in part to increase in the number and percent of youth. These data indicate that the suicide rate for young people age fifteen to nineteen leveled out and may even have declined in the 1980s as the size of the youth group declined (Tugend 1986; Wynne and Hess 1986).

Other causes cited in accounting for increase in suicide among youth include the infectious effects of media coverage (Viadero 1986b; 1987a), the diminishing role of religion, increased family disruption, and general rapidity of social change (Tugend 1986). In any case, school officials in some locations have become concerned with the problem and have begun to work with mental health agencies in trying to alleviate it (Tugend 1984), and some educators, such as Pfeifer (1986), have outlined a survival curriculum through which schools might help young people learn coping skills to avert suicide.

Youth and Employment

Major questions exist concerning how society should provide employment training for youth who do not graduate from high school or who do not obtain rewarding employment or go on to colleges and technical schools after high school. The problem of helping youth prepare for and enter productive employment is particularly difficult with respect to minority youth in concentrated poverty neighborhoods within the inner city. But it has become increasingly severe for many other youth as well, as up-grading of skill and certification requirements for employment have reduced opportunities for obtaining unskilled employment leading to subsequent acquisition of skills and promotions. Rist (1981) has summarized the overall problem:

> *For most of the youth who want to work when they leave high school—with or without a diploma—they are simply on their own. There is no social net below them as they attempt to make their way. There is no social infrastructure to which they can turn for assistance. Youth have no ombudsman in the United States, as they do in New Zealand and Sweden, to whom they can turn for advocacy on their behalf as they seek housing, employment, training opportunities, social welfare, and health benefits. In America, unless one is sponsored by one's friends, or neighbors, finding adult roles is a lonely endeavor. (Rist 1981, 5–6)*

The National Commission on Youth established by the Charles F. Kettering Foundation undertook a comprehensive examination of the problem of providing preparation for employment within the larger challenge of ensuring an effective transition to adulthood for all youth. Its final report published in 1980 included the following ten recommendations (pp. 1–6) for improving the transition of youth to adulthood.

- *Develop community-based educational programs.* Schools should become "action-rich" and develop community-based programs to provide a variety of opportunities for learning.
- *Give credit for community-based education.* Academic credit should be awarded for learning in community-based programs that help students master basic knowledge and skills.
- *Create a National Youth Service.* The Congress of the United States should provide all youth an opportunity for at least one year of full-time service.
- *Advocate National Youth Service as a condition of employment.* One year of service experience should be a condition for employment.
- *Provide educational entitlements.* Youth should receive vouchers that grant one year of educational entitlement for each year of service.
- *Establish Youth Transitional Planning Councils at the local level.* Such councils should function in every community to facilitate the transition to adulthood.

- *Revise child labor laws.* Employment opportunities should be opened through revision of outdated laws and regulations.
- *Develop youth policy at the state level.* The governor of each state should appoint a cabinet-level special assistant to improve coordination of youth policies and programs.
- *Establish transition schools.* Transition schools for the final years of secondary education should be operated by the public school system to provide youth an opportunity to pursue special interests, explore career options, and learn new skills in internships and apprenticeships in a community-based environment.
- *Establish optional learning centers.* Such centers operated independently of the public school system should be established to provide jobs, service opportunities, and vocational apprenticeships in the community.

One approach that appears to have had some success in helping youth prepare for and obtain employment is the Jobs for America's Graduates (JAG) program, which began in Delaware in 1979 and expanded to a number of other states in the 1980s. In the JAG approach, a single professional person works with about 35 high-school seniors to improve their skills in finding and keeping jobs and to identify and develop jobs in which students are placed (Wichess 1984). Research on the employment status of seniors from four states (Delaware, Massachusetts, Missouri, Tennessee) that participated in 1981–82 indicated that only 16 percent were unemployed the following autumn, as compared with 41 percent of students in a comparison group. In addition, 81 percent of the employed JAG students had jobs rated as "positive placements," as compared with 67 percent of the comparison students (Newitt et al. 1984).

Disadvantaged Minority Youth

Unemployment rates among young people in the United States are substantial, particularly among minority youth in the inner city. As shown in Figure 6.1, the unemployment rate for white males between sixteen and twenty-four years of age increased from about 7 percent in the late 1960s to the range of 16 to 18 percent in the 1980s. The comparable rate for black males between the ages of sixteen and twenty-four generally has been from two to three times as high as the rate for white males during the past thirty to forty years and has been above 30 percent in the 1980s.

The pattern for females sixteen to twenty-four years of age is somewhat similar: for white females, the unemployment rate increased from 7 percent in 1955 to the 12 to 14 percent range in the 1980s, while the rate for black females generally was two to three times higher and increased to the mid-30 percent range in the 1980s.

High rates of unemployment remain persistent among black youth: among black males sixteen to nineteen years of age, 42 percent were unemployed in 1986, and 35 percent of black females in this age group were unemployed.

Hahn and Lerman have reviewed these data for the National Planning Association's Committee on New American Realities and concluded that although

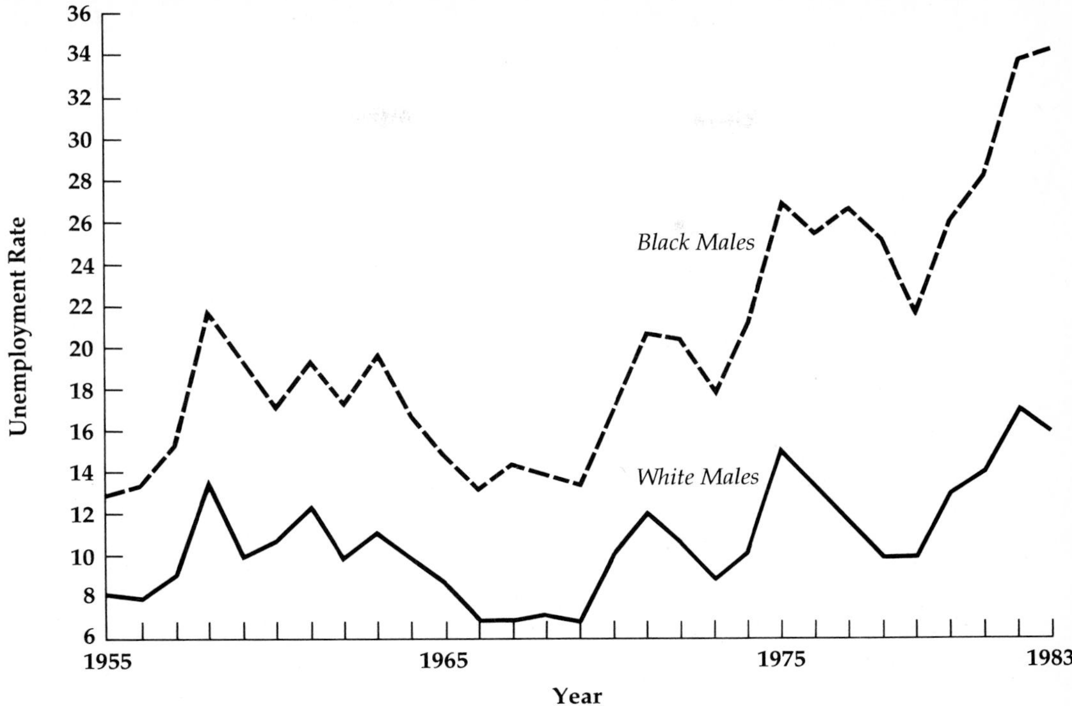

Figure 6.1 ***Unemployment Rates for White and Black Males between Sixteen and Twenty-Four Years of Age, 1955 to 1983*** (*Source*: Andrew Hahn and Robert Lerman, *What Works in Youth Employment Policy?* Washington, D.C.: National Planning Association: Committee on New American Realities, 1985, p. 3.)

the U.S. economy was able to create millions of jobs for the large cohorts of young people who were entering adulthood in the 1960s and 1970s, a "devastating job situation . . . has hit poor and black youth" (1985, 2). Other conclusions they reached included the following:

> *Unemployment is highly concentrated among . . . poor and minority youth who had dropped out of school . . . or graduated from high school [but] are ill-prepared for the bulk of available jobs. . . . The job problems of disadvantaged youth are of particular concern because of their close association with crime, teenage pregnancy, poverty, and long-term unemployment. . . . Failure to cope with the problems of these youth tends to perpetuate an underclass with the all too common mix of family instability, involvement in or exposure to crime, poverty, unemployment, and a difficult home environment for children. . . .*
>
> *The evidence clearly points to low educational achievement as one of the primary factors contributing to the employment problems of low income and minority youth. . . . Family factors also complicate the ability of low income youth to*

> *take advantage of increased job opportunities. Many disadvantaged youth live with nonworking adults, which limits their connections to jobs and the world of work. . . . Many of these factors . . . are the result of complex social problems not easily addressed through employment policies. However, employment policy can lessen some of the problems and help overcome the effects of others.* (Hahn and Lerman 1985, 2, 7, 31)

Other researchers who have studied the problem of unemployment among low-income minority youth have reached similar conclusions. For example, Williams and Kornblum studied inner-city communities in Cleveland, Louisville, Meridian (Mississippi), and New York City, and concluded that "adolescents who fail in school, work in marginal (at best) employment, or drop out of the labor market as teenage parents, all need structures of opportunity within which they can realize their potential" (1985, 113). Freeman and Holzer (1985; 1986) examined the research on black youth unemployment and concluded that "the overall picture . . . is one in which black youth clearly want to work, but only at jobs and with wages that are comparable to those received by their white counterparts. Unfortunately . . . with increased job market competition from women and other groups . . . the youths have had trouble obtaining such jobs . . . [and] many have been led into alternative modes of obtaining money 'on the street' and to leisure activities that will not get them back on track" (1985, 30–31).

With regard to the specific problem of improving employability and employment of economically disadvantaged youth, much has been learned through national and local programs that have attempted to identify the types of approaches that are most successful. Robert Taggart, who played a major part in designing and evaluating a number of national demonstration projects for disadvantaged youth, has assessed their results and concluded that

> *jobs can reduce the likelihood and consequence of negative events such as crime. Findings from work programs featuring intensive support services for youth in the criminal justice system suggest a noticeable in-program decline in arrests. Findings from another federally supported experiment guaranteeing jobs to low-income youths who stay in high school or return indicate that jobs can be used to lure youth back to school and to forestall early leaving. It is estimated that . . . one-third of eligible dropouts have been lured back to school.* (Taggart 1982, 259)

Taggart also concluded that programs that are well designed and well implemented to provide linkages between education and training, skilled supervision, and adequate materials and funding can substantially improve the employability and subsequent employment history of disadvantaged youth. He further concluded that employment experience can help prevent disadvantaged youth from becoming more alienated and that postsecondary training can provide them with skills and knowledge that lead to significant employment gains.

Other lessons Taggart identified as resulting from various national and local projects included the following: (1) one must provide careful structuring of career-entry experience to assure multiple steps and subsequent access to regular jobs; (2) youth who have left school may need some "aging" before they are ready to return to the classroom; those who have left and return voluntarily do better than those who are enrolled immediately; (3) alternative settings should be available to provide educational remediation through self-paced learning and individualization; (4) basic employability skills should be developed through job search assistance, counseling, vocational exploration, and other means; and (5) work activities should be structured and demanding, but second and third opportunities should be provided for youth who do not meet meaningful performance standards (Taggart 1982, 264–271).

Generalizations that are supported most frequently by persons who have been assessing programs to prepare disadvantaged youth for employment include conclusions regarding the importance of (1) integrating or coordinating basic learning skills and job training education, and (2) providing a comprehensive set of services in the overall training program. Regarding the first point, a Congressional Budget Office staff member who reviewed the research on a variety of federal projects concluded that "the major problem with youth employment programs is their failure to provide an integrated curriculum of skill training and vocational experience" (Green 1982, 58–59).

It should be emphasized that recommendations such as those described generally are based on the results of demonstration-type programs that tell us what can be achieved through successful implementation of well-planned approaches. In practice, however, many or most programs do not appear to have been successful, even when based on the findings of previous theory and research. As in the case of federal funding for compensatory education (e.g., Title I) in the public schools, as a society we know a lot more about what is required to make an employment or school program for disadvantaged youth successful than we have been able to put into practice on a widespread basis. As one example, analysts of employment training programs long ago recognized that linking training to the prospect of a guaranteed job with subsequent advancement opportunity can be highly motivating for disadvantaged youth or adults, and the U.S. Department of Labor's $222 million Youth Incentive Entitlement Pilot Projects program was designed to determine whether this type of approach would induce disadvantaged youth to remain in or return to school and to reduce their rate of unemployment. However, the U.S. General Accounting Office investigated implementation of Entitlement projects and concluded that many sponsors experienced "serious operational problems" regarding job quality, supervision, job development, counseling, worksite monitoring, and other matters, and in the end questioned "whether sponsors are capable of implementing complex programs such as Entitlement" (U.S. General Accounting Office 1980, i–ii). "Real world" improvements in implementation, the report concluded, would require much more oversight, monitoring, and technical assistance than usually are provided in most youth employment training projects.

In this context, the important underlying question regarding social policy in the United States is whether the nation can develop the will and know-how to provide effective elementary and secondary education and employment training for disadvantaged youth throughout the country. As we note in Chapter 7, neo-Marxist and other critics of United States society do not believe our existing political and economic arrangements are capable of providing effective opportunity for underclass and working-class students. Developments in education and related fields during the 1970s demonstrated that we now can specify the types of programs and approaches that can deliver effective education and employment training. On the other hand, billions of dollars are spent each year on programs and approaches (e.g., in substantial summer jobs) that do not result in any measurable improvement in fundamental learning skills and employability. The result of this situation, as summarized by Julia Wrigley of the University of California at Los Angeles, is reinforcement of a cycle of lack of opportunity that provides alienated, disadvantaged youth with further "daily evidence of their superfluity." Thus, our national efforts to date have not come to grips with the problems of youth whose experience has taught them a "message of marginality." As long as this remains the case, many such youth will continue to remain at the end of the labor queue, "on the edges of the productive institutions of the economy" (Wrigley 1982, 256–257).

It also should be noted that employment training programs generally have accomplished very little in combatting the isolation from mainstream culture and economic activity that severely hamper opportunity for disadvantaged inner-city youth in large metropolitan areas. Stated differently, growing up in a depressed poverty neighborhood in a big city in itself constitutes a major handicap in terms of learning about and gaining productive employment, particularly in many metropolitan areas with large central city-suburban distances and limited public transportation. Part of this pattern that restricts employment for inner-city youth has been summarized in testimony before the U.S. Civil Rights Commission:

> *What are the industries that employ large numbers of young people? . . . [These are] the retail establishments and the restaurants and that kind of activity. . . . The growth of retail business in our society is in the suburbs. . . . The McDonalds and the Kentucky Fried Chickens, they are not in the middle of the ghetto; they are on the periphery, on the border. But when you really go out down Rockville Pike and you see a hundred fast-food places, the majority of the youngsters that work there are white, the vast majority of them, and those are the youth industries.*
>
> *Where you get the babysitting money is the suburbs. Youth are also able to get some income mowing lawns. No one is paying, I don't think, in the inner city barrio to have their lawns mowed. . . . I really cannot say what the impact of working at an early age is. But I would venture to say that at least that youth is getting some notion of the world of work, getting some income, some positive reward. (U.S. Commission on Civil Rights 1982b, 32–33)*

Possible Negative Effects among High School Students

Before the 1940 to 1950 period, few high school students had paid employment, but part-time employment of students has increased enormously in the past forty years. Today a majority of high school students over sixteen years of age have part-time jobs, and national surveys indicate that more than one-fourth of seniors work more than twenty hours per week (Viadero 1987c).

Employment of high school students frequently has been perceived to be desirable because it provides young people with additional income, offers them an opportunity to learn about work and develop dependable habits and transferable skills for later employment, and reduces the dependency associated with prolonged adolescence in modern society. In recent years, however, some educators, social scientists, and other observers have begun to question whether the overall consequences are generally positive for most young people and for society.

For example, Jerald Bachman of the Survey Research Center believes that employment may be encouraging adolescents to place too much emphasis on cars and other material possessions, and some school superintendents have reported that employment of students not only results in low academic performance in many cases, but also may be stimulating teachers to require less homework and otherwise decrease academic standards. In addition, many observers wonder whether most students are acquiring transferable skills and positive work habits in jobs typical of the fast-food industry and other low-level employment (Viadero 1987b).

In general, many school officials as well as other concerned citizens are concluding that action should be taken to limit the number of hours students work and to ensure that jobs are meaningful and productive.

Delinquency

As adolescents pass through the period of youth on the way to adulthood, many of them engage in delinquent behavior, and most outgrow it. One might see it as a kind of contagious disease, like mumps, that most youth catch and get over, with few permanent disabilities. But to treat delinquency so lightly would be a mistake, for two reasons: first, it hinders a youth from developing into a competent adult, even though he or she does not become a criminal; and second, some youths become seriously delinquent and go on into an adult life of crime or serious maladjustment.

Boys are delinquent much more frequently than girls. In all societies for which delinquency data are available, boys outnumber girls in the delinquency statistics by a ratio ranging from between 4 to 1 and 10 to 1. Boys at the beginning of adolescence are likely to do some mischief to property in the neighborhood and may be warned by the police.

Table 6.2 *Percentage Rates of Self-Reported Delinquent Behaviors during the Previous Twelve Months for National Sample of Youth Age Eleven through Fifteen and for Utah Sample of Youth in Corrections and Probation Programs*

Type of Delinquent Behavior	Percentage for National Sample	Percentage for Utah Youth in Corrections and Probation Programs
Felony assault	.3	20.7
Minor assault	1.2	32.3
Robbery	.1	8.5
Felony theft	.4	34.8
Minor theft	1.1	80.3
Damaged property	.6	53.6
Alcohol use	44.5	73.7
Sold marijuana	3.2	33.2
Sold hard drugs	1.2	6.8
Bought liquor as minor	1.6	13.1
Drunk in public	6.1	20.2

Note: Percentages for the Utah sample are unweighted averages for data on the corrections and probation subsamples.
Source: Adapted from Austin 1984.

There has been a large increase of juvenile and young adult arrest rates since 1960. Total annual arrest rates for juveniles under age 18 approximately tripled between 1960 and 1985. Worse still, arrest rates for youth 18 to 24 years of age approximately quadrupled during this period (Wynne and Hess 1986).

Patterns involving delinquency are apparent in the data reported in Table 6.2, based on a national longitudinal sample of youth 11 through 15 years of age and information on young people in this age group in corrections and probation programs in Utah (Austin 1984). For the national sample, self-reported delinquency rates are relatively low except for alcohol use and public drunkenness. For the delinquent sample in Utah, however, there are multiple infractions including relatively high percentages of serious offenses. Much of the delinquency among young people seems to be due to a small proportion of youth who are frequently involved in a variety of delinquent behaviors.

Generalizations about Juvenile Delinquency

1. Although a large majority of young people are not delinquent (Austin 1984), there is significant delinquency among youth from all social classes. Tittle, Villenez, and Smith (1978) reviewed research on crime and delinquency and concluded that if one considers the fact that middle-class delinquents are less likely to be arrested and punished than are working-class delinquents, then

the relationship between social class and delinquency has been declining for forty years and is now negligible.

2. However, violent delinquency is much more common among working-class youth than among middle-class youth (Glaser 1979). In addition, low-status youth in low-status neighborhoods are more likely to be delinquent than are low-status youth in other neighborhoods (Strasburg 1978).
3. A large proportion of crimes is committed by youth under the age of twenty-five. However, most youthful offenders settle down to a stable adult work life.
4. Much of the delinquent behavior of male youth is not for material gain but consists of violence or gang fighting.
5. Violent delinquency is associated with participation in a violent subculture and tends to be perceived by participants as neither illegal nor immoral (Austin 1980).
6. There is probably a relation between youth crime and unemployment. Idleness and the need for money combine to favor money-making forms of crime (Williams and Kornblum 1985). Regarding this relationship, Daniel Glaser has summarized research on factors affecting delinquency among young people and concluded with the following statement: "To combat youth crime is largely futile unless an effort is also made to assure legitimate employment for youths. To deal effectively with both youth crime and youth unemployment in the United States today, however, major social, cultural, and political developments must be taken into account" (1979, 79).
7. The best predictor of serious delinquency is association with delinquent peer groups (Austin 1984; Elliott, Huizinga, and Ageton 1985).

Causes of Delinquency

It is clear that juvenile delinquency is not one single pattern of behavior but a complex phenomenon that takes a variety of forms and has a variety of causes. One can see different sets of causes, some of which may combine to produce delinquent behavior.

Delinquency as Restricted Opportunity. According to this view, a lack of legitimate opportunities to secure income and to get satisfactory jobs causes many working-class youth to seek illegal means of achieving their goals. Delinquent acts are expressions of frustration, such as vandalism directed at schools, and various forms of theft. This view has been advanced by Cloward and Ohlin (1960) and by Stinchcombe (1964). Glaser (1979) attributed the growth in violent delinquency in the inner city in part to a growth in perceptions of restricted opportunity among minority youth in the big cities:

Theodore Lownik Library
Illinois Benedictine College
Lisle, IL 60532

> *To claim a full understanding of this upsurge in violent crime would be presumptuous, but it seems reasonable to infer that it was in large part a consequence of a growing sense of relative deprivation among ghetto youths. Their frustration at*

> *the inaccessibility of legitimate ways to realize the 'American dream' Dr. King had portrayed evoked an anger that usually was directed at the most convenient targets—other blacks. (1979, 73)*

Delinquency as a Subcultural Phenomenon. The most common type of juvenile delinquency in the United States and other industrialized countries seems to arise from certain disjunctions in the society itself. People in power in the society regard certain types of behavior as undesirable and they label it "delinquent," although the same behavior may appear natural to other people who belong to special subcultural groups. From this point of view, delinquent acts are primarily carried out by subgroups of youth who are at odds with the value system of the greater society in which they live. In a sense, these young people are alienated from society and, feeling rejected by the community at large, they do not wish to obey its rules.

According to this theory, working-class boys grow up with standards of behavior that get them in trouble with the authorities who represent middle-class standards. Kvaraceus and Miller (1959) favor this theory and list the following characteristics of working-class culture that tend to get a boy in trouble with the authorities: high value placed on toughness, outsmarting others, seeking excitement, maintaining one's autonomy, and attributing events to fate. In contrast, the middle-class culture places high value on the following traits: achievement through hard work, responsibility, desire for education, respect for property, cleanliness, ambition, belonging to formal organizations, and ability to defer present pleasure in favor of future gratification.

Since most working-class boys do *not* become delinquent, Kvaraceus and Miller (1959) concluded that not all working-class families have typical working-class values and that some boys from working-class families learn middle-class modes of behavior in school, in church, or in recreational settings. With the aid of education, these boys move out of the working class.

Prolonged Adolescent Dependence and Denial of Autonomy. This is the view of Coleman and the Panel on Youth (1974). When young people cannot meet their needs for autonomy and responsibility, they may turn to illegal activities or to protest activities.

Family Failure and Delinquency. Much delinquency is related to problems in the family (Wilson and Herrnstein 1985). The classic studies by Sheldon and Eleanor Glueck (1950, 1968) found the following five family characteristics to be closely related to delinquency:

- Overstrict, erratic, or lax discipline of boy by father.
- Lack of supervision of boy by mother.
- Lack of affection of father for boy.
- Lack of affection of mother for boy.
- Lack of cohesiveness in the family.

School Failure and Delinquency. There is certainly a positive correlation between failure in school and delinquency; but it is not certain which is the cause and which is effect. Some students of the problem believe that youth with learning problems tend to become delinquent. For instance, the Comptroller General of the United States in 1977 reported that there is growing "evidence, being established by experts in education, medicine, law enforcement, and juvenile justice . . . [indicating] a correlation between children experiencing academic failure (learning problems) and children demonstrating delinquent behavior" (p. 2). The report went on to say that the research did not definitely establish a causal link between learning problems and delinquency.

Related research also has supported the conclusion that delinquency is associated with the existence of learning disabilities (LD) among male teenagers. Based on a three-part study initiated by the National Institute for Juvenile Justice and Delinquency, Dunivant (1982) reported a significant relationship between learning disabilities and delinquent behavior among teenage boys in Baltimore, Indianapolis, and Phoenix, after taking account of socioeconomic differences between learning disabled and nondisabled subjects. Youth with LD reported more acts of violence, theft, alcohol and marijuana use, and school misbehavior and had more contact with the criminal justice system. The study provided support for the "susceptibility" hypothesis, which argues that personality characteristics (e.g., lack of impulse control) that are associated with LD contribute directly to increases in delinquency.

An experimental study in which adjudicated delinquents were randomly placed in remediation and control conditions showed that a relatively large amount of instruction (at least 40 to 50 hours) to improve basic skills reduced the recidivism of black youth, of teenagers with a relatively mild history of official delinquency, and of participants whose performance IQ was below average. The investigators concluded that this reduction in delinquency probably was due to bonding with the LD specialists who provided remediation.

The Peer Group Interacting with Other Causes. The various causes of delinquency have been studied and delineated systematically in research Elliott, Huizinga, and Ageton (1985) conducted using longitudinal data from the National Youth Survey. The authors found support for a causal model in which problems involving socialization and social disorganization in the home, neighborhood, and school lead to involvement with delinquent peers. In particular, they concluded that "bonding to delinquent peers is the most proximate cause of delinquency and drug use," while "strain" and low "conventional bonding" in the family and the school have indirect effects mediated by the level of bonding to delinquent peers (p. 142). "Strain" involves the "discrepancy between a set of cultural expectations endorsed by the subject as important" in the home and the school and "his or her perceived realization of these goals." Youngsters who perceive themselves as not meeting important goals of the home and school experience strain. "Conventional bonding" involves the "amount of time spent with the family and on academic concerns at school" and the belief that one must not violate the rules of the home and school in order to achieve personal goals or aspirations (Elliott, Huizinga, and Ageton 1985, 95–96). Youngsters who experience strain and low conventional bonding in the family and the school are more likely to develop strong bonding with delinquent peers and then engage in delinquency and drug use (Thornberry 1987).

Genetic Factors. James Wilson and Richard Herrnstein (1985) argue that some crime and delinquency is genetically based. Others such as Jencks (1987) reject this explanation but agree that genetic factors may predispose some individuals to be highly aggressive, and in some cultures aggressiveness is channeled into antisocial outlets.

Inequality. Evidence presented by Currie (1985) indicates that inequality in wealth and power is positively correlated with crime and delinquency in working-class populations. This relationship is not present in all societies and cultures.

Cause and Treatment of Violent Delinquency

Although much research has been conducted on both the extent and causes of violent delinquency, social scientists have not been able precisely to identify the forces that lead some young people to do serious harm and lead others to remain nondelinquent or nonviolent. However, Paul A. Strasburg (1978, 82–83) has reviewed the research on this issue very carefully and concluded that both a "subculture of violence" and unusually severe social stress are implicated in developing patterns of violent delinquency, particularly among underclass youth in big cities.

Robert L. Woodson of the American Enterprise Institute has been studying programs to reduce delinquency among underclass youth in big cities and has come to the conclusion that most efforts made through traditional agencies have been largely ineffective. He summarizes the situation:

> *The crime problem is real and growing. It is highly concentrated in the minority urban youth group. Moreover, among minority populations at least, youth crime is resistant to or outside of the scope of programs guided by trained human services specialists. Typically, black delinquents receive no effective help from the justice system and remain unchanged. . . . Various alternative treatments have been devised by human services professionals in response to the juvenile court mandate to 'save the children.'*
>
> *However well meant these efforts have been, the record of performance remains disappointing. No clear, significant relationship has yet been discovered between any institutional youth program and the subsequent life history or criminal activity of youth treated in these programs. Whatever success there is seems to be achieved with white, middle-class status offenders. (1981a, 4, 6)*

Woodson also has identified a number of local-neighborhood efforts that appear to have reduced violent delinquency and crime among youth in some inner-city neighborhoods. Successful approaches have been developed and car-

ried out by local residents who formerly were street leaders or have been able to influence crime-prone youth in their neighborhoods. Examples of such efforts include the antigang activities carried out at the House of Umoja in Philadelphia and community development activities of the Ching-A-Ling Corporation in New York City. Woodson's books titled *Youth Crime and Urban Policy* (1981b) and *A Summons to Life: Mediating Structures and the Prevention of Youth Crime* try to identify the factors that can make this kind of approach successful.

Drug Abuse

A major aspect of the life of youth since about 1955 is the so-called drug culture—the vastly increased use (or abuse) of psychedelic (consciousness-expanding) and other drugs by youth. Data on drug use among youth have been provided annually since 1975 in national surveys of high school seniors conducted by the University of Michigan Institute for Social Research (Johnston et al. 1985). Major findings from the surveys include:

- As indicated in Figure 6.2, use of marijuana by high school seniors has declined in the 1980s. The percentage of seniors who report having used marijuana within the previous year fell from a peak of 54 percent in 1978 to 46 percent in 1985. This decline probably was due in part to an increasing concern about the effects of marijuana on health. The percentage of seniors who attributed "great risk" to regular marijuana use increased from 35 percent in 1978 to 58 percent in 1981.
- *Cocaine.* As indicated in Figure 6.2, the percentage of seniors who reported using cocaine during the previous year increased from 7 percent in 1975 to 17 percent in 1985.
- *Illicit drugs other than marijuana and alcohol.* Figure 6.2 also shows that the percentage of seniors who used illicit drugs other than alcohol and marijuana (cocaine, heroin, opiates, tranquillizers, stimulants, sedatives) without a physician's supervision increased from 26 percent in 1975 to 34 percent in 1981 and 1982, and then dropped back to 27 percent in 1985.
- *Alcohol.* Sixty-six percent of 1985 high school seniors reported using alcohol during the previous month. Use and abuse of alcohol by young people continues to be a very serious problem, and the average beginning age for alcohol drinking has dropped to 12.5 years.

Even though recent declines in use of marijuana and other illicit drugs (except cocaine) have been encouraging, the increase in use of cocaine has been troubling, particularly since evidence has been accumulating concerning serious negative effects of cocaine on mental and physical health, and cocaine has become much more easily available in the form of crack. Lloyd D. Johnston of the Institute for Social Research has summarized some findings and implications of the Institute's surveys on cocaine use:

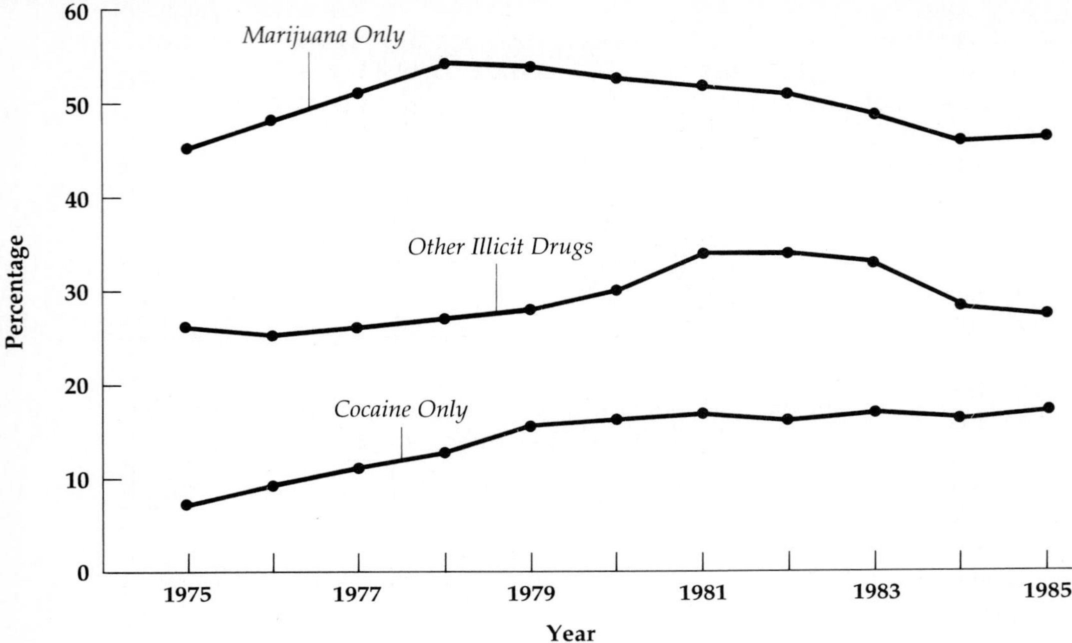

"Other illicit drugs" include hallucinogens, heroin, cocaine, and opiates, tranquillizers, stimulants or sedatives not under a physician's supervision.

Figure 6.2 ***Percentages of High School Seniors Using Marijuana, Cocaine, and Other Illicit Drugs during the Previous Twelve Months, 1975 to 1985*** (*Source*: Adapted from Johnston et al. 1985 and other surveys conducted by the University of Michigan Institute for Social Research.)

> *It is important for the general public to recognize the insidious way in which a severe cocaine dependency develops, or we are going to see an already serious epidemic expand even further. . . . We have suggested to those in policy positions that changing people's complacency about experimental and occasional use of cocaine may be an important step toward controlling the rising casualty rate of this drug. . . . Trying to publicize the vast network of corruption and human suffering associated with cocaine may be an effective way of getting potential users to think twice. (quoted in "Cocaine Use Rising" 1985–86)*

The Institute for Social Research surveys of high school seniors also showed that illicit drug use was highest in large metropolitan areas, in the Northeast, among males, and among students who do not plan to go to college. In addition, the surveys found that the great majority of students say their friends do not condone the use of illicit drugs other than marijuana, and three-fourths say their friends do not approve of regular marijuana use. The data further indicated that the rise that had been occurring in peer approval of marijuana use was sharply reversed in 1980–81. The researchers concluded that the decline they found in marijuana use among seniors was due to greater recognition of both the physical and the psychological damage that may accompany abuse of this drug.

Both alcohol and marijuana are not just widely used but also are widely abused by many adolescents and youth. Evidence of widespread abuse of alcohol among adolescents has been reported in national studies that indicate that approximately 70 percent of high school seniors consume alcohol at least once a month (Snider 1987c). In addition, recent data indicate that use of alcohol has been increasing among young persons younger than fifteen years of age (Desmond 1987).

Concern with marijuana, alcohol, or other relatively mild drugs arises partly from the possibility that they may stimulate or reinforce alienation from major social institutions and hinder the transition to adulthood among many adolescents and youth. Thus, a report on marijuana by the Secretary of Health, Education and Welfare points out that many "of the factors which have been found to be related to drug use—low academic performance, rebelliousness, depression or criminal activity—appear more often to precede rather than to follow the use of drugs." There is reason to be concerned about increased use among adolescents, especially "when such use become an escape from the demands of preparing for later life" (National Institute on Drug Abuse 1977, 9, 11, 27). Recent research regarding the effects of marijuana supports the conclusion that frequent use has a variety of detrimental consequences including impairment of learning ability and memory, damage to the body's immune system, and infertility. Some authorities now believe that contrary to earlier conclusions, heavy use of marijuana frequently is a stepping stone to use of other drugs such as heroin and cocaine (Mills and Noyes 1984).

Several researchers have been trying to identify the forces that lead to or are associated with the use of illicit drugs (Stein, Newcomb, and Bentler 1987). For example, Huba and Bentler (1980) surveyed 1,634 students in the seventh, eighth, and ninth grades and concluded that adolescents become more susceptible to peer encouragement to try various drugs as they proceed through these grades, and that the relative effects of peer and adult influences depend on the student's age and sex and on the type of drug considered. Jessor, Chase, and Donovan (1980) have analyzed data on seventh- through twelfth-grade students who participated in the National Study of Adolescent Drinking Behavior, Attitudes, and Correlates, and concluded that proneness to marijuana use

> *appears to consist of a rather coherent and integrated pattern of psychosocial attributes: in the* personality system, *greater value on independence than on academic achievement, lower expectations for academic achievement, greater tolerance of deviance, and less religiosity; in the* perceived environment system, *less compatibility between the adolescent's two major reference groups—parents and friends, less influence of parents relative to friends, and greater approval for and models for marijuana use and other problem behaviors; and in the* behavior sys-

> tem, *greater actual involvement in other problem behaviors and less participation in conventional activities.* (p. 610)

Jessor and his colleagues also found that essentially the same pattern accounted for problem use of alcohol, that marijuana involvement and abuse of alcohol were highly correlated, and that these patterns held regardless of sex, age, or ethnic group. After noting that similar conclusions have been reported with respect to adolescent vandalism, stealing, and other forms of deviance, they further concluded that prevention approaches should consider the syndrome or cluster of problem behaviors, rather than trying to deal with adolescent problem behaviors in isolation from one another.

Concern for drug abuse among adolescents and teenagers probably should be somewhat tempered by recognition that most users apparently do not suffer long-range harm from participation in youth subcultures that sanction drugs. In this regard, Ramos (1980) has examined research on the drug subcultures of the 1960s and 1970s and concluded that one should not underestimate the "extent to which illicit drug users naturally reform once the adolescent peer group supporting the deviant behavior matures, weakens, and inevitably disbands" (p. 242). After citing research indicating that most young drug abusers eventually "mellow out" or "mature out," he concluded that "it is of some consolation, no doubt, to recognize that . . . going straight, not staying deviant, is the rule rather than the exception" (p. 244).

Nevertheless, drug and alcohol abuse among youth is a serious national concern. As mentioned, cocaine use involves a vast network of corruption and human suffering that increasingly afflicts the young. In addition, the spread of smokable cocaine in the form of crack appears to be increasing the number of youth addicted to cocaine (Snider 1987c). Use of other drugs is still substantial and frequently has harmful physical and psychological effects on young people.

As is true with delinquency, teenage pregnancy, and several other youth problems, drug use is particularly a problem with underclass youth in big cities. Inciardi (1980) has examined research on this aspect of the drug problem and concluded that at least since the 1940s, most inner-city communities "have maintained large populations of drug users that are heavily involved in crime" (p. 199). Because youth crime in the inner city has a number of causes other than drug addiction (e.g., high rates of unemployment and poverty), one cannot say that delinquency and crime are caused primarily by drugs. Rather, illicit use of hard drugs is both a manifestation of underclass environments and a cause, for some users, of additional deviance. Unless this environment is changed, youth drug abuse will continue to be characteristic of inner-city communities in the future, with occasional epidemic use occurring as social, political, and economic forces escalate the underlying conditions that lead to abuse.

Much of the responsibility for education about drug use and its prevention has been given to the schools, but educators apparently have not been very successful in providing effective programs to prevent drug use (Buscemi 1985; Miller 1988). Thus, Hanson (1980) has provided the following summary of conclusions from research on drug education:

> *Research has demonstrated that while it is relatively easy to increase drug knowledge, it is more difficult to modify attitudes. A number of studies have reported greater changes in knowledge than in attitude, or have reported changes in knowledge unaccompanied by changes in attitude. . . . By far the largest number of studies have found no effects of drug education upon use. (p. 273)*

However, there also are indications that some antidrug programs devised in the 1980s have been more effective than earlier programs (Viadero 1986a). In general, such programs place greater emphasis on younger students in accordance with data showing that the age of first use has significantly declined, on helping students learn to resist peer pressure to use drugs, and on coordination between efforts of the school and the community (Buscemi 1985; Rose 1986). On the other hand, this also means that successful antidrug education tends to be relatively complex and expensive, in contrast to ineffective earlier programs that frequently consisted of little more than occasional lectures and provision of information (Viadero 1986a; Rose 1986).

National concern about the negative effects of drug use among young people and adults greatly escalated in 1986, perhaps in part because many observers felt that cocaine use had reached epidemic proportions and was having increasingly detrimental effects on individuals and society. In this context, the President's Commission on Organized Crime issued a report stating that the "menace of drugs" has become "a threat to national security," the president proposed to divert $100 million from higher education to antidrug programs in the schools, and the National Association of Secondary School Principals issued a statement referring to drug abuse as the most "pernicious and persistent" problem faced by contemporary youth (Rose 1986).

Teen Pregnancy

The teenage pregnancy rate has risen significantly during the past few decades. In 1974, the estimated pregnancy rate per thousand women between the ages of fifteen and nineteen was 99; by 1982 the rate had climbed to 112—an increase of 13 percent. Even though the number and rate of births among all teenagers fell during this period due to decline in the youth population, availability of abortion, use of contraceptives, and other causes, the percentage of births to unwed mothers among babies born to teenagers increased explosively from 15 percent in 1960 to 54 percent in 1983 (Select Committee 1986).

The Select Committee on Children, Youth, and Families of the U.S. House of Representatives examined these trends in the context of other information bearing on teenage pregnancy and identified six related problems:

- Families headed by young mothers are seven times more likely to be living below the poverty level than are other families.

- In 1975, nearly two-thirds of women receiving AFDC (Aid to Families with Dependent Children) had their first child during their teenage years.
- Teen mothers suffer higher rates of marital separation and divorce than do women giving birth at later ages. In 1983, 35 percent of all divorces involved women who married in their teens. The risk of marital dissolution is carried on through later life, showing up in increased risks of marital dissolution in second marriages.
- Infants born to teenage mothers, particularly those under age 17, are much more likely to have a low Apgar score—the summary measure used to evaluate the newborn infant's overall physical condition—than are babies born to older mothers.
- In 1983 only 52 percent of all pregnant teens who gave birth received prenatal care in the first trimester of pregnancy, while 75 percent of all mothers received early prenatal care.
- Children of teenage parents tend to be less healthy on the average than do other children and to exhibit learning difficulties more frequently in school. These effects result principally from the severe social and economic consequences of early childbearing. (Select Committee n.d., p. 1)

Kingsley Davis (1980) has studied the data on teenage pregnancy in the United States and stressed the following four conclusions: (1) teenage births constitute a higher proportion of births in the United States than in other industrial nations; (2) this proportion is particularly high in the black population and in the younger ages; (3) the proportion of out-of-wedlock births is nearly five times greater for women under 20 than for older women; and (4) out-of-wedlock fertility has risen steadily for adolescents while falling for older women. Davis attributes the rise in illegitimacy among teenagers to such interrelated considerations as wider availability of contraceptives, earlier and more frequent sexual intercourse, decline in parental and community influence over the behavior of youth, changes in ideology that no longer require or pressure the father to marry a pregnant teenager, assumption by society and social agencies of responsibility for assisting young mothers with out-of-wedlock children, and greater community and societal acceptance of teenage sexuality and illegitimacy.

Regarding international comparisons, a study conducted for the Guttmacher Institute (Jones et al. 1986) found that the teenage pregnancy rate for white females in the United States is much higher—in some cases two to five times higher—than the rates reported for Canada, England, France, the Netherlands, Sweden, and other industrialized nations. The authors' analysis concluded that "two factors are key to the location of the United States with regard to teenage fertility: an ambivalent, sometimes Puritanical attitude toward sex [which discourages fertility control], and the existence of a large, economically deprived underclass" (Jones et al. 1986, 230).

As mentioned, the teenage pregnancy rate in the United States is higher among black females than among white females (Chase-Lansdale and Vinovskis 1987). In addition, the rate of out-of-wedlock births among women under 20 is much higher for blacks than for whites: in 1984, 90 percent of the births to black women under age twenty were out-of-wedlock, as compared with 42 percent for white women. (These figures were substantially higher than the corresponding 1950 rates of 37 and 6 percent, respectively.) Because a higher percentage of the black population is relatively low in socioeconomic status, one can assume that the racial discrepancy in illegitimacy is due partly to this social class difference.

Although research has not systematically examined or distinguished racial differences taking account of social class, Davis (1980) and other observers believe that some of the differences probably involve racial factors; that is, that oppression and discrimination associated with race have produced social conditions conducive to relatively high illegitimacy rates among black Americans. After reviewing research on the very high rates of teenage pregnancy among black youth in the United States, Moore, Simms, and Betsey (1986) reached the following conclusions:

> *Many of the factors found independently to predict early childbearing—less information, more poorly educated parents, school dropout, poor employment prospects, single-parent families—are found to be concentrated in those neighborhoods in which black children are particularly likely to be growing up. The aggregate influence of these separate factors may be greater than the single sum of the separate effects. . . . A realistic approach to the problem of early pregnancy in the black community will need to confront the attitudes of contemporary black youth which seem to be relatively accepting of early sex and out-of-wedlock parenthood. However, it is important to recognize that blacks, like other social groups, are very heterogeneous and that the adult generation does not support or encourage early sexual activity or pregnancy. (Moore, Simms, and Betsey 1986, xii, 136–137)*

In any case, it appears that pregnancy and illegitimacy are particularly likely to cause other problems and to be symptomatic of destructive social environments among black youth in inner-city communities (Sonenstein 1985). The association between teenage motherhood and later-life disadvantage is well established, and many observers believe this association is bidirectional: young women who are poor and have limited opportunity are more likely to have babies at an earlier age, but having a baby also reduces the future opportunities of many young women. Furstenberg (1980; 1988; Furstenberg, Brooks-Gunn, and Morgan 1987) has conducted longitudinal research working with low-income, teenage, black females in Baltimore and has found that in many cases motherhood had a negative impact on their subsequent careers:

> *Early pregnancy created a distinct set of problems for the adolescent parent that forced a redirection of her intended life course. In particular, we established a number of links connecting early childbearing to complications in marriage, to disruption in schooling, to economic problems and, to some extent, to problems in family size regulation and childbearing as well. . . .*

> *Some women had been able to repair the disorder created by an untimely pregnancy. . . . Still other participants were not so successful in coping with the problems caused by precipitate parenthood. . . . Poorly educated, unskilled, often burdened by several small children, many of these women at age 20 or 21 had become resigned to a life of economic deprivation.*
>
> *. . . Almost all the young mothers in our study wanted to complete high school, but most were not so inspired to remain in school whatever the difficulties. . . . Similarly, with few exceptions, the young mothers wished to avoid a rapid repeat pregnancy, but few were so anxious not to conceive that they continued to use birth control methods when events in their lives made contraception difficult or frightening. (Furstenberg 1980, 297–298)*

Furstenberg provides a portrayal of young inner-city women trapped in a destructive environment in which a variety of forces generate and reinforce underclass status; teenage pregnancy and childbearing constitute one force that frequently is a devastating hurdle for all but the most supermotivated young women. He also points out that although the federal government emphasizes that pregnant teenagers have a right to continue their education and although many programs have been initiated to reduce or eliminate teenage pregnancy and related problems, opportunities and programs vary in scope and effectiveness, and services generally are too timid and fragmented to deal with the inner-city situation. Jaffe and Dryfoos (1980) studied fertility control programs in the United States and concluded that it was not yet possible to determine whether preventive educational services (family life, population, or sex education) have any substantial effect on adolescent sex patterns, fertility control practices, pregnancy experience, abortion use, or childbearing.

However, subsequent research has reported encouraging results concerning the efficacy of school-based clinics and other public-school programs to help prevent or alleviate the problems associated with teenage pregnancy (Sonenstein 1985; Zabin et al. 1986; Buie 1987). On the other hand, these problems seem to have become increasingly severe and widespread in the 1980s, and public recognition of their importance expanded rapidly in the mid-1980s. For example, popular journals carried articles with such provocative titles as "Children Having Children" and "Children As Parents" (Hulbert 1984); and the National Education Association published a paperback book (Compton, Duncan, and Hruska 1986) emphasizing the widening scope of teenage pregnancy problems and recommending that, among other responses, schools expand sex education and related staff development activities, bolster antidropout programs for pregnant adolescents, help sponsor advocacy and day-care programs, and offer appropriate prenatal care and social support services. The U.S. House of Representatives Select Committee on Children, Youth, and Families surveyed the situation and reported that "there is no focused approach to solving the complex problem of teen pregnancy. . . . The efforts that do exist are too few, uncoordinated, and lack significant support. In short, the system is broken" (Select Committee 1986, ix).

Shortly thereafter, a National Research Council Panel appointed by the National Academy of Sciences and the National Academy of Engineering issued a 337-page report recommending widespread distribution of inexpensive contraceptives to teenagers, beginning sex education at an early age, establishment of more school-based clinics, and life-planning courses as part of the curriculum, media help to emphasize "sexual responsibility," and availability of abortion to teenagers (Panel on Adolescent Pregnancy and Childbearing 1986). The Panel's report drew attention to controversial aspects (e.g., information about contraceptives and abortion) of school-based clinics established or proposed in many school districts, and highly publicized conflicts over school-based clinics took place in several cities (Montague 1986a).

National Service

Although several study groups and a number of educational leaders have recommended systematic expansion of service opportunities and/or obligations for youth and young adults, relatively little attention was paid to such possibilities in the 1970s and early 1980s (Lewis 1987). In the past few years, however, support for national/community service programs appears to have grown substantially (Hamilton 1988).

In 1984, for example, the Youth Policy Institute issued a report advocating that service opportunities be expanded sufficiently to constitute a national system with a "demonstratable impact" on society. Pointing out that the United States already operates an ad hoc program including the Peace Corps and VISTA (Volunteers in Service to America), the authors of the report described a model system based in part on programs in West Germany, Nigeria, and Israel and incorporating components such as the following (Foley, Manaker, and Schwartz 1984):

- Voluntary opportunities for all young people past the age of compulsory schooling.
- Inclusion of a wide variety of opportunities such as military service, care for the elderly, and tutorial assistance to children.
- Contributions to goals unmet by the marketplace, such as support for health care and conservation of public lands.
- Involvement of all sectors and every level of society in planning and operation of a national service.

Two years later, a study conducted for the Ford Foundation analyzed four approaches to national service, including a mandatory school-based program, a national draft, a federally supported volunteer service, and universal service with income-tax penalties for nonparticipants (Danzig and Szanton 1986). Among the most important benefits, the authors concluded, would be promotion of a sense of citizenship as well as personal development and socially useful activity on the part of youth and young adults.

Surveying developments as of 1987, Anne Lewis reported that sentiment favoring some kind of national service seemed to be expanding on a widespread basis. Pointing to increasing support for reinstitution of a military draft, introduction in both houses of Congress of legislation to create a national service system, support from political leaders such as Gary Hart and educational leaders such as Ernest Boyer (1987), Lewis expressed the personal hope that "the political leadership of the nation understands the need for young people to believe that their hearts are as important to the nation's future as their heads" (Lewis 1987, 573).

Schools in a Constructive Program for Youth

To be constructive and realistic at the same time is the goal we must set for ourselves as we consider the situation of youth in the 1990s. The transition from adolescence to adulthood is more difficult than it has been in earlier periods. The weight of helping young people make this transition has been shifting away from the family and the employers toward the secondary schools and colleges.

Several committees of responsible citizens who have studied the interaction of schools and colleges with other community agencies that might serve youth have arrived at a kind of consensus. (Some of these study groups are named and described in the Suggestions for Further Reading at the end of this chapter.) Professor Harry Passow of Teachers College, Columbia University, has summarized a number of common themes that guide the way toward a constructive program in which the high school and the community college are the central educational agencies. His conclusion can be summarized as follows:

1. The objectives of youth education go beyond the acquisition of mental skills and vocational training—with goals as indicated in the statement by the President's Youth Panel.
2. High schools and community colleges alone cannot supply an adequate environment for youth development. They must work with other community agencies.
3. The segregation of youth by age should be reduced, through more arrangements for youth to associate with adults in socially useful and intellectually stimulating activities.
4. A program combining education with work experience should be promoted in high schools and community colleges. The existing cooperative work-study programs should be expanded, and a variety of mixtures of part-time work and part-time schooling should be encouraged. The program of Action-Learning sponsored by the National Commission on Resources for Youth should be extended.
5. Laws governing the movement of youth into the labor force should be reconsidered. The National Manpower Institute advocated establishment of Community Education-Work Councils, which might facilitate the channeling of youth into appropriate careers.

6. Citizenship education should be provided through involving youth in community agencies—social and governmental—where they could supplement their academic studies.
7. Alternative educational programs should be provided by the school system, using space and time in ways that enhance the quality of education—open schools, magnet schools, metro-schools, internships, and apprenticeships. The community college should also move toward this kind of flexibility.
8. Compulsory school attendance laws should be reconsidered. The age might be lowered, with perhaps a category of work-study with pay as early as age 14, monitored by the school system.
9. All individuals should be given vouchers usable for a range of skill-training as well as for academic studies. The Brown Committee Report proposed that state and federal legislation should be drawn so as to entitle every youth to fourteen years of tuition-free education, only eight of which would be compulsory. The remaining six years might be available for use at any later age, though most people would use the vouchers to go through high school and two years of college work.
10. Youth should be given the opportunity to leave school and then return some months later, having pursued travel or employment or some other useful learning experience. This would require a highly flexible program at some Learning Centers, since the ordinary high school course program might not be sufficiently flexible.
11. Somewhat less agreement was given to the proposition that the high school should assume primary responsibility for the intellectual development and mental skill training of youth, with some kind of competency-based diploma for meeting those standards. Nonschool agencies would be given greater responsibility for work experience, citizenship education, and experience with the arts.

Generally similar recommendations subsequently were offered in a major report from the Carnegie Council on Policy Studies in Higher Education (1979). The report included the following recommendations regarding the role of high schools and postsecondary institutions in facilitating the transition from adolescence and youth to adulthood:

High Schools
- Modify the fundamental structure of high schools by making them smaller or by creating more diversity within them, and by creating full-time or part-time specialty schools for education-related work and service.
- Emphasize out-of-class activities and work and service opportunities.
- Stop tracking students.
- Locate applied skill training in the private sector; instead emphasize literacy, numeracy, and good work habits.
- Finance needy students through work-study programs.
- Establish job preparation and placement centers in the high schools, and provide follow-up assistance for two years after graduation.
- Encourage earlier entry into college.

Postsecondary
- Concentrate most applied skill training at the postsecondary level.
- Create programs, particularly in the community colleges, where students can be prepared for jobs and can work part-time.
- Revise student aid programs to target them more to low-income students.
- Help students find off-campus work or service opportunities.

It is clear that most of these changes would make the secondary schools and the community colleges into much more diversified institutions than they now are. Some school and college administrators and teachers would prefer to avoid these programs, leaving them to be established and operated by a State or Area Youth Authority, supported with public funds. Then the schools and colleges could maintain academic programs aimed primarily at the development of cognitive skills and preparing students for the professions. Also, some social scientists and some policy makers doubt that the school and college personnel can carry on these nonacademic operations. The need is to develop educative institutions that ordinary people can run.

James Coleman and Torsten Husen (1985) have provided an analysis somewhat similar to Professor Passow's, but their work and conclusions are broader in the sense that they deal with other industrialized nations in addition to the United States and they place greater stress on coordinating the activity of institutions responsible for assisting youth and young adults. Published internationally by the Organization for Economic Co-operation and Development and titled *Becoming Adult in a Changing Society*, the analysis by Coleman and Husen points out that the historic "conventional triangle" wherein

> *the economy produces, the family consumes, and the State redistributes, is not adequate any longer. The traditional meanings have changed. The economy educates as well as produces, the family produces (with most women in the labour force), and the State is drawn into the productive system as a major provider of services. This also means that the relationships between the three have changed profoundly. . . . However, the shift . . . does not take place without problems: the process of transition from youth to adult appears to be increasingly taken over by youth-oriented commercial interests. . . . It is evident that if the difficulties are not to increase, society as a whole must, especially through its educational institutions, devise new mechanisms for aiding youth entering the labour market. (Coleman and Husen 1985, 9, 47)*

Conclusion

Trends reviewed in this chapter indicate that the transition to adulthood has become more difficult for many young people than was true earlier in the twentieth century. The prolonging of adolescence is a problem for many youth. In the past few decades it has been associated with substantial increases in unemployment, suicide, crime and delinquency, drug use and abuse, teenage pregnancy, and out-of-wedlock birth rates. These problems have been particularly evident and devastating among economically disadvantaged minority youth in the inner city.

Wynne and Hess (1986) have documented most of the trends described in this chapter. These authors present data demonstrating that youth suicide and homicide rates, drug use, and out-of-wedlock birth rates have increased sharply since about 1955. They also point out, however, that most of these trends stabilized or even declined slightly in the 1980s. They then speculate that these "improvements in levels of disorder" may be due to a "moderate shift" in the

> *values structure prevailing in America. . . . The improvement is surely not due to the lessening of poverty, which apparently has gotten worse over the years. . . . Perhaps the shift, insofar as it directly relates to education and youth issues, partly occurred because of widespread public recognition that the youth situation was basically very unwholesome. (Wynne and Hess 1986, 306)*

Whatever the reasons for some recent encouraging developments, the problems young people encounter in their transition to adulthood and the high incidence of destructive behavior such as crime, drug abuse, and teenage pregnancy are causes for serious concern. This chapter also identified the kinds of national and local programs and actions that governmental and nongovernmental agencies and the schools might take to address the problems systematically and comprehensively. Many such programs and actions are required in the future if more youth are to make a successful transition to productive adulthood.

EXERCISES

1. Write a paper arguing for or against the following proposition: Education at the secondary school and college levels should be mainly concerned with the development of knowledge and intellectual skills necessary for the professions and for business leadership.
2. Assuming that everybody at age 16 was given a voucher, equivalent in value to the average cost of education through four years of college, to be used at his or her discretion for schooling or skill acquisition at any subsequent time, describe how you think four quite different persons, two women and two men, might use these vouchers.
3. From your observation and experience in your own institution, what is the drug situation?
4. Read what you can find on delinquency among girls. What differentiates it from delinquency among boys?
5. Find an example of a work-experience program for predelinquent or delinquent boys; describe and evaluate it.
6. Is it valid to say that youth are less mature now than they were two or three decades ago? What arguments support this conclusion, and what arguments counteract it? Which arguments do you think are most defensible?

SUGGESTIONS FOR FURTHER READING

1. For students who want to get further into the subject of this chapter, the books recommended are *Youth and Dissent* by Keniston; *Youth: Transition to Adulthood* by Coleman; *Adolescence to Adulthood* by Bachman, O'Malley, and Johnson; and Yankelovich's *Changing Values on the Campus*.
2. The 1975 Yearbook of the National Society for the Study of Education, entitled *Youth*, is an extensive treatment of the theme of this chapter.
3. A set of essays on the transition from youth to adulthood has been edited by Ralph W. Tyler. Entitled *From Youth to Constructive Adulthood*, these essays describe and analyze the situation of youth from the points of view of educators and social scientists.
4. A thought-provoking four-year longitudinal study of high school and college students has been made by Richard and Shirley Jessor, entitled *Problem Behavior and Psychosocial Development*. This study reveals a great deal of deviant behavior in a middle-sized college town.
5. For a look at youth unrest and youth culture in several modern societies, see the collection of essays edited by Allerbeck and Rosenmary, which contains articles from writers in England, France, Germany, Italy, the Soviet Union, and the United States.
6. The values of a work-experience program for boys in the prevention of delinquency are explored thoroughly in the book *400 Losers* by Ahlstrom and Havighurst, which describes a five-year experimental study in Kansas City.
7. Much of the analysis in James Q. Wilson's *Thinking about Crime* (1983) is devoted to juvenile delinquency and drug abuse.
8. *Student Pregnancy* by Compton, Duncan, and Hruska (1986) offers many suggestions regarding how the schools might help address problems related to teenage pregnancy.
9. *Finding Work* (1986) edited by Ray Rist provides information and analysis regarding youth employment and training in Australia, England, Japan, the United States, and other countries.
10. A report on *Student Service* (Harrison 1987) prepared for The Carnegie Foundation for the Advancement of Teaching describes many programs providing voluntary and assigned community service for high-school students and also offers suggestions for initiating and conducting such programs.

7

Mobility and Education

In a complex, democratic society, many people will move upward from one social class to another during the first half of their lifetime. This kind of movement is implied in the ideal of equality of opportunity. However, social movement downward from one class to another is also implied for some people.

A substantial amount of upward mobility is evidence of the existence of opportunity. Education is widely believed to help young people move up the social scale by preparing them for a higher status occupation than that of their parents, by increasing their earning power, and by giving them more of the general knowledge of the past and the present that marks middle-class people.

In a democratic society, there is bound to be much competition for the prized middle- and upper-class positions because they have so much that most people desire. Children born to upper- and middle-class families have some advantage in this competition, because they probably learn much in the family that will help them maintain the family position. Children from lower-status families may be able to compete successfully for some of the higher-status positions if they have certain favored qualities of mind and personality and if they get sufficient help from the educational system.

It is widely believed that democratic societies reward young people on the basis of merit, where *merit* is defined as ability plus effort. Such a society is called *meritocratic* and should display a good deal of upward social mobility for its young people. However, difficulties do block the path of upward mobility for children of lower-status families and for children of some minority groups.

This chapter examines the nature and amount of social mobility and the relationships of education to social mobility. First, we report on the actual amount of social mobility and on several aspects of this general phenomenon. Then, major research studies on the relations of education to social mobility are described. This chapter also describes major controversies among researchers on the relationship of education to the socioeconomic structure of the United States.

The Nature and Amount of Social Mobility

Even though much upward social mobility today occurs through education, other channels also are important. The self-made businessman whose wife guides him up the social ladder is one example of an alternative pattern of mobility. Athletic prowess in a boy often provides a good base for mobility, as when a boy becomes a professional baseball or football player. Although there are notable exceptions, in most cases athletic ability combines with a college education if the young man is to become a successful middle-aged man. The mobility patterns of girls have increased in variety as the world of business and professions opened more widely to women in the 1970s.

The people who rise on the social scale are those who have talents, abilities, and motives their society values. In the highly instrumental and materialist society of the past 100 years, these values were ambition, economic foresight, habits of industry, and verbal or mechanical intelligence. Today's period of rapid technological and social change is likely to see a change in the human qualities that gain favored status for people. It is difficult to predict the future, but we should keep this possible change in mind as we examine the mobility data for recent decades.

Mobile Youth

Teachers and other observers often feel confident that they can spot the talented or the ambitious students and that they can predict which ones will and will not get further in life than their parents. At the same time, there are relatively few studies in which a large group of youngsters have been followed to find which ones actually do, in adulthood, follow patterns of upward mobility and thus to identify the characteristics leading to mobility.

One such study was carried out on a group of boys and girls who in 1951–52 constituted all the sixth graders in the public schools of a community called River City. They were followed until 1964, when they were approximately 23 years old. Some of the original 450 left the city and were lost to the study, but fairly adequate data are available on almost 400 of the group (Havighurst et al. 1962).

Table 7.1 shows the social and intellectual characteristics of the group when studied at age 23. By this time, almost all of those who expected to go to college had at least started. Of those who had not gone to college, the men and some of the women had been working for four to seven years. Most of the women had married and were homemakers.

Each person in the group was evaluated in comparison to family of origin with regard to educational level, occupation, occupational performance, and reputation in the community. On this basis he or she was identified as upwardly mobile, stable, or downwardly mobile. (The women who had married were assigned the status of their husbands; those who had not married were evaluated in the same way as the men.)

The data on *intelligence* are based on a battery of tests administered when the group was in the sixth grade. The data on *social effectiveness* came from sociometric tests and teachers' descriptions obtained when the students were in the sixth grade and again when they were in the ninth grade. The combination measure shown in Table 7.1 includes popularity, friendliness, and leadership as evaluated by both teachers and peers.

Among the men, the upwardly mobile as compared to the socially stable had been markedly superior in high school on measures of intelligence, school

Table 7.1 *Characteristics of Mobile and Stable Twenty-Three-Year-Olds in River City (N = 399)*

		Mean Percentile Scores*		
	N	*IQ†*	*High School Grades*	*Social Effectiveness‡*
Upwardly mobile:				
Men	52	71	59	70
Women:				
Not married	11	75	75	77
Married between ages 21 and 24	18	65	75	77
Married by age 20	36	50	51	64
Total	117			
Stable:				
Men	101	42	45	42
Women:				
Not married	10	86	66	80
Married between ages 21 and 24	17	59	71	57
Married by age 20	72	42	47	46
Total	200			
Downwardly mobile:				
Men	44	28	26	40
Women:				
Not married	4	42	41	44
Married between ages 21 and 24	4	34	52	—
Married by age 20	30	50	48	42
Total	82			

* Based on the entire group of students.

† Based on a number of tests given in sixth grade.

‡ A combination measure including popularity, friendliness, and leadership as evaluated by both teachers and peers.

grades, and social effectiveness. The downwardly mobile had been the poorest on these measures. Thus, a teacher who knew this group of students could have predicted with considerable accuracy which boys would be upwardly mobile and which would be downwardly mobile.

For the women, however, predictions would have been more difficult. Although the upwardly mobile women had been superior in high school to the stable and to the downwardly mobile, the patterns were complicated by differences related to age at marriage. With a few exceptions, in the stable and upwardly mobile groups the late-marrying women (those who had not yet married by age 23) had been superior to those who married between 21 and 24; the latter, in turn, had been superior to those who married early (before age 20).

At the same time, the woman who was upwardly mobile as the result of an

early marriage to a higher-status man was higher on social effectiveness than were other early-marrying women, though not higher in intelligence or school grades. The early-marrying downwardly mobile women had the same IQ as the early-marrying upwardly mobile women. In short, social effectiveness, but not IQ, differentiated between early-marrying women who married "above" and early-marrying women who married "below" their own social status levels.

All in all, the River City study clearly showed two main paths of social mobility. Men, and some women, will climb the social ladder by making use of superior intelligence and superior social effectiveness to succeed in school and college and on the job. The more frequent path for women (as of 1960) was by marrying a relatively successful young man. Today, the path for upwardly mobile women probably is much more similar to that of men than was true in 1960.

The data and case study just described appear to indicate that education is a means to upward mobility for some young people, but not for others. Some people are downwardly mobile, and others achieve upward mobility through social resources other than education and through abilities other than intelligence, or through a combination of education or intelligence with other resources and personal qualities.

Group Mobility

The preceding section considered the phenomenon of individual social mobility, one mark of democracy in our social-class system. Group mobility affects and qualifies individual mobility. Group mobility occurs when a social group moves as a whole in relation to other groups. The mobile group may be a large or a small one. For example, skilled workers in the United States have gained greatly in economic status relative to minor white-collar workers and relative to farmers. The wages of electricians, plumbers, railroad men, and others of the so-called aristocracy of labor have risen more since 1900 than have the incomes of clerical and retail sales-workers, teachers, farmers, and other groups. This economic gain has enabled many of these blue-collar workers to move up, using their money to purchase the symbols of lower middle-class living.

Upward group mobility tends to favor upward individual mobility of members of the group, but the two movements are not identical. Thus, as the standard of living has risen, some working-class people have come to enjoy fancy automobiles, the newest home appliances, high school educations, and paid vacations, all of which would have marked them as middle class in 1920. Indeed, this phenomenon has caused some foreign observers to refer to the United States as a nation of middle-class people. However, those working-class people who now possess certain material and nonmaterial goods that in 1920 would have symbolized middle-class status have not thereby been turned into middle-class people. This is true because many of the symbols of middle-class status have changed in the interim. Today, middle-class people quite generally have a college education rather than the high school education characteristic of the middle class in 1920. Quite a few travel to Europe. These things have now become symbols of a middle-class life-style, a life-style not shared by working-class people. Thus, the system of rank continues in a changing society even though the bases or signs of rank are shifting.

Mobility of Ethnic, Racial, and Religious Groups

There has been a great deal of group mobility among the various ethnic and religious groups that have come to this country: first, English, then Irish, German, Scandinavian, French, Dutch, Polish, Hungarian, Italian, Bohemian, Serbian, Rumanian, Armenian, Chinese, Japanese, and Spanish American. People came in groups and made settlements either in the new lands on the frontier or in the cities. Gradually, they joined the main cultural stream of life in the United States. The schools hastened this process by teaching the new language and the new ways to their children.

Generally, a new immigrant started at the bottom of the social scale and worked up. For example, the Irish, the lowest status group in the midnineteenth century, were employed in digging canals and building railroads in the expanding country. They moved up, leaving room at the bottom for Scandinavians, Italians, and Bohemians, who in turn worked their way up.

Some immigrant groups came into the social system at a level above the bottom, either because they possessed capital, or because they brought with them a culture that was enough like that of the middle class to enable them to participate at once at that level. For example, numerous Germans came after 1848 because of political unrest and persecution in Germany. Some of them were middle-class people who started businesses and built up cities such as Milwaukee, St. Louis, and Cincinnati.

The Jews came with their religion and with a compound Jewish ethnic culture from Holland, France, Germany, England, Poland, and Russia. Some, with business skills and a willingness to go alone into new communities, moved into small towns and cities, where they rapidly rose to middle-class status, though their religious culture set them apart from other middle-class people. Many others remained in big cities, where, although they now occupy a wide range of social-class positions, a significant proportion work mainly as factory workers. Today, the Jewish people themselves comprise a variegated set of cultural subgroups. Some have become liberal in their religious views; others have remained orthodox.

The Jews have probably made more use of education as a means of moving up in the social-class structure than has any other immigrant group, although education alone does not account for their mobility. According to studies by Sowell (1981), even when education is held constant, Jews as a group still outdistance non-Jews in occupational mobility.

Upward mobility among black Americans also has been substantial in recent decades. However, although the black middle class has greatly increased, many blacks are trapped in the big-city underclass. This situation is discussed extensively in Chapters 2 and 10 and also elsewhere in this book.

Japanese immigrants who settled on the Pacific coast and who had lived in islands of Japanese culture were dispersed by the relocation measures of World War II. Possessing personal habits that were acceptable to our middle class and having valuable skills, they moved into the cities of the Midwest at lower middle-class and upper working-class levels.

The displaced persons who fled into Germany at the close of World War II from Lithuania, Estonia, and Latvia and later came to the United States, were mainly middle-class people. So also were the Hungarian refugees of the mid-1950s. Although they took whatever working-class jobs they could get, they quickly integrated themselves into the culture of the United States. Their children adopted middle-class ways of life relatively quickly.

During the 1960s, 1970s, and 1980s, there was substantial in-migration of Hispanics and Asians. Most Hispanic immigration has been from Mexico and Cuba, but some has been from South America. Asian immigrants have come particularly from Southeast Asia—Vietnam, Laos, and Cambodia; but significant numbers of in-migrants have also come from Korea and the Philippines. Mexican immigrants have tended to be low status and unskilled, whereas many of the immigrants from Cuba and the various Asian countries have been persons with relatively high levels of education and occupational skills. In the 1970s, immigrants from Russia, Israel, and other countries also had relatively high skill levels. Because the immigration laws generally require that applicants possess skills or contacts likely to result in gainful employment, immigrants who enter the United States legally tend to be in a relatively good position to pursue social mobility for themselves and their children, compared to most who came during the high tide of immigration before 1920.

Thomas Sowell (1981) has studied the research on ethnic patterns of immigration and mobility in the United States. He cites many studies and historical records to support the following conclusions:

> *Perhaps the most striking pattern among American ethnic groups is their general rise in economic conditions with the passage of time. . . . In many parts of the world, people still live at an economic level not much above that of their ancestors. But in addition to absolute rises in living standards . . . American ethnic groups have typically also risen in relative terms.*
>
> *Every ethnic group has encountered obstacles to its progress. But the obstacles and suffering they experienced before arriving here usually exceeded anything experienced on American soil. Anti-Semitism in the United States meant encountering snobbery and occupational restrictions, but not living under the threat of mass expulsions and massacres. Even . . . slavery was worse for Africans enslaved to the Arabs or in the rest of the Western Hemisphere, where slaves died off faster than they could reproduce. In short, America has never been exempt from the age-old sins that have plagued the human species. What has been distinctively American is the extent to which other factors have also been at work, usually for the better. (p. 275)*

Differences in Group Status and Mobility

Various ethnic groups have differed in the rates with which they have moved up the social scale. Among immigrant groups in the northeastern section of the United States, for instance, the Greeks as well as the Jews attained middle-class status more quickly than did French Canadians or southern Italians (Strodtbeck 1958; Rosen 1959).

There are probably several reasons for such differences. One is the extent to which the immigrant group possesses certain work skills that are valuable in the economy; another is the degree to which the dominant group is willing to permit newcomers equal access to jobs, housing, and schooling; another is the differences between the immigrant groups in psychological and cultural orientations toward achievement. In a study of six ethnic and racial groups (Rosen 1959), historical and ethnographic data showed that differences between the groups in achievement motivation, values, and aspirations existed before these groups arrived in the United States, and that these differences tended to persist. The differences are related to the variations among the groups in rates of upward mobility.

Demographic and cultural considerations also play a part in determining the amount and rate of a group's mobility. Some of these considerations include the following:

Age structure. Groups that have a relatively high proportion of young people, as do Mexican Americans and Puerto Ricans today, are likely to have lower than average mobility because many members are just getting started in occupations and careers;

Region. Although differences in wealth, education, and other indicators of status in regions of the United States are diminishing, these differences are still important; thus, groups such as Mexican Americans that are concentrated in the southwest will score lower on many socioeconomic measures;

Fertility. Historically and still today, high fertility rates and large numbers of children per family not only reflect poverty but also help perpetuate it (Kasarda and Billy 1985). Groups such as black Americans and Hispanic Americans, which have higher than average fertility rates and relatively low incomes, will have problems transmitting socioeconomic advantages to their children;

Circumstances involving in-migration. Those groups that have been in the United States longest will have had more time to become mobile, and those that enter under favorable conditions will have relatively greater opportunities for mobility. In this regard, Sowell (1978a, 1978b, 1981) has pointed out that black Americans from the West Indies rank above the United States average in social status, whereas "native" blacks rank far below. Sowell believes that the reasons for this difference involve historical patterns wherein slaves in the United States were made dependent on external support and were deprived of opportunities to obtain educational and occupational skills. Even though slavery in the West Indies was in some ways even more harsh and brutal, he argues, its effects were not so systematically perpetuated in terms of dependency and related cultural patterns. In addition, blacks who migrated to the United States from the West Indies were among the most ambitious and motivated persons in their original communities, a pattern that also has characterized other ethnic groups.

Geographic concentration. Differences in the degree to which ethnic groups are concentrated in a geographic area or are in high- or low-density settlements may also have effects on mobility. These effects can vary according to group history and circumstances. For some groups, concentration in a community can contribute to mobility through reinforcement of intergroup contacts and support, provided that opportunities for mobility are present in the society and group cohesion is not stressed to the exclusion of contact with the mainstream. For other groups, effects may be largely negative, particularly if the group is low in status and geographic concentration reinforces its separation from the larger society (Hacker 1988).

Consistency among socializing institutions. Many social scientists believe that the degree to which there is consistency among institutions that socialize children and youth plays an important part in determining whether the group will be successful in the educational system and the society. For example, De Vos (1982) has studied the family and the peer group in several cultures and concluded that consistency among the peer group, the family, and the school is a major force in determining whether youth will take advantage of educational and economic opportunities in postindustrial society. "What one sees in contemporary Japan as well as in many Japanese-American children in the United States," De Vos observes, "is a peer-group orientation that mutually reinforces" an intense educational commitment developed in the family and the school (p. 97).

De Vos further points out that the development of and interactions between socializing institutions reflect an ethnic group's relationships to the larger society. If adults in the group are powerless or discriminated against in the larger society, then young people may be relatively less willing to follow their parents' entreaties to work hard in school and the economy; in this case, the peer group may be especially at odds with the family and the school (also see Ogbu 1978; 1982). If both family and peer group encourage teenage males to be aggressive but the school stresses passivity, education may not function effectively as a route to economic mobility. These types of inconsistencies—particularly among disadvantaged minority groups—are described more fully in Chapter 5 and elsewhere in this book.

The preceding examples raise the question of how group characteristics involving ethnicity and race are related to social class in affecting status and mobility. Clearly, a group's opportunity for mobility reflects its participation in and situation as an ethnic or racial group in the larger society. Just as clearly, a group's social class standing influences its participation and opportunity in society.

Stephen Steinberg (1981) has been studying this issue and has reached the conclusion that social class interacts with race and ethnicity in determining group status and mobility. Steinberg's book *The Ethnic Myth* points out that the historic position of ethnic and racial groups within the social class structure has played a major part in determining whether they would succeed economically. Black Americans, for example, were denied opportunities to own land in the rural South and to compete for industrial employment in the nineteenth and early twentieth centuries. Other groups, such as Jews from Eastern Europe, were not as hampered by social forces that maintained low social class status among blacks in the United States. Some of Steinberg's major conclusions in this regard are as follows:

> *Where the class theory differs from the cultural theory is in its emphasis on the* primacy *of class factors . . . cultural factors have little independent effect on educational outcomes, but are influential only as they interact with class factors. Thus, to whatever extent a reverence for learning was part of the religious and cultural heritage of Asians and Jews, it was . . . given existential significance by their social class circumstances . . . without which it is hardly conceivable that these groups could have sustained their traditional value on education. . . . Had immigrant Jews remained in poverty and deprived of educational opportunities, it is unlikely that Jewish intellectual life would have advanced beyond the archaic scholasticism . . . carried over from Europe. Conversely, other immigrant groups that started out with less favorable cultural dispositions with respect to education rapidly developed an appetite for education once they achieved a position in the class system comparable to that of Jews a generation earlier. . . . As in the case of Jews, Catholics had to secure an economic foothold before their children could make significant advances up the economic ladder. (Steinberg 1981, 132, 138, 144)*

Differences in group status are evident in Table 7.2, which shows whether groups are above or below the national average as measured by the occupational status scores on a scale of 2 (coal miner) to 96 (physician) of men ages twenty-one to sixty-four in a national study conducted in 1973 (Featherman and Hauser 1978). Hispanic groups and blacks were far below the national average of 40; men whose background was from English-speaking countries, Russia, and China or Japan were substantially above the average. However, taking account of years of schooling, father's occupation, and generational status (number of generations in the United States) greatly reduces group differences from the national mean. This finding means not only that groups low in social status generally are low in social background (as measured by father's occupation), education, and generational status; it also indicates that low status is transmitted by or through low status background, low educational level, and recency of immigration to the United States. The implications of this pattern are analyzed and discussed in the next chapter and elsewhere in this book.

Table 7.2 shows that several racial-ethnic minority groups—namely, the black and the Hispanic populations—are seriously disadvantaged in socioeconomic status. One must keep in mind that a large proportion of both groups is

Table 7.2 *Occupational Status of National Heritage Groups, U.S. Men Aged Twenty-One to Sixty-Four, 1973*

Group	Difference from the National Mean	
	Gross Difference	*Considering Education, Father's Occupation, and Generational Status*
Mexican	−16.01	−4.60
Puerto Rican	−14.70	−3.09
"Other" (includes blacks)	−7.10	−2.14
Italy	−.36	−1.03
Ireland	.96	1.21
Germany	1.92	.61
Poland	3.12	.83
England, Scotland, Wales	7.03	2.74
USSR (includes Jews)	15.04	3.20

Source: Adapted from Featherman and Hauser 1978.

now urban but was living in rural poverty only one or two generations ago. As regards black Americans, Sowell (1981) has pointed out that massive movement from the rural south to cities in the 1940–1970 period constituted the kind of "traumatic social change" that required generations of adjustment among other ethnic groups: "The social pathology that other groups experienced—violence, alcoholism, crime, delinquency—all reappeared in the transplanted black populations of the cities" (p. 211). Sowell also points out that established middle-class black families in the cities tended to separate themselves from the newly urbanized migrants, but forces generating segregation have concentrated both middle- and low-status blacks in racial ghettos in the core parts of metropolitan areas. Results and implications of this pattern are analyzed in detail in succeeding chapters.

The Extent of Mobility in the United States

Returning now to individual mobility, its extent can be studied by measuring the degree and kinds of mobility that have occurred within the lifetimes of adults.

Several studies have been made of the family socioeconomic origins of certain occupational groups. For example, a major study has been carried out by Featherman and Hauser (1978), using data from two large national surveys in 1962 and 1973. Both surveys included men from 21 to 64 years of age, thus the time period included in the study spanned the entire twentieth century. The focus of the study was on occupational status, as measured by Duncan scale scores ranging from 2 to 96 and by 17 groupings of occupations arranged hierarchically. Socioeconomic status (i.e., social class) was designated by five groupings of occupational strata including these seventeen occupation categories:

I. *Upper Nonmanual:* 1) Professionals, self-employed; 2) Professionals, salaried; 3) Managers; 4) Salesmen, other.
II. *Lower Nonmanual:* 5) Proprietors; 6) Clerks; 7) Salesmen, retail.
III. *Upper manual:* 8) Craftsmen, manufacturing; 9) Craftsmen, other; 10) Craftsmen, construction.
IV. *Lower manual.* 11) Service; 12) Operatives, other; 13) Operatives, manufacturing; 14) Laborers, manufacturing; 15) Laborers, other.
V. *Farm:* 16) Farmers; 17) Farm laborers.

There are many difficulties in conducting this type of research, including problems in collecting data and measuring occupations, ambiguity in measuring "mobility," uncertainty in interpreting floor and ceiling effects, and selection of statistics to analyze and portray complicated situations. Featherman and Hauser worked out sophisticated methods that seem to be an improvement over previous research and reported the following data as regards mobility for men in 1962 and 1973 across the five social-class strata and the seventeen occupational-status categories: in both years, approximately 51 percent of the men had moved up across stratum boundaries and 60 percent had moved up in occupational categories. Fifteen percent of the men in 1962 and 17 percent in 1973 had moved down in stratum level, and 24 percent in 1962 and 26 percent in 1973 had moved down in occupational category. Among the major conclusions Featherman and Hauser drew from their data and analysis were the following:

— there has been a trend toward greater occupational mobility in the United States. Although there was little change between 1962 and 1973 from the father's job to the son's first job, mobility from the first job to current occupation has increased.

— upward mobility is much more common than is downward mobility.

— trends in mobility are partly but not entirely explained by change in occupational distribution. That is, though some mobility has occurred largely because there are relatively more high-status jobs than there used to be, some mobility seems to be due to opportunity for sons to advance beyond their fathers' occupations.

— there is great immobility at the top and bottom of the occupational hierarchy, among the upper nonmanual and the farm occupations, respectively. (Relative immobility at the top is not unexpected since children of upper-status families have nowhere to move but down.) According to Featherman and Hauser, this immobility is "far more extreme than had heretofore been supposed by most students of the mobility process; it may even be consistent with the beliefs of the most extreme critics of rigidity in the American class structure" (p. 179).

— there is also considerable immobility into or out of occupations adjacent to the top and bottom. "In this sense," Featherman and Hauser conclude, the data "suggest the existence of barriers to movement across class boundaries" (p. 179).

— on the other hand, there is very little immobility in the middle range of occupations, from upper blue-collar through middle-class, white-collar jobs. In particular, there is "no evidence" of class boundaries "limiting the chances of movement to or from the skilled manual occupations" (p. 180).

— historically, mobility rose for groups entering the labor market from the 1920s to 1940, declined during the war years, rose again after World War II, and then gradually dropped to the pre-Depression level in the early 1960s.

Studies reviewed here indicate that there has been considerable upward mobility in the United States during the twentieth century. Although there has been relatively less upward mobility from the lowest social class positions and although opportunities for mobility have increased or decreased in accordance with economic conditions, technological change, population growth or decline, and other factors, it may generally be concluded that the social structure in the United States is not hardening in the sense that class lines have become systematically and consistently more rigid at all levels of the social structure.

Net Mobility versus Exchange Mobility

In an open society with relatively free educational opportunity and with a tradition favoring social mobility, the amount of individual mobility is relatively high. Upward and downward mobility, considered together, can be called *exchange mobility*. The amount of one kind of mobility over the other can be called *net mobility*.

The amount of exchange mobility may be a better index of equity in a society than is the amount of upward mobility. Exchange mobility signifies openness to individual mobility and therefore signifies that people succeed in relation to their ability and effort. A society may have considerable exchange mobility and yet, if industrialization is not rapid and if upward and downward mobility are approximately equal, there may be very little net upward mobility. Glass (1954) found this condition to exist in Great Britain between 1920 and 1950. During that time, given the more rapid economic and industrial expansion in the United States, it probably required less intelligence, drive, and social effectiveness to be upwardly mobile in the United States than it required to be upwardly mobile in Great Britain. For the same set of reasons, those who were downwardly mobile in the United States were probably less able and less ambitious than those who were downwardly mobile in Great Britain.

Reviewing Featherman and Hauser's 1973 data on social-class movement across five occupational strata, the rate of exchange mobility was 68 percent (51 percent up and 17 percent down); the net rate of upward mobility was 34 percent. Goldthorpe (1980) and his colleagues have carried out a similar analysis using 1972 data from a national survey in Great Britain. After classifying occupations into seven social class categories and then determining the amount of mobility into and out of three larger groupings (classes 1 plus 2; 3, 4, and 5; and 6 plus 7), they found that 32 percent of the men in their sample had been upward mobile and 17 percent had been downward mobile. Thus, the exchange mobility rate was 59 percent, and net upward mobility was 15 percent.

Caution must be exercised in comparing these figures with data from the United States due to differences in collecting, analyzing, and interpreting the information; however, the data do suggest that while there has been substantial mobility in both the United States and Britain, there probably has been greater exchange mobility and net upward mobility in the United States. The American situation has involved a substantial degree of technological mobility. Future decades may see less upward mobility due to technology, and therefore less net upward mobility in the United States. This would signify a decrease of opportunity, though it need not mean that equity will decline if opportunity is based on ability and merit.

Recent trends suggest that economic recession combined with increasingly rapid computerization and automation in the late 1970s and 1980s may now be generating a significant increase in downward mobility. Some observers believe that many blue-collar workers have lost relatively high-paying jobs as manufacturing industry has declined, and that many middle-class employees are being squeezed out of well-paid jobs by technological change. For the first time in our history, the next generation of workers may end up in lower status positions than their parents. Michael Harrington, author of an influential 1964 book that generated support for the federal antipoverty programs of the late 1960s, has been examining recent trends and has reached the following conclusions:

> *Upward social mobility has been, in theory and even in practice, the American answer to the problem of inequality. Even when there was no change in social position, a growing national product made it possible for almost everyone to make some gains.*
>
> *The people in McKeesport and throughout 'smokestack' America are discovering that this postwar pattern no longer holds. But what if middle-class people—those who had been confidently heading for the professions and executive suites—make the same bitter discovery?*
>
> *The real middle class would be foolish to observe these events as if they were a play staged by working people. The social insecurity of these times is going to hit the suburbs as well as the mill towns. We, dear reader, are 'they'; our slope is getting more slippery by the day.* (Harrington 1983, 53)

A low degree of net or upward mobility is interpreted as a hardening of the social structure and a lessening of opportunity. On the other hand, too high a degree of mobility may indicate a revolutionary or chaotic quality in the society. The latter may be unhealthy because people cannot count on holding and passing on to their children the gains they have made. No one can say what precise degree of individual mobility would be most desirable in a modern society, but there would probably be general agreement that the present amount of mobility in the United States generally should not decrease and should be enhanced for the working class and, particularly, for the underclass.

Education, Opportunity, and Mobility

Confirmation that there is still substantial upward mobility in the United States does not in itself indicate whether the United States is now a meritocratic society in which most young people have realistic opportunities to succeed socioeconomically in accordance with their abilities and efforts. The facts are clear that the social-class position held by a young person growing into adulthood is determined to a significant extent by how the parents rear the child and by what economic assistance is given. Parents who are in middle- or upper-class positions naturally do a great deal to pass their favored status on to their children. Many working-class parents also are of significant help to their children, though they cannot give much economic assistance.

The school system seeks to help young people from lower-status families rise on the social scale, and the extent to which a society is meritocratic depends partly on how effective the educational system is in this effort. Thus, the social class of young adults is determined partly by what they make out of their schooling, and partly by their social class origins. The preceding sections present evidence indicating that many young people do use education to overcome disadvantages associated with their family background, but a more systematic examination of the issue and of the role of the schools in advancing or retarding opportunity requires additional analysis.

Sociologists have been active in conducting research on these topics, especially since about 1960. Research has attempted to find out how mobility is related to the socioeconomic status of an individual's family, mental ability, level of school achievement, and the kind of schools he or she attends. Researchers also have attempted to determine whether the schools and other social institutions function to provide opportunities on a meritocratic basis.

An extensive review of the research on social mobility and education was reported in 1976 by Shea, with a set of approximately 150 references. Shea summarizes the consensus of these studies as follows: "An increasing body of evidence suggests that schooling is indeed meritocratic, i.e., operates in a classless way to make destination status independent of origin status" (p. 511). Featherman and Hauser's studies (1976, 1978) of 1962 and 1973 data on the occupational status of adult men further support the conclusion that education increasingly is functioning to provide mobility for many persons. However, the authors found that education also is implicated in the transmission of low status from one generation to the next: although more Americans are acquiring more years of education and although more education yields more occupational status, the greatest payoff now comes from acquisition of a college education, and individuals from low-status families are less likely to go to college than are those from high-status families:

> *Demands for a more highly skilled labor force, rising GNP, and more favorable social origins combined . . . to enable ever larger fractions of each cohort to attend high school. But . . . the historical educational differentials by socioeconomic status have not disappeared. Rather, they have shifted from the precollege to college years. (Featherman and Hauser 1978, 302)*

On the other hand, Featherman and Hauser also stress the conclusion that the relationship between social origins and college attainment is far from perfect (p. 251). In addition, it should be kept in mind that gains in higher education for the disadvantaged that may have been associated with open admissions policies, increasing federal support for students, and other equalizing measures in the 1970s could not have had much effect on the 1973 data.

Jencks and his colleagues (1972, 1979) also have been studying the relationships between family background, education, and occupational attainment and additionally have tried to delineate relationships of these variables with data on the earnings of adult men. Using the 1962 and 1973 data sets analyzed by Featherman and Hauser as well as nine other major United States sources of data collected in the 1960s and 1970s, Jencks's 1979 book, *Who Gets Ahead? The Determinants of Economic Success in America*, concluded that family background accounts for nearly half of the variation in occupational status and somewhere between 15 and 35 percent of the variation in earnings, depending on the nature of the data available and the statistical approach used in analysis. Family background and amount of education, which, of course, is related to family background, together explain 55 percent of the variation in occupational attainment. Other conclusions involving the relationships between family background and education on the one hand and occupational attainment and earnings on the other included the following.

1. Men from advantaged families have more cognitive skills and noncognitive traits valued by employers.
2. Comparing men with similar cognitive and noncognitive traits, those from advantaged families have more education than do men from disadvantaged families.
3. Men from advantaged families are relatively successful economically partly because they obtain more education than do men from disadvantaged families.

In addition to confirming Featherman and Hauser's conclusion that higher education has become the more important factor (as compared to acquisition of a high school diploma) in influencing later career success and in translating high status background into occupational attainment, Jencks and his colleagues analyzed data on cognitive skills (e.g., IQ scores) and noncognitive traits (such as are measured in teachers' ratings of students' personality traits) in examining the question of whether the schools and society are providing equal opportunity on a meritocratic basis for talented and motivated students. Their major conclusions included the following:

> *If we define 'equal opportunity' as a situation in which sons born into different families have the same chances of success, our data show that America comes nowhere near achieving it. . . . But . . . in contemporary America . . . inequality between families or individuals is acceptable so long as it derives from 'merit' of some sort. We doubt that merit runs in families to anything like the extent necessary to reconcile our results with 'meritocracy.' But our data do not speak on this issue directly.*
>
> *We have shown, for example, that a nontrivial fraction of background's effect on success derives from the fact that background affects cognitive skills. But it is not clear that cognitive skills are, or should be, synonymous with 'merit.' . . . The same logic applies to educational attainment. Educational credentials are essential for obtaining some lucrative jobs. But it does not follow that educational credentials* ought *to be essential for these jobs. . . . Our surveys do not measure these attitudes or values [associated with success in obtaining top jobs]. . . . Without evidence on this, our data constitute neither an indictment nor an endorsement of the status quo. (Jencks et al. 1979, 82–83)*

It should be noted that Jencks and others who have been studying relationships between family background, education, and occupational or economic attainment have been examining data collected before the mid-1970s. Thus, *Who Gets Ahead?* concludes with the statement that "past efforts" through education and other efforts aimed at "equalizing the personal characteristics known to affect income have been relatively ineffective." As pointed out in Chapter 8 and elsewhere in this book, compensatory education to overcome the disadvantages of low-status students has been relatively unsuccessful on a national basis, but much has been learned concerning the changes needed to make it more successful in providing more effective and equal educational opportunity. Definitive conclusions about the equity and adequacy of education in helping accomplish the fundamental goals of United States society therefore will depend on the success of efforts to improve compensatory education in the future.

Results of mobility studies in other Western nations also indicate that the structure of society is stable enough to encourage people to expect to pass on their social-class position to their children, while there is enough individual social mobility to change the composition of the social classes as many individuals move from one class to another. Assessing studies conducted in the 1950s in Britain and in the 1960s in France, Boudon (1973) concluded that both a "meritocratic and a social heritage effect appear very clearly. . . . Let us be content to note that both effects seemed to be relatively important" in both societies.

A major analysis of family background, education, and occupational attainment in Great Britain has been conducted by Halsey, Heath, and Ridge (1980); conclusions were basically similar to those reported above. However, the authors also conclude that whereas higher education in the United States is now the attainment point that best distinguishes the advantaged from the disadvantaged, in Great Britain the comparable dividing line is still at the secondary level:

> *Cultural capital influences selection for secondary school, but thereafter its importance is minimal. . . . This picture of unequal access to the superior secondary schools has remained depressingly constant over time. For the selective schools as a group, chances of access rose at all levels in the middle of our period, leading to some slight narrowing of class differentials, but then they fell back again to levels like those of a generation earlier. . . . In summary, school inequalities of opportunity have been remarkably stable over the forty years which our study covers. Throughout, the service [white-collar] class has had roughly three times the chance of the working class of getting some kind of selective secondary schooling. (Halsey, Heath, and Ridge 1980, 200, 203, 205)*

Schools Both Perpetuate and Modify the Social Class Structure

The preceding sections indicate that many young people use education to become upwardly mobile, but we also have seen that many lower-status students are disadvantaged before they ever enter school and are not able to achieve much success through the schools or other social institutions. There is no logical reason to believe that the schools cannot function both as a route to mobility for some students and a barrier for others, even though some social scientists and educators habitually speak of the "educational system" as being either a force for meritocracy and egalitarianism or a means by which the existing social structure perpetuates itself.

Nor is there a logical contradiction in the conclusion that the schools are becoming more of a force for upward mobility than they have been in the past and at the same time are becoming more of a barrier to the mobility of some segments of the population. Indeed, this is exactly what one would expect if the schools are playing a larger part in the mobility process than they did before. In this case, both the mobility generating and the mobility limiting roles of the school could be simultaneously more pronounced. We shall see that there is evidence for accepting both propositions.

Preceding sections have noted that the educational system as a whole does appear to be an increasingly important part of the social mobility process. This is not surprising inasmuch as industrial society places growing emphasis on the attainment both of the skills acquired in elementary, secondary, and higher education and on the education credentials that presumably provide short-hand certification that a person has acquired the skills for a given job. Evidence for the growing importance of education has been provided by a variety of studies in several western nations, particularly the United States.

However, it is still true that the family also helps determine the amount of education its children receive, more in some countries than in others. For instance, in Great Britain, family status has been more closely linked to educational level of the children than in the United States. A 1972 British study conducted at Nuffield College (Halsey 1976) suggests that the effects of education on mobility in recent decades may have been as much or more in the direction of perpetuating as unfreezing the social class structure.

> *Clearly there are both ascriptive and achievement forces at work in the passing of occupational status between generations. We live neither in a caste society nor one in which the generations are severed from each other by random reallocation of status. . . . What has happened is the weighting of the dice of social opportunity according to class, and "the game" is increasingly played through strategies of child rearing refereed by schools through their certifying arrangements. The direct effect of the class hierarchy of families on educational opportunity and certification has* risen *since the war. And at the same time the articulation of education to the first entry into the labor market has been tightening. Thus education is increasingly the mediator of the transmission of status between generations. It commands the passage from school to work more completely than it did a generation ago, and it is a mediator with power independent of the family. Institutionally, education is the principal agent of achievement. (p. 184)*

The school's role in bringing about mobility and/or transmitting status appears to depend on a variety of factors, such as the characteristics and development of the society in which it functions, the definition of mobility and status attainment, and the social subgroups that are studied. For example, Tinto (1981) studied the 1968 occupational status of 1961 male college graduates and found that variables such as father's status and type of college attended accounted for much of the variation in status of men in professional occupations but almost none for the men in business-managerial occupations.

The Transmission of Status

How is social status transmitted from one generation to the next? This can be seen both as a simple process involving mainly the family and a more complicated process involving schools and the economic and political systems of a society (Holmes 1988). Practically everyone realizes that growing up in a low-income environment is not conducive to attaining higher social status later and that high-status families pass on certain advantages to their children. The resources that families and society make available to promote the development of children and youth and that are related to their success in the school and other institutions are clear in their broad outlines. These resources include:

- Material resources, useful or necessary for success in later life.
- Values and attitudes, which help determine how one behaves in social institutions.

- Knowledge and understandings, required for success in socializing institutions, particularly the school.
- Cognitive and verbal skills, required for success in the school.

Material Resources. Much of the process of status transmission involves the transfer and use of material resources that help young people get a good start toward achieving or maintaining middle- or upper-status positions in society. Material resources can take such forms as funds spent on helping children do well in school through tutoring or the pursuit of intellectually enriching hobbies, financial support to remain in high school or attend college, assistance in establishing a business or entering a profession, or availability of time to work with teachers in establishing positive home-school relationships (Lareau 1987). Resources include contact with adults who can provide a youngster with a part-time job, family acquaintances who can help gain admission to professional training or full-time employment when jobs are scarce, and guidance or role models in deciding what career to pursue and how to go about preparing for it.

Values and Attitudes. Children in differing social classes grow up not only with different levels of material support but also with different attitudes toward society and the schools. An important description of the overall process by which low status is transmitted through values and attitudes passed on from one generation to another has been worked out by sociologist Melvin L. Kohn, who collected and analyzed data on the values, status, and child-raising orientation of men and women in Washington, D.C., and in Turin, Italy. Kohn began by asking parents to pick the characteristic they valued most highly in their children and then compared the responses of parents of differing social classes. The data showed that middle-status parents placed relatively more value than did low-status parents on having their children demonstrate interest in how and why things happen, whereas low-status parents placed relatively more emphasis on children being obedient and well mannered (Kohn 1969; 1987).

Kohn also found that middle-status men attached more importance than did low-status men to how important their work is, the amount of freedom they have at work, and the chance to use their abilities fully on the job. Understandably, low-status men attached relatively more importance than did middle-status respondents to pay, fringe benefits, and job security. "Self-direction," Kohn concluded, "is a central value for men of higher class position, who see themselves as competent members of an essentially benign society. Conformity is a central value for men of lower class position, who . . . [have] an orientational system premised on the dangers of stepping out of line." (Kohn 1969; 1987).

Kohn interpreted his data along with information he and his colleagues have collected since the original studies to mean that the conditions of middle-class life, particularly on the job, tend to place a high value on self-direction and intellectual flexibility. Middle-class parents not only perceive that these qualities are important for success but also become committed to them as values in their own right. Their methods of child-rearing reflect these values, with emphasis on rearing children to function independently in an intellectually complex world.

Working-class parents, by way of contrast, tend to emphasize obedience and conformity to accepted opinion, placing little stress in their child rearing on the development of intellectual flexibility and self-direction. The demands of the job thus generate values and attitudes that parents strive to pass on to their children (Kohn and Schooler 1973).

The conclusions regarding middle-class versus working-class emphasis on the value of self-direction versus conformity agree with the results of decades of research on differences in child-raising practices between classes. As long ago as 1958, Bronfenbrenner summarized twenty-five years of research on this theme:

> *The data on the training of the young child show middle-class mothers, especially in the postwar period, to be consistently more permissive toward the child's expressed needs and wishes. The generalization applies in such diverse areas as oral behavior, toilet accidents, dependency, sex, aggressiveness, and freedom of movement outside the home. . . .*
>
> *In matters of discipline, working-class parents are consistently more likely to employ physical punishment, while middle-class families rely more on reasoning, isolation, appeals to guilt, and other methods involving the threat of loss of love. At least two independent lines of evidence suggest that the techniques preferred by middle-class parents are more likely to bring about the development of internalized values and controls. . . .*
>
> *Over the entire 25-year period studied, parent-child relationships in the middle class are consistently reported as more acceptant and equalitarian, while those in the working class are oriented toward maintaining order and obedience. (See Maccoby, 1958, 424–425)*

There is reason to believe that working-class values and child-rearing practices have shifted slightly away from a stress on order and obedience since the 1940s and 1950s. This is not very surprising inasmuch as Bronfenbrenner found that working-class values in child-rearing tended to be influenced by middle-class patterns becoming dominant in the mass media, reflecting the recommendations of prominent authors of books on child care. For example, a general shift toward greater emphasis on self-direction in parental values for children was reported in 1976 by Wright and Wright based on a national sample of data collected in 1973. It is not clear to what degree this shift represented changes in the occupational and educational structures of the United States population (a relatively higher proportion of middle-class population) or some actual change in values within social classes, but in any case the overall results clearly confirmed Kohn's original conclusions regarding differential emphasis on self-direction and on conformity across social classes.

Knowledge and Understanding. Socialization for success in an industrial society can be seen as learning to participate in an ever-expanding social environment. The social environment, in turn, can be viewed in terms of the life space in which a child or an adolescent lives and grows. The concept of life space, as used here, involves physical space and the objects contained within that space, the people who inhabit that space, and the psychological sense of freedom or constraint in exploring and expanding one's social and intellectual environment.

The life space of the growing individual expands—from the crib, to the living room, to the street in front of the house, to the neighborhood, and then to the community. From here, it enlarges partly through the child's travel experience and partly through vicarious experiences by way of movies, television, magazines, books, maps, and geography lessons. At the same time, the child's psychological and intellectual life space expands to include new ideas, new attitudes, and new values.

It is obvious that neighborhoods and communities vary in the extent to which they provide a variety of opportunities for learning. Cohen (1981), for example, has shown how English parents moving from working-class neighborhoods to a new middle-class housing estate developed a "collective estate culture and life-style" conducive to the academic success of their children, and how mothers both adapted their child-raising methods and worked with the local elementary school to achieve this goal. Sociocultural patterns developed by the parents included segregating children from nearby working-class neighborhoods, grooming children for success beginning at an early age, sharing of responsibility for education-oriented child-development activities, and providing a variety of growth experiences for children.

In a study of families who live in a large public housing project in Chicago, mothers often reported to the interviewers that their ten-year-olds were not allowed out of the apartment alone, except to go back and forth from school; or they were limited to playing on the small balcony of the apartment. Often these children were not allowed even to play in the playgrounds below, because, as one mother said, "I can't keep my eyes on him all the time, up here on the tenth floor; and he might get into trouble with some of the bad kids that live in this project."

Another mother said, "I tell her she can't walk through this neighborhood. It isn't safe. Especially she is *not* to play in the elevators or on the stairs of this building. That means she can watch television, and she can do her school work, and she can wait for me or her daddy to take her out. Of course I don't get out much because of the younger kids. . . ."

One interviewer reported an extreme case in one of these families: "There are four children, all under five. Each time I arrived, all four were lined up on the bed, watching television and not moving. I couldn't get even the oldest one to respond to me, even after several visits and after I tried repeatedly to bribe him with candy. I couldn't lure him from the fixed position on the bed."

A middle-class mother, on the other hand, living within several blocks of the same housing project, described to the same interviewer the activities of her ten-year-old daughter: "She has to check in after school, of course, but then she usually goes down the block to play with her friend . . . or else the two get on their bicycles. (Interviewer: Where do they go?) Oh, around the neighborhood. Sometimes they ride over to the lake. They have to stay on the streets, of course, and they have to be home by five o'clock. They don't go into any deserted areas. But they're sensible by this age, and I don't worry. Then one day a week she takes the bus after school and goes to her piano lessons . . . and on Saturdays she goes down to the Art Institute for her art class. . . ."

These considerations indicate that young middle-class children are likely to acquire more knowledge of the world outside their home and immediate neighborhood than are working-class children. This knowledge becomes important when children enter school and when they are required in later years to make choices concerning their educational and vocational careers.

Cognitive and Verbal Skills. The child-rearing practices of the middle class favor a more rapid development of cognitive skills than do those of the working class. This is a conclusion reached by Edward Zigler, who ended a systematic review of social class influences on cognitive development (1970) with the statement: "There are real class differences in intellectual functioning and these are produced by class differences in environment." According to Zigler, there is a general developmental sequence in cognitive function that is common to all social classes, but the middle-class children move along this sequence more rapidly than do lower-class children; and lower-class children may end up at a lower level as adults.

In addition to being at a disadvantage in mastering cognitive skills, which are needed to understand the increasingly abstract material children encounter as they proceed through school, working-class children tend to lag behind middle-class children in mastering standard English, or, in other countries, whichever formal language is the primary medium of communication for learning in the classroom. Moreover, mastery of verbal skills in the language of the school probably is related to development of cognitive skills inasmuch as the student whose linguistic preparation does not allow for clear understanding of classroom material is placed at an additional disadvantage in trying to understand and manipulate concepts inherent in the material (Heath 1983; Heath and McLaughlin 1987).

How verbal patterns handicap students from working-class families has been studied by Bernstein (1961, 1975, 1986), who has analyzed the language used by working-class and middle-class children and found considerable differences. Children of both classes learn adequately the language of ordinary conversation, which is grammatically simple, uses stereotyped expressions, does not permit precise statement of ideas or emotions, and relies on gestures, inflection, and further explanation to make meaning clear. Bernstein calls this language "public," or "restricted." Middle-class children learn, in addition to the restricted language, what Bernstein calls the "formal" or "elaborated" language—the grammatically complex language of the schoolroom, which permits precise expression and provides greater potentiality for organizing experience than does the restricted language.

The elaborated language characteristic of many middle-class children is based on general principles that are relatively context-independent, as compared with the restricted language more typical of working-class children (Holland 1981). The child who learns only the restricted language, in Bernstein's view, is limited in his or her ability to learn new things and to interact with other people because one's language restricts the ability to organize experience. The child who masters the elaborated language possesses a tool that permits expression of complex ideas and distinctions between feelings and ideas.

In an effort to understand why some children learn a more elaborate language than others, Hess and Shipman (1965) studied the ways in which mothers teach their own four-year-old children. They found that the techniques used by mothers vary by the amount of education the mothers have had—and thus also by social class. The middle-class mothers, as compared with the working-class mothers, talked almost twice as much to their children in teaching them, and used more abstract words, more adjectives, more complex grammar, and longer sentences. Furthermore, they more frequently gave explicit instructions, let the children know what was expected of them, and praised them for their accomplishments. The children from the middle-class homes learned much better than did the children from the working-class homes; and the middle-class children were more frequently able to explain correctly the principle behind the task they had learned.

Later studies further specified some ways in which working-class children are disadvantaged because of language development in the home. Snow, Dubber, and De Blauw (1982) have found that middle-class mothers are more likely than working-class mothers to establish intellectually productive conversational *routines* and to provide *responsive talk* that is semantically contingent on the child's own speech. Snow summarizes these differences in concluding that middle-class youngsters are more likely than working-class youngsters to learn "impersonal" and "relatively complex" language forms (1983, 185).

Analysis by Feagans (1982) and others indicates that school-like narratives and dialogues may be relatively infrequent in the homes of poverty children, thus placing them at a disadvantage when they enter school. In addition, Snow, Dubber, and De Blauw believe that problems associated with poverty may be even more important than are parent-child language interaction style *per se* in retarding the verbal development of children from low income homes: "Social class is a *package variable*, a shorthand term for describing many differences" in income, financial security, parental education and occupation, goals for children, access to interaction with parents, and parents' style of interaction with children. "It is not yet clear," they concluded, "to what extent and how these different components of social class differences may interact; whether, for example, a particular style of interaction with children is caused by financial insecurity or by the parents' ideology" (Snow, Dubber, and De Blauw 1982, 70).

The preceding analysis indicates that working-class children tend to be educationally and socially disadvantaged relative to middle-class children. Their families possess fewer material and nonmaterial resources that could help them succeed in school and later in life, and their attitudes, cognitive and verbal skills, and early experience in the world also tend to place them at a disadvantage in school and society. An excellent summary of the nature and implications of social class differences in child-rearing has been provided by John and Elizabeth Newson, based on their intensive study of 700 children and their parents in Nottingham, England:

> *Parents at the upper end of the social scale are more inclined* on principle *to use democratically based, highly verbal means of control, and this kind of discipline is likely to produce personalities who can both identify successfully with the system and use it for their own ends later on. At the bottom end of the scale . . . parents choose* on principle *to use a highly authoritarian, mainly non-verbal means of control, in which words are used more to threaten and bamboozle the child into obedience than to make him understand the rationale behind social behavior. . . . Thus the child born into the lowest social bracket has everything stacked against him* including his parents' principles of child upbringing *(1976, 406).*

In addition, differences in socialization by social class almost certainly are much more pronounced among parents who live in predominantly working-class or middle-class neighborhoods, as contrasted with relatively heterogeneous neighborhoods. Since metropolitan areas have become relatively more stratified (i.e., middle-class and working-class families live in different locations), social-class differences in socialization may be a more potent determinant of future success than was true in earlier periods.

Schools in the Upward Mobility Process

The process by which social mobility is attained through schools and other institutions has been painstakingly investigated by Alex Inkeles and his colleagues, who have been studying modernization in six developing countries (Argentina, Chile, East Pakistan, India, Israel, and Nigeria) as well as in other parts of the world. Inkeles has been trying to identify characteristics of the "modern man" and to determine how and why some people acquire the skills needed for upward mobility in an industrial or industrializing society and others do not. Even though he has carried out most of his research in developing nations, Inkeles and many other social scientists believe that the same process has occurred earlier and is still occurring among some segments of the population in industrialized nations. Inkeles and Smith (1974) have summarized the characteristics of the "modern man":

> *The modern man's character . . . may be summed up under four major headings. He is an informed participant citizen; he has a marked sense of personal efficacy; he is highly independent and autonomous in his relation to traditional sources of influence . . . and he is ready for new experiences and ideas, that is, he is relatively open-minded and cognitively flexible. . . . Our results provide definite evidence that . . . modern man is not just a construct in the mind of sociological theorists. He exists and can be identified with fair reliability within any population where our test can be applied. (p. 290)*

It is apparent that the "modern man" as defined by Inkeles and Smith tends to be well educated and resembles the middle-class or upwardly mobile type of individual whom Kohn portrayed as valuing and exemplifying self-direction and intellectual flexibility in his attitudes and his work. After examining the forces that seem to be most important in producing modernity and mobility, Inkeles and Smith summarized their conclusions:

> *Some of the institutions most commonly associated with the process of modernization failed to substantiate their claim to standing as important schools for making men modern. Most notable of these was the city, whose failure to qualify as an important independent modernizing influence was not corrected by taking into account either the size or the cosmopolitanism of different urban centers. . . .*
>
> *Since a whole set of institutions, including the school, the factory, and the mass media, all operated to make our men modern, the question arises: Must a nation be able to bring* all *these forces to bear, and do so simultaneously, in order to stimulate the development of individual modernity?*
>
> *. . . Our experience suggests that it is not necessary that all, or even most, of the more effective agencies be available and working simultaneously . . . any one modernizing institution seems to be able to operate independently of the others. (p. 311)*

Inkeles and his colleagues thus stress the conclusion that although the schools are not the only modernity-generating institution in modern society, they can have an effect even when nonschool conditions work against the acquisition of attitudes and behaviors associated with middle-class status and upward mobility (Inkeles et al., 1983). In addition, the conclusion that living in cities is not in itself a very potent generator of modernity implies that educational and economic opportunity and other social resources are needed to improve the condition of working-class people in big cities. These points are considered further in a later section of this chapter on mobility and the underclass, but first there is need to review some ways in which schools may function to help transmit low status from one generation to the next.

Schools in the Perpetuation of Low Status

We have seen that the schools appear to function effectively in helping many middle-class youth acquire skills and attitudes they will need later and that historically they have helped many working-class youth in the United States and elsewhere become upwardly mobile. This means that many working-class youth use the schools to retain respectable upper working-class status. Working-class children tend to enter school lacking some of the knowledge, attitudes, and skills that would help them succeed there; afterward, many of them are sorted at one or another level into career lines leading to blue-collar jobs similar in status to those of their parents. Middle-class students, by way of contrast, tend to enter school with a head start that they maintain in later years and then enter college to prepare for white-collar and professional jobs for which family and school have worked to prepare them.

In addition, there are other ways in which the schools may be thought of as actively helping to lock low-status youth into the same social class as that of their parents. To the extent that what is taught in school is not adapted as fully as possible to the special learning problems that many working-class students encounter in the classroom, the schools become as much a cause as a conduit of low status transmitted from generation to generation. To the extent that educators do not do everything they can to help working-class students develop their talents to the fullest in accordance with the demands and opportunities of a modern economy, the schools can be viewed as making an unnecessary and gratuitous contribution to the transmission of low status. These considerations are discussed much more fully in Chapter 13, but at this point we want to emphasize how the educational system helps reproduce low status if it groups working-class students into relatively homogeneous low-status schools and thereby helps isolate them from the wider society in which they will have to function later.

The issue of whether predominantly working-class schools handicap working-class students over and beyond the disadvantages associated with their family background has been extensively investigated in research examining attitudes and achievement of students in differing types of schools. Although some researchers disagree, most have reached the conclusion that working-class students who attend a middle- or mixed-class school tend to achieve more and develop more productive aspirations than do students of equivalent background who attend working-class schools. James S. Coleman and his colleagues (1966) reached this conclusion in carrying out one of the largest studies ever conducted on the schools or other social institutions. A number of other researchers have reached the same conclusion based either on their own data (e.g., Wilson 1967) or on years of additional analysis of the data collected by Coleman and his colleagues (Mosteller and Moynihan 1972; Mayeske et al. 1971).

Why is it that students in working-class schools tend to perform less satisfactorily than do working-class students in other types of schools? In part, the answer seems to involve a tendency for working-class students in middle-class or mixed-status schools to develop more adequate motivation than do working-class students in low-status schools. Researchers have shown that the influence of other students who are significant others in the sense of influencing a young person's attitudes and behaviors is nearly as important as the influence of parents in predicting school-related attitudes and behaviors (Alexander and McDill 1976; Shea 1976); thus, it seems probable that the influence of middle-class peers can make a valuable contribution to mobility among working-class youth.

Other ways in which predominantly working-class schools may hamper the status attainment process for their students involve the attitudes students develop in attending such schools and the classroom behaviors of students and teachers. At one time it was thought that students in working-class schools achieved poorly because they received fewer resources per pupil (books, teachers, etc.) than did mixed- or middle-class schools, but the Coleman report tended to discredit this as the only or major explanation, and federal as well as state funds for low-income schools have helped somewhat in equalizing the resources available in differing types of schools. The school's social environment is as important as or even more important than differences in physical resources in accounting for very low performance levels in working-class schools.

Negative social environments appear to be particularly problematical in inner-city schools attended by minority students: Coleman and his colleagues found that among black and Hispanic students, a sense of control over one's future and one's chances in life was more highly related to learning than was one's view of oneself as a competent learner; the reverse was true among white students. The latter pattern is what educators would predict, given the established fact that students who believe they can learn tend to perform better, other things being equal, than do students who say they are not capable of learning much in their classroom. It is reasonable to conclude that for minority students in working-class schools, and probably also for white students in the inner city as well, growing up in a predominantly low-status environment and/or attending a low-status school tends to generate feelings of exclusion and powerlessness that inhibit success both in school and later life.

In addition, teacher expectations for students tend to be lower in working-class than in middle-class schools. For a variety of reasons, it appears that students in working-class schools are not required to perform at a level as high as are students of comparable background in other types of schools (Payne 1984). Related to differences in student behavior patterns and teacher expectations (i.e., requirements), educational climates in schools differ according to the socioeconomic composition of the student body. These differences are explored more fully in Chapter 8, but at this point it is important to notice that there tends to be a much greater emphasis on external discipline in low-status schools than in high-status schools, whereas teachers in the latter schools stress independent work and self-discipline to a much greater extent than do teachers in low-status schools.

For example, Wilcox (1978) studied classrooms in so-called open elementary schools and found that despite the use of instruction emphasizing such approaches as multiple learning centers and individualized contracting with students, teachers used more "authoritarian control mechanisms" in working with lower-status than with higher-status classes. Similarly, Anyon (1980, 1983) studied students' work tasks in five elementary schools that differed greatly in social class: two working-class schools in which the majority of fathers were unskilled or semiskilled; a mixed-status school (which she called "middle class") in which most parents were well-paid blue-collar workers or were white-collar workers; an "affluent professional" school in which parents were predominantly upper middle-class professionals; and an "executive elite" school in which most of the fathers were high-level executives. Her descriptions of task assignments and activities in mathematics, language arts, social studies, and other subjects included the following portrayal of modal tendencies:

> *[In the* Working-class Schools] *work is following the steps of a procedure . . . usually mechanical, involving rote behavior . . . the children . . . [copied mathematical terms] in their notebooks. . . . Work in language arts is mechanics of*

> *punctuation, . . . capitalization, and the four kinds of sentences. . . . [In history, the teacher] put information . . . on the board and the children copied it. . . .*
>
> *[In the* Middle-class School] *work is getting the right answer. . . . One must follow the directions . . . but there is . . . some choice, some decision making. . . . [In math] one may do two-digit division the long way, or the short way. . . . In social studies the daily work is to read the assigned pages . . . and answer the teacher's questions. . . .*
>
> *[In the* Affluent Professional School] *work is creative activity carried out independently. The students are continually asked to express and apply ideas and concepts. . . . [In history, children] wrote and exchanged a letter in hieroglyphics. . . . [In language arts, the students] wrote editorials [and] radio plays . . . to read on the school intercom. . . .*
>
> *[In the* Executive Elite School] *work is developing one's analytical intellectual powers. Children are continually asked to reason through a problem, to produce intellectual products that are both logically sound and of top academic quality. A primary goal . . . is to conceptualize rules by which elements may fit together. (Anyon 1980, 73–85)*

Using Kohn's terminology for analyzing education in the status attainment process, one might say that middle-status schools tend to receive youngsters who have been prepared at home to work independently, and then the schools help them develop their skills further so youngsters can pursue self-directed jobs in the economy. Working-class schools, by way of contrast, receive students who have not been prepared or are otherwise not ready to work independently in the classroom, and then use external discipline of the kind students are familiar with at home to provide guidance in the classroom.

Based on the results of the studies cited above, the Chicago School Survey (Havighurst 1964), and other sources (e.g., Bernstein 1975), schools can be distinguished according to the types of students they enroll and the kinds of discipline they stress or exemplify. As shown in Table 7.3, discipline in middle-class schools tends to be relatively informal, whereas teachers in schools with a large proportion of working-class students attempt to impose strict discipline in the hope that this will facilitate instruction in basic skills. The descriptions in Table 7.3 are, of course, prototypical: not all schools can be placed in such clear-cut categories, and disciplinary emphasis will vary from teacher to teacher and according to the age of students, the type of leadership, and other conditions in a given school. There is enough truth in the descriptions, however, to make them useful summaries of the disciplinary emphases that exist in differing types of schools. There also is empirical support in research such as that conducted by Anyon (above) and by Howell and McBroom (1982), who found significant correlations between emphasis on "openness" versus control in the family patterns and the school experience of a national sample of high school students. These findings underline how elementary and secondary schools reinforce family background in preparing or not preparing young people for upward mobility in a modern economy.

There also is reason to believe that many community colleges and other

Table 7.3 *Disciplinary Approaches Emphasized in Differing Types of Schools*

Type of School	Economic Background of Students	Disciplinary Emphasis
Middle class	Upper- and lower-middle class	Students work independently in the classroom; discipline is informal; emphasis is on developing a variety of scholarly and creative skills.
Mixed	Lower-middle class and working class	Emphasis is on developing self-discipline and greater capacity to work independently.
Working class	Upper- and lower-working class	Emphasis is on obedience to authority; students work in structured situations with stress on developing mastery of basic academic skills.

higher-education institutions that are disproportionately working class in student composition extend the emphases on control and on low-level learning into the postsecondary level. Richardson, for example, cited evidence indicating that "open-access" colleges—including many community colleges and other colleges and universities in big cities—minimize "activities involving the synthesis or comprehension of large issues," thereby detracting from development of "students' abilities to read and write" (1985, 45). He also concluded, however, that "urban areas are threatened by the absence of critical literacy skills among high percentages of their population. Urban universities and colleges represent the best hope for interrupting the channeling process through which those who lack such literacy skills gain credentials as teachers and return to perpetuate their own inadequacies through the public school system" (1985, 49).

Social Mobility, Education, and the Underclass

Our analysis to this point suggests that schools along with other social institutions provide successful routes to upward mobility for a substantial percentage of the population by equipping talented and ambitious young people with skills and opportunity to enter and advance in the economic system (Holmes 1988). However, another segment of the population—particularly the big-city underclass—has relatively little realistic opportunity to succeed because the family, the schools, the economy, and other social institutions serving this population apparently are not functioning successfully to generate mobility. This is not to say that none of the underclass achieves upward mobility. Some members of the underclass are able to escape from extremely disadvantaged circumstances and enter the stable working class or the middle class. Many others, however, are not succeeding, and their numbers have become sufficiently large to make the inner core part of our cities a social tinderbox.

If this analysis is correct, our conclusions should be reflected in data showing that education for the underclass is not working as effectively to generate upward mobility as it is for the national population as a whole. To our knowledge, social scientists have not framed and pursued this question precisely in these terms, but several lines of research do suggest that this is exactly what has been happening in the United States during the past three decades.

This research generally examines differences between the white and black population. Since the black population until fairly recently included only a small middle class, research comparing whites and blacks tends to constitute a comparison between a mixed-status population (whites) and a low-status population (blacks). Some research conducted during the past few years also has singled out the black population of big-city ghettos for special study, thus focusing more directly on the urban underclass. Other studies have begun to focus on social-class differences emerging among the black population, to an extent thereby highlighting the black underclass (e.g., Landry 1987). The results of these studies provide indirect support for the conclusion that the schools and other mobility-generating institutions are not working as well for the underclass as for the population as a whole.

1. In a 1972 study using 1966 data on education and employment in urban ghettos, Harrison found that "ghetto blacks seem to have achieved about the national nonwhite average for years of school completed" (1972a, 799). Although the gap between the school completion rates of young whites and blacks had nearly disappeared, blacks in urban ghettos were not benefiting as much from schooling as were other segments of the population. Harrison speculates that this difference may reflect the strong influence of a "street culture" among the black underclass: "Clearly, education has a very high opportunity cost for nonwhites living in the urban ghetto. There are any number of (largely illegal) activities out 'on the street' which are capable of returning more money than can be obtained through a high school diploma" (p. 806).

2. We already have mentioned the studies by Featherman and Hauser (1976, 1978) that found that the occupational status attainment of whites had become more meritocratic between 1962 and 1973. Featherman and Hauser also examined attainment for blacks and concluded that the pattern for blacks had begun to resemble the pattern for whites:

> *In 1962, black men of all ages, except those 35–44, were not able to advance in the status hierarchy much beyond the position of their family heads. . . . [In 1973] black men were far more likely to be upwardly mobile than their counterparts a decade earlier . . . black men recently have begun to experience status mobility in their life cycles which more closely duplicates the circumstances of whites. (1976, pp. 629–630)*

However, Featherman and Hauser also stress that the increasing utility of education in the status attainment process for blacks is linked to the emergence of clearer social-class lines among the black population. Before the 1960s, the great majority of the black population was either working class or underclass; but economic classes are more visible among the black population now than in 1962. "Black families seem increasingly able," they concluded, to "transfer their socioeconomic statuses to sons" (1978, p. 381). We interpret this situation as indicating that it is the black middle class that is translating educational attainment into social mobility, while large segments of the black population still are immobilized in the working and underclass groups, particularly in big cities and metropolitan areas.

3. Portes and Wilson (1976) have examined black and white differences in educational attainment and have come to conclusions that shed further light on the role of education in the status attainment process for both groups. Analyzing data collected in the late 1960s and early 1970s from a national probability sample of 87 high schools, they stressed the "crucial fact" that

> *for the white majority academic grades, apart from the psychological effects, appear to "carry along" individuals toward predictable levels of achievement. Black grades . . . appear to be more irrelevant as marks of achievement within the schools themselves and as criteria of selection for higher education. Institutional administrators seem to do so much "discounting" of the value of inner-city and other black school grades as to render their importance for admission almost nil. (pp. 428–429)*

"Discounting" of the grades of inner-city students could operate in either or both of two directions. High grades might be discounted because it is felt that they do not represent very high achievement levels, or low grades might be disregarded because it is believed that their possessors can perform more adequately if given opportunity and support in undertaking a career after high school. It is probable that both tendencies are at work in the status attainment process for students in low-status schools, but for our purposes here the most important point is that educational attainment as measured by grade point average does not seem to be as accurate an indicator of academic achievement among inner-city students as it is among the population as a whole.

The same generalization can be made for educational status as measured by attainment of a high school diploma or number of years completed in the public schools. Much research has indicated that for the population as a whole, number of years of schooling completed is an excellent measure for characterizing educational attainment. Based on an extensive survey of the literature, Shea (1976) summarized the justification for this generalization as follows: "Those who attain more years of schooling score higher on most measures of achievement anyway, including intelligence tests, grade point averages, and achievement test scores" (p. 477). As noted earlier, however, neither grade point average (Portes and Wilson) nor attainment of a high school diploma (Harrison

1972a) seem to represent very useful measures of attainment for the ghetto segment of the black population. In our view, this means that partly due to inadequate school performance, blacks in the underclass are highly dependent at this time on nonschool routes to mobility, but they also are in a poor position to take advantage of even these channels because they tend to be cut off geographically and socially from opportunities to become mobile through the job market (Hacker 1988).

4. Analyses of the status attainment process for whites and blacks have provided additional data to support the conclusions enumerated above. For example, J. P. Smith (1982) reviewed census information on educational attainment collected in 1940, 1970, and 1979 and related this information to data on income and literacy among men and women born in five-year groups from 1865–1870 to 1946–1950. His overall conclusion was as follows:

> *The tale being woven in this paper is a relatively optimistic one of slow progress. It is also a story of the long lags before changes in the home and school are reflected in outcomes in the labor market. . . . The long-term historical process has been one in which black incomes have risen relative to whites in all schooling classes. . . . The largest black gains relative to whites [now] are concentrated among black college graduates. But the most intriguing trend documented . . . is the post-1973 deterioration in relative black incomes among new entrants with a high school diploma or less. This deterioration represents the first significant reversal in the gradual trend toward income convergence between the races that has occurred in the last few decades. . . . We may be picking up the first signals of problems with the relative quality of Northern inner-city black schools. A substantial part of the well-documented improvement in the quality of black schooling in the twentieth century reflected black migration from the South to the better schools of the North and also the overall rise in the quality of Southern schools. These factors having largely run their course, further improvement in black schooling depends critically on what is taking place in Northern urban black schools. (J. P. Smith 1982, 29–30)*

This pattern also suggests that the public school system is not operating very effectively to help the underclass achieve mobility. Students who are sufficiently motivated tend to finish high school, but even among this group many are not acquiring adequate academic and occupational skills. Neither grades nor a diploma appear to represent much achievement in schools enrolling high proportions of poverty students, apparently because students are able to move along from one grade to another without actually learning much.

This critical situation is discussed in more detail in succeeding chapters, but at this point it is important to emphasize that schools and society in the United States appear to be generating too little mobility for underclass students in big-city school districts.

Education and the Socioeconomic Power Structure: The Neo-Marxist and Revisionist Critiques and Critical Theory

A number of economists and political scientists have challenged the conclusion that schools and society in the United States and in other western nations really function to provide meaningful opportunity for the working class. Because their major conclusions are that education in a capitalist society is bound to work against the interests of the poor and that reforms within the capitalist system fail to provide adequate opportunity for the working class, their point of view can be described as Marxist or neo-Marxist. (Much of the analysis involving or related to the neo-Marxist critique is sometimes referred to as critical theory.) Henry Levin, a leading advocate of this position, has described its basic thrust in the following summary of the central arguments on both sides:

> *The role of education in creating a just and productive society is very much a topic of controversy today. On the one side are those who see the educational system as that institution of modern society which develops, sorts, and selects persons according to their productive proficiencies to fill the hierarchical positions of modern, large-scale bureaucratic organizations in a rational and meritocratic manner (Inkeles, 1975; Bell, 1973).*
>
> *On the other side are those who see the schools as agencies for reproducing the social relations of production for monopoly capitalism and its supportive state structures (Bowles and Gintis, 1976).*
>
> *. . . In their view the schools serve the role of preparing wage-labor for capitalist enterprise with its attendant needs for docile and disciplined workers who are socialized and certified for particular places in the work hierarchy with an awareness only of their individual relations to the enterprise rather than of solidarity with other workers as a class. . . .*
>
> *While other important versions of the role of the school exist, the poles of the present debate are represented by the functionalists who see schooling as the essential institution for preparing competent members of a modern, rational, efficient, and meritocratic society and the Marxists who see schooling as one of the most important instruments of the state for supporting the capitalist hegemony over the worker. (Levin 1976, 148–149)*

As described by Levin, the neo-Marxists view the schools as part of a larger system designed primarily to produce "disciplined" workers certified for a position at the bottom of the social structure. The schools do this partly by emphasizing external discipline in teaching working-class children, in the same manner as does the family in which they grow up and the factories in which many work as adults. The neo-Marxists frequently refer to this arrangement as the *correspondence principle:* the social relations of schooling and of family life correspond to the social relations of production; the social relations of the larger society are reproduced in the school in a way that tends to reproduce the social class structure later.

In other words, the economic and technological characteristics of a society cause the families and the schools to take on characteristics that fit in with the socioeconomic structure. Bowles (1975) develops this idea:

> *I will argue that the social division of Labor—based on the hierarchical structure of production—gives rise to distinct class subcultures. The values, personality traits, and expectations characteristic of each subculture are transmitted from generation to generation through class differences in family socialization and complementary differences in the type and amount of schooling ordinarily attained by children of various class positions. . . . This outline, and what follows, is put forward as an interpretation, consistent where testable with the available data, though lacking as yet in firm empirical support for some important links in the argument. . . .*
>
> *These personality attributes are developed primarily at a young age, both in the family and, to a lesser extent, in secondary socializing institutions such as schools. Because people tend to marry within their own class (in part because spouses often meet in our class-segregated schools), both parents are likely to have a similar set of these fundamental personality traits. . . . The children of managers and professionals are taught self-reliance with a broad set of constraints. The children of production-line workers are taught obedience.*
>
> *Although this relation between parents' class position and child's personality attributes operates primarily in the home, it is reinforced by schools and other institutions. Thus, . . . the authoritarian social relations of working-class high schools complement the discipline-oriented early socialization patterns experienced by working-class children. The relatively greater freedom of wealthy suburban schools extends and formalizes the early independence training characteristic of upper-class families. (pp. 58–60)*

Carnoy (1974) has a similar view of the educational system in the United States, which he calls a system of "cultural imperialism." He writes that

> *schooling in capitalist societies* does *serve as a means to higher status for a* small percentage *of the urban poor and an even smaller number of rural poor, and it also may contribute to dissent and original thinking, which may be important intellectual forces for societal change. Nevertheless, these are not the* primary purposes *or functional characteristics of school systems. They are by-products of schooling which occur as its attempts to achieve its main function of transmitting the social and economic structure from generation to generation through pupil selection, defining culture and roles, and teaching certain cognitive skills. (p. 13)*

Bowles, Gintis, and some other neo-Marxists recently have somewhat moderated their views on the correspondence principle by recognizing that the schools can and sometimes do function to develop habits of independent thought among disadvantaged students, rather than simply reproducing labor market relations aimed strictly at obedience and acceptance of the status quo (Bowles and Gintis 1981; Carnoy 1982). Similarly, Michael Apple—a prominent critical theorist who concentrates on implications for curriculum—has pointed out that "progressive elements within the content of curriculum" sometimes function to help working class students recognize their disadvantage in society (quoted in Papagiannis, Klees, and Bickel 1982, p. 256).

Recent works of some neo-Marxist analysts also have given more adequate attention to other disjunctions between the educational system, the economic system, and the larger social system. These disjunctions indicate that schools do not simply reproduce the existing social order through the mechanical operation of a universal correspondence principle. For example, *Schooling and Work in the Democratic State* by Martin Carnoy and Henry Levin (1985) recognizes that although schooling functions partially to reproduce the unequal class relations of a capitalist economy, it also is "more democratic and equal than the workplace for which it prepares students" (p. 4). Specific contradictory tendencies in the relationships they describe between the educational system and the economy include the effects of schooling in (1) alienating students, thereby undermining the school's role "as a producer of trained labor" (p. 156); and (2) deprofessionalizing the teaching force, thereby making teachers less effective in training the labor force. In addition, Carnoy and Levin conclude that conflicts over spending on education may result in improved funding to enhance the performance of disadvantaged students. Thus, in contrast to some of their previous writing, Carnoy and Levin's recent analysis allows for greater progress toward economic equality through reform of the educational system.

The discussion in this chapter has shown that some criticisms of the neo-Marxists and other critical theorists have a certain amount of validity. Many working-class children have little realistic opportunity for mobility through the schools and other social institutions; this problem has become particularly acute among the underclass population of big cities.

However, if the neo-Marxist position that schooling mainly reproduces the existing social order through an underlying *correspondence principle* is correct, then there should be very little social mobility upward and downward between the working class and the middle class, and most working-class children should be attending predominantly working-class schools and be enrolled in vocationally oriented programs in which they are being indoctrinated in the discipline of the capitalist order. But we have seen that the evidence available from a large number of studies suggests not only that there is considerable mobility occurring in the United States and in other western societies, but also that these societies seem to be growing more meritocratic and education seems to be accounting for an increasing share of mobility.

In addition, there also is reason to question the extent to which working-class children are additionally disadvantaged by being shunted into vocationally oriented programs or by attending predominantly working-class schools in which consistent emphasis is placed on external discipline. For one thing, the climate in working-class schools varies to an extent from one school or classroom to another. Second, it is far from true that all working-class children are enrolled in different courses based on their vocational aptitudes or attend schools that are predominantly working-class in socioeconomic composition.

Table 7.4 *Social Class Composition of High Schools in the 1970s*

Type of School	Socioeconomic Status of Students Percentage Distribution					Number (000)	Percentage of Total
	I(HI)	*II*	*III*	*IV*	*V(LO)*		
Middle class	33	33	29	5	—	2,000	13.1
Independent	45	50	5	—	—	100	0.7
Working class: urban	3	10	28	46	13	1,200	7.9
Vocational	—	5	50	40	5	400	2.6
Comprehensive-mixed: urban	12	20	36	28	4	6,300	41.5
Small city & rural	3	14	30	38	15	4,000	26.3
Church-related	8	17	34	35	6	1,200	7.9
Total American high school students	11	19	33	30	7	15,200	100

Note: The five Socioeconomic Categories are *not* identical with the five social classes we have defined previously. The categories are based on a specially devised scale of socioeconomic status used with high school seniors in the Kansas City metropolitan area. Class I is actually mainly upper middle-class students and Class V is students from very low-status families.

Source: Adapted from Levine, Mitchell, and Havighurst 1970.

There has been some research on the social class composition of secondary schools in the United States, and this is summarized in Table 7.4. First, small-city and rural high schools serve the entire community without regard to the socioeconomic status of the students. They do not have vocational education courses much beyond agriculture and home economics. Approximately one-fourth of our youth attend such schools. Elsewhere in the United States, the "comprehensive" high schools of cities larger than 50,000 population serve perhaps about 40 percent of youth. In these schools, working-class and middle-class youth take the same courses, except for a small minority who take vocational education courses. An ambitious and reasonably successful working-class youth will attend the same classes and go on to a university in company with the middle-class youth. It is certain that many upwardly mobile working-class youth learn the same material and associate intimately with middle-class youth in these comprehensive schools. The case studies of youth in River City illustrated this process.

This leaves two relatively small social class-related types of schools. The urban high schools in working-class neighborhoods and the big-city vocational high schools tend to serve working-class and lower middle-class youth—perhaps 10 percent in all; and the middle-class and independent schools tend to serve upper- and upper middle-class youth, while a substantial group of upper middle-class students are in comprehensive-urban and small city-rural high schools. To take a specific example, in the metropolitan area of Kansas City, only 22 percent of the total number of students of working-class families were attending predominantly working-class schools (Levine, Mitchell, and Havighurst 1970). On the other hand, only one-third of upper-class and upper middle-class students were attending middle-class or independent schools. This kind of evidence throws doubt on the sweeping propositions advanced by the neo-Marxist group.

Other research also has countered some arguments of the neo-Marxist position regarding the correspondence principle. For example, Olneck and Bills (1980) analyzed information from a study of Kalamazoo youth and found that among men from middle-class families, those who were rated uncooperative by their teachers had higher initial occupational status than those who were rated cooperative. In addition, there was no relationship between teachers' ratings of cooperativeness and initial job status among working-class youth. The authors conclude that these findings are inconsistent with Bowles and Gintis's contention that the same behaviors are rewarded at work as in school.

Part of the problem in the neo-Marxist critique seems to be that many of its proponents tend to take an either-or position on issues involving social mobility. As Levin himself states in describing the Marxist point of view, functionalists such as Inkeles and critics such as the Marxists are seen as representing "the poles of the present debate." Once debate has been polarized to force a choice among contending positions, one tends to lose sight of the evidence indicating that although education is reinforcing the low status of too many working-class students, it also is serving as a route to mobility for substantial numbers of others. Thus, even though the neo-Marxists have added a useful and important perspective to the debate on education and social mobility, their overall conclusions are too limited and one-sided to yield a validated position on what should be done to provide more equal opportunity in schools and society.

On the other hand, preceding sections indicate that the schools and other institutions do not seem to be functioning at all adequately for the underclass in big cities. Children from this group generally are enrolled in predominantly low-status schools, and the schools thus appear to be reinforcing their isolation from the larger society. Evidence presented in later chapters indicates that there is a real question whether schools are working or can be made to work effectively for underclass students in the cities.

The Revisionists: Who Controls the Public Education System in the United States?

Another important strand of critical theory explores the relation of education to the contemporary economy; a school of revisionist historians of education emerged in the 1960s. The general thesis of this group is that historically the public schools in the United States have systematically miseducated citizens in ways that serve the interests of the upper middle (capitalist) class. They argue that, since 1850, the public schools have served to make the children of the poor and of ethnic minorities satisfied with failure in school and with low-status occupations. If this proposition is true, it might be supported by data indicating that the children of the poor have now and have had in the past very little upward social mobility, that education has not and does not lead to upward social mobility, and that the teaching of United States history and social studies in the schools has been systematically false in many respects.

There has been much controversy over the work of the revisionists; the student can find and read the books and articles that carry on the controversy. One problem in the revisionists' writings is that a reader looks in vain for a consideration of this question: What amount of upward and downward social mobility is viable in a democratic society in which middle-status families believe they have the right and the obligation to help their children maintain the same or a higher social status? The basic problem of a balance between social fluidity and social stability seems to be ignored. Do the revisionist historians favor a complete social revolution every generation, so that every child of a new generation stands on an equal basis with every other, with respect to economic support and to home support for school achievement? If not a revolution, how do they propose to equalize the differential opportunity that comes from different home backgrounds?

A useful summary and analysis of the arguments of the neo-Marxist writers on education and society and of the revisionist historians can be found in the monograph *The Revisionists Revised: Studies in the Historiography of American Education* by Diane Ravitch. Professor R. Freeman Butts of Teachers College, Columbia University, published a thoughtful review in 1974 of the revisionist position in *The History of Education Quarterly*, and Henry J. Aaron (1977) has prepared a short review of the evidence for and against the neo-Marxist revisionists. In addition, Donald Warren has put together a set of articles that report the contributions of history to the broader study of education and public policy in the United States. Historian Sol Cohen has summarized some problems in the methods and conclusions of the revisionists (whom he calls the "new reconstructionists"):

> *To the new reconstructionists the function of history of education is clearly to serve the cause of social reconstruction. . . . Novel canons of historical writing are introduced. Katz ingenuously states: "Our concerns shape the questions that we ask and, as a consequence, determine what we select from the virtually unlimited supply of facts," and, "in any event, the burden of proof no longer lies with those who argue that education is and has been unequal. It lies, rather with those who would defend the system. . . . The new reconstructionists ask such loaded questions of the evidence that they can be pretty sure at the beginning what answer they will emerge with at the end. There is a finality and rationality about their work that terribly oversimplifies the ambiguity, the incompleteness, the complexity of historical events. . . . Karier has said that history speaks only very cautiously and modestly to the present, that in history one seldom finds answers which are completely satisfying. But despite these caveats, the ideological commitment of the new reconstructionists has become a strait jacket." (Cohen 1976, 327–329)*

Resistance Theory

A third major strand of critical theory involves what some observers call "resistance" theory. This theory seeks to explain and interpret the genesis and meaning of working-class students' tendencies to resist participating in learning opportunities available to them in the typical public school. Robert Connell and his colleagues (1982) interviewed working-class teenagers and some of their teachers and parents in Australia and concluded that resistance is the "*main* relation to the school" for many working-class students who struggle against "oppressive futures" (p. 88).

Resistance to the school arises partly because many working-class students reject the authority of both their parents and their teachers (Connell, Ashenden, Kessler, and Dowsett 1982, 172), partly because school rules and norms contradict working-class students' definitions of and emphasis on masculinity and femininity (p. 98), and partly because an "oppositional peer life" reinforced by the mass media stimulates them to resist being treated as children by adults in the school (p. 164). Equally important, these authors concluded, many working-class students have little or no interest in the "hegemonic" traditional curriculum of the schools, which "marginalizes" the knowledge acquired by working-class students in daily life. "The main form of dissent" in the school thus reflects the

> *working-class tradition of resistance to power and authority . . . [and is] pitted* against *the bearers of knowledge. It becomes anti-intellectual, and, partly for that reason, open to commercial exploitation. Everyone comes to agree that the resisters are 'stupid'—that's even a word they use themselves for what they do in classrooms and outside the school with their friends. . . . [Thus mass education] is a mechanism of hegemony in class relations: it divides the working class, [and] undermines its self-confidence. (Connell, Ashenden, Kessler, and Dowsett 1982, 172, 197).*

Robert Everhart (1983), in a study of a similar group of working-class students attending a junior high school in the United States, reached much the same conclusion as did Connell and his colleagues in Australia. In particular, Everhart studied the behavior and attitudes of three teenagers named Don, Steve, and Roger; he summarized some of his observations as follows:

> *Don, Steve, and Roger were finding the requirements of school to be unfulfilling and alienating. They resisted teacher attempts to involve them in the classroom because to become so involved would be tantamount to admitting that the reified knowledge of the school was legitimate. . . . Don and his friends were interested in the present, not the future, and no amount of cajoling or ridiculing by teachers could convince them that this alienative work was for the better. Their goals were simply to consume as much of the products that liberal capitalism had produced as possible. (Everhart 1983, 115)*

Henry Giroux has been analyzing the implications of resistance theory for improving the education of working-class students. Giroux believes that resistance theory is useful and potentially liberating because it "redefines the causes and meaning of oppositional behavior," and in so doing "points to a number of assumptions and concerns about schooling that we generally neglect in both traditional views of schooling and radical theories of reproduction" (Giroux 1983, 289). The theory of resistance, he says, calls attention to the need to "unravel the ideological interests embedded in the various messages of the school, particularly those embedded in its curriculum, systems of instruction, and modes of evaluation" (p. 292). It further suggests taking seriously the "counter-logic that pulls students away from schools into the streets, the bars, and the shopfloor culture" (p. 293). In this and other papers, Giroux argues that improving education for working-class students is dependent on developing curriculum and instructional approaches that are relevant to them in terms of their own experience, interests, and personal knowledge, and also that their education should assist them in developing a "critical consciousness" of the part the schools and other institutions play in reproducing their low social status (Giroux and McLaren 1986; Giroux 1988).

Important recent research involving key aspects of resistance theory also has been carried out by Lois Weis. After a year as a participant-observer at a big-city high school, Weis (1987) concluded that changes seem to be occurring in the attitudes and behaviors of working-class white students. She reported that working-class males generally resist institutional authority in the school and "attempt to carve out their own space . . . which can then be filled with *their* fundamentally anti-school meanings" (p. 87), as had working-class secondary students in several other studies in the United States and Great Britain. However, Weis also found that the male students she interviewed perceived schooling as offering utilitarian opportunities for acquiring skilled jobs and thus were willing to "put in their time" in school and even go to college (p. 93). Noting that this finding differed from earlier research, Weis viewed this change in attitudes as reflecting students' recognition that unskilled manual labor provides decreasing opportunity for success in postindustrial society.

Regarding females, Weis reported that the working-class girls she interviewed generally did not aim for a marginal "wage labor identity" (p. 113) as had girls in earlier studies. Instead, they had a positive perception of the usefulness of education and wanted to prepare themselves for high-paying jobs that would provide a measure of independence and autonomy. Rather than pursuing romantic fantasies focused on the traditional family, as working-class females in previous research had done, the girls in this study challenged a "fundamental premise of patriarchy—that woman's primary place is in the home-family sphere" (p. 114). Because the boys she studied still held to this traditional premise, Weis concluded that changes in "female culture" may "therefore hold the greater promise of challenge to the traditional role and conception of the working class" (p. 116).

Conclusion

The educational system in the United States helps both to change and perpetuate the existing social class structure. The social structure probably is even more fluid now than it has been at some times in the past, and education—which is increasingly a prerequisite to upward mobility in modern societies—is a major route to status advancement for many young people, including working-class youth. However, the public schools and other social institutions are not providing sufficient mobility for the underclass population in big cities.

Research on developing countries suggests that living in cities is not enough to generate modern attitudes and behaviors associated with upward mobility among working-class populations. Educational and economic opportunity and other social resources are required to improve the conditions of life of the working class. Because education in modern societies is a more important route to mobility than it was in pre-modern societies, effective education is required to generate mobility for the working-class in the United States.

On their own, the public schools cannot provide equal opportunity in life for underclass students, or for working-class students in general, but together with other institutions the schools may be able to help them succeed in accordance with their talents and ambitions. The role of the schools in working with other institutions for this and other purposes is analyzed in more detail in succeeding chapters.

EXERCISES

1. In what ways is a youngster with high academic ability better off in a modern society than a premodern society? What considerations determine whether high ability will be translated into success later in life?
2. If there is a low-status school nearby, interview several students and/or teachers to determine the extent to which grades that students receive reflect high levels of performance. Do teachers in this school give good grades for low-quality performance? If they do, is it because they do not care about the quality of performance? What problems would teachers encounter if they graded more directly according to performance?
3. Interview several parents to determine the kinds of child-rearing practices they advocate and use with their children. To what degree do these practices agree with the information in this chapter on differences between the social classes?
4. Describe the group mobility of one subgroup in your own community during the past 100 years.
5. Interview a dozen adults, selected more or less at random, asking them what they think is happening to social mobility in the United States. Is it increasing or decreasing, and why?

6. Identify three or four people who have been upwardly mobile and interview them to determine whether education has helped them achieve this mobility. What other factors or qualities played a part in their success? How do their goals for the education of their children compare with their own educational backgrounds?
7. Analyze the want ads in the employment section of a Sunday newspaper to determine what kinds of educational background are required for differing jobs. Do some of the ads list or assume the completion of high school or college? To what degree do you think some of the skills required could be learned on the job?
8. *Choosing Sides* by Cary Goodman and *Muscles and Morals* by Dominick Cavallo present contrasting interpretations of the movement to establish playgrounds and leisure activities for urban children from 1875 to 1925. Goodman emphasizes reformers' motives involving preparation of young people for "industrial discipline" (e.g., stress on punctuality, team play, following rules and regulations), while Cavallo stresses broader goals involving development of positive mental and moral habits. Which author provides better evidence for his conclusions and interpretations?

SUGGESTIONS FOR FURTHER READING

1. *Power, Ideology and Education* (1977), edited by Jerome Karabel and A. H. Halsey, includes a number of chapters bearing on the schools and the social structure. The volume contains a wide range of viewpoints on issues involving education and mobility in different societies. Various authors report the results of research on these issues, and others analyze the implications and adequacy of this research.
2. In *Class and Merit in the American High School*, Richard A. Rehberg and Evelyn R. Rosenthal report the results of a longitudinal study indicating support for the meritocratic position that scholastic ability, educational ambition, and academic performance are at "least as important as social class in the determination of ultimate educational attainment" (1978, 250). The book also contains a useful summary of both the meritocratic and revisionist viewpoints, basic research approaches that are being used to examine the issues, and previous research conducted by other investigators.
3. In *The Training of the Urban Working Class*, Paul C. Violas reviews the history of urban schools in the United States during the first part of the twentieth century. He concludes that a number of developments associated with the "progressive" movement actually were intended to enable working-class children "to adapt more easily to the assembly lines and production teams in the modern factory" (1978, 15). He argues that compulsory attendance laws, the establishment of playgrounds, "learning by doing," and the development of extracurricular activities, differentiated curricula, and vocational guidance were all designed to develop disciplined and obedient work-

ers for business and industry. For example, he argues that the "playground movement implanted in the child behavior patterns appropriate for an industrial worker" (p. 14). Whether or not one accepts this neo-Marxian revisionist interpretation, the book contains useful historical information on the social purposes of United States schools.

4. Christopher J. Hurn's *The Limits and Possibilities of Schooling* includes concise summaries of the neo-Marxist and meritocratic positions (which he calls "radical" and "functional," respectively) and a thoughtful analysis emphasizing an alternate explanation of the role of education in modern society. Hurn believes that the importance of formal education is best explained by "shared beliefs" that it yields occupational status and "high quality people" (1978, 261) rather than by its actual accomplishments in achieving these goals (the functional explanation) or its role in reproducing inequality (the radical explanation). Hurn offers many thoughtful insights and perspectives in the course of his analysis.
5. Arthur M. Cohen's 1977 paper on "The Social Equalization Fantasy" reviews some of the research on the meritocratic versus neo-Marxist positions regarding the functioning of the educational system at the postsecondary level.
6. We have concluded in this chapter that there is substantial mobility in United States society but that many individuals are now trapped in a big-city underclass. Some evidence also suggests that there is relatively little mobility in or out of the upper status segment of United States society, at least as regards the role of education in contributing to mobility. A study supporting this conclusion is reported in Tinto's 1978 review of research on the effects of schooling.
7. The November 1980 issue of the *American Journal of Education* includes several articles reviewing and critiquing *Who Gets Ahead?* by Jencks et al., as well as some of the research and conclusions reported by Bowles, Gintis, and other neo-Marxists.
8. Several books by Michael Apple (1981, 1982a, 1982b, 1985) provide an analysis emphasizing neo-Marxist perspectives on curriculum. Neo-Marxist and revisionist scholars are well represented in the book he edited on *Cultural and Economic Reproduction in Education*.
9. Based on participant observation and interviewing of working-class youth in England, *Learning to Labour* by Paul Willis describes how working-class culture and the larger society lead students to adopt counter-school attitudes that devalue education and how educators develop a custodial orientation in responding to the problems of teaching in working-class classrooms. David Hogan's essay on social-class formation and reproduction in the United States also provides perspectives on the development of working-class attitudes toward school and society.
10. *The Language of Children Reared in Poverty* edited by Lynne Feagans and Dale Farran analyzes and discusses recent studies and intervention projects dealing with language development of low-status children.
11. *The Hidden Curriculum and Moral Education* edited by Henry Giroux and David Purpel (1983) describes and discusses differing viewpoints on a number of

issues involving neo-Marxist and revisionist analysis of education. Many of their points are updated in Giroux (1988) and Purpel (1988).

12. *Ideology and Practice in Schooling* (1983), edited by Michael W. Apple and Lois Weis, provides a variety of perspectives on reproduction of the social classes through education. The chapter by Weis on students at a black community college in the United States provides a useful analysis related to higher education and an interesting contrast with white working-class youth in England. Compared to white youth described in *Learning to Labour* by Willis, black college youth studied by Weis seemed much more willing to cooperate with teachers and administrators, provided that the latter groups were perceived as being sincerely concerned with the interests and goals of their students.
13. The book by Coleman and Neugarten, *Social Status in the City*, is an empirical study of the social-class structure of a large midwestern city, with special attention to social mobility.
14. *The Social Order of the Slum* by Gerald Suttles discusses some of the reasons that various ethnic and racial groups have found it more or less easy to attain social mobility in the United States.
15. A wealth of important and fascinating information on the history and status of ethnic groups in the United States is provided in *American Ethnicity* by Bahr, Chadwick, and Strauss, and in *Ethnic America* by Sowell.
16. Two essays in the *Harvard Educational Review* (Giroux 1983, Giroux and McClaren 1986) summarize and extend much of recent critical theory and its implications for education.
17. *The Politics of School Reform 1870–1940* by Paul Peterson (1985) and *The Origins of Public High Schools* by Maris Vinovskis (1986) criticize much of the data and interpretations of the revisionist historians.
18. An essay by Mark Holmes (1988) provides useful perspectives and analyses regarding education and mobility in contemporary society.

8

Low-Status Students and Compensatory Education

The material in the preceding chapters helps explain why many students from low-status homes are not well prepared for success in a modern school and why it is important to improve their performance in the educational system. One purpose of this chapter is to identify some reasons that low-status students continue to perform poorly in school despite efforts made recently and in the past to improve their academic performance.

At the outset, it is important to emphasize several points to avoid misleading conclusions or implications. First, much of the discussion is concerned in one way or another with the reasons that schools have not been sufficiently effective in helping low-status students achieve at a more satisfactory level and what can be done to make them more effective in this regard in the future. In considering these questions, we necessarily consider what makes schools or schooling relatively effective or ineffective in general.

Second, it should be clear by now that such terms as *working-class students* and *inner-city schools* are meant to describe differences that exist between differing groups of students and schools but not to imply that all students with similar background or all schools with similar student composition are necessarily alike. Thus, our concern is with averages and modal patterns; but exceptions can be found to any generalization involving relationships between social class or other sociological background variables and achievement in the schools.

Reasons That Low-Status Students Perform Poorly

We already have described some ways in which schools differ with regard to student control patterns and the kinds of behaviors emphasized in working with students. Schools in working-class neighborhoods tend to emphasize conformity and order in the classroom, whereas schools in middle-class neighborhoods tend to provide less external structure and to emphasize the development of self-directed learning. Students who do not eventually acquire self-directed learning skills experience increasing difficulty as they proceed to higher levels of education. We also noted that teachers in working-class schools sometimes confuse order with learning; that is, teachers have had a relatively difficult time maintaining order, and once this goal has been accomplished, many have been unwilling or unable to move beyond it toward the development of self-directed learning skills. This latter phenomenon helps account for the low-achievement patterns found in most working-class schools, but it provides only a partial explanation of the widespread failures teachers have experienced in working to improve the performance of low-status students.

1. *Inappropriate curriculum and instruction.* Because their home environment frequently has not exposed them to the kinds of materials teachers have been trained to use in instruction (see Chapter 7), many low-status students respond uncomprehendingly to the lessons teachers try to develop in the classroom. This is true in the early grades, when teachers are introducing terminology and concepts with which low-status students may have little familiarity; it frequently becomes even more of a problem in later years when teachers introduce more advanced vocabulary and concepts dependent on earlier understandings that students did not master in earlier grades.

Lack of congruity between disadvantaged students' cultural background and the school's expectations in curriculum and instruction involves not just vocabulary and terminology but also general linguistic patterns important for successfully functioning in the classroom. In this regard, Judith Green of the University of Delaware has surveyed the research on linguistic process in the classroom and concluded that "surface-level" linguistic problems may be less important than "pervasive linguistic patterns" that inhibit many students' "acquisition of strategies for participating in school activities . . . and learning how to learn." She also concluded that successful students not only know "academic information" but also know "how and when to display this information. Being accurate or right was not enough; students needed to present information in appropriate form at the appropriate time" (Green 1983, 207, 227). Many low-status students are disadvantaged in school because they lack knowledge and experience involving such linguistic expectations.

2. *Lack of parental and peer reinforcement of school norms and learning experiences.* We have seen that the home environment in early childhood among working-class families generally is less intellectually stimulating than among middle-class families, and that relatively many working-class parents encounter serious difficulty protecting children from educationally distracting external influences. These tendencies continue to hamper preparation for and interest in school as the child grows older, and their effects make it difficult for the school to function effectively with working-class children.

In many cases, working-class parents physically punish their children or ask the school to use corporal punishment when their children misbehave or do not pay attention, but this approach frequently is not as effective as the middle-class approach emphasizing understanding and internalization of school behavior and academic achievement norms. Working-class parents who are too busy earning a living or are otherwise not able or inclined to visit the school and work closely with teachers in solving their children's problems frequently find that neither physical punishment nor verbal exhortation has much permanent effect. Working-class youth who get into trouble in school or drop out before completing high school frequently mention an early involvement in antischool peer groups as the crucial turning point in their educational careers. This tendency is most likely to be manifested in predominantly low-status schools, in which it is most likely that a student's peers will be other working-class students.

3. *Mismatch between classroom expectations and students' behavioral and learning styles.* Although they have not been adequately researched, explanations involving a mismatch between students' behavioral and learning styles and school expectations may help account for the relatively low academic performance of many low-status students. For example, Boykin (1978) has examined the research on home and school behavioral characteristics of black children and concluded that the "psychological/behavioral verve" that he believes many black youngsters display interacts with the typical classroom environment to produce failure and misbehavior in school. According to this interpretation, many black children show a higher-than-average "chronic activation level . . . through exposure to more constant high and variable stimulation" in homes characterized by "televisions on continuously, stereos constantly blaring, a steady stream of people coming in and out of the home, [and] a greater number of people per living space" (p. 346). (Recall Aries's description in Chapter 3 of preindustrial community in England.)

Boykin believes that the increased "behavioral vibrancy" and "psychological affinity for stimulus change" produced in many children in such an environment place them at a disadvantage in classrooms that are "relatively unstimulating, constraining, and monotonous" (p. 347). In support of this conclusion, he cites research such as that of Greenberg and Davidson (1972), which showed a high correlation between school achievement and orderliness of the home among inner-city black students, and research by Guttentag and Ross (1972), which concluded that low-status black students learned verbal concepts better through an instructional method that used movement than through traditional passive learning. Morgan (1980) also described classrooms in which "management for docility" appears to lead many black children, particularly males, to "disengage from the mainstream of academic tasks" (p. 51). The schools' failure to take children's activity level into account may thus be an example of "blaming" or "victimizing" the child for the institution's failure to make appropriate adaptations in classroom practice. (Also see Gilbert and Gay 1985.)

Although Boykin limits his consideration to black students and refers to "certain cultural and ancestral" factors that may result in high behavioral verve, we believe that his description of their home environment is not accurate for many or most middle-class black children but is characteristic of the family setting of many underclass children whatever their racial or ethnic group. For example, descriptions by Oscar Lewis (1961) and Piri Thomas (1967) of the environment of underclass Hispanic children indicate that many probably will encounter classroom problems related to a relatively high activation level. In addition, the fact that regardless of racial-ethnic background, many more boys than girls experience school problems associated with hyperkinetic behavior may indicate that underclass boys generally face more severe problems in adjusting to traditional school environments than do underclass girls.

It should be noted that some researchers believe that overstimulation in the home environment frequently interferes directly with learning by making students unusually distractible and inattentive. But whether analysis places emphasis on ways in which high activity level may detract from cognitive learning or on behavioral problems that many low-status students experience in a traditional classroom, there is little doubt that mismatch between home environments and classroom environments and expectations plays an important part in accounting for the low academic performance of many low-status students. Social class differences in nutrition, such as a greater working-class dependence on junk food, may also play a part in producing unusually high activity levels that detract from learning in traditional classrooms. Elsewhere in this book, we discuss the need to structure learning conditions for economically disadvantaged students, but this does not mean that structure should force students to be unnaturally inactive, fixate student and teacher attention on discipline as opposed to development of independent learning skills, or detract from emphasis on abstract thinking skills.

Another perspective on possible learning style differences that may affect the development and achievement of disadvantaged students has been provided by Barbara Shade and others who have been studying cognitive patterns among black children. Shade (1982) has reviewed research bearing on the cognitive style of black students and has concluded that part of their achievement deficit involves an "Afro-American cognitive or perceptual style preference" that emphasizes a *person* rather than an *object* orientation (p. 236). Such an orientation, which appears to be relatively common among economically disadvantaged students in general, may in turn create or magnify difficulties experienced by disadvantaged students in elementary and secondary schools:

> *For Afro-American learners . . . [there appears to be] a preference for people-oriented situations and for spontaneous and novel stimuli and situations . . . and a highly affective orientation toward ideas, things, situations, and individuals. . . . [which may be associated with a relatively great need for] constant encouragement, recognition, warmth, and reassurance in order for them to continue participating in the schooling process. . . . It is postulated that an enhanced ability in social cognition may work to the detriment of individuals within an object-oriented setting such as the school. (Shade 1982, 237–238)*

4. *Lack of previous success in school.* Failure to learn adequately in the early grades is damaging not just to a student's chances to understand later material but also to the student's perceptions of himself or herself as a capable learner and his or her confidence in having a chance to succeed later in school and in life. Partly for this reason, many low-status students have a low self-concept as a learner and low feelings of control over what happens to them in the school (Broderick and Sewell 1983). Other things equal, such feelings will be associated with even more failure later, because students who feel they cannot or do not have a chance to learn are less likely to work hard toward this end than are students who feel confident about their learning capabilities.

5. *Difficulty of teaching conditions and lack of adequate preparation for teachers in low-status schools.* As implied in the preceding discussion, it is difficult to teach low-status students because many need extra help and assistance to function effectively as learners. Middle-status students tend to benefit from traditional

curricula more than do low-status students, and in any case they generally make some academic progress even if the quality of their instruction is poor. Low-status students, in contrast, tend to fail academically, and their teachers, like the students themselves, are frustrated and defeated by lack of success in the classroom. As students fall further behind in their classwork, they tend to lose interest in school and many cause behavior problems in the classroom. Teachers become still more frustrated dealing with both academic and behavioral problems and experience difficulty establishing a productive learning environment in the classroom.

The problem is compounded by the fact that few teachers have had adequate preparation for solving the learning or behavior problems they encounter among low-status students, since neither preservice nor in-service training programs generally develop much practical skill in dealing with these types of problems. As a result, some teachers either give up trying to teach low-achieving students or try to obtain less frustrating positions teaching higher achieving students who may present fewer overt problems.

The difficult problems encountered by a teacher—particularly a new teacher—in working-class schools have been illustrated by Binzen in an account of his experience as a new fourth-grade teacher in a predominantly white working-class school. Binzen describes how he received a note from a teacher next door, who said:

> *"Will you please keep your kids quiet? We can't hear ourselves think!" Very funny. Well, I couldn't think either. The kids simply ran roughshod over me. . . . Somehow it became two o'clock. Time for physical education. The gym instructor awaited my little band of hardened criminals. The class lined up raggedly and, on my signal, raced down the stairwell as though shot from a cannon . . . the class came trooping back. The physical-education teacher had refused to accept such a disorganized, uncontrolled horde. I really couldn't blame him. (Binzen 1970, 178–179)*

6. *Teacher perceptions of student inadequacy.* Related to the frustrations and failure experienced both by students and teachers, teachers of low-status students easily can conclude that their pupils are inadequate learners and have little capacity for attaining academic success. This perception tends to become a self-fulfilling prophecy because teachers who believe their students cannot learn are less likely to work hard in designing appropriate learning experiences than are teachers who believe that their pupils can perform much better if properly taught (Good 1981, 1982; Brophy and Good 1986). In addition, students tend to be influenced by the views and treatment of their teachers and other significant figures in their lives, such as parents and peers; students whose significant others treat them as inadequate learners will tend to internalize this perception and perform still more poorly in the future. It was this probability that led a U.S. Office of Education Task Force on Urban Instructional Strategies (1977) to conclude that too many "teachers and administrators in communities with high concentrations of poor children believe these children cannot learn.

All too often this has become a self-fulfilling prophecy. . . . The need to create positive teachers' attitudes about and responses to the learning styles and aptitudes of the urban pupil cannot be overemphasized" (p. 8).

7. *Homogeneous grouping, tracking, and differential treatment of low-status students within schools and classrooms.* Related to the lack of success and problems in self-concept as a learner that low-status students experience in school is the tendency to set low-achieving students apart in special classes or in separate classroom groups, generally as part of an effort to provide special instruction appropriate to their current level of performance. However, as noted in Chapter 2, many educators believe that separate grouping of low-achieving students tends to create more problems than it solves, and that it is better to individualize instruction within heterogeneous groups rather than risk reinforcing feelings of incompetence generated by singling out low achievers to be part of a group of so-called dummies. Rist illustrated some of these problems in his study of classroom dynamics in a predominantly low-status elementary school in which he found that some teachers tended to fail with the lowest-status students and wound up focusing most of their energy helping the few high-achieving students who they perceived would benefit most from instruction:

> *The class was divided into groups: those expected to succeed ("fast learners") and those expected to fail ("slow learners"). . . . this categorization had the following results:*
>
> *(1) Differential treatment was accorded the two groups in the classroom, the group designated as "fast" learners receiving the most teaching time, rewards, and attention from the teacher. Those designated as "slow learners" were taught infrequently, subjected to more control, and received little if any support from the teacher.*
>
> *(2) The interactional patterns between the teacher and the various groups in her class became increasingly rigidified, taking on caste-like characteristics, during the course of the school year. . . .*
>
> *(3) The consequence of the differential experiences of the children within the same kindergarten classroom was that they were differentially prepared for the first grade. The first grade teacher grouped the children according to the amount of "readiness" material they had completed in kindergarten. (Rist 1973, 91)*

This kind of development occurs frequently in working with low-status students, but sometimes an opposite pattern develops. In some cases, teachers confronted with a significant number of low-achieving students concentrate their efforts on this group and as a result tend to neglect the higher-achieving students, hoping that the latter group will make progress without much guidance from the teacher. In a few instances, this approach may work out satisfactorily; but much more frequently, it results in unsatisfactory performance among both groups.

Although the hazards of homogeneous grouping of low-achieving students are clear, implications for practice are not at all clear. On the one hand, some degree of individualized instruction in heterogeneous classes may make it possible to provide effective instruction for both low- and high-achieving students. On the other hand, it is both difficult and expensive to provide individualized instruction effectively (Bennett and Desforges 1988), and efforts to do so in schools with a high percentage of poverty students generally have not been very successful. Instead, teachers confronted with heterogeneous classes in the inner city typically have not been able to work effectively with relatively large numbers of low achievers.

One possible solution is to group low achievers for reading and language arts instruction but to make sure these groups are small and are taught by skilled and well-trained teachers (Slavin 1987). This alternative is in line with recent studies indicating that unusually successful inner-city elementary schools have particularly effective arrangements for teaching low achievers (Levine and Stark 1982; Levine, Levine, and Eubanks 1985), and that "restrictive" school settings (i.e., separate or "isolated" settings for low achievers) may have either positive or negative outcomes, depending on what is done to make instruction effective (Leinhardt and Pallay 1982).

8. *Ineffective delivery of services in classrooms with many low-status students.* The preceding discussion suggests that instructional services generally are difficult to deliver effectively in classrooms with a significant number of low-status students. Although few studies have been conducted bearing directly on this question, those that have examined differences between low-status and middle-status schools suggest that for whatever reason, instruction in low-status classrooms generally is not being carried out as effectively as in predominantly middle-status classrooms. One study was conducted by Deutsch et al. (1964), who found that teachers in low-status schools spent only about half as much time actually teaching as did teachers in middle-status schools, apparently because a much greater proportion of their time was spent dealing with the diversity of classroom problems that arose in the former group of schools as compared with the latter.

A more recent series of studies conducted by Behr and Hanson (1977) carefully examined the degree to which differing schools actually implemented a common instructional program in terms of placing pupils "into the proper point" in the program and then delivered "appropriate program instruction that the pupil . . . [could] complete or receive" (p. 4). It was concluded that "differential access to instruction is afforded in schools where pupils have different biosocial characteristics" (p. 12). "Biosocial" characteristics were defined to include income level, ethnicity, school location, and other variables, and in this regard it was found that students in low-status schools tended to be "underplaced" in the instructional program (i.e., placed at a level below their appropriate starting point, leading to wasted time in working toward program completion). For this and other reasons, including greater delays in implementing the program, they received a lesser "amount of instruction" than did pupils in higher-status schools.

9. *Low standards of performance.* By standards of performance, we mean the requirements for promotion or advancement from one level to another either within a classroom, as when students are moved to a more difficult unit of work

without having mastered earlier skills, or within a school or educational system, as when students are promoted to the next highest grade or from elementary school to high school without having accomplished as much as their abilities would allow.

There are many reasons that low-achieving students are advanced from one level to another without having been required to achieve adequately at the earlier level. These reasons include "sympathy" for students who do not appear to be succeeding; low expectations among teachers who believe that low-status students cannot meet minimum standards; doubt whether retaining students at a current level would stimulate them to perform better in the future; recognition that repeating a given level might involve wasted time going over material already found to be not stimulating or useful; higher financial costs seemingly involved in retaining students at an earlier grade level; and, of course, difficulties encountered in trying to "force" students to work harder in school when they reject teacher demands or live in an environment that is not conducive to study. For reasons such as these, schools have tended to promote students from one level to another without requiring them to do their best work inside the classroom or to complete assignments for outside work, with disastrous results on academic performance.

At the high school level, evidence is available indicating that low-status students tend to be expected and required to accomplish very little, and that they frequently are led to believe that low performance is acceptable to their teachers. This tendency probably is most pronounced in schools with a preponderance of low-status students, because students then reinforce each other in resisting demanding requirements and teachers are most likely to lower standards when they have many pupils who are not meeting them. Whether in a working-class or mixed-status school, however, many low-status students appear to be making very little effort to meet demanding academic requirements by the time they reach the secondary level. Wrigley (1982) has summarized the way in which student-teacher interactions reinforce low standards of performance:

> *[Low-track students] dislike teachers who do not trouble to maintain educational illusions. . . . The frequency with which even students who are doing very poorly in school say that they aspire to middle-class professional occupations indicates that it is difficult to give up the idea of success through schooling; the student may well have given it up in a practical, day-to-day sense . . . but it is far more devastating to have teachers who . . . have already given up. . . .*
>
> *. . . As academic work requires steady application in the absence of much immediate return . . . it is hard for many ghetto youth to muster this application in the face of the unemployment and low earnings that are pervasive in their milieu. Educational ambivalence is essential to the functioning of many ghetto schools; if the students lose faith entirely, they become impossible to control, yet the teachers do not want to foster hopeless illusions about their students' possible success. Thus, students are praised for work that might actually be below par, even while a climate of failure and misdirected application hangs over the entire school. (pp. 242, 245)*

Massey, Scott, and Dornbusch (1975) studied student attitudes at eight high schools in San Francisco and provided data indicating that academic requirements for low-status students were very low and that low standards appeared to have detrimental effects, overall, on student attitudes. These authors compared the attitudes of black, Spanish surname, other white, and Asian-American students and found that black students seemed to be most frequently victimized by systematically low expectations; hence, they titled their report "Racism without Racists: Institutional Racism in Urban Schools." However, it is likely that their black sample was lower in status than were the other three groups, so that their findings can be attributed as much or more to classism as to racism, and in any case they found the low standards pattern operating among low-status students whatever their racial or ethnic group:

> *A curious irony is presented. Black students . . . were doing the least amount of work in school. Yet . . . they believed they were trying extremely hard. How is it possible . . . that black students are allowed to kid themselves on their level of effort . . . given their low academic achievement and grades?*
>
> *. . . About half of the students believed they would not usually get poor grades if they did poor work or did not try. . . . The students did not feel that grades operated as mechanisms of control to encourage greater effort. (Massey, Scott, and Dornbusch 1975, 8–9)*

Attitudes and Performance in School

Conclusions enumerated above regarding expectations for students and their response to these expectations underline the importance of examining student attitudes in conjunction with conditions in the schools they attend when trying to identify the reasons pupils fail in the classroom. In general, it is desirable that students feel they are competent learners in the classroom, but this feeling of competency should be based on actual accomplishment; otherwise high self-concept as a learner may be an inflated perception that does not signify high motivation to succeed. High self-concept as a learner is not very useful unless it signifies attainment of learning goals in the past and understanding of what is required to attain more difficult goals in the future. From this point of view, one of the most damaging effects of segregating students by social class and race may be that such segregation frequently causes low-status students to develop an unrealistically high self-concept as a learner. In the terminology of Massey, Scott, and Dornbusch, this is part of the process wherein low-status students "are allowed to misinterpret feedback on their level of effort and achievement."

These considerations help to explain why research relating self-concept to achievement tends to report only a small association between measures of the two variables (Ligon, Hester, Baenen, and Matuszek 1977). In the first place, it is difficult to measure self-concept accurately, since respondents tend to give positive responses even if they have considerable doubt about their abilities. In addition, there are many aspects or dimensions of self-concept, including self-image in general and competence in social activities and athletics. A child's self-concept also may change substantially from day to day or year to year, in accordance with maturational factors or with things that happen to the child inside or outside the classroom. But probably as important as any of these in accounting for low relationships between measured self-concept and achievement is the tendency for self-concept scores to be grossly inflated among low-achieving students who are led to believe their performance is adequate even when they are allowed to perform far below their capacity.

Self-concept also is related in complex ways to other aspects of attitude and behavior in the classroom. It is likely, for example, that a student who has a low self-concept as a learner due to previous failure in the classroom also will feel that he or she has little chance to do better in the future, and these feelings may result in reduced effort and still lower self-concept and sense of control. If, on the other hand, the student's self-concept is lowered due to higher demands for performance but higher demands result in higher performance, then self-concept, a sense of control, and other attitudes toward school may all improve later. In addition, sense of control involves a number of important dimensions that interact with self-concept in influencing subsequent effort and achievement.

For example, attribution theory suggests that students who take responsibility for their failures may benefit from having a high sense of control over what happens to them in school, whereas students who blame "unfair" teachers or other outside forces may not work harder to achieve success even if their teachers look for ways to encourage success and build a feeling of confidence in the future (Maehr 1983). "Internal attributions for success," according to Weiner (1976), "augment pride in accomplishment and thus magnify the reward for goal attainment . . . [also increasing] the probability of future achievement-related actions" (p. 197), but students who are high in self concept tend to interpret success in terms of their own ability, whereas low self-concept students are less likely to react in terms of "personal causation" (Ames and Felker 1977). All these considerations also may be related to the inferences a student may make concerning his or her worthiness as a person and the opportunity to be successful in life based on the fact that he or she lives in a segregated, low-status community or attends a segregated, low-status school.

The preceding discussion has shown that student attitudes, teacher expectations, and previous failure in school play an important part in limiting the academic performance of low-status students. These and other considerations such as inappropriateness of learning materials interact in complex ways in reducing motivation to succeed and reinforcing initial disadvantages associated with home and family background, particularly in schools in which the overall school climate exemplifies low expectations for students and a sense of futility that anything can be done to improve achievement. This type of climate is not inevitable in a low-status school or classroom, but it does tend to be prevalent in situations where students have experienced repeated failure in the past.

Implications for Instruction

The most important implication of the preceding discussion is that it is critically important to structure the learning experiences of low-status students so they succeed in school and develop a substantively based sense of competence as learners who are able to perform at an acceptable level in the classroom. This need was mentioned in Chapter 3, and its importance is underscored when we consider what happens to low-achieving students from nonstimulating home environments after they enter the schools.

Does this conclusion suggest that low-status students should be given high grades in order to bolster their sense of adequacy in the classroom, regardless of whether their actual effort or achievement is high or low? Keeping in mind the evidence indicating that automatic promotion policies have been detrimental to the performance of students in the public schools, it is better to conclude that success must follow from meaningful effort and achievement if it is to generate a cycle also characterized by improved performance and a positive but realistic self-concept as a learner. Teachers should work in any way they can to strengthen the academic and nonacademic self-concepts of low-status students, but their foremost effort should be to stimulate and help students master academic skills in the classroom.

Does it then follow that teachers should fail to promote low-status students from one academic level to another in order to encourage them to work harder, achieve success, and thereby raise their academic self-concept and later performance? This solution, too, is unsatisfactory, because failure generally helps a child very little and may destroy his or her motivation to succeed in the future. Just as the arguments in favor of automatic promotion have been one-sided in taking into account the negative effects of retention in grade on a failing pupil but not considering the effects on others in the classroom when a student who makes little or no effort is promoted from one grade to the next (Levine 1966), so, too, it is simple-minded to believe that merely failing to promote students whose effort or achievement is below their capacities will help many of them attain higher levels of performance later.

It should be noted, in this regard, that recent efforts to depart from what have become traditional automatic promotion policies in United States schools generally are adopting a more sophisticated and promising approach than did some earlier efforts simply to "flunk them out if they can't or won't learn." For example, school officials in Greensville, Virginia, rejected the automatic promotions policy in 1973, and 800 out of 3,750 students were retained in grade (Owen and Ranick 1977). The following year, after an achievement-based promotion policy had been explained to the public, 1,100 were not promoted. In the succeeding year, the number of nonpromoted students dropped to 695, and achievement scores meanwhile began to increase dramatically. For example, average scores in seventh-grade reading rose from the twenty-sixth to the sixty-fourth percentile.

These developments have made the Greensville approach synonymous with punitive education in some circles but a praiseworthy example of desirable change in other quarters, particularly among people advocating a return to the basics in education. What has often been overlooked on both sides is that the Greensville program included not just a rejection of automatic promotions but also a number of concomitant changes such as new organizational arrangements for conducting instruction, emphasis on diagnosis and correction of individual learning problems, staff development and a system of teacher accountability, close cooperation with parents and the community in implementing the new policies, and development of alternative curricula based on student interests. In other words, the Greensville approach involves a new *system* of organization and instruction of which achievement-based promotions is only one important part. By itself, rejection of automatic promotions probably would have accomplished little in improving the performance of low-achieving students.

What this discussion does suggest, then, is that to improve the academic performance of low-status students requires the development and implementation of new systems of instruction and organization that carefully structure learning experience to ensure successful mastery of academic skills required for later academic work. One alternative for doing this is the *mastery learning* approach, which is being developed and tested in many types of schools at various educational levels. The mastery learning approach has been described at length in a 1976 book on *Human Characteristics and School Learning* by Benjamin S. Bloom. His central argument is that 95 percent of students can "master" what the schools have to teach at practically the same level of mastery, with the slower 20 percent of students needing 10 to 20 percent more time than the faster 20 percent. Though slower students require a longer period of time than others to achieve mastery, they can do so if their knowledge level is diagnosed accurately and if they are taught the material with appropriate curriculum and methods of teaching in a sequential manner beginning with the level where they are now.

To do this, it is necessary to focus attention on a smaller unit rather than on an entire course or curriculum. An entire course such as fifth-grade reading is too complex to be studied all at once with the detailed attention to basic facts that is needed. Many students have difficulty keeping up with their work because they do not have the "entry skills" to master the material they are asked to learn. Bloom says that in this situation the teacher's job is to find out which students lack the knowledge and skills expected of students at their grade level, and then to teach them systematically from the base of their present level of entry skills and knowledge.

Bloom and his colleagues believe that quality of instruction should be defined in terms of the cues or directions provided to the learner, the reinforcement that the learner secures, and the feedback or corrective system instituted for overcoming problems that arise in the learning process. He and his colleagues have found that individual assistance to the slower students in the early stages of a new learning experience helps more than does the same amount of assistance at a later stage. They cite several research studies that show substantial achievement gains by classes using these procedures (Bloom 1988). Several of these studies have been carried out with low-status students in big cities, and reports of successful implementation of mastery learning programs are present in the literature on research and evaluation in big-city schools (Smith and Wick 1976; Levine 1985; Levine and Eubanks 1986/87; Abrams 1988).

Even before data on these projects were available, Rosenshine (1976; 1986) had surveyed the research on the effectiveness of various teaching methods and concluded that the most successful approach for students of low socioeconomic status uses "direct instruction," which he defined as including "a drill pattern consisting of questions that the students could answer, followed by feedback and subsequent questions," and a "pattern of direct instruction, consisting of small steps at the students' level and a great deal of work mediated by either the teacher or workbooks" (1976, p. 368).

However, we also should emphasize that improving the academic performance of low-status students is likely to require (1) a broader approach than simply working on basic skills, in order to develop students' capacity for learning increasingly abstract subject matter as they proceed through the grades; and (2) explicit "matching" of learning experiences with the individual "style" of students who are at somewhat different stages in conceptual development.

1. *Abstract thinking skills.* Direct instruction seems to be effective in helping low-status students master essential skills such as word recognition in reading, but later they will have to acquire more abstract skills if they are to remain successful in school. Lack of development of abstract thinking skills may be one reason that many special preschool and primary programs for low-status students have been successful in improving academic achievement but that gains made by students at these levels disappeared later when students entered higher grades (Bronfenbrenner 1974).

A number of educators working with low-status students are aware of this problem and are trying to find ways to develop abstract thinking skills, in addition to basic skills such as word recognition in reading and fundamental operations (multiplication, division) in mathematics. For example, Kessler and Quinn (1977) have found that instruction in hypothesis testing, which they refer to as an "inquiry approach" to "cognitive development," improved the language development of sixth graders both high and low in social status. After working to develop skills in Spanish as well as English in a bilingual population, they reported that there is a

> *correlation between the ability to generate hypotheses and the level of language development as measured in terms of syntactic complexity. This correlation is independent of socio-economic variables, indicating that this is a generalized principle operating for all children. And . . . the principle may be expected to apply in any type of language acquisition situation, either first or second. (Kessler and Quinn 1977, 20)*

2. *Matching instruction with student's conceptual level.* We have mentioned that direct instruction in a structured learning environment appears to be the most effective approach for improving the academic performance of low-status students. However, this generalization should not be applied mechanically, because any group of students is likely to show considerable variation in conceptual

development and in responses to differing types of instructional approaches. For this reason, efforts should be made whenever possible to provide a learning environment that is appropriate to each student's learning needs and stage of development.

Researchers who have been studying the relationships between student characteristics and learning environments believe that appropriate matching of environments and students can result in improved academic performance, whatever the ability level or social background of the student involved. David E. Hunt, for example, has been investigating students' "conceptual level" in relation to the learning environments that are most effective in the classroom. By "conceptual level," Hunt refers to "both cognitive complexity (differentiation, discrimination, and integration) as well as interpersonal maturity (increasing self-responsibility)" (Hunt 1975a, 218). A person at a higher level, according to Hunt, is "more structurally complex, more capable of responsible actions, and, most important, more capable of adapting to a changing environment." Hunt's studies also indicate that conceptual level is significantly higher in middle-class groups of students than in working-class groups at the same grade level, though working-class groups tend to have more variability than do middle-class groups (Hunt 1965).

Over the years, Hunt and his colleagues have conducted a number of studies to identify the effects of differing learning environments categorized by the "*degree of structure*, or the degree of organization provided by the learning environment. In high structure, the environment is largely determined by the teacher, and the student himself has little responsibility, whereas in low structure, the student is much more responsible for organizing the environment" (Hunt 1975, 219). In one early study conducted at junior high schools in Syracuse, Hunt and his colleagues showed that low conceptual level students placed in classes in which teachers were requested to provide a structured environment learned more than did low conceptual level students in unstructured classes, whereas high conceptual level students learned more in classes where teachers provided low structure than they did in structured classes. Hunt also has found that students low in conceptual level "can develop skill in self-directed learning," but only if their learning environment provides "step-by-step instructions" to a much greater degree than is needed by high conceptual level students (Hunt et al. 1974, 29).

Concentrated Poverty Schools

Earlier in this chapter, we mentioned that there is reason to believe that instructional services are delivered less effectively in low-status schools than in mixed- or middle-status schools, apparently because the concentration of learning and behavioral problems in low-status schools makes teaching and learning problems particularly difficult there. This generalization suggests that low-status schools tend to be dysfunctional compared to other types of schools. Social-class

segregation in the schools makes it more difficult to provide an adequate education for students from low-status families.

This phenomenon can be seen most clearly by looking at inner-city schools, which we have defined as schools located in concentrated poverty neighborhoods in big cities. Poverty in these neighborhoods is more concentrated on a larger scale than is true in most other low-status neighborhoods; families and students there tend to be particularly isolated within a distinctive urban subculture, and schools tend to face particularly severe problems related to the difficult living conditions that characterize these neighborhoods.

Levine and his colleagues (1979) studied achievement patterns in big-city schools and found that there appears to be a so-called threshold point involving the concentration of urban poverty beyond which the schools as presently organized are unable to function effectively. Evidence for this conclusion was found by examining measures of poverty status among students in elementary schools or poverty-related characteristics of neighborhoods they serve and relating these scores to average reading achievement for students in grades three through six. For each elementary school in a given district, the poverty score was plotted on a graph that also showed the average achievement for a particular grade level. For example, Figure 8.1 shows the percentage of students eligible for subsidized lunch in 1976 (an indicator of poverty) and average sixth-grade reading achievement scores for each of sixty-one schools in Kansas City, Missouri.

As shown in the figure, there appears to be a threshold point of 35 to 40 percent poverty pupils beyond which none of the schools have high achievement scores. None of the forty-two schools that had 40 percent or more of their students eligible for subsidized lunch had achievement scores above 5.7, whereas thirteen of nineteen schools with less than 40 percent poverty pupils had scores higher than 5.7. This means that at least half the pupils in the forty-two schools with 40 percent or more poverty pupils scored below 5.7, which in turn is more than a year below the national norm of 6.8 for the date the test was administered. Clearly, a significant number of the students in these concentrated poverty schools are not learning to read. Similar patterns regarding reading comprehension have been found for Chicago, Cincinnati, Cleveland, Houston, Los Angeles, Milwaukee, Rochester, and other big cities for which Levine and his colleagues obtained appropriate data.

Other socioeconomic factors related to poverty also characterize the neighborhoods in which school achievement is low. For example, the schools with lowest sixth-grade reading scores were in neighborhoods with the highest percentage of households with 1.51 or more persons per room. Similarly, almost all schools in neighborhoods in which 3 to 5 percent or more of the adult women were separated from their husbands had low reading scores.

The authors of this study interpreted their indicators of neighborhood socioeconomic status as measuring not just concentrated urban poverty but also high social and family disorganization in the neighborhoods that had a high proportion of poverty residents. Crime rates, for example, were highly correlated with poverty and were related to achievement in the same way as was

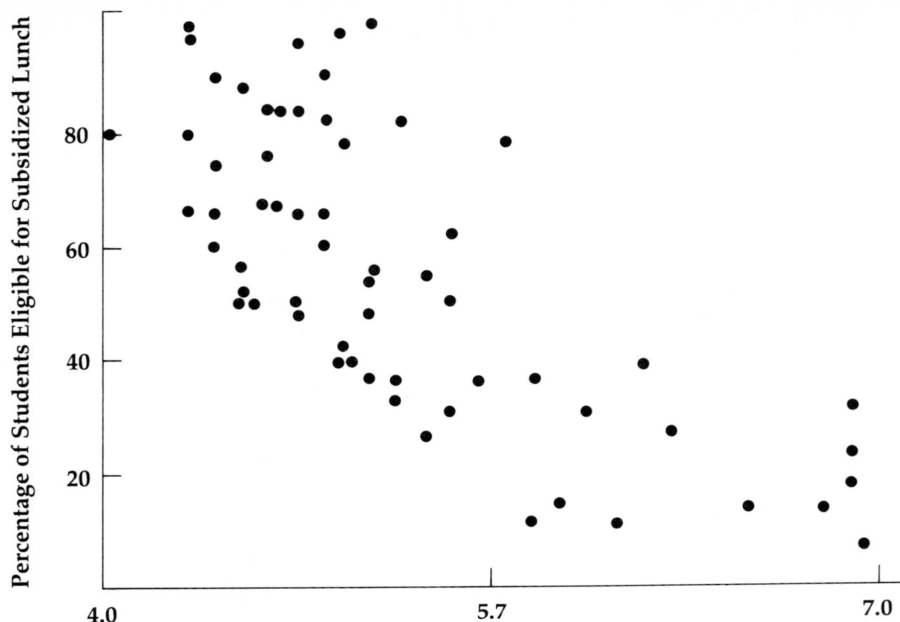

Figure 8.1 *Average Sixth-Grade Scores Plotted against Percentage of Students Eligible for Subsidized Lunch, Sixty-One Kansas City, Missouri, Elementary Schools, 1976* (*Source*: Kansas City, Missouri Public Schools.)

percentage of poverty students. High density (people per room), housing deterioration (percentage of year-round vacant housing units), and family disorganization (separated females; female-headed households) were interpreted as indicating general social disorganization in a neighborhood. Measures such as percentage of separated females were interpreted not as measuring the "adequacy" of individual female-headed families but as denoting the existence of socially disorganized communities. (There was little relationship between percentage of separated females and achievement either above or below the threshold point that isolated the concentrated poverty schools from other schools in the six cities.)

Three additional aspects of this research should be emphasized in considering the relationships between concentrated urban poverty and school achievement. First, although a large proportion of the concentrated poverty population in many big cities are racial minorities, there also are concentrated poverty schools that are predominantly white. These schools meet the concentrated poverty criteria specified above, such as having a threshold percentage of their students eligible for subsidized lunch, and also have reading scores in the bottom part of the achievement distributions in their respective cities.

Table 8.1 *Actual and Predicted Third-Grade Reading Comprehension Scores for St. Louis Elementary Schools, 1970–1971*

School Number	Actual Third-Grade Reading Achievement, 1970–1971	Predicted Third-Grade Reading Achievement, 1970–1971	Difference
1	3.3	3.8	−.5
2	3.3	3.5	−.2
3	4.0	4.0	.0
4	4.7	4.5	.2
5	3.6	3.8	−.2
6	3.5	3.4	.1
7	3.9	3.8	.1
8	3.3	3.4	−.1
9	3.7	3.3	.4
10	4.3	4.1	.2
11	3.1	3.3	−.2
12	4.1	4.2	−.1
13	3.4	3.4	.0
14	3.6	3.4	.2
15	4.1	4.0	.1
16	4.4	4.3	.1
17	4.2	3.9	.3
18	4.0	4.1	−.1
19	4.2	4.0	.2
20	3.5	3.5	.0
21	3.1	3.4	−.3
22	3.3	3.8	−.5
23	3.2	3.5	−.3
24	3.5	3.3	.2
25	4.3	4.2	.1
26	3.3	3.3	.0
27	4.2	4.2	−.1
28	4.4	4.3	.1
29	4.3	4.3	.0
30	3.2	3.6	−.4

Source: St. Louis Public Schools and authors' calculations.

Second, threshold points can be found among groups of schools that are predominantly minority in the same manner as they are found in the samples for the cities as a whole. Among a group of sixty-four predominantly black schools in Chicago, for example, none of the thirty-six in neighborhoods in which 3 percent or more of households had 1.51 or more people per room had sixth-grade reading scores above 5.2 in 1969, as contrasted with nineteen of twenty-eight schools with lower density scores that had achievement scores above 5.2. This finding suggests that socioeconomic status and concentrated poverty, not race and ethnicity, are the key determinants of low achievement in big-city schools.

Third, in line with what one would expect given the relationships enumerated above, achievement scores in big-city schools are highly predictable based on information about the socioeconomic and concentrated poverty status of the neighborhoods in which they are located. Table 8.1, for example, shows the actual third-grade reading scores and the scores statistically predicted for the first thirty schools in a sample of sixty-five schools in St. Louis. The predicted scores are based on the following four types of information: percentage of students from families receiving public assistance; percentage of adult females separated; percentage of owner-occupied housing units lacking plumbing; and number of separated females per residential acre. The statistics used in predicting achievement scores took into account the threshold points denoting concentrated urban poverty. As shown in the table, all of the actual scores were within one-half grade level of the predicted scores. Predictions for the remaining schools not shown in the table were equally accurate.

Threshold Phenomena in Inner-City Schools and Society

If it is true that concentrated urban poverty is associated with the existence of threshold points beyond which inner-city schools do not function effectively, it is important to understand why this may happen and what it may mean in terms of implications for the improvement of academic performance in the inner-city school.

No research has been conducted explicitly to determine at what point learning and behavior problems in low-status schools may make it extremely difficult to deliver instruction effectively, but research by Deutsch and by Behr and Hanson, cited earlier in this chapter, does indicate that teachers in low-status as compared to middle-status schools tend to spend relatively more time on non-instructional tasks and have greater difficulty providing appropriate instruction at each student's current level of performance.

If this is so, as seems likely in view of the relatively high incidence of learning and behavior problems among low-status students, it probably also is true that teachers in low-status schools experience growing difficulty as the number of problems to be solved approaches and exceeds a point at which problems are being compounded faster than they are being solved. For example, where a teacher in a middle-status school may have two or three academically retarded students, a teacher in a low-status school may have eight or ten such students and may have to spend so much time helping this group that the majority of students in the class are neglected.

Similarly for administrators, counselors, and other school personnel, concentrated urban poverty appears to be associated with a proliferation of problems beyond the point at which educators are able to carry out their jobs successfully and the schools are able to function effectively. High school counselors, for example, will be unable to discharge responsibilities such as providing personal advice for students or guiding high school students into appropriate postsecondary careers if most of their time is spent keeping track of truancies and suspensions (as frequently happens in inner-city schools). In other words, doubling the number of problems in a school may triple or quadruple the difficulty of dealing with them and may result in dysfunction throughout the institution.

The much greater incidence of problems at schools with a substantial percentage of low-status students than at schools with few such students is shown graphically in Figure 8.2. This figure shows the percentage of low-income students in relation to teachers' perceptions of certain problems at high schools in the Milwaukee metropolitan area in 1984. The average for the central-city high schools is represented by a "C"; suburban high schools are represented by "S." The problem score is based on teachers' responses to four types of problems following the question, "To what degree do you consider each of the factors below to be a problem that detracts from your ability to do the best possible job of teaching your students?" The four problems dealt respectively with "inadequate student preparation," "students cannot read," "classroom discipline," and "English is students' second language." A higher score on the problems scale represents a perception that problems are severe rather than unimportant.

Figure 8.2 shows the clear tendency for teachers at high schools with a higher proportion of low-income students to report a greater incidence or degree of problems present in their schools than do teachers at schools with higher-income students. (The percentages of low-income students at the suburban schools are slightly exaggerated because they enroll small percentages of transfer students from the city school district.) In addition the high schools in the city of Milwaukee exceed the suburban high schools both in percentage of low-income students and in teachers' perceptions that problems involving student preparation and discipline interfere with the effectiveness of their teaching.

Knowledge of the high incidence and severity of teaching/learning problems at concentrated poverty schools helps us understand why many researchers have concluded that socioeconomic rather than simple racial integration can improve educational opportunities for low-income minority students. For example, Coleman and his colleagues (1966) and O'Reilly (1969) reviewed research on desegregation and concluded that schools with predominantly low-status students do not provide a positive educational environment. When carried out effectively, socioeconomic desegregation can reduce the number of students who attend concentrated poverty schools.

These speculations also help explain why enormous expenditures to improve the performance of students in inner-city schools frequently appear to have had little discernible impact on the academic achievement of students in these schools. Pouring additional money into these schools for whatever purpose—more materials, more teachers, new equipment—may make little difference if the school as a whole is not changed sufficiently to deal successfully with learning and behavior problems in the classroom. Fiddmont (1976) studied a group of seventeen Kansas City elementary schools eligible for federal assistance for low-income students and found that 25 million dollars in special federal,

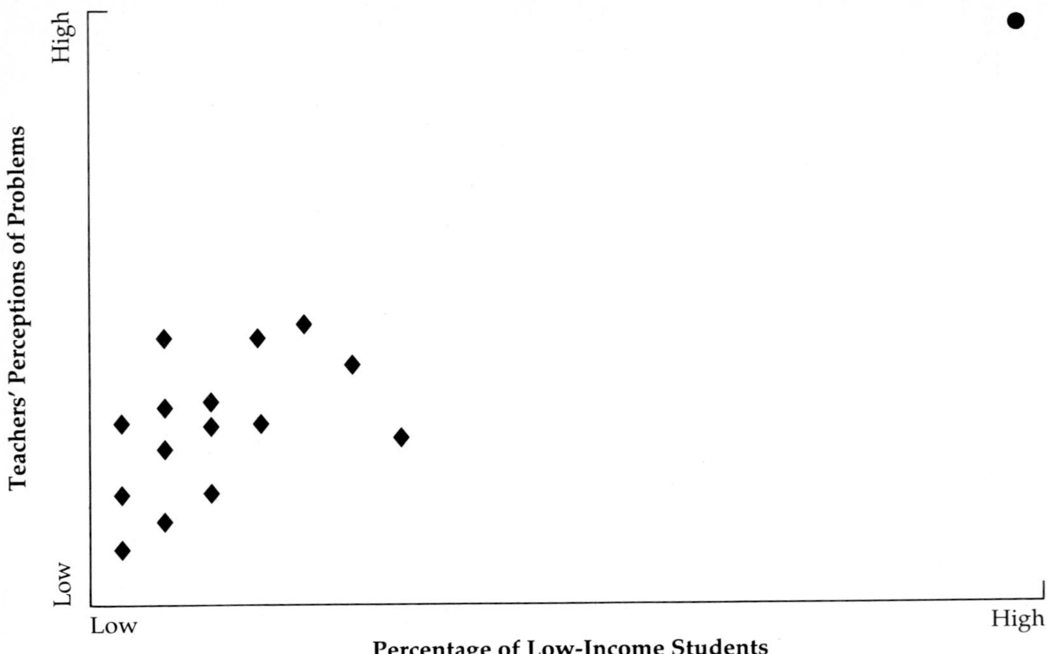

● = City; ◆ = Suburban. Each symbol represents the location of one school on each axis. Problems that teachers assessed included "inadequate student preparation," "students cannot read," "classroom discipline," and "English is students' second language."

Figure 8.2 ***Relationship between Teachers' Perceptions of Problems and Percentage of Low-Income Students at High Schools in the Milwaukee Metropolitan Area, by City and Suburb*** (*Source*: Authors' analysis of data available from the Study Commission on the Quality of Education in the Metropolitan Milwaukee Public Schools.)

state, and local funds were spent to improve education between 1965 and 1975 in addition to regular per pupil expenditures, but achievement levels in these schools changed hardly at all in this ten-year period. Similarly, Rand Corporation researchers analyzed eleven inner-city schools in New York City that had received forty million dollars in federal money over a period of four years and found no improvement at all in academic achievement or truancy rates.

It should be stressed that other social institutions in the inner city face comparable problems in handling the multiple problems characteristic of concentrated poverty neighborhoods (Wilson 1982). As regards the law enforcement system, for example, police and other personnel faced with a particularly high incidence of crime have less time to deal effectively with any given offense; partly as a result, their morale tends to deteriorate, offenders are apprehended and punished relatively less frequently than in low crime areas, young people do not perceive that there is much connection between crime and punishment, and conditions favorable to the spread of delinquency then become as destructive as the most virulent physical epidemic.

Institutions concerned with maintenance of the physical environment are similarly impacted by conditions in the inner city. Savings and loan associations, for example, may be unable to make a profit when the default rate on home loans doubles from 2 or 3 percent to 5 or 6 percent; one result is that residents of the inner city are unable to obtain loans to maintain or improve their property, except, perhaps, at exorbitant interest rates that lead to still more defaults. Once a few properties on an inner-city block become deteriorated and unsalable, property values nearby go down and lending institutions become still more reluctant to approve loans. Before long, a threshold point has been reached beyond which occurs a spiralling cycle of further deterioration and deflation in the capital stock of the neighborhood.

Furthermore, it also should be recognized that dysfunctioning in one inner-city institution such as the school tends to lead to dysfunctioning in others, such as the law enforcement system or the housing maintenance system. A full analysis of institutional functioning in the inner city would consider the interrelationships between differing institutions and urban systems, as when abandoned housing provides a breeding ground for delinquency among teenagers or when students who can barely read drop out of school and begin looking for work that requires a higher level of literacy. Inner-city schools, for their part, are faced with the problem of teaching large numbers of students whose main concern frequently is that of survival in the neighborhood outside the school. Overloaded with too many students who themselves are overloaded with a multitude of individual and family problems, the public schools as traditionally organized and operated sometimes then may all but cease functioning educationally.

Violence in the Schools

One of the most serious problems confronting many schools in concentrated poverty neighborhoods is the tendency for violence in the community to affect teaching and learning conditions in the schools. Violent and other antisocial behavior of one sort or another is more prevalent there than in most other neighborhoods, and it is difficult if not impossible to prevent problems in the community from impinging on the schools. At the elementary level, vandalism and extortion against younger students are frequent problems, and physical assaults against students and teachers frequently constitute additional problems at the secondary level. At either level, a climate of violence outside the school is not conducive to study or learning on the part of students whose attention is bound to be distracted by this type of detrimental environment (Rubel 1980).

Violence in and around big-city schools has constituted a growing problem since the early 1960s. Part of this trend is reflected in an increase in assaults on teachers, particularly in urban schools (Leff 1980). The National Education Association estimated that 3 percent of public school teachers had been assaulted in 1974, compared with 1.4 percent in 1964, and that rates for urban teachers increased from 2.5 percent in 1964 to 5.4 percent in 1974 (Stalford 1977). Violence in the schools appeared to escalate particularly rapidly in the early 1970s, after which time the U.S. Senate Subcommittee to Investigate Juvenile Delinquency (1977) estimated that in school districts with more than 10,000 students, assaults on teachers increased by 77 percent between 1970 and 1973, assaults on students increased by 85 percent, weapons confiscations increased by 54 percent, and rape or attempted rape increased by 40 percent (Marvin et al. 1976). Rates of violence in the public schools have remained relatively stable since the mid-1970s (Baker 1985).

Increasing violence in the schools appears to be closely associated with parallel increases in the size and severity of problems in concentrated urban poverty neighborhoods during the past two decades (Viadero 1987). There is no doubt that these trends are most apparent in big cities in general and in poverty neighborhoods in particular. By 1975, the average annual per pupil cost of vandalism was $5.22 in school districts with 25,000 or more pupils, as compared with $3.18 in districts with 10,000 to 24,999 pupils and a little over $1.50 in districts with less than 10,000 students (Marvin et al. 1976). Violence in and around schools in big cities also is associated with a series of related problems that are particularly characteristic of poverty neighborhoods in these cities, namely, the operation of gangs of teenagers and young adults, the infiltration of schools by intruders and trespassers, and high rates of absence and truancy among students. As regards the functioning of gangs in and around the schools, a 1973 study on youth groups "as a crime problem in major American cities" concluded that although this problem had waxed and waned for decades, there was reason to believe that it became very severe in the 1970s particularly in terms of effects on the schools:

> *In many instances, several gangs, often rivals, operate within the same school—often two or three, in extreme cases eight or more. This creates a high potential for intergang conflict.*
>
> *Gang members above school age or out of school for other reasons customarily frequent school environs, impeding or interdicting passage or entry by non-gang students, attacking rival gang members leaving or going to school, engaging in gang combat, and defacing and destroying school property.* (Miller 1973, 52–53)

Violence in the schools also is related to the extremely high absence and truancy rates now characteristic of low-status secondary schools in big cities. The Executive Secretary of the National Association of Secondary School Principals told the U.S. Senate Subcommittee to Investigate Juvenile Delinquency that absence rates that traditionally had been 4 to 5 percent in city schools had jumped closer to 15 percent in many cities and were approaching 30 percent in some others. At schools with the poorest attendance, he continued, "faculty members would be delighted if they could claim better than 50 percent attendance on any given day" (U.S. Senate Subcommittee 1977, 23). Thus, a study of Chicago high schools concluded that a "culture of cutting" of late morning and early afternoon classes not only was prevalent at the schools studied but had been institutionalized at one school by assigning students to nonexistent study halls (Wells and Prindle 1986).

There obviously are many reasons for absence rates of this magnitude, which signify a breakdown in the functioning of the inner-city high school; one cause is simple fear of going to school. Along these lines, Lalli, Savitz, and Rosen conducted a three-year study of one thousand male students in the Philadelphia Public Schools and reported that nearly half the black students and one-fourth of the whites "viewed the streets to and from school as extremely dangerous" (quoted in Delaney 1975).

Since the mid-1970s, school officials have moved vigorously to contain violence in big-city schools and to make them more secure places in which to teach and learn. Steps taken to accomplish this have included (1) the provision of elaborate security systems, and creation of safety corridors to provide protected access to and from the street; (2) intensification of counseling services for students in trouble; (3) programs to help students acquire basic skills in the classroom; and (4) organizational modifications such as dividing a school into five independent communities (Ianni 1980). In 1976, a study conducted for the National Institute for Juvenile Justice and Delinquency Prevention reported that the overwhelming majority of school administrators who had initiated a combination of these four types of approaches for reducing school violence felt that these actions had been helpful in attaining their goal (Marvin et al. 1976, 46). Nevertheless, the overall effects on education of violence and related problems in concentrated urban poverty neighborhoods were still generally detrimental to learning, as summarized in this eloquent statement by Chicago Superintendent of Schools Manford Byrd:

> *The losses . . . cannot be measured in terms of dollars. No one has measured the immediate and long term effects on the education of children resulting from the climate of fear generated by these conditions. Many hours of education are lost because of false fire alarms and bomb threats. Much harm is done to educational programs when classroom windows are shattered, teaching materials destroyed or stolen, and schools damaged by fire and other acts of vandalism. When students and teachers are fearful of going to school . . . a healthy environment for learning is lost. (U.S. Senate Subcommittee 1977, 17)*

The existence of threshold phenomena and the problem of violence in and around inner-city schools suggest that the goal of improving the education of students in these schools is related to the larger goal of improving general social conditions and opportunities for the underclass residents of concentrated poverty neighborhoods. Unless radical improvements are made in the education available to students in these neighborhoods, and unless systematic national efforts also are made to attack both the structural and cultural causes of underclass status, the typical difficulties of teaching and learning in low-status schools will continue to be compounded in concentrated poverty schools, and achievement in these schools may continue to be extremely low even after sub-

Table 8.2 ***Percentage Distribution of Students by Poverty Status of Their Schools and Race/Ethnicity, 1984***

Race/Ethnicity	Poverty Status of School (average income of students' families)		
	Very Poor (less than 50 percent of poverty line)	*Poor (50–100 percent of poverty line)*	*Nonpoor (Above poverty line)*
Black	26	22	52
Hispanic	15	23	62
Non-Hispanic white	06	08	86

Source: Adapted from Kennedy, Jung, and Orland, 1986.

stantial sums of money are spent to conduct compensatory education programs there.

National information about the incidence of problems that characterize concentrated poverty schools is provided as part of the congressionally mandated National Assessment of Chapter 1. The assessment reported that U.S. schools in the highest quartile on percentage of poverty students (i.e., schools with 25 percent or more poverty students) had higher rates of vandalism and physical violence than did schools in the middle quartiles, which in turn had higher rates than schools in the bottom quartile (Kennedy, Jung, and Orland 1986). It also confirmed that large urban school districts have a much higher percentage of concentrated poverty schools than do smaller districts, and that black and Hispanic students are much more concentrated in poverty schools than are non-Hispanic whites (see Table 8.2). While results regarding the independent effects of concentrated poverty on achievement were complicated and somewhat contradictory, the authors' overall conclusions stated that "achievement scores of all students—not just poor students declined as the proportion of poor in a school increases" and that poverty concentration negatively influences "learning between full grade 1 and full grade 2 as well as at all later time points" (Kennedy, Jung, and Orland 1986, 107, D–32).

The Status of Compensatory Education

It had become clear, by 1965, to most educators that the majority of children from low-income families, particularly from low-income black families, were achieving poorly in the schools and were probably headed for a lifetime of poverty. There was also convincing evidence that these children were severely handicapped by the time they reached school age. Hence, there arose a number of proposals and experiments for working with such children to help compensate for their unfavorable start in life and for their disadvantages in school. The federal government put relatively large sums of money into this field, first through the War on Poverty and the Office of Economic Opportunity, beginning just before 1965, and then through Title I of the Elementary and Secondary Education Act of 1965. By 1976, nearly 6 million low-income children in public elementary and secondary schools were receiving a variety of compensatory education services through Title I or through special state government support for educating disadvantaged students (Frechtling and Nyitray 1977).

It was then, and still is, uncertain what balance of effort should be placed on preschool children as compared with school-age children, and how much relative emphasis should be placed on working to improve the home environment as compared with the school in providing compensatory education.

Those who emphasize the family factor wish to expand preschool classes for socially disadvantaged children, educational work with their mothers and fathers, spread of birth-control knowledge among lower working-class people, and a variety of other forms of assistance and support. Those who emphasize the school factor demand new forms of education, not merely more of the old forms. They call for radical changes in the schools and ask that the schools find new ways of teaching working-class children. Research has identified approaches to improve the effectiveness of schools for disadvantaged students, but most inner-city schools are not yet systematically providing effective education for the urban poor.

Here, we review the status of compensatory education efforts at various levels including the preschool, elementary, secondary, and postsecondary levels. Particularly successful projects for each level are described in order to illustrate the kinds of improvements possible in outstanding programs for improving the academic performance of low-status students.

Preschool Compensatory Education

Several variants of preschool programs have been tried, in which children in the experiments are matched with similar children in comparison groups. The age of children ranges from infancy to five. Some experiments involve training the mothers; others take the children to a preschool site where a variety of educative procedures are used. The most widespread program is Head Start, which has operated in some areas on a six- to eight-week summer basis but now generally functions on a year-round basis and provides two years of preschool instruction for most participants. Children are tested for mental ability as well as for physical health when they enter Head Start programs. They are tested again at the close of a program, and the results are reported to state and federal agencies.

Between 1965 and 1987, Head Start served about 10 million children, approximately one-fifth of the population from families below the income level that determines eligibility for the program. In recent years Head Start has had a budget of about one billion dollars and has served approximately 4,000,000 disadvantaged students per year. Over the years, a progressively greater emphasis developed on helping parents provide a more positive home environment for achievement.

The director of the office of Child Development from June 1970 through July 1972 was Edward Zigler, professor of psychology at Yale University. In 1973, he wrote an article entitled "Project Head Start: Success or Failure?" in which he gave a limited positive evaluation. He argued that Head Start's main goal was social competence, and that this had been improved substantially:

> *Whether Head Start is seen as a success or a failure is determined by the factors one chooses to weigh in making such an assessment. . . . If one assesses Head Start in terms of the improved health of tens of thousands of poor children who have been screened, diagnosed, and treated, Head Start is clearly a resounding success. . . . I believe that a realistic and proper assessment of Head Start demonstrates that is has been a success. (Zigler 1973, 3)*

However, several major evaluations of Head Start have indicated that it is not generally successful in terms of bringing about lasting improvement in students' IQ scores (Caruso and Detterman 1981) or academic achievement (C.S.R. 1985). This conclusion has generated widespread pessimism concerning the potential of preschool efforts to enhance cognitive functioning. On the other hand, educators and researchers have continued to develop and evaluate preschool programs designed to achieve this goal. In 1974, Bronfenbrenner examined the impact of those programs that appeared to have incorporated the most promising approaches for this purpose and had been most carefully implemented and evaluated; he concluded that some of these programs were resulting in significant IQ gains among the students who participated. His review of these and other projects suggested that those that failed to show much "cumulative effect of intervention" generally were programs that employed "traditional nursery school" approaches and hence failed "to employ the kind of structured curriculum" characteristic of the programs that successfully improved cognitive development (Bronfenbrenner 1974, 17).

Bronfenbrenner's 1974 review of preschool compensatory education led to encouraging conclusions about the potential of such efforts, but it was not enough to dispel the pessimism that had become widespread as a result of the Head Start evaluations. Although widely cited, Bronfenbrenner's conclusions were drawn mostly from study of programs that improved the IQ scores of participating students, but little evidence was available to indicate that these gains could be sustained after the children graduated from them and entered regular school classes. In addition, there was considerable uncertainty over whether it was necessary to have a parent-centered component in these programs, in order to help parents learn how to improve the home environment for learning in the early years of life.

Since Bronfenbrenner's review of research on early intervention, even more encouraging results have been reported concerning the effects of outstanding preschool programs to enhance the cognitive development of low-status students. In general, these data suggest that low-status students who have participated in cognitively oriented preschool programs subsequently perform substantially better in school than do children of comparable background who did not participate.

For example, one of the most carefully developed and evaluated programs for disadvantaged youngsters was the cognitive-development oriented Perry Preschool Project conducted by David Weikart and his colleagues in Ypsilanti, Michigan, between 1962 and 1967. Since 1967, longitudinal analysis of the subsequent performance of participants and comparable "control" group children has been carried out, with initial results leading to the discouraging conclusion that substantial IQ gains participants showed at age three and four disappeared by the third grade.

However, subsequent research showed that scores of participants in reading, language, and arithmetic began to exceed those of the control group beginning at grade three. By grade eight, the children who had been in the preschool, although still averaging more than two years below grade level, were more than a year ahead of the control group. (Schweinhart and Weikart 1977). By the time students had graduated from high school, 39 percent of the control group as compared with only 19 percent of the preschool students had required special education services for at least one year, and still later data showed that the preschool group was more likely to find and hold jobs or enroll in college and less likely to be on welfare or to be arrested (Schweinhart and Weikart 1980; Farnsworth, Schweinhart, and Berrueta-Clement 1985). Similar results have been reported for the Syracuse Preschool Project operated in the early 1970s (Neinhuis 1986).

This phenomenon, sometimes referred to as the sleeper effect, also has appeared in other longitudinal studies of the subsequent school careers of low-status students who had received preschool compensatory education. For example, Francis H. Palmer has been studying the subsequent performance of black youngsters in Harlem who had participated at age two or three in preschool programs respectively emphasizing *concept training* and *discovery training*. ("Concept training" emphasized teacher presentation of concepts. "Discovery training" encouraged students to learn concepts through inquiry methods.) Both groups attended one-hour sessions twice a week for eight months. After an intensive search to locate the children nearly ten years later, he found that the fifth-grade reading scores of children who had received concept training were significantly higher than those of children in discovery training or a control group, and that training at age two was more potent in improving reading than training at age three (Palmer n.d., 24). Average differences between the two groups in some cases were substantial, as in the results for students in the fifth grade in 1975: 47 percent of concept training students were reading at or above grade level, as compared with 37 percent of the discovery training students, and a little more than 30 percent of students in comparison groups.

Longitudinal gains in achievement also have been reported for children whose mothers participated in special training and assistance programs for the parents of infants in low-status families. For example, the Florida Parent Education Project conducted by Ira J. Gordon and his colleagues began work with poverty-level mothers of children who were three months old in September 1966. Families were randomly assigned to experimental and control groups, and those in the experimental group participated for either one, two, or three years. The intervention consisted of home visits approximately once a week by paraprofessional parent educators. They demonstrated home learning activities to the parent so the parent in turn would engage in instructional interaction with her child. Children in the experimental group at age two also were enrolled in home learning centers in their neighborhoods, where five children at a time spent eight hours a week working with the parent educator. Three to five years later, children in the experimental groups were found to score seven or eight points higher in IQ than did control children (Guinagh and Gordon 1976, 20).

Thus, a number of preschool programs such as Weikart's, Palmer's, and Gordon's appear to have had encouraging longitudinal results. Summary conclusions also have been reported by Irving Lazar and other researchers who examined the results found in studies of twelve early childhood programs for youngsters who participated in the early and mid-1960s and were subsequently studied at ages nine to eighteen (Lazar et al. 1977; Darlington et al. 1980). Lazar and his colleagues reported that for most of the twelve programs, students who had participated in the compensatory education preschools had IQ scores generally about four to eight points higher three to six years later than did students in the control groups. They also found that this trend was higher for the preschool children than for the control children.

However, some researchers have challenged the validity of data available or the results of well-known preschool programs, particularly those data dealing with IQ gains (see Spitz 1986). Also, keep in mind that programs reporting positive results appear to have been unusually well-implemented. One cannot assume that the average program has been run well or has had permanent effects (Schweinhart 1987).

In general, there still is considerable uncertainty about the extent to which early intervention in the family is necessary for improving the cognitive performance of low-status students. Research indicates that preschool compensatory education can improve the later academic performance and, sometimes, the IQ of participating students, but researchers are unsure how much emphasis should be placed on ecological (i.e., family) intervention. Intensive family intervention to help disadvantaged youngsters beginning in infancy probably can compensate substantially for the cognitive disadvantages suffered by many youngsters in a concentrated poverty environment. However, it does not provide a simple answer to the questions that sponsors of preschool compensatory education are still struggling with in the 1980s.

Important unresolved questions also include the problem of determining the proportion of children from the most severely damaging environments who require ecological intervention in order to be able to function effectively in school and whether the costs of ecological intervention are politically prohibitive if this type of approach is necessary on a sizable scale. Intensive preschool projects that provide continuous work with parents as well as formal instruction beginning in infancy may cost as much as $6,000 or $7,000 per child per year. It is not at all certain that the public is willing to support compensatory education for large numbers of children on this scale even though the later costs of subsidizing retarded adults probably are much higher.

Elementary- and Secondary-Level Compensatory Education

Research reported in the previous section regarding the sleeper effect of some preschool programs in generating academic gains found years after the programs ended should not be interpreted as indicating that later support is unnecessary to ensure sustained gain of a substantial nature. Few early childhood educators believe that these gains are sufficient to ensure continuing success in school for most participating students. The Head Start evaluations along with data from big-city school districts showing consistent later declines among students with improved academic performance in kindergarten or even first and second grade (Fuerst 1977) both indicate that it is desirable to continue compensatory education after early childhood.

Nor should the consensus that high-quality compensatory education is desirable in the earliest years of life be interpreted to mean that school-age programs are of no value for students who have not had the opportunity to participate in an effective preschool program. One can conclude that early intervention may be necessary for maximum compensatory effect, but this does not mean that programs for students in the schools will have no effect at all. This section presents evidence indicating that school-based compensatory education frequently does serve to improve the academic performance of low-status students.

Primary Grades and Follow Through. Data from a number of school districts show that compensatory education in some locations has been effective in raising the academic performance of low-status students to the national average in the primary grades, even in some inner-city schools in which achievement deficits generally have been most sizable. For example, primary grade achievement very close to national norms was reported for inner-city schools in Chicago's subdistrict ten in 1974 (Fuerst 1976), and citywide achievement in the third and fourth grades in Philadelphia was reported as "approaching national norms" in 1977 (Philadelphia Public Schools 1977, 11).

Research on the results of Follow Through projects also shows that compensatory education can be effective in improving the performance of low-status students in the primary grades. These projects were initiated in 1967 to "follow through" on Head Start after evaluation indicated that gains from early childhood programs frequently were not being maintained after kindergarten and first grade. President Lyndon Johnson requested 120 million dollars to conduct Follow Through programs for 200,000 low-income, primary grade students in 1968, but only 14 million was made available by Congress. Appropriations increased to 70 million dollars in 1970 but declined to a much lower level in subsequent years.

Follow Through has been organized and implemented on a national "planned variation" basis. A number of different instructional approaches (models) have been tried in a variety of locations, with an unusually thorough evaluation to determine which approaches are most effective. Local parents and educators have selected among twenty-two approaches ranging fom the Cognitive Curriculum model stressing teaching of concepts, to responsive education using the so-called talking typewriter, and a behavior analysis approach emphasizing positive reinforcement through award of tokens for success.

The Follow Through evaluation, like the program itself, has been difficult, expensive, and controversial. By 1977, more than 30 million dollars had been spent on evaluation, and the difficulties encountered in reaching firm conclusions were exceeded only by the difficulties encountered in administering the program in many different settings spread throughout the United States. Major problems in carrying out the evaluation included questions involving the comparability of groups of students of somewhat different socioeconomic status (severely versus moderately disadvantaged), high attrition of students, teachers, and sites, complicated technical issues involving comparison of gain scores at differing levels of performance, and uncertainty whether a given model at a particular site was implemented well enough to be considered a good test of its potential effects. "It's safe to say," one U.S. Office of Education official commented in 1977, "that evaluators did not know what was implemented in the various sites. Without knowing what was implemented it is virtually impossible to select valid effectiveness measures" (Tucker 1977, 11).

Despite such problems, evaluations of Follow Through have yielded useful knowledge about instructional approaches for improving the performance of low-status students. Tucker (1977) reviewed the results of many Follow Through studies and derived a set of conclusions including the following:

> *Educational philosophies based on a well defined curriculum with emphasis on the development of basic skills generally produce meaningful gains over a variety of cognitive and affective outcome measures. . . .*
>
> *Models based on the use and development of the . . . language [used in the child's home] and culture produced meaningful effects over the range of outcome measures. Models with a definite set of instructional objectives in the cognitive and conceptual domains produced expected outcomes. (p. 17)*

It should be emphasized here that although Follow Through research has helped identify the characteristics of successful compensatory education in the primary grades, this research does not indicate that the problem of improving the academic performance of low-status students at this level has been definitively solved, particularly in concentrated poverty schools. Richard Anderson of Abt Associates, which conducted a major Follow Through evaluation, has examined the effectiveness of differing models in terms of enhancing the performance of low-achieving students. He concluded, "The most successful model, in this respect, achieved this heroic level with only a minority of groups. If educators know how to close the performance gap between disadvantaged children and the nation in general. . . . Follow Through has not proved that they can do it reliably'' (Anderson 1977, 4). It also is known that much of the Follow Through gain, where it does occur, is lost when students enter the middle grades, just as Head Start gains frequently are lost when students enter the primary grades. This failure to maintain gains is sometimes referred to as the fade out effect.

Compensatory Education through the Middle Grades. Although many school districts are reporting substantially improved academic achievement in the primary grades, few schools or programs have been able to sustain these gains through the middle grades. Examination of achievement data in these situations suggests that there frequently is a third- or fourth-grade dropoff in the achievement of students attending low-status schools. This pattern is particularly obvious in the case of concentrated poverty schools in big cities, where middle-grade achievement levels almost always are very low.

One reason that achievement levels for low-status students who gained in the primary grades tend to fall in the middle grades may be insufficient attention given in their previous compensatory education to developing abstract thinking skills that become important in the middle grades. As pointed out in Chapter 7, direct instruction seems to be most effective in developing basic learning skills such as decoding of words and computation in arithmetic, but other instructional emphasis such as inquiry training also may be necessary to develop cognitive thinking abilities that become more important later. This explanation suggests that it is easier—as one would expect—to improve basic learning skills than to develop abstract thinking abilities. It also suggests that preschool and primary compensatory education programs have not yet identified the optimal mix between direct instruction and emphasis on more complex cognitive skills.

However, there also are other plausible explanations for the dropoff in achievement of low-status students in the middle grades, including two such possible reasons as the following: (1) much less has been done in the middle than the primary grades to improve instructional materials and approaches, train teachers in how to use them, or otherwise provide effective compensatory education; and (2) academically negative influences from peer and neighborhood sources may become much more important in the middle grades than in the early years of school. Systematic research is needed to determine which of these or other factors are most important in producing a plateau in achievement where compensatory education seems to have been effective through the primary grades. Even without such research, it is apparent that new instructional approaches are needed if early academic gains are to be extended into the middle grades.

Until recently, about all that could be said with confidence about this goal was that substantial academic gains in the middle and upper grades would need the same educational components required to make any innovation work successfully, namely, outstanding administrative leadership, large-scale staff development, systematic organizational changes in support of the innovation, and competent planning and evaluation. Fortunately, much has been learned during the 1980s about how to make instruction more effective for economically disadvantaged students beyond the primary grades. The status of efforts to improve the achievement of disadvantaged students in the middle grades and high schools is described in the section on effective schools research in Chapter 13.

Title I/Chapter 1. Since the Elementary and Secondary Education Act of 1965 was passed by Congress, nearly 30 billion dollars have been spent to improve the academic achievement of low-status students in elementary and secondary schools. Approximately 70 percent of all public elementary schools in the United States receive some Chapter 1 funding for this purpose. Originally called Title I, these funds were re-titled Chapter 1 in 1981. Nearly 4 billion dollars were budgeted for Chapter 1 in 1987.

Every school district that receives Chapter 1 money must collect evaluation data, and surveys of these school district reports have formed the basis for most of the national evaluations. One frequently used criterion for attainment of the academic objectives of Chapter 1 programs has been the goal of having participants achieve one month of gain on standardized achievement tests for every month in the program. Such month-to-month gains would mean that low-status students no longer were falling progressively further behind national averages each year in school.

Early evaluations of Chapter 1 during the late 1960s were similar to the Head Start evaluations in suggesting that compensatory education was not very effective in improving the performance of disadvantaged students. Students in Chapter 1 programs did not appear to be achieving normal month-to-month gains or to be catching up with higher-status students during the late 1960s and early 1970s. However, it also became apparent that one reason Chapter 1 programs were having little impact was because funds were being dispersed on a variety of services and activities that often were clearly incapable of improving participants' mastery of basic skills. Federal, state, and local guidelines for the conduct of Chapter 1 programs were revised to concentrate funds on students with the greatest learning deficiencies, to introduce planning and monitoring procedures in order to ensure more effective service delivery, and to incorporate instructional approaches aimed particularly at improving academic performance. In 1973, the Department of Health, Education and Welfare initiated a systematic review of the effectiveness of Chapter 1 and other compensatory education programs. Some of the conclusions reached were that

> *children receiving compensatory help show very small but consistent improvement in learning compared with matched children without compensatory help; and, the more disadvantaged the children are, the more effective this compensatory help has been in improving their academic performance compared with similar children not receiving any help. (Lynn 1973)*

Since 1973, several additional studies of Chapter 1 achievement effects have been carried out by analyzing data from state department of education reports to the federal government. Findings by Thomas and Pelavin (1976) replicated the conclusions of other researchers who reported that students in Chapter 1 programs by that time generally were meeting or exceeding the month-to-month gain standard within a given school year. Hendrickson (1977) reviewed the history of Chapter 1 evaluations and concluded that they "justify cautious optimism" in the capacity of Chapter 1 to raise the achievement of disadvantaged children within a given school year.

On the other hand, national data clearly indicate that although Chapter 1 has had some positive impact, it has not substantially improved the achievement of disadvantaged students on a long-range basis. For example, studies conducted by the National Assessment of Educational Progress showed that the difference between the reading performance of black nine-year-olds in schools eligible and not eligible for Chapter 1 services declined by less than 1 percentage point between 1971 and 1980, and that the reading scores of low-income thirteen-year-olds in cities with more than 200,000 population increased only minimally (from 48.4 to 52.1) in the same time period (National Assessment of Educational Progress 1981b). Continuing inadequacies in the achievement of students at Chapter 1 schools in part reflect that many students who improve in achievement do not receive help the following year and many others are not helped at all due to national funding limits (Kennedy, Jung, and Orland 1986).

In addition, the final report of the national Chapter 1 evaluation (i.e., the Sustaining Effects Study) found that even though Chapter 1 students gained in mathematics in grades one through six and in reading in grades one through three, reading scores of students beyond grade three did not improve (Stonehill and Anderson 1982; Mullin and Summers 1983; Carter 1984). A second national evaluation released in 1987 came to the same conclusion, reporting that Chapter 1 students appear to make small gains in reading and math but that these gains do relatively little to offset their large learning deficits (Kennedy 1987). The fact that millions of poverty students are still entering high school each year with very low scores in reading, mathematics, and other basic skills also indicates that Chapter 1 and other compensatory programs have not yet generally succeeded in overcoming the academic problems experienced by disadvantaged students in the United States.

Secondary-Level Compensatory Education. Since some of the projects included in the national Chapter 1 evaluations were in junior and senior high schools, evidence is available supporting the conclusion that compensatory education can be effective in improving the academic achievement of low-status students beyond the middle grades. This conclusion has been explicitly confirmed by a study the U.S. Office of Education commissioned to separate out and assess data on the effectiveness of programs for secondary students. One purpose of this study was to provide data for policy makers struggling with the question of whether to set aside more funds for secondary programs on the grounds that low-status students at this level have a very large achievement deficit, or to continue to concentrate Title I funds on early childhood and elementary programs in order to prevent learning problems that many educators believe become insoluble among older students.

The study (Larson and Dittmann 1975) found that achievement gains equal to or greater than the month-to-month criterion were attained in a number of projects, but critics suggested that much of this gain represented a "rebound" effect that appears when older students enter a skills development program in which they reacquire skills and knowledge they had previously forgotten. However, the study concluded that this type of explanation did not account for most of the gain and that there was no basis

> *for the claim that compensatory projects for adolescents are less effective than those for children in primary grades. Grade equivalent gains in reading skills are consistently higher for students in grades 7–12, with both mean and median gains of over one month per month. . . .*
>
> *Other data show with equal clarity that there are large numbers of adolescents who vitally need special assistance if they are to achieve basic skill levels and to function effectively as adults. The present concentration of compensatory funds on the early grades is neither eliminating nor meeting these needs. (Larson and Dittmann 1975, xii, 53)*

Larson and Dittman also examined the characteristics of the most successful secondary programs in California and found that these programs generally did more than provide individual instruction from remedial education specialists, which is the typical approach used in most Chapter 1 programs. In addition, the successful projects included an intensive effort to "involve regular teaching staff, through in-service training" and attempted, in some cases, to redirect the whole curriculum in the school "so as to create a more central place for basic skills, and to legitimize the learning of them for all students, not just the slower" (p. 59).

This conclusion helps explain why national evaluations of Chapter 1 and other compensatory educational programs have found that low-status students seem to gain a good deal while participating but frequently are found to be falling further and further behind national averages as they proceed through school. Because most Chapter 1 secondary students are dropped from the program after they are judged to have made enough progress to function adequately in regular classes, and because few secondary schools have made systematic adjustments to address their learning needs after they return to regular classes, whatever they gained during Chapter 1 is soon washed out.

Secondary compensatory education also has been provided through the federally sponsored Upward Bound Program and similar efforts to offer special help to disadvantaged students at the senior high level. The goal of Upward Bound programs is to improve participants' preparation and motivation for post-secondary education. Recent analysis of data on Upward Bound students indicates that the program "continues to enhance youths' preparation for post-secondary education. . . . [UB students are] more likely to be planning to attend and complete college, and more likely to have made concrete plans for attending college" (Steel and Schubert 1983, 18).

Open Admissions and Compensatory Education in College

By 1970, there was a broad movement toward admissions procedures that would admit at least a substantial minority of students who could not qualify by the earlier aptitude test or high school course record requirements. For example, the City College of the City University of New York (CUNY), long known as even more highly selective than some Ivy League colleges, in 1970 adopted an open admissions policy that admitted any applicant with a high school diploma. This policy applied to the four-year senior colleges of CUNY as well as to the two-year community colleges. The CUNY consisted of nineteen colleges, all with free tuition in 1970.

It should be understood that open admissions is standard practice in many state-supported colleges and universities, which are required to admit any graduate of an accredited high school. However, it is well known that this form of open admissions frequently results in a kind of so-called revolving door phenomenon, with a considerable number of entering students failing in their first-year course work and dropping out of the college.

The New York City College faculties undertook to meet this situation with a number of remedial courses and arrangements for tutoring students who were below average in reading and in mathematics. There was substantial growth in enrollment, indicating that the policy was drawing youth who could not have gained admission under the earlier requirements. For example, from 1969 to 1974 the undergraduate enrollment at four-year state universities in the State of New York increased by 33 percent, while the enrollment increase at CUNY four-year colleges was 60 percent. And enrollment at state two-year institutions increased 36 percent while the two-year colleges of CUNY increased 103 percent. Blacks comprised 14 percent of the freshman class in 1969, and 31 percent in 1977. Puerto Ricans represented 6 percent of freshmen in 1969 but 16 percent in 1972. It was also found that the numbers of applications and admissions of students from poverty families more than doubled.

Based partly on earlier programs that had been initiated to provide remedial services for disadvantaged students entering New York City institutions of higher education, City College initiated and expanded a variety of efforts to help poorly prepared applicants succeed. Students in the Search for Education, Elevation, and Knowledge (SEEK) program constituted about 13 percent of the entering class of 1,500 in 1977. (Approximately one-third of the students who had graduated high school with honors averages above 85 were placed in remedial English.) Other special program adjustments included placement of many students in ESL (English as a Second Language) courses; assistance to minority students in science, engineering, and health sciences; and establishment of urban-oriented centers for academic skills, biomedical education, legal education, and performing arts.

Robert E. Marshak, President of CUNY from 1970 to 1979, reviewed developments in connection with open admissions at CUNY. In a two-part article in *Change* magazine (Marshak 1981; 1982), he reported data suggesting that CUNY generally and CCNY in particular have maintained high-quality education. For example, CCNY students have continued to score at or above national norms on all national college exit exams, and high percentages of graduates still gain acceptance into graduate schools. Marshak offered the following "general statements" about the achievements of the open admissions program:

> *One must first acknowledge that the open admissions experience brought about invaluable educational changes at the college. Many of the remedial programs added measurably to the college's ability to bring poorly prepared high school students through the difficult transition to the intellectual demands of a college education that would meet traditional graduation requirements. The relaxation of 'entrance' requirements was not accompanied in any significant fashion by a relaxation of 'exit' requirements. What is true is that the attrition rate before graduation increased substantially—especially in the freshman and sophomore years—not a surprising result if graduation standards were to be maintained.*
>
> *. . . The experiment must be judged a success. Given the emergency conditions under which open admissions was instituted, the constant underfunding of the program, the lack of experience of faculty dealing with large numbers of underprepared students, the economic, physical, and social handicaps of the students, the problems of overcrowding on campus, the constant sniping by a vocal minority of the faculty, the disproportionate burden assigned to City College through CUNY's allocation policies, the college not only survived open admissions but showed how to turn it to academic innovation as well as social good. (Marshak 1981, 52)*

Later evaluations of the CUNY open admissions program by David Lavin and his colleagues (1981; 1986) also support the conclusion that it has been successful in several respects. The authors conclude that minority students were not disproportionately channeled into dead-end community college careers as a result of open admissions, and that opportunities for students from low-income families were substantially increased and improved. Their overall assessment is that

> *the open-admissions policy probably has altered forever historic patterns of ethnic access to the University. . . . Open admissions substantially boosted the number of graduates from every group, but its contributions were critical to the proportion of black and Hispanic graduates. . . . The program more than doubled the number of black students who received a degree of some kind and . . . nearly doubled the number of black students placed on the threshold of graduate or professional school. . . .*
>
> *But at the same time that many minority students were gaining the opportunity for a college education under open admissions, so were even more whites. (Lavin, Alba, and Silberstein 1981, 271, 276–277)*

It has been understood from the outset that an open admissions policy requires a special program of instruction to help compensate for the disadvantages of the low-scoring students. This has been done in various ways at many colleges and universities and has met considerable opposition from some outstanding scholars who argue that relaxation of admissions standards will either lower the intellectual quality of higher education or will cause a great deal of frustration for students who are first admitted and then failed.

However, the director of research for the American Council on Education, Alexander W. Astin, has made a thorough study of the relation between test scores, high school grades, and college dropouts, and has come to the conclusion that a considerable fraction of students do make it in college in spite of low aptitude scores or low high school grades. He concluded, furthermore, that "the model of selective admissions based on test scores and grades is inappropriate for institutions of higher education. Presumably, educational institutions exist in order to educate students. They should strive in their admissions practices to select those applicants most likely to be favorably influenced by the particular educational program offered at the institution" (Astin 1969, 69).

By 1970, lessons of the early college compensatory education programs were beginning to be apparent. Such programs could and did work, but they generally included only a small number of students, tended to accept only the most highly motivated low-status students, and required extensive changes in normal higher-education arrangements. Social psychologist Theodore N. Newcomb addressed these points in a major address delivered to a national conference sponsored by the American Association for Higher Education in March of 1970:

> *The dilemma, for both student and institution, can be simply stated. If the previously inadmissible students are expected to take the present array of courses, and to be judged by present standards, a great many of them will not make the grade. And, if, on the other hand, their academic menu consists primarily of "watered down" or remedial courses, they will be regarded both by themselves and others as second-class citizens. Neither alternative represents a constructive educational experience. In short, for institutions to invite new breeds of students without changing themselves is an invitation to debasement in one way or another. (Newcomb 1970, 1–2)*

Early experience and research on college compensatory education also indicated that although low-status students who participated certainly were greater risks than the average student who was admissible under the usual standards, they generally had attained fairly high grades in high schools. In other words, they seldom were among the hard-core disadvantaged but came from low-status families that had been relatively successful in motivating and preparing them for higher education. As found in one study of special programs for disadvantaged students in the late 1960s, the students who were succeeding in these programs "seemed to have a pervasive middle-class orientation, and in most cases a parent, brother, sister, or other close relative who had college experience. For such students, even what seemed to be severely limiting personal circumstances—for example . . . living at home with four younger brothers under miserably crowded conditions, and without a means of convenient transportation—did not prove to be a roadblock" (Klingelhofer and Longacre 1972, 7).

After about 1975, a growing volume of research on college compensatory education was providing a degree of positive evaluation. Edmund W. Gordon, director of the Clearinghouse on Urban Education at Teachers College, Columbia University, has been periodically reviewing research on this topic and has provided the following 1976 summary of research on "the confused state of compensatory education at the collegiate level":

> *Where programs have been implemented with full systems of student support services (financial aid, adjusted curriculum, tutorial support, remediation where necessary, and counselling and continuous social/psychological support), special opportunity students showed equal or higher grade-point averages than regular students of comparable abilty and showed equal or higher retention than regular students. . . . Where programs with full systems of student support services have been implemented special opportunity students show increased self-esteem and motivation. (Gordon 1976, 12)*

Positive experience with a remedial program has been reported from Chicago State University, with 7,000 students, mainly from minority groups. In 1977, 36 faculty members were teaching remedial reading, composition, or mathematics to 1,069 students. Of every 100 students who took remedial courses, 77 passed the competency test they had failed on entering the university. Research also indicates that the number of black students (many of whom are disadvantaged) studying engineering has tripled and that many colleges and universities have provided compensatory education and successfully doubled the retention rate for these students (Foster 1982).

A systematic review of evaluation studies of college compensatory education also supports the conclusion that such programs frequently result in substantial gains for participants. Kulik, Kulik, and Shwalb (1982) examined evaluation on sixty special college programs for high-risk students and concluded that in general these programs "had basically positive effects" (p. 1). Students who participated had higher grade-point averages and completed more years of college than comparable students who did not participate. Although differences in the majority of programs were small, some programs had large positive effects. The investigators also reported that compensatory education appeared to be more successful in four-year colleges than in community colleges.

Social Policy and Compensatory Education

The discerning reader may have noted that the preceding discussion introduced a variety of criteria for determining the goals and success of compensatory education. At some points, early childhood programs seem to have been considered successful if they resulted in any longitudinal gain beyond what low-status children would have attained in the absence of compensatory intervention. At other points, the implicit goal was to help inner-city youth become sufficiently literate to obtain a good job; and at still others, it was to prevent disadvantaged students from falling further and further behind middle-status peers as they proceed through school.

Lack of clarity and agreement regarding the goals of compensatory education is an important issue because definition of the goal to be sought has important implications for the design of compensatory programs. If the major goal is to be functional literacy, then programs that stress direct instruction may be successful in developing basic skills subsumed under this goal.

However, Resnick and Resnick (1985) have examined the history of efforts to develop literacy and concluded that the criterion of *comprehension*—which is a step beyond the mastery of basic skills required for functional literacy—may not be attainable through traditional methods emphasizing basic skill development. Moreover, Singer (1977) has reviewed the research on instructional strategies and skills development and concluded that although "guided" learning is appropriate in developing a basic skill, some form of "discovery" or "problem-solving" learning may be necessary to develop the capacity to apply the skill in new situations (p. 494). These conclusions suggest that methods to develop comprehension skills and high-cost early ecological intervention focusing on conceptual development may need to receive much more stress in compensatory education programs if their goal is to develop a high level of literacy and the ability to become a self-directed learner.

One reason the goals of compensatory education tend to be shifting and poorly defined is that compensatory education is a major national issue involving fundamental values in society. As education has become more important in determining a person's chances for success in life, greater stress has been placed on ensuring that low-status students really do have a chance to succeed educationally in accordance with their inherent talent and ability. Everyone can agree on the goal of equal educational opportunity stated at this level of generality, but disagreement occurs as soon as the goal is stated in operational terms. Is society responsible for providing low-status children a chance to proceed as far in the educational system as middle-status children, even though parents of the latter expend a great deal of their own time and money to give their children educational advantages?

One group of researchers has computed the money value of the mother's educational services to her child in relation to the extent of her education. They concluded that the school system should devote about twice as much money to the education of a working-class child, compared with an upper-middle-class child. This would tend to compensate the working-class child for the lower value of his or her mother's educational services (Levin et al. 1971). However it is not clear that society can afford to pay or will agree to pay for compensatory education of this magnitude.

In addition, unanswered questions regarding the conditions necessary for successful compensatory education make it difficult to work out comprehensive social policies for more effective compensatory education in the future. We have seen that compensatory education can achieve at least some of its goals at any level from preschool through college, and this research has led to concomitant changes in social policy. For example, many Head Start programs now stress work with parents in accordance with research suggesting that home-based components are vital in the early years. Follow Through was established after research suggested that Head Start participants lost ground following entry into regular primary classes. Nevertheless, uncertainties involving the design and implementation of compensatory education still make it difficult to work out a coherent national approach.

One uncertainty involves the degree to which *massive ecological intervention* in the early years may be prerequisite to later success. It seems clear that many youngsters, particularly those in concentrated poverty neighborhoods, require this type of intervention in order to have a real chance to succeed later in life, but no one knows just what proportion of disadvantaged students fit in this category or how much continuing intervention they may require after the preschool years.

A second and related uncertainty involves the issue of *costs*. It is easy to see that massive early intervention is expensive, but the costs of successful compensatory education in elementary and secondary schools generally have been underestimated in practice. Expenditures per child from Chapter 1 and other sources typically amount to six or seven hundred dollars per student per year, but we have presented evidence suggesting that compensatory education may have to continue at the same intensity as Head Start and Follow Through (which are considerably more expensive than Chaper 1), and that secondary schools may need to provide a consistently improved learning environment for low-status students rather than merely providing short-term remedial instruction. Many authorities believe that it requires two or three times as much money per student to provide effective compensatory education at the elementary and secondary levels as it does to educate nondisadvantaged students (McLure and Pence 1971, 26), whose education already costs well over $3,000 per student per year in many big cities. How much would this figure be decreased if early childhood compensatory education were more effective? The answer is not known, and meanwhile the problems of paying for compensatory education on an adequate scale in big cities have been compounded by fiscal crises that have forced schools in Chicago, Cleveland, Detroit, Los Angeles, New York, and many other big cities to cut back their general instructional programs.

On the other hand, it seems clear that effective compensatory programs at the preschool level can more than pay for themselves in terms of a variety of social and economic costs that otherwise would be incurred later. For example, cost analysis of the Perry Preschool Project indicated that the two-year program cost $5,984 per child expressed in 1979 dollars, but it produced $10,798 per child in increased lifetime earnings projected from improved educational attainment and $4,021 in other benefits such as greater earnings of the mothers who worked while their children attended preschool (Weber, Foster, and Weikart 1978; Schweinhart and Weikart 1985).

Also related to the issue of ecological intervention is that of *racial and socioeconomic integration in the public schools*. One purpose of desegregation is to provide equal opportunity for minority students and, presumably, thereby help improve the academic performance of low-status or low-achieving minority students. Since the 1960s, compensatory education has tended to be seen as an alternative to integration. From our point of view, desegregation—particularly socioeconomic desegregation—should be viewed as an ecological intervention designed to improve the environment of the school, by reducing the number of low-status students who attend classes in a dysfunctional environment.

Another issue regarding compensatory education involves the extent to which *alternatives outside the regular educational system* may be necessary to provide effective educational opportunities for low-status students at the secondary and postsecondary levels. We have discussed compensatory education in the educational system at these levels, but other alternatives also have been or can be made available to improve opportunity for disadvantaged students. One of the most important of these has been the Job Corps, originally established as part of the War on Poverty to provide low-income youth sixteen to twenty-one years of age with educational and vocational skills required to escape from poverty.

The Job Corps is an ecological intervention designed to remove young people from poverty neighborhoods in the hope that this together with suitable instruction will enable them to function effectively in a job training program and, afterward, the economy. Assessments of the first few years of the Job Corps were discouraging, indicating that costs were running $8,000 per trainee per year and that graduates were not clearly more successful than were control group youth who had not participated (Levitan and Mangum 1969). Later evaluations, however, have been considerably more positive, indicating that the Job Corps has had some success recruiting and retaining hard core disadvantaged youth, and that graduates of some centers had made significant gains in acquiring basic academic and vocational skills that helped them make an improved entry into the economy (Mallar 1979; Burbridge 1983). Even though it is still a relatively expensive program, the Job Corps appears to be paying for itself on a cost-benefit basis to the degree that it is helping some participants avoid life-long dependence on the public welfare system (Mallar 1980; Dervarics 1985).

Financing of Central-City Schools

A particular problem in working to improve education for disadvantaged students in most metropolitan areas is the inequality of financial support for schools between the central city, on the one hand, and the wealthier suburbs, on the other hand. Where public schools are paid for mainly by local property taxes, it happens that some wealthy suburbs have twice as much taxable property for each pupil as does the central city. Thus, one district may support its schools with $4,000 or $5,000 per pupil, while a neighboring district in the same metropolitan area, although it taxes its property owners at a higher rate, still provides only $2,000 or $2,500 per pupil.

At the same time, central city school districts generally have greater financial needs than do other metropolitan school districts. Reasons for this differential include the following:

1. *Greater proportion of low-status students.* Effective compensatory education for working-class students is expensive because it requires, among other things, purchase of a range of diversified learning materials, intensive staff development and specialized personnel such as reading supervisors, counselors, and school security officers. Because most central city school districts have a much higher proportion of low-status students than do most suburban districts, their financial requirements are correspondingly greater (National School Boards Association 1988).

2. *Teacher salaries.* Because the teaching staff in big-city districts tend to be more militant than is true in most suburban districts, salaries in the central city tend to be among the highest in the metropolitan area. Teacher salaries typically constitute from 75 to 85 percent of a school district's overall budget.

3. *Cost for buildings and maintenance.* Central city school districts have had relatively high costs because land values historically have been higher than in most of the suburbs, and because older buildings are relatively expensive to maintain.

4. *Difficulty of increasing property taxes.* Central city school districts generally have had even more of a problem gaining approval for property tax increases than have suburban school districts. Part of the reason is that a higher proportion of voters in the central city tend to live on low or fixed incomes. In addition, central city residents tend to suffer from what political scientists have called "municipal overburden." This means that central city taxpayers tend to pay proportionately more than most suburbanites for fire, police, and other municipal services, thus making it difficult to obtain approval for additional school taxes.

5. *Enrollment decline and higher absence rates.* Enrollments have declined in most suburban as well as central city school districts, but overall the central cities have lost enrollment even faster than the suburbs (Odden and Vincent 1976). A major reason for enrollment decline is the low birthrate; in addition, central cities are still losing middle-class and white population to the suburbs. Also, central cities with large numbers of low-status students have much higher absence rates than do most suburban districts. Because state funding for public schools generally is based on the number of pupils in average daily attendance, both these tendencies result in reduced operating budgets for central city schools. Central city schools, like their suburban counterparts, are struggling to close unneeded school buildings and reduce the size of the teaching staff in line with falling enrollment, but a variety of obstacles make this difficult to accomplish very quickly.

One solution is for the state to take more of the financial responsibility for public education and to pay 50 percent or more of the school bill. Most states have reviewed or are reviewing their school finance arrangements, in several cases such as California and New Jersey because courts have required them to reduce inequities in per pupil expenditure levels. The general trend has been toward a school finance formula that brings about power equalization in the sense that impoverished districts with tax rates set above a designated minimum level receive additional state funds so that per pupil expenditures approach those of wealthier districts.

However, this basic reform in state school finance arrangements does not address the differential caused by higher costs and special needs in central city districts. Equality in per pupil expenditures does not take into account the factors leading to significantly higher per pupil needs in the central city. Federal funds for compensatory education and instructional improvement provide central city schools with some of the additional money they need for these and other purposes; but as noted above, the financial condition of many city school districts remains precarious.

In addition, depressed economic conditions and reductions in federal funding for elementary and secondary schools further magnified the financial problems of central city school districts in the 1980s. St. Louis, for example, lost 86 percent of its federal funding between 1982 and 1983. Reduced federal appropriations for education in 1982 resulted in an average reduction of 16 percent in the total operating budget of twenty-eight of the nation's largest school districts and in elimination or curtailment of compensatory education services provided for several hundred thousand students in these districts. Problems involved in providing effective education in the big cities thus were intensified in Boston, New Orleans, Philadelphia, and other big cities (Roberts 1982).

Conclusion

Low-status students face many problems in the schools in addition to initial learning disadvantages associated with their home and family background. Problems of teaching and learning in working with low-status students include inappropriate curriculum and instruction, lack of parental and peer reinforcement of school norms and learning experiences, loss of motivation associated with lack of previous success in school, teachers' lack of preparation for solving the learning and behavior problems of low achieving students, teacher perceptions of student inadequacy, homogeneous grouping of low achieving students, ineffective delivery of instructional services, and low standards of performance.

These problems begin to be apparent in the earliest grades in school and generate a cycle of failure characterized by poor academic performance, low or inaccurate self-concept as a learner, and lack of a sense that one can succeed in school by trying harder in the future. Implications for instruction include the conclusion that schools must provide structured success experience for low-status students by developing systems of instruction that address each student's individual problems in the classroom. Because low-status students tend to lack essential academic skills, some "direct" instruction should be provided to develop these skills. Research on teaching low-status students supports this conclusion, but theory and research also suggest that additional goals such as development of self-directed learning skills, enhancement of conceptual skills through an inquiry approach to learning, and appropriate matching of teaching methods with students' conceptual level must be given much attention in working to improve the academic performance of low-status students.

Schools in concentrated poverty neighborhoods confront teaching and learning problems that are even more difficult to solve than those in other low-status schools or classrooms. Evidence from research in a number of big cities suggests that academic performance in concentrated poverty schools almost always is very low, possibly because the schools and other social institutions in these neighborhoods are unable to function effectively in the face of multiple problems that exceed their capacity to handle successfully. Violence in a variety of manifestations including assaults on students and teachers, operation of gangs in and around the schools, and invasion by intruders and trespassers makes the teaching and learning environment even more difficult than in other low-status schools. For reasons such as these, there is a real question whether compensatory education can be made to work effectively in inner-city neighborhoods in the absence of successful efforts to improve general economic and social opportunities, reduce social disorganization, and deconcentrate the poverty population that lives there.

Many efforts have been made throughout the United States to improve the academic performance of low-status students in general and inner-city students in particular. These efforts have had some success at the preschool, elementary, intermediate, secondary, and postsecondary levels. However, the general level of achievement among low-status students is still inadequate, particularly among students in concentrated poverty schools.

A number of problems, including value disagreements, high costs, and inadequate information for key policy decisions, make it difficult to work out and implement a comprehensive program for compensatory education. This goal is particularly difficult to attain in a large, relatively decentralized country like the United States, where most educational decisions are made at the local level and a tradition of individualism conflicts with some actions that might have to be taken to make compensatory education effective on a carefully planned and sequenced national basis. The United States is still far from having attained a rational system of compensatory education wherein each child who needs massive ecological intervention receives it in the early years, thereby minimizing the costs of school-age programs later, and appropriate funding and alternatives are available to ensure that effective compensatory education is provided at each educational level from preschool through postsecondary.

EXERCISES

1. If data are available on achievement in a nearby big-city school district, examine the results to determine whether a threshold effect appears to be op-

erating. In addition to reasons listed in this chapter, what other causes could help account for the threshold effect? How would one go about determining whether these causes actually are present in low-status schools?

2. Read Jonathan Kozol's *Death at an Early Age* or James Herndon's *The Way It Spozed to Be,* both of which describe the experience of relatively successful inner-city teachers, and make a list of the understandings and abilities needed to be successful in teaching in an inner-city school.
3. In what ways and situations would high self-concept as a learner probably contribute to improved academic performance as a learner? When might high self-concept contribute to poor performance? What, if anything, do you think educators should do to improve the academic self-concept of low-status students?
4. As discussed in this chapter, a basic skills or minimal competency approach to grading requires that students obtain a minimum score on an examination before being promoted from one grade to another or receiving a diploma. What are the advantages and the dangers in this type of approach? What types of policies and practices are required to make it work successfully?
5. In recent years, there has been a trend to place learning-handicapped students in regular classrooms (i.e., "least restrictive environments") as much as possible, while gifted and talented students more frequently are separated in special classes or learning activities. Are these trends in conflict? Why are these differing grouping arrangements frequently prescribed for "slow" and "fast" students? What do you think is the best policy for each group?
6. It is sometimes said that by the time a child enters school it is "too late" to make any real changes in his or her personality. A teacher may say, especially of a lower-class child, "I can't undo what the family has done." Do you agree with this point of view, generally speaking? Why or why not?
7. What are the main arguments for and against spending more money for compensatory education at the secondary level? Interview local school officials to find out how effective such programs have been in nearby schools.
8. Make a list of the most important actions or guidelines needed to make compensatory education effective. Visit a school that receives Chapter 1 funding and analyze its programs in terms of your list of guidelines.
9. If a nearby school district has a compensatory education program for economically disadvantaged students under Chapter 1 of the Elementary and Secondary Education Act, ask to see the evaluation reports that have been submitted to the federal government. Has any progress been reported in raising the achievement of eligible students? If yes, what types of programs or program elements seem to have been effective? How do these results fit with the data and conclusions in this chapter?

SUGGESTIONS FOR FURTHER READING

1. Much of Bronfenbrenner's review of research regarding the effectiveness of compensatory education is easily accessible in his article titled "Is Early In-

tervention Effective?" which appeared in the October 1974 issue of the *Teachers College Record.*

2. *Reforming Metropolitan Schools* by Ornstein, Levine, and Wilkerson includes a chapter on the history of compensatory education in the United States and an analysis of the most important issues the schools have encountered in trying to implement it.
3. An excellent short summary of the research on Follow Through is available in Mary M. Kennedy's paper describing the problems encountered in carrying out and evaluating the program.
4. Wesley C. Becker's paper on "Teaching Reading and Language to the Disadvantaged: What We Have Learned from Field Research" includes a description of the DISTAR program and discusses ways to extend direct instruction methods in improving the achievement of disadvantaged students. Much of what was learned in the Follow Through program has been summarized in W. Ray Rhine's *Making Schools More Effective: New Directions from Follow Through.*
5. *Handbook for Successful Urban Teaching* by Johanna K. Lemlech, *Does Anybody Give a Damn?* by Nat Hentoff, and *The Culturally Deprived Child* by Frank Riessman all contain a good deal of material dealing with instructional strategies for teaching low-status students.
6. *Reaching the Disadvantaged Learner,* edited by A. Harry Passow, includes a number of papers presented at a conference on educating economically disadvantaged students. Passow also has edited several other volumes from conferences on this topic held at Columbia University Teachers College. Papers delivered at these conferences dealt with a wide range of issues and problems involving the education of low-status students.
7. The functioning—and dysfunctioning—of inner-city high schools are convincingly described and analyzed in *Getting What We Ask For* by Charles Payne. Mary Haywood Metz (1986) and James Herndon (1968) each describe comparable situations at inner-city elementary and middle schools.
8. *Implementing Mastery Learning* by Guskey (1985) is written primarily for teachers and administrators who may want to use mastery learning. *Improving Student Achievement through Mastery Learning Programs* edited by Levine (1985) provides information on the theory and practice of mastery learning and includes case studies dealing with implementation at inner-city schools.

9

Desegregation

In 1954 the U.S. Supreme Court ruled in *Brown* v. *Topeka Board of Education* that "separate but equal has no place" in education, and that government-imposed or government-supported segregation unconstitutionally violates the rights of black students. Effects of the *Brown* decision soon became apparent in many areas of U.S. society, including voting, employment, and all public services. After Rosa Parks refused in 1955 to sit at the back of a bus in Montgomery, Alabama, protests against segregation were launched in many parts of the nation. Reverend Martin Luther King, Jr., along with other civil rights leaders, emerged to challenge deep-seated patterns of racial discrimination. Fierce opposition to civil rights made the headlines in the late 1950s and early 1960s as dogs and fire hoses were sometimes used to disperse peaceful demonstrators. After three civil rights workers were murdered in Mississippi, the U.S. Congress passed the 1964 Civil Rights Act and other legislation that attempted to guarantee equal protection under the laws for minority citizens.

The Status of School Desegregation

The history of public-school desegregation since 1954 can be divided into three major phases. Little desegregation was accomplished during the first phase through about 1965. Much desegregation was accomplished in the South and in smaller cities and towns during the second phase, between 1966 and 1973. Since 1973, some progress has continued to be made outside the largest cities, and desegregation plans in big cities with many segregated minority students have included an increasing emphasis on improvement of instruction, particularly for minority students in segregated schools.

The courts have been petitioned by parents and by civil rights organizations to step in and order desegregation of the schools in ways that will be helpful to minority racial and ethnic groups. There is a language problem here, since the so-called minority groups that need assistance are mainly blacks and Hispanic or Spanish-speaking children. These are minority groups in terms of national population, but generally they are segregated locally so that they are majorities in many schools. The white children are really in the majority of the national school population, but they are a minority of students in many schools that are mainly black or Hispanic.

Our practice in this book, as in the literature on school desegregation, is generally to use the term *minority* to refer to nonwhite children and to Hispanic children, and to refer to white children of the majority group as *nonminority* or sometimes as non-Hispanic white.

Phase I: 1954–1965

The Supreme Court decision in the *Topeka* case rested in part on the argument that segregation had damaging psychological effects on black children, even when the school facilities themselves were supposedly equal to those of white schools. The consensus of social scientists was—and is, still—that segregation of blacks has been an obstacle to their competence in an urban, industrial, democratic society. This conclusion is based on research on the social psychology of race relations (summarized by Katz 1964). The research conclusion is that where the races are systematically segregated, black children are taught by their parents that they cannot expect to be treated as equals by most white people. Their teachers, whether black or white, tend to look on them as slow learners and therefore lower their standards of expectation.

These researchers argue that black children, in order to overcome or avoid a self-concept of inferiority, should associate with white children as early as possible in life, in situations where they will sometimes be superior and sometimes inferior. They should be taught by a biracial school staff.

These propositions, when read today, have a dated quality. They report the thinking that prevailed at the time of the Supreme Court decision of 1954. The economic and educational situation of the black population has changed so much during the 1960s, 1970s, and 1980s that a substantially different set of propositions has now come to the forefront. These propositions are developed in this chapter.

Initially, after 1954, the focus of attention by educators and by government officials was on the process of desegregation. There were two aspects of this problem—*de jure* segregation and *de facto* segregation. *De jure* segregation refers to segregation brought about in one way or another by government action. This was clearly the situation in southern states, where state laws long prevented white and black children from attending the same schools. *De facto* segregation is caused by private decisions rather than government action. This is one major cause of the problem in big cities, where, because most blacks live in segregated housing areas, many schools are attended entirely by black children.

Although the Supreme Court in 1955 ordered school districts to desegregate with "all deliberate speed," desegregation proceeded slowly. The U.S. Office of Education reported that at the beginning of the 1965 school year, at most only 7.5 percent of black students in the South were attending schools with white children. In most parts of the North and West, some black students who lived in integrated neighborhoods continued to attend desegrated schools, but there was little additional desegregation because the official policy in most school districts was that the schools should be "color blind." This meant that the school system would take no formal notice of the color of pupils or teachers but would strive to do the best job possible of educating all children in accordance with their needs and abilities.

Phase II: 1966–1973

The second phase of desegregation was a period during which much desegregation was accomplished in the South. At the same time, major efforts were begun elsewhere to improve public schools for economically disadvantaged students regardless of their race.

The major legislative forces were the Civil Rights Act of 1964 and the Elementary and Secondary Education Act of 1965, which together gave government officials and public school educators a great deal of power. The Civil Rights Act of 1964, among other things, required all state and local agencies as well as private persons or agencies *who receive federal government funds* to give written assurance that "no person shall be excluded from participation, denied any benefits, or subjected to discrimination on the basis of race, color, or national origin." The requirement that school systems receiving any federal payments must submit "assurance of compliance" with the law had the effect of stimulating desegregation in the schools.

The Elementary and Secondary Education Act of 1965, by providing large sums of federal monies to local school systems, strengthened the pressures enormously and provided financial incentives for compliance. In particular, Title I provided billions of dollars each year for improving the education of economically disadvantaged students (see Chapter 8).

The Deep South. Given these new legislative changes, most school systems of the South had begun the process of integration by 1966. The *New York Times* of September 4, 1965, reported, "Under the threat of a loss of Federal assistance, the South is admitting probably 7 percent of its Negro children to classes with white children this fall—a percentage that compares reasonably well with the national average. And for the first time school desegregation has come to the Black Belt and to hundreds of rural southern towns, with virtually no violence or resistance." Faculty desegregation also got under way in some southern cities.

Border Cities and Northern Cities. The drive for desegregation in the border cities and northern and western industrial cities also was accelerated in this period. Civil rights organizations joined together and were aided by federated church groups acting through such agencies as a Council on Religion and Race. Civic organizations became involved. The most prominent domestic issue in the country during this period was the issue of change in the schools. Most big cities saw school boycotts aimed at inducing the board of education to take more active measures to hasten desegregation.

The majority of school boards, while issuing statements saying that they favored integrated school experience for as many pupils as possible, added, however, that there were limits beyond which the school system would not go in fostering integration. They said the major limiting factor was the "neighborhood school policy," which places a high priority on the pupil's attending school near home. Because the big cities have a great deal of residential (i.e., *de facto*) segregation by race, the neighborhood school policy makes it difficult to get integrated schools, especially at the elementary level.

Nevertheless, during the latter half of the 1960s, the more positive forms of integrative procedure were being pushed forward and tried in some locations. This was partly due to a mounting series of court decisions, for after 1965 the courts were increasingly throwing their weight against *de facto* segregation or were beginning to define government action such as building new schools in segregated neighborhoods as *de jure* segregation. In New York and New Jersey, the courts upheld the actions of school boards in fixing boundary lines of schools so as to produce an ethnic balance among students. In 1965, Massachusetts went further than any other state had gone up to that time by passing a law aimed at the *elimination* of racial imbalance in the public schools.

In spite of efforts made in a number of cities to reduce segregation, the proportions of black pupils in schools that were all-black or nearly so continued to increase in the big cities. Table 10.2 makes it clear that the black population was becoming more densely concentrated in many of the cities. Between 1950 and 1980 the black population increased between 100 and 300 percent in New York, Chicago, Los Angeles, Oakland, Detroit, Boston, and other cities. It simply was not possible to get a racial balance in more than a few of the schools in these large cities, unless mass transportation of as many as a third of the pupils was to be undertaken. The migration of white families to the edges of the cities and to the suburbs was defeating the policy of school desegregation.

Desegregation in Small Cities. Many small cities successfully desegregated their schools as students from formerly segregated schools were reassigned to schools with a stable racial balance. An example of this type of city is Evanston, Illinois, a predominantly middle-class suburb north of Chicago. The black minority in Evanston was less than 25 percent—large enough to fill several elementary schools before desegregation was carried out. Many black families in Evanston are working-class families whose adult members work at nearby industrial plants that employ a large part of the local population. Few, however, are lower-working class, and the median income for black families in Evanston in the 1960s was about double that of all black families in the United States. Thus, cities like Evanston did not have the high concentrations of very low-status minority students as did many of the big cities.

Phase III: 1974–1988

During the third phase of desegregation, emphasis shifted significantly to large urban school districts. Much desegregation had been accomplished successfully in the South and in small cities and towns throughout the nation, but desegregation of minority students in big cities was infrequent and segregation was increasing as their minority population increased.

Much of the impetus toward desegregation efforts in urban school districts with widespread *de facto* segregation was supplied in 1973 by the U.S. Supreme Court's decision in *Keys* v. *School District No. 1, Denver*. Plaintiffs charged that the school board had followed policies that intentionally brought about segregation (i.e., *de jure* segregation caused by foreseeable government action) in the Park Hill section of Denver. They also argued that segregation of black and Hispanic students in some schools and of non-Hispanic whites in others throughout the district was caused partly by the segregated patterns originating in Park Hill and partly by "purposeful and systematic" action of the school board. Where there has been intentional segregation of students in "substantial" portions of a district, they concluded, it is likely that segregation throughout the district is intentional, if only in the sense that the school board could have taken action to reduce or eliminate segregated attendance patterns.

Even though the Supreme Court did not directly rule that *de facto* segregation is unconstitutional, it did accept much of the plaintiffs' argument and concluded that clear evidence of intentional segregation in one part of a district suggests that other instances of segregation also are intentional, and the burden is on the school board to prove they are not. In ordering district-wide reassignment of students in Denver, the Supreme Court provided a spur for desegregation suits in other cities in which it could be shown—as it usually can—that there has been some intentional segregation that helped generate or reinforce larger patterns of residential segregation.

The recent situation with respect to desegregation of black students is shown in Table 9.1, which reports U.S. Department of Education surveys of racial and ethnic enrollments. Table 9.1 shows less segregation of black students in the South than in other parts of the United States. This condition is the result of school districts' actions in the southern states to combine formerly all-black and all-white schools into mixed schools that reflect the local population ratios. Because many schools were in rural counties that had long transported pupils by bus, there was no major change in the school-attendance routine for most families except that the children would now attend a biracial school. As Table 9.1 shows, 43 percent of the southern black pupils attended schools in 1984 where they were in the minority. During the 1970s and 1980s, all regions except the Northeast reduced segregation of black students to some degree. The Northeast, with many large urban concentrations of black population, increased in segregation of black students and is the most heavily segregated region in the United States. Gary Orfield examined these data and concluded that "as the United States becomes an increasingly multiracial society, racial segregation remains the prevailing pattern in most regions with significant minority populations. Progress in desegregation for blacks in the South is offset by increasing segregation in the North" (1982, 9).

As the percentage of Hispanic population in U.S. schools and society has increased during the past three decades, segregation of Hispanic students has

Table 9.1 ***Percentage of Black Students in Public Elementary and Secondary Schools More Than 50 Percent and 90 Percent Minority, 1968 to 1984, by Region***

	Percentage of Black Students in Schools 50 Percent or More Minority			Percentage of Black Students in Schools 90 Percent or More Minority		
	1968	*1976*	*1984*	*1968*	*1976*	*1984*
National	77	62	64	64	36	33
9 Northeast states	67	73	73	43	51	47
11 Midwest states	77	70	71	58	51	44
11 West states	72	67	67	51	36	29
6 border states and D.C.	72	60	63	60	43	37
11 Southern states	81	55	57	78	22	24

Note: National figures are for the continental United States (i.e., excluding Alaska and Hawaii). The definition of *minority* is the official federal classification, which includes the following groups: Black (Negro); American Indian; Spanish-surnamed; Portuguese; Asian (Oriental); Alaskan; and Hawaiian.

Source: Orfield and Monfort 1987.

become a growing problem for the educational system and the nation. The percentage of Hispanic students in public school enrollment increased from 5 percent in 1968 to 9 percent in 1984, while the percentage of non-Hispanic white students declined from 80 percent to 71 percent. Increase in Hispanic enrollment was particularly pronounced in the western states, where the percentage of Hispanic students increased from 12 percent in 1968 to 21 percent in 1984 (Orfield 1987).

In tandem with the increase in Hispanic enrollment, the percentages of Hispanic students in schools more than half minority and more than 90 percent also steadily increased (see Table 9.2). By way of contrast, segregation of black students decreased substantially in the early 1970s and then held mostly steady (see Tables 9.1 and 9.2). Both patterns reflect the fact that Hispanic and black enrollment has become increasingly concentrated in large metropolitan areas, particularly in central city school districts that are most difficult to desegregate (see also Tables 2.9 and 10.2).

The problem of desegregating schools in the practical sense—that is, of putting white and minority pupils in the same school building with both groups having at least 20 to 30 percent of the enrollment—is now particularly a problem for the large cities, where residential segregation has developed to such an extent that a minority child who attends a neighborhood school is likely to be in a school that is nearly all black or Hispanic. Given the segregated housing patterns and the high percentages of minority students in many big-city school districts, most minority students in these locations still attend segregated schools. Possibilities for desegregation of students in big-city school districts are discussed more fully in a subsequent section of this chapter.

Table 9.2 ***Percentage of Black and Hispanic Students in Public Elementary and Secondary Schools More Than 50 Percent and 90 Percent Minority, 1968 to 1984***

	Percentage in Schools More Than 50 Percent Minority		Percentage in Schools More Than 90 Percent Minority	
	Black Students	*Hispanic Students*	*Black Students*	*Hispanic Students*
1968	77	55	64	23
1972	64	57	39	23
1980	63	68	33	29
1984	64	71	33	31

Note: National figures are for the continental United States (i.e., excluding Alaska and Hawaii). The definition of *minority* is the official federal classification, which includes the following groups: Black (Negro); American Indian; Spanish-surnamed; Portuguese; Asian (Oriental); Alaskan; and Hawaiian.

Source: Orfield and Monfort 1987.

Development of Desegregation Planning

Another important development during the past two decades was the accumulation of knowledge concerning approaches to successful desegregation. Educators and researchers have learned a great deal about the types of programs and policies most likely to produce stable desegregation in which both minority and nonminority students benefit from integration in the school and classroom. Much of this knowledge has been summarized in studies by Willis Hawley and his colleagues at Vanderbilt University (Hawley et al. 1982; Hawley 1983; Subcommittee on Civil and Constitutional Rights 1982). Hawley and his colleagues have concluded that the following actions are particularly important in designing and implementing effective pupil reassignment plans:

- Begin desegregation as early as possible.
- Implement a mandatory plan but provide educational options within and among schools. Magnet schools and programs are most effective in the context of a mandatory plan for the school district as a whole.
- Enrich and improve curriculum and instruction in all schools, not just magnet schools.
- Implement a plan for all ages of children at one time rather than phase in desegregation at different educational levels.
- Take account of special needs (e.g., bilingual education, development of pride in one's culture, instruction for the handicapped) of different racial and ethnic groups.
- Encourage stability in student-student and teacher-student relationships, and otherwise reduce or eliminate uncertainties parents have about where their children will attend school and who will be responsible for their education.
- Provide a safe school environment.

- Retain a "critical mass" (15 to 20 percent) of students of any racial or ethnic group at a given school.
- Allow the percentage of minority population to vary in accordance with the nature of residential patterns and other factors.

Considerations that were cited as helping to improve achievement and race relations as part of a desegregation plan included the following:

- Create schools and instructional groupings within schools of limited size that provide a supportive environment in which teachers know students personally and can provide continuity in learning.
- Develop multiethnic curricula.
- Make human relations a fundamental component involving everything that is done in a school.
- Maximize direct parental involvement in the education of their children.
- Discourage interstudent competition while holding high and attainable expectations for individual students.
- Maintain discipline through clear rules of student behavior that are consistently and fairly enforced.
- Maximize participation in extracurricular programs that provide opportunities for interracial interaction.

Most of these as well as some additional recommendations also have been supported by other researchers, such as Genova and Walberg (1981) and Crain, Mahard, and Narot (1982), who have conducted research on successful desegregation. Several of them are considered further in the section below on effects of desegregation on student achievement and attitudes.

Desegregation Goals and Obstacles

The desegregation programs and procedures ordered by courts or by state or local boards of education, and some of the problems connected with them, can be summarized as follows:

1. *Racial isolation and racial balance.* There should not be one-race schools. Local school boards should draw school boundary lines to achieve a mixture of students from various racial and ethnic groups. School boards should use buses to transport pupils to schools that have been mainly attended by one racial or ethnic group.

There is no universal definition of a *one-race school,* but in some school districts the courts have ruled that schools that are 80 or 90 percent or more minority or nonminority are one-race schools that must be eliminated through all practicable means, including reassignment of students. This must be done even though the arrangements to eliminate segregation may seem administratively "bizarre," as in the 1971 court case of *Swann* v. *Charlotte-Mecklenberg Board of Education*. Transportation of students frequently is required if this will eliminate one-race schools without busing students more than about forty-five minutes one way.

In seeking to eliminate one-race schools, judges frequently have required a more balanced racial composition than is found in a school 80 percent or more minority or nonminority. Some courts have required that each school be within about 15 percent of the district-wide racial composition. Applying this guideline in a school district that has 55 percent minority students, each school must have between 40 and 70 percent minority students. The federal executive branch, particularly the Department of Health and Human Services, the Justice Department, and the Office of Civil Rights, is obligated to work toward the elimination of segregation in accordance with laws passed by Congress and the rulings of the courts. No school district may receive federal funds if it is not in compliance with constitutional mandates for desegregation.

It is clear that in a big-city school system where the school population has a majority of black and Hispanic pupils, such as Chicago or Los Angeles, there are severe limits on the extent of desegregation practicable. Such a school system will continue to have many one-race schools unless desegregation is carried out on a regional or metropolitan basis including suburban schools.

2. *Increase in segregation.* The percentage of minority students in many school districts has been steadily increasing for decades. Due to white suburbanization, minority migration to urban areas, and other factors, schools in some districts first have been desegregated and then have become resegregated as nonminority enrollment decreased and minority enrollment held steady or increased. As noted elsewhere in this chapter, there also is reason to believe that desegregation sometimes has accelerated white and middle-class withdrawal in school districts with a high percentage of low-status, minority students. Thus, steps that have been taken to desegregate the public schools frequently have been only temporarily successful, particularly in large urban school districts in which underlying trends toward segregation have continued to operate.

In 1976, the Supreme Court ruled in *Pasadena City Board of Education* v. *Spangler* that school districts do not have to take new action each year to desegregate schools that have become resegregated following implementation of a constitutionally acceptable desegregation plan. As long as the population shifts that cause resegregation are not attributable to segregative action on the part of the school system, the system need not take continuous action to maintain racial balance.

3. *White flight.* The Supreme Court has said that school district desegregation plans must "promise realistically to work." School officials frequently have tried to minimize student reassignment and transportation on the grounds that larger efforts would result in the withdrawal of whites and thereby defeat the purposes of desegregation. The courts generally have been alert to the possibility that potential white flight will be used as an excuse to avoid desegregation and have insisted that the right of minority students to attend desegregated schools should not depend on whether desegregation is convenient for nonminority students

or on the cooperation of families that threaten to leave the schools if constitutional guarantees are extended to minorities. The counter-arguments on this issue have led to a delicate legal and practical balance: school district officials are allowed to take the possibility of white withdrawal into account in formulating a desegregation plan which has a reasonable chance to succeed, but this possibility cannot be the only major consideration in determining the extent to which busing or other techniques will be used to desegregate the schools.

The outcome of these difficult legal decisions has been considerable uncertainty regarding the types of court-ordered desegregation plans appropriate in big-city school districts. One type of relatively comprehensive plan has been put into effect in Boston, Denver, Memphis, and several other cities where courts have ruled that nearly every school must be within 10 to 20 percent (depending on the city) of the overall racial composition of the district, even if this requires extensive pupil reassignment and transportation. At the other end of the continuum, courts have allowed Dallas, Houston, and some other cities to implement plans involving much less student reassignment, with substantial numbers of schools remaining one-race on the grounds that additional desegregation would be impractical. Most one-race schools remaining in this latter situation are minority schools, because courts generally require action to desegregate schools that have a preponderance of nonminority students.

During the first half of the 1970s, big-city desegregation orders appeared to be going in the direction of the first type of plan. Recognizing that millions of minority youngsters still attended segregated schools twenty years or more after the *Brown* decision, the courts along with concerned officials at various levels of government tended to push for the complete desegregation of big-city school districts. In general, it was not difficult to show that government action had played a major part in segregating the schools, and courts in a number of locations ordered the preparation and implementation of comprehensive plans to eliminate these patterns "root and branch." Boston's comprehensive plan was implemented in the fall of 1975, and similarly comprehensive plans were advanced by courts in San Francisco, Denver, and other cities.

At the same time, however, the potential pitfalls of implementing extensive student reassignment plans in big cities with a high proportion of minority students also were becoming clear. Analysis of desegregation plans in Detroit and some other cities suggests that large-scale reassignment of students sometimes would involve the transportation of minority students from schools 90 percent or more minority to schools 60 to 90 percent minority, with unclear benefits for any of the participants. Recognizing the dilemma, many desegregation planners systematically began to reexamine the possibilities and prospects for big-city school desegregation.

In this context, viewpoints regarding alternatives for big-city desegregation were undergoing inevitable change. On the one hand, it was apparent that the courts could and sometimes did take a legalistic approach to desegregation. The constitution would be satisfied either by making the racial composition in each school similar to the district as a whole or by reassigning students such that every minority student was enrolled in a school with 10 percent or more nonminority students assigned to it. White or middle-class families might continue to withdraw from schools with a majority of minority and working-class students thus assigned to them, leaving working-class minority students still more racially and economically isolated, but the courts and other government bodies could then walk away from the problem because the constitution had been upheld.

On the other hand, it was apparent that less extensive student reassignment plans also would leave many working-class minority students racially and economically isolated, and that other alternatives would have to be pursued if segregation and stratification were to be reduced. For example, magnet schools might be helpful in retaining white or middle-class students in big-city schools, and desegregation pursued on a metropolitan basis would be more stable than plans limited to the central city (see below). Armor (1980) has reviewed the research on white withdrawal from school districts undergoing desegregation and concluded that desegregation can accelerate the withdrawal of nonminority students, particularly in larger school districts with accessible white suburbs. Acceleration of white withdrawal is most pronounced in large central city districts in which there is a high concentration of minority students and the desegregation plan calls for substantial two-way busing of students. Some recent research (Rossell 1987) indicates that voluntary plans including magnet schools and other nonmandatory components can bring about more desegregation than do large-scale mandatory plans.

4. *Mandatory busing.* During the 1970s, many big-city desegregation programs were going in the direction of extensive pupil reassignment to schools often some distance from the local neighborhood school and requiring transportation by bus as much as half an hour or more one way. There was a growing opposition to mandatory busing on the part of parents and also of many members of the general public. An example of this was the referendum called for in California by a member of the California legislature. This referendum called for an amendment to the state constitution that would bar mandatory busing for the sake of desegregation. (However, federal courts could still require mandatory busing in California.) In 1979, voters approved the referendum by a large margin. However, civil rights organizations charged that such an amendment to the state constitution was contrary to the United States Constitution and appealed to the U.S. Supreme Court for a ruling.

The U.S. Supreme Court in 1982 ruled that the proposed amendment to the state constitution was acceptable under the U.S. Constitution. Also, at about the same time in the early 1980s, the United States Congress passed several laws that would deny federal government financial support for desegregation programs that included mandatory busing of students.

Thus, in the late 1970s and early 1980s, it became clear that additional assignment of pupils to schools outside of their own neighborhoods would not be widely supported by mandatory busing. Consequently, many districts that were highly segregated turned to a variety of procedures that were acceptable to many pupils and their families and involved freedom of choice and voluntary transportation if distances of travel were great. In addition, while racial or ethnic desegregation was still emphasized in some programs, others placed equal or

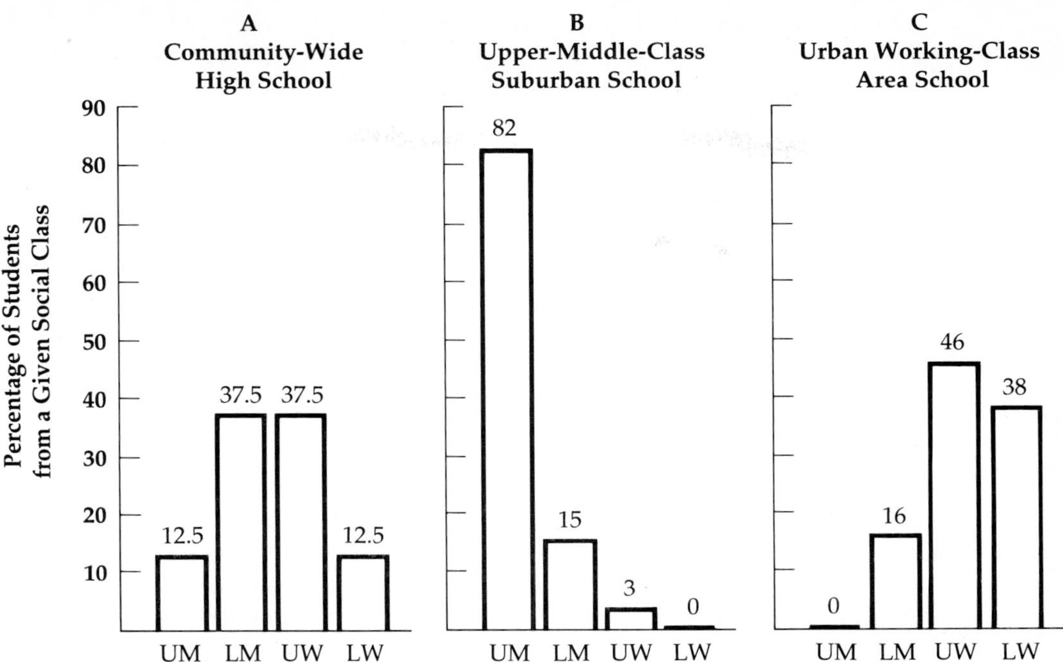

UM = upper-middle; LM = lower-middle; UW = upper-working; LW = lower-working

Figure 9.1 *Social Class Composition of Various Types of Secondary Schools* (*Source*: Authors' estimates.)

greater emphasis on improving the quality of instruction in segregated minority schools and/or desegregated schools.

For example, court orders in Chicago, Detroit, Los Angeles, St. Louis, and several other cities placed as much or more emphasis on improving instruction in minority schools as on reassigning minority students to desegregated schools. In most cases, state government was required to pay half the cost of both the instructional improvement and the student reassignment components in this type of desegregation plan. Instructional improvement components of desegregation plans are discussed more fully in a later section of this chapter.

Socioeconomic Mixture and Middle-Class Withdrawal from the Schools

Figure 9.1 shows the social compositions of three general types of high schools. School A is a typical high school in a town or small city that has only one high school; it therefore receives all the children of secondary school age. Most of the students are lower middle- and upper working-class, but there also are significant numbers of upper middle- and lower working-class students.

School B is a high school in an upper middle-class suburb, where there are very few working-class people. This type of school is sometimes called a "comprehensive" high school because it offers several curricula, including commercial and vocational courses, but it is not representative in the sense that its students represent a cross section of the social structure.

School C is a big-city high school with mostly working-class students. It serves a community in which there are no upper middle- and only a few lower middle-class families. In such an area there may be a majority of lower working-class residents, but since their children tend to drop out of school early, the composition of the high school shows a preponderance of pupils from upper working-class homes.

There is probably a critical point involving the socioeconomic mixture of most big-city schools, a point at which middle-class parents are likely to become anxious and will consider removing their children from the school and moving to a higher-status area. If the proportion of working-class students increases beyond this point, middle-class parents may fear there will be a drop in the academic standards of the school, or changes in curricular offerings, or unwelcome influences on their own children's motivation for school achievement.

We should note that such attitudes on the part of parents are not altogether unfounded. A study by Wilson (1959) supports the generalization that when student bodies vary in their proportions of middle and working class, students develop different educational and vocational aspirations. The study showed that in predominantly lower-status schools, *higher*-status children have lower educational and occupational aspirations than in predominantly higher-status schools, and in predominantly higher-status schools, *lower*-status children have higher aspirations than in predominantly lower-status schools. Wilson says, "The *de facto* segregation brought about by concentrations of social classes in cities results in schools with unequal moral climates which likewise affect the motivation of the child . . . by providing a different ethos in which to perceive values" (Wilson 1959, 845).

The point at which a school becomes undesirable in the eyes of middle-class parents is subjective and variable, depending on the attitudes and experience of a particular parent, and depending also on such factors as the tradition of the school, the racial composition of the school, the type of curriculum, and the quality of the teachers. However, in practice there seems to be relative consensus among middle-class parents on the question of when a school becomes a "poor" school and when they begin to move out of the school district. As this happens in big-city school districts, a higher proportion of the schools become predominantly working-class.

The phenomenon of middle-class withdrawal from schools that have a substantial number of working-class students appears to be as characteristic of black neighborhoods as of white neighborhoods. One primary reason that middle-class black families have been moving to the suburbs has been to remove their children from concentrated poverty schools and neighborhoods (Wolman 1976). Middle-class black families that remain in the city typically send their children to parochial or other nonpublic schools if there is no predominantly middle-class public school nearby.

White Withdrawal from Desegregated Schools

Just as middle-class families rapidly withdraw their children from schools they perceive are becoming predominantly working-class, nonminority families (i.e., non-Hispanic white families) tend to withdraw their children from schools that have a substantial proportion of minority students. These two tendencies frequently are difficult to disentangle, because many minority students are from working-class families and because nonminority parents often have confused socioeconomic status and race, that is, they have assumed that minority students entering their children's schools are from lower working-class homes. However, the two phenomena can be distinguished both conceptually and in practice, as is shown by some cases in which middle-class black families withdraw from schools with an increasing proportion of working-class students and other cases in which working-class nonminority families withdraw from schools that have become racially balanced.

There is some uncertainty concerning the possible existence of a so-called tipping point at which schools that are growing in minority percentage tend to become rapidly resegregated. Some studies such as one conducted in Kansas City by Levine and Meyer (1977) have indicated that big-city schools that reach about 30 percent in minority enrollment subsequently tend to become resegregated at a rapid rate, but other studies such as one in Baltimore (Stinchcombe, Medill, and Walker 1969) suggest that schools with a small percentage of minority students subsequently experience continuing nonminority withdrawal with no discernible point at which the process is accelerated. Either conclusion suggests that it has been difficult to prevent the segregation of big-city schools.

However, most big cities also have had a few schools with a relatively stable minority percentage ranging from 30 to as much as 70 percent, indicating that it is possible to prevent the segregation of big-city schools. As in the case of socioeconomic integration, much depends on such aspects of the situation as the degree to which parents have confidence that the student composition of local schools will remain stable, the availability of alternatives such as private schools or affordable housing in the suburbs, and the leadership of educators in maintaining attractive instructional programs.

It is certain, however, that middle-class families still were leaving schools in many big cities at a rapid rate during the 1980s. In addition to unwillingness to send their children to increasingly working-class schools, middle-class families leave big-city schools for a variety of reasons, including dissatisfaction with instructional offerings in financially distressed districts, deterioration of local neighborhoods, and general unhappiness with conditions in the city (Abravanel and Mancini 1980). In general, school and other government officials not only have failed to intervene effectively to stop this process of segregation and deterioration but in some ways have also aided it through policies that helped to concentrate low-status population in the central city.

Instructional Improvement Components in Desegregation Plans

The situation in the 1970s forced educators to define the goals of desegregation in larger terms. Emphasis began to be placed on improving instruction in an effort to reduce the achievement gap between minority and nonminority students and courts began to include more instructional components in desegregation plans designed to overcome the effects of past and current racial isolation of minority students. (Components of this kind frequently are referred to as *ancillary relief components*.) This trend was particularly apparent in the big cities, where it had become clear that many minority students would continue to attend predominantly minority schools in the absence of metropolitan remedies involving nonminority students outside the central city.

Judicial insistence on improvement of instruction as part of desegregation plans was particularly evident when Judge Robert E. DeMascio, Jr., issued a 1975 desegregation order requiring, among other things, that "the Detroit Board of Education and the General Superintendent, together with a staff unit appointed by such Superintendent, shall design, develop and institute a comprehensive instructional program for teaching reading and communication skills. Such educational program shall be characterized by excellence and shall be instituted in every school in the system." Judge DeMascio further ordered that the state government, which with the board of education was responsible for segregation in Detroit, should pay half the costs of carrying out the remedial program. The Supreme Court opinion upholding Judge DeMascio's order said the Detroit schools had been so "pervasively and persistently segregated" that the constitutional violation could not be remedied by student reassignment alone.

Since 1975, Detroit has implemented a desegregation plan limited almost entirely to ancillary relief components designed primarily to improve the effectiveness of instruction in its predominantly minority schools. Major components in the plan have dealt respectively with reading, in-service training, guidance, testing, student conduct, bilingual education, vocational education, and school-community relations.

A good example of a central-city district attempting to implement an ambitious program of ancillary relief is Kansas City, Missouri, which designed many of the components in its first court order (1985) to improve the effectiveness of instruction for minority students throughout the district. (Seventy-two percent of enrollment was minority in 1985.) As shown in Table 9.3, ancillary relief components were designed to make funds available for individual school needs; reduce class size; provide additional staff development; expand summer school; meet state standards for art, music, physical education, libraries, and teacher planning time; conduct all-day kindergartens; carry out early childhood

Table 9.3 *Ancillary Relief Components in the Three-Year Court Order for Desegregation of the Kansas City, Missouri, Public Schools, 1985–1987*

Component	Three-Year Expenditures
Discretionary school funds*	$17,175,000
Reduction in class size	12,000,000
Staff development	500,000
Summer school	1,131,500
Meet state standards**	5,207,750
All-day kindergarten	1,638,000
Early childhood development***	1,850,022
Capital improvements	27,000,000

* Discretionary school funds to improve student achievement were provided for 1985–86 on the basis of $50,000 per school less than 90 percent black and $75,000 per school 90 or more percent black, with the respective allocations increasing to $120,000 and $100,000 per school in 1987–88.

** Standards addressed include minimal provisions for the highest State of Missiouri classification with respect to art, music, and physical education teachers, libraries and librarians, and teacher planning time.

*** Early childhood development refers to a variety of preschool programs including expansion of Head Start–type activities, screening of young children for learning problems, and parental education to improve home learning environment.

Source: Eubanks and Levine 1987b.

education; and improve capital facilities. In general, these components were designed to enhance desegregation by making the district more effective and attractive.

Effects of School Desegregation

There have been considerable disagreement and confusion concerning the effects of school desegregation on students. Some observers, including researchers familiar with the fairly extensive literature on this topic, firmly believe that desegregated schools provide an indispensable means for improving the achievement of minority students or for developing positive interracial attitudes. Others, also including researchers familiar with the literature on desegregation, confidently state that desegregation either has not generally had positive effects on achievement or attitudes or has not been shown to have positive effects. Conclusions differ a good deal according to one's selection and reading of the research and its meaning.

Effects on Achievement of Minority Students

In addition to the larger disagreement on whether desegregation has had a positive effect on the achievement of minority students, there has been a dispute over the reasons that achievement gains occur where they do appear to have been documented. Some observers believe that such gains are primarily or entirely due to socioeconomic mixture; achievement gains are brought about when low-status minority students attend schools with middle-status nonminority students. Other observers, however, believe that racial desegregation sometimes improves the achievement of minority students apart from the effects of socioeconomic desegregation. (It should be noted that most desegregation research deals with black students; very little deals specifically with Hispanics or other minorities.) Most researchers agree that desegregation has not harmed the achievement of nonminority students, but it also should be noted that middle-status white parents generally withdraw their children from predominantly minority and working-class schools in which their achievement might decline. Where some research has indicated that desegregation is associated with lower achievement among nonminority students, the major reason appears to be that teachers and administrators in schools with a high percentage of black students "tend to lower their expectations of, and demands upon, students" (Patchen 1982, 347).

Disagreements regarding achievement effects underline the complexity and difficulty of school desegregation research. Problems arise in measuring and controlling for the effects of socioeconomic status, in distinguishing between students who improve in achievement and those who do not, in measuring changes that may be relatively small but meaningful over a one- or two-year period, in comparing results for students who participate in different types of desegregation settings (e.g., voluntary transfer programs or mandatory assignment; urban or rural), and in assessing gains in different subject areas such as reading or mathematics. Among these and many other methodological problems, probably the most important involves the comparison of results in situations in which desegregation has been well implemented with results in situations—probably the vast majority—in which little has been done to prepare teachers to work with students of diverse performance levels and backgrounds.

Given these problems, it is not surprising that scholars have reached such differing conclusions concerning the achievement effects of desegregation. St. John (1975) carefully reviewed the major studies on school desegregation and concluded that due to methodological weaknesses and problems in data interpretation, one could not say that desegregation had been either successful or unsuccessful in terms of raising minority students' achievement. Weinberg (1977) also has analyzed this research and concluded that overall, desegregation does have a positive effect on minority achievement. Bradley and Bradley (1977) analyzed studies that had been reported through 1976 and concluded that there are "well designed" studies both supporting and disconfirming "the use of school desegregation as an intervention strategy" (p. 444). Their general conclusion was that "the data collected since 1959 regarding school desegregation has been inconsistent and inadequate" (p. 444).

A later review by Krol (1980) of 129 studies dealing with effects on minority-student achievement also raised questions about the effectiveness of desegregation. Krol concluded that even where desegregated minority students made greater achievement gains than did comparable groups of segregated students, these gains generally were small and not statistically significant.

However, Crain and Mahard (1982) also reviewed available research on desegregation effects and came to somewhat different conclusions. (To a substantial degree, conclusions in this type of research review frequently depend on the studies one selects as worth review, the methods used to assess them, interpretation of the research design and statistics in a given study, and other considerations.) After analyzing 93 studies reporting on 323 samples of black students, Crain and Mahard selected 45 that met the standards they had established for adequate research design. Their main conclusions included the following:

> *Studies that avoided . . . [major] methodological errors show consistent results. We found positive effects of desegregation in 40 of 45 such studies. . . . the effect of desegregation, when measured properly, is a gain of about .3 standard deviations (about one grade-year). . . . The 93 studies of black achievement after desegregation were used to identify the most successful types of desegregation plans. These are metropolitan plans, either voluntary or mandatory, which result in schools that have a minority, but not a small minority, of black students—in the North, schools that are 10 to 20 percent black; in the South, schools that are 10 to 30 percent black. These estimates cannot be considered precise, but they clearly imply that schools should have a majority of white students and more than a token number of black students.*
>
> *. . . These findings are quite consistent . . . with the hypothesis that the benefits of desegregation are the result of socioeconomic desegregation. . . . [In addition, studies of Hispanic achievement suggest] that any low-income group will benefit academically from attending a school whose students are predominantly higher status, regardless of the ethnicity of either the higher-status or the lower-status group. (Crain and Mahard 1982, v, vi, 35)*

Taking account of the reported discrepant research interpretations, it is not possible to offer either conclusive generalizations about desegregation or facile predictions that desegregation will improve the achievement of minority students in the future. However, in view of the facts that some well-designed studies have reported positive outcomes from desegregation and that desegregation typically has not been combined with effective systematic efforts to improve instruction for students of differing performance levels, we believe the research literature supports the following two conclusions.

1. Desegregation accompanied by instructional improvement efforts can be an effective technique for raising the achievement of low-status minority stu-

dents. The National Evaluation of the Emergency School Aid Act (ESAA), which provided hundreds of millions of dollars to facilitate desegregation, has shown that some local ESAA projects were quite effective in improving both basic skills and school racial relations, though the success of those projects was obscured by the failure of other projects (Coulson 1976). This evaluation also indicated that successful programs had the following characteristics: there was a greater focus of resources on attaining the goals of the program; administrative leadership was stronger and more assertive; classroom lessons were more highly structured; parents were more heavily involved in the classroom; and administrators and teachers made greater efforts to promote positive interracial attitudes. Several of these characteristics resemble those identified in Chapter 8 as being required for successful compensatory education.

The similarity between characteristics of successful compensatory education and successful desegregation projects makes it difficult to determine whether desegregation has a separate impact beyond effectively implemented compensatory education. In addition, the finding that desegregation projects that were successful in raising achievement also tended to improve interracial attitudes may mean either that minority students who feel accepted in the school may become more motivated and improve in achievement or outstanding leadership accounts for both achievement gains and improvements in interracial attitudes. In view of these difficulties in interpretation, it probably is best to view desegregation as a condition facilitating the implementation of compensatory education or other instructional reforms.

This conclusion is congruent with the fact that compensatory education has not been very effective in concentrated poverty schools. Although some gains have been reported during the past few years, for the most part achievement in concentrated poverty schools continues to be very low above the primary grades, regardless of whether their enrollment is white or black or integrated. Thus, positive effects of desegregation on minority students' achievement probably are due much more to socioeconomic mixture than to racial desegregation per se. Several major studies, such as a five-year experiment in Israeli elementary schools (Klein and Eshel 1980), indicate that socioeconomic desegregation *plus* instructional improvement can improve the achievement of low-status minority students.

2. However, it is possible that racial desegregation also can help improve minority achievement beyond the effects of socioeconomic desegregation. Arguments in favor of this conclusion depend on the premise that racial isolation has a negative effect on minority students' motivation separate from the effects of socioeconomic isolation among low-status minority students, perhaps by reinforcing feelings of powerlessness associated with racial segregation or by shielding minority students from competitive pressures and stimuli that support high achievement among nonminority students. Supporting this conclusion, Anthony Pascal (1977) of the Rand Corporation reviewed the research on desegregation and found that even after socioeconomic status and previous achievement are taken into account, the "gains for minority students are real" (p. 4). However, Pascal also concluded that gains from racial desegregation per se are

modest and contribute little to narrowing the achievement gap between the races.

It should be emphasized that few if any scholars studying the effects of school desegregation believe that it can totally eliminate achievement differences that exist between low-status minority students and higher-status nonminority students. A typical estimate of the potential effect of desegregation is that offered by Pettigrew (1973), who believes desegregation by itself can close approximately only one-fourth of the achievement gap between minority and nonminority students. On the other hand, gains of this magnitude represent one or more years of achievement on standardized performance tests. For many students, such gains constitute the difference between functional literacy and illiteracy. It also should be kept in mind that contact with middle-status students frequently appears to have an important positive influence on the academic aspirations of low-status students. (Evidence for this conclusion is presented in Chapter 5 and elsewhere in this book.) Together with effective compensatory education programs beginning in the early years, desegregation may prove to be an indispensable precondition for bringing about widespread improvement in the academic performance of low-status minority students.

We also should emphasize that the impetus for desegregation does not depend primarily on whether research has demonstrated it has been consistently effective in raising minority achievement. Courts have reviewed the complicated and sometimes contradictory research on this topic, and judges have found the results as difficult to interpret as have other observers. Faced with this complex literature, judges have had little recourse but to begin from the starting point established in *Brown et al.* v. *Board of Education of Topeka, Kansas,* in 1954 and elaborated in subsequent Supreme Court decisions: state action that places minority students in segregated schools is unconstitutional because segregated schools are inherently unequal and discriminatory.

Effects on Interracial Attitudes and Relations

Research on the race-relations effects of desegregation has not shown a consistent tendency for results to be positive. Pascal (1977) reviewed the studies that have been carried out on this issue and reached the following conclusion:

> *Race relations consequences encompass inter-racial attitudes and feelings, cross-race friendship, and the degree of tension between the races in a school. Research findings suggest that desegregation* per se *rarely produces positive change for both races in attitudes and friendships. The positive outcomes which do occur appear to be most frequent in elementary schools and scarcest in junior high schools. . . . Middle class and high achieving students tend to respond more than others. (pp. 5–6)*

However, as is true with respect to research on achievement effects, there is reason to believe that this conclusion understates the potential utility and efficacy of desegregation in improving interracial attitudes and relationships. Desegregation typically has not been implemented very well, so it is not surprising that it has frequently been ineffective. In cases in which it has been well implemented, it frequently appears to have some positive effects in terms of interracial relationships.

Recognizing this need to distinguish between successful and unsuccessful desegregation efforts and to determine why some are more successful than others, Forehand, Ragosta, and Rock of the Educational Testing Service (1977) conducted a systematic study to identify successful ESAA projects and the factors responsible for their success. Data for the study were obtained from a 1974 survey of 96 elementary schools and 72 high schools and a 1975 follow-up in 22 elementary schools and 21 high schools. Data collection methods included site visits and interviews to obtain information on successful school practices and problem-solving techniques. Like the National Evaluation Study, this examination of successful desegregated projects showed that these projects tended to have outstanding administrative leadership, achievement gains among minority students, and improved interracial attitudes and relationships. The ETS study examined teaching and administrative practices in considerable depth and reported the following three major conclusions:

1. Low-status black students often attend desegregated schools whose faculties do not provide appropriate leadership for desegregation. These schools are characterized by negative teacher attitudes and by absence of teaching practices to improve race relations. At both the elementary and secondary levels, teacher attitudes toward race seemed to be the crucial determinant of white students' attitudes.
2. Successful schools have adopted specific practices and policies effective in improving race relations among students. Examples include use of multiracial curriculum materials, teaching of minority group history and culture, open classroom discussions on race, and assignment of black and white students to work and to play together in organized activities.
3. High schools that have good race relations tend to have principals supportive of both black and white teachers. A principal's impact in improving student race relations results from leadership to adopt effective practices and policies and the effects this leadership has on teachers. This happens because principals' racial attitudes have a direct effect on the attitudes of teachers, and because desegregation appears to be most successful when the principal demands unbiased behavior of the staff, regardless of whether they believe in it.

It should be noted that these findings concerning the kinds of instructional practices that lead to successful school desegregation are well in line with decades of research in which social psychologists have identified some conditions necessary for producing positive attitude and behavior change as a result of intergroup or interracial contact. Psychologist Gordon Allport and others have studied this issue in some detail and concluded that personal contact is much more important than is information in generating change in attitudes and behavior, but contact can have either positive or negative results depending on its nature and quality. Positive change (i.e., favorable toward members of other groups) is most likely to occur when contact is "equal status"; an "authority" and/or the social climate are in favor of and promote it; the contact is sustained and intimate rather than fragmented and casual; it is pleasant and rewarding; and the members of interacting groups cooperate in functionally important activities or develop common goals or superordinate goals that are more important than individual goals (Amir 1969).

Desegregated schools provide an opportunity that did not previously exist for positive intergroup contact, but they also provide an opportunity for neutral or negative contact (Hallinan and Teixeira 1987). Depending partly on the leadership in a school, contact may tend to be unpleasant or unrewarding for many students and teachers, and it may result in little meaningful interaction in working on common goals. In many situations, minority students enter desegregated schools or classrooms far below nonminority students in academic achievement, and partly as a result they may be placed in separate learning groups where there is relatively little personal contact. If low-achieving minority students are placed in desegregated classrooms, stereotypes and negative perceptions and self-perceptions regarding their ability may be reinforced rather than alleviated. Unless desegregation is implemented to avoid these outcomes, its effects on race relations and interracial attitudes may be more negative than positive. Scott and McPartland (1982) have reviewed the research on this topic and concluded that "although desegregation under some conditions may foster more positive race relations, favorable conditions may not exist in all schools, in all classes of the same school, or for both races in the same class. . . . The different ways in which desegregation has been implemented and is practiced from one community to the next virtually insures that the quality and amount of face-to-face contact cannot be predicted from racial composition alone" (pp. 399–400).

Scott and McPartland also examined data from the National Assessment of Educational Progress 1976 survey of nine-, thirteen-, and seventeen-year-olds, in order to identify relationships between desegregation and interracial attitudes. Racial tolerance was assessed with items inquiring about willingness to engage in interracial contact. They found that despite vast differences in implementation of desegregation among schools in this national sample, desegregation is positively associated with racial tolerance for both blacks and whites. They also found that although both black and white nine-year-olds responded less tolerantly than did the older students, desegregation had a stronger relationship with tolerance among the younger students.

Curriculum and instruction researchers have been working to develop systematic approaches for achieving the goals of desegregated education. By organizing instruction and other school activities to bring about equal status contact and cooperative work on common educational goals, they hope to generate positive interracial interrelationships and also to improve the achievement of low-achieving students who otherwise tend to be frustrated by competitive practices of the traditional classroom. For example, Lucker et al. (1976) found that a classroom technique called the jigsaw method, in which students work interdependently as members of teams, increased the academic achievement of black and Mexican-American students. Rosenholtz (1977) has found that the self-fulfilling prophecy wherein students low in reading performance tend to withdraw from instruction and hence continue to perform poorly can be altered by a "multiple abilities curriculum" wherein every student is provided with some degree of competence in at least one skill and is expected to improve in subsequent performance. Emphasis in the multi-ability classroom involved the installation of groupwork, task activities that do not make reading a prerequisite for success, use of multi-ability definitions of the situation, individualization of academic tasks, private evaluation of students, and reduction in comparative and competitive marking and grading. Cohen (1980) reported that use of small groups and multi-ability activities has led to a dramatic increase in the classroom participation rates of low-achieving students in desegregated classrooms.

Much work along these lines also has been done by Robert E. Slavin and his colleagues at the Center for Social Organization of Schools at Johns Hopkins University, where researchers are developing the Teams–Games–Tournament (TGT) approach and the Student Teams–Achievement Divisions (STAD) approach for equalizing probability of success in learning. Using the TGT approach, students compete as individuals to contribute points to their teams in three-person competitive situations in which the highest three students in past performance compete with each other, the three next highest compete with each other, and so on. Using the STAD approach, team points are earned based on competitions in which student scores on twice-weekly quizzes are compared to the scores of other students of similar past performance. Thus, both TGT and STAD contain a (cooperative) team component and a comparison-among-equals component. Slavin (1977b) reports an experiment using STAD in a 70 percent black junior high school in Baltimore in which black student achievement was improved more markedly than white student achievement. He speculates that this difference may have been due to a tendency for black participants to be lowest in social class and for low-status students to be more peer oriented than are middle-status students.

Slavin also reports a comparative study (1977a) in three junior high schools in which it was found that STAD methods were more effective than were control methods in increasing academic achievement, peer support for academic performance, liking of others, and number of students cited as friends. The study also indicated that there were team effects at the two schools that were overwhelmingly white but team effects were most apparent at the predominantly black working-class school. Slavin concluded that the "present study joins a steadily growing body of literature supporting the use of student teams in classrooms to achieve multiple outcomes, including increased time on task, academic performance, and most dramatically increased interpersonal attraction among class members . . . including friendships across racial lines" (p. 18).

These findings are not surprising inasmuch as research consistently indicates that cooperative learning arrangements in the public schools contribute to the improvement of student achievement and the attainment of other goals such as social and physical development, positive school attitudes, and good interpersonal relationships (Leming and Hollifield 1985; Slavin 1980, 1983). David and Roger Johnson also have been developing and studying cooperative learning arrangements and reached the following conclusion based on an analysis of available research: "Cooperation is considerably more effective than are interpersonal competitive and individualistic efforts in promoting achievement and productivity. . . . It is the cooperative goal structure that especially promotes the positive interaction among students" (Johnson and Johnson 1981, 78).

Opportunity Networks

Another major purpose of desegregation is to help minority youth enter so-called opportunity networks that can help them gain access to social and economic resources in mainstream society. Thomas Pettigrew of the University of California at Santa Cruz has summarized research on opportunity networks:

> *Labor economists . . . have long noted that blue-collar workers, clerical workers, engineers, lawyers, and even college professors typically secure their positions through such indirect methods as personal contacts . . . rather than such direct methods as employment agencies and advertisements. The important thing is to be in the informational flow about jobs, to hear about openings and new occupational possibilities.*
>
> *Earlier work on this problem assumed that it was close ties with relatives and intimate friends that were crucial for this network phenomenon. But Mark Granovetter found that job information flowed typically through 'weak ties.' . . . Two-thirds of these contacts were work-related rather than family members or social friends. . . . Granovetter reasons that the importance of weak ties in the flow of job information is related to the fact that they are maximally informative because the networks minimally overlap, while relatives and close friends are likely to share much the same knowledge of the world. (Pettigrew 1978, 44–45)*

The possible role of desegregation in providing minority students with access to opportunity networks has not been widely researched. A study by Robert Crain (1970) that examined the postsecondary experience of blacks who had attended segregated compared with desegregated schools indicated that the latter group was more fully in the white-dominated job information flow than the former, but Crain's study did not address the issue systematically. Henry Becker of Johns Hopkins University examined the research related to desegregation and opportunity networks and concluded that existing research does not provide enough evidence to allow for firm conclusions. He also stressed, however, that the hypothesized relationship between desegregation and opportunity networks "remains plausible. Obtaining a job requires much more than having certain attributes like the ability to read and write. . . . To the extent that racial segregation in housing, schooling, and employment continue to prevent young blacks from having access to the information channels used to fill job vacancies and to the extent that employers continue to demand greater degrees of sponsorship for unknown black youth than for whites, the gap between the employment prospects of white and black youth will remain" (Becker 1979, 22–23).

Subsequent Desegregation Participation

One of the most important benefits of desegregation is that it appears to generate greater willingness and capacity to participate in additional subsequent desegregated experiences. Increasing minority students' likelihood of participating in subsequent desegregated experience may be particularly important in encouraging their attendance at schools and colleges with high academic standards and high levels of student aspirations, as well as subsequently enlarging their socioeconomic opportunity networks. Jomills Braddock II (1987) has reviewed the research bearing on this potential benefit of desegregation and reached the following four conclusions:

1. Individuals who grow up in largely segregated environments are "more likely to lead their adult lives in segregated situations . . . be it in education, residential location, employment or informal social contacts." The research provides "impressive evidence that segregation is perpetuated from elementary-secondary schools to colleges, neighborhoods, jobs, and other adult social settings. . . . Earlier desegregated schooling breaks this self-perpetuating cycle."
2. School desegregation generates "positive reactions among blacks and whites to future interracial situations."
3. School desegregation helps develop "interpersonal skills that are useful in interracial contexts."
4. Desegregation of schools thus may be a "uniquely necessary ingredient to open up fairer career opportunities, to penetrate barriers to adult desegregation, and for students to develop skills at working successfully in multiracial settings." (Braddock 1987, 8, 14, 15, 18, 31).

Desegregation of Urban Schools

As noted at the conclusion of Chapter 2, declining cities and metropolitan areas cannot be renewed successfully without attractive, high-quality public schools. Smaller metropolitan areas are likely to proceed through the same stages of deterioration as have older and larger areas unless central city schools remain attractive and can provide effective instruction for children of all social classes, particularly for lower working-class students who otherwise may constitute a segregated underclass. This section discusses what can be done to make urban schools a positive force for desegregation in the long-range development of metropolitan society.

We also note earlier in this chapter that desegregation is closely related to the issue of social class in the schools. The academic benefits of desegregation for minority students tend to be associated with socioeconomic mixture, that is, with situations in which low-status minority students go to school with higher status nonminority students. Desegregation also is primarily a social-class issue to the degree that withdrawal of middle-class families from desegregated schools follows from fear that instructional standards will decline as schools become increasingly working class.

Despite the importance of socioeconomic mixture, courts and school officials have given little systematic attention to it in formulating and carrying out plans for desegregation of the public schools. In part, this is because the Supreme Court has ruled that economic discrimination is not prohibited by the federal constitution. There is no recognized constitutional requirement that the poor must have a chance to attend economically desegregated schools.

Big-City School Districts

After about 1950, the black areas of large cities experienced a very rapid increase in child population that soon overcrowded the schools in these areas. By the early 1950s, schools that had formerly stood partially empty in many central cities were full to overflowing with black children. The rapid in-migration of black population into central cities ended during the late 1960s in most parts of the country, but suburbanization of whites continued at a steady pace; as a result, black Americans have constituted a steadily increasing proportion of the population of central cities. The percentage of the black population residing in central cities increased from 44 percent in 1950 to 56 percent in 1980, while the comparable percentages for non-Hispanic whites declined from 35 percent to 24 percent (see Table 10.2).

During the 1960s the Hispanic population of the cities began to increase rapidly in many parts of the United States. As shown in Table 10.2, the Hispanic population is concentrated in central cities almost as heavily as is the black population, and the percentage of Hispanics is still increasing at a rapid rate in many cities. The result of movement of blacks and Hispanics to big cities together with non-Hispanic white movement to the suburbs is that the largest central cities and their school systems now have high proportions of minority population and enrollment (see Table 2.9). With most big cities now enrolling a large majority of minority students, the general pattern is that most of their minority students attend predominantly minority schools.

Big-city school officials have been trying to find policies that might result in sustained movement to reduce segregation. We discuss key elements of plans that have emerged in several cities, with special emphasis on the situation in Dallas, Texas, where more has been done than in most other localities to develop a plan systematically addressed to the goal of improving the quality of education in the central city. We believe that plans similar in some respects to the Dallas plan, but adapted to the situation in individual cities, provide a promising approach for advancing the goals of big-city school desegregation in the remainder of the 1980s and thereafter.

Student Assignment Patterns

The court-ordered plan for desegregation in Dallas was implemented in 1976. The plan does not reassign students in grades K–3, on the grounds that it is inappropriate to transport young students beyond a nearby school and that emphasis at this level should be mostly on developing basic skills so students are prepared to participate fully in instructional programs offered in desegregated settings at the middle-grade levels. Effective compensatory education programs emphasizing parent involvement along with improvement in instruction must be introduced to make this goal attainable.

Working within this broad policy, it may be desirable to pair or cluster K–3 enrollment in nearby schools in some cities, in situations where predominantly minority schools are adjacent to predominantly majority schools. Pairing and clustering involve "pooling" of students from such schools and reassignment to campuses with desegregated enrollment. Care should be taken in these circumstances to make sure that travel times are short and that each campus has a potentially stable racial mixture (i.e., generally not more than 40 to 60 percent minority students). In addition, middle-status students should not be assigned to schools with more than 30 to 40 percent working-class students. Few middle-status parents—white or black—will send their children to this type of school for very long.

At the middle-grades and above, students should be reassigned wherever practical to schools with a desegregated student body. Reorganization of the schools at these levels provides an opportunity to improve education greatly for older children and young adolescents, with special emphases on providing multicultural experience to prepare students for life in a pluralistic society and on introducing students to career possibilities in the wide society. The Dallas plan, which established intermediate schools for students in grades 4–6 and grades 7–8, is a good example of movement in this direction on a district-wide basis.

Within this policy, it is important to maintain a potentially stable racial balance in desegregated schools and to offer options to parents who might otherwise withdraw their children from the public schools. Schools in integrated neighborhoods that already are 40 to 60 percent minority should be basically left alone, since natural desegregation of this sort can provide a nucleus for expanding neighborhood and school desegregation on a stable foundation. Leaving them undisturbed also may begin to give parents a vested interest in living in integrated communities, because middle-grade students in predominantly minority or nonminority neighborhoods will have to be transported to schools outside their communities for purposes of desegregation.

Particularly in school districts that have more than 50 or 60 percent minority students, implementation of this type of policy means that some students will remain racially isolated in schools more than 80 or 90 percent minority. The initial Dallas plan left many students in one of the school system's six administrative subdistricts racially isolated in this way, and some judges elsewhere have accepted similar arrangements in districts where there appear to be too few nonminority students to achieve anywhere near an even racial balance in most schools.

In addition, emphasis should be placed on reducing racial isolation through the establishment of magnet schools and programs. There is an important difference between a magnet *school* and a magnet *program*. As defined here, a magnet school is a desegregated school that students voluntarily attend on a full-time or half-time basis in order to participate in instructional programs not available in their local school. A magnet program is a part-time educational experience, as in the case of a two-week assignment at a science center with special instructional resources. As defined here, a magnet program also can be a course or set of courses that students from a variety of schools voluntarily attend for one or two hours a day at a desegregated magnet location.

Voluntary magnet arrangements should be particularly stressed at the secondary level. In many big cities, some or most high schools already have 30 to 50 percent minority students, making it difficult to assign minority students to them much more extensively without upsetting their stability. In addition, as demonstrated in the next section, magnetization is a particularly promising approach to improving the quality of instruction for secondary students. By establishing magnet schools and programs at the high-school level, school officials hope to increase the minority percentage at each school to at least 35 to 40 percent and to reduce the number of minority students at racially isolated schools. Magnet schools are discussed at more length later in this chapter.

Variations on the Larger Theme

The emerging desegregation pattern described above can be summarized as follows:

1. Little or no mandatory reassignment of students in grades K–3, with emphasis at this level on improving basic skills through instructional reform and parent involvement.
2. Substantial reassignment and transportation of students in grades 4–8 or 4–9, with emphasis at this level on multicultural experience and programming but not so much student reassignment as to disturb schools that already have 40 to 60 percent minority students. This approach leaves many minority students in racially isolated schools in school districts that have more than 50 or 60 percent minority students.
3. Establishment of voluntary magnet schools and programs to increase desegregation and reduce racial isolation at the high school level, with mandatory

reassignment of students if necessary to ensure there are at least 35 to 40 percent minority students at each school.

Within this larger pattern, there are many variations developing in line with the situation, issues, and possibilities that characterize a given school district. Several of these variations and considerations are as follows:

1. *Desegregation goals.* The goal implicitly being used to develop the kind of desegregation plan described above is to reduce racial isolation of as many minority students as possible without precipitating further withdrawal of white or middle-class families. In a few cities, this goal has been stated explicitly and has even been enlarged to aim at attracting students back from suburban and nonpublic schools. Minimum and maximum percentages of minority enrollment to be aimed at in desegregated schools may vary somewhat from city to city, but generally the minimum is set at about 30 percent and the maximum at about 70 percent.

2. *Nonblack minority groups.* The size and status of nonblack minority groups in a school district also affect the formulation of desegregation plans. Except in a very few cities, the largest groups of this type are Hispanic—Puerto Ricans on the East Coast and in some midwest cities, Cubans in Miami, and Mexican Americans in the West and Southwest. Hispanic students are the largest racial-ethnic group in some cities such as Los Angeles, where there were nearly 335,000 Hispanic students (57 percent of the overall enrollment) in 1988.

The presence of relatively large numbers of Hispanic or Asian students obviously is a complicating factor in striving to desegregate big-city schools. Members of these groups tend to be located in ethnically distinct neighborhoods. Desegregation thus requires bringing students together from three or four rather than from two neighborhoods if black and non-Hispanic whites also are present and are to be mixed on a multiethnic basis. Additional complications arise because Hispanic groups tend to be more divided than do blacks on the steps that should be taken to advance desegregation. Although only about 50 percent of black parents indicate much enthusiasm for transporting their children to reduce segregation, and although some community groups in most black neighborhoods oppose busing for desegregation, predominantly black organizations and the most respected leaders in black communities generally have continued to support vigorous action toward desegregation. Hispanic communities, by way of contrast, appear to be much more divided on this issue. As a result, local political circumstances appear to be much more influential among Hispanics than among blacks in determining the extent to which there is pressure for desegregation.

In addition, the status and history of Hispanics in a given city influence their participation in a desegregation plan. If the proportion of Hispanics in the school population is relatively small, there is a tendency to stress nonparticipation, partly from fear that dispersal in a large number of schools will work against the maintenance of cultural and political identity. If Hispanics are a relatively large group that was isolated by state action (e.g., construction of new segregated schools) in the same manner as were blacks, the courts will tend to require that their ethnic isolation be eliminated to the same degree as is true for black students.

3. *State and federal initiatives.* Actions at the state and federal executive levels also continue to play a large part in shaping big-city desegregation efforts. For example, disposition of desegregation suits in some cities depends partly on whether they are filed under the state or federal constitution. Suits such as the Los Angeles case brought under the California constitution are governed by state supreme court decisions, which place greater emphasis on long-range reduction of *de facto* segregation (not caused by governmental action) than have most federal courts. Decisions in many cities are affected by congressional limitations on magnet school expenditures. The impact of these limitations varies a great deal according to the circumstances in local communities.

This analysis of student desegregation patterns emerging in big cities describes the situation as it developed in the 1980s. We believe that in some respects these developments were positive inasmuch as they opened up possibilities for reducing metropolitan segregation and stratification, rather than continuing the historic process which reinforced these harmful trends in earlier decades. In particular, emerging desegregation trends in some cities appear to be taking account of the need to strengthen instructional programs and to retain multiracial and economically diverse populations in central city schools and neighborhoods.

Magnet Schools

We have defined magnet schools and programs as voluntary approaches in which there is an attempt to attract a desegregated student body to schools that offer instructional opportunities not available at local neighborhood schools. Magnet-type schools have been operating in some cities for many years, although they generally were not so designated until recently. New York has long had specialized district-wide high schools in science and in the arts. Boston's Latin School traditionally has attracted top students from throughout the city. Rochester, San Diego, and other school districts have provided specialized, magnet-type programs for elementary students for a number of years, sometimes for decades. Many cities have offered advanced vocational programs at schools similar to some high schools now being established as magnet schools.

Because magnet-type schools are well established in many cities, it is appropriate to ask whether there is anything new about the current magnet-school movement, which has seen magnet schools established in Cincinnati, Dallas, Dayton, Houston, Milwaukee, St. Louis, Seattle, and many other cities. For four reasons, we believe this movement is distinctive.

First, it places definite emphasis on attracting desegregated student enrollment, if necessary using quotas to facilitate the attainment of this goal.

Second, the magnet-school movement aims to serve a much larger clientele than the selective magnet-type schools of the past. (This seems to be true of alternative schools in general; see Raywid 1987; 1988). Opportunities are offered for average-achieving students and for students whose special talents were generally ignored until recent developments in diversified programming. At the high-school level, a much greater range of specialized topics is pursued in greater depth than was true in magnet-type vocational schools operated years ago. The range and depth of a good district-wide magnet program are shown in Table 9.4, which lists the magnet high schools and fields of study operating in 1978 in the Dallas Independent School District. Similarly, Milwaukee established the

Table 9.4 *Magnet High School Enrollment and Selected Fields of Study in the Dallas Independent School District, 1978**

Jobs for which high school students are fully or partially prepared by the school progran

Arts High School
Art Gallery Employee
Window Designer
Interior Decorator
Internship with: Musician, Sculptor, Potter, Jeweler, Dancer
Enrollment: 670 (44% NM; 49% B; 7% H.)

Health Professions High School
Dental Hygienist
Medical Lab Technician
Dental Technologist
X-Ray Technologist
Practical Nurse
Medical Office Assistant
Enrollment: 837 (28% NM; 64% B; 8% H.)

Human Services Center
Social Work Assistant
Media Aide
Rehabilitation Assistant
Child Care Aide
Mental Health Assistant
Child Welfare Assistant
Recreation Assistant
Geriatrics Aide
Enrollment: 108 (32% NM; 56% B; 12% H.)

Business-Management Center
Bank Teller Aide
Stenographer
Legal Assistant
Administrative Assistant
Office Assistant
Machine Transcriber
Real Estate Sales Aide
Enrollment: 1,226 (13% NM; 73% B; 14%

Transportation Institute
Auto Sales Assistant
Equipment Sales Assistant
Parts Distributor
Body Repair Aide
Front-End Aide
Tune-Up Specialist Aide
Enrollment: 518 (26% NM; 55% B; 19% H

Law and Public Administration
Police Officer Aide
Law Clerk Aide
Security Officer Aide
Probation Officer Aide
Tax Collector Assistant
Enrollment: 206 (34% NM; 45% B; 21% H

Skyline Career Development Center
(A magnet-type high school opened in 1971) 27 Career Clusters including Architecture, Aviation, Cinematography, Computer Technology, Cosmetology, Electronics, Horticultur Plastics.
Enrollment: 4,329 (55% NM; 37% B; 8% H.)

* Abbreviations following enrollment figures denote racial-ethnic members, NM = Nonminority; B = E
H = Hispanic

Source: Dallas Public Schools.

following specialty (magnet) high school programs in 1977: Visual and Performing Arts; Applied Technology; Marketing and Business Communication; Small Business Management; College Preparatory; Finance and Commerce; Communications and Media; Medical, Dental, and Health; Transportation; Government and Community Services; Tourism, Food Service, and Recreation; Computer Data Processing; and Law, Law Enforcement, and Protective Services.

At the elementary level, magnet schools and programs also offer a variety of distinctive educational options for students of varied ability levels. Whereas earlier magnet-type schools such as Boston Latin usually had rigorous entry requirements, many or even most of the magnet schools established since 1970 place greater emphasis on students' interests than on test scores or previous academic record. District emphases in the elementary grades can include themes as divergent as foreign language, the Montessori approach to preschool and primary grade instruction, and systematic organizational patterns for individualizing instruction. Houston is operating magnet elementary schools specializing in such subjects as music, literature, math, and science; and other school districts are establishing their own or comparable variants providing specialized instruction and resources in areas of particular concern to parents and students. Opportunities of this nature have been offered here and there in the past for a few elementary students, but they seldom were available for substantial numbers of students and they frequently lacked the specialized staff and resources to make them successful. Some big-city school districts are aiming to enroll a substantial proportion of their students—both elementary and secondary—in magnet alternative programs. As of 1982, for example, about one-third of the students in Houston were participating in magnet schools or programs (McIntire, Hughes, and Say 1982).

A third feature of the magnet school movement is its frequent emphasis on using resources in the wider community to a much larger extent than has usually been the case in public education. This is particularly true at the high-school level, where some outstanding magnet schools are organized and operated in conjunction with business or professional leaders and resources in the fields of study available in the school. In Dallas, for example, the first director of the Arts Magnet High School was one of the metropolitan area's most respected leaders in that field, and students have facilities and equipment unmatched in schools elsewhere in the city. The Business and Management Center, similarly, has equipment—much of it donated by business—more advanced than is available in regular high school business or commercial courses. Students develop their skills using the latest equipment for word and data processing and also have a chance to attend training programs conducted by employers for their own employees. In their senior year, students are placed in appropriate, supervised internships paying anywhere from the minimum wage to $5 or $6 per hour. It is hoped that opportunities such as these will attract enrollment from regular high schools.

The fourth major distinguishing characteristic of the magnet school movement is its emphasis on retaining middle-status population in central city schools. Even though this goal is seldom if ever stated explicitly in these terms, it is clearly an important objective in cities in which a variety of educational options or alternatives are being made available as part of an effort to reduce withdrawal associated with desegregation. Establishing an attractive magnet school may retain white and black middle-class students whose parents are unwilling to send them to a local neighborhood school, whether racially segregated or desegregated. Magnet schools also attract upwardly mobile working-class students who are dissatisfied with educational opportunities or security arrangements in inner-city schools. From this point of view, some magnet schools may be thought of as the big city's attempt to compete with suburban and nonpublic schools.

Levine and Campbell (1978) have examined data on magnet-school programs in cities (mainly Boston, Cincinnati, Dallas, Houston, and Milwaukee) that were early leaders in the movement and concluded that magnet schools in these cities did appear to be attracting multiracial enrollment in many cases and that school administrators in several of them felt magnets were helping reduce white and middle-class withdrawal. In addition, there was no doubt that some magnet schools were offering a variety of outstanding educational opportunities for students of varying ability levels and interests in some locations. For example, former University of Chicago Dean of Education Francis S. Chase studied the first four magnet high schools established in Dallas in 1976 and along with Marjorie Buchanan reported that

> *the Arts Magnet High School is drawing on the full range of artistic talents and opportunities in the Dallas area. Museums, theatre and dance companies, musical groups, and other artists are making resources available to students. . . . The High School for the Health Professions is drawing on a wide variety of professional services and resources in the adjoining Baylor hospital. Other hospitals and the medical and dental professions are providing additional opportunities. . . . The automotive industry has provided invaluable models and materials for students in the Transportation Institute; and dealers and automotive shops are cooperating fully in field trips and on-the-job employment. (Quoted in Levine and Campbell 1978, 46)*

However, even though it was clear that some magnet schools are desegregated and are offering superior education, it is not possible to say that district-wide magnet programs will accomplish the larger goals set for them or to predict that the magnet-school movement will have widespread national success in helping counteract or reverse trends toward deterioration in big cities and their public schools. Uncertainties affecting the success and future of magnet schools include questions involving local, state, and national funding, acceptability under judicial and executive standards for desegregation, and interpretation of data dealing with school district enrollment trends and projections. In addition, there is little evidence suggesting that magnet school planning generally is being coordinated with city planning to bring about constructive urban renewal.

Nevertheless, the limited research available on magnet schools has been generally encouraging. For example, the two-year, federally funded Survey of

Magnet Schools (Blank et al. 1983; Blank 1984) concluded that magnet schools can improve the quality of education while offering expanded choices to students and parents and enhancing desegregation. One author summarized some of the survey's specific findings:

> *A large majority of magnets rate very well on commonly used standards for school effectiveness. On a composite measure of instruction, curriculum, student-teacher interaction, and educational climate, a third of the magnet schools received 'high' ratings and over half received 'good' ratings. . . . Although magnets typically serve only a minority of the student population . . . [successful districts] have found increased public support and confidence to be a by-product of the plan. (Blank 1984, 72)*

Controlled Choice in Small Urban Districts

During the 1980s several school districts in small cities have introduced or begun to consider initiation of controlled-choice plans that allow students to select the school they will attend within the district, with free transportation provided. Parents are required to designate three or four schools of choice for each child, and the district attempts to place every student in a school selected by the parents. Enrollment in each building is controlled in order to enhance or maintain desegregation. This approach is somewhat analogous to a magnet plan in that each school must function like a magnet in order to attract students to meet its enrollment goals.

The controlled-choice approach was first adopted in 1981 in Cambridge, Massachusetts. Data on implementation indicate that in 1985 70 percent of parents received their first choice of schools, and another 21 percent received their second, third, or fourth choice. Research on the Cambridge controlled-choice plan indicates that it appears to be stimulating improvements in instruction and school climate, that a significant number of students have been attracted from nonpublic schools, and that the positive impact on desegregation has been substantial (Snider 1987a).

Controlled choice appears to be most feasible in relatively small districts in which minority enrollment is not more than 40 or 50 percent and distances between schools in the plan are not too large to dampen parents' willingness to select a school outside their immediate neighborhood. Elements of the controlled-choice approach are now being implemented in Buffalo, Little Rock, San Jose, and also in several other urban school districts.

Desegregation in a Central-City District: Seattle

The Seattle Public Schools began voluntary efforts to desegregate in 1963, but the percentage of minority students in the district and in segregated schools increased steadily in the 1960s and 1970s. By 1977, civil rights groups and many civic leaders were urging district officials to take more vigorous action to desegregate the schools. The Board of Education responded by issuing a statement specifying that no school should be more than 20 percent above the district-wide average in percentage minority (then 35 percent), and initiating six months of activities involving the community in planning for desegregation.

The desegregation plan adopted in December 1977 includes both voluntary and mandatory components to desegregate the schools. When voluntary efforts such as magnet schools and permissive transfer prove ineffective, schools are desegregated through pairing and clustering and through mandatory transportation. Nonminority enrollment in Seattle decreased from 85 percent in 1963 to 65 percent in 1977, and then declined further to 48 percent in 1987. Although there apparently has been significant white withdrawal associated with the plan, desegregation has been maintained in most of the district (Hittman 1981; Egan 1988).

Several efforts were made to block implementation of the mandatory component of the Seattle plan. The most serious was a statewide referendum in which Washington voters supported prohibition of mandatory transportation to bring about desegregation in education. However, in 1982 the U.S. Supreme Court ruled that such a prohibition is not constitutional when a state intervenes in local school board decisions in a manner inconsistent with the fourteenth amendment to the Constitution. Because the explicit goal of the referendum was to prevent desegregation, the Supreme Court ruled, the State of Washington could not prevent the Seattle Board of Education from implementing mandatory action to provide more equal opportunity for minority students.

As shown in the contrast between the following description of the status of school desegregation in Chicago and the situation in Seattle, desegregation is much easier to attain in moderate-sized cities than in very large districts with a very high proportion of minority students. Short of a metropolitan or regional remedy, many minority students in the latter districts will remain in predominantly minority schools no matter how much emphasis is placed on mandatory student reassignment. In smaller urban districts with a moderate percentage of minority students, by way of contrast, it is possible to provide desegregation for most or all minority students.

Limited Desegregation in a Very Large Central-City District: Chicago

A good example of the development of a desegregation plan in a very large urban school district is provided in the case of Chicago. Like Detroit, Houston, Los Angeles, New York, Philadelphia, and other very large districts enrolling a preponderance of minority students, Chicago has been unable to provide desegregated education for most of its minority students. Many of the larger urban school districts in the South and the West have been able to provide desegregated education for most minority students, because school districts there tend to be county-size units that include relatively large proportions of nonminority students. However, although there is great variation nationally in the degree to

Table 9.5 *Racial-Ethnic Composition of the Chicago Public Schools, 1950–1987*

Year	Percentages				Total Enrollment
	White	*Black*	*Hispanic**	*Asian/Pacific Is.*	
1950	62	36	—	0	372,000
1960	55	42	—	0	480,000
1970	35	55	1	1	578,000
1978	22	61	16	2	495,000
1981	17	61	20	2	443,000
1987	14	60	23	3	429,000

* Nearly all Hispanics are included in the white category before 1970. Numbers may not add to 100 percent due to rounding.

Source: Chicago Board of Education.

which desegregated education has been attempted and attained, in general there is a tendency for desegregation to be most limited in very large Northern and Midwestern districts with a high proportion of minority students.

The percentage of non-Hispanic whites in the Chicago Public Schools decreased substantially, declining from 62 percent in 1950 to 14 percent in 1987 (see Table 9.5). The percentage of black students grew rapidly from 1950 to 1978, and Hispanic enrollment rose explosively in the 1970s.

To a considerable extent, the increase in black enrollment reflected the fact that Chicago experienced an economic boom in the decade of the 1950s, which brought a large number of black in-migrants seeking work. The immigrants found housing in areas already heavily black in population. Also, in the 1950s, a number of high-rise buildings were constructed by the City of Chicago with funds from the federal government, and these were mostly located in areas that were predominantly black. In 1960, it was noted by concerned observers that there was a growing number of elementary schools with 90 percent or more black pupils.

The Chicago Urban League, an organization that worked to improve the economic and educational condition of the black population, began to exert influence against school and residential segregation. From this time, the Chicago Board of Education came under increasing pressure to adopt procedures that would reduce the racial-ethnic segregation.

In April 1976, the Illinois Board of Education placed the Chicago Public Schools on Probationary Recognition Status. The State Board of Education was in a position to cancel or reduce state financial aid and asked for action by the Chicago Board of Education sufficient to show that some progress was being made to reduce segregation. Early in 1977, Superintendent Joseph Hannon appointed a City-Wide Advisory Committee to produce a desegregation plan that might satisfy the State Board of Education. CWAC, as it was called, produced a 200-page report entitled *Equalizing Opportunities: Proposed Plan* and delivered it to Superintendent Hannon on January 12, 1978.

This Plan contained sixteen components aimed at substantially reducing segregation. A crucial question was whether the desegregation program would produce enough desegregation if the movement of students to desegregated programs was voluntary on the part of students and their parents. The CWAC plan included the following statement: "*Voluntary/Mandatory Process*. This component provides for each component in the plan to become mandatory if the voluntary process fails to bring about the amount of integration expected."

Superintendent Hannon appointed an Administration Management Committee of members of his staff to study the CWAC Plan. This committee produced an alternative plan entitled *Access to Excellence*, which contained material from the CWAC Plan but did not have a mandatory clause. The Board of Education approved the *Access to Excellence* plan by a vote of six to five.

Access to Excellence was put into action in the autumn of 1978. There was evidence of some progress toward desegregation in the spring of 1979. During this period, Superintendent Hannon requested the federal government to provide money to support the cost of Access to Excellence under the Emergency School Aid Act. This was part of a continued attempt by the Chicago Public Schools to secure federal government assistance, which had been denied several times on the ground that the Chicago Schools had not satisfied all the criteria stated in the Emergency School Aid Act. An exchange of letters and consultation between Superintendent Hannon and staff of the Office of Civil Rights of the Department of Health, Education and Welfare did not produce agreement.

The year 1980 saw a complicated series of events in which Governor James Thompson and Mayor Jane Byrne worked out a plan that created a Chicago School Finance Authority to take charge of the finances of the Chicago schools. The superintendent and the board of education could not spend money without the approval of the Finance Authority. The Finance Authority ordered the board of education to reduce expenditures substantially, which meant a number of difficult money-saving actions by the board of education and some savings at the expense of teachers' salaries.

At this point, the Department of Justice of the federal government filed a complaint in the United States District Court of Northern Illinois alleging that the Chicago Board of Education had engaged in acts of discrimination in violation of federal laws. A series of conferences between representatives of the Department of Justice and members of the board of education and lawyers for the board resulted in a *Consent Decree* signed by the Justice Department and the Chicago Board of Education in September 1980.

Essentially, the consent decree established a procedure whereby the board of education would create an aggressive desegregation program and the federal government would provide financial assistance. The federal government provided a substantial sum of money to enable the board of education to hire outside consultants to help forge a desegregation plan, with Chicago parents and citizens included to contribute to the preparation of such a plan.

In October, the board voted to employ as chief desegregation consultant Robert L. Green, dean of the College of Urban Development of Michigan State University, a black educator with broad experience in the field of school desegregation. From December 1980 until May 1981, a series of public meetings and conferences was conducted by Green and his staff. These meetings resulted in a plan for desegregation, which was submitted to Judge Milton Shadur of the Federal District Court. A desegregated school was defined as one with an enrollment between 30 to 70 percent non-Hispanic white. This would leave many schools all or nearly all black or Hispanic; they would receive additional federal funds to improve instruction. It was proposed that voluntary desegregation measures be attempted during the school years 1981–82 and 1982–83; then, mandatory measures, if needed, would be put into action in September 1983.

In December 1981, the board of education issued a major report entitled *Student Assignment in the Program of Desegregation*, which was put into action in the spring of 1982. Clearly, one difficult task was to desegregate the heavily white schools in the southwest and northwest areas of Chicago, which had mostly white populations. The plan's most important components were to (1) desegregate predominantly white schools (more than 70 percent non-Hispanic white) through a variety of techniques including voluntary transfering of minority students, pairing and clustering of schools, redrawing of attendance areas, and closing of old buildings; (2) expend approximately 25 million dollars extra per year for improvement of instruction (i.e., compensatory education) at more than 400 predominantly minority schools; (3) allocate an additional $72,000 per school to target schools high in minority percentage and very low in achievement; and (4) continue to create and expand magnet-type schools and programs.

In January 1983, Judge Shadur accepted the board's desegregation proposal, even though it would leave approximately two-thirds of the district's schools predominantly minority. Judge Shadur's ruling stated that district-wide desegregation did not seem feasible in a system with nearly 85 percent minority students. He further stated that "it would be tragic if a well-intentioned desegregation plan" that involved extensive student reassignment and busing in Chicago "were to cause accelerated resegregation—so that the common desegregation goals of the board and its critics were defeated" (Mirga 1983).

By the fall of 1983, the Chicago school district had 50 magnet schools in operation and had also initiated 50 magnet programs that provided some part-time desegregation. In addition, nearly all the district's approximately 600 schools were more than 30 percent minority, and hundreds of schools more than 70 percent minority were participating in a variety of compensatory-education programs.

Metropolitan Arrangements for Desegregation

It is obvious that central city school districts that have 70 to 80 percent or more minority students and a high proportion of concentrated poverty schools are not going to achieve full racial or socioeconomic desegregation within the confines of their own boundaries. No matter how elaborate or well worked out their overall desegregation plans or how successful their magnet school programs, such districts will have a significant percentage of their students' attending racially isolated and concentrated poverty schools. Most big-city school districts are now approaching or have passed the 70 percent minority figure (see Table 2.9). Many have half or more of their students in concentrated poverty schools. Full racial and socioeconomic desegregation in these districts will require arrangements on a metropolitan area scale involving white and middle-status students from a region larger than the central city.

Metropolitan arrangements fostering desegregation can take either of two forms. They can be brought about through *court orders requiring regional solutions* to problems of unequal educational opportunity in the metropolitan area or they can be accomplished through voluntary *cooperation* between the central city school district and surrounding suburban districts. Levine and Levine (1977) have identified two reasons that metropolitan arrangements are desirable in addition to the fundamental goal of counteracting deterioration in the central city and its public schools:

1. Some inner suburbs in large metropolitan areas are now becoming heavily minority as black families escape the inner city. Unless a regional approach to desegregation is formulated and implemented, some of these suburbs will become an extension of the inner city and the pattern of central-city decay will be repeated in the suburbs. Regional arrangements can help achieve or maintain desegregation in these suburbs.
2. Metropolitan arrangements for desegregation frequently are more feasible than are plans limited to the central city. In situations where predominantly white suburbs adjoin minority sections of the central city, it is much more efficient to transport students a couple of miles across the city border than to bus them ten or fifteen miles between a nonminority neighborhood at one end of the city and a minority neighborhood at the other end. The greater feasibility of desegregation arrangements when suburbs are included has been demonstrated by the fact that city-only plans proposed in Cleveland, Kansas City, Los Angeles and some other cities either have to bus city students *across* suburban districts, route buses along inconvenient detours to avoid leaving the city, or leave unnecessarily large numbers of minority students in racially isolated central-city schools.

Court-Ordered Regional Solutions. Prospects of mandatory action to reduce big-city and metropolitan school segregation through the courts were being explored in a number of other metropolitan areas in the late 1970s and 1980s. Earlier efforts to bring about regional solutions received setbacks in 1973, when the Supreme Court in a 4–4 decision refused to approve District Judge Robert R. Merhige's order consolidating the Richmond Public Schools with adjoining districts in Henrico and Chesterfield Counties and in 1974, when the Supreme Court voted 5 to 4 in *Bradley* v. *Milliken* to reverse U.S. District Judge Stephen J. Roth's decision requiring cross-busing of students between Detroit and fifty-two suburban districts. In the *Milliken* decision, the Supreme Court stated, "Before the boundaries of separate and autonomous school districts may be set aside by consolidating the separate units for remedial purposes or by imposing a cross-district remedy, it must first be shown that there has been a constitutional violation within one district that produces a significant segregative effect in another district."

However, the *Milliken* decision did not completely close the door on suits petitioning for regional solutions. In subsequent years, the Supreme Court approved lower-court orders requiring merger of the Louisville Public Schools with the surrounding Jefferson County Public Schools and interdistrict remedies for the segregation of minority students in the Wilmington, Delaware, Public Schools and the Indianapolis Public Schools. Evidence submitted and judicial decisions in these court cases suggested that constitutional violations justifying an interdistrict remedy for big-city segregation can include such government actions as the following:

1. Required transportation of minority students into central-city schools where southern and border states practiced *de jure* (legally mandated) segregation before 1954. Where school district boundary lines were disregarded for the purpose of segregation, they cannot be considered as impermeable boundaries to prevent desegregation.
2. State laws that had the effect of exempting segregated city schools from plans to improve the organization of school districts in the metropolitan area.
3. Housing practices supported by state and local governments that had the effect of establishing or reinforcing segregated residential patterns on a multijurisdictional basis. Included under this heading might be actions that concentrated public housing for minorities within the central-city school district, state support of restrictive housing covenants that forced minority families to settle in segregated city neighborhoods, and zoning practices that intentionally prevented minority families from moving to integrated locations.

Depending on subsequent court decisions, it is possible that regional remedies eventually may be ordered in a number of metropolitan areas, particularly in southern and border states in which it can be shown that substantial numbers of minority students were transported across school district lines before 1954 for the purpose of segregation. For most of the United States, however, regional approaches to reduce segregated schooling in the big cities and their metropolitan areas during the next ten years will come about as a result of voluntary cooperation between cities and suburbs, if they come about at all.

Metropolitan Cooperation. If there are to be regional arrangements aimed at preventing further deterioration in large metropolitan areas and big cities during the next ten years, they generally will come about as the result of voluntary cooperation between central-city and suburban school districts. Given the strength of forces that work against cooperation between city and suburbs, there would not be any hope of achieving this goal in most large metropolitan areas except for the fact that developments during the 1970s and 1980s were such that cooperative arrangements now can contribute directly to the solution of serious problems in suburban schools. Primarily this is true because:

1. Many suburban districts are losing enrollment. Rather than close schools or maintain undersized classes, it frequently may be more efficient for districts to work together with central-city schools when allocating space for the future. At the middle-grade level, this means an emphasis on placing limited but significant numbers of low-status, central-city students in mixed-status schools in the suburbs.

2. Magnet high schools in the central city can offer educational opportunities far superior to those now available anywhere in the metropolitan area. The best suburban high schools are outstanding institutions, but few of them can draw on a sufficiently large and heterogeneous population base to offer the types of curricula that a regional magnet high school can make available for youth throughout the metropolitan area. For example, few, if any, suburbs are in a position to establish a magnet high school devoted to science or the performing arts. Conversely, inclusion of the suburban population base for the central-city, magnet high schools will improve their chances of attracting a desegregated student body with enough enrollment to be cost-effective. This suggests that magnet high schools should be planned and operated on a regional basis, with some located inside and others outside the central city, but all easily accessible to both city and suburban students from a wide geographic area.

However, regional cooperation for desegregation and related purposes is not likely to come about—no matter how desirable it may be objectively—without strong leadership and incentives from the state and the federal government. It is true that school districts in many metropolitan areas already have cooperative arrangements for providing services such as special education, teacher training, and instructional television, and that these arrangements provide a model, and in some cases an existing mechanism, for further cooperation involving desegregation. In addition, a few metropolitan areas such as Boston, Hartford, Milwaukee, and Rochester have had city-suburban transfer programs for fifteen years or more, with significant numbers of central-city minority students transported to suburban schools on a voluntary basis. On the other hand, it also is unlikely that most suburban districts will cooperate voluntarily on thorny and controversial issues like desegregation unless incentives for doing so are strong and obvious.

Wisconsin. Leadership on the issue of city-suburban cooperation for desegregation has begun to emerge in a few states and at the federal level. Probably the best example of what can be done at the state and local level has been provided in Wisconsin, where in April 1976 the state legislature passed a law providing incentives for intra- and interdistrict transfer of students for desegregation. Financial help is given both for transfer of minority students from districts or schools 30 percent or more minority to districts or schools less than 30 percent minority and for transfer of nonminority students following the same formula in reverse. In the case of interdistrict transfers, the sending district receives the normal amount of state aid per student and the receiving district also receives additional state aid for each student plus a bonus of 20 percent if more than 5 percent of its enrollment are transfer-in students. The state also pays transportation costs. In 1977, eight suburban districts transferred in 321 minority students from Milwaukee and received an average of $1,880.00 per pupil from the state as compared with normal state aid of $280.00 per student.

Results in Milwaukee. Court action accusing Milwaukee Public School officials of unconstitutional segregation began in 1965. As in many other cities, the case (*Armstrong* v. *Brennan*) dragged on for years, until in 1976 Judge John Reynolds issued a ruling finding the district in constitutional violation. Judge Reynolds also directed public school officials to formulate and implement a plan to desegregate the schools. The court defined a desegregated school as one that is between 25 and 45 percent black. (Hispanic students have not been defined as minority students who must be desegregated in Milwaukee.) The board of education responded by indicating an intention to use voluntary approaches and incentives to bring about as much desegregation as possible.

Between 1976 and 1979, the court set annual targets for increasing desegregation in the Milwaukee Public Schools, and the school district made modifications in school attendance areas and grade organization, established elementary and secondary magnet schools and developed a voluntary city-suburban transfer program, and encouraged both minority and nonminority students to attend desegregated schools. These steps appear to have been relatively successful inasmuch as the number of desegregated schools (redefined in 1978 to be 25 to 50 percent black) increased from 14 in 1976 to 101 in 1978 (Bennett 1979), and the percentage of black students in desegregated schools increased from 16 percent to 71 percent.

In May 1979, the court accepted a five-year settlement in which the plaintiffs and the school district agreed to withdrawal of the litigation as long as desegregation goals are met as specified in the agreement. The board of education agreed to have at least 75 percent of the district's black students in desegregated schools as long as the percentage of black students in the district as a whole remains 50 percent or less. (If the district exceeds 50 percent black, the goals may be readjusted.) The district also agreed to continue notifying students still in segregated schools that they have the right to free transportation to attend desegregated schools, and to make instructional and organizational improvements in schools remaining predominantly black. It was not difficult for the district to make this commitment because it had nearly reached the desegregation goal the year before.

The magnet-school component in Milwaukee's desegregation plan has grown to include twenty elementary and middle schools, five senior high schools, and twenty-five career specialty programs at the remaining ten high schools. Ten percent of the seats in the magnet programs are set aside for suburban students. By 1987, nearly 800 suburban students were attending schools in the city, and 3,074 minority students from the city (including 2,629 black students) were attending suburban schools.

The ancillary relief component to improve education for black students choosing to remain in segregated schools in the inner city also has had some success at the elementary level. Implemented primarily through the RISE project at sixteen elementary schools, efforts to improve the achievement of students at inner-city schools resulted in a gain in average fifth-grade reading scores from the 43rd percentile in 1979 to the 68th percentile in 1984. The comparable gain in fifth-grade math scores was from the 57th to the 79th percentile (McCormack-Larkin 1985).

However, natural decline in the white population base in Milwaukee is making it increasingly difficult to maintain desegregated environments for 75 percent of the district's black students. (By 1985, student enrollment was 48 percent black and 45 percent white.) "Looking ahead to 1990 and beyond and seeing a growing minority student population and isolation in the city," and also concerned with the quality of education provided for minority students who transfer to suburban schools, members of the Milwaukee Board of Education initiated litigation in 1984 requesting a mandatory interdistrict remedy for school desegregation in the Milwaukee metropolitan area (McMurrin 1985, 32). A voluntary settlement reached in 1987 requires the suburban districts to work with the city district in order to increase interdistrict transfers substantially in the future.

Massachusetts. Massachusetts also has been a leader in providing financial incentives and other forms of suport (e.g., in planning and communications) for city-suburban cooperation on desegregation. In 1976, the Massachusetts legislature appropriated up to $3 million to support magnet schools and programs, many of which involve cooperative exchange and transfer of students in the Boston and Springfield metropolitan areas. These funds supported such activities as the Metropairways program, in which approximately 500 city and suburban elementary and middle-school students were in paired groups studying environmental science, ethnic history, and other subjects. Also, under the METCO program (Metropolitan Council for Educational Opportunities), approximately 3,000 minority students from racially unbalanced schools in Boston have attended suburban schools each year since 1976.

St. Louis. St. Louis also has implemented a plan to provide desegregation for many black students, largely through cooperation with suburban districts. (The plan is only semivoluntary in that a federal court required suburban districts to accept sufficient black students from the city to reach a minimum percentage of 15 percent black.) The St. Louis desegregation plan also includes emphasis on instructional improvement and on establishment of the city magnet schools to attract suburban students. Implemented in 1981, the plan has been expanded each year so that approximately 12,100 black students from the city were attending suburban schools and more than 600 suburban white students were attending city schools during the 1987–88 school year. Altogether, approximately 10,800 city black students were attending either predominantly white suburban schools or desegregated city magnet schools (Levine and Eubanks 1986).

San Diego. Probably the best example of successful voluntary desegregation on a metropolitan scale involves the multifaceted desegregation plan in the San

Diego Unified School District. (Although San Diego is a city school district, it is a very large regional district that includes a number of suburban areas that would be separate school districts in many other parts of the United States.) Desegregation of the San Diego schools has been carried out almost entirely on a voluntary basis.

After initiation of a court-ordered desegregation plan in 1978, 41 magnet schools were established in San Diego between 1978 and 1986 (among 130 schools in the district), and more are being opened each year. As of 1983–84, 7,193 minority students who otherwise would have attended segregated schools attended desegregated magnets, and another 4,770 participated in a voluntary program through which they transferred to predominantly white outlying schools in the district. Altogether, 61 percent of the minority students living in racially isolated attendance areas participated in these two desegregation programs in 1983–84. The percentage of minority students attending racially isolated schools was reduced from 35 percent in 1977 to 24 percent in 1984, despite a large natural decline in enrollment of white students and a continuous Hispanic in-migration during this period (Levine and Eubanks 1986).

In addition, San Diego's court-ordered plan for improving instruction at inner-city, minority schools has had outstanding success. Components and effects of the instructional-improvement plan are described in the last chapter of this book.

Magnet Schools in Urban Development: The Webster Magnet School

One example of the use of a public school as a major factor in the strategic redevelopment of a deteriorating neighborhood close to the downtown area of a large city is the Webster School in St. Paul, Minnesota. Slum clearance and housing rehabilitation had been carried on for several years in the roughest and most socially disorganized section contiguous to downtown St. Paul.

In 1975, St. Paul school officials designated the Webster Elementary School as a desegregated magnet school as part of the overall plan for desegregation of the schools in the district. At that time, enrollment at Webster was 74 percent minority. Most pupils were economically disadvantaged, the neighborhood was considered so unsafe that students had to ride a bus only a few blocks to school, and there was a question whether Webster could retain any middle-class or nonminority students. There is no doubt that Webster was a typical inner city school that would have trouble attracting students from other neighborhoods.

Planning for the desegregation program at Webster was carried on during 1975–76 with the aid of a citizens' committee and publicity for the program. New students were bused to Webster on a voluntary basis, with 25 minutes as the longest bus ride. A $600,000 addition to the school building was constructed and opened in 1978. During this time enrollment increased from 362 to 975, with minority students constituting 34 percent of the student body and 575 pupils bused.

According to the principal of the Webster, the main attraction for parents was an outstanding instructional program that involved a split-day schedule according to which approximately one-half of a student's day is devoted entirely to basic skills instruction and the other half is spent in application of skills. Basic skills instruction in reading and mathematics is provided by assigning students into "accelerated," "mainstream," and "alternative" (significantly below normal achievement range) groups, with great efforts made to avoid racial segregation within this grouping. The applied skills part of the program allows for a variety of enrichment activities building on the particular learning interests and requests of students. Thus, the overall program can be equally attractive both to parents who want what they call "the basics" stressed for their children and for those whose greatest stress is something they refer to as "openness" or "humaneness." Subjects that have been taught in minicourses as part of the applied skills program include Arts and Crafts; Heritage—Many Lands and People; Ceramics; Photography; Creative Writing; Classical Literature; Children's Theater; Performing Arts; Creative Drama; Dance; Vocal Music; Instrumental Music; Spanish; French; Computer Logic; Typing; Business; and Environmental Science.

At the same time that the Webster School was being improved, neighborhood redevelopment was being promoted by community groups, a number of substantial old homes were rehabilitated, and a Control Data Corporation plant was located there.

The construction of a new building at a school that previously had been underenrolled seems to have helped convince middle-class parents that the magnet school would not be a predominantly working-class school. Before 1975, a high proportion of the students at Webster were from poverty families, and there was little likelihood that many middle-class parents would send their children to Webster even if it had an attractive magnet program. Addition of the new building, however, suggested to parents that there would be a "critical mass" of new students when the magnet school opened, and this perception probably helped make it possible to obtain a large enough nucleus of nonpoverty students to reopen Webster as a mixed-class school.

Housing Desegregation and School Desegregation

Both educators and lay leaders recognize that school desegregation is much easier to achieve when blacks and whites live in the same community served by a naturally integrated neighborhood school. Conversely, school desegregation can contribute to desegregation in housing, particularly if schools are desegregated on a metropolitan or regional basis so that there is no point in nonminority parents' moving to avoid sending their children to desegregated schools (Pearce 1980).

Gary Orfield has been studying the relationship between desegregation in schools and housing and has concluded that although there is much to be gained by coordinating school and housing policies in an effort to maximize stable desegregation, relatively little has been done to develop and implement coordinated policies. After studying the situation in twelve communities that had relatively effective school desegregation plans and a reputation for relatively progressive leadership on racial issues, Orfield (1981) reached the following six general conclusions:

1. School and housing officials agreed on the need for coordinating policies for desegregation but had done little to formulate or carry out effective coordinated action.
2. Most school desegregation plans and orders neglect possibilities for encouraging desegregation in housing.
3. In most cases, there has been no serious attempt to stabilize existing integrated neighborhoods.
4. The common assumption that subsidized housing in the suburbs automatically will lead to desegregation is incorrect.
5. The urban revitalization process that is bringing middle-class whites back to some central city neighborhoods has not generally resulted in much desegregation of schools.
6. However, solutions for parts of the problems have been found in a few cities, and officials elsewhere express strong interest in learning about such possibilities.

Orfield's discussion of possibilities for coordinating desegregation in schools and housing emphasizes three major policy goals: (1) achieving stable integration in communities that already have both minority and nonminority residents; (2) opening nonminority neighborhoods, schools, and jobs to blacks and Hispanics; and (3) maintaining desegregation in neighborhoods where revitalization is forcing out low status, minority families. He describes many actions such as the following, which can be taken and in a few communities are being taken to achieve or maintain desegregation in schools and neighborhoods: penalize realtors who steer clients to segregated neighborhoods; establish housing counseling centers that emphasize desegregation; exempt integrated neighborhood schools from busing; give preference to integrated neighborhood schools in closing schools; provide scattered-site subsidized housing for families; provide loans to maintain and improve housing in desegregated neighborhoods; guarantee the safety of children in desegregated schools; improve the quality of instruction in desegrated schools; and carry out school desegregation on a regional or metropolitan basis. Orfield also noted that provisions of the 1980 court-ordered desegregation plan for the St. Louis Public Schools can be a model for coordinating policies to desegregate schools and housing:

> *The May 21, 1980, St. Louis court order embodied the most fully developed approach so far to the school-housing relationship. . . . It exempts integrated neighborhoods from busing and guarantees any neighborhood that becomes integrated in*

the future a neighborhood school as long as it remains integrated. The plan provides integrated schools for the reviving neighborhoods that were attracting whites but still had all-black neighborhood schools. Any integrated neighborhood that becomes virtually all black or any reviving neighborhood that becomes virtually all white will have to resume busing. An incentive is thus created for an integration-stabilization policy in both kinds of areas.

Any white neighborhood that accepts sufficient subsidized housing to produce a 20 percent black public school enrollment will get back its neighborhood school. (Other children can still be bused in if necessary.) . . .

The novel feature of the St. Louis order, however, is the directive that the city government, the school board, the state government, and the federal departments of HUD and Justice devise a plan to administer federal housing programs in the St. Louis metropolitan area in a way that will support integrated schools. (Orfield 1981, 25)

When Inner-City Families Are Relocated in the Suburbs

One of the potentially most important social developments occurring in the United States involves the movement of inner-city families from Chicago to its suburbs. This movement followed the 1977 decision in *Hills* v. *Gautreaux*, in which the U.S. Supreme Court ruled that black families had been unconstitutionally concentrated in inner-city public housing. To remedy this constitutional violation, the federal government made rent subsidies available for black families who would move to the suburbs. By the early 1980s, approximately 1,300 families had taken advantage of this opportunity to relocate in more than fifty Chicago suburbs.

James Rosenbaum and his colleagues at Northwestern University have been collecting data on black families participating in the Gautreaux remedy and have prepared several reports dealing with the experience of people relocated in the suburbs. Rosenbaum has reported that there were no differences in the number of friends made by children and youth in these families when compared with a city control group (Rosenbaum 1985) and that they were as "well-integrated in their new neighborhood as in their former neighborhood, or as the city control group was" (Rosenbaum, Rubinowitz, and Kulieke 1985, 10/12).

In addition, the mothers of the suburban black students reported that peer influences were significantly more positive than in the city, that the students had more positive attitudes about their suburban schools than about their former city schools, and that peer influence was strongly and positively associated with the grades students received in school (Rosenbaum, Kulieke, and Rubinowitz 1987). The authors summarized much of the school experience of the relocated black students:

The mothers reported that their children's academic performance relative to their classmates did not change from the city to the suburbs. Despite the greater de-

> *mands of the suburban schools, teachers also offered more help in the suburbs and this sometimes had great benefits, according to the reports of some mothers. (Rosenbaum, Rubinowitz, and Kulieke 1985, 10/16–10/17)*

Rosenbaum and his colleagues also have reported that mothers' sense of control over their fate is strongly associated with their aspirations for their children. That is, among black families in the Gautreaux study, mothers who responded that they had some control over their future have higher educational expectations for their sons and daughters than did mothers perceiving less control over their future. In addition, mothers who perceived relatively low amounts of physical danger in their environment had higher educational aspirations for their sons than did those who perceived greater danger (Kulieke, Rosenbaum, Rubinowitz, and McCareins 1985). These generally encouraging findings indicate that relocation to the suburbs may provide an improved setting for inner-city families and for the social and educational development of their children. Relocation to the suburbs may be one of the most potent and successful social policies for alleviating the plight of underclass children and youth growing up in concentrated poverty neighborhoods in big cities.

Conclusion

Considerable desegregation of elementary and secondary schools has been attained in much of the United States, particularly in rural areas and in small towns and cities. However, segregation is still prevalent for many minority students, particularly in large Northern and Midwestern cities that have many concentrated poverty schools enrolling a substantial proportion of the nation's black and Hispanic children and youth.

Research on desegregation, although somewhat ambiguous, indicates that it can help improve minority students' achievement, motivation, and aspirations and can also help improve subsequent social and economic opportunities and outcomes. One major mechanism for explaining this result appears related to the fact that socioeconomic desegregation frequently removes minority students from poorly functioning, concentrated poverty schools.

Some big-city districts with a relatively small minority enrollment or that serve a regional population are providing desegregated education for most minority students. Other urban districts with a high percentage of minority students have enhanced desegregation through magnet schools and cooperative arrangements with suburban districts. In addition, instructional improvement has become a major emphasis in many big-city desegregation plans.

However, given the existing widespread pattern of segregation of minority students, much more remains to be accomplished in order to help alleviate the plight of the underclass, to reverse metropolitan trends toward segregation and stratification, and thereby to bolster the health of the city and the metropolis as a whole. Attaining these goals will require metropolitan arrangements for dealing with the segregation of millions of minority students within the educational system in accordance with perspectives articulated by President Lyndon Johnson in a 1965 message to Congress on "The Problems and Future of the Central City and its Suburbs":

> *We begin with the awareness that the city,* possessed of its own inexorable vitality, has ignored the classic jurisdictions of municipalities and counties and States. That organic unit we call the city spreads across the countryside, enveloping towns, building vast new suburbs, destroying trees and streams. Access to suburbs has changed the character of the central city. The jobs and income of suburbanites may depend upon the opportunities for work and learning offered by the central city. Polluted air and water do not respect the jurisdictions of mayors and city councils, or even of Governors. Wealthy suburbs often form an enclave whereby the well-to-do and the talented can escape from the problems of their neighbors, thus impoverishing the ability of the city to deal with its problems.*
>
> *The interests and needs of many of the communities which make up the modern city often seem to be in conflict. But they all have an overriding interest in improving the quality of life of their people. And they have an overriding interest in enriching the quality of American civilization. These interests will only be served by looking at the metropolitan area as a whole, and planning and working for its development. (Johnson 1965)*

EXERCISES

1. What are the arguments for and against stressing desegregation of schools in the primary grades? What arguments can be made for giving it particular stress for high school students?
2. Talk to some of your relatives or neighbors about their views on school desegregation. To what degree do you think they make a distinction between racial-ethnic and socioeconomic integration? To what degree do they assume that desegregation automatically assumes mixing working-class minority students with high-status nonminority students?
3. What do you think are the major obstacles in persuading students to attend magnet high schools? How do you think these obstacles might be overcome?
4. The Supreme Court has ruled that school segregation must have been caused by intentional state action to justify a court order for desegregation. Consult a law library to see if you can find any material on the legal definition of *intent*.
5. What are the reasons that school desegregation seems to have been achieved much more widely in towns and small cities than big cities?

* In this message, the word *city* is used to mean the entire urban area—the central city and its suburbs.

6. What part do you think private elementary and secondary education play in the development of social and geographic patterns in the metropolitan area? In what ways might private schools contribute to stratification and segregation? In what ways might they contribute to reducing or minimizing the effects of stratification and segregation?
7. Investigate a school that has had a successful program of racial integration. Talk with some teachers and parents as well as with the principal. Analyze the reasons for success.
8. Investigate a school in which efforts at racial integration have been unsuccessful. What are the reasons for failure?
9. Contact city or regional planning officials in a nearby metropolitan area to obtain information on the movement of black families to the suburbs. Is such movement occurring on an integrated or segregated basis? How rapidly is such movement taking place? What do local planning officials see as its most important implications?

SUGGESTIONS FOR FURTHER READING

1. *School Desegregation in Metropolitan Areas: Choices and Prospects,* edited by Ronald D. Henderson and Mary von Euler, includes papers and discussion originating at a 1977 conference dealing with most major aspects of desegregation in central cities and metropolitan areas. The topic is examined from a number of vantage points ranging from legal and political to instructional and financial.
2. *The Future of Big-City Schools,* edited by Daniel U. Levine and Robert J. Havighurst, includes chapters dealing with desegregation policies and developments, magnet school programs, and related topics in urban education. Major sections are devoted to describing developments in Cincinnati and Dallas.
3. *The Integration of American Schools* by Harris, Jackson, Rydingsword et al. reviews a wide range of data and viewpoints on desegregation in the 1970s.
4. *School Desegregation: Past, Present, and Future,* edited by Stephan and Feagin (1980), includes chapters on a variety of topics involving desegregation.
5. B. Smith's book, *They Closed Their Schools,* tells the story of the closing of public schools in Prince Edward County, Virginia, an extreme example of a community that attempted to avoid, then delay, school integration. The story is told in the personal terms of the people involved.
6. A conservative analysis of school desegregation rationales and effects is provided in *The Burden of Brown* by Raymond Wolters.
7. A positive view of the St. Louis desegregation plan is described in "Country and city transfers," a 1987 paper by Willie and Uchitelle. A negative interpretation is put forward in *A Semblance of Justice* by Daniel Monti.
8. Case studies of urban magnet schools are provided in *Different by Design* by Mary Haywood Metz.

9. Methodological issues in studying desegregation are described and discussed in *School Desegregation Research,* edited by Jeffrey Prager, Douglas Longshore, and Melvin Seeman.
10. *Cooperative Learning* (1983) by Robert Slavin describes and analyzes several cooperative learning approaches and summarizes research dealing with achievement effects for disadvantaged minority students.

10

Cultural Pluralism and Minority Education

Even though Anglo-Protestants have constituted the largest subgroup, the population of the United States has always included a number of different national, racial, and religious groups. The diversity of population in the United States today is underlined in Table 10.1, which provides an enumeration of the population of the racial groups and selected subgroups designated in the 1980 Census.

Relationships between groups in the United States population frequently have been antagonistic, but the expressed ideal of many Americans historically has been to anticipate and support reduction of group differences through various forms of common activity within a framework of a democratic society. Thus, it was common to speak of the United States as a "melting pot."

However, in recent years the attitude toward the continued existence of subgroups and subcultures has become more approving and more appreciative. Educational systems are now expected to help various groups maintain their cultural differences and achieve their cultural goals within a cooperative framework. Thus, James E. Allen, Jr., former United States Commissioner of Education, in recommending support for ASPIRA, a Puerto Rican organization, wrote:

> *The day of the melting pot is over. No longer is it the ideal of each minority to become an indistinguishable part of the majority. Today, each strives to maintain its identity while seeking its rightful share of the social, economic, and political fruits of our system. Self-help and self-determination have become the rallying cries of all minorities.*

Separate and different group cultures and traditions are now generally regarded as healthy in a complex democratic society. They enrich the society. At the same time, the mainstream of the society is open to new recruits and offers many rewards to members of minority groups who join the mainstream and who consequently reduce their participation and allegiance to a minority group. Thus, there is an inherent tension between the societal forces that push for a democratic cultural pluralism and those that work toward a democratic social integration.

In the period since 1965, the slogans of pluralism have been popular, but integration continues to be an important social goal. By *social integration* we mean the mixing of various racial and cultural groups through association in business, education, government and cultural affairs, and some degree of intermarriage with the goal being one common culture. By *democratic cultural pluralism* we mean the amicable coexistence of a variety of racial, ethnic, religious, and economic groups, each group keeping its subculture partially intact.

Table 10.1 *Population of Racial Groups and Selected Subgroups Designated in the 1980 Census*

Group	Population	Percentage of Total Population
White	188,340,790	83.61
Black	26,488,218	11.76
American Indian	6,756,986	03.00
Chinese	806,027	00.36
Filipino	774,640	00.34
Japanese	700,747	00.31
Asian Indian	361,544	00.16
Korean	354,529	00.16
Vietnamese	261,714	00.12
Hawaiian	167,253	00.07
Laotian	47,683	00.02
Thai	45,279	00.02
Eskimo	42,149	00.02
Samoan	42,050	00.02
Guamanian	32,132	00.01
Cambodian	16,044	00.01
Pakastani	15,792	00.01
Aleut	14,177	00.01
Total	225,267,754	

Source: U.S. Bureau of the Census 1980.

If equal respect and equal opportunities and privileges are accorded to all groups, then a condition of democratic pluralism may be said to exist, as it does in Switzerland, with its French, German, and Italian cantons, and in Holland, where religious subcultures set themselves apart in political and civic as well as social and religious affairs. The dynamics of the burgeoning pluralism and diversity characteristic of contemporary society and education in the United States have been captured and celebrated by Otto Friedrich in a special *Time* magazine issue dealing with immigration:

> *The American schoolroom has traditionally provided a hopeful glimpse of the nation's future. . . . Come for a moment to the playground of the Franklin elementary school in Oakland, where black girls like to chant their jump-roping numbers in Chinese. 'See you manana,' one student shouts with a Vietnamese accent. 'Ciao!' cries another, who has never been anywhere near Italy. And let it be noted that the boy who won the National Spelling Bee . . . was born in India . . . and speaks Tamil at home. . . . Graffiti sprayed in a nearby park send their obscure signals in Farsi. . . . Such changes require adaptation not only in the schools and the marketplace but throughout society. The Los Angeles County court system now provides interpreters for eighty different languages from Albanian and Amharic to Turkish and Tongan. (Friedrich 1985, 29)*

Pluralism in Nineteenth-Century America

The United States was a pluralistic society from its very beginning, with the thirteen colonies representing a variety of European nationalities and a variety of religious groups, with Indians who were being pushed out of their lands, and with Africans who were held and sold as slaves. This pluralism could hardly be called democratic. For many of the European immigrants who came to this country in the nineteenth century, there was blatant discrimination. For example, the large Irish immigration between 1840 and 1860, resulting partly from famine in Ireland, produced a lower class of Irish in the United States, who were given only the most menial jobs. Advertisements in the newspapers for an office boy or for a parlor maid often carried the letters "NINA" (No Irish Need Apply). Subsequent to this period, immigrant Hungarians, Poles, Italians, Croatians, and Russian Jews arrived and lived in poverty under brutal conditions of employment.

What saved the situation for the newcomers and led to their upward mobility were the constant demands for unskilled and semiskilled labor in the expanding economy, the free schools that enabled many immigrant children to move into white-collar jobs, the almost free land on the frontier, and the expansion of local government and business, which created roles into which many of the immigrants could move with little formal schooling. A mixture of social integration and cultural pluralism was at work. Each wave of European immigrants who arrived without money or position improved its status rapidly, although leaving behind in its rise, after one or two generations, some members who were not so fortunate.

Several groups, however, did not share equitably in the nineteenth-century blend of democratic pluralism and social integration: the American Indians, who were pushed into inferior lands and decimated by the U.S. Army if they chose to fight; and the freed African slaves. Smaller groups in some regions also were virtually excluded from participation.

The period of United States social history up to about 1900 was dominated by a policy that sociologist Milton Gordon calls *Anglo-conformity*. This policy assumed the desirability of maintaining the social institutions of England, the English language, and English-oriented cultural patterns as dominant in American life (Gordon 1964, 88). The society was also heavily Protestant, and there was much prejudice against Catholics and new Catholic immigrants. The German, Scandinavian, and Irish immigrants who predominated during the 1840 to 1890 period were accepted with some misgivings. Most of the Irish and some of the Germans were Catholic. The Scandinavians were regarded as clannish and they maintained their home languages. Still, the country was large, a growing industry needed labor, and the frontier was open. The society became in fact more pluralistic than before.

The Melting Pot

Around the beginning of the twentieth century, there developed the concept of a new, composite nationality being formed through the agency of frontier life as it spread across the middle of the country and onward to the west. The historian Frederick Jackson Turner in his influential book, *The Frontier in American History*, said the western frontier acted as "a solvent for national heritages and separatist tendencies" of the European immigrants (Gordon 1964, 118). Yet the vast flow of immigration from southern Europe after 1880 made it clear that neither Anglo-conformity nor the frontier life could be a feasible social or political model. The eastern cities were filling up with a polyglot population. This reality had to be reckoned with in any conception of the structure of American society.

An English Jewish writer, Israel Zangwill, stated the new theory through his popular drama, *The Melting Pot*, first produced in 1909. The hero of the play is a Russian Jewish immigrant who falls in love with a Gentile girl. The hero, in the rhetoric of his day, procaims that

> *America is God's Crucible, the great Melting Pot where all the races of Europe are melting and re-forming! Here you stand, good folk, think I, when I see them at Ellis Island, here you stand in your 50 groups, with your 50 languages and histories, and your 50 blood hatreds and rivalries. But you won't be long like that, brothers, for these are the fires of God you've come to—these are the fires of God. A fig for your feuds and vendettas! Germans and Frenchman, Irishmen and Englishmen, Jews and Russians—into the Crucible with you all! God is making the American. (Zangwill 1909, 37)*

The melting pot theory accepted the eastern and southern European immigrants as good material for making Americans, just as good as the English and north European stock.

Education and the Melting Pot Theory

About the middle of the nineteenth century, free public education became widespread, in theory aiding the Americanization process by teaching everybody English and American social ideals. Although the public school system was influential, it was probably not as effective as claimed by some public school leaders of the 1880–1920 period. Many children of immigrant families achieved poorly in school and dropped out as early as possible to work at unskilled jobs. Furthermore, Roman Catholic parish schools were established that taught not only the Catholic religion but taught also the European ethnic culture of the particular parish being served.

Integration and Pluralism after 1920

After the close of World War I, the socioeconomic condition of the country changed markedly. Restrictions were placed on immigration, thus opening the job market in heavy industry to migrants from the South and the Appalachian states and to Mexican Americans from the Southwest. Puerto Ricans came to the eastern cities. These groups did not integrate readily into the mainstream. At the same time, technological development reduced the proportion of jobs that required high-school and college education. Industrial productivity increased so much that after 1950 the economic-industrial complex could not employ all the available labor, thus producing a substantial group of unemployed who had to live on welfare payments.

In effect, socioeconomic changes since about 1920 have worked to restrict opportunities for groups with the lowest incomes to integrate themselves into the mainstream of economic, social, and civil life. This was occurring at the same time that the United States was becoming in some respects more of a melting pot than it had ever been. Overt racial and ethnic discrimination was reduced on an historically dramatic scale after World War II. Laws restricting opportunities for blacks, Jews, Japanese, and other groups were eliminated, and many minority citizens moved into the mainstream of United States society.

Social practice also changed; racial intermarriage became if not common at least thinkable: the percentage of Japanese men marrying non-Japanese women increased to 40 percent, and more than half of all Irish-American, German-American, and Polish-American men were married outside of their respective ethnic group by the 1970s (Sowell 1978a).

The effect of these changes, however, was to make it clear that the melting pot had its limits. Many members of the various minority groups prefer not to be too assimilated within dominant patterns in the larger culture, and in any case millions of minority citizens who are economically and racially isolated from the larger society did not realistically have the option of assimilation. It thus became clear that socially or economically disadvantaged groups would have to organize within their own communities to work for improved economic and social opportunity.

The Rise of Cultural Pluralism

The idea of the melting together of many diverse cultures into a single culture was not widely approved by leaders of American thought, nor was it clear that it was actually happening. Horace M. Kallen criticized the melting pot theory in his book *Culture and Democracy in the United States* (1924). He used the term *cultural pluralism* to describe his program for the United States as a democracy of nationalities cooperating voluntarily. Other social philosophers, social scientists, and popular writers favored this concept. Among educators, the field of *intergroup relations* assumed considerable importance. Teaching units on intergroup relations and recommendations for more favorable treatment of minority groups found their way into high-school social studies and history courses. The late 1940s and early 1950s saw much activity along these lines, supported by such organizations as the National Conference of Christians and Jews and the American Jewish Committee.

Then came the 1954 Supreme Court decision against racially segregated public schools, followed in the 1960s by the Civil Rights Act and by the Civil Rights movement, which broke down many political and economic barriers against blacks. As noted in Chapter 9, however, the blacks were not brought into the melting pot. With the exception of a few middle-class families, they were segregated residentially in the large cities and their children continued to be segregated in school. Nevertheless, the 1960s saw substantial improvement in the economic, educational, and political situation of the black population. These improvements were obtained largely, it seemed, by black organizations asserting their rights and using political and legal measures to influence the government and the business community.

The relative success of the early civil rights movement stimulated other minority groups to organize for group action—especially the Mexican American and Puerto Rican and American Indian groups. The middle 1960s saw the creation of several Hispanic groups: Cesar Chavez developed the United Farm Workers Organizing Committee in California; Reies Lopez Tijerina started the Alianza Federal de Mercedes in New Mexico; Rodolfo Gonzales organized the Crusade for Justice in Denver. These groups worked for better housing, better wages, better health and educational services. Among the Puerto Ricans, ASPIRA worked for better educational and social conditions. Several small Indian groups were organized, including the American Indian Movement, which came to public attention with the occupation of the Bureau of Indian Affairs building in Washington in 1972, and with the occupation of the village of Wounded Knee in South Dakota in 1973. Meanwhile, the Black Muslims also grew strong in several cities, with separate schools and separate business activities alongside their religious institutions.

European Ethnic Movements

By 1940, the eastern and southern European immigrants had generally established themselves securely in upper working-class and lower middle-class positions. Most of them lived in the large cities and in the industrial north central and northeastern regions.

After World War II, the migration of blacks, Chicanos, and Puerto Ricans to the big cities began to crowd the European ethnics, both in terms of housing and in jobs. Middle-class people moved to the suburbs or to middle-class enclaves in the central city, leaving the working-class whites to come to terms with the new in-migrants. Tensions arose, with white ethnic working-class people appearing as opponents to the expansion of residential areas for blacks and for Spanish Americans. Mark Krug pointed to this rivalry as a partial cause of the emergence of white ethnic group activism. "Encouraged by the example of the black community and strengthened by their unity of interests, white ethnic minorities have become more united and more militant in protesting their grievances" (Krug 1972, 322).

An eloquent voice on behalf of the ethnics of southern and eastern Europe was Michael Novak in his book *The Rise of the Unmeltable Ethnics*. He spoke of the 1970s as the "Decade of the Ethnics" and regarded the rise in ethnic consciousness as part of a more general cultural revolution in America. His basic proposition is that ethnic identity has similar elements from one ethnic group to another and it is a desirable antidote to the poisons of the modern industrial society: "The rise in ethnic consciousness is, then, part of a more general cultural revolution. As soon as one realizes that man is not mind alone, and that his most intelligent theories, political decisions, and works of genius flow from 'intelligent subjectivity,' attention to the roots of imagination, value, and instinct is inevitable. When a person thinks, more than one generation's passions and images think in him" (1971, p. 37).

The ethnic group, for Novak, lives within the individual in a mystical, nonrational way. He defines an *ethnic group* as "a group with historical memory, real or imaginary. . . . Ethnic memory is not a set of events remembered, but rather a set of instincts, feelings, intimacies, expectations, patterns of emotion and behavior; a sense of reality; a set of stories for individuals—and for the people as a whole—to live out" (p. 56).

Recent research suggests that ethnic identification continues to be an important consideration for many Americans from European background and other ethnic groups. For example, Andrew Greeley and his colleagues at the National Opinion Research Center have been collecting data on ethnic groups in the United States and have found that the majority of Irish, Italian, and Jewish respondents rank their ethnic background as either "extremely important" or "very important," and that the adolescent members of these ethnic groups are more likely than their parents to rank their ethnicity as important. Greeley concludes that "the NORC research shows that both unconscious transmissions of ethnic subcultures and conscious ethnic identification are important features of American life" (1980, pp. 148–149).

What Is Cultural Pluralism?

The racial minorities and the white ethnic minorities who make up about one-third of the population of the United States have become actors on the stage of cultural pluralism. The action has become so vigorous since 1960 that it is a major concern in domestic politics, in social ethics, and in education. Some functions of a viable cultural pluralism are:

1. To provide substantial opportunity to the members of each subculture to achieve life satisfaction in their own lifestyle.

2. To provide education and training for every member of every subculture of a kind and quality that will enable the individuals to earn a fair living—to avoid poverty.
3. To provide employment or access to the labor force on equal terms to all members of the society.
4. To provide opportunity and encouragement for the youth of every subculture to associate with youth of other groups in activities of mutual interest.
5. To maintain freedom of individuals and groups to practice separatism, though perhaps at some sacrifice in terms of material standard of living.
6. To permit subgroups to maintain a separate economic system as long as this does no damage to the general welfare of the society.
7. To permit subgroups to carry on their own separate educational systems, though they must bear the extra expense.
8. To make all subgroups responsible for contributions to the general welfare of the society.

This definition agrees with the answers Milton Gordon secured from officials of eight agencies for intergroup relations when, in 1963, he asked them, "What would you say is meant by cultural pluralism?" (Gordon 1964, 16–17).

Integration, Pluralism, Separatism

Cultural pluralism lies between integration on the one hand and separatism on the other. The boundaries are not clear. Although the melting pot concept is the extreme of integration, cultural pluralism can shade into a stable form of integration in which various subcultures are quite distinct in some areas of life but are merged together in other areas of life. At the other extreme is a multigroup society characterized by separatism in which each group keeps itself apart through laws and customs that prevent intermarriage and through a rigid limitation on the extent of its relations with other groups. Individuals and groups that advocate or lean toward separatist policies include the following:

1. Those who want to be left alone to work out their own lifestyles, which they see as superior to others. This position is characteristic of certain small religious sects such as the Amish, the Hutterites, the Seventh Day Adventists, and the Black Muslims. They attempt to keep separate schools and to do as little business as possible with the mainstream society. In 1884, when the Roman Catholic bishops made a decision that Catholic children were not receiving proper religious education and called for every parish in the country to set up and operate its own parish school, this was a separatist act.
2. Those with a distinct and visible racial-ethnic identity, who participate fully in the educational and economic mainstream but tend to maintain a separate social life. Some Asian-Americans have taken or been pushed into this condition.

3. Many American Indians and Eskimos—a numerically small but historically significant group, who have been kept in a separate status by historical events and by basic cultural differences from the European majority.
4. Those who want to use separatism as a temporary means for building strength and identity within the minority group, after which the group will be ready to move into a pluralistic situation with power and confidence. This is the position of spokespeople for some subgroups of low-income blacks, Puerto Ricans, and Mexican Americans. It grows out of a conviction that the existing form of pluralism is not satisfactory and will not become more satisfactory unless certain minority groups can gain the power and the self-assurance with which to negotiate with other groups for a fair distribution of the opportunities and privileges of the larger society.

Black Separatism or Integration?

As described in Chapter 9, there was widespread disappointment among the black population when, during the 1960s and 1970s, so little progress was made toward racial desegregation in the cities of the North and West, and when black children were not improving much in their school performance, even with substantial increase of expenditures under the Elementary and Secondary Education Act. By 1970, there was a considerable sentiment in the black community for "black schools, with black teachers and administrators, and a fair share of the school dollar." This argument holds that meaningful integration—with true equality of the races—can only occur when blacks have achieved a group identity, pride in their race, and bargaining power based on unified black communities. Consequently, blacks in the United States should stay to themselves, study African culture and history, learn that they come from African centers of civilization and high culture that flourished at a time when much of western Europe was inhabited by savages. They should have black teachers for black schools, and they should demand separate black colleges and universities.

Black separatism was strengthened in the period from 1965–1970 by the rise to power of black politicians in the northern and western cities, and by their need to maintain a black voting constituency. Many black aldermen, state legislators, and congressmen, elected to office by the growing black populations in the cities, accepted the fact of segregation and strove to improve segregated communities, including improvement of segregated schools. This position came to the fore in 1972, when black political leaders of the country met in Gary, Indiana, in a National Black Political Convention and adopted a platform statement that included an anti-integration and antibusing resolution. Their statement was quickly repudiated by the Black Caucus of the U.S. Congress in its own Black Bill of Rights. Thus, while the separatist groups were pushing for black schools, congressmen in the Black Caucus stood behind integration and busing to achieve integration.

The case for integration was put forth by the Kerner Commission, (the National Advisory Commission on Civil Disorders appointed by President Johnson). This commission, which included both blacks and whites, reported in 1968, "Our nation is moving toward two societies, one black, one white—separate and unequal." Saying that improvement of the black part of the society is effectively blocked by racial discrimination, the report said the black ghetto is a responsibility of the white society: "White institutions created it, white institutions maintain it, and white society condones it" (National Advisory Commission, 1968, 225–226).

The commission went on to argue, however, that separatism can never produce equality for blacks. It "could only relegate Negroes permanently to inferior incomes and economic status." The goal of the United States, the commission said, "must be achieving freedom for every citizen to live and work according to his capacities and desires, not his color."

Pluralistic integration is the position of most black leaders and is generally supported by liberal whites. A vocal proponent of this position is Bayard Rustin, who has argued that the well-being of America's blacks is tied to the well-being of whites and other groups and depends primarily on improvements in the economy that produce more jobs and higher incomes for all people. In an article entitled "The Failure of Black Separatism," Rustin concluded that blacks cannot be effective working alone. They should join with other minorities and with the trade union movement to give political power to the democratic Left in America. The leaders of the Urban League and the NAACP have consistently taken a position for social and political integration, although they do not stress the trade union aspect.

A leading social psychologist, Thomas Pettigrew, in an address entitled "Racially Separate or Together?" analyzed the various points of view held by both blacks and whites and pointed out that many of both races favor a policy of separatism, but for different reasons (Pettigrew 1971). The white separatist, he says, believes:

1. That both racial groups are more comfortable when separated.
2. That blacks are inferior to whites—perhaps by heredity, but in any case, in fact. Therefore integrated schooling and other forms of integrated interaction will lower the standards for whites.
3. Strife and unrest can be kept at a minimum by separation of the races.

The black separatist believes:

1. That both racial groups are more comfortable when separated.
2. The central problem is white racism. White liberals should fight against this, and black leaders should work in separate institutions, such as schools, businesses, and churches, to improve the situation for blacks.
3. Equal and mutually beneficial relations with whites are possible only when blacks have gained personal and group autonomy, self-respect, and power.
4. Equality and interdependence are goals that cannot be achieved until blacks have a period of separatism during which they can develop themselves.

Pettigrew disagreed with both sets of beliefs, instead concluding that:

1. Separatism is a cause, not a remedy, for dissatisfaction and discomfort in interracial situations.
2. The belief of whites in their racial superiority is decreasing, as shown by scientific studies during the past three decades. The recent confrontations between whites and blacks have resulted in further reduction among whites of a belief in racial superiority.
3. Studies of the results of desegregation in jobs, restaurants, and hotels, and in churches and schools, show that increased contact reduces racial friction and strife.
4. Doing nothing about integration means leaving the present institutional arrangement (segregated schools, housing, and churches) to continue to cause discrimination and prejudice.

For these reasons Pettigrew argued against black separatism and urged a strong program of social integration.

Hispanic Separatism?

Separatist tendencies among Hispanics—primarily among Mexican Americans in the Southwest—may turn out to be much stronger than they have been among black Americans. Hispanic Americans have not encountered overt barriers to participation in the larger society quite as strong as those that historically hampered blacks in the United States. The stress that many Mexican Americans place on retention of Spanish within their homes and communities, together with the growing size of predominantly Mexican-American communities in the Southwest, may result in a greater relative stress on separate development. Carlos Arce of the University of Michigan Institute for Social Research has been studying data on the attitudes of Mexican Americans and has found that respondents typically cited Spanish as the single most important aspect of Mexican culture for their families to maintain and were "virtually unanimous in wanting their children to know and speak Spanish." He concluded that the data show a "movement toward ethnicity and away from the 'melting pot'" (Arce 1982, 7).

Movement away from melting pot concepts does not, of course, in and of itself mean that Mexican Americans will move very far toward separatism rather than cultural pluralism. On the other hand, it is possible that insistence on bilingual as against desegregated education, isolation from the mainstream of large numbers of Mexican Americans in relatively self-contained "barrios," and political antagonism between Mexican Americans and other groups may result in systematic movement toward separatism. Such a movement might resemble separatist tendencies that have been developing among the French in Canada (Garreau 1982). The next two or three decades will determine whether such tendencies become a major force among Mexican Americans in the United States.

Black Americans and Education

Relations between blacks and whites have been a major problem for society throughout United States history. These relations have been changing rapidly since the mid-1950s, when black migration to the cities began to reach massive proportions and the U.S. Supreme Court outlawed government-imposed segregation in the historic case *Brown* v. *Topeka Board of Education*. In one way or another, these changes have affected every major social institution, including family, business, industry, education, religion, government, sports, and communications. Education has been particularly critical in defining and reflecting the status and problems of the black population.

To understand the educational situation of a minority group, we need to know something about the group in terms of numbers, residence, and socioeconomic status. The black population has been growing at a slightly more rapid rate than the white population. It was 9.9 percent of the total United States population in 1950, 10.5 percent in 1960, 11.1 percent in 1970, and 11.6 percent in 1980.

During the period since World War I, the black population has become urbanized, and it is now more urbanized than the white. In 1910, 73 percent of blacks lived in rural or semirural settings; but this situation is now reversed, with 76 percent living in metropolitan areas in 1980 (Table 10.2). Urbanization has taken place with about equal speed in all regions of the country except the South. Blacks have moved from the South to the North, East, and West and have moved into industrial centers.

The urbanization of blacks and their migration to industrial centers have posed new problems in intergroup relations. As long as most blacks lived at a subsistence level in the rural South, they tended to be ignored by the rest of the country. As soon as they moved into the cities, they became more highly visible. Many became integrated into the social and economic life of the cities. They followed the familiar pattern of other immigrant ethnic groups. They worked hard and saved their money; they secured as good an education as possible for their children; their children moved up the socioeconomic ladder into professional and business occupations. Thus, a black middle class developed.

However, a large proportion of newly urbanized blacks have not been able to succeed in this way and instead have become a sizable underclass in concentrated poverty neighborhoods. They and their children are still set aside from the mainstream of life. They are segregated residentially, they are discriminated against with regard to housing and jobs, and their children attend segregated schools. This larger group of blacks has become a burden on the conscience of a democratic society (Alter 1988; Ellis 1988).

We also should note that a significant proportion of black Americans consists of immigrants from other countries. Nearly 1 million black Americans were born

Table 10.2 *Selected Characteristics of Hispanic, Black, and White Populations in the United States*

Characteristics	Black	Hispanic	White
Metropolitan location (1980 percentage distribution)			
Central city	56	49	24
Suburban	20	35	42
Nonmetropolitan	24	19	34
Median family income (1984)	$15,432	$18,833	$27,686
Fertility rate (1980)	2.4	2.5	1.7
Poverty rate (1982)	33.0	27.0	10.0
Occupational distribution (1979 percentages)			
White collar	35	33	53
Blue collar	38	47	33
Service	24	16	12
Farm	2	4	3

Note: White collar grouping includes professional and technical, managers and administrators, sales, and clerical; blue collar includes crafts and kindred, operatives, and nonfarm laborers; service includes private household and other. Persons of Hispanic origin may be of any race.

Sources: U.S. Department of Labor 1981; U.S. Bureau of the Census 1981; *Statistical Abstract of the United States* 1984.

in Africa, Central or South America, the Caribbean, or elsewhere outside the United States. The percentage of foreign-born immigrants in the black population is higher than the comparable figure for the U.S. population as a whole.

Economic Development

The occupational distribution of whites and nonwhites in 1980 can be compared from the data in Table 10.3. Smaller proportions of nonwhites are found in the higher-status occupations (professional, technical, and managers) and higher proportions in the lower-status occupations.

Another index of the relatively disadvantaged position of blacks is the fact that unemployment has long been, and continues to be, higher than among whites. Since 1950, the unemployment of blacks aged twenty and over has been about twice as high—roughly 6 to 10 percent as compared to 3 to 5 percent for whites. The differences have been particularly striking among young people aged sixteen to nineteen, where unemployment among whites since 1960 has fluctuated from 11 to 15 percent, but among blacks, from 24 to 45 percent. The unemployment rate among black teenagers has averaged about 40 percent in the 1980s.

In addition, the percentage of blacks classified as below the poverty level continues to be much higher than the corresponding figure for whites. In 1982, 34 percent of blacks were classified as poor under U.S. Department of Labor

Table 10.3 *Changes in the Occupational Distribution of Nonwhite and White Workers, 1958–1980*

	Percentages			
	Nonwhites		*Whites*	
	1958	*1980*	*1958*	*1980*
Professional and technical	4	13	12	17
Managers and administrators except farm	2	5	12	12
Clerical	6	18	15	19
Sales	1	3	7	7
Craft and kindred	6	9	14	13
Operatives	20	19	18	14
Nonfarm laborers	15	7	4	4
Service workers	33	23	10	12
Farm workers	13	2	8	3

Percentage totals vary from 100 due to rounding.
Note: Blacks make up 90 percent of nonwhites. The next largest group are Asian Americans.
Sources: U.S. Department of Labor 1977; 1981.

income guidelines, as compared with 11 percent of whites. Median family income of blacks declined in the 1970s and 1980s from 61 percent of white family income in 1973 to 59 percent in 1984 (Danziger and Gottschalk 1986).

On the other hand, the occupational status of blacks improved markedly from 1958 to 1980. As we saw in Chapter 7, studies of the 1962–1973 time period showed a clear increase in occupational and educational attainment among blacks, as a sizable black middle class formed and the status attainment process for blacks became much more similar to that of the white population. This result also is clear in Table 10.3, which shows that the proportion of black workers in higher-status occupations more than doubled between 1958 and 1980.

How should one interpret the data indicating that blacks have been gaining in occupational status but falling further behind whites in median family income since 1971? Several major developments help account for these differences. First, income gains that were registered in the 1950s and 1960s for the black population as a whole were not sustained in the 1970s; instead black family income fell relative to whites. Second, economic recession and, possibly, declining emphasis on affirmative action slowed or reversed trends toward socioeconomic gains among blacks. Third, dissolution of two-parent families placed an increasing percentage of the black population in low-income, female-headed families (Sternlieb and Hughes 1988). Fourth, the black population apparently became more polarized into middle-class and underclass components than it had been before (Landry 1987; Coughlin 1988). That is, many blacks moved from working-class to middle-class status (as indicated by the occupation figures), but many others became part of the black underclass. Growth of the underclass occurred in conjunction with the urbanization of the black population, which located large numbers of black children and youth in big-city poverty neighborhoods characterized by a high percentage of female-headed families and unattached (single, separated, divorced) males. This interpretation is supported by data such as the following:

- The income of black, two-parent families with children relative to similar white families increased by 4 percent between 1973 and 1984, but the relative income of black, female-headed families declined by 13 percent (Danziger and Gottschalk 1986).
- There were fewer black, middle-class families in 1980 than in the mid-1970s (McAdoo 1981).
- In 1980, 47 percent of black families with children under eighteen were headed by females, as compared with 13 percent in 1970. In central cities of metropolitan areas with more than 3 million people, 59 percent of black families with children were single-parent families in 1982. This change more than accounted for the 1970s decline in black median family income relative to whites (Auletta 1982; Kimmich 1985).
- Out-of-wedlock births in the black population rose from 24 percent of all births in 1962 to more than 50 percent in the 1980s, and in some big-city poverty neighborhoods this figure reached 80 or 85 percent (Magnet 1987).
- Between 1970 and 1982, the percentage of black men classified as not in the labor force increased from 5 percent to 13 percent. The comparable increase for white men was from 3 percent to 5 percent (Farley 1984).

Thus, recent demographic trends among black Americans seem to have further magnified a 1970 trend that Federal Reserve Board member Andrew Brimmer referred to then as a "deepening schism" among blacks, "between the well-prepared and those with few skills." Problems described in 1975 by Eleanor Holmes Norton, then director of the federal Equal Employment Opportunity Commission, clearly became even more severe in the late 1970s and early 1980s: "Raising black children in today's cities, fraught with social danger, requires the maximum in physical and psychological support. Particularly in the nation's ghettos, where blacks are increasingly concentrated, it is simply too much to ask black mothers without a husband at home to raise the children of the black nation" (quoted in Auletta 1982, 263).

It also should be noted that the black middle class may be experiencing greater problems in the 1980s than during the 1970s. Deteriorating economic conditions in the early 1980s hampered progress among those whose income and status were precarious, and fewer gains probably were registered through affirmative action. (Some economists such as Thomas Sowell believe that no real economic gains have been made through affirmative action even in the 1970s.) In addition, 1979 data examined by Robert Staples and Alfredo Mirandé indicate that a "dramatic increase" among blacks in teenage pregnancies, out-of-wedlock births, single-parent households, and marital dissolution appears, to some extent, to be cutting across social classes. Staples and Mirandé believe that such trends, which also are occurring among whites, may "presage a need to undergo a revolution in theory and research on the family as a viable institution for all groups in society" (1980, 892).

The Plight of Underclass Black Males

Evidence supports the conclusion that the plight of the urban black underclass has much of its roots in the problems experienced by males in the inner city (Wilson 1987). In a 1986 crisis report titled "The Black Male in Jeopardy," Kenneth Jones informed readers of *The Crisis* (the monthly magazine of the NAACP) that statistics on crime and delinquency, unemployment, and other indicators of social disorganization among black males had reached new highs. For example, the homicide rate among black males twenty-five to forty-four years of age has risen to 125 per 100,000, compared with a rate of 14 per 100,000 for whites. Available data also show that the percentage of black males between twenty-five and thirty-four years of age who are married and living with their wives declined from 74 percent in 1940 to 56 percent in 1980, compared with a decline from 72 percent to 69 percent for white males (U.S. Commission on Civil Rights 1987).

Connected with this high level of social disorganization, Jones pointed out, the percentage of females in the adult population of the inner city is much higher than the percentage of males (Jones 1986) because many black males drop out of the labor force, are incarcerated, enter the military, or otherwise are excluded or exclude themselves from mainstream institutions.

Among the indicators and results of this exclusion are the facts that approximately 60 percent of black college students and more than 70 percent of black college graduates are female (Hatchett 1986; Office of Educational Research 1988), that the percentage of adult black females in managerial and professional occupations is more than 50 percent higher than the comparable percentage for adult black males, and that there are fewer than 60 employed black males per 100 employed black women between the age of twenty and thirty-four (Christensen 1987). These aspects of imbalance between black men and women further exacerbate social disorganization, for example, by generating divorce and separation in families composed of relatively successful women and relatively unsuccessful men, by placing black women in competition with each other for a limited supply of relatively successful men, and by making it more difficult for black men to assume or discharge family responsibilities. (For an extended discussion of these dynamics, see *Too Many Women?* by Marcia Guttentag and Paul Secord (1983), and *Crisis*, "Interviews Dr. Nathan Hare."*) Thus, research has

* Hare describes one of the dynamics of male-female relationships in the inner city as follows:

> Bitterness among black boys too often surfaces as dysfunctional behavior through the emulation of pushers and pimps, who have ready access to material goods. This trips up the black girl, too, in the choice of a mate, because she may select the young man who achieved the loftiest status (by whatever means), even if this status is short-lived. In the meantime she's ignoring the young man who is in the library studying. . . . Of course, it's at the precise point where the latter youngster succeeds and achieves a material advantage that he becomes attractive to women. (*Crisis* 1986, 45)

indicated that a 1-percent increase in the ratio of black women to black men results in an increase of more than 6 percent in the odds that black families will be female-headed (Darity and Myers 1984) and that "the problems of male joblessness . . . could be the single most important factor underlying the rise in unwed motherhood among poor black women" (Wilson and Neckerman 1984, 15).

From this perspective, the plight of the inner-city black male can be viewed as both a cause and a consequence of the larger syndrome of low school achievement, crime and delinquency, teenage pregnancy, unemployment, serious drug addiction, and other indicators of deterioration and disorganization in concentrated poverty neighborhoods documented elsewhere in this book. "The urban core," as Wilson and Aponte have summarized this point of view, "has spawned a sizable and growing black underclass of marginally productive and unattached men, and of women and children in female-headed homes" (Wilson and Aponte 1985, 241).

Much of the material in this book is concerned with social policies and practices that might help alleviate the plight of underclass children and youth in the inner city. For example, improvements in employment training (Chapter 6), compensatory education (Chapter 8), desegregation (Chapter 9), and school reform (Chapter 13) can make significant contributions in improving educational and social/economic opportunities for underclass children and youth. In addition, many concerned citizens and civic leaders are considering or exploring other actions that might be particularly responsive to the plight of underclass black males. Proposals for reform include action in the areas of family policy, governmental tax policy, job training, and housing (e.g., Cross 1984; Kasarda 1985, 1986; Magnet 1987). Regarding education, some advocates of comprehensive reform in social institutions are discussing possibilities such as the following, which David Hatchett described in a review of some recent thinking among black social scientists and community leaders:

> *Most of the authorities I interviewed concluded that the solution to the black male's difficulties in the educational process lies with the development of separate black educational facilities. Perkins says that churches and other institutions need to begin a process where older black men help to teach black male teenagers how to conduct themselves as men. The Hares advocate the development of alternative schools similar to those in Jewish and Asian communities, where after the conclusion of the regular school day, black children can be trained in a more specialized manner by black professionals. . . . [In addition] individual black parents must make more of an effort to educate their children. (Hatchett 1986, 46–47)*

Is There a Black Subculture?

In thinking about the educational situation of the black population in the United States, it is important to understand the relative importance of two bases for grouping: one based on social class and the other based on race. According to one view, blacks and whites of a given social-class level are very similar in lifestyles and therefore social class is the major determinant of subcultural differences. The contrasting view is that color or race is a primary factor; that blacks behave and think differently from whites, no matter what their economic status; and thus that race is a major determinant of subcultural differences.

The data on this question are not easily disentangled, but the answer is beginning to be clear. It appears that at very low income levels blacks are different from whites with regard to cultural values and attitudes. As we go up the income or social-class scale, blacks and whites become more similar, even though certain attitudinal differences persist. A study of the low-income population of Pittsburgh illustrates this point. Three "poverty neighborhoods" in Pittsburgh were studied in 1968. Persons were grouped into two economic levels: the "poor," having a median family income of $4,143, and the "not-poor," having $6,764. To determine whether there were differences in subculture, the following questions were asked:

—When you think about the future, how far ahead do you have a clear idea of what your life will be like? (Future orientation)

—Can you count on most people you meet? (Trust in people)

—Which of the following statements do you think is the primary cause of poverty?

Lack of an individual's effort?
Circumstances beyond an individual's control?
Both have equal weight?
Neither are primary reasons? (Work ethic)

The researchers found striking differences between the black and white groups, but little difference between the nationality groups among the whites (Irish, Italian, Anglo-American). Concerning the three value themes stated above, blacks were lower on "trust in people," "future orientation," and "individual responsibility for poverty."

At the same time, the racial differences were substantially less among the "not poor" group than among the "poor." The authors conclude that

> *there are many Black and White people whose response patterns are very similar. There are several instances where racial differences diminish with higher income levels. Large proportions of those calling themselves Colored give responses similar to the White pattern. Many in the White poor group conform to the typical Black response pattern. (Johnson and Sanday 1971, 141)*

Comparisons of blacks and whites at middle-class levels have not been made so systematically, but it appears that there is relatively little difference. Values appear to be much the same for both middle-class groups, especially those that have to do with the education of children.

John Ogbu (1978, 1982, 1988) has pointed out that the "castelike" history of blacks in the United States has had an effect in producing cultural patterns that diverge from the mainstream. Ogbu defines a "castelike minority" as a group in which membership "is acquired more or less permanently at birth. Members . . . generally have limited access to the social goods of society by virtue of their group membership" (1982, p. 125). Enslavement and, later, forced segregation of black Americans prevented them from taking advantage of social opportunities; as a result, cultural patterns arose that reflected their oppressed status. Ogbu indicates that some of these patterns arising out of many decades of blocked opportunity include development of

> *a coping lifestyle shared by members of all social classes but most pronounced among lower-class blacks because of extreme poverty and fewer chances for advancement. . . . [Castelike minority children] live in a world in which they daily observe unemployed and underemployed adults as well as drug abuse, alcoholism, and crime. Although ghetto black parents tell their children that it is important to get a good education, they may also subtly convey to them the idea that society does not fully reward blacks. . . . The children increasingly learn to blame the system as their parents do. Eventually the children become disillusioned about their ability to succeed . . . [and] become less and less interested in school, less serious about their schoolwork, and less willing to exert the efforts necessary to do well in school. (Ogbu 1982, 125, 128, 132)*

Some consequences of these cultural patterns have been described in a study that Signithia Fordham (1988) conducted at an inner-city high school in Washington, D.C. After analyzing the attitudes and behaviors of high achievers at this mostly low-achieving school, Fordham concluded that they used "racelessness" as a strategy to succeed in their academic endeavors. Students striving to succeed in school were ridiculed as being "un-Black" and sometimes as "brainiacs" who identified with the dominant society; in turn, they "adopted personae that indicate a lack of identification" with their peers and with "indigenous Black American culture" (1988, 57–58). Fordham further concluded that this situation creates considerable ambivalence that "drains the energy" of both high and low achievers, and that although racelessness may be a pragmatic strategy that works for some people, it is not producing acceptable academic performance for most students (1988, 81–82).

Even though attitudes opposing the school as portrayed by Ogbu and Fordham appear to be widespread among students not only at inner-city black schools but at working-class white schools as well (e.g., see Willis 1979), it is not clear whether this rejection of traditional school curricula and academic demands is typical of black students or of working-class students elsewhere. Gerald Grant (1988) recently studied a desegregated school in Syracuse and found that black students who study no longer are called "whitey" by other blacks, as their predecessors were in the late 1970s. Middle-class black students probably are less likely to exemplify such behavior or to succumb to ridicule then are their working-class peers, and desegregation presumably can help reduce perceptions of hopelessness arising from caste barriers and thus can enhance minority students' motivation to succeed in school and society.

On the other hand, desegregation may reinforce unproductive reactions among black students if they are low achievers and do not receive adequate assistance to meet rigorous academic demands in desegregated settings; in this case, black students might be inclined to reject academic values and school work as a psychological defense mechanism in an effort to alleviate feelings of personal failure or ambivalence. One implication is that educators should find ways to demonstrate respect for minority students' background and culture while also strengthening their self-esteem and capacity to succeed in school. An example of such an approach has been described by E. Wayne Harris (1988), who initiated a successful approach to accomplish these goals in the Fairfax County Public Schools, Virginia.

Black English

One area of behavior in which the existence of a black subculture is apparent involves the use of so-called Black English—a particular dialect that differentiates many black Americans from other cultural groups in the United States (Dillard 1972; Adler 1979). Like other aspects of black culture, Black English appears to be much more characteristic of working-class than middle-class blacks. Black Americans who have grown up in middle-class homes or attained middle-class status typically speak standard English for their region most of the time but occasionally use some elements of Black English. Research also indicates that dialect has little association with school performance in the absence of social-class disadvantage (Schacter 1979; Williams 1987).

Because Black English appears to be the basic form of speech for many working-class black children who are not succeeding in reading and other academic subjects, it frequently has been proposed that the school teach such students in Black English until they learn to read and can shift to standard English. Other proposals have suggested teaching English as a foreign language to students who speak Black English, capitalizing on similarities between Black English and standard English, emphasizing students' personal experience in teaching language, and various other transitional teaching techniques. These types of proposals generally reflect a belief that early instruction in standard English for students who are not prepared for it interferes with cognitive development and also communicates nonacceptance of a student's person and culture to students who grow up speaking Black English.*

Harber and Bryan (1976) have reviewed the research dealing with Black English and language interference and found that the existence of this phenomenon has not been sufficiently demonstrated to support a systematic effort to use teaching techniques other than direct instruction in standard English. The authors reached the following three conclusions:

---

* It should be noted that some educators favor special instructional approaches that take into account the "mountain English" dialect of disadvantaged white students in Appalachia. In this regard, Adler (1979) has reported some success with a "bidialectical" approach in which Headstart students were taught to understand differences between mountain English and standard English.

> *First, even though there is substantial evidence that black low-SES children experience dialect interference when reading orally in Standard English, there is no clear-cut evidence that the children's use of Black English interferes with the entire reading process.*
>
> *Second, there is, as yet, no conclusive empirical evidence in the literature supporting the belief that using any of the methods which purport to minimize the interference of Black English on reading performance . . . is more successful than the traditional standard instructional materials. . . .*
>
> *Third, experimentation with beginning reading materials that purport to minimize . . . [interference] has been resisted by many community leaders and parents. (pp. 397–398)*

In 1979 a federal judge ruled that the Ann Arbor, Michigan, school district must recognize that students who speak Black English may need special help in learning standard English. Following lengthy court hearings including the testimony of numerous experts in teaching, psychology, and linguistics, Judge Charles Joiner ruled that though speaking Black English may not constitute a language barrier in and of itself, "If a barrier exists . . . it exists because in the process of attempting to teach the students how to speak standard English the students are somehow made to feel inferior."

Judge Joiner's decision further stated that though there was no direct evidence that teachers in Ann Arbor had "treated the home language of children as inferior," neither had teachers taken the child's home language into account in helping them learn to read standard English. The judge then pointed out that Ann Arbor teachers had testified to treating black English-speaking students "just as they treated other students," but concluded that requiring a student to switch without even recognizing that he or she is switching "impedes the learning of standard English." Based on this reasoning, the court ordered the school district to submit a plan defining the steps it will take to identify children who speak Black English and then to take their dialect into consideration in teaching them to read.

Educational Attainment and Achievement

As shown in Table 10.4, black students, along with the largest Hispanic subgroups (Mexican and Puerto Rican) and American Indians, have the lowest average achievement scores among major racial-ethnic groups in the United States. These achievement patterns are closely related to the fact that black and Hispanic Americans tend to be disproportionately concentrated in poverty neighborhoods in big cities, as described in Chapters 1 and 2 and elsewhere in this book.

Dropout rates among black students are relatively high (see Chapter 2) and, as shown in Figure 10.1, the average black seventeen-year-old has a reading proficiency score about the same as the average white thirteen-year-old. In addition, black young adults (twenty-one to twenty-five years of age) have an

Table 10.4 ***Standardized Tests Scores and Socioeconomic Status of Secondary School Sophomores and Seniors, by Racial/Ethnic Group: Spring 1980***

Level and Subject	Standardized Scores by Group								
	Total	*White*	*Black*	*All Hispanic*	*Mexican*	*Puerto Rican*	*Cuban*	*Asian American*	*American Indian*
Sophomores									
Vocabulary	50.0	52.0	42.4	44.9	44.2	44.0	48.1	51.6	45.0
Reading	50.0	51.7	44.2	45.1	44.6	44.5	48.6	51.6	46.2
Math part 1	50.0	51.8	43.1	44.9	44.5	43.9	48.0	55.7	44.6
Math part 2	50.0	51.3	44.9	46.2	45.7	45.5	49.3	55.5	46.2
Science	50.0	52.1	41.6	44.5	44.0	42.9	46.3	51.5	46.1
Writing	50.0	51.8	43.3	44.9	44.8	43.3	46.8	53.7	46.0
Civics	50.0	51.3	45.7	45.9	45.7	46.0	45.6	51.0	45.5
Socioeconomic status	50.0	51.3	46.1	46.0	45.0	44.2	47.3	51.7	47.2
Seniors									
Vocabulary part 1	50.0	51.4	43.6	44.8	44.5	44.3	48.5	50.2	45.2
Vocabulary part 2	50.0	51.3	43.9	45.2	44.8	45.4	48.3	50.5	46.6
Reading	50.0	51.5	43.4	43.7	43.6	43.7	46.4	50.3	46.6
Math part 1	50.0	51.5	42.8	44.1	43.8	43.4	48.2	54.2	45.2
Math part 2	50.0	50.9	45.4	46.1	46.2	46.0	48.4	55.4	46.0
Socioeconomic status	50.0	51.2	45.1	45.7	44.9	41.9	47.6	51.9	47.2

Note: Scores are standardized to a mean of 50 points and a standard deviation of 10 points.

Socioeconomic Status (SES) composite computed from father's occupation, father's education, mother's education, family income, and household item index.

Source: Data avaliable from the National Center for Education Statistics *High School and Beyond* study.

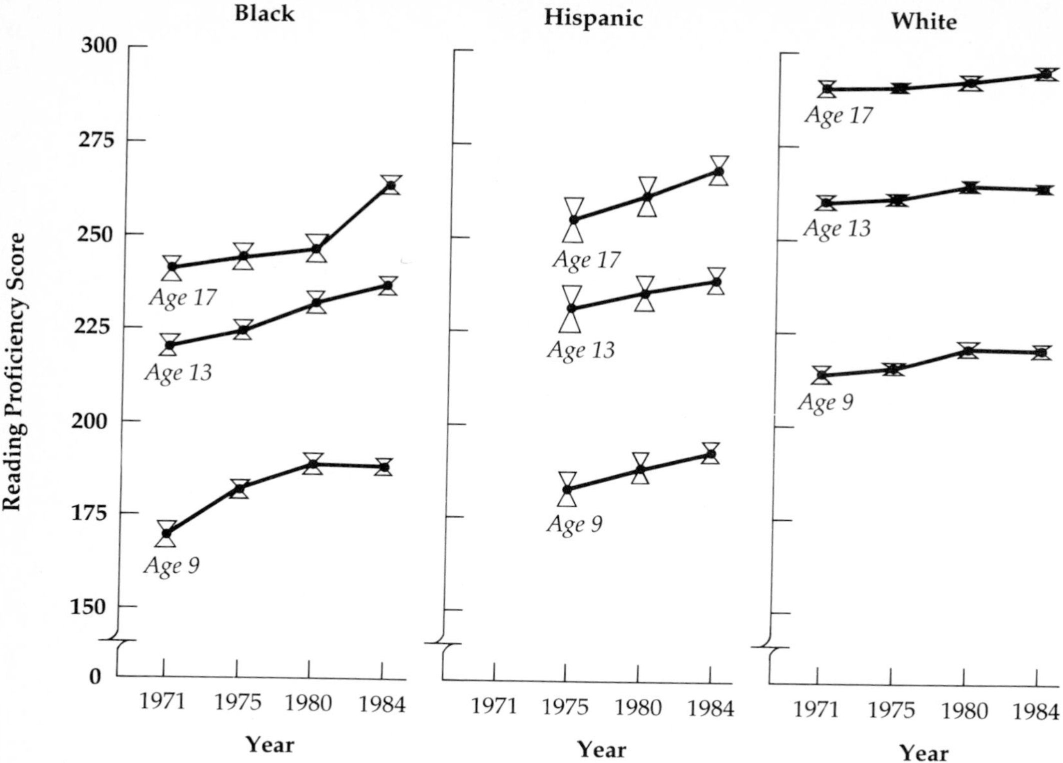

Figure 10.1 ***Average Reading Proficiency Scores for Black, Hispanic, and Non-Hispanic White Students, 1971 to 1984 by Age*** (*Source*: National Assessment of Educational Progress [NAEP] 1985.)

average reading score far below that of white or Hispanic students (see Figure 10.2). These patterns constitute an important part of the crisis in selecting and sorting that has developed in our postindustrial metropolitan society (see Chapter 2).

However, important gains have been registered in the educational attainment and achievement of black Americans. In 1960, only 13 percent of black Americans over age twenty-four had completed high school; in 1980, slightly more than half (51 percent) had done so. This compares with an increase from 26 percent to 71 percent among non-Hispanic whites during the same time period. And, as shown in Table 10.5, more than half the black-white gap in educational attainment was eliminated between 1940 and 1980 among Americans under forty-five years of age.

In addition, achievement gains among black Americans have been substantial. As shown in Figure 10.1, reading scores for black nine-, thirteen-, and

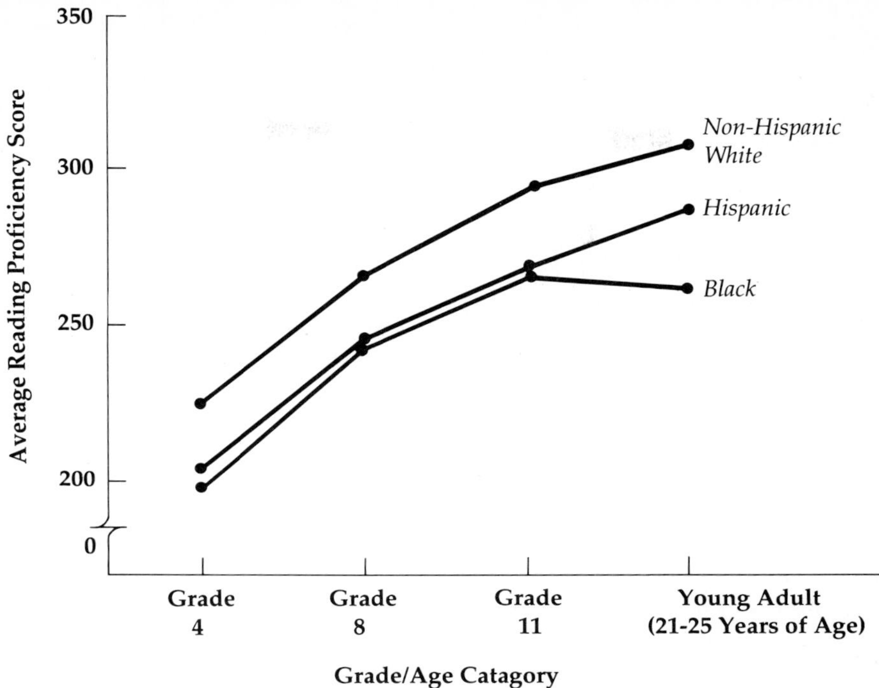

Figure 10.2 ***Average Reading Proficiency Scores, 1984, by Grade/Age and Race/Ethnicity*** (*Source*: National Assessment of Educational Progress [NAEP] 1987.)

seventeen-year-olds improved impressively between 1971 and 1984. The sharp gain among black seventeen-year-olds between 1980 and 1984 may be translated into gains among black young adults in future years.

On the other hand, data presented in Chapter 2 and elsewhere in this book indicate that black students are concentrated in large central-city school districts with very low achievement and very high dropout rates and that unemployment among black high-school graduates is as severe as it is among black dropouts. In addition, educational attainment among black students and other disadvantaged groups may not represent as much achievement as it does for white students (see Chapter 7). Researchers at the National Assessment of Educational Progress (NAEP), which collected the data portrayed in Figures 10.1 and 10.2, view the patterns of black (and Hispanic) achievement shown in these figures as still indicative of a "considerable disadvantage" in a postindustrial society that now requires "advanced literacy skills" (NAEP 1987, 22). The somewhat conflicting patterns indicating that the educational attainment and achievement of black Americans have increased substantially while the overall levels of attainment and achievement are low is consistent with the conclusion that the gains have been most pronounced for a subgroup of the black population—those who have attained or are beginning to attain middle-class status.

Table 10.5 *Differences in Average Educational (in Years of School) Levels of Non-Hispanic Whites and Blacks, 1940 to 1980*

Age Group	Year		
	1940	*1960*	*1980*
26–35	3.9	2.5	1.4
36–45	3.8	3.1	1.8
46–55	3.7	3.5	2.4
56–64	3.7	3.6	3.0

Source: Smith and Welch 1986.

Black Students in Higher Education

As pointed out, there has been a substantial improvement in the educational attainment of black Americans. As part of this trend, black enrollment in colleges and universities increased substantially after 1964. The percentage of black students among college and university undergraduates increased from 5 percent in 1966 to 10 percent in 1974 and has since remained at approximately this level. Thus, the percentage of black students among undergraduates is only slightly below the percentage of blacks in the population. In line with this increase in black participation in higher education, the percentage of black youth completing four years of college more than doubled between 1967 and 1982 (Marks 1985).

The difference that still exists between blacks and whites in college attendance and completion is partly due to differences in family socioeconomic status (Thomas, Alexander, and Eckland 1977). Some studies have indicated that when account is taken of differences in socioeconomic status, blacks have higher aspirations to attend college than do white students (Portes and Wilson 1976). Thus, the increase in black attendance in institutions of higher education probably reflects the increase that has occurred in the size of the black middle-class as well as efforts made by colleges and universities to recruit more minority students and a reduction in the barriers that limit black access to higher education.

As in the case of undergraduate enrollment, gains were made in black graduate and professional school enrollment in the late 1960s and early 1970s. Black enrollment in medical schools grew from 2.8 percent in 1969 to 6.7 percent in 1978, and black enrollment in law schools increased from 3.1 percent in 1969 to 4.7 percent in 1977.

However, some of the encouraging trends for black students in higher education most evident in the 1960s and 1970s were reversed in the 1980s. The proportion of black high-school graduates enrolling in college peaked at 34 percent in 1976 and then fell steadily to 27 percent in 1983—a decline of 21 percent.

The percentage of black students in higher education enrollment fell from 9.1 in 1980 to 8.8 in 1984 (Fiske 1987), and black enrollment in graduate and professional schools declined by 12 percent, compared to a 1-percent drop for white students (Wilson and Melendez 1986). These negative developments at every level of higher education led Leonard Hynes of Southern University to observe that "the number of blacks in the professional ranks is down dramatically and slipping. . . . [The United States may be witnessing] the last wave of blacks finishing graduate and professional schools" (quoted in Ranbow and Sirkin 1985, 13). Among the causes cited as responsible for these negative trends in the participation of black (and other disadvantaged) students in higher education are:

- Shifts in federal aid from grants to loans combined with rising tuition have disproportionately impacted disadvantaged students.
- Many colleges and universities have reduced or eliminated special recruiting and counseling programs and remedial services.
- Entrance standards have been raised at many institutions.
- Some students may have concluded that higher education will not help them obtain high-paying jobs.
- Reduced federal emphasis on affirmative action may have inhibited minority enrollment.

Overall Progress and Lack of Progress among Black Americans

The black population of the United States has become clearly polarized between a significant middle class, which substantially expanded as a result of social economic, political, and educational developments following World War II, and a very large underclass that is now heavily concentrated in poverty neighborhoods in big cities and metropolitan areas (Wilson 1987). Thus the overall indicators of progress among black Americans are mixed—some encouraging signs of impressive progress contradicted by other data reflecting severe problems associated with concentrated poverty in large urban areas (Alter 1988; Coughlin 1988).

Much of the discrepancy in the underlying forces responsible for these apparently contradictory trends was captured and interpreted in a major longitudinal study of black economic development that James Smith and Finis Welch carried out for the Rand Corporation. The authors first noted that "dramatic" gains were registered between 1940 and 1980. For example, the gap in educational attainment between whites and blacks was substantially reduced, and whereas in 1940 only one in twelve black men earned as much as the average white man, income distributions "sharply converged" in the next forty years. However, they also reported that in 1980 more than 20 percent of black men were "still part of the black underclass, a reminder that many blacks remained left out and left behind" (Smith and Welch 1986, viii). Their overall conclusions included the following observations:

> *These last forty years . . . provide us with both optimistic and pessimistic glimpses of black America's future. The most fundamental reason for optimism is the emerging and growing size of the black middle class and particularly the black elite. . . . Unfortunately, there are also reasons for concern about the future, especially for the still large black underclass. . . . The contrasting economic progress of intact and female-headed families is an excellent illustration of an increasingly segmented black experience—growing numbers of black families participating in an affluent America while distressing numbers are left behind in the ravages of poverty. (Smith and Welch 1986, xxii–xxv)*

The Declining Significance of Race?

In 1978, University of Chicago sociologist William Julius Wilson published a book titled *The Declining Significance of Race*, in which he noted occupational gains among blacks and concluded, from these and other data, that economic barriers now constitute central barriers to further black progress:

> *In earlier years the systematic efforts of whites to suppress blacks were obvious to even the most insensitive observer. Blacks were denied access to valued and scarce resources through various ingenious schemes of racial exploitation, discrimination and segregation. . . . But the situation has changed. However determinative such practices were for the previous efforts of the black population to achieve racial equality, and however significant they were in the creation of poverty-stricken ghettoes and a vast underclass of black proletarians . . . they do not provide a meaningful explanation of the life chances of black Americans today. . . .*
>
> *In the period of modern industrial race relations, it would be difficult indeed to comprehend the plight of inner-city blacks by exclusively focusing on racial discrimination. For in a very real sense, the current problems of lower-class blacks are substantially related to fundamental structural changes in the economy. A history of discrimination and oppression created a huge black underclass, and the technological and economic revolutions have combined to insure it a permanent status. . . .*
>
> *As a result, for the first time in American history class issues can meaningfully compete with race issues in the way blacks develop or maintain a sense of group position. (Wilson 1978, 1, 21–23)*

Wilson's book set off a storm of controversy among social scientists. For example, fourteen members of the Association of Black Sociologists voted to condemn the book because they believed it to be a "misrepresentation of the black experience" that "obscures the problem of the persistent oppression of blacks." They also expressed the fear that opponents of programs to help black Americans would use Wilson's argument to influence government policy (quoted in Willie 1979, 71).

Although most critics granted that Wilson did not claim race to be unimportant in affecting the status and mobility of black Americans, many felt that his emphasis was misleading and dangerous. Social psychologist Thomas F. Pettigrew argued that Wilson's book should have been called *The Changing Significance of Race,* because Wilson's title "risks adding unsubstantiated support to the dominant ideological myth . . . that racial problems were basically solved during the 1960s, and thus there is no continuing need for such measures as affirmative action and metropolitan approaches to public school desegregation" (quoted in Willie 1979, 116). Harvard sociologist Charles V. Willie (1979) argued that because a high percentage of blacks now live in underclass poverty neighborhoods that are both racial and economic ghettos, Wilson's title actually should have been *The Inclining Significance of Race.*

There are many data and arguments that might be used to support the conclusion that race is or is not declining as a factor in affecting opportunity for black Americans. For example, Wilson argues that the rise in underclass female-headed families among blacks reflects relatively low levels of training and education (i.e., low social-class indicators) among black males who have increasingly restricted opportunities for high-income employment as structural changes in the economy require higher levels of skill (1979, p. 163). Other considerations that might be used to support Wilson's position on the growing importance of class relative to race include the following points.

1. Analysis by Jencks et al. (1979) and by Featherman and Hauser (1978) indicates that the status attainment process for blacks is becoming more like that for whites. For example, Featherman and Hauser found that after controlling for socioeconomic background, race had less than half as much an effect on occupational status of adult men in 1962 as in 1973. They concluded that black families "seem increasingly able to transfer their socioeconomic statuses to sons," and that occupational and earnings benefits to schooling—especially college education—have risen sharply for blacks (1978, p. 381).

2. A study on trends in the aspirations of black and white youth found that social class had become relatively more important than race in accounting for the data. After analyzing information collected in 1966 and 1971, Gottfredson (1979) concluded that "social background is becoming more importanat *compared* to race in determining the fate of blacks." This pattern was interpreted as indicating that a large proportion of low-status black youth "still face enormous handicaps" (p. 17). Studies of academic achievement (e.g., Coleman et al. 1966) also indicate that social class consideration largely accounts for low achievement patterns among blacks and some other minority groups.

3. A 1982 study by Chiswick of racial and ethnic patterns in educational attainment indicated that the sharp group differences that exist "are not easily explained by . . . discrimination against minorities" (p. 24). Chiswick cautioned that his findings do not mean that racial discrimination has been unimportant, but rather that other factors such as attitudes and behavior regarding fertility control, which operate separately or interact with discrimination, also affect educational attainment. He concluded that racial and ethnic minorities that were most successful in overcoming barriers to educational attainment frequently

place a special emphasis on fertility control and on providing a productive environment for child development.

On the other hand, a variety of data and arguments support the argument that race remains the fundamental factor in blocking progress among black Americans. Considerations that can be cited here include the following points.

1. Segregation of many black children and youth within the schools and other institutions such as the metropolitan labor market makes it difficult or impossible for them to acquire mainstream cultural patterns and personal contacts that play an important part in affecting mobility (Hacker 1988).

2. Analysis by Featherman and Hauser (1978) found that large racial differentials still exist with regard to economic returns to education—below the college level, blacks benefit less from a year of schooling than do whites. These researchers concluded that "discrimination in the labor market, although perhaps smaller in absolute size, is not significantly less as a proportion of the total distance that separates the races socioeconomically" (1978, p. 381). They also note that even as young blacks in the labor force have gained ground relative to whites, the likelihood of young blacks being out of the labor force (either unemployed or not seeking work) has been increasing.

3. A review of the literature by Pettigrew (1985) found support for the conclusion that the interaction between race and social class has become an increasingly important determinant of socioeconomic and educational opportunities and outcomes. Pettigrew concluded that

> *the main effects of race and class together do not adequately account for the growing complexity of modern race relations . . . Racial phenomena generally operate differently across class lines just as class phenomena generally operate differently across racial lines. (Pettigrew 1985, 337)*

No matter what position one takes on the class-caste controversy, it is clear that the largest part of the problem posed for black Americans as a group involves the development of a large black underclass in big cities. As we concluded in Chapter 8, several lines of research during the past decade suggest that big-city public schools are not functioning effectively for the black underclass, and other institutions such as the youth labor market and the traditional youth-serving agencies (see Chapters 5 and 6) also appear to have lost some of their effectiveness in concentrated urban poverty settings within a postindustrial setting.

From this point of view, whether race or class was originally or continues to be most potent in affecting opportunity is less important than is the fact that the two have become inextricably intertwined in the evolution of metropolitan areas. Stated differently, racism has become "institutionalized" in the functioning of modern urban society. Bayard Rustin has remarked on this new form of racism:

> *The old form of racism was based on prejudging all blacks as somehow inherently undeserving of equal treatment. What makes the new form more insidious is its basis in observed sociological data. The new racist equates the pathology of the poor with race, ignoring the fact that family dissolution, teenage pregnancy, illegitimacy, alcohol and drug abuse, street crime, and idleness are universal problems of the poor. They exist wherever there is economic dislocation and deterioration—in the cities, for example, dotting Britain's devastated industrial north. They are rampant among the white jobless in Liverpool as well as among unemployed blacks in New York. (Rustin 1987, 21)*

Once racism has become institutionalized in this way, social policies that appear to be racially neutral will tend to have a clear racial impact (Hacker 1988). For example, social welfare policies that encourage family break-up (by reducing payments when males are in the home), and reductions in expenditures for social welfare are not racially discriminatory in a direct manner. However, since a disproportionate percentage of black Americans is below the poverty level, such developments may have a disproportionate racial impact in terms of limiting black mobility. Similarly, reductions in federal support for public schools can be expected to disproportionately harm black Americans.

Our analysis does not imply, however, that the race-class controversy is unimportant. In the real world where government expenditures necessarily cannot be open-ended, one must decide whether to allocate funds to combat discrimination directly (e.g., affirmative action programs), to overcome class-related disadvantages (compensatory education, job training for the poor), or to strike a balance between the two. Of course, there are also some possibilities such as desegregation of schools on a socioeconomic as well as racial basis that give considerable attention to both objectives.

An additional conclusion that can be drawn from the race-class controversy is that the well-publicized statement of the National Advisory Commission on Civil Disorders (the Kerner Commission) probably should be reworded. The commission's final report in 1967 warned that "Our nation is moving toward two societies, one black, one white—separate and unequal." To some degree, events since 1967 indicate that this admonition would now be more accurate reworded to read "To a significant extent, the United States has become two separate nations, one white, plus minority middle class, and one minority underclass (largely black and Hispanic)." The future will indicate whether this type of division is more viable than one based entirely on race.

Hispanic Americans and Education

After blacks, the largest minority group in the United States is the Spanish origin or Spanish surname group, more generally referred to as Hispanic. *Hispanic* refers to persons whose ancestry is primarily Iberian or Latin American. Hispanics officially comprised 6.4 percent of the total U.S. population in 1980.* The estimated number of people and their percentage in the overall population** among the ethnic groups that made up this Hispanic minority were as follows:

• Mexican	7,326,000	(3.2%)
• Puerto Rican***	1,748,000	(0.8%)
• Cuban	794,000	(0.4%)
• Central and South American	840,000	(0.4%)
• "Other Spanish" descent	1,371,000	(0.6%)
• Subgroup not determined	2,521,000	(1.1%)

However, these population percentages underestimate the actual size of the Hispanic minority. Officials of the U.S. Immigration and Naturalization service estimated that there were at least 3 million or more illegal aliens in the United States during the early 1980s. A high proportion of these undocumented aliens were Mexicans, due in part to the facts that Mexico has the fastest growing population in the world, a high unemployment rate, and a border shared with the United States. Many of these aliens are becoming U.S. citizens as a result of 1986 changes in immigration law. Recent estimates indicate that the Hispanic population of the United States increased by 30 percent between 1980 and 1987 and that Hispanics now constitute nearly 8 percent of the U.S. population.

In addition, the Hispanic population of the United States is much younger than the total population. In 1987, almost 33 percent of the Hispanic population was under sixteen years of age, as compared with 23 percent of the non-Hispanic population.**** Fertility rates among Hispanics also are much higher than those in the total population (see Table 10.2). This high rate means that there will be proportionately more Hispanic children growing up and forming families during the 1990s than is true for the United States population as a whole.

Long-term results of these developments will have a significant impact on the composition of the United States population. The federal government is trying to reduce illegal immigration from Mexico and other countries, but difficulties in border security make it unlikely that this effort will be completely successful. Illegal, as well as legal, immigration together with natural growth in the Hispanic population make it certain that its percentage in the United

* The U.S. Census uses the phrase *Spanish origin* for people in the states of California, Arizona, New Mexico, Texas, and Colorado who report a Spanish or Mexican family relationship. The Census category "Spanish surname" applies to people, wherever they reside, with such surnames. The latter category therefore omits people who may have a parent or grandparent of Spanish-American lineage but who have non-Spanish names because of intermarriage, just as it includes people who have no such parental lineage but who are married to persons with Spanish surnames.

** Percentages total slightly more than 6.4 due to rounding.

*** Unless otherwise indicated, the term *Puerto Rican* is used in this chapter to refer to Puerto Ricans on the United States mainland.

**** The term *white* is used in this chapter to refer to non-Hispanic whites. The Hispanic group includes people whose racial background is white, black, Indian, or other racial groups.

States population will increase in the future (Russell 1983). Some authorities predict that the census will show Hispanics as constituting 9 or 10 percent of the population in the year 2000 and much more than that in future years (Exter 1987). The percentage of Spanish-origin population in California increased from 12 percent in 1970 to 19 percent in 1980. Growth of this magnitude among the Hispanic minority underlines the increasing importance of government-designated "minority" groups in the United States. A 1986 report by the Population Reference Bureau predicted that these groups will constitute a majority of the population in Southern California in about the year 2005. By 2030, a majority of California's total population may be Hispanic (Schreiner 1986).

Socioeconomic and Educational Development

As shown in Table 10.2, Hispanics as a group are more highly concentrated in metropolitan areas than are blacks and whites but less highly concentrated in central cities than is the black population. Family size among the Hispanic group is bigger than among blacks and whites, reflecting its relatively young age distribution and high fertility rates; and average family income, although higher than for blacks, is much lower than for whites. In 1982, 27 percent of Hispanic families were below the poverty level, as compared with 10 percent of the non-Hispanic white population. The occupational distribution of Hispanic workers is somewhat similar to that of blacks, except that a higher proportion of Hispanics are skilled workers and a lower proportion are service workers.

As might be expected given the relatively low socioeconomic status of the Hispanic population, school attainment and achievement levels among Hispanic students are lower than average for United States schools. As shown in Table 2.2, Hispanic students are less likely than black students to enroll in college, and, as shown in Table 10.4, achievement levels of Hispanic secondary students generally are similar to those of black students and far below those of white students.

Some data indicate that educational attainment and achievement have been increasing among Hispanic Americans. For example, national surveys conducted by the National Assessment of Educational Progress (see Figure 10.1) showed that reading scores of Hispanic students improved substantially between 1971 and 1984. The number and percentage of Hispanics in undergraduate institutions rose steadily between 1970 and 1984.

However, the 1984 data collected by the NAEP (see Figures 10.1 and 10.2) indicate that the average reading proficiency score of Hispanic seventeen-year-olds is still only slightly above that of white thirteen-year-olds. In addition, some data indicate that little or no gain has been recorded in Hispanic educational attainment in recent years. For example, the percentage of Hispanic eighteen- and nineteen-year-olds completing high school fell slightly between 1979 and 1984, and the percentage of bachelor's degrees earned by Hispanics increased only slightly: from 2 percent in 1976 to 2.3 percent in 1981. The percentage that Hispanic students constitute in graduate schools has held steady in the 1980s, despite a rapid increase in the number of Hispanic youth and young adults. In 1984 only 605 Hispanic students among 24,536 U.S. citizens received doctorate degrees.

Part of the problem that Hispanic students encounter in school involves the fact that many are classified as non-English speaking or proficient (NES or NEP), or limited-English speaking or proficient (LES or LEP). (In recent years, greater emphasis sometimes has been placed on English *proficiency* as compared with English *speaking*, because many students who speak English are not sufficiently proficient to succeed in school.) Studies conducted by the National Center for Education Statistics indicate that students with Spanish-language backgrounds enrolled in grades 5 to 12 are about twice as likely to be two or more grades below the grade levels expected for their ages as are those with English-language backgrounds. These studies further concluded that one in ten children six to eighteen years old has non-English background, and that 60 percent of this latter group are Hispanic (Waggoner 1978). The National Center has concluded that the number of LEP Hispanic students in United States elementary schools may increase from 1.8 million in 1976 to 2.6 million in the year 2000 (National Center for Education Statistics 1982).

Nationally, Hispanic students are as segregated in predominantly minority schools as are black students (see Table 9.2). Moreover, the percentage of Hispanic students attending predominantly minority schools increased between 1968 and 1984 in all sections of the United States, so that by 1984 71 percent of Hispanics compared with 64 percent of blacks were in schools 50 percent or more minority (Orfield and Monfort 1987). Thus, it appears that Hispanic students in big cities are segregated in much the same way as are black students. Gary Orfield reviewed the 1980 data for both blacks and Hispanics and concluded that to a significant degree, "The remaining problems of segregation are really problems of large metropolitan areas in the large states" (1982, p. 10). Data collected by the National Opinion Research Corporation indicate that the children of recent Hispanic immigrants may do better in school than the children of Hispanic families that have been in the United States for a few years. Some observers believe this difference reflects the fact that many Hispanics—particularly Puerto Ricans and Mexican Americans—are segregated in "ethnic ghettos" in the United States (Robey 1983; Arias, 1986).

This pattern of segregation of the Hispanic group raises the question of whether many of its members are part of the big-city underclass. If *underclass status* is defined in terms of severe poverty in neighborhoods with a prominent street culture and substantial family disorganization, it is obvious that significant numbers of Hispanics are part of the underclass. Forty percent of Puerto Rican families lived in big-city neighborhoods such as New York's East Harlem and South Bronx, areas that are high on indicators of social disorganization. Among Mexican Americans, less than 20 percent of families were single-parent families, but other measures of disorganization such as crime and drug abuse are very high in many Mexican-American communities. As is true with respect to the black population, the existence of a significant underclass among Hispanics poses grave problems for the educational system and other social institutions in the United States.

Segregation of Hispanic students also raises questions about how they should be treated in desegregation plans. Some plans, such as that in San Francisco, have required representation of every major group (white, black, Hispanic, Asian) in formulating the definition of a desegregated school; but in other cases (e.g., Los Angeles), Hispanics have been combined with blacks as a minority to be desegregated or have not been classified as a minority at all for purposes of racial balance.

Due partly to the relatively high percentage of Hispanic students in Los Angeles, Judge Paul Egly employed several social scientists to help him consider important issues including the definition and treatment of Hispanic students in desegregation planning. Beatriz Arias examined this issue for Judge Egly and tried to determine which Hispanic students should be given priority to attend desegregated schools because they "suffered the effects" of racial segregation, and which might not require desegregation because "they are sufficiently acculturated into 'mainstream' Anglo-American culture" (Arias 1978, 34). She proposed that consideration be given to constructing a weighted scale including both socioeconomic dimensions (poverty, housing value) and cultural dimensions (language handicap, traditional Hispanic family patterns and values), with emphasis placed also on identifying students in communities that magnify their "sociocultural isolation."

Thomas Pettigrew also struggled with this issue and concluded that Hispanic and other minority students might be given preference for desegregation according to whether they were "connected" or "disconnected" with mainstream society. Since one major purpose of desegregation is to help minority youth learn to function successfully within the wider society, he reasoned, middle-class minority students who reside in largely white neighborhoods possibly should be treated "in the same manner as Anglo children" (Pettigrew 1978, 61). Pettigrew also pointed out that due to the increasing percentage of Hispanic students and the declining percentage of "network connected Anglos" in the Los Angeles schools, the purpose of desegregation might be best accomplished in the future by desegregating working-class and middle-class Hispanic students. In the absence of a metropolitan remedy that would include more non-Hispanic whites, assigning working-class minority students to socioeconomically desegregated minority schools might help "put minority members into the larger networks of opportunity, whereupon *their* children can provide the vital network links for future generations of minority children in America" (Pettigrew 1978b, 54, 135).

Several national studies tend to support the conclusions that status and mobility patterns for the Hispanic population are much like those for the black population, and that growth of an underclass group is an important characteristic of these patterns for both groups. Featherman and Hauser's study (1978) of the occupational status and earnings of United States men in 1962 and 1973 showed that Hispanic Americans are at a greater disadvantage than are other major ethnic groups, after taking account of education, father's occupation, and generational status (see Table 7.2). Featherman and Hauser also reached the following two conclusions regarding the status of Mexican Americans:

1. The comparatively slow gains among Mexican Americans may be "important to understand" because they may be due to discriminatory barriers that no longer apply to other major groups (except blacks), and/or they may mark "lingering incompatibilities between the sociocultural experiences" of Mexican Americans and United States society as a whole (Featherman and Hauser 1978, 476).
2. Second-generation Mexican Americans improved their socioeconomic status compared with the first generation, but the third generation did not continue this improvement. However, this latter finding may be due to the relatively young age of the third generation; thus, firm conclusions are not yet possible.

Hispanic Subgroups

The Hispanic minority is made up of a number of subgroups that differ in some important respects such as age, income, and regional location. This section describes the most visible of these groups, with emphasis placed on their socioeconomic characteristics and the educational situation of their children. Following these descriptions, attention is given to the topic of bilingual/bicultural education and to related issues involving segregation of the Hispanic minority and its place within United States schools and society.

"Old" Americans of Spanish Descent in the Southwest. Within fifty years of the discovery of North America by Columbus, expeditions of Spanish soldiers and priests explored the Rio Grande country. Later, the Spaniards moved north from Mexico along the coast of California, setting up missions and military outposts, as well as large *haciendas* owned by wealthy families. What is now the southwestern corner of the United States was a part of Mexico until the Mexican War of 1848. After the war, which resulted in annexation of Texas and the southwestern territory to the United States, the Spanish and Mexican settlers who remained there became United States citizens.

Thus, there is an "old" population of Spanish origin that has as long a history of residence in this country as the New England colonists. Some of these people became business and professional leaders and legislators, so that Spanish surnames figure prominently in the history of the past hundred years in the Southwest. Cities such as Albuquerque, Santa Fe, San Antonio, El Paso, Los Angeles, and San Diego indicate by their names the Spanish influence; and many Spanish surnames are carried on the rosters of the Chamber of Commerce, the upper middle-class service clubs, and the country clubs. In New Mexico, Spanish and English are both official languages. This "old" population of Spanish origin constitutes a large proportion of the group labeled "Other" in Table 10.6 and number about 1 million. They are relatively older in age, and their higher educational level testifies to a relatively high socioeconomic status.

Table 10.6 ***Characteristics of Hispanic Groups in the United States***

	Location (1979 percentages)	
	Central City	*Suburban*
All Spanish Origin	48	32
Mexican American	43	34
Puerto Rican	75	15
Other (includes Cuban)	44	37

	Income in Dollars (1984)	Percentage of Families in Poverty (1985)
All Spanish Origin	18,883	25
Mexican American	19,184	24
Puerto Rican	12,371	42
Cuban	22,581	13
Other	21,423	15

	Broad Occupational Groupings of Employed Persons 16 Years of Age and over (percentage) 1985			
	White Collar	*Blue Collar*	*Service*	*Farm*
All Spanish Origin	55	21	22	1
Mexican American	55	21	22	2
Puerto Rican	56	20	23	1
Cuban	56	27	16	0
Non-Spanish Origin	70	11	18	1

	Percentage 4 Years or More College (1985)	Percentage under 17 Years old (1985)	Percentage Adults Married (1985)
All Spanish Origin	9	36	58
Mexican American	6	39	60
Puerto Rican	7	37	50
Cuban	14	20	63
Central and South American	16	31	58
Other	15	28	55
Non-Spanish Origin	20	26	59

* *Notes*: Percentage sums differ from 100 due to rounding.
White-collar grouping includes professional and technical, managers and administrators, sales and clerical; blue collar includes crafts and kindred, operatives, and nonfarm laborers; service includes private household and other.

Sources: U.S. Bureau of the Census 1985; *Statistical Abstract of the United States* 1987.

There have also been some isolated Spanish communities that did not move into the mainstream but led an impoverished existence in the mountains of New Mexico and on the dry farms of the areas near the Mexican border. They retained their language and religious customs and have only recently come into close contact with the Anglo culture. This group is small in number.

Mexican Americans (Chicanos). By far the largest group of Spanish Americans are those who identify themselves to the census taker as being of Mexican origin. More than 7 million strong by 1980, they provided almost half of the 540,000 students in the Los Angeles public schools. Most Mexican Americans live in the Southwest, but there also are large numbers on the West Coast and in the Midwest. A large majority are United States citizens, but many are illegal immigrants and are liable to deportation if discovered by immigration officials.

The name *Chicano* probably comes from the colloquial term *mechicano* (Mexican), which frequently has been used by Mexican Americans in the Southwest to refer to themselves. Many Mexican Americans now use the term to refer to their ethnic group, but some others reject it because they believe it has working-class connotations or introduces other stereotypes.

The majority of the adults of this group are semiskilled and unskilled workers (see Table 10.6). In many cases, their parents have had experience as agricultural workers, often as migratory workers following the crop cycle through the states of the west coast and mountain regions. In the past twenty-five years, they have tended to settle permanently in the large and middle-sized cities of the Southwest, partly because much of their work of planting and harvesting crops has been taken over by machinery, and partly because they were able to get steady employment and, thus could give up the migratory life. With 7 percent of adult males still working as farm laborers in 1979, the Mexican-American group is the most rural of the Spanish American population.

Because many Mexican Americans are or have been migratory laborers, our system of education has not provided regular schooling for their children. The local school districts tended either to set up temporary classes for these children for a few months each year, or to ignore them. Before school desegregation began in the 1950s, there was a tendency to place these children in segregated schools. For example, Mexican-American children were formally segregated in California until 1947, and in Texas until 1948.

Since a considerable proportion of Mexican-American families use Spanish as their home language, many of their children come to school with little or no facility in English. Chicano children of low socioeconomic status have the poorest knowledge of English. On the other hand, many Mexican-American pupils, especially from high-status families, speak English quite well.

School authorities in the Southwest responded to this situation initially by barring Spanish speech from the school classes and playgrounds as much as possible. They argued that pupils would benefit from the no-Spanish rule. However, due to strong objections of parents and pupils and changing attitudes on the part of educators, this rule has now been moderated or dropped in most districts. For example, one Texas district reported, "Effective September 1, 1968, students were allowed to speak correct Spanish on school grounds and classrooms if allowed by individual teachers. Teachers may use Spanish to 'bridge a gap' and make understanding clear'' (U.S. Commission on Civil Rights 1972, 15). We return to this issue of bilingual education later in this chapter.

The United States Commission on Civil Rights summarized its study of the education of Mexican-American students as of 1974:

> *Entrance into public school brings about an abrupt change for all children, but for many Mexican-American children the change is often shattering. . . . The language which most Chicano children have learned—Spanish—is not the language of the school and is either ignored or actively suppressed. Even when the Spanish language is deemed an acceptable medium of communication by the schools, the Chicano's dialect is often considered ''substandard,'' or no language at all. . . .*
>
> *The curriculum which the schools offer seldom includes items of particular relevance to Chicano children and often damages the perception which Chicanos have gained of their culture and heritage. It is a curriculum developed by agencies and institutions from which Mexican Americans are almost entirely excluded.*
>
> *Chicano children also are taught primarily by teachers who are Anglo. Generally, these teachers are uninformed on the culture that Chicanos bring to school and unfamiliar with the language they speak. . . . [the teachers'] training and practice teaching do little to develop in them the skills necessary to teach Mexican-American children. (United States Commission on Civil Rights 1974, 67–68)*

Puerto Ricans. The socioeconomic status of Puerto Ricans in the United States reflects the economy of the island. That economy has grown greatly over recent decades due to the investment of mainland capital and rapid industrialization. Nevertheless, the per capita income of the island is much less than that of the United States as a whole. There has been a relatively high unemployment rate among the working classes in Puerto Rico, due largely to the modernization of agriculture, which resulted in large numbers of rural people moving to the cities in search of work. Thus, the average Puerto Rican immigrant to the mainland has been a rural person with relatively little education. Racially, the Puerto Ricans include persons with 100 percent Spanish ancestry to persons (a minority) with African ancestry.

More than half of the mainland Puerto Ricans live in the New York City metropolitan area, and there are large populations in Philadelphia, Newark, Washington, D.C., and Chicago. By 1974, there were more than a quarter of a million Puerto Rican students in the New York City public schools.

As has been true with many other immigrant groups, including Italians, Jews, Mexican Americans, Poles, and Slovaks, accommodation to life in the United States has involved difficult problems that call into question traditional cultural patterns and tend to cleave the generations. These problems probably have been accentuated among Puerto Ricans because so high a proportion of them are located in big-city poverty neighborhoods in which traditional family patterns have become increasingly difficult to maintain. Joseph P. Fitzpatrick has described these difficulties in discussing the efforts of Puerto Rican parents to maintain traditional practices such as chaperonage of young girls and emphasis on respect for age and adult authority:

> *Puerto Rican families have frequently lamented the patterns of behavior of even good boys in the United States. . . . American children are taught to be self-reliant, aggressive, and competitive, to ask "why," and to stand on their own two feet. A Puerto Rican child is generally much more submissive. When the children begin to behave according to the American pattern, the parents cannot understand it. A priest who had worked for many years with migrating Puerto Ricans remarked to the writer: "When these Puerto Rican families come to New York, I give the boys about 48 hours on the streets of New York, and the differences between his behavior and what the family expects, will have begun to shake the family."*
>
> *. . . The parents are living in the Puerto Rican culture in their homes. The children are being brought up in an American school where American values are being presented. The parents will never really understand their children; the children will never really understand the parents.* (Fitzpatrick 1972, 116–117)

Table 10.4 shows the standing of Puerto Rican pupils in 1980 relative to Chicano and other minorities. The data are drawn from the High School and Beyond study referred to earlier. Puerto Rican students were slightly but consistently below Mexican Americans. The problems Puerto Rican children encounter in school appear to be related most closely to their low socioeconomic status, with some intensification due to ethnic and cultural differences. This mixture of socioeconomic and ethnic factors is clear in the following description of problems in predominantly Puerto Rican schools with which Francisco Cordasco and Eugene Bucchioni introduce their book *The Puerto Rican Community and Its Children on the Mainland*:

> *Teachers like to teach students . . . who study a great deal, and who will follow obediently whatever instructions are given. Teaching is less difficult and students seem to be learning with ease. When lower-class Puerto Ricans are taught, however, the teachers are confronted with many different social and cultural patterns of behavior. . . . To many Puerto Rican students, much of North American middle class teaching is uninteresting and unrealistic. . . . In the high school there may be talk of future work as doctors or lawyers. But Puerto Rican students are not always motivated by these techniques, partly because of the seeming impossibility of attainment of these goals. . . . For many Puerto Rican students the urban school becomes a marketplace of unreality and alienation.* (Cordasco and Bucchioni 1972, 17)

Cubans. Emigration of Cubans to the United States was small until the Castro-led revolution in the late 1950s put property owners at an economic disadvantage and led to a major migration to the United States. Many of the 1960s immigrants from Cuba were well-educated middle-class persons who generally settled in the Miami metropolitan area. In later years, however, Cuba expelled significant numbers of working-class citizens with criminal records, who then were granted asylum in the United States.

Nearly half a million Cuban Americans were living in the area of South Florida by 1980. Other groups of Cubans numbering in the thousands are living in New York, Philadelphia, Chicago, Milwaukee, and Indianapolis. Their median age as of 1980 was thirty-six, considerably older than the other Spanish-surname groups. Approximately 56 percent of employed Cuban adults were in white-collar jobs in 1985 compared with more than 70 percent for Anglos. Even though the Cubans as a group may have economic handicaps, many have business and professional skills, and many have become relatively prosperous in the United States economy. The median income for a Cuban family in 1984 was $22,581, compared with $18,883 for the total Hispanic population.

Due probably to the fact that the Cuban immigrants have a higher average socioeconomic status than most immigrants, their children tend to do better in school, in spite of the fact that most of them speak Spanish at home. Achievement test data in Chicago and Miami show the children of Cuban families to score higher than other children of Spanish descent.

The Non–Spanish-Speaking Hispanic Child

As the proportion of Hispanic students in the United States rose rapidly in the 1960s and 1970, there was growing concern regarding the low achievement level of many Hispanic students. Most frequently, this concern involved the educational needs of students who are not proficient in English but are fluent in Spanish and might benefit from bilingual education. In recent years, growing concern has been expressed concerning Hispanic students who are not proficient in Spanish (e.g., Burt and Dulay 1980). González (1980) has identified some of their needs:

> *[Hispanic] children may appear to be proficient in the English language and may seem to operate mainly in dominant traditional American culture. . . . Teachers often say, 'But these children* do *speak English; they know no Spanish. . . . Why are they consistently behind academically'?*
>
> *. . . The Hispanic child who is English dominant may have developed in a bilingual/bicultural environment in which the English language was not the pervasive, intensive force needed to mold fluent English speakers. Learning a first and only language in a non-native speaking environment may serve to limit the speaker's degree of proficiency. . . . The standard curriculum does not make allowances for language limitations. . . .*
>
> *. . . [In addition, if] the standard curriculum evolves around the behaviors, artifacts, and values of traditional 'American' culture, omitting those of Hispanic culture, the effect on the child may be both conceptual and emotional. Conceptual interference may occur when a cultural concept is presented that is completely unfamiliar to the learner. . . . Emotional interference may occur if the child feels that the family's and community's lifestyle is not valued by the school's curricu-*

lum. . . . The act of omission may cause the child to feel unworthy and this is detrimental as the child attempts to succeed in the existing curriculum. (González 1980, 3–5)

González and others have attempted to spell out some of the implications of these problems for curriculum and instruction. Among the recommendations frequently made in this regard are the following: emphasize the development of language facility and conceptual development in working with Hispanic students; institute activities that reflect the cultural and linguistic lifestyle of Hispanic communities; recognize the special contributions of Hispanic and other groups; enhance students' self-concept; avoid using or misusing tests that may be culturally biased; use peer tutoring and community volunteers to assist in instructional activities; and recognize possible ethnic group differences in cognitive style (see the section below on bicognitive style).

Bilingual/Bicultural Education

One primary goal of education for Hispanic students with little or no knowledge of English is to teach them to function in English so they can take advantage of opportunities available in the larger society. This goal is now being pursued to a large extent through bilingual education, which provides instruction in students' native languages at least until such time as they are able to learn in English. Federally sponsored bilingual education has expanded fairly rapidly since being initiated for low-status children with limited English skills in Title VII of the Elementary and Secondary Education Act of 1965 and the Bilingual Education Act of 1968, with appropriations increasing from $7.5 million in 1969 to $143 million in 1987. Revisions of the Bilingual Education Act in 1974 opened participation to nonpoverty students.

Although the federal government sponsors bilingual projects for more than sixty language groups speaking various Asian, Indo-European, and Native American languages, the large majority of children in these projects are Hispanic. California, Colorado, Massachusetts, and other states as well as local school districts also fund a variety of bilingual programs.

Bilingual education has been expanding partly because the federal Office of Civil Rights (OCR) has been insisting that opportunities be improved for limited English-proficient (LEP) and non–English-proficient (NEP) students, and the Supreme Court has backed up this insistence in the 1974 *Lau* v. *Nichols* case. Since 1970, OCR has required that schools take "affirmative steps" to correct English language deficiencies of minority children in order to receive federal funds in accordance with the Civil Rights Act of 1964. Its authority to enforce this requirement was upheld by a unanimous Supreme Court vote in the *Lau* case, which involved language problems experienced by Chinese students in San Francisco. The Court held that steps had to be taken to help students who "are certain to find their classroom experiences wholly incomprehensible" because they do not understand English. However, it did not spell out a solution but instead stated, "Teaching English to the students of Chinese ancestry is one choice. Giving instruction to this group in Chinese is another. There may be others."

Since 1975, federal guidelines for protecting the rights of LEP and NEP children have required that schools provide special bilingual opportunities where a school district has twenty or more students who have a primary language other than English, unless a school district could demonstrate that another approach would be effective in providing a meaningful opportunity to learn. Most programs approved and funded under federal guidelines for LEP and NEP students have used the Transitional Bilingual Education (TBE) approach, in which students are to be taught wholly or partly in their native language only until they can function adequately in English. Other major approaches include Teaching English as a Second Language (TESL); Immersion, in which students are placed full-time in an English-language learning environment; and bilingual maintenance, in which some effort is made to maintain or improve the native language. (Immersion and TESL are not usually defined as bilingual techniques.)

Some scholars believe these approaches should not be defined as antithetical. For example, a bilingual program might provide both for maintenance and transition, provided that one is not defined as excluding the other, and it may be desirable to include a TESL component in any bilingual program whether it emphasizes transition or maintenance (Troike 1981). The overlap between approaches and the difficulties of clearly distinguishing differing approaches were underlined in a U.S. Department of Education report that found that 72 percent of the instruction in bilingual classes was in English, and 42 percent was in English only (Lewis, 1986).

In 1980, U.S. Secretary of Education Shirley Hufstedler proposed regulations that would have continued to place primary emphasis on TBE as the preferred approach for teaching NEP and LEP students. Her successor, Terrel Bell, withdrew this proposal in 1981 and directed that new regulations be prepared that would give states and local school districts more leeway to use other approaches provided that they are based on expert advice concerning the most suitable program in a particular situation. The proposed new regulations, released in 1985 under William Bennett, Bell's successor, provided school districts with much more discretion in selecting from among immersion, bilingual education, TESL, and other approaches for helping NEP and LEP students. Congress, however, refused to approve these proposals (Crawford 1987) and finally in 1987 worked out a compromise with the executive branch. Thus, reauthorization of Title VII in 1988 provided continuing support for transitional bilingual education but did somewhat expand opportunities for school districts to use other approaches.

As indicated, considerable uncertainty exists over the kinds of bilingual programs that can or should be offered. Josué González, former director of the U.S. Office of Bilingual Education, has described major alternatives in bilingual programming as ranging from relatively short-term programs aimed at transitional preparation of LEP and NEP students for study in English, to continuing programs requiring that all students learn to function in two languages and cultures.

Some characteristics of five of these alternatives are as follows:

- Type A—*Transitional Bilingual Education* programs, which provide native language instruction to help non–English-speaking students learn to function in English.
- Type B—*Bilingual Maintenance* programs in which there is an additional emphasis on maintaining or developing the native language skills of LEP and NEP students.
- Type C—*Bilingual/Bicultural Maintenance* programs in which there also is an emphasis on maintaining the culture and teaching the history of the language group of the participating students.
- Type D—*Bilingual/Bicultural Restorationist* programs that also enroll students who have lost their native language due to assimilation, in order to "restore . . . the language and culture of their ancestry."
- Type E—*Bilingual/Bicultural Culturally Pluralistic* programs in which all students regardless of their ethno-linguistic group learn to function in two languages and benefit from "an active participation in and appreciation of each others' backgrounds." (Adapted from González 1975, 14–15)

It should be noted that there are two types of bilingual programs and three types of bilingual/bicultural programs according to González's definitions, which he points out are themselves oversimplifications of the overlapping goals and characteristics of differing approaches. It also should be noted that other definitions frequently are explicitly or implicitly formulated by other observers, so that it is very important to examine any given program in order to identify its major goals and characteristics. One of the most widely used definitions of bilingual/bicultural education is that offered by a group of bilingual education leaders in May 1973: "a process of total self-development by which a person learns and reinforces his or her own language and culture while at the same time acquiring the ability to function in another language and behave on occasion according to patterns of the second culture" (Rodriguez 1975, 3). This definition is most similar to González's Type C.

Controversies Regarding Bilingual/Bicultural Education

Bilingual/bicultural education has become one of the most controversial topics in United States education. Decisions made regarding its future are likely to play a major part in determining the subsequent history of the United States. The magnitude of the immediate problem it deals with is suggested by the fact that the Los Angeles public schools classified more than 100,000 students as LES or NES in 1978. (Most are Hispanic, but more than 100 language groups are represented.) The underlying problem is much larger, involving general social policy toward linguistic minority groups. Although it is impossible to summarize briefly all the interrelated arguments made by various observers, the following pages provide a general overview of some of the most essential issues.

What type of program should be offered? The type of program advocated by a particular observer depends partly on one's ideology concerning the kinds of experience that will be most helpful in preparing children to function productively in society, and on one's views concerning the government's responsibility for fostering such experience.

Toward one end of the continuum on this issue are people who believe that preservation of the language and culture of minority-language groups is a vital necessity that must be systematically attended to in public education if children from these groups are to maintain or develop positive individual and group identity and to cooperate productively with other groups in building an equitable society. This point of view regarding the Mexican-American minority has been summarized by Leonard C. Pacheco:

> *The thousands of Spanish-speaking people of the United States—concentrated for the most part in the American Southwest—are beginning to give voice to feelings that are only barely understood by the dominant Anglo-Saxon culture of the United States. These people feel that their culture should not be submerged or assimilated beyond recognition by American society. The language of these people is a facet, and an important one, of a culture that seeks to be an equal partner in the dominant culture. (1977, p. 170)*

Toward the other end of the continuum are people who believe that minority children will be better prepared to compete in society if they are immersed as soon as possible in English-language instruction, or that public schools should provide transitional bilingual education but should not require participation in programs emphasizing the maintenance of minority language and culture. This type of position has been taken by Noel Epstein, whose 1977 study of bilingual/bicultural education concluded that maintenance programs are neither necessary nor effective in preparing cultural minorities for participation in United States society and should not be sponsored by the federal government because they may be socially separatist and divisive:

> *If developing and maintaining literacy in the native language is the goal, that would not require giving the native tongue the kind of equal status in the curriculum envisioned by many bilingual/bicultural supporters. It could be accomplished by continuing to teach these pupils one or two classes in the native language for the rest of their school careers. . . . The central issue . . . [is not] the unquestioned importance of ethnicity in individuals' lives . . . [nor] the right or the desirability of groups to maintain their languages and cultures . . . [but] the federal role. Is it a federal responsibility to finance and promote student attachments to their ethnic languages and cultures, jobs long left to families, religious groups, ethnic organizations, private schools, ethnic publications and others? (1977, p. 7)*

Tension between these two types of positions has appeared in local communities in which minority parents disagree among themselves on whether their children will be best prepared to participate in United States society through immersion-type experiences that force them rapidly to acquire competence in English or through programs that conduct instruction in their native language. In Chicago, for example, residents of Greek-speaking neighborhoods have been bitterly divided on this issue, and in some other communities, Chinese, Puerto Rican, Mexican-American, and Native American parents have been similarly divided internally.

Uncertainty on this issue also extends to the language used in federal legislation (Rotberg 1982). The Bilingual Education Act of 1974 emphasizes the transitional goal of "providing for children of limited English-speaking ability instruction designed to enable them, while using their native language, to achieve competence in the English language" but also defines bilingual education as instruction given "with appreciation for the cultural heritage of such children." The legislation allows for instruction in the native language "to the extent necessary to allow a child to progress effectively through the educational system." Since no time limit is specified and programs may continue indefinitely if English is introduced slowly and standards for English proficiency are set high, it is possible to establish what are basically language and cultural maintenance programs under the Bilingual Education Act.

What types of programs are being offered? Partly due to lack of adequate data and partly due to difficulties in defining terms and classifying programs, it is not certain how many of the hundreds of bilingual projects supported through federal and state funds are mainly transitional and how many have a predominant language- or culture-maintenance emphasis. González states that the most "cursory examination of bilingual education programs created through legislation" shows "in general, they are *transitional* in their emphasis and regard the learning of English as the ultimate goal. Little emphasis is placed on language *maintenance* and the corollary assumption that cultural and linguistic pluralism is a desirable condition in the society" (1975, p. 12). However, Epstein also has examined a variety of programs and concluded that there is "no question that Washington has been financing language and cultural maintenance programs at least through elementary school." He also quoted Manuel D. Fierro, president of El Congreso, the National Congress of Hispanic American Citizens, as saying it is fair to conclude that "a great number of programs are using it [Title VII money] for maintenance" (Epstein 1977, 25–26).

Research has not completely settled this question. As of 1988, the major national study on participation in bilingual education was a 1977 report prepared by the American Institutes for Research (AIR) on 150 schools and 11,500 students, 75 percent of whom were of Spanish descent. Teachers in the study judged that about 70 percent of their Hispanic students were dominant in English, not Spanish, thus indicating that many of them may be in programs that are primarily maintenance-type rather than transitional. However, many experts in bilingual education such as José A. Cárdenas dispute this conclusion and criticize the AIR study on various grounds, including classification of students on the part of non–Spanish-speaking teachers "in spite of a body of research which points to the unreliability of teacher judgment as an indicator of the language characteristics of students" (1977, p. 74). Cárdenas and others also argue that instruction in the native language constitutes so small a part of the day in most bilingual programs that it is incorrect to consider them maintenance-type.

To what extent do students who might benefit from special language instruction actually receive such services? A 1985 study for the Educational Testing Service found that only 16 percent of Spanish-dominant fourth graders and only 9 percent of Spanish-dominant eighth graders were receiving bilingual or TESL services (Olson 1986a). Officials of the U.S. Department of Education responded by providing data indicating that the number of LEP students between the ages of five and fourteen had declined from 3.6 million in the late 1970s to less than 1.7 million, thus suggesting that special programs to help students acquire English were proving basically sufficient. However, many observers were skeptical about the adequacy and intepretation of these data, and some believed that the department's definition of English proficiency incorrectly minimized the extent of the problem (Crawford 1986a).

Does bilingual/bicultural education improve student academic performance? The situation regarding bilingual research appears to be similar to that regarding desegregation research: it may be misleading to reach a general conclusion based on mixing together a large number of unsuccessful programs with a few that may be particularly well designed and implemented and, consequently, unusually successful. Practically every observer agrees that many bilingual education projects have not been very well implemented. Qualified teachers are scarce, appropriate materials are in short supply, and diagnostic instruments to help in teaching are still somewhat primitive. For this reason, federal legislation has placed substantial emphasis on training staff and on the development and dissemination of exemplary approaches to bilingual education, but it is still too early to determine whether superior programs can be successfully developed and implemented on a widespread scale in the future.

Research on bilingual education, immersion, and other techniques for teaching students a second language has been complicated, controversial, and, to say the least, contentious. Research on immersion indicates that middle-class students generally perform well when immersed in a second-language environment, provided this approach is well implemented. (Much of this research has involved Anglo students in French schools in Canada.) However, research also has indicated that disadvantaged students generally do not learn well when thrust into a totally new language setting, that mental development is more advanced when students learn higher-order skills in their native language rather than rudimentary skills in a second language (Eddy 1978; Troike 1981; De Avila and Ulibarri 1980; Krashen 1981; Hakuta 1986), and that bilingual approaches have been more successful for disadvantaged students than has immersion (Dobson 1985).

On the other hand, one systematic review of research on immersion concluded that it can be helpful for students from "lower socioeconomic backgrounds and from minority ethnic groups" when it is designed and implemented well (Genesee 1985, 359). Also, data on "structured immersion" (in which care is taken to ensure that instruction is understood by students) suggest that "immersion can and does work with low-income Hispanic and Asian children and that the effects seem to endure even after students enter the mainstream" (Gersten and Woodward 1985, 78).

Various reviews of the literature on research dealing explicitly with bilingual approaches have reached radically different conclusions. For example, a review prepared for the U.S. Department of Education (Baker and De Kanter 1981) concluded that based on the results of twenty-eight studies that met the reviewers' standards for methodological adequacy, bilingual approaches were not consistently successful and "structured immersion" sometimes was more successful than TBE. The authors concluded that the

> *commonsense observation that children should be taught in a language they understand does not necessarily lead to the conclusion they should be taught in their home language. . . . There is no reason to assume a priori that the same approach that is applied to a rural Southwest Texas district with a large proportion of second-generation Hispanic children should also be applied to a district with a small group of Lao refugees in a Northern city. (Baker and de Kanter 1981, 13, 16, 17)*

On the other hand, Dulay and Burt (1982) also reviewed studies on the effectiveness of bilingual education; after identifying twelve methodologically acceptable studies on bilingual programs conducted in the United States in the 1970s, they concluded that "despite the recentness of this complex innovation, more than half of the findings show that bilingual education worked significantly better than monolingual programs" (p. 2). Willig (1985) reviewed and synthesized the results of twenty-three studies and concluded that "participation in bilingual education programs consistently produced small to moderate differences favoring bilingual education for tests of reading, language skills, mathematics, and total achievement when the tests were in English, and for reading, language, mathematics, writing, social studies, listening comprehension, and attitudes toward school or self when tests were in other languages." She also cautioned, however, that "methodological inadequacies in the synthesized studies render the results less than definitive" (p. 269).

Controversies over the findings of research on bilingual education have continued into the latter part of the 1980s. Hakuta and Gould (1987), for example, systematically analyzed the available research and concluded that "programs with substantial native-language components may be very effective" (p. 40). Their conclusions included the following five observations:

1. Even though NEP and LEP students may acquire some English proficiency through instruction in their native language in as little as two years, it may take five to seven years to master the "decontextualized" language skills necessary to function well in English.
2. Prematurely mainstreamed students "run the risk of being diagnosed as slow, disabled, or even retarded because of their language handicap" (p. 41).

3. Both immersion* and bilingual programs vary widely in the extent to which they provide support in English, the instructional methods used and the quality of instruction, effectiveness of implementation, and whether or to what extent students learning a second language are in classes with other students who function in the language.
4. Children learning a second language will need several years before their English "is as good as that of children who have been speaking it since birth . . . [although] starting to speak English as late as high school is no barrier to learning to speak it very well" (p. 42).
5. Bilingual programs should be designed in accordance with conditions in a given community but generally should aim at "additive" language-learning (i.e., students acquire an additional language) rather than "subtractive" goals that aim at replacing a child's first language with English.

On the other hand, Chester Finn, Jr., assistant secretary for Education, has interpreted the available research as indicating that bilingual education is not consistently more effective than immersion. He therefore concluded that government should allow "diversity, innovation, experimentation, and local options" in providing for the education of NEP and LEP students (Crawford 1987). However, the Government Accounting Office assembled a panel of ten experts to examine major studies as well as statements of Department of Education officials and reported that most panelists interpreted the research as supporting the efficacy of bilingual rather than other approaches for educating NEP and LEP students (Crawford 1987).

Rotberg examined both positive and negative studies dealing with bilingual education as of 1982 and offered the following partial explanation of their frequently conflicting results:

> *Programs that teach initially in the second language may be more likely to succeed when:*
>
> - *Children come from middle- or upper-class homes*
> - *Children's linguistic development in the native language is high*
> - *The home language has high status in the community*
> - *There is a strong incentive for the children to learn a second language. . . .*
> - *Program quality is high and is specifically designed for children who are learning a second language.*
>
> *Conversely, some observers suggest that initial learning in the native language might be more desirable, both academically and psychologically, for children who come from low-income families and also are not proficient in their native language. . . . These generalizations, if not taken too literally, can be helpful to com-*

* Hakuta and Gould have distinguished between *immersion*, which they define as carefully planned English-only instruction in classes composed entirely of NEP and LEP students, and *submersion*, in which language-minority students attend classes with native English-speaking students. Also see Wong (1987) for additional distinctions between immersion and submersion.

> *munities considering alternative educational programs for language-minority children. (p. 35)*

Regardless of whether one believes that bilingual education in the United States has been more or less effective or ineffective, it is clear that bilingual programs for linguistic-minority students from economically disadvantaged families will have to do more than simply provide transitional or continuing instruction in the native language if it is to improve their achievement substantially in English and other subjects. Bilingual education research indicates that LEP and NEP students who have the greatest problem learning English or another second language in the school also tend to have problems mastering their native language. Conversely, children who perform well in their own language—many Chinese and Mexican-American students, for example—tend to learn English and other school subjects very rapidly (Schacter 1979). If working class subcultures among Anglo, Chicano, Filipino, Puerto Rican, and other groups impede learning in the school, then bilingual instruction may make little difference. Thomas Iiams, adjunct professor of bilingual education at the State University of New York, summarized this point in a paper on "The Gathering Storm over Bilingual Education":

> *Whereas Spanish-surnamed pupils—Spanish monolinguals, for the most part—are now filling up "bilingual" classrooms, the problem is not one of communicating with these English-handicapped immigrants but of overcoming years of inadequate schooling in their native villages and bringing them up to grade level in one language or another. . . .*
>
> *Needless to say, this is not the sort of argument one is likely to hear in the Office of Bilingual Education. For the time being at least, it would be impolitic for anyone there to admit that bilingualism is producing a group of semiliterates in two languages. . . . (Iams 1977, 227)*

Joshua Fishman, distinguished research professor at Yeshiva University, also has studied the research on bilingual education and reached essentially the same conclusion. "On the whole," he says, bilingual education is

> *too frail a device in and of itself, to significantly alter the learning experiences of the minority-mother-tongue-poor in general or their majority-language-learning-success in particular. It is of course true that foisting a language other than their own upon such children is equivalent to imposing an extra burden upon those least able to carry it. However, precisely because there are so many other pervasive reasons why such children achieve poorly . . . removing the extra burden . . . does not usually do the trick, particularly when the teachers, curricula, and materials for bilingual education are as nonoptimal as they currently usually are. (Fishman 1977, 5)*

Needless to say, both the skeptics and the proponents of bilingual/bicultural approaches tend to agree that a good deal more research and experimentation are needed if such programs are to be more successful in the future. Research is needed particularly to identify the specific bilingual and bicultural approaches that work best with differing groups of children and to avoid possible mistakes such as using "Standard" Spanish to teach low-status Puerto Rican students whose dialect is quite different. In particular, research is beginning to examine the characteristics of schools and/or classrooms in which bilingual education appears to have had considerable success in improving the academic performance of disadvantaged language-minority students.

For example, Tikinoff (1985) has reported the results of a systematic effort (the Significant Bilingual Instructional Features Study) to identify successful bilingual classrooms enrolling Puerto Rican, Cuban, Mexican, Navajo, and Chinese students and to assess the reasons for their success. The first part of the SBIF study found that successful bilingual instruction involved

1. "Active teaching" in which teachers communicated subject matter and tasks clearly, obtained and maintained students' engagement on instructional tasks, and monitored students' progress while providing appropriate feedback.
2. Effective use of both the native language and the second language, "alternating between the two when necessary."
3. Coordination and integration of English-language development with academic skills development.
4. Appropriate use of information about the students' home culture.
5. Communication of high expectations to students (Tikinoff 1985, 3).

The second part of the SBIF study examined classroom dynamics and processes in greater depth. Among the varied and somewhat complicated conclusions were that

1. Effective bilingual instruction is adapted within the classroom in accordance with the language problems and deficiencies of different students.
2. Emphasis on the native language as compared with the second language should vary with the time of the year and the nature of the subject matter.
3. The frequency and use of language alternation should vary with the instructional context.
4. The quality of instruction in basic skills is more important than the amount.
5. A variety of instructional arrangements can be used to attain similar instructional goals.
6. LEP students who do not understand instruction in English should receive translation and other assistance in their regular classroom while responding to class tasks.
7. Confusion and other negative effects of pulling students out of regular classes must be avoided.
8. TESL strategies can be used while still coordinating bilingual language development strategies with regular instruction in content areas (Tikinoff 1985).

Many of these SBIF conclusions about successful bilingual education are strikingly similar to those provided by general research on effective teaching and effective schools. Of course, it is not surprising that factors associated with successful instruction in regular classrooms are also present in bilingual classrooms. Further confirmation of the conclusion that key considerations for providing effective instruction in regular classes are also necessary for bilingual education to be successful can be found in an analysis of SBIF data in which Courtney Cazden (1985) concluded that great heterogeneity in the bilingual classroom makes it difficult to teach effectively, that the pace of instruction can be unproductively slowed by concurrent translation, and, in particular, that many bilingual classrooms are not successful in avoiding tendencies toward minimizing stress on comprehension and application of skills beyond literal understanding.

In addition, Carter and Chatfield (1986) studied unusually effective bilingual schools. They found that many characteristics of schools, such as positive climate, a safe and orderly environment, and high opportunity to learn, have been identified in the general effective schools literature. The findings presented by Cazden and by Carter and Chatfield are in line with conclusions regarding teaching and school effectiveness described briefly in Chapter 8 and returned to at greater length in the final chapter of this book.

Will bilingual/bicultural education impede school desegregation or be otherwise socially divisive? Uncertainty about the degree to which emphasis on bilingual/bicultural education may impede school desegregation follows partly from the fact that educators have not been able to work out systematic plans for successfully combining the two approaches, as well as recognition that there is likely to be continuing tension between their major objectives. On the one hand, it is clear that placing students of a given language group in separate classes for native language instruction all or part of the school day effectively segregates them even if they are enrolled in a racially and ethnically mixed school. On the other hand, it also is clear that desegregation plans may limit opportunities for bilingual/bicultural education by dispersing LES and NES students in a large number of schools at which it is difficult to deliver native language instruction economically.

Many advocates of bilingual/bicultural education believe it is possible and desirable to devise programs that can be implemented in a desegregated setting. For example, José A. Cárdenas, executive director of the Intercultural Development Research Center in San Antonio, has stated (1975) that in-class grouping of students according to their individual needs, exchange or regrouping of students and teachers across classes for special instruction part of the school day, and staffing patterns that draw on resources other than the regular classroom teacher should all be part of a bilingual program. Such approaches also could facilitate the implementation of bilingual education in desegregated settings. School administrators in Los Angeles and other cities are trying to develop ways of doing this. Castellanos (1980) assessed the tensions that arise between bilingual and desegregation goals and concluded that "bilingual education and school desegregation will conflict only to the extent that the staffs of both programs do not take cognizance of each other, are inflexible in their demands, or insist on quarreling over turf" (p. 8).

The situation with respect to bilingual/bicultural education and desegregation is complicated by the differing conditions and legal rulings that govern developments in differing communities. In many school districts, particularly those in the Southwest, Hispanics are counted as minority in drawing up a student desegregation plan, but in others such as Cleveland they have not been designated by the courts as minority victims of *de jure* segregation. Some school districts count Hispanics along with blacks in developing a desegregation plan, but others have developed plans specifying a multi-ethnic balance in every school. In some locations such as Denver and Detroit bilingual programs have been mandated as part of court desegregation remedies in either desegregated or ethnically isolated schools, but in some other districts this has not been true. In addition, Hispanic leaders differ from district to district on whether to push hardest for bilingual alternatives or desegregation, or for both equally.

Related to the desegregation issue is the possibility that bilingual/bicultural education will reinforce or stimulate separatist trends that may prove divisive and harmful to the development of a pluralistic society. Public attitude surveys indicate that the majority of Hispanic citizens favor desegregation in schools and other major social institutions. However, some observers such as Epstein (1977) fear that bilingual or bicultural maintenance programs may contribute to greater emphasis on ethnic separateness and thereby reduce movement toward desegregation in the future. The director of the New York City Board of Education Division of Community Affairs described this kind of possibility:

> *While on the one hand, we can accept intellectually the need to improve educational opportunity by breaking out of the ghetto and joining the mainstream . . . we also are wary of the loss of power—political and economic—that would result from a diffusion of the Puerto Rican community. This dilemma faces us constantly. A case in point is the bilingual movement. While bilingualism . . . is meant to foster the Puerto Rican/Hispanic identity and consequently encourages concentrations of Hispanics to stay together and not be integrated, one also has to be wary that it not become so insular and in-grown that it fosters a type of apartheid that will generate animosities with other groups, such as Blacks, in the competition for scarce resources, and further alienate the Hispanic from the larger society. (Mathews 1978, 47)*

On the other hand, there is little hard evidence to support the conclusion that bilingual/bicultural maintenance programs generally have had much of an independent effect in stimulating separatist tendencies among racial or ethnic groups in the United States or elsewhere. Joshua Fishman has reached the following conclusions concerning the potentially divisive effects of bilingual approaches:

> *Very few, if any, secessionist movements have been spawned thereby or related thereto, and it would seem to me to be more wicked than wise to raise any such*

> *bugaboo in conjunction with discussions of bilingual education in the U.S.A. today. . . . When coterritorial groups move toward separatism, it is almost never because of conflicts over bilingual education.* (1977, p. 6)

It also should be noted that many scholars such as Fishman (1977), Iiams (1977), González (1975), Hakuta (1986), and Orfield (1977) believe that bilingual education ideally should be provided for most or all students whatever their ethnic background, and that participation in such programs could reduce social divisiveness by bringing students into contact with one another and their respective cultures. Helping all students acquire sufficient skill to function successfully in another language might be an important step toward maintaining a constructive pluralistic society in the United States. Thus, a group of government officials and civic leaders concerned with bilingual education has recommended the following six actions and emphases to make bilingual education a positive force for constructive pluralism in the 1980s (Academy for Educational Development 1982):

1. Overall emphasis on development of a "language-competent" society.
2. A "no-holds-barred insistence on full mastery of English."
3. Emphasis on real multilingual competence rather than just on remediation in English.
4. Emphasis on parent-school partnership; parents should not have to rely on private schools as their only means of developing language competence in their children.
5. Bilingual programs should expand to include English-speaking children, so that non-English speakers and English speakers can help each other learn.
6. Increased attention to the international political and economic advantages of multilingual competence.

Bicognitive Development

In recent years, attention has been given to developing instructional approaches that take into account possible differences in learning styles and preferences among students of differing cultural background. Manuel Ramirez III and Alfredo Castañeda have been particularly systematic in examining such possibilities with respect to Mexican-American children and have written a book (1974) in which they describe instructional approaches designed to help students function "bicognitively" (i.e., using more than one cognitive style).

The basis for the Ramirez and Castañeda approach is the finding that Hispanic children are more "field dependent" or "field sensitive" than are Anglo children. Field dependence-independence usually is measured with perceptual tests that ask a respondent to identify subpatterns within a larger pattern. Field-sensitive students are described as being more influenced by personal relationships and by praise or disapproval from authority figures than are field-independent students. Based on their own as well as other research, Ramirez and

Castañeda argued that instruction for field-sensitive Mexican-American students will be more successful if it is adapted to their cognitive style. Among the many suggestions they make for conducting instruction in this way are the following:

> *Field-sensitive curriculum is humanized through use of narration, humor, drama, and fantasy. . . . Emphasis is on description of wholes and generalities; the overall view or general topic is presented first. . . . The curriculum is structured in such a way that children work cooperatively with peers or with the teacher in a variety of activities. (Ramirez III and Castañeda 1974, 142)*

Ramirez and Castañeda also emphasize research suggesting that other things being equal, students tend to be most successful when taught by teachers with the same cognitive style. The ultimate goal of such instructional adaptation and student-teacher matching is not to remove field-sensitive students from field-independent mainstream environments requiring abstract analytic skills but to prepare them to function well in these environments (Ramirez III 1976, 13).

A bicognitive approach such as that advocated by Ramirez, Castañeda, and some other educators is not yet of proven value in working to improve the performance of low-status students of Mexican-American or other background. Some instructional components such as emphasis on friendly, understanding teacher behavior have been regarded as important for decades, but educators still have trouble translating this admonition into effective teacher behavior. De Avila and Ulibarri (1980) have examined the research on field dependence and concluded that field dependence is not consistently related to academic achievement among either urban or rural Hispanic students, and that Mexican-American students are not consistently more field dependent than are non-Hispanic whites. They also worry about the possibility that too much stress on using one teaching style with Hispanic students may be educationally destructive.

Asian Americans and Education

Eight groups of immigrants from Asia and the Pacific Islands are present in substantial numbers in the United States, although they represent only a small percentage of the total population. As indicated in Table 10.1, these groups are the Asian, Indian, Chinese, Filipino, Hawaiian, Japanese, Korean, and Vietnamese. In 1980 these eight groups comprised 1 percent of the U.S. population.

Asians have constituted a substantial proportion of immigration to the United States since 1960, and their increase in some locations has been explosive. For example, the Asian-born population of Chicago more than tripled between 1970 and 1980, from 35,341 to 128,293. Nationally, the Asian-American population grew by 142 percent during this period. It is continuing to grow rapidly and is expected to reach about 8 million by the end of the century. Asian Americans may constitute 3 percent of the national population by 2000 and 6 percent

Table 10.7 ***Metropolitan Location of American Indians/Eskimos and Asian Americans/Pacific Islanders, 1980***

	Group Percentages	
	American Indian and Eskimos	*Asian and Pacific Islanders*
Inside SMSAs	48	91
Inside central cities	21	46
Outside central cities	27	44
Outside SMSAs	53	10

Percentages do not add to 100 due to rounding.
Source: Statistical Abstract of the United States, 1984.

by 2050. By the turn of the century, one-tenth of California's population will be Asian. (Bouvier and Agresta 1985).

Status of Asian Americans

Asian Americans have tended to settle in urban areas (see Table 10.7) on the West Coast, but since about 1950 there has been significant distribution of Asian population in all regions of the United States. The Japanese Americans, Korean Americans, and Chinese Americans have a higher percentage in white-collar jobs than the national average. All three groups are relatively high in educational attainment compared to other ethnic groups in the United States. For example, nearly 90 percent of third-generation Japanese Americans have attended college (Takei 1981). Although some problems have been evident in California and New York with respect to in-migration of low-status population from Cambodia, Hong Kong, and other locations, the once-sordid Chinatowns in several big cities have become relatively prosperous and stable communities.

Asian Americans now constitute more than 20 percent of undergraduate enrollment at the Berkeley and UCLA campuses of the University of California, and they also are disproportionately well represented in the enrollments of several highly selective big-city high schools. For example, Stuyvesant High School in New York City had 41 percent Asian students in 1988 (Schwartz 1988). Twelve of the forty high-school seniors identified in the Westinghouse Science Talent Search in 1983 were Asian Americans.

Staples and Mirandé (1980) have reviewed research on family patterns among Asians in the United States and concluded that their relative success in the educational and economic systems is associated with cultural values that overcome the disadvantages of poverty and discrimination typically experienced by new immigrant groups. Their overall assessment is as follows:

> *In sum, culture seems to be the key element in Asian family life. Their traditional culture stressed the importance of the family unit at the expense of the individual,*

Table 10.8 *Selected Characteristics of Asian-American Subgroups, 1980*

Subgroup	Median Age	Percentage of Families in Poverty	Mean Annual Earnings of Males 25–54	Median Years of School Completed by Persons 25 or Older	High-School Graduation Rate
Chinese	30	11	$17,777	13.8	90
Filipino	29	6	16,973	14.1	89
Japanese	34	4	21,466	12.9	96
Korean	26	13	18,978	13.0	94
Vietnamese	22	35	11,303	12.4	76

Sources: U.S. Commission on Civil Rights 1985; various U.S. Census Bureau documents.

and socialization processes in the family created patterns of self-control which facilitated the achievement of societal goals. These cultural values were very consonant with traditional American values and made them adaptable to the American family system. Class membership does not seem as important since many of the Asian immigrants brought with them values associated with the middle class: i.e., an emphasis on education and a capitalist orientation. (Staples and Mirandé 1980, 897)

Disparities in the status of Asian-American subgroups are shown in Table 10.8. The Filipino and Japanese groups have a low percentage of families in poverty, and the recently arrived Vietnamese have a very high poverty rate. Among all five subgroups shown in Table 10.8, the average adult has completed at least twelve years of school.

The fact that Asian-American subgroups generally score relatively high on indicators of socioeconomic status and education does not mean that they do not experience special problems as do other nonwhite minority groups. A 1980 study by the U.S. Commission on Civil Rights indicated that despite their comparatively high figures on educational attainment, Asian Americans as a group also rank relatively low on income and relatively high on unemployment. They also have a relatively high proportion in low-status occupations (see Table 7.2). The commission concluded that "Asian Americans as a group are not the successful minority that the prevailing stereotype suggests. Individual cases of success should not imply that the diverse peoples who make up the Asian-American communities are uniformly successful. . . . Asian Americans earn far less than majority Americans with comparable education" (p. 24). Some of this disadvantage probably is due to the relatively recent in-migration status of many Asian Americans and to language barriers associated with immigration, but some probably can be attributed to discrimination in employment and to lack of political power among small ethnic groups. Some Japanese Americans are still suffering from loss of property that was associated with their forced internment at United States detainment camps during World War II.

Southeast Asians

Representation of Asians in the U.S. population has been increased substantially by in-migration since 1975 of nearly 1 million persons from Southeast Asia. Among these in-migrants, approximately 65 percent were from Vietnam, about 20 percent were from Laos, and the remainder were from Cambodia. Approximately 40 percent of Southeast Asians have settled in California.

The first wave of Vietnamese immigrants in 1975 and 1976 consisted primarily of well-educated persons of high socioeconomic status. Many in this group could speak English. The Southeast Asian immigration since 1976 has been of refugees heterogeneous in cultural, linguistic, and educational background. Relatively few in this group knew English.

Given the low social-class background and the language barriers experienced by many Southeast Asian in-migrants in the 1970s and 1980s, it is not surprising that many also experienced economic problems. Nearly two-thirds who arrived after 1980 were receiving public assistance in 1986. Data collected by the federal government indicate that the subsequent status and success of Southeast Asian immigrants to the United States has been highly correlated with proficiency in English. Among those who possessed or had acquired fluency in English, the unemployment rate in 1985 was 19 percent, compared with 32 percent for those speaking no English. Overall, however, the data provided encouraging indications that most were acquiring some English and also were improving in economic status (Jaeger and Sandhu 1985).

As a group, the children of Southeast Asian in-imigrants have done well—frequently exceedingly well—in U.S. public schools. For example, a study conducted by Nathan Caplan and his colleagues at the Institute for Social Research found that among children of Southeast Asian families who entered the United States after 1978, 47 percent had a math grade point average above 3.5 (on a scale of 4), 27 percent scored at or above the 90th percentile in math achievement, and 79 percent had an overall grade point average (including English) above 2.5. The authors also found that the "highest-achieving children are from families that embodied what are traditional Confucian cultural values, emphasizing the family as a cohesive unit working to achieve shared goals, and encouraging a strong respect for education" (Caplan 1985, 7).

School Performance of Asian Pupils

As shown in Table 10.4, Asian-American pupils do as well as or better than white pupils on standard tests of school achievement. They do much better in mathematics. Their performance on tests of reading and of vocabulary is about equal to that of white pupils, and this is in spite of the fact that many Asian pupils speak little or no English at home. These data are particularly impressive given that approximately 15 percent of Asian students were classified as limited-English-speaking in 1980 (Tsang and Wing 1985).

Other data on Asian students also are generally positive. For example, although they constituted 5 percent of public school enrollment in 1980, Asian students accounted for less than 2 percent of suspensions from school. Conversely, approximately 5 percent of Asian students were participating in instructional programs for the gifted and talented, compared with less than 3 percent of white students. In addition, information from the High School and Beyond data set shows that Asian students are earning significantly more credit in science and math than are students from other racial-ethnic groups (Tsang and Wing 1985). After entering college, the percentages of Asian students majoring in engineering, life science, and physical science are respectively twice, four times, and twice as great as those for white students (Peng 1985).

However, many Asian-American students experience special school problems arising from their distinctive cultural patterns. For example, as pointed out in a paper prepared for the Education Commission of the States, children from Vietnamese families frequently have been encouraged to learn by rote memory and thus may find it difficult to apply analytic skills in the classroom, and students from each Asian group may find it difficult to express their own opinions when asked to do so by their classroom teacher because this might be viewed as disrespect toward adults.

In addition, the concept of counseling has not been a part of Asian cultures, thus making it unusually difficult to conduct counseling programs for Asian students. Mizokawa and Moroshima (1979) have identified seven other school-related problems that many Asian-American students encounter:

1. Low self-concept possibly related to lack of material on Asians in the curriculum.
2. Lack of native-speaker fluency in English.
3. Linguistic differences such as the greater emphasis on intonation in Asian languages.
4. Speech anxiety.
5. "Loaded" words, images, and stereotypes such as those that portray Asians as exotic, overly passive, inscrutable, or sinister.
6. Lack of attention to or recognition of differences between various Asian- and Pacific-origin groups, including groups from differing parts of China.
7. Relatively nonassertive and nonverbal behavior in the classroom, particularly in the presence of authority figures.

Native Americans (American Indians and Eskimos)

The 1980 census reported that there were about 1.4 million American Indians. (However, nearly 7 million Americans report that they have some Indian ancestry.) There are also more than 50,000 Eskimos and Aleuts living in Alaska who are placed in a similar status with Indians by the state and federal governments. Indians have grown rapidly in numbers in recent decades, due partly to the fact that the U.S. Public Health Service has brought modern health services to most of the Indian communities. With their numbers almost tripling between 1950 and 1980, they are one of the fastest growing ethnic groups in the country.

Indian people are diverse in tribal customs, religious beliefs, and ways of earning a living. When white men first came into contact with Indians in the various geographical areas that are now the United States, there were about 200 tribes that formed several different language groups. The Eastern Indians were generally farmers; the Plains Indians were buffalo hunters; the Southwest Indians were dry-land farmers, food gatherers, or small-game hunters. Along the Pacific coast, the people were fishermen; and in Alaska, they were hunters of seal and caribou and salmon fishers.

When the warfare between Indians and whites came to an end about 1870, the government took the role of guardian over the Indian people. It recognized each tribe's ownership of land but tried to teach the adults better farming and cattle- and sheep-growing practices. At the same time, Indian children were placed in boarding schools, where they were expected to learn white American culture. It was hoped that Indians would soon become like other Americans and would become assimilated into the surrounding society.

This policy did not work. Only a minority of American Indians accepted the ways of white society. Most held to Indian ways and to tribal identifications. Because they were confined to reservations and ruled by agents of the federal government, their ways of life changed and were no longer Indian in the traditional sense, but neither were their ways of life American. Indians became marked by poverty, primarily because they were generally given poor and infertile land for their reservations.

American Indians today are a disadvantaged minority group. On the average, they are low in income, educational level, and occupational levels, and their children are low on school achievement (see Table 10.4). Twenty-seven percent of American Indians were below the poverty level in 1980, and unemployment rates for Indians, particularly for those on reservations, frequently exceed 50 percent (Karoniaktatie 1986). Among some tribes, such as the Navajo, less than 20 percent of students complete high school (Crawford 1986b), and only seventy-three American Indians received doctorate degrees in 1984.

Indians have a moral claim on the public conscience somewhat different from the moral claims of other minority groups because they are the original Americans, whose lands were taken from them by force or by shady bargaining. For this reason, the American Indians might now expect the best possible treatment from the wealthy society that surrounds them. There is a real desire on the part of most government leaders in the United States to make up for past mistakes by giving the Indians better treatment. But there is no general agreement on what is the best program for improvement of Indian life.

Educational Policy before 1925

Because official government policy after 1870 was for the assimilation of Indians into the dominant white culture, both in schools run by the federal government and in schools run by churches and missionaries, the aim was to teach Indian children to be like white children. Consequently, the schools at first were almost entirely boarding schools, with the Indian child living away from the family and tribe. The Carlisle Indian School founded in 1878 at Carlisle, Pennsylvania, to serve children from midwestern and western tribes was typical. The curriculum was designed to teach Indian children to speak, read, and write English, to live like white people, and to practice a trade. Part of the educational program was the "outing system," which provided an Indian youth a three-year apprenticeship with a white family after completion of school training. The government paid $50 a year for his medical care and clothing; his labor in the home or on the farm was expected to compensate for his room and board.

By the early 1900s, there was a good deal of opposition to the boarding school as the principal institution for educating Indian children, opposition based partly on the resistance of Indian parents to having their children moved away from the family. Accordingly, a number of federally operated day schools were opened on the reservations. At the same time, many Indian children were encouraged to attend local public schools on or near the reservations. By 1920, more Indian pupils were in local public school than in federal schools, and by 1928, the number of federal schools was less than in 1910.

Following World War I, federal appropriations for Indian education were increased, efforts were made to increase the proportions of Indian children attending school, and secondary school work was made more available at schools near reservations.

Indian Education, 1925–1965

The New Deal of the 1930s saw a change in Indian education toward relating schools more closely to Indian life, with the new commissioner of Indian Affairs, John Collier, exerting a decisive influence. In 1934, the Indian Reorganization Act was passed, giving more power and more responsibility for self-government to Indian Tribal Councils. A large number of day schools were built by the federal government on reservations, and the native language was used in the early grades. More emphasis was placed on learning about native Indian culture and history, and on arts and crafts.

Because the Indians were wards of the federal government, reservations were not subject to state or local taxation, and they were given very limited services by the states in which they were located. Educational costs were paid by the federal government, except for Indians who moved to towns and cities, where they paid rent and property taxes just like other citizens.

World War II had a great influence on Indian life. Some 25,000 Indians served in the armed forces. Older Indian men and women left reservations to take jobs in war industries or other jobs in towns and cities. The end of the war brought Indians back to the reservations with more knowledge of outside affairs and more interest in education, especially high school and vocational education. For example, the Navaho tribe, containing about one-fifth of all Indians and previously the most isolated tribe, moved explicitly to get literacy training for its teenage youth, many of whom had never been to school.

Indians in Urban Centers

Since 1950, there has been substantial migration of Indians into urban centers of the United States. Like other urban migrants, many Indians leave their home communities because of limited employment opportunities. And like many other migrant groups, Indians find urban communities to be alien environments. Their cultural background, with its strong emphasis on close personal interrelationships and strong traditional family and tribal values, does not prepare Indians for depersonalized and sometimes hostile encounters with other urban residents. Their educational and vocational skills are, in many cases, inadequate or inappropriate for the available job opportunities. When they seek those few jobs for which they are prepared, they often face bigotry and discrimination. However, with increasing numbers of Indians already in the city, with improved job training and housing, and with personal advisory service provided by the Bureau of Indian Affairs and private agencies, many Indians are making good adjustments.

As noted in Table 10.7, 48 percent of Indians were living in metropolitan areas in 1980. The largest urban Indian concentration is in the Los Angeles area, where about 3,000 children and youth are in schools in the Los Angeles School District. Other cities with 5,000 to 15,000 Indian population are Minneapolis, Oklahoma City, Tulsa, Phoenix, and Chicago.

Contemporary Policy of Education for Indians

The federal government moved during the 1960s toward official adoption of a policy of Indian self-determination. This was laid out in detail in President Nixon's message to Congress on July 8, 1970, and was then incorporated in the Indian Education Act of 1972. Before this date, there had been much action by individual tribes in their negotiations with the Bureau of Indian Affairs. Most thoroughgoing was the series of contracts made by the Zuni Tribe of New Mexico earlier in 1970, which empowered the tribe to administer all the programs formerly operated by the Bureau of Indian Affairs. The president's message commenced with such general statements as "It is long past time that the Indian policies of the Federal government begin to recognize and build upon the capacities and insights of the Indian people." The four main points of the Message were:

1. The Indian tribes should have self-determination over their own affairs without termination of their reservation status and their tribal unity. The Indian tribes should have the right to control and operate federal programs, including schools.

Table 10.9 *Schools Attended by Indians, Aged Six to Eighteen*

	Enrollment	Precentage of Total Group
A. Schools with practically all Indian enrollment:		
BIA-operated boarding and day schools	56,000	17
Indian-Controlled School Boards: Contract with BIA (est.)	3,500	1
Mission or other private schools	10,000	3
Public schools operating on or contiguous to reservations	37,000	11
B. Public schools with 50 to 90 percent Indian enrollment:		
Contiguous to Indian reservations or in native communities	125,000	38
C. Public schools with 10 to 50 percent Indian enrollment:		
Mainly in rural communities and small cities	60,000	18
D. Public schools with 1 to 10 percent Indian enrollment:		
Mainly in large cities	37,000	11

Source: Fuchs and Havighurst 1972.

2. The Federal Government should assist financially in projects for economic development of Indian groups.
3. A substantial increase in funding of the U.S. Public Health Service for Indians.
4. Assistance to urban Indians through the operation of service centers in major cities.

The commissioners of Indian Affairs, who directed the Bureau of Indian Affairs, under President Johnson and his successors were for the first time Indians: Robert Bennett, a member of the Oneida Tribe; Louis R. Bruce, Mohawk-Sioux; Morris Thompson, Athabascan from Alaska; and Forrest Gerrard, Blackfoot.

In 1978, about 330,000 Indian and Eskimo youth were enrolled in public elementary and secondary schools in the United States, with the largest numbers distributed in seven western states (Alaska, Arizona, California, Montana, New Mexico, Oklahoma, and South Dakota) and in North Carolina.

Table 10.9 shows the distributions of Indian pupils, age six to eighteen, among various types of schools as of 1972. These figures show that about 80 percent of the six to eighteen age group were enrolled in school. There are four categories or types of schools. Except for the first category, these figures are not official and there are no official data on the numbers of students, but they can be estimated with reasonable accuracy.

Thus, the educational picture is very complicated. But one thing should be clear. Practically all native Americans between the ages of six and seventeen have access to schools and attend schools almost as fully, in terms of proportions attending school by age, as do the Anglos, the Spanish descent groups, and the blacks. The proportion of Indians who graduate from high school is smaller than the proportion of all American students, but this is more a matter of socioeconomic status than of ethnicity, and the proportion of Indians graduating from high school is approximately the same as the proportions of other ethnic groups that have a similar socioeconomic or income composition.

Available data also indicate that the Indian Education Act (IEA) of 1972 has had significant success in improving educational opportunities for Indian Americans. Evaluation of IEA activities dealing with elementary and secondary education concluded that many programs have been effective in responding to students' special needs, and evaluation of the higher education section concluded that it has been effective in improving opportunity for Indians. These evaluations specifically have indicated that much has been accomplished in providing tutoring, bilingual/bicultural education, guidance counseling, basic skills remediation, dropout prevention, and career education for Indians at all levels in the educational system (Ryan 1982).

Contemporary Problems of Indian Education

As seen by most observers, the primary problem of Indian education is that Indian pupils as a group fall well below the national averages on standardized tests of school achievement. This has been true ever since school tests were first given in Indian schools. For example, a nationwide testing program carried on by the BIA in 1951–1954 showed Indian children to be below national norms after the fourth grade. Table 10.4 shows that the 1980 achievement level of American Indians at the secondary level was slightly better than that of black and Hispanic students but substantially below the national average.

This low school achievement is *not* because Indian children are less intelligent than white children. Several studies based on intelligence tests that do not require reading ability show Indian children to be at or slightly above the level of white children. For example, on the Goodenough Draw-a-Man Intelligence Test, a test of mental alertness that does not require language facility, Indian children show about the same level of achievement as white children. The 1,700 Indian children who took this test in 1969 under the auspices of the National Study of American Indian Education showed an average IQ of 101.5, slightly superior to the average of white children (Fuchs and Havighurst 1972).

The problem of Indian education has a good deal in common with the problems of education of other economically disadvantaged minorities. Many Indian children live in homes and communities where the cultural expectations are different and discontinuous from the expectation held by school teachers and school authorities. Although there are exceptions, the average Indian family teaches its children many valuable attitudes and skills, but it is not effective in teaching them the skills of school-learning.

Early in the decade of the 1970s, the federal government provided funds to help native Americans reform and direct their educational systems. The Indian Education Act of 1972 and its successor, the Indian Self-Determination and Educational Assistance Act of 1975, provide money and require Indian direction and Indian responsibility for the design of programs. The Bilingual Education Act, part of the Elementary and Secondary Education Act since 1967, provides funds for the employment of teaching staff who speak the local home language in Indian and Eskimo communities.

The Indian community is itself divided on the kind of education it wants for Indian youth, recognizing that this is central to the establishment and maintenance of a viable cultural pluralism. The two extremes of assimilation and separatism each have their proponents.

One of the most important problems with which educators and native American leaders struggle in attempting to improve schools for Indian students is the very high rate of alcoholism and drug abuse among adolescents and young adults. Substance abuse has long been a serious problem among American Indians and has been described as "the primary reason" for Indian students' dropping out of high school and college (Monaghan 1987).

More than forty Indian tribes and bands from across North American have joined together since 1982 to initiate the Four Worlds Development Project, which aims to reduce alcoholism and drug abuse among native American youth by the turn of the century. This project, based largely on community development techniques compatible with traditional Indian values, includes an emphasis on providing children with an improved awareness and understanding of their heritage as native Americans (Monaghan 1987).

The Alaska Native Land Claims and Education

December 18, 1971, marked the most comprehensive and favorable legal settlement of native people's claims to land and its resources yet seen—the Alaska Native Claims Settlement Act. The educational implications and results of this Act have great significance for Alaskan natives and for the question of the viability of a policy of cultural pluralism for Indians.

Here, for the first time, very large economic resources are placed in the hands of native people with very few external controls over the way they use those resources. The United States Congress recognized the right of Alaskan natives to land and mineral resources, restored forty million acres of land to native ownership, and promised to pay $962.5 million for land taken over by the state and federal governments. There are approximately 55,000 Eskimos, Aleuts, and Indians living in Alaska, and another 20,000 living outside of Alaska, and having one-fourth or more Alaska Indian, Aleut, or Eskimo ancestry. As of the date of passage of the Act, there were approximately 76,500 Alaskan natives of all ages entitled to equal shares of the land and money. These people as individuals will not receive large money grants. Over the twenty-year period from 1971 to 1991, most of them will receive less than $1,500 apiece. The valuable thing they receive is 100 shares in one of twelve Native Regional Corporations that take title to the land and that keep for investment purposes 90 percent of the money paid under the Act. Also, the Regional Corporations must distribute almost half of their income to some 200 native villages, which form corporations to select land, possibly invest money, or use money income to provide services to village residents.

The Regional Corporations were formed as quickly as possible after the passage of the Act and used the approximately $200 million they received from the government in the first five years to invest in productive enterprises—such as hotels, supermarkets, mineral exploration, reindeer herds, and fish canneries.

The stock in the Regional Corporations cannot be sold in the market until 1991, twenty years after the passage of the Act. At that time, the youngest stock holder will be twenty years old (having been born on or before the day of the passage of the Act by Congress). The money value of the stock will then depend on the investment experience of the corporations, just as it does for any other business corporation. Since every Indian, Aleut, and Eskimo in Alaska has become a capitalist by virtue of the Act, there will be a need to understand this complicated process. One educational consequence has been the publication of a high-school textbook, *Alaska Native Land Claims*, by economist-educator Robert D. Arnold, sponsored by the Alaska Native Foundation.

Educational effects of the Act have included the training of employees of the Regional and Village Corporations and in the Corporations' selection of officers who have some business or technological experience or training. Several vocational schools have come into existence—such as the school at Barrow, farthest north settlement in the United States and capital city of the Arctic Slope Regional Corporation. Furthermore, an Eskimo university, Inupiaq University, was founded at Barrow, to serve as a kind of community college, with representatives in a dozen villages on the Arctic Slope, and with courses taken by correspondence for those who could not get to a class.

Informed opinion is divided concerning the cultural and educational consequences of the Land Claims Settlement. Some say that this inevitably means the assimilation of the Alaska native people into the economic and cultural mainstream. Others say that the Eskimo culture, with its emphasis on community action and cooperation, will be active in the form of a cooperative society culture, and that the Eskimo language will be kept alive in the villages, which will not grow very much because life in them requires hunting, fishing, and adjustment to the arctic climate, a life-style that few Anglos will choose.

Rural Appalachian Students

Although not conventionally considered a minority group, rural students in Appalachia (and other economically debilitated rural communities in the Ozarks and elsewhere) can be viewed as a disadvantaged minority group in the sense that their social environment is isolated from mainstream society and helps generate poor performance in the education system.

Many rural students in Appalachia are the descendants of Anglo-Saxon and Scotch-Irish pioneer families that settled in mountainous or hilly parts of the region in the eighteenth and nineteenth centuries (Keefe, Reck, and Reck 1983). Like other racial-ethnic minority groups discussed in this chapter, their performance in school has been hampered by language and/or dialect differences as well as by other cultural patterns that led to their being defined as distinctively outside the larger society. Thus, "Appalachian children who do best in school are those most alienated from their cultural roots and identity" (Keefe, Reck, and Reck 1983, 215). Some observers view Appalachian students' relative lack of success in school and in the economy as arising from an internal colonialism that made Appalachians simultaneously ashamed of their cultural heritage and also intent on maintaining it in the face of mainstream values and expectations encountered outside their families and immediate community (Lewis, Kobak, and Johnson 1978).

Keefe, Reck, and Reck (1983) have reviewed the limited data available on ethnic background and its interaction with other factors in the lives of rural Appalachian students and concluded that cultural considerations related to ethnicity combine with socioeconomic and demographic characteristics in hampering their progress in traditional educational settings. For example, cultural patterns stressing resistance to authority, sex-segregation, and suspicion of modern life that are reinforced by poverty and rural location place Appalachian students at a severe disadvantage in the typical classroom. One overall conclusion is that "it is the powerful combination of Appalachian ethnicity, lower class status, and rural residence which seems to ensure that students drop out" (p. 218).

A number of educators and social scientists who work with Appalachian schools and communities have been trying to identify ways in which teachers can adapt curriculum and instruction constructively in accordance with the cultural and social background of rural Appalachian students. David Mielke (1978), for example, has edited a volume to help teachers modify commercial materials and traditional classroom practices in an effort to take account of Appalachian culture and circumstances. Also, the well-known *Foxfire* approach (Wiggington 1986) has been designed to use oral history and other local cultural materials to help improve students' motivation and understanding. In addition, possibilities exist for matching instruction with students' learning styles, initiating cooperative learning techniques, and using other interventions discussed elsewhere in this chapter and in Chapter 8.

The Looming Crisis in Employment of Minority Teachers

As documented in Chapter 1 and elsewhere in this book, the minority population of the United States and its public school system is increasing rapidly and is expected to continue increasing for the foreseeable future. At the same time, however, an alarming decline has been occurring in the percentage of minority teachers in the nation's teaching force.

The percentage of black enrollment in the public schools is expected to rise to about 16 percent in 1990, but the percentage of black public-school teachers has declined from 8 percent throughout the 1970s to 7 percent in 1986 and is projected to fall even more in the future (Gifford 1986; Graham 1987; Office of Educational Research 1988). The situation is similar for Hispanic students and teachers, thus raising serious questions regarding the availability of positive role models for black and Hispanic students.

Major reasons for the declining percentage of minority teachers include the following:

1. As discussed earlier in this chapter, college-attendance rates for black students have declined in the 1980s.
2. Opportunities for minority students and for women have expanded in such fields as business, law, natural sciences, and engineering, thus reducing the percentage of black students preparing to be teachers.
3. The growing movement to use standardized tests in selecting candidates for teacher education and in licensing both new and currently employed teachers has had a disproportionate impact in terms of eliminating minority candidates.

The latter development—widespread testing for teacher education and for employment in teaching—appears to have had a particularly negative impact in terms of reducing the percentage of minority teachers in the teaching force. Available data on passing rates for licensing a new teacher indicate, for example, that only 41 percent of black candidates and 36 percent of Hispanic candidates passed Arizona's test for new teachers in 1983, compared with 70 percent for whites. Similar patterns have been reported in Alabama, California, Connecticut, Florida, Georgia, Louisiana, Mississippi, New Mexico, Oklahoma, Texas, and other states. In Louisiana, state institutions have been producing only 55 certified black teachers per year since the initiation of teacher competency testing, and Florida certified only about 200 new black teachers in 1981, among an overall total of 5,500 new teachers receiving certificates (Smith 1986).

Bernard Gifford (1986), Patricia Graham (1987), G. Pritchy Smith (1986), and others have provided analyses of the developing crisis in preparation and employment of minority teachers and its implications for all levels of education. These four suggestions are among the actions identified as constituting positive and perhaps necessary responses to the problem:

1. Improve the academic achievement of minority students in elementary and secondary schools, in order to increase the percentage entering college and the likelihood that they will pass tests for new or prospective teachers.
2. Recruit more minority candidates for teacher education, including adults with or without a college degree, and provide sufficient academic and financial assistance to help them succeed in obtaining teaching certificates.

3. Review and modify testing policies and practices, particularly in order to reduce or eliminate cultural inequities in standardized tests used to select candidates for teacher education and new teachers.
4. Ensure that teacher salaries and other aspects of employment are sufficiently attractive to recruit minority candidates who have expanded opportunities in other fields.

Learning Styles of Minority Students

There is reason to believe that adapting instruction to the cultural background of students—particularly disadvantaged minority students—can help improve their performance in school. As we point out in Chapter 8, disadvantaged black students may benefit by considering what some observers perceive to be an unusually high activity level (Boykin 1978; Gilbert and Gay 1985), and promising opportunities may exist to match students' learning styles with teachers' instructional practices (Hunt 1975). Chapter 9 cites evidence that cooperative learning arrangements may be particularly beneficial for economically disadvantaged black students, and earlier in this chapter we describe the bicognitive theory offered by Ramirez and Castañeda.

Probably the best-known example of adaptation of instruction to recognize the cultural background of minority students is the Kamehamaha Early Educational Program (KEEP) initiated in 1971. Designed to improve reading among disadvantaged Hawaiian students in kindergarten through grade three, KEEP has been refined and modified to include the middle grades. Following unsuccessful initial attempts to teach through phonics, KEEP instruction was redesigned to emphasize comprehension of text, criteria-referenced objectives and questioning, integration of language development and reading instruction, small reading groups, and classroom learning centers. In addition, program personnel developed and introduced the experience-text-relationship method to help students learn to function independently of the teacher by drawing on their cultural experience, language, and personal knowledge (Au and Kawakami 1985).

By 1985, KEEP was being implemented in six schools by nearly seventy teachers working with approximately 1,800 students. Data on the reading performance of KEEP minority students indicate that they have been achieving at about the national average through the third grade, compared with much lower scores for similar students in control classes (Jordan 1984; Au 1985; Steinberg 1988). Program personnel have stated that "there is now good evidence that with two years of in-service training and consultation, most teachers can learn to operate the program effectively so that their Hawaiian pupils achieve at norm levels," and schools can improve the achievement of "at-risk ethnic minority children by training teachers to use methods designed for and suited to the particular student population" (Jordan 1984, 69).

Other promising practices also have been proposed or reported concerning possibilities for adapting instruction in accordance with cultural background.

Regarding the education of native American students, for example, Havighurst (1971a) and Cole (1985) have pointed out that American Indian students are more concerned than Anglo students with peer reactions in the classroom to the extent that Indian children may not respond to a teacher for fear of shaming other children. Similarly, Erickson and Mohatt (1982) have found that Indian students tend to reject being singled out as individuals for public praise or censure and so remain silent when asked to answer questions in the classroom.

Erickson and Mohatt also have proposed classroom rules of participation consisting of a functional blend of traditional U.S. practice and native American discourse styles that they believe will enhance instruction in Indian classrooms. Erickson (1985) subsequently reported on the results of an effort to introduce native teachers in schools for Alaskan village children. Participant observation and videotape analysis indicated that achievement rose "dramatically" after closer rapport was established with parents, and the native teachers

> *organized instruction and interacted with students in ways that were culturally appropriate. Exercise of social control was for the most part very indirect, and the teachers usually avoided public reinforcement—not only avoiding negative reinforcement . . . [but] positive reinforcement as well. These patterns are typical of child-rearing in the community. (Erickson 1985, 55)*

Many educators working with native American children also are attempting to integrate Indian culture into the curriculum. For example, some teachers are teaching the shape of the triangle by comparing it to a tepee, having students read stories with Indian characters, and incorporating symbols from Indian culture into mathematics story problems (NWREL 1987).

Related observations also have been offered regarding other ethnic groups. Kim (1977), for example, has pointed out that Korean children are taught at home not to be "overtly expressive with their emotions, feeling and thoughts" and consequently "find it extremely difficult to express them in American classrooms. They would consider it rather rude to challenge a teacher by asking questions" (p. 16). Cultural characteristics of this kind can lead to failure if teachers are not familiar with their origins and meaning.

Pluralistic education that recognizes cultural differences among racial and ethnic minorities will not be easy to implement. Relatively little is known about how teachers can adapt instruction to such differences. Above all, it is not at all clear how the schools can respond to cultural differences without further segregating or isolating students of a given minority group. Conversely, working out methods and approaches to give minority youth a chance to participate in the larger culture while helping them maintain ethnic pride and identity will require an extraordinary effort on the part of U.S. educators and public officials.

Constructive Cultural Pluralism in Education

This chapter documents the cultural diversity of ethnic and racial and socioeconomic groups in the United States. The American society is pluralistic. Pluralism is democratic if it succeeds in providing equal rights and equal opportunity for the variegated cultural groups that make up the society.

The democratic goal of fair shares needs to be combined with the right of each subgroup to refuse to assimilate itself in the mainstream of economic and cultural life. This combination is constructive cultural pluralism. It respects the right of a cultural subgroup to hold itself aloof from the rest of the society even if this means giving up some of the advantages of full participation in the economic and social mainstream.

The critical areas of life for the success of cultural pluralism during the remainder of this century are the labor force and the educational areas. Economic opportunity must be increased for the economically disadvantaged groups in the society, especially blacks, Hispanics, and American Indians. These groups will work through political activity to enhance their access to jobs and to welfare benefits. At the same time, they will seek better education and more education to give them access to better jobs.

Education and Constructive Pluralism

The educational system in the United States inevitably reflects a degree of pluralism in its structure of private and public schools and colleges and in its teaching of history and social studies. However, there has been serious criticism of the lack of accuracy of textbook presentations of the history and status of minority cultures. Also, during the period of melting-pot dominance of public educational policy, there was a tendency through the public schools to encourage Americanization to an extent that discouraged pluralism. Minority-group students who were successful in school achievement as measured by promotion in school and high school and college graduation were rewarded by upward socioeconomic mobility to jobs and income well above the level attained by their fathers. But a large proportion of minority-group pupils did not succeed very well in school work and tended to remain at the lower or upper working-class levels in which their fathers were located.

Constructive pluralism faces the major problem of working through education to help minority-group members retain their identity and their pride in cultural group membership, and at the same time to increase the socioeconomic status of the economically disadvantaged minority groups (Banks 1988). Helping minority children retain a positive identity may be achieved to some degree through the schools by working to ensure that instruction reflects their racial or ethnic heritage and does not require them to reject their background in order to succeed. As we discuss in this chapter, it is possible that bilingual/bicultural education will help achieve this goal for some groups. However, it is far from certain that minority group members will retain an ethnic identity as they improve their social status except in communities or regions of the United States where they participate in almost a separate culture, as among Mexican Americans in some parts of the Southwest or Eskimos in Alaska.

The goal of improving academic performance and thereby promoting socioeconomic mobility among economically disadvantaged minority students probably will not be accomplished solely through bilingual/bicultural or similar approaches. At present there is little solid evidence suggesting that transitional approaches for teaching low-status black students in Black English or teaching non– or limited-English-speaking students in their native language are sufficient to improve their academic performance very much. Rather, the major changes needed to improve the performance of low-status students of whatever group include those outlined in Chapters 8 and 9—namely, early intervention to improve their preparation for school together with desegregation and reform of the school to improve its effectiveness with low-achieving students.

Constructive educational pluralism as described in this chapter is similar to a concept that Nicholas Appleton refers to as the "new pluralism" in an important treatise titled *Cultural Pluralism in Education* (1983). Appleton describes this approach as one in which schools and government agencies should acknowledge the relevance of ethnicity but should not

> *actively promote or reinforce ethnic associations. . . . Individuals [should] determine for themselves to what extent they wish to remain as members of a group and partake of its cultural offerings. . . . Schools would play an important part in this process by teaching students to respect and tolerate diversity; to develop understanding of their own ethnicity, as well as alternate life styles, values, and beliefs; and to decide for themselves how they wish to assert or accept their ethnicity or if they should do so. (Appleton 1983, 92)*

Appleton also proceeds to point out that pluralism in education should not be viewed as requiring exactly the same mixture of policies and practices in all communities or for all students. This means that how schools should respond to learning style differences, how and how much they should stress multi-ethnic curriculum and intergroup-relations activities, what stress should be placed on desegregation and how it should be advanced, and other educational responses to other issues involving cultural pluralism in education necessarily will vary in their development and application depending on local and temporal circumstances. "It should be evident," he concludes, that the "contextual variables" in Puerto Rico differ radically from those in San Francisco, that settings for native Americans in urban areas differ from those for native Americans on reservations, and that the problems of urban blacks are not exactly the same as those of Mexican Americans: "If the spirit of pluralism is to be followed, we should expect to develop not one national model, but a number of regional and local models that meet the needs of various groups" (Appleton 1983, 153). But however policies and practices differ with community context, he further concludes, pluralistic multicultural education should follow a general set of guiding principles that include the following eight ideas (1983, 208–217):

1. Interethnic hostility and conflict should be defused and depolarized.
2. Implementation should be treated as a long-range process.

3. Multicultural concepts and perspectives should be incorporated in the total curriculum.
4. Changes should be produced not just in the curriculum but in teaching methods and classroom social structure.
5. Emphasis should be on affective as well as cognitive aims of education.
6. Teaching approaches and materials should be sensitive to students' background and experiences.
7. Parental involvement in education of their children should be increased.
8. Students should gain a better understanding of such issues as racism, sexism, and social class inequality.

Conclusion

We see in this chapter that in the United States, blacks have made substantial progress toward equality as regards mobility in the economic system and attainment in the educational system. Thus, the Black Revolution of the 1960s and 1970s has had some impact in improving opportunity for many members of the nation's largest minority group. However, gains that have been made frequently are precarious and are not sufficiently widespread to ensure continuing positive developments in the future. Economic gains signify the development of a substantial black middle class, but many blacks are locked into a destructive underclass environment.

The growing Hispanic minority is in much the same position educationally as is the black minority. A relatively large percentage of its Mexican-American and Puerto Rican members are working class, and many are segregated in concentrated poverty schools and neighborhoods in much the same way as are blacks. In addition to disadvantages associated with socioeconomic background, many low-status Hispanic students also experience problems related to linguistic and cultural discrepancies between the school and the home. It is logical to believe that bilingual/bicultural education and other approaches that take these cultural differences into account may help Hispanic students succeed in school and society, but relatively little is known concerning the approaches that might be most effective or how to implement them in the public schools.

In general, many Hispanic youngsters are likely to experience considerable strain between their ethnic and national cultures. Underlying this situation is the paramount need to provide effective education for low-status Hispanic students without isolating them in segregated bilingual programs but also without ignoring their needs as members of a culturally different ethnic minority. This dilemma is similar to that faced by blacks, American Indians, and other minority groups in trying to build viable communities as a base for productive participation in the larger society. In trying to do this, minorities face the problem of deciding how to combine emphasis on separate group identity with stress on individual and group participation in a society composed of a variety of competing and cooperating groups.

Cultural pluralism in the United States is now at a point at which it can be used constructively to make a great improvement in intergroup relations in this country and at the same time to increase the economic and civic opportunity of the minority groups with lowest socioeconomic status. Movement in this direction will require careful educational planning, particularly in the large cities. What is needed is a complex system of pluralism adapted to each of a variety of subcultures and maintaining a strong opportunity structure that facilitates economic success for members of low-income groups.

The ultimate goal of constructive pluralism in schools and society should be to nurture and draw on the talents and distinctive contributions of all groups in the nation while also ensuring that opportunities to participate are equitable and common interests and goals are developed and addressed through participation in desegregated environments.

EXERCISES

1. Write a paper that either supports or opposes a program of bilingual education aimed to assist the children of a particular non–English-speaking minority. What are the advantages and disadvantages?
2. Collect information on a bilingual program in a nearby school district. Is it primarily a transitional or a maintenance program? What criteria can be applied in making this determination? How do local administrators and teachers classify the program?
3. What ethnic groups besides the Hispanic minority are included in nearby bilingual programs? What other ethnic groups are included nationally? Consult local or federal government sources to obtain additional information on the variety of ethnic groups for which bilingual education programs are being offered.
4. *Hunger of Memory* by Richard Rodriguez describes his early years in a Spanish-speaking home in California and the personal uncertainties he experienced later in becoming an intellectual. Rodriguez has said he hopes these memoirs "can serve as preface to future deliberations" about policy in bilingual education. Read *Hunger of Memory* and discuss its implications for bilingual policy.
5. What are the principal intergroup conflicts (economic, ethnic, religious, or racial) in your community? In your school or college? Interview members of each of the groups in question and obtain their views regarding the ways in which conflict could be alleviated.
6. Write a paper describing your own position on the integration-pluralism-separatism continuum and indicating how you think this area of human relations will develop over the next ten years.
7. Select a particular minority group in which you are interested and write a paper on the treatment of this group in the public schools in your com-

munity. Include a description of the strategy (explicit or implicit) of this group for achieving its goals in the community.

8. If you are a member of a minority ethnic group, describe your own experience in the schools.
9. Andrew Greeley (1980) cites evidence indicating that ethnicity and ethnic culture continue to be important considerations for many white ethnic groups in the United States. Stephen Steinberg summarizes evidence indicating that ethnicity is of declining importance in the lives of white Americans, particularly in comparison with social class influences. To what extent do these two scholars disagree? Which point of view is closer to the truth about ethnicity in United States society today?
10. What progress has been made at local colleges and universities in increasing the enrollment of black students? What are the major obstacles preventing further progress?

SUGGESTIONS FOR FURTHER READING

1. To get some perspective on the extent of democratic pluralism in the United States at various times within the past century, read one of the following: *Up from Slavery*, by Booker T. Washington; *The Americanization of Edward T. Bok*, by Edward T. Bok; *Giants in the Earth*, by Rölvaag; *Twenty Years at Hull House*, by Jane Addams; *The Newcomers*, by Oscar Handlin.
2. Students with an interest in white European ethnic groups will be interested in Michael Novak's book, *The Rise of the Unmeltable Ethnics*, which is a spirited defense of the "hardhat ethnics," who he feels are put down by the middle-class intellectuals.
3. The book by Milton Gordon, *Assimilation in American Life*, gives a good historical and sociological treatment of intergroup relations in the United States.
4. An extensive study of American Indian education is given in the book by Estelle Fuchs and Robert J. Havighurst, *To Live on This Earth: American Indian Education*.
5. A useful treatment of cultural pluralism from the point of view of education is provided in the book *Cultural Pluralism*, edited by Edgar G. Epps. His concluding essay on "Schools and Cultural Pluralism" is especially good for clarification of the issues.
6. James A. Banks's *Teaching Strategies for Ethnic Studies* (1984) and *Multiethnic Education: Theory and Practice* (1988) include materials on concepts, strategies, and materials for teaching students from most of the largest racial and ethnic groups in the United States.
7. The last section of *Philosophy and the American School* by Van Cleve Morris and Young Pai provides a philosophical analysis of cultural pluralism in education.

8. The last five chapters of *American Ethnicity*, by Bahr, Chadwick, and Strauss, review and discuss the history and future of cultural pluralism in the United States.
9. The *Comparative Education Review* regularly includes papers on bilingual education in the United States and other countries.
10. *Educating English-Speaking Hispanics*, edited by Leonard Valverde, Rosa Feinberg, and Esther Marquez, provides information and discussion on a topic that received little explicit attention before 1980.
11. *Clamor at the Gates*, edited by Nathan Glazer, discusses many contemporary aspects of immigration and its implications for the United States. The chapter by Peter Rose, "Asian Americans: From Pariahs to Paragons," is particularly recommended.
12. *The Black Power Imperative* by Theodore Cross concludes with a comprehensive section on "The Shape of a Black Agenda."
13. The entire issue of the *American Journal of Education* for November 1986 is devoted to the education of Hispanic Americans.
14. Nicholas Appleton's thoughtful book *Cultural Pluralism in Education* is well worth reading for its insightful analysis and the breadth of its concepts and documentation.
15. A paper by Sau-ling Wong (1987), "The Language Needs of School-Age Asian Immigrants," provides much excellent material on several topics discussed in this chapter.
16. A paper by Shirley Stennis Williams (1987), "The Politics of the Black Child's Language," provides a useful history and analysis of black English and its implications for education.
17. *The New Black Middle Class* by Bart Landry provides an unusually well written and thought-provoking analysis of data on this important topic.
18. A 1982 paper and a 1978 book by John U. Ogbu provide detailed explanations of the racial (as contrasted with the socioeconomic) disadvantages experienced by low-status blacks in segregated schools and communities.

11

Women and Education

In recent years, people in the United States have experienced a resurgence of interest in feminism unparalleled in scope and fervor since the first major wave of concern for women's rights, which developed concurrently with the abolitionist movement of the nineteenth century. Indeed, now, as before, feminists can trace their changing perceptions of the position of women in society partly to their experience in the civil rights movement.

The first major surge of feminism in the United States occurred in the 1840s, when the movement to abolish black slavery was becoming an important political force. The Woman's Rights Convention held at Seneca Falls, New York, in 1848 passed twelve resolutions that included statements that "woman is man's equal" but has "too long rested satisfied in the circumscribed limits which corrupt customs . . . have marked off for her." The Convention also resolved that "the speedy success of our course depends upon the . . . untiring efforts of both men and women . . . for the securing to women an equal participation with men in the various trades, professions, and commerce." It thus inaugurated a national effort to counteract belief in the inferiority of women and the confinement of women to domestic roles (the "cult of domesticity").

After the Civil War, Elizabeth Cady Stanton, Susan B. Anthony, and other leaders of the feminist movement founded the National Women's Loyal League (1865) and worked to gain support for women's rights—particularly the vote—along with constitutional amendments (13, 14, and 15) designed to enfranchise black Americans. When some leading opponents of slavery refused to support voting rights for women out of fear that this would detract from the movement to help blacks, feminist leaders formed separate groups to improve the status of women (e.g., the National American Woman's Suffrage Association, 1869). Efforts along these lines finally reached fruition with ratification in 1920 of the Nineteenth Amendment, giving voting rights to 26 million women.

However, the vote proved of limited value in improving the status of women in the United States; and after World War II, many women became increasingly dissatisfied with their situation and opportunities. Civil rights and other strains of social activism again served as a spur for the women's movement: as women participated in efforts to eliminate discrimination against blacks or took part in student movements to gain greater control over educational institutions during the 1960s, feminists became sensitive also to inequities between men and women. Betty Friedan's 1963 book *The Feminine Mystique*, which eloquently describes the problems in many women's lives associated with their virtual confinement to home and family roles, marked the emergence to prominence of the modern feminist movement.

Many complex factors come together to affect the contemporary women's movement. One is the increase in level of education of women; another, the changes in concepts of marriage and parenthood, hastened by the development of modern methods of contraception and the increased control over fertility. Changing concepts of sex roles have brought with them an increasing minority of women who no longer look to motherhood as the necessary core of feminine identity (Walsh 1986). Also, there has been an increasing demand for women in the labor force, particularly as the service occupations have expanded. Now, a majority of women work outside the home at one or more periods in their lives, and a growing proportion enter and stay in the work force throughout their adult lives, thereby creating new role models for their daughters.

The women's movement has given rise to a wide range of advocacy positions focusing on a variety of issues, and there has been rapid growth of literature, both scientific and popular, written by, for, and about women. Some feminist organizations have worked primarily for changes in education, in the law, and in the workplace to create more equality of opportunity for women. Others have taken more extreme views, calling for new sex roles and new forms of family organization. The latter groups believe that important changes in the direction of equality between the sexes cannot be accomplished without fundamental changes in society whereby women will be freed from their primary responsibility for childcare.

Despite the wide range of views it has produced, the feminist movement that took shape in the late 1960s focuses overall on the special characteristics and needs of women and the promotion of social, economic, and political changes that will support their development. Most leaders in the feminist movement agree that women occupy a minority status in contemporary society. They also tend to agree that the so-called feminine traits and motivations so widely accepted in the past are due only in small part to underlying biological differences, but instead are due in large part to our socialization practices—that is, to what girls are taught directly or indirectly as they grow up.

Although perhaps the sharpest criticisms are reserved for the socialization experiences that occur within the family, most feminists also see the schools as part of the problem, and they accordingly look to the schools to become part of the solution. It is often alleged, for instance, that most of our educational institutions maintain a division between masculine and feminine subject matter, encouraging women to enter the humanities and certain social sciences, while encouraging men to enter science and technology, the major professions, business, and engineering. Many people believe that this is only one of the ways our formal education system, as it carries out both its socialization and its sorting and selecting functions, helps create what they perceive as the sexist society. Even though such allegations ignore or blur over the very real changes in the education of women that have been occurring over the past century, there is evidence, some of it presented in this chapter, that supports these views in their general outline.

Theodore Lownik Library
Illinois Benedictine College
Lisle, IL 60532

Whatever the speed of social change that lies ahead, and whatever the opinions set forth, the feminist writers and their supporters have clearly succeeded in bringing to public attention a range of issues that have broad implications for educational theory and practice. In turn, educators are looking to the broader social context when they deal with the changing educational needs and demands of women. The latter point is well illustrated in the opening statement of the report by the Carnegie Commission on Higher Education, *Opportunities for Women in Higher Education* (1983, 2):

> *The second most fundamental revolution in the affairs of mankind on earth is now occurring. The first came when man settled down from hunting, fishing, herding, and gathering to sedentary agricultural and village life. The second is now occurring as women, no longer so concentrated on and sheltered for their childbearing and childrearing functions, are demanding equality of treatment in all aspects of life, are demanding a new sense of purpose.*

The Work Roles of Women

Women who devote their time to homemaking and mothering are workers, no less than women who work outside the home. Yet the terms *women workers* or *women in the labor force* have come to refer only to the latter group, those who work outside the home for remuneration. For the sake of convenience only, we shall use the terms in the ways that have become customary.

Fifty years ago, one out of five persons in the labor force was a woman; now, it is more than two of five. The woman of today as compared to her mother or grandmother has many more years of life when she is free from the responsibilities of childcare. On the average, mothers are now in their midthirties when they see their last child off to school, and they then have more than forty years ahead of them, or more than half their lives. Increasingly, they use their time to work outside the home. Studies conducted by the U.S. Department of Labor indicate that nine out of ten women are in the labor force at one or more times in their lives, although whether a given woman will be working outside the home in any given year depends on her age, level of education, racial or ethnic background, marital status, age of her children, and, if she is married, her husband's income. In the year 1987, of all women between sixteen and sixty-five, nearly two-thirds were in the labor force.

Not only the numbers but also the characteristics of women workers have changed dramatically. For one thing, in addition to single women, it is now married women, and women with children, who are working outside the home. In 1940, one out of ten mothers in the United States was in the labor force; in 1980, it was five out of ten. Although the presence of young children in the family has an important effect on whether the mother works, approximately one-third of all working mothers have children under the age of six.

The ages at which women are most likely to be working have also changed. If we look at the composition of the labor force in 1920 and compare it with 1987, then at both periods women were most apt to be working when they were age twenty to twenty-four. But then the patterns diverge. In 1920, only a small percentage of women age forty-five to fifty-four were employed, whereas in

1987, it was nearly two-thirds of this group. Today, middle-aged women are working in proportions nearly as high as younger women.

All this means that increasing millions of women have chosen to marry, raise children *and* work, and to work at more than one time in their lives. This change is part of what Neugarten and Neugarten (1987) call the "fluid life cycle" and describe as follows:

> *Adults of all ages are experiencing changes in the traditional rhythm and timing of events of the life cycle. More men and women marry, divorce, remarry and divorce again up through their seventies. More stay single. More women have their first child before they are fifteen, and more do so after thirty-five. The result is that people are becoming grandparents for the first time at ages ranging from thirty-five to seventy-five. More women, but also increasing numbers of men, raise children in two-parent, then one-parent, then two-parent households. More women, but also increasing numbers of men, exit and reenter school, enter and reenter the work force and undertake second and third careers up through their seventies. It therefore becomes difficult to distinguish the young, the middle-aged and the young-old. (Neugarten and Neugarten 1987, 30)*

New Family Patterns

In addition to changes in timing and increased fluidity, significant numbers of women coming to maturity are moving away from traditional family patterns in other ways. New forms of the family unit include the couple who live together without marriage, the husband and wife who have had previous marriages, the couple who choose to remain childless, the never-married or divorced parent raising children alone, and the communal family group. It is true that about 80 percent of all families in 1987 were husband-wife families, and only a fraction of all couples had been identified as living together and maintaining a quasi-familial relationship outside marriage. Still, the percentage of female-headed households has increased substantially (see Chapter 4). In addition, the number of women living alone increased rapidly during the 1970s and early 1980s, reflecting the increasing numbers of women who postpone marriage, the increasing divorce rate, especially for first marriages, and the increasing numbers of older widowed women who live alone.

We cannot yet assess the long-term effects of the women's movement, of improved methods of family planning, of changes in the education of women, or of changing economic conditions and work patterns as these factors affect the family cycle. This assessment is difficult because social change seems to be affecting younger women more than older and because we cannot predict the eventual patterns for women who are presently young. Nevertheless, it is clear that more women of all ages are spending more and more time in work roles and in community roles that lie outside the traditional roles of mother and

Table 11.1 *Change in Percentage of Women Twenty-Five to Thirty-Four Years of Age in the Labor Force, by Educational Level, 1960 to 1980*

	1960	1970	1980
Less than high school graduation	33	39	49
Four years of high school	34	44	62
One to three years of college	36	46	70
Four years of college	42	53	75
Five or more years of college	59	71	80

Source: Bianchi and Spain 1986.

homemaker. Only about 10 percent of adult women are now nonemployed housewives with children at home (Russell 1985).

The major reasons that women work, whether they are married or not, whether they are mothers or not, whether they are young or middle-aged, are economic reasons (just as is true for men). It is significant that the greatest growth in women workers in the past few years has taken place among well-educated wives from families with incomes that are moderate but insufficient to maintain the desired pattern of consumption. Before World War II, married women workers came almost exclusively from low-income families, but this picture has changed so that by now it is about as likely for a middle-class wife to be employed as for a working-class wife.

There is a direct relationship, furthermore, between women's levels of education and their levels of employment. The more education a woman has, the more likely she is to be in the labor force, as shown in Table 11.1. The table refers to all women as a group, but the same general trends are present if the data are broken down for different age groups. Whether women are in their twenties or in their fifties, it is still true that the more education they have, the more likely they will be working outside the home.

The latter finding, as well as findings from other studies of why women work, make it clear that reasons other than economic also propel women into the labor force. Especially at higher educational levels, women work for intellectual and social stimulation, for opportunities for service, for self-development, and because they find the work intrinsically satisfying and rewarding. More than 70 percent of the United States population approves of a married woman working even if her earnings are not required to support her family (Cherlin and Walters 1981).

It is similarly true, of course, that there are other than economic reasons that propel women into higher education. Women seek education for self-enrichment, to become better wives and mothers, to contribute to community betterment—in short, not only for its value in the marketplace, but also for its value in enhancing the quality of life.

Table 11.2 ***Women as Percentage of All Workers, by Occupation Group, 1985***

Occupation Group	Percentage
Total	44
Professional and managerial	43
Technical, sales, and administrative support	65
Craft	08
Operators, fabricators, and laborers	25
Service	61
Farming, forestry, and fishing	16

Source: Statistical Abstract of the United States, 1987.

Occupational Status

Table 11.2 indicates what percentage of all workers in each occupational group in 1980 were women. Table 11.3 shows the changing proportions of women in various occupational categories since 1950. Although the overall proportion of women workers has increased substantially, a few major occupational groups still have a concentration of women. Well over half of all women were working in relatively low-paying clerical, operative, or service positions in 1979 (see Table 1.1). In fact, a higher proportion of employed women were clerical or service workers in 1979 than in 1910.

It is worth taking a closer look at the professional-managerial category, since it includes occupations that are closely tied to higher education and are frequently used as the barometer of the status of women workers. As suggested in Table 11.3, the large majority of women in the professional and managerial category are employed in the normally lower-paying occupations within the category—for example, as registered nurses and as elementary and secondary schoolteachers. Women have made substantial inroads in some specific occu-

Table 11.3 ***Women in Selected Professional and Managerial Occupations***

Occupation	Percentage of All Workers in Occupation			
	1950	*1970*	*1980*	*1985*
Accountants	15	25	36	44
Engineers	1	2	4	7
Lawyers, judges	4	5	13	18
Physicians, osteopaths	7	9	14	17
Registered nurses	98	97	96	95
Teachers	75	70	71	73
College faculty	23	28	34	35

Sources: U.S. Bureau of Labor Statistics 1977, 1982; *Statistical Abstract of the United States, 1987.*

pations; for example, as accountants, lawyers, physicians, bank officials, sales managers. Two occupations that remain heavily male are engineering and architecture.

Women's employment patterns described here do not as yet fully reflect the impact of the educational changes occurring in recent years. The proportions of women now entering medical, law, or business school, and the numbers being awarded degrees in such fields as the physical sciences and mathematics have been increasing. Similarly, data on the career choices of entering college freshmen show that women are increasingly choosing to enter the fields traditionally regarded as men's fields (Lyson 1981; Hafner 1985). Thus, the occupational distribution of men and women is shifting markedly, as younger women—those who are probably being most affected by the feminist movement—finish their schooling and move into the labor force.

But just as is true of predictions regarding rates of marriage and childbearing, it is too soon to assess fully the effects of the women's movement as it interacts with other social and economic factors in influencing the work lives of women. It can be said with certainty, however, that insofar as work decisions are governed by educational preparation, women will no longer be handicapped to the extent they have been in past years.

The Earnings Gap

In spite of a relatively optimistic outlook for women who will be working in the future, at the present time women workers make much less money than men do. The gap widened somewhat during the 1970s, even in the midst of feminist activity, so that fully employed women earn only about seventy for every one hundred dollars earned by fully employed men (Goldin 1985). A woman with a college degree on the average earns less than a man who is a high school dropout.

It is not clear to what extent the earnings gap between women and men reflects discrimination, and to what extent it reflects other factors—for instance, that in many occupations, women work more sporadically than men and therefore accumulate less seniority (Lloyd and Niemi 1979). The gap is present, however, even among women and men with the same amount of education, and it exists in every major occupational group. Women fare best in professional and technical occupations and worst in sales, where their earnings are less than half of men's (Waite 1981; Schwartz 1988).

Careful studies indicate that the earnings gap between women and men is closely associated with the segregation and concentration of women in less skilled, low-paying, dead-end jobs—that is, after differences in age, education, race, residence, experience, unionization, turnover, absenteeism, hours worked, and so on, are all taken into account (Bridgman 1986). The fact that women are concentrated in low-paying jobs appears to be partly a product of discrimination, both institutional and individual (U.S. Commission on Civil Rights 1982; Bergmann 1986). Institutional discrimination includes recruitment policies and informal networks of hiring and advancement. Discrimination by individuals—who discriminates (personnel officers, managers, others) and why (because of personal preference, assumptions about female turnover rates, or other reasons)—is difficult to assess, but it undoubtedly plays a role, also.

At the same time, the fact that women are concentrated in low-paying jobs is voluntary in part, at least insofar as traditional socialization patterns have led women to set low levels of aspiration for themselves as workers (Corcoran and Courant 1985). Thus, motivational factors constitute another important factor in understanding why large numbers of women fail to move up the occupational ladder. As women become educated for and move into higher-level occupations, and particularly as they begin to think in terms of careers, building up consistent and strong attachment to work in a single or related occupation over long time periods, their earnings vis-à-vis men's should change for the better.

A factor that has great potential for improving the status of women workers is the antidiscrimination legislation enacted by Congress in recent years. An important example is the Equal Pay Act of 1963, which provides that where equal skill, effort, and responsibility are required to perform jobs under similar working conditions, an employer may not discriminate in wage payments on the basis of sex. This Act was extended in 1972 to cover executive, administrative, and professional workers, as well as outside sales persons. Another example is Title VII of the Civil Rights Act of 1964, which prohibits discrimination in employment based on sex, among other characteristics; and a 1972 amendment, which extends coverage to state and local government agencies and public and private schools. In addition, in 1967 Presidential Executive Order 11246, which had earlier established a policy of nondiscrimination in government employment, was amended by the addition of sex as a prohibited type of discrimination. At present, all firms doing business with the government are required to prepare and use affirmative action plans for increasing the representation of women in job categories in which they are underrepresented. Finally, Title IX of the Education Amendments of 1972 forbids sex discrimination in employment in any education program or activity receiving federal financial assistance.

Sex Differences in Achievement and Ability

Overall sex differences in achievement and attainment appear to be diminishing, but there is considerable controversy concerning the degree to which differences in specific subjects such as mathematics may be due to differences in biological functioning as contrasted with socialization and sex-role stereotyping.

Differences in Achievement

Cross-national studies providing data on educational achievement show that males have had higher overall achievement and have attained more years of

Table 11.4 ***1984 Reading Proficiency Scores, by Age and Sex, and 1982 High School Seniors' Mathematics Scores, by Sex***

	Mathematics		Reading Proficiency		
	Basic Skills	*Problems Solving*	*Age 9*	*Age 13*	*Age 17*
Female	11.7	2.9	216	262	293
Male	13.0	3.3	210	254	283

Note: Mathematics scores are 1982 averages for high-school seniors in the High School and Beyond Study. Reading proficiency scores are 1984 averages for students in the National Assessment of Educational Progress.

Sources: National Assessment of Educational Progress (NAEP) 1985; National Center for Educational Statistics 1985.

schooling than have females. For example, Finn, Dulberg, and Reis (1979) surveyed the research in this area and concluded that "on a global basis, the deficiencies in the educational achievement of women are obvious. According to 1970 figures, an estimated 34.2 percent of the world's population is illiterate: 28.0 percent of the male population and 40.3 percent of the female population" (p. 496).

Among the best sources of United States data on school achievement by sex are the surveys and reports prepared by the National Assessment of Educational Progress (NAEP). Recent reports released by the NAEP (1981a; 1985) provide data on reading achievement by sex and age from four national surveys conducted in 1971, 1975, 1980 and 1984, respectively. These assessments indicated that females have slightly higher reading achievement than do males at all three ages (see Table 11.4).

The NAEP reports also show that mathematics achievement of United States males differs very little from that of females at ages nine and thirteen, but that males have slightly higher scores than do females at age seventeen. As have several other large-scale studies, the NAEP surveys concluded that by age seventeen, males score significantly higher than do females on higher-order cognitive skills in mathematics, though females score nearly as high in computation and other lower-order skills (see Table 11.4).

A special survey conducted by the Education Commission of the States also was noteworthy in finding no large sex differences in participation in mathematics courses (Armstrong 1985). No difference by sex was found with respect to Algebra I and Geometry. Though a higher percentage of males than females took Algebra II, Probability/Statistics, Trigonometry, Pre-Calculus, and Calculus, these differences were small and, in the latter three subjects, were nonsignificant.

Similarly, research indicates that girls participate in mathematics at the middle-school level as much as do boys (Lockheed et al. 1985), and data from the National Longitudinal Study of high school seniors graduating in 1980 show that the percentage of females taking two or more years of mathematics in high school is nearly as high as the comparable percentage among males (Peng, Fetters, and Kolstad 1981). Thus, it appears that female enrollment in mathematics courses has increased in recent decades. There probably still are many schools and school districts in which female participation in mathematics is substantially less than male participation, but this is no longer a pervasive national pattern as in earlier periods.

However, mathematics achievement and participation among women continue to involve important problems in that females are still much less likely than males to take advanced math courses in high school and college (Chipman, Brush, and Wilson 1985) and thereafter less likely to choose and enter careers in engineering, physics, and other fields that depend on math. This pattern not only represents a diversion of women (compared with men) from relatively well-paid to relatively low-pay occupations, but also functions to restrict development of the nation's pool of scientific talent and skill.

Research indicates that remaining sex differences in mathematics performance and careers are due to the complex and poorly understood interaction of variables involving motivation and attitudes toward math and science, previous performance, exposure to learning opportunities, socialization and sexual stereotyping, verbal and quantitative abilities, and other factors (Fennema 1982; Chipman, Brush, and Wilson 1985; Ethington and Wolfle 1986). Motivational and attitudinal considerations include greater math anxiety among females than among males, lower expectations for females on the part of teachers, and girls' perceptions that math is relatively unimportant for their future careers (Tobias and Weissbrod 1980; Wigfield and Meece 1988). Summarizing the meaning of some of these research findings, Chipman and Wilson (1985) pointed out that implications go beyond the problem of improving math opportunities for girls and women:

> *Poor preparation in mathematics is not just a problem of women: many believe that it is a very general problem in the United States today. . . . Most students know only that mathematics is required to enter the career they desire, not why it is required or how it will be used. . . . There are indications that something about the style of teaching or classroom interaction in high school mathematics may be unattractive to students. Lecturing, with low student involvement, appears to be more common in mathematics classes. . . . In addition, student confidence in ability to learn mathematics declines in high school. Thus, many of the changes that seem to be needed to improve opportunities for female students actually seem to be needed for all students. (Chipman and Wilson 1985, 325)*

Differences in Ability

Regarding general academic ability, sex differences are nonexistent or inconsequential. Stated differently, males and females differ little or not at all in total IQ scores (Feingold 1988). This conclusion is not surprising inasmuch as IQ tests are deliberately constructed so as to eliminate sex differences (Stockard 1980).

Most recent controversy concerning possible sex differences in ability has centered on whether a higher percentage of males than females have very high aptitude in mathematics or in higher-order cognitive skills in general. A widely cited comprehensive review of research on sex differences (Maccoby and Jacklin 1974) indicated that there is more variability in ability among males than females: males are more likely than females to be either very low or very high in ability. Several later reviews of research have concluded that there probably is a greater percentage of mental "defectives" among males than females, and that this pattern may occur because young boys are more vulnerable to serious disease and other physical problems than are girls (Sherman 1977; Featherstone 1988). In addition, some research indicates that males have higher scores than females on tests of spatial ability (Bock and Moore 1986; Hannay and Levin 1987) and that these differences are related to males' higher scores in mathematics (Halpern 1986).

As regards the possibility that more males than females may have very high intellectual ability, most support for this position in recent years has been provided in longitudinal analysis of SAT mathematics scores (Feingold 1988) and in the Study of Mathematically Precocious Youth (SMPY) conducted at Johns Hopkins University. Data on the SMPY indicate that among more than 10,000 seventh- and eighth-graders who scored higher than 660 on the mathematics section of the Scholastic Aptitude Test, the ratio of boys to girls was approximately fourteen to one (Benbow and Stanley 1980). Males and females in the study were approximately equal in verbal ability. Partly because males and females in those grades generally have had similar participation in mathematics instruction, the authors concluded that there is a substantial difference in the percentages of males and females who are high in mathematical reasoning ability. After reporting that students' attitudes toward math and its importance were related to their achievement but not their ability scores, the researchers summarized their conclusions:

> *We favor the hypothesis that sex differences in achievement in and attitude toward mathematics result from superior male mathematical ability, which may in turn be related to greater male ability in spatial tasks. This male superiority is probably an expression of both endogenous and exogenous variables. We recognize, however, that our data are consistent with numerous alternative hypotheses. (Benbow and Stanley 1980, 1264)*

Some other researchers, however, have disputed the conclusion that the SMPY patterns probably are due to biologically rooted sex differences. Pointing to differences in socialization and expectations for boys and girls other than differential participation in classroom mathematics instruction, they believe that factors such as greater opportunity to engage in active manipulation of concepts among males than females may account for differences found in the Hopkins data (Kolata 1980; Pallas and Alexander 1983).

Possible Biological Causes of Ability Differences

A number of psychobiological causes have been proposed to account for possible sex differences favoring females in verbal ability or achievement and favoring males in spatial ability or mathematics ability and achievement. Sherman (1977) examined several possible causes, including (1) hereditary differences linked to the X-chromosome, (2) sex differences in serum uric acid (the "gout" hypothesis), (3) hormone differences, and (4) differences in brain lateralization and cerebral organization (e.g., specialization in left- and right-hemisphere functioning). It should be noted that causes grouped under these headings are not necessarily exclusive. For example, differences in brain lateralization may be due to hormonal influences, and both may be generated by the X-chromosome.

After examining each explanation in some detail, Sherman concluded that the only one that has solid research support involves sex differences in brain lateralization. Among right-handed persons, females appear to handle spatial functions more with the left hemisphere (relative to males), whereas males show less hemispheric specialization. There is also some evidence that females may "have more right hemisphere involvement in verbal function," as compared with males. It is "a very viable hypothesis," she concluded, that "more females than males may be oververbalized and lean too heavily on left-hemisphere, verbal analytic functioning to solve tasks that would benefit from more right hemispheric participation. . . . [This preference] may have a biological basis in the earlier development . . . of linguistic facility and left-hemisphere dominance for verbal function in women . . . [and in] later maturation that may favor right hemisphere development" in males (Sherman 1977, 181–182).

Anne Petersen (1980) also has reviewed the research on biological processes and sex differences in ability, with specific attention to the role that hormones may play with regard to brain functioning. Her general conclusion is somewhat similar to Sherman's:

> *The manifestation of genetic potentials may also require certain moderate levels of androgen influence (or perhaps the appropriate ratio of androgen to estrogen or some other endocrine mechanism). These sexually-differential levels may be important at the so-called critical period of development (prenatal in humans) to function in brain organization, hemispheric lateralization, and perhaps prefrontal development. . . . Brain organization may in turn serve to extend cognitive differences to verbal-versus-spatial skills. . . . The appearance at adolescence of sex differences in these skills may be caused by increased sexually differential socialization at this time and/or by the activational influences of hormones at puberty, perhaps on the termination of brain lateralization. (Petersen 1980, 45)*

Research on hormones and their possible association with brain-related sex differences in ability is continuing (Gallagher 1988). For example, research on laboratory animals has shown that male-female differences in the wiring of neurons reflect the functioning of sex hormones (Carter and Greenough 1979). This finding fits well with much previous research indicating that sex hormones affect the brain in producing sex-differentiated and sex-typed behaviors in a variety of species (Weintraub 1981; Witelson and Swallow 1987; Holland 1988). Research on prenatal development in human beings indicates that the effects of sex hormones are "dramatic," but also that effects on ability depend greatly on what abilities are being considered (Kimura 1985).

However, caution should be exercised in assessing the meaning and implications of possible sex differences involving biology and intellectual ability. As pointed out by Shepherd-Look (1982), hormone research is beset with difficult problems involving measurement of hormone levels and their effects, and researchers in this area are beginning to give more emphasis to interactions and contingencies. In many cases, sex hormones may not have a universal influence but may have an effect dependent on situational factors. There is evidence, for example, that the relationship between high levels of testosterone and aggression in males is mediated by psychological stress. Furthermore, there appears to be wide variation across individuals in the effects of hormones, brain lateralization, and other biological factors, so that sex is a "poor screening device for intellectual assessment (Kimura 1985, 58). Research on possible sex differences in spatial abilities indicates that such differences tend to be relatively small and inconsistent across subskills (Caplan, MacPherson, and Tobin 1985; Hannay and Levin 1987). In addition, several studies indicate that spatial abilities scores of girls and women can be improved through education (Halpern 1986).

The Education of Women

The changing patterns of work and family life for women have been both the cause and the effect of changes in the education of women that have occurred over the past century. In focusing now on the educational system and on the role of education in shaping women's lives, we should look first at socialization experiences that occur within the school setting.

Socialization

It should be said first that there is an enormous scientific literature on sex differences and socialization practices, a literature that grows out of biology, psychology, sociology, and anthropology as well as education, and a literature that cannot possibly be summarized here. Suffice it to say that while nobody doubts the presence of important biological differences between the sexes, there is a wide variety of interpretations regarding which, if any, of these biological differences make a significant difference in the way boys and girls learn or in the abilities that are needed to fulfill most occupations of modern society. Whatever the inherent biological differences, much of the difference in behavior observed between boys and girls, and later between men and women, stems from differences in the socialization experiences that occur from earliest infancy onward. In short, in most families boys are treated differently from girls from their first days of life, when hospitals give boy babies a blue bracelet and girl babies a pink one. These differences become reinforced over time as the child meets the expectations of parents, teachers, and peers, and as these expectations become internalized.

To quote only one example of what is meant by differential socialization experiences, a study of mother-infant interactions during the first and third months of life showed that mothers tend to stimulate male infants significantly more than female infants and to arouse them to a higher activity level. On the other hand, they imitated girl babies significantly more frequently than boy babies, especially their vocalizations (Moss 1967). Perhaps such differences in the treatment of infants in the nursery are involved in the differences observed later when youngsters reach school age, when boys show higher general activity levels than girls and when girls frequently demonstrate greater verbal skills than boys.

One author summarizes some of the studies concerning parents' differential socialization of boys and girls, as follows:

> *Mothers maintain physically close and affectionate relationships with girls for a longer period of time. Mothers expect girls to be more dependent and give them more physical attention. On the other hand, boys are given more independence training, more punishment and are encouraged more in intellectual curiosity. Mothers place a greater degree of pressure for achievement and punish dependency more in boys than in girls of pre-school age. In addition, boys' aggression is rewarded as appropriate masculine behavior while girls' aggression is never rewarded, though indirect expressions are tolerated. Mothers place pressures on girls for "feminine" neatness, obedience and conformity, while pressure on boys is for independence and achievement. Mothers of girls . . . demand obedience and control verbal protests by using withdrawals of love, while mothers of boys use negative sanctions (deprivation of privileges) to control verbal protests from boys. (Constantina Safilios-Rothschild, quoted in the report of the Advisory Committee on the Rights and Responsibilities of Women 1975, 34)*

Parental and childhood experiences feed into society's attitudes toward men and women; and schools tend to reflect these attitudes in the ways teachers and counselors deal with students, and in the choice of curriculum materials. We return to socialization and gender roles in the schools later in this chapter.

Vocational Education

Until the 1970s, students reaching the high school level sometimes found themselves segregated by sex, either in different schools or within a given school. In some large cities, for example, a specialized science and math school would admit only boys; and boys' vocational schools taught electronics, plumbing,

Table 11.5 *Vocational Education Enrollments by Sex, 1979*

Field of Study	% Male	% Female
Agriculture	83	17
Distributive	48	52
Homemaking and consumer	29	71
Occupational home economics	24	76
Office	28	72
Technical	80	20
Trade and industrial	82	18
Health	25	75

Source: Division of Vocational and Technical Education 1979.

carpentry, printing, and other supposedly male trades, while girls' schools prepared students to be homemakers, secretaries, beauticians, and health aides. Although sex discrimination in enrollment is now illegal and the patterns of vocational preparation can be expected to change, it was still the case as recently as 1972 that half of all women registered in vocational education courses were enrolled in homemaking and consumer education classes not designed to prepare them for employment, and another 30 percent were being trained for office work. As shown in Table 11.5, in 1979 women still constituted less than one-quarter of the enrollment in agriculture, technical, and trade and industrial courses. Many educators thus believe it is important to guide more women into these so-called nontraditional fields in which they will have improved opportunities to earn higher incomes (Landers 1988).

College Attendance

In 1900, about 6 percent of all persons eighteen years old were high school graduates; in 1940, almost 50 percent; and by 1980, about 74 percent. Throughout these years, a higher percentage of women than of men in the relevant age group has graduated from high school. The opposite has been true for college entrants, for through the years a noticeably higher proportion of men than of women have entered or have completed college. Although women have made great progress toward achieving educational parity, equality in higher education has not yet been fully attained. The educational distributions of persons twenty-five to twenty-nine years old clearly illustrate the changes. (Because most persons of these ages have recently completed their schooling, their educational attainment can be used as an indicator.) Among persons twenty-five to twenty-nine years old in 1950, there were 66 women who had completed four years of college for every 100 men who had done so. By 1980, the corresponding ratio was almost 80 to 100.

Differences between the sexes at these and higher levels of educational attainment in 1983 are given in Table 11.6.

Table 11.6 *Percentage of Academic Degrees Awarded to Women*

	1964	1983
Bachelor's degrees	42	51
Master's degrees	34	50
Doctor's degrees	11	33
First professional degrees	3.5	30

Source: Adapted from Randour, Strasburg, and Lipman-Blumen 1982; *Statistical Abstract of the United States, 1987*.

Regarding the handicaps that women face in their efforts to acquire education, a brightening picture is shown by the changes in college enrollment of women and men. In 1977, for the first time, college women outnumbered college men in the eighteen- and nineteen-year-old population group. In 1983, 51 percent of the freshmen at United States colleges were women, as compared with 40 percent ten years before. If these trends continue, it is projected that by 1990 a higher proportion of women than of men in the age range thirty to forty-four will be college graduates, a situation that would be unprecedented.

Fields of Study

If we examine sex distribution of college students by major field of study, it appears that women have been moving in increasing numbers into traditionally men's fields. Although women continue to be overrepresented in fields such as education, English, and the health professions, their educational interests are rapidly becoming more diversified. The percentage majoring in mathematics and statistics has increased, as has been true in business administration and management, in the physical sciences, and in agriculture and forestry.

Women have also begun to enroll in educational institutions to which they have never had access in the past. In 1975, legislation was enacted to permit women to apply for appointment to the Army, Naval, and Air Force Academies for the first time, and the U.S. Coast Guard and Merchant Marine Academies have recently been opened to women. All but about one hundred of the private schools that formerly limited enrollment to men, including Yale, Princeton, Dartmouth, and Notre Dame, are now coeducational, and others, like Harvard and Columbia, have joined administrative forces with their sister schools, Radcliffe and Barnard.

As college women continue to move into nontraditional educational programs, especially those that increase their eligibility for graduate or professional school programs, they are clearly increasing their options for the future. We can expect that women graduating from college in the 1990s will follow more heterogeneous career lines than have the women of the past.

Graduate and Professional Education

As seen in Table 11.5, sex differences at the graduate level have been even greater than those at the college level. These differences persist even though women are improving their position. By 1983, women earned 50 percent of master's degrees but only 33 percent of doctorates.

Women in graduate schools are more likely than men to be single, more likely to be in their thirties or older, and more likely to be enrolled as part-time students. A large proportion expect to take terminal M.A. degrees rather than to proceed toward the doctorate, a function of the fact that more women than men are taking graduate work in such fields as education and social work, where the M.A. is the important credential.

With regard to other professional degrees, recent changes in enrollment have resulted in increased proportions of degrees granted to women. For example, the percentage of women among business-school graduates increased from 10 percent in 1970 to 40 percent in 1986; in medical schools, the corresponding increase was from 9 percent in 1970 to 30 percent in 1985.

Graduate school attrition rates for women historically have been higher than for men. It is difficult to document the extent of discrimination against women in graduate and professional schools, but many researchers who have studied the problem believe it has existed to a significant degree, not only in admissions practices, but also in financial aid practices and in the rigidity of institutional regulations that fail to accommodate the needs of many women for flexible schedules. The situation is complicated; applicants are usually selected and rules made by individual departments, making it difficult to maintain a common standard across a university; the cost of educating a graduate student in many universities (especially in such fields as medicine) greatly exceeds the tuition charge and creates a greater concern lest places be taken by women who will not finish because of marriage or motherhood or who will not pursue subsequent careers as effectively as men; some faculty believe women graduate students are therefore not as "dedicated" as men; and so on.

Even though such attitudes are changing, and the recent laws prohibiting discrimination are having their effects, it is probably still fair to say that women are somewhat disadvantaged as compared with men in pursuing higher degrees. In part, the disadvantage stems from factors that taken together can be called discrimination, but in part it stems also from the personal decisions made by women themselves. Even though the latter are often explained by the fact that women have been taught to set their standards unnecessarily low, it must also be said that most women in their twenties and thirties face a genuine range of options regarding the balance they wish to create between family and career responsibilities, and related thereto, the financial commitments they wish to make to continued education. Thus, the lack of motivation for graduate work may be a more significant factor for women than for men.

Motivation is, of course, a complicated question. Attention has been given to the possibility that women students, rather than fearing failure, fear success (Horner 1969; Tobias and Weissbrod 1980). Some studies indicate that in addition to the obvious social rejection that a competitive and achieving girl may experience, there is also an internal anxiety and a fear, conscious or unconscious, that outstanding academic or other achievement may be equated with a loss of femininity (Safilios-Rothschild 1979). Girls who have this fear are not likely to pursue higher education.

At the same time, there is good reason to believe that women's gains in higher education will continue and perhaps be accelerated. For one thing, young women are facing less social and institutional resistance in their efforts to gain access to advanced education than did earlier cohorts of women. In addition, older women are finding themselves welcomed back on campus as universities face future enrollment declines that will result from smaller cohorts of college-age persons. More women can be expected to continue their education for longer periods than ever before in our history, and more women will eventually achieve graduate and professional degrees.

Instructional Materials

A number of studies have indicated that instructional materials frequently have reflected sexual stereotypes and that such materials have played a part in generating and maintaining disadvantages that girls and women experience in schools and society. For example, one study conducted in the 1970s showed that among 134 stories in children's reading texts, men were shown in 147 different jobs, but women in only 26; all the work done by women in the stories fell into the traditional concept of women's jobs. The texts included biographies of 88 different men but only 17 women, suggesting that the authors found fewer interesting women to write about. And the central figures in stories dealing with ingenuity, creativity, bravery, perseverance, achievement, adventuresomeness, curiosity, autonomy, and self-respect were boys four times as often as they were girls (U.S. Dept. of HEW, "Sex Stereotyping in Children's Readers" 1975).

Kathryn Scott and Candace Schau (1985) reviewed the literature on instructional materials and sex bias and reached the following four general conclusions:

1. Sex-biased language distorts students' perceptions of reality.
2. Sex-equitable instructional materials can broaden attitudes about sex roles and also increase motivation to learn.
3. Sex-equitable instructional materials influence students' sex-role behaviors. "When children hear stories or see films that contain sex role behaviors, both traditional and nontraditional, they may imitate these behaviors" (p. 224).
4. Many commonly used instructional materials are sex biased.

The problem of sexism in elementary and secondary textbooks has been significantly alleviated since 1972, when Scott, Foresman and Company was the first publisher to take action by issuing "Guidelines for Improving the Image of Women in Textbooks." By 1978, the National Education Association reported that almost all major textbook publishers, nearly forty, had issued such guidelines. Although much progress has been made, more remains to be done. Scott and Schau (1985) have offered a number of recommendations for pursuing further reduction of six bias and inequity in instructional materials, including guidelines for publishers, consumers, and researchers.

Testing

Testing policies and practices also can lead to or reinforce and support sex inequities. Much of the recent concern regarding this possibility has focused on potentially inequitable or otherwise negative effects of interest inventories and vocational guidance instruments used in education and counseling. Esther Diamond and Carol Tittle (1985) examined the research on this issue and reported the following general conclusions:

> *Since the early 1970s . . . more research has been done on the question of gender differences in interest inventory responses and the extent to which they contribute to sex inequities in education, than in the 50 years preceding. . . . It is difficult to tell to what extent the bias exists in the inventories themselves—the item content and context—and to what extent their results reflect the bias in society, including that of parents, the media, and other societal influences. It may be a long time before the socialization process catches up with the social changes that have taken place at the legal, theoretical, and legislative levels. (Diamond and Tittle 1985, 182)*

Socialization and Gender in the Schools

As noted earlier in this chapter, gender-related socialization of children and youth beginning in the home and family extends to and affects the treatment and performance of both boys and girls in the educational system. Research (e.g., Eccles and Blumenfeld 1985; Brophy 1985; Irvine 1986; Sadker and Sadker 1985) supports the conclusion that differentials in gender roles and treatment in the schools include the following three conclusions:

1. Teachers interact more with boys than with girls. Much of this differential interaction involves greater negative feedback given to boys and boys' greater success, compared to girls, in gaining the attention of teachers. According to Sadker and Sadker, these patterns indicate that boys thereby are "being trained to be assertive; girls are being trained to be passive—spectators relegated to the sidelines of classroom discussion" (1986, 513). However, Eccles and Blumenfeld have reviewed research on differences in gender-related interactions and cautioned that most such differences are small, that greater similarity in treatment "may not yield equitable outcomes for both boys and girls," and that differential treatment seems to be as much a consequence of preexisting differences in student behavior as of teacher bias. Nevertheless,

they conclude that when differences do occur, they appear to be "reinforcing sex-stereotyped expectations and behavior" (1985, 112).

2. Sex interacts with race, age, grade level, and other factors in generating differentials in instructional practice and treatment. For example, one sizable study of elementary schools found that although white females in both the lower- and upper-elementary grades received less feedback from teachers than did other students classified by sex and race, black females particularly stood out as receiving fewer opportunities to respond in the classroom as they proceed through the grades (Irvine 1986).
3. Differences in teaching style associated with sex of the teacher probably play a part in reinforcing differential treatment of boys and girls in the classroom. Brophy reviewed the literature on this topic and concluded that female teachers tend to be less teacher-centered and more supportive of students than are male teachers. He also speculated that these patterns may have different consequences for the achievement of boys and girls. However, he also concluded that "the data continue to indicate that male and female teachers are much more similar than different," that teachers "do not systematically discriminate against students of the opposite sex," and that "teachers do not seem to be major reasons in causing or broadening student sex differences (1985, 137).

Sex-role stereotypes are present in the schools in other ways, also; in the arrangement of physical space, as when kindergartens have a corner for the dollhouse, which girls are expected to use, and another corner for building blocks, which boys are expected to use; in music activities, when boys are offered the drums to play and girls are offered the triangles; in social studies, when only traditional family roles are portrayed; and so on. The stereotypes are also reinforced when children see that it is only women teachers who deal with the youngest children and that men teachers are usually to be found only in the higher school grades, and then usually as teachers of science or vocational courses, or as athletic coaches, or as principals.

One should also keep in mind the special sex-related problems that males experience in elementary and secondary schools. As pointed out above, many studies indicate that males have lower verbal achievement than do females, and the school's emphasis on verbal learning places many boys at a serious disadvantage beginning in the early grades. Restak (1979) has noted that high percentages of hyperactive children and of learning disabled children are male and has linked this phenomenon to school expectations that require boys to display fine motor coordination and to sit attentively for long periods at an age when many are not physically ready or able to meet such demands: "the classrooms in most of our nation's primary grades," he concludes, "are geared to skills that come naturally to girls but develop very slowly in boys" (p. 235). McGuiness (1979) has pointed out that the greater distractibility of boys—whether due to biology, socialization, or some combination of the two—interferes with the concentration required to learn to read and write, and Skovholt (1978) concluded that male aggressiveness is frequently associated with behavioral problems and poor performance in the schools. Findings such as these suggest that schools should do much more than they do now to provide instruction in a manner that takes account of both male and female disadvantages in ability and behavior.

Using participant observer methods, Raphaela Best (1983) studied peer-group dynamics in a group of children moving from the second through the fifth grades and then into junior high school in an affluent but increasingly diverse suburban community. After reviewing research underlining the importance of peer groups in the development of children's attitudes and behaviors, Best distinguished among three different curricula that students learn at school: a first or academic curriculum, a second or "gender-role" curriculum that teaches children the traditional role behavior for their sex, and a third curriculum that involves how boys and girls relate to each other. Best referred to the third curriculum as "self-taught" because the children worked on it by themselves with little help from adults.

After noting that the first curriculum is particularly troublesome for boys, in part because they have relatively more difficulty than do girls in meeting classroom expectations for passive behavior, Best concentrated on studying and then trying to intervene in the second and third curricula.

We've All Got Scars, Best's report on her research, describes the somewhat separate and differing expectations and experiences of boys and girls in their peer groups. One of the clearest patterns in the second grade was that boys began learning the "most fundamental second-curriculum rule for male sex-role behavior" (p. 13): they distanced themselves from the girls, and they began to attach more importance to acceptance by male-oriented peer groups than to rewards and affection from the teacher. Best also found that the boys' reading scores were strongly associated with their peer status, and that causality worked in both directions: rejection harmed academic performance and, in some cases, high performance seemed to help generate acceptance.

Best (1983) proceeded to describe what she termed the positive and negative "canons" that peer relationship and behaviors helped teach boys inside and outside the classroom. The positive canon emphasized a need to "be strong" and "be first," while the negative canon stressed "don't associate with a sissy," "don't play with a cry-baby," "don't do housework," and "don't show affection." Girls, Best found, also learned sex roles through the peer group, but "entering the girls' world was like moving from a dark and fearful forest into a sunny valley" (p. 88) where there was little or nothing that stressed or reinforced fighting and winning; instead, emphasis was on having fun rather than winning and on cooperation more than competition. Best also was struck by the greater leeway allowed to girls; that is, girls could compete and otherwise emulate some aspects of boys' roles without being rejected by other girls, but boys who violated the negative canons were strongly rejected.

The concluding chapters in *We've All Got Scars* describes Best's efforts to reduce and overcome sex-role stereotyping through discussion with her students and the changes that appeared to occur as they moved through elementary school and later, after some intensification in the seventh grade of gender stereotypes involving boy-girl relationships, through junior high school. To "clear the way," she reported, "it was essential that the children learn to see the world around them as it really was rather than . . . the stereotypes . . . [denoting] the passive, incompetent girls they saw in their textbooks, library books, and the media" (p. 130). Although Best is uncertain whether her efforts had much or any impact compared with changes in social influences taking place outside her classroom, she believes that the boys and girls she studied made real progress in overcoming gender stereotyping and its frequently pernicious effects that limit the aspirations of girls, restrict the emotional growth of boys, and establish a nonegalitarian pattern of relationship between the sexes (p. 6).

Interventions to Improve Sex Equity in Education

During the past thirty years a variety of actions and programs have been initiated to improve sex equity in education. Some of these efforts involve policies and practices to counter discrimination and improve the status of women in general; others involve interventions targeted specifically at the educational system.

Among the most fundamental changes that have taken place are those involving public policy, which provides the legal framework for further situational modification. These changes include legislative and administrative actions such as the federal Equal Pay Act of 1963 and Title VII of the 1964 Civil Rights Act. Of direct importance to educators is the Higher Education Act of 1972, which provides in its Title IX for sex equality both in employment in educational institutions and in education itself. The Act applies to all schools receiving federal grants and loans—preschools, elementary and secondary schools, vocational and professional schools, and both public and private undergraduate and graduate institutions.

The National Advisory Council on Women's Educational Programs (1982) reviewed developments in education following passage of Title IX and concluded that real progress had been made nationwide in improving educational opportunity for women. In addition to changes such as those described in the preceding pages, the Council cited improvements in student services (counseling, health, financial aid) and in conducting athletics and other extracurricular activities on an equitable basis. It also concluded, however, that there have been some "major disappointments," particularly with respect to the goal of women "gaining positions as principals, superintendents, and full professors" (p. 11). In addition, a 1984 Supreme Court decision (*Grove City College* v. *Bell*) reduced the applicability of Title IX by limiting its operation to campus programs that receive federal funds directly.

Some other developments that facilitate the participation of women in educational programs and support them as they attempt to cope with multiple roles include continuing education programs, the "open" university and "external degrees," women's committees or caucuses in professional associations, and women's studies programs.

Continuing education programs have had special benefits for women who have interrupted their education to marry and rear children but who wish to prepare to enter the labor force. Although the design and focus of such programs vary from college to college, they generally include one or more of the following features: enrollment on a part-time basis, flexible course hours, short-term courses, counseling services for adults, financial aid for part-time study, limited residence requirements, removal of age restrictions, liberal transfers of course credits, curriculum geared to adult experiences, credit by examination, refresher courses, reorientation courses, information services, child-care facilities, relaxation of time requirements for degrees, and job placement assistance.

Many activities have been initiated to extend women's entrance into the so-called male professions as well as to strengthen women's status in all professional fields. For example, many professional associations have established official committees concerned with the status and special problems of women in their respective fields. Generally, these associations seek to abolish dual standards of admission and quota systems and to increase financial assistance to women who wish to acquire a professional education.

In the past twenty years, women's studies have emerged as a special field in higher education. Hundreds of institutions of higher education have established formal women's studies programs, and many others offer a variety of courses and services that emphasize women's roles in education and society. Howe (1982) studied the development of feminist scholarship in higher education and identified the major curriculum emphases emerging in the women's studies movement as involving an understanding of the following topics:

1. Patriarchy in historical perspective.
2. The "still chaotic area" of biological and psychological sex differences.
3. Socialization and sex roles.
4. Women in history.
5. Women as represented in the arts they have produced.
6. The impact of post-Freudian psychology on women.
7. Female sexuality.
8. The history and function of education related to women.
9. The history and function of the family.
10. Women in the workforce.
11. Legal and social changes affecting women.

In addition, many activities have been initiated to counter sex-stereotyping and to raise the career and occupational aspirations of girls and women (Klein 1985; Carelli 1988). For example, teacher-training approaches such as the Gender Expectations and Student Achievement Program have been developed to improve classroom participation of female students and to enhance their aspirations and have been used in both preservice and in-service teacher training (Grayson and Martin 1986). Jacquelynne Eccles (1986) has reviewed the theory and research dealing with efforts to broaden the occupational and educational aspirations of girls and women and pointed out that their *perceived career options can be increased by programs targeted to their beliefs that train them to (1) associate different attributions and expectations with various occupations, (2) assess the value they attach to occupations, (3) reevaluate their stereotypes of various occupations and life-roles; and (4) reassess the compatibility between various career options and one's adult-role plans. Actively socializing young women and men to recognize the need to be able to support oneself and one's family is probably as important as helping them select the most 'appropriate' profession. (Eccles 1986, 19)*

Development of Androgyny

The changing occupational structure of the American society plus what may be loosely called the Feminist Movement have generated consideration of a theoretically and practically important concept called *androgyny*. The word *androgyny* comes from two Greek words—*andros* (male) and *gyne* (female)—and might be defined as "being both male and female" or "being sex-role flexible."

The concept is useful in the study of adults of all ages over the age of eighteen. Researchers in this developing field suppose that nearly all adults are either masculine, feminine, or androgynous in personal-social characteristics.

To grasp the differences between these three categories, we need a method of defining and measuring them.

A self-rating method for the measurement of androgyny has been created by Sandra Bem. She compiled a list of 200 personality characteristics that seemed to her and some of her students to be socially desirable and either masculine or feminine in tone. She compiled an additional list of 200 characteristics that seemed to be neither masculine nor feminine in tone. Of these neutral characteristics, half were socially desirable and half were socially undesirable.

She then asked 100 Stanford undergraduates to rate the desirability in American society, for one sex or the other, of each of the approximately 400 personality characteristics. Those judges were to use a 7-point scale, ranging from 1 (Not at all desirable) to 7 (Extremely desirable). For example, "In American society how desirable is it for a man to be cheerful?" "In American society, how desirable is it for a woman to be forceful?" Each individual judge was asked to rate the desirability of all 400 personality characteristics either "for a man" or "for a woman." No judge was asked to rate both. In both groups of judges, half were male and half were female.

A personality characteristic qualified as masculine if it was independently judged by both males and females to be significantly more desirable for a man than for a woman. Similarly, a personality characteristic qualified as feminine if it was independently judged by both males and females to be significantly more desirable for a woman than for a man. Of those characteristics that satisfied these criteria, 20 were selected for the Femininity Scale and 20 were selected for the Masculinity Scale. Another 20 items, which were judged to be neutral, were selected. These 60 items comprise the Bem Sex Role Inventory (BSRI).

Table 11.7 *Percentage of Subjects Self-Classified as Masculine, Feminine, and Androgynous*

Category	Bem Sample			
	Stanford University		*Foothill Junior College*	
	% Males (444 total)	*% Females (279 total)*	*% Males (117 total)*	*% Females (77 total)*
Androgynous	34	27	44	38
Masculine	36	8	22	8
Near masculine	19	12	17	7
Feminine	6	34	9	40
Near feminine	5	20	9	8

Source: Studies conducted by Sandra Bem and her colleagues at Stanford University.

The BSRI asks a person to indicate on a 7-point scale how well each of the 60 masculine, feminine, and neutral personality characteristics describes himself or herself. The scale ranges from 1 (Never or almost never true) to 7 (Always or almost always true), with a descriptive label for each of the 7 points. On the basis of the responses, each person receives three major scores: a Masculinity score, a Femininity score, and an Androgyny score. The Androgyny score is a measure of the relative amounts of masculinity compared with femininity that the person includes in his or her self-description. People who are high on both Masculinity and Femininity are Androgynous.

To secure data on a representative sample of college students aged about eighteen to twenty, in the winter and spring of 1973 Bem administered the BSRI to 444 male and 279 female students in a course of introductory psychology at Stanford University and to an additional 117 male and female paid volunteers at the neighboring Foothill Junior College. The results are shown in Table 11.7. It can be seen that a few persons of both genders rate themselves higher on the opposite-sex characteristics than on the characteristics of their own gender.

Androgyny as an Ideal for Human Development. A powerful essay with the foregoing title has been written by Ann Ferguson (1977). She says: "I shall argue that male/female sex roles are neither inevitable results of 'natural' biological differences between sexes, nor socially desirable ways of socializing children in contemporary societies."

Ferguson attempts to demolish the Natural Complement Theory of male/female human nature. This theory rests on the biologically based differences between men and women. Because men are stronger than women and have higher amounts of the male hormone androgen, which is linked to aggressive behavior, it is natural for men to produce the physical commodities needed by society and to make war when necessary. Women should stay at home, raise their children, and minister to the emotional needs of their men and children.

Instead of this simplistic theory, Ferguson says it is useful to recognize that human nature is plastic, and that we should ask: "What traits are desirable and possible to teach people in order for them to reach their full individual human potential? And how would our society have to restructure its productive and reproductive relations in order to allow people to develop in this way?" (p. 57).

Elise Boulding (1979; 1987) has pointed out that strong trends toward androgyny have been present in the later stages of the life cycle, at which time the "androgyny of aging" is apparent when men "become gentler, more person- and family-oriented, and women become more assertive, more ready to test out what they know about how the world works" (1987, 131). Boulding believes that further movement toward androgyny would be desirable at earlier ages, but she also points out that such transitions do not occur on a smooth path and are affected by many social and historical influences.

Recent Directions in Feminism in the United States

Modifications in sex roles and related reductions in sex-differentiated norms that viewed aggressiveness as ideally masculine and passivity as ideally feminine have constituted major changes in United States society during the past thirty years. Associated with the feminist movement, these changes involved a combination of interrelated economic and cultural developments. Political developments in the early 1980s have been forcing redirection in the philosophy and goals of the feminist movement. Failure to ratify the Equal Rights Amendment in enough states to modify the U.S. Constitution and political fragmentation among various segments of the feminist movement have generated changes in emphasis among many of its leaders and supporters (Kramer 1986).

Probably the best-known statement of some of these changes has been provided by Betty Friedan, whose influential earlier writings in *The Feminine Mystique* played an important part in enlarging opportunities for women and freeing them from the "cult" of domesticity. Friedan's 1981 book, *The Second Stage*, described the agenda she believes should be most important in working to advance women's rights in the 1980s. She argues that the feminist movement will be most successful if it deemphasizes issues that divide liberals and conservatives and men and women and instead places greater emphasis on developing and supporting policies that help women (and men) pursue success in both the family and the labor market.

Friedan calls this direction the "second stage" because she believes it can help overcome some of the disquieting developments in first-stage efforts to improve opportunities for women. Thus, she stated that supporters of women's rights should avoid "getting locked into obsolete power games and irrelevant sexual battles" and, by emphasizing family policy, should recognize the reality of each woman's "childbearing, her roots and life connection in the family" (pp. 29, 51). Much of the discussion in *The Second Stage* deals with possibilities for making job arrangements more flexible, modifying housing design to reduce homemaking burdens, instituting maternity and paternity leaves, and providing day care and other family services in order to accommodate parents' difficulties in juggling economic and family goals. After describing research indicating that enlarged opportunities for employment have been associated with improved mental health among United States women but that many women are having difficulty reconciling job and family "choices" in contemporary circumstances, she concluded that

> *part of the conflict over motherhood today—and part of the conflict that feminists feel about the family and that younger women feel about feminism . . . is a hangover from the generations when too great a price was paid. But part of the conflict is realistic: the price of motherhood is still too high for most women, the stunting of abilities and earning power is a real fear. . . . The enemies of feminism insist that woman's move to equality, self-realization and her own power in society is destroying the family, which they feel is woman's real locus of power. Many feminists insist that the family was, and is, the enemy, the prime obstacle to women's self-realization. There are pieces of the truth in these interlocking fears. . . . Part of the problem comes from the lack of real economic measures or political attention to the previously private woman's work, in home and family, an irreducible minimum of which is necessary for human and society's survival. (Friedan 1981, 87, 95, 111)*

It should be noted that emphasis on family considerations in the women's rights movement fits in well with recent thinking regarding the social psychology of sex differences. In particular, Carol Gilligan (1982) and other social scientists (e.g., Lyons 1983) have been re-examining data on female development and concluded that some important generalizations in social science do not quite fit for female respondents because they are based largely or entirely on male samples. Thus, Gilligan concludes that women tend to emphasize "ongoing attachment" with others as a "path to maturity" and "interdependence of self and other" to a greater extent than do men (p. 170). According to Gilligan, this emphasis tends to create problems for women because in modern society it may lead to self-definition through "relationships with others" and then to severe midlife crises when such relationships prove fragile or vulnerable. Gilligan further concludes that

> *in view of the evidence that women perceive and construe social reality differently from men and that these differences center around experiences of attachment and separation . . . the major transitions in women's lives would seem to involve changes in the understanding and activities of care. When the distinction between helping and pleasing frees the activity of taking care from the wish for approval by others, the ethic of responsibility can become a self-chosen anchor of personal integrity and strength. . . . The inclusion of women's experience brings to developmental understanding a new perspective on relationships that changes the basic constructs of interpretation. The concept of identity expands to include the experience of interconnection. The moral domain is similarly enlarged by the inclusion of responsibility and care in relationships. (Gilligan 1982, 171, 173)*

In a related and somewhat similar analysis, Jane Martin (1986) has advocated joining Plato's view that gender roles are not fixed by nature with Rousseau's insight that behavioral traits have been genderized. After pointing out that constructive sexual equity may not be attainable merely by placing more emphasis on the masculine virtues of "rationality and independent judgment" in educating women, she concludes that education also should include development of feminine virtues involving nurturance and care. In addition to counteracting in this way the "negative messages [about women and their roles] transmitted by the standard curriculum," Martin also concludes that the curriculum should advance equity by attending to "women's lives, work, experiences, and relationships" and should help diffuse "generation love" by joining "reason to feeling and self to other" (Martin 1986, 10).

Conclusion

A stable and relatively unchanging society uses the process of socialization to teach its young members the social roles they must perform in order to maintain the society in generally satisfactory shape. With respect to sex roles, they are taught the socially appropriate masculine and feminine roles, by their family, school, neighborhood, and community.

Attitudes and behavior regarding sex roles in United States society have been changing significantly in the period since 1950. Women have been entering the labor force to an extent that would have been almost unimaginable fifty years ago, and they also have been pursuing higher education in unprecedented numbers. Although the majority of women still are preparing for and entering traditionally so-called white-blouse occupations, a growing proportion are entering traditionally male fields.

Both as a cause and a result of these changes regarding occupational and educational opportunities for women, attitudes and practices involving the socialization of children—particularly girls—also have been changing. For example, parents are less likely today than forty or fifty years ago to stress future homemaking roles in raising girls, and they are more likely to insist that their daughters receive a good education so they can compete on an equal basis in the economy. There is some evidence that middle-class youngsters are somewhat in advance of working-class youngsters in stressing equal opportunity for girls and women (Holland, 1980; Christensen 1987), but opportunities opening up for women certainly have not been limited to the middle class. Over the past forty years or so, our society has redefined what is meant by masculinity and femininity.

The first chapter of this book began with a recognition of the fact that the United States is becoming a postindustrial society in which provision of services—particularly information—is replacing manufacturing and extraction of goods as the primary economic activity. This change in the economy has been one factor generating changes in sex roles in United States society, but it is difficult to predict whether future economic change will hinder or further improve opportunities for women. From one point of view, the movement to a postindustrial economy benefits women because women can carry out most tasks in such an economy as well as men. On the other hand, computerization and other forms of advanced technological change may reduce the availability of many jobs such as teacher and secretary that are now filled by women. Much will depend on the educational opportunities available to women and on how well women take advantage of these opportunities to prepare for highly skilled jobs in the economy of the future.

EXERCISES

1. Obtain copies of the readers used in the first and second grades of a nearby school system. Analyze their content with regard to images of women and men.
2. Interview your mother and your grandmother regarding their life histories. What were the attitudes toward women's roles that prevailed when they were young women? What were their own views? Have those views changed recently?
3. Interview several of your instructors. What do they report regarding the status of faculty women in your institution?
4. Talk with three or four mothers of young children. What are their aspirations for their sons? For their daughters? Do these mothers report agreement or disagreement with their husbands on these issues?
5. Construct a sociogram of a fifth-grade class. Do boys have "gangs" whereas girls have "best friends"?
6. Read Charles Derber's *The Pursuit of Attention*. How do men and women differ in conversation?

SUGGESTIONS FOR FURTHER READING

1. Schneir's *Feminism: The Essential Historical Writings* is, as indicated by the title, a collection of major writings on the feminist movement.
2. For historical perspective, Mabel Newcomer's *A Century of Higher Education for American Women* is an excellent reference.
3. The women's liberation movement of the 1960s and 1970s gave rise to a flood of books and magazine articles setting forth a wide range of views. Friedan's *The Feminine Mystique* was an early and highly influential book. Others include Firestone's *The Dialectic of Sex: The Case for Feminist Revolution*, Morgan's *Sisterhood Is Powerful*, Millett's *Sexual Politics*, Komisar's *The New Feminism*, and Chafe's *The American Woman*. Betty Friedan's *The Second Stage* (1981) describes major concerns of feminists in the 1980s.

4. *Comparative Perspectives of Third World Women* edited by Beverly Lindsay includes papers dealing with the status and role of women in racial minority groups.
5. *Beyond Her Sphere* by Barbara Harris traces the development of the feminist movement in the United States from precolonial times to the present.
6. *The Economics of Sex Differentials* by Lloyd and Niemi and *The Economic Emergence of Women* by Bergmann provide a thorough review and well-balanced assessment of research on why women earn less than men and of the implications of this research for social policy.
7. Constantina Safilios-Rothschild's *Sex Role Socialization and Sex Discrimination* includes a comprehensive review of the research on sex differences in socialization. Particular emphasis is given to the family and the school.
8. *Too Many Women?*, by Marcia Guttentag and Paul Secord, argues that the ratio of men to women in society has an important influence on social, economic, cultural, and political developments. If there are many more men than women, the authors argue, men compete for women by emphasizing marriage and the family, and women have more opportunity to participate fully in society. If there are many more women than men, marriage and the family are deemphasized and women are devalued. Guttentag and Secord support their conclusions with data from ancient and medieval as well as contemporary societies.
9. *Women and Mathematics: Balancing the Equation*, edited by Chipman, Brush, and Wilson, reviews a wide range of previous research and also presents and analyzes original research dealing with mathematics achievement and participation of girls and women.
10. *The Handbook for Achieving Sex Equity through Education*, edited by Susan Klein, includes chapters on curriculum and instruction, school organization and administration, early through postsecondary education, teacher education, testing, and other topics. The volume concludes with eighteen pages of recommendations for improving sex equity through the educational system.
11. Diane Halpern's thoughtful review of research in *Sex Differences in Cognitive Abilities* examines and assesses a number of studies dealing with differentials in performance and their possible causes.
12. Based on interviews with women, Mary Belenky and her colleagues (*Women's Ways of Knowing* 1986) speculate that "educators can help women develop their own authentic voices" by emphasizing "connection over separation, understanding and acceptance over assessment, and collaboration over debate" and by according respect to the "knowledge that emerges from first-hand experience" (p. 229).

12

Additional Topics Focusing on Educational Equity

This chapter provides information on and discussion of three important topics that have major implications for attainment of educational equity: computers in elementary and secondary schools, rural education, and nonpublic schools. Each topic constitutes a large and specialized field of study in itself. We do not try to discuss or analyze all of the important considerations involving these themes; instead, we are concerned largely with recent developments that have direct implications in terms of providing equal and adequate educational opportunity and, perforce, the public policies that might or should be formulated to ensure provision of equitable opportunity.

Computers and Equity in Elementary and Secondary Schools

Computers are becoming an important tool in elementary and secondary schools because they hold promise for improving many aspects of the educational process. Computers can contribute to education by

1. Enhancing student performance through computer-associated instruction (Kulik 1983; Vargas 1986).
2. Improving student motivation (Lepper and Chabay 1985).
3. Improving disadvantaged students' social and economic opportunities by providing access to modern technology and also to enhanced academic performance.

Between 1981 and 1985, the number of computers in elementary and secondary schools increased from less than 25,000 to more than one million (Becker 1986a). John Lipkin of the Bureau of Social Science Research reviewed the data on computers in education as of 1982 and found that developments in information technology appeared to be advancing what he called the "Matthew Effect": "For whosoever hath, to him shall be given." Lipkin reported that schools and school districts enrolling mostly wealthy students were much more likely to have obtained microcomputers and to be teaching computer literacy than were schools and districts with mostly poverty students (Lipkin 1982, 7). Worse, Lipkin also found data indicating that where computers were being used to deliver instruction, there was a tendency for middle-class students to concentrate relatively more on higher-order skills and for working-class students to concentrate relatively more on lower-level skills. Lipkin summarized the situation:

> *It is the urban, low-income minority student who is most likely to be provided with drill and practice usage of computers while middle class students are more likely to use it for more creative purposes relating to problem-solving and discovery. . . .*
>
> *It has been suggested that the effect of this distinction in computer use is to produce benefits of a different kind along class lines, with the upper classes cast in the mold of leaders and the lower classes, followers.*
>
> *Evidence of an analogous dichotomy of computer instruction at the secondary level is beginning to appear with the emergence of a vocationally oriented curriculum for innercity or low-income students which is set apart from the higher level uses of the computer which pertain in the precollege curriculum. (Lipkin 1982, 7)*

It should be noted that both commercial and school-initiated resources and projects that involve home use of the computer also favor wealthier students, who are most likely to possess a personal computer (Teske 1988). For example, many excellent computer programs dealing with thousands of educational topics can now be purchased for home use, and several school districts have introduced arrangements that allow students to use home computers to review vocational guidance information obtained by the district. Many more projects of this kind will be introduced in the future. Students whose families cannot afford a computer will be at a serious disadvantage in competing with those who have access to a microcomputer at home (Rothman 1988).

Although developments involving computers and technological change thus threaten to widen achievement gaps between middle-class and working-class students, it is possible that these developments can have the opposite effect. Computers and other technological developments such as the videodisc can help reduce differences in achievement and opportunity between advantaged and disadvantaged students. In particular, the computer and the videodisc may help low-achieving students master fundamental skills required for later success, and in the future they may help disadvantaged students master abstract thinking skills if adequate software is developed to accomplish this purpose.

Virtually the same observation can be made concerning the education of girls and women: females have been disadvantaged in learning math and some other subjects in the past; introduction of the computer may either magnify this disadvantage or help reduce it, depending on how the computer is used and the efforts made to improve opportunity for females (Kiesler, Sproull, and Eccles 1983). Much will depend on how well and how widely the new technologies are introduced in schools and classrooms, and on how great an effort is made to advance rather than retard the goals of equity for low-income students and for women.

Data collected since 1982 provide a somewhat mixed picture regarding equity considerations in the use of computers in elementary and secondary schools. On the one hand, major national data sets indicate that inequities involving economically disadvantaged students and females may not be as severe as suggested by information available in the early 1980s. For example, Henry Becker and his colleagues working on a national survey of computer use found relatively

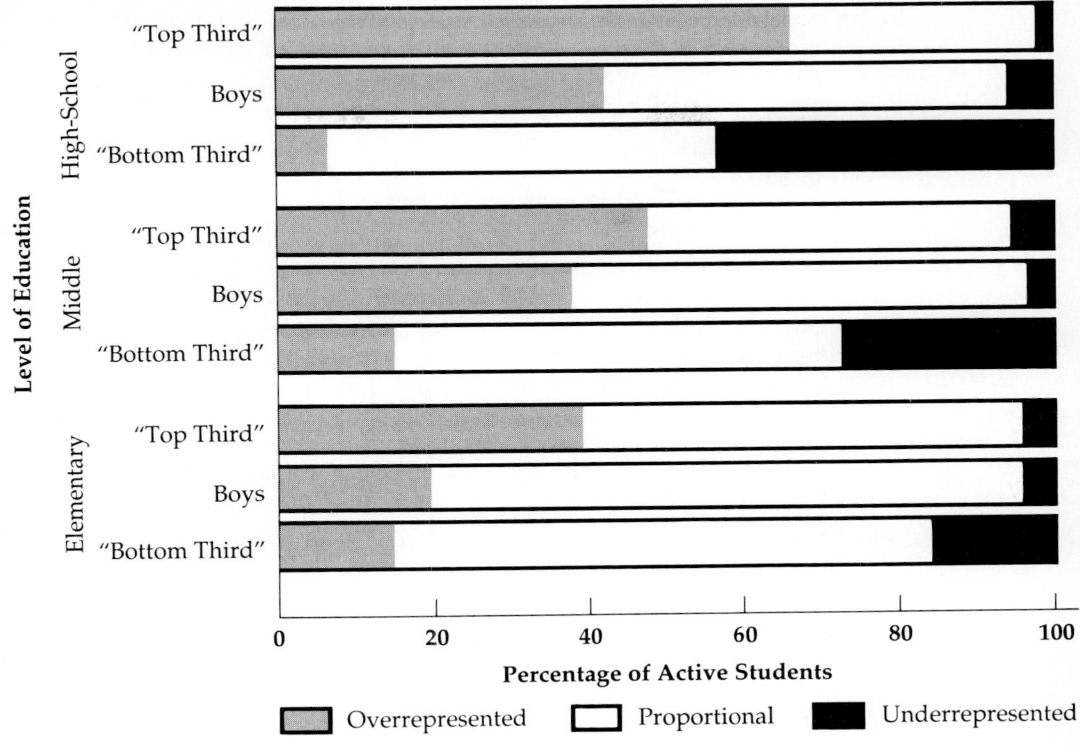

Figure 12.1 ***The Most Active Student Users of Computers, by Sex, Academic Ability, and Level of Education, 1985*** (*Source*: Becker 1986b.)

little variation by metropolitan location in the percentage of high schools with fifteen or more computers (Becker 1986b). Marianne Lockheed analyzed 1984 data collected by the National Assessment of Educational Progress and reported "few consistent gender or ethnic differences" in computer course enrollment or use in the fourth, eighth, or eleventh grades (Lockheed 1986).

On the other hand, Becker and Lockheed also found some indications that inequities involving computers in the public schools may be more serious than was suggested by other information in their data sets. For example, Lockheed reported that schools with less than 50 percent white students have fewer computer resources and are less likely to use computers for instruction than are schools with a majority of white students (Lockheed 1986, 47–48). Becker reported that computer-using teachers at schools high in socioeconomic status have "more expertise than those at other high schools" (Becker 1986b, 10). In addition, Becker and his colleagues found that boys were disproportionately represented among the "most active" student users of computers at all levels of education and that students in the top third on academic ability were much better represented in the group of active users than were those in the low third (see Figure 12.1).

Both Becker and Lockheed suggest that some of the discrepancies in their findings may be reconciled by taking account of differences in participation in computer education according to whether use is formally scheduled by the school or exemplifies enrichment and other student-determined activities. That is, socioeconomically disadvantaged students and girls generally appear to be participating as frequently as advantaged students and boys in programming courses and computer-assisted instruction classes, but the advantaged students and boys are making more use of computers in such independently motivated activities as out-of-class enrichment and application of school computers in pursuing personal interests and problem solving.

But regardless of how one resolves the differing implications of specific findings, the data on disproportionate use by sex and the differentials reported above by socioeconomic status, race/ethnicity, and ability suggest that serious equity problems have been developing and that schools should do more to ensure productive and equitable results for disadvantaged students and girls. The National Task Force on Educational Technology (1986) considered how the schools could productively transform elementary and secondary education in general in order to improve learning and increase "equity of opportunity, access, and quality" through computers and technology. The Task Force reported to Secretary of Education William Bennett that schools should begin to plan for a "computer-managed learning environment . . . [that] will allow students to progress at varying speeds according to their individual abilities" and should plan for the "orderly acquisition of both the hardware and software needed to serve the school's educational goals" (p. 14).

Rural Education

Even though rural schools enroll a significant proportion of students in the United States, their status and problems have received relatively little attention during the twentieth century. This neglect has been corrected to some extent during the past few years by groups and individuals endeavoring to analyze the problems of rural education and to identify approaches for improving the quality of education in rural schools.

As we point out in Chapter 10, many students in rural areas are from low-income families and have relatively low achievement, particularly in such economically impoverished regions as Appalachia and the Ozarks. In addition to educational disadvantages associated with poverty background and dialect differences (Keefe, Reck, and Reck 1983), many rural students historically have had relatively low educational aspirations in circumstances in which advanced education was not perceived as necessary or even desirable for youth preparing to become farmers or farm laborers (Fuller 1985).

Although academic performance is high in some rural communities and students' aspirations certainly have escalated as farming has become highly technological, the relatively low status and economic difficulties experienced by many rural youth probably still function to generate relatively low aspirations. Thus, Oneida Martin (1987) recently found that a sample of rural high school students had lower educational aspirations than did a comparison group of disadvantaged urban students.

One problem analysts encounter in trying to delineate and find solutions to educational problems in rural areas is that rural locations are very diverse and the characteristics of rural schools and society are difficult to define and generalize (DeYoung 1987). This problem was addressed by educators trying to build a network to share information on common problems through the National Rural and Small Schools Consortium. Members of the consortium attending a national conference agreed that rural school districts could be defined as districts that have fewer than 150 residents per square mile and are located in counties in which at least 60 percent of the population lives in communities with fewer than 5,000 inhabitants. They also pointed out that more than 300 separate rural subcultures have been identified, based on such characteristics as ethnic composition, degree of remoteness, and economic infrastructure (Montague, 1986b). The diversity of rural schools has been illustrated and underlined by Jonathan Sher:

> *Reliable hard data about the quality of small rural schools are scarce. . . . The fact that small rural schools are so diverse, especially when viewed internationally, only compounds the problem. Indeed, one can find evidence to support nearly any characterization. Someone who wishes to describe these institutions as ineffective, stifling, third-rate, or worse will have little trouble finding schools that fully deserve such criticism. However, another person who wishes to portray rural schools as innovative, high-performing, delightful places will have equal ease in justifying such a glowing assessment. (Sher 1983, 259)*

Despite the great diversity found in rural schools and society, several key problems appear to be particularly widespread. Among the most severe of these contemporary educational problems in rural areas are lack of financial resources, which has been intensified by economic recession in recent years; shortages of teachers; and difficulty in meeting the higher academic standards that increasingly have been mandated by state governments throughout the United States (Miller and Sidebottom 1985; Montague 1986b; Killian and Byrd 1988).

Financial Limitations

Given their small population and frequently impoverished economic base, rural districts historically have had a difficult task obtaining the financial resources needed to provide a comprehensive educational program. Severe financial limitations thus constitute a recurring theme throughout Wayne Fuller's (1982) history of rural education in the Middle West. In addition to the inadequate financial base characteristic of many rural communities, according to Fuller, difficulties in supporting public education also arose from farmers' social situation in an industrializing society:

> *[Farmers] could scarcely help feeling that educating their sons and daughters would either lure them away from the farm, where their labor was needed, or make them discontented with a life in which the monotony of morning and evening chores was broken mainly by bone-wearying work. . . . They [also] seemed instinctively to fear that education, at least too much education, went hand in hand with wealth, luxury, and leisure and ended in corruption and decadence. (Fuller 1985, 37–38)*

Recent economic trends affecting rural areas appear to have magnified the financial difficulties that historically have hampered the operation of many rural districts. Thus, a case study conducted in rural areas in Minnesota found that low commodity prices, falling land values, and curtailed mining operations have produced negative effects beyond "normal business cycle fluctuations" and are producing both decline in enrollment and "reduced capacity for local tax support" of rural education (Sederberg 1986, 19–20). Conversely, various observers have pointed out that economic recession has made public education an even more important force than it has been traditionally in providing jobs and skilled personnel for rural areas and in promoting the development of rural communities (e.g., Hobbs 1982; Sederberg 1986).

Teacher Shortage

Due in part to financial difficulties and concomitantly low salaries, many rural districts face recurrent problems in attracting and retaining qualified teachers, even when there is a nationwide oversupply in most subject areas (Miller and Sidebottom 1985). According to a study conducted by the National Rural Project, for example, nearly half of seventy-five rural school districts polled in seventeen states reported problems in recruiting and keeping teachers. In addition to low salaries, cultural and social isolation was noted frequently as a reason for high rates of turnover and insufficient numbers of candidates for teaching positions in rural areas (Helge and Marrs 1981; Miller and Sidebottom 1985).

On the other hand, many rural communities also have distinctive features that can be advantageous in attracting and retaining teachers. As Miller and Sidebottom (1985) pointed out, these features include friendly relationships in the community and high potential for achieving respect, scenic and easygoing environments with little traffic or pollution and attractive recreational opportunities, small enrollments that allow teachers to give individual attention to students, and availability of libraries and university extension branches (pp. 15–16).

William Mathes and Robert Carlson (1986) have studied differences among newly certified teachers who accepted positions in differing types of communities and found that many of those teachers in rural school districts were particularly concerned with settling and fitting in to their new communities and work environments. Mathes and Carlson concluded that successful recruitment of rural teachers depends not just on competitive salaries but also on "a sense of support and the presence of a pleasant school climate" (p. 9). Based on similar data and considerations, Miller and Sidebottom recommended a number of actions, such as the seven following, that might help rural schools acclimate their staff and improve professionally:

1. Initiate a colleague support program by pairing new and established teachers.
2. Provide district services or referrals to help with personal problems.
3. Publicly recognize new staff members and their accomplishments.
4. Help teachers obtain external grants for scholarships, travel, and other professional development.
5. Assign faculty only in their areas of certification.
6. Provide such staff development incentives as university credit, released time, and certification renewal.
7. Promote activities to reduce stress, including social functions and exercise.

Instructional Improvement

Due partly to resource limitations and to their low enrollment, rural districts traditionally have had difficulty in providing comprehensive, high-quality programs of curriculum and instruction and in meeting state government standards for minimal programming and services. This problem has become particularly acute as education has come to play an increasingly central role in postindustrial society and as state governments have increased minimum standards during the 1980s.

The problem is not, of course, a new one. As documented in Wayne Fuller's history of rural education, nineteenth-century educators criticized many country schools for their insufficient tax base and programs and for glaring inequities between one school or district and the next:

> *To most Midwestern professional educators the small school was ipso facto a poor school. Supported by only a handful of taxpayers it was too poor to employ a good teacher, to build a good schoolhouse, to buy school apparatus, and to stay open longer than the minimum number of days required by state law. . . .*
>
> *Some districts were populous and could easily afford a good school, while others, sparsely populated, could not, even with the greatest effort. (Fuller 1985, 111–112)*

Distance Education. Improvements in transportation, government initiatives to reduce inequalities, growing awareness of the limitations of extremely small schools and districts, and other forces have coalesced to bring about an enormous reduction in the numbers of rural school districts and one-room schools (see Table 12.1). However, many rural districts with low enrollment and very

Table 12.1 *Numbers and Sizes of School Districts Since 1930*

	1931–32	1961–62	1967–68	1973–74	1982–83
Number of public school districts	127,244	35,555	22,010	16,730	15,747
Number of public schools	270,000	107,000	97,890	90,976	82,039
Total public school enrollment below college level (in thousands)	26,300	38,253	44,140	45,652	39,328
Average enrollment per school district	207	1,075	2,000	2,700	2,479

Source: U.S. Department of Education, 1985–86.

small schools still find it difficult to provide a full range of instructional services and a comprehensive curriculum. To address this problem, rural educators are trying to make use of advanced technology. This approach, frequently referred to as *distance education,* includes use of such technological developments as the following five techniques (Wall 1986):

1. Videotape lessons.
2. Audio teleconferencing, using telephones or other one-way or two-way audio technologies.
3. Interactive television, involving real-time, two-way audio, and visual contact.
4. Interactive video, blending microcomputers with video storage units.
5. Computer networks.

Used effectively, distance education can serve a variety of functions, including provision of specialized courses and instructors to isolated schools, facilitation of interaction among students at differing schools, dissemination of timely information, and delivery of staff development services. Recent examples of the promising use of distance education include development of an Agri Data Network for students studying agriculture at fifteen rural schools in Wyoming; delivery via satellite of instruction in Spanish, Japanese, and precalculus to eighteen school districts in Washington state; provision through teleconferencing of required foreign-language instruction at rural schools in Nebraska; and delivery of foreign language and physics instruction in Oklahoma, Texas, and Utah through multistate telecommunications networks (Pipho 1986b; Wall 1986; Batey and Cowell 1987; Gudat 1988).

Smith Holt (1985) has pointed out that distance education can be very cost effective and also can draw on the best and most current resources to deliver outstanding and exciting instruction. Milan Wall (1986) and others have pointed out that effective distance education requires sharing resources and responsibilities across school districts and that the "major roadblocks are usually political, not technological" (p. 51).

Innovative Projects. Paul Nachtigal (1982) has examined several innovative efforts made to improve instruction in rural schools. Nachtigal concluded that some approaches, such as the Teacher Corps and the Experimental Schools Project, did not work well in rural locations, primarily because they did not take adequate account of the special circumstances that differentiate rural from urban situations and the diverse circumstances that make one rural situation different from others. Some other projects, however, do appear to be effective because they allow for extensive adaptation to local rural settings. Nachtigal concluded that one such project is the National Diffusion Network, which provides school districts with information and follow-up support in selecting among and then implementing successful approaches for improving curriculum and instruction.

Nachtigal and his colleagues also have tried to identify strategies that "if properly implemented" would "go far in creating a development capacity in rural education." Among the strategies he viewed as most promising are to emphasize "people development" by helping participants in leadership development programs visit and work with others in similar situations and to stress the provision of follow-up support, both technical and psychological, for innovative efforts. He also suggests that "acceptance of rural reality" requires a "critical look" at the current organization and delivery of rural education to develop "new models" that "fall somewhere between the country school of days past and the urban-style school that has taken its place" (Nachtigal 1982, 307–309).

Nonpublic Schools and Public Policy

Church-supported and other nonpublic schools have been an important part of the education system in the United States, both at the elementary-secondary levels and the higher education level. In some towns and rural areas with a population relatively homogeneous in religion, such schools have outshadowed the public schools. They also have constituted a very large enterprise in cities with a high proportion of Catholics. In the Chicago area, for example, enrollment in Catholic elementary schools peaked at 182,262 in the city in 1960 and grew to 127,295 in the suburbs in 1965 (Sanders 1977, 4–5). In 1987 nearly 700,000 students attended Catholic elementary and secondary schools in the five systems operated in Brooklyn, Chicago, Los Angeles, Manhattan, and Philadelphia (National Catholic Education Association 1987).

As shown in Table 12.2, a majority of students in nonpublic elementary and secondary schools are in Catholic schools, and the vast majority are in church-related schools. The number of nonpublic students declined by 19 percent between 1966 and 1979. This decrease was accounted for by Catholic schools, in which enrollment dropped primarily because of the decline in the size of the youth population, the movement of population out of central cities, and increased operating costs. Enrollment in Catholic schools has decreased further to approximately 2.8 million students since 1979 (Pavuk 1987). The percentage

Table 12.2 *Enrollment Trends in Nonpublic Elementary and Secondary Schools, 1966–1979, by Type of School*

Type of School	Enrollment 1966	Enrollment 1979	Percentage Change
Roman Catholic	5,481,300	3,269,800	– 40
Lutheran	188,500	217,400	15
Seventh Day Adventist	62,600	148,200	137
Baptist	25,200	204,100	710
Jewish	52,600	101,800	94
Episcopal	48,600	76,500	57
Methodist	5,600	11,200	100
Presbyterian	4,800	12,800	167
Friends (Quaker)	10,600	14,600	38
Other church-related	83,700	281,200	236
Not church related	341,300	746,700	54
Total nonpublic	6,304,800	5,084,300	– 19

Source: National Center for Education Statistics, 1981.

of elementary and secondary students enrolled in Catholic schools ranged from a high of 31 percent in the Mideast region to a low of 7 percent in New England (see Table 12.3).

Enrollment in church-related schools other than Catholic generally increased rapidly in the 1970s, as was true for Baptist schools and for evangelical groups (included in the "other church-related" in Table 12.2). Reasons for increasing enrollment in church-related schools frequently involved dissatisfaction with the public schools (including unhappiness with achievement levels and discipline), perceived lack of teaching of moral values, and/or desegregation of public school districts (Lines 1986). Enrollment in nonpublic elementary and secondary schools represented 12 percent of total public and nonpublic enrollment in 1985, as compared with 14 percent in 1964.

Table 12.3. *Catholic School Enrollment as a Percentage of Total Elementary and Secondary School Enrollment, 1983 to 1987 by Region*

Region	1983	1985	1987
Great Plains	25.6	25.7	15.9
Mid-Atlantic	32.1	31.7	31.0
New England	7.1	7.0	6.9
Plains	8.7	8.8	9.0
Southwest	11.2	11.4	11.6
West/Far West	15.3	15.4	15.6

Source: National Catholic Education Association, 1987.

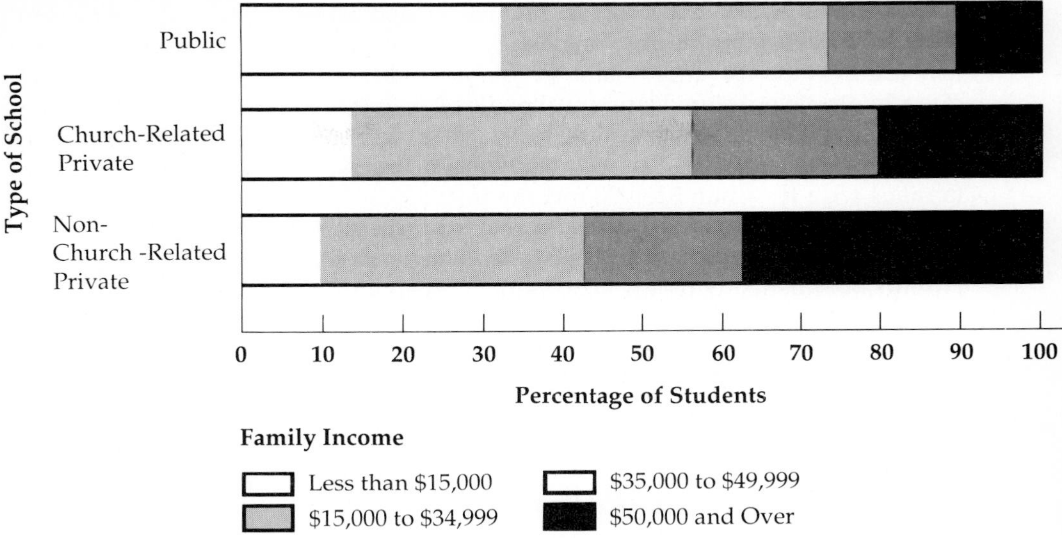

Figure 12.2 ***Proportion of Elementary and Secondary Students by Family Income and Control of School, 1985*** (*Source*: Center for Education Statistics 1986.)

In part due to the relatively high socioeconomic status of most students attending prestigious independent private schools and to the withdrawal of many middle-class families from some urban public schools, the average social class of students in nonpublic schools is higher than that of students in public schools. More than 30 percent of public-school students were from families with annual income less than $15,000 in 1985, as compared with 12 percent of nonpublic-school students (see Figure 2.2). Related data on parents' education also show that in 1982, 94 percent of students whose parents did not have high-school diplomas attended public schools, compared with only 81 percent for students whose parents have four or more years of college (*Statistical Abstract of the United States, 1987*).

One notable trend in nonpublic schools involves their enrollment of minority students. Although enrollment in Catholic schools declined by more than 40 percent between 1971 and 1987, the number of minority students (black, Hispanic, Asian, American Indian) increased slightly, and the percentage of minority students increased from 11 percent to 22 percent (National Catholic Education Association 1987). Growth in minority enrollment of Catholic schools was largest in the big cities. By 1982, for example, minority students constituted 44 percent of the enrollment in Catholic schools in Chicago (Lanier 1982).

In line with public-nonpublic differences reported above, the families of minority students in nonpublic schools generally are higher in social class than are those of minority students in public schools (Goldberg 1986). This is not surprising inasmuch as nonpublic schools charge tuition—frequently, a substantial amount. On the other hand, many nonpublic schools provide scholarships or have low tuition because they receive church subsidies, pay relatively low salaries, and/or have relatively high pupil-teacher ratios. Thus, they frequently do have a significant enrollment of students from low-income families (Cibulka, O'Brien, and Zewe 1982). As shown in Figure 12.2, nearly 15 percent of the students in church-related elementary and secondary schools were from families with less than $15,000 income in 1985.

Some observers view the trend toward increased nonpublic enrollment of minority students in big cities as a "new strategy for upward mobility" among parents dissatisfied with low achievement levels and severe discipline problems at many urban schools enrolling high proportions of poverty students (Goldberg 1986). As noted above, much of the Catholic school enrollment is in big cities, and students who are black or Hispanic now constitute 20 percent of Catholic enrollment. Only about one-third of the black students in Catholic schools are Catholic—an indication that many black students fled the public schools and also that Catholic and other nonpublic schools appear to be providing important educational services for many urban minority students.

Achievement in Nonpublic Schools

Whether nonpublic schools are more effective than public schools in raising academic achievement and accomplishing other educational goals has become an important issue in the past few years. The debate was spurred particularly by publication of research conducted by James Coleman, Thomas Hoffer, and Sally Kilgore (1981). This research analyzed 1980 data collected from 58,728 students in 1,016 high schools as part of the High School and Beyond study sponsored by the National Center for Education Statistics. After comparing data on achievement and other variables for students in public and nonpublic schools, Coleman, Hoffer, and Kilgore reached the following conclusions. Presented under the heading of "premises," these conclusions indicate whether nonpublic schools should or should not receive additional government aid or other support (Coleman, Hoffer, and Kilgore 1981, 224–233):

Premises Underlying Policies That Would Increase the Role of Private Schools:

1. Private schools provide better cognitive outcomes than do public schools. . . . When family background factors that predict achievement are controlled, students in both Catholic and other private schools are shown to achieve at a higher level than students in public schools. . . .
2. Private schools provide a safer, more disciplined, and more ordered environment than do public schools.

   The evidence is strong that this premise is true. . . .
3. Private schools are more successful in creating an interest in learning than are public schools.

   There is little evidence to confirm or disconfirm this premise.

4. Private schools encourage interest in higher education and lead more of their students to attend college than do public schools with comparable students.
   The evidence on this premise is toward a positive answer, but it is not extremely strong evidence.
5. Private schools are smaller and thus bring about greater degrees of participation in sports and other activities than do public schools.
   The evidence shows that this premise is true for other private schools, but not for Catholic schools. . . .
6. Private schools have smaller class sizes, and thus allow teachers and students to have greater contact.
   The other private schools have sharply lower student-teacher ratios than the public schools, while the Catholic schools have slightly higher ratios. . . .

Premises Underlying Policies That Would Decrease the Role of Private Schools:

1. Private schools are socially divisive along income lines, creaming the students from higher income backgrounds, and segregating them into elite schools.
   The evidence on this premise works in two directions. First, among the three major sectors, the other private schools contain students from somewhat higher income backgrounds and the Catholic schools contain students from slightly higher income background than the public schools. The differences are primarily at the highest and lowest income levels, with all three sectors having a majority of students in a broad middle income category. . . .
2. Private schools are divisive along religious lines, segregating different religious groups into different schools.
   The evidence is strong that this is true. . . .
3. Private schools are divisive along racial lines, in two ways: They contain few blacks or other minorities, and thus segregate whites in private schools from blacks in public schools; and the private sector itself is more racially segregated than the public sector.
   The evidence shows that the first of these premises is true with respect to blacks but not with respect to Hispanics and that the second is not true with respect to blacks or Hispanics. . . .
4. Private schools do not provide the educational range that public schools do, particularly in vocational and other nontraditional courses or programs.
   The evidence on this premise is that it is correct. . . .

Following publication of the major report, Coleman summarized his interpretation of the data on differences between public and nonpublic schools:

> *The major measured differences . . . [are] in disciplinary climate, in academic demands, and in student behavior. Further, even when the backgrounds of students are statistically controlled, much of these differences remains—differences in homework, in student attendance and in-school behavior, and differences in the disciplinary climate perceived by students. These differences can reasonably be attributed to differences in school policy rather than student background.*
>
> *When we examined, wholly within the public sector, the performance of . . .*

> *the average public school sophomore, [at schools] with the levels of homework and attendance . . . and disciplinary climate and student behavior attributable to school policy in the Catholic or other private schools, the levels of achievement are approximately the same as those found in the Catholic and other-private sectors. (Coleman, Hoffer, and Kilgore 1981, 19–20)*

Because the data analyzed by Coleman, Hoffer, and Kilgore were part of a major government-financed study, they are available for further analysis and reanalysis by other researchers. Several researchers did this and reported results that differ from those of Coleman and his colleagues. In addition, a number of social scientists and educators have challenged conclusions of the study on a variety of technical research grounds and on the basis that it did not fully take account of home background and other differences between public and nonpublic students and schools.

For example, Samuel Peng (1982) has analyzed data from the High School and Beyond study and found that controlling for students' ability on entering high school eliminates achievement differences between seniors in public and nonpublic high schools, thus indicating that differences in "input" are responsible for measured achievement differentials. Page and Keith (1981) took account of estimated differences in family background not measured in High School and Beyond and found that this explained the achievement difference between public and nonpublic students. Willms (1982) reanalyzed data from High School and Beyond and reported that when one takes account of family background, there is no difference in achievement of public and nonpublic students in "academic courses of study," though there is a small difference between those in the general track. Goldberger and Cain (1982) carefully reexamined the data and methods used by Coleman, Hoffer, and Kilgore and concluded that there is "no basis for accepting their conclusions and no merit in their analysis" (p. 121). Keith and Page (1985) reanalyzed the data further and concluded that after accounting for background differences, black and Hispanic students have achievement scores little if any higher in Catholic schools than in public schools. Raudenbush and Bryk (1986) reported that although students low in socioeconomic status who attend Catholic schools have achievement somewhat higher than those in public schools, for high status students the pattern is reversed.

Thus, critics of the research reported by Coleman and his colleagues generally have concluded that unmeasured home background variables involving greater motivation and home support are higher among nonpublic students whose parents are willing to pay tuition than among public school students of the same social class and income level, and that these differences account for most or all of the achievement differences between public and nonpublic schools. They also argue that the reason nonpublic schools are more orderly and disciplined is that they do not have to accept disorderly or difficult students, and that other research such as a study by the National Assessment of Educational Progress (1981c) indicates there is little or no difference in achievement between public and nonpublic students after taking account of background differences.

Coleman and his colleagues as well as other researchers also have carried out additional analyses that they believe confirm and extend the original conclusions. For example, Coleman and Hoffer (1987) and Lee and Bryk (1988) have reported that nonpublic schools enhance achievement by placing a higher proportion of students in academic tracks than do public schools; and Bryk, Holland, Lee, and Carriedo (1984) found that students in Catholic schools had higher achievement associated with such factors as positive discipline, greater emphasis on academics, and less separate grouping of students low in socioeconomic and/or minority status. The latter variable in turn is related to the smaller concentration of poor and minority students in Catholic schools than in public schools. In addition, Coleman and Hoffer (1987) analyzed data on the performance of High School and Beyond students after 1980 and concluded that Catholic schools produce greater achievement gains and lower dropout rates among low-income, black, and Hispanic students than do other nonpublic schools or public schools.

One major reason so much difference of opinion exists concerning achievement differentials between nonpublic and public schools is that it is so difficult to determine whether family and home environment differences in student's background, social-class mixture in student bodies, and other input factors have been adequately identified, measured, and statistically taken account of in assessing school outcomes. The research provides strong evidence that orderly school environment, homework, emphasis on college prep courses, internal tracking, and other related school variables are associated with differences in student performance, but that these variables are themselves related to student background and social-class mixture variables that may or may not have been adequately accounted for in a given data set. In addition, the small magnitude of the average achievement gains registered by students in either public or nonpublic schools makes it difficult to identify effects associated with schools or sectors (i.e., public/nonpublic) or to attach much importance to such effects when they are detected (Haertel 1985). Thus, researchers probably will continue to argue over the relative effectiveness of public and nonpublic schools.

If nonpublic schools are more successful than public schools in promoting high achievement among comparable students and student bodies, one important reason may be that they tend to function with more independence and less bureaucracy than do many public schools. This latter generalization has received substantial support from research by John Chubb and Terry Moe of the Brookings Institution. Based on data from the National Administrator—Teacher Survey, which collected follow-up data and expanded on the High School and Beyond Study, Chubb and Moe (1985) found that "public schools, relative to private, live in environments that are complex, demanding, powerful, constraining, and uncooperative. As a result, their policies, procedures, and personnel are more likely to be imposed from the outside" (p. 41).

In particular, as reported by Chubb and Moe, principals of public schools are much more constrained than are nonpublic principals in hiring and firing teachers. In addition, constraints on public-school principals result in their providing "less instructional leadership for teachers and less clear signals about school objectives," as well as less opportunity for teachers to work collegially and exert influence over their own work (p. 42). These latter characteristics,

Chubb and Moe also point out, have been associated with effectiveness of instruction in research on successful schools.

A subsequent version (1986) of Chubb and Moe's report also cautions, however, that organizational and bureaucratic problems that impede the effective functioning of public schools cannot be solved simply by demanding or legislating that these schools operate more like nonpublic schools. Their concluding comments in this regard include the following remarks:

> *The public schools . . . are subordinates in a hierarchic system . . . in which myriad interests and actors use the rules, structure, and processes of democracy to impose their preferences on the local school. It is no accident that public schools are lacking in autonomy, that principals have difficulty leading, and that school goals are heterogeneous, unclear, and undemanding . . . [nor that] weak principals are tenured. . . . [This organizational syndrome is] deeply anchored in democratic control as we have come to know it. . . .*
>
> *If this is essentially correct, the standard proposals for reforming public schools are misconceived. It is easy to say, for instance, that schools should have greater autonomy or that principals should be stronger leaders, but these sorts of reforms cannot simply be imposed. . . . A maverick principal who comes on as a strong leader . . . would quickly tend to get into hot water with political and bureaucratic superiors, teachers, and unions.* (Chubb and Moe 1986, 43–46)

From one point of view, the question of whether minority students in nonpublic schools have better achievement than those in public schools is analogous to issues involving the establishment of public magnet schools. Magnet schools frequently have been viewed (see Chapter 9) as a means to retain middle-class nonminority and minority students in big-city school districts with high concentrations of poverty students and to provide opportunity for upwardly mobile working-class students who do not want to attend poverty schools. As Denis Doyle has pointed out, private schools in big cities also have provided an "escape" from the problems perceived to be prevalent in big-city districts: "The issue . . . is educational quality, for it is precisely 'good' [private] schools that enroll those students that the 'bad' [public] schools 'push' into the market. . . . It appears that in the 1980s, at least, private schools are increasingly being viewed as the good alternative, and urban public schools as schools of last resort" (Doyle 1982, 17).

In part, the argument that private schools, like public magnet schools, provide an important alternative for middle-class and upwardly mobile working-class students depends on the assertion that they have a more productive and effective educational environment than do the public schools. As we have seen with respect to studies cited above on private and public high schools, private schools do seem to provide a more conducive environment for learning than do public schools, but there is no agreement that this advantage is due to superior educational policies and practices rather than to greater selectivity. The same point can be made comparing magnet and nonmagnet public schools. Just as research on a nonpublic elementary school enrolling high-achieving poverty students indicated that these students had much higher home environment scores than did low-achieving poverty students at a nearby public school after taking account of social class (Levine et al. 1972), so research on poverty students in an elementary magnet school indicated that they have higher home environment scores than do poverty students of similar social class who elected to remain in their neighborhood schools (Levine, Eubanks, and Roskoski 1980). Such research supports the conclusion that it is extremely difficult if not impossible to disentangle "selectivity" effects from "school quality" effects in trying to determine whether private schools are more effective than public schools.

Tuition Tax Credits

The debate over the relative effectiveness of public and nonpublic schools has taken place in a larger social context in which political leaders have considered providing tuition tax credits for the parents of students in nonpublic schools. A tax credit allows for a reduction in taxes according to the percent of tuition deductible for federal income tax purposes. In August 1982, President Reagan proposed that families earning less than $50,000 per year be allowed a tax reduction equal to 50 percent of nonpublic school tuition, with a maximum limit of $100 per nonpublic student in 1983, $300 in 1984, and $500 in 1985 and thereafter. The president pointed out that the federal government already was spending approximately $350 per child for the education of children in public schools.

Public policy debates concerning tuition tax credits for nonpublic students have been vigorous and emotional. Opponents have argued that such credits would provide unconstitutional support for church-related schools, would undermine the public school system by supporting and encouraging the movement of students to nonpublic schools, would result in a large drain on the U.S. Treasury, would reduce the likelihood of obtaining voter support for public-school tax increases, and/or would contribute to additional racial and socioeconomic segregation and isolation of low-status students in the public schools.

Debate over provision of tax credits and other forms of aid for nonpublic schools also is concerned with policies and practices at the state level. As shown in Table 12.4, only three states (Iowa, Louisiana, and Minnesota) currently provide tax benefits to assist students in nonpublic schools, but many states do provide assistance in the form of provision of transportation and/or loans or grants to help nonpublic schools provide instructional materials and testing or counseling services.

Supporters of tuition tax credits argue that such credits are not unconstitutional (e.g., McGarry 1982) and would not severely reduce federal revenues or hamper public-school tax levy efforts. Often pointing to the research of Coleman and his colleagues (above), they also argue that tax credits would provide wider opportunities for disadvantaged students and would not contribute to and might even reduce racial and socioeconomic isolation. In addition, many supporters believe that tax credits not only would provide parents with a choice

Table 12.4 *Forms of Government Assistance to Nonpublic Schools, by State*

	Loans or Grants for Textbooks and Other Materials	Transportation	Testing or Counseling Services	Tax Benefit for Tuition Payment
Alaska		x		
Arkansas			x	
California		x		
Colorado	x			
Connecticut	x	x	x	
Delaware		x		
Florida			x	
Georgia			x	
Illinois	x		x	
Indiana		x		
Iowa	x	x	x	x
Kansas		x		
Kentucky		x		
Louisiana	x	x		x
Massachusetts		x		
Michigan		x	x	
Minnesota	x	x	x	x
Mississippi	x			
Montana		x		
Nebraska		x		
New Hampshire	x	x	x	
New Jersey	x	x		
New Mexico	x	x	x	
New York	x			
North Carolina			x	
North Dakota		x		
Ohio	x	x	x	
Pennsylvania	x	x	x	
Rhode Island	x	x	x	
Washington			x	
West Virginia	x	x		
Wisconsin		x		

Note: This table does not include states that provide none of the assistance listed. A number of states allow for part-time enrollment of nonpublic students in public schools.

Sources: U.S. Department of Education data provided by the Education Commission of the States in 1983 and state education agencies in 1986.

in selecting schools but also would stimulate reform efforts in the public schools. This latter point of view has been articulated by Robert Hawkins, Jr., as follows:

> *President Reagan's support for tuition tax credits has again raised the issue of educational reform. The outcry from the education establishment has been both intense and predictable: tuition tax credits will destroy public education and aid the*

> *rich. While the latter statement is false on its face, the former provokes comment. The very notion that tuition tax credits can destroy public education says something about the state of public education. Cynics might well say that public education is doing an adequate job of destroying itself, needing no help from tax credits. . . . Increasing numbers of parents are choosing, at great cost to themselves, to send their children to private schools. These two factors demonstrate how important education is to parents and that they will withhold support from public education until they begin to receive the type of education they want from their public schools. (Hawkins 1982, 9–10)*

As we pointed out in the preceding section, research does not allow for a confident conclusion regarding the question of whether nonpublic school students have higher achievement than do public school students with the same family and home background. Therefore, it is very difficult to predict achievement or other output effects of a tax credit that might shift some or many students from public to nonpublic schools. Similarly, researchers disagree on whether tax credits would increase or decrease racial and socioeconomic isolation in the public schools, and the effects of a tax credit with respect to segregation certainly would depend on the policies (if any) instituted to guard against negative outcomes. For example, a policy requiring that transportation be provided free along with a tax credit would enhance the likelihood that poverty parents would send their children outside the inner city to mixed-class schools, as would policies stipulating that poverty families that paid no taxes would receive the tax credit as an income payment.

Lacking agreement concerning the validity of available data, proponents and opponents will continue to cite findings and conclusions favorable to their own position. Meanwhile, research can help identify some of the probable effects of tax credits and their implications for the educational system. For example, David Longanecker (1982) of the Institute for Research on Educational Finance and Governance has calculated that given current enrollment, a maximum credit of $250 per student based on deductions of 50 percent of tuition would reduce federal tax revenues by about one billion dollars per year in 1982 dollars. Data collected by the Council of Great City Schools indicate that President Reagan's proposal would have increased federal aid per nonpublic school student from $43 per student in 1980–81 to $329 per student in 1984–85, at the same time that aid per public school student based on federal budget estimates would have declined from $206 to $105. On the other hand, any associated movement of students from public to nonpublic schools could increase the amount of local and state revenue available per student in the public schools. Needless to say, we believe that additional research is necessary to help policy makers struggling with the larger issue of public support for students who attend nonpublic schools.

Education Vouchers

Another way by which nonpublic schools may receive public financial support is through the use of *education vouchers*, a device that has been much discussed and debated since about 1968. This idea grew in part out of the movement for *alternative schools,* which had developed vigorously in the big cities. With so much dissatisfaction over the existing school system, it was natural to ask for a substantial amount of experimentation with new schools, and this might be better done by people outside the present school system than by those who have adjusted and perhaps are tied down to the usual procedures (Raywid 1987; Hume 1988).

One obvious way to promote experimentation and new methods is to support with public funds an array of new schools developed by innovators and favored or accepted by parents and students. This led to the voucher idea. Basically, this idea is that parents and students are best judges of the kind of education they need, and that public funds should be entrusted to them, to use for their education in an open market where they have a choice among schools. This should provide better education than the present system, which gives the educational bureaucracy a monopoly.

The voucher method would give a family a voucher for each school-age child, which is worth a certain amount of money—approximately the amount that is spent on the average pupil in the public schools. The family then shops around among schools that meet certain criteria and assigns the voucher to the school of their choice. The school is supported by the vouchers it collects, plus any other money it can obtain from private sources. Parents could send their children to the local public school by giving their vouchers to that school, but the public schools would have to compete in the market with a variety of nonpublic schools as well as with other public schools.

This idea aroused active support and active opposition from people with a wide variety of attitudes toward education. Vouchers were approved by very conservative people, and also by very radical people, because the scheme could presumably free them to find or create the kind of education they most desired.

The federal Office of Economic Opportunity, in its role as supporter of educational experiments designed to reduce poverty and to increase educational opportunity, made several grants of money to support tryouts of the voucher idea in the 1970s. Also, the OEO supported an analysis by Professor Christopher Jencks of Harvard University of the pros and cons of the voucher concept. This analysis explored seven possible voucher plans, or sets of ground rules for distributing money to voucher schools. Jencks points out the probable advantages and disadvantages of each plan. The simplest plan, advocated by free-market conservatives, would provide every child with a flat grant, which his or her family could use to pay tuition at the school of its choice. The school could select pupils freely among applicants and therefore could reject applicants because of low IQ, behavior problems, ethnicity, or any other criteria.

The OEO made grants for feasibility studies of vouchers to school systems in Seattle, Gary (Indiana), San Francisco, and San Jose (California). The only study that concluded that the plan was feasible was the San Jose study. An elementary school district (Alum Rock) in that metropolitan area concluded that a plan limited to public schools was worth trying. Accordingly, the OEO made a grant to fund the Alum Rock voucher program for two years—1972–1974. This experiment was limited to public schools in the Alum Rock School District. Parents chose between twenty-one competing school programs, not schools. They allocated their vouchers (equal to the average per-pupil expenditure in the district, plus a supplement of one-third for children who are eligible for federal school lunch programs and who come from low-income families). Several schools offered three or four different programs, giving some choice to parents who prefer the local neighborhood school. Children were bused (at OEO expense) to any other school with a program they wanted. Names of some of the school programs were Cultural Arts, Multicultural (bilingual), Math-Science, Open-Activity Centered, Individual Learning, Continuous Progress Nongraded, Three R's Plus, Basic Skills, and School 2000. The voucher program was made available to 4,000 pupils, and some 40 percent chose nontraditional programs for the 1972–73 school year.

The OEO also provided substantial funding to evaluate the results of the Alum Rock experiment. Cohen and Farrar (1977) reviewed the data on the voucher experiment at Alum Rock and reached the conclusion that it "produced mixed results, and that several views are plausible. As an effort to reform the nation's schools, the voucher demonstration left much to be desired." Relatively few parents took advantage of the opportunity to select an innovative school for their children, and students' academic performance did not improve. On the other hand, Cohen and Farrar also point out that "Alum Rock increased professionals' ability to choose and design their work settings, and made it possible for parents to select among alternatives. If choice and diversity are good, then schools in Alum Rock were better places" (1977, pp. 96–97).

The Alum Rock demonstration constituted only one small test of one version of the voucher approach in one small school district. After the Office of Economic Opportunity was abolished by President Richard Nixon, the voucher approach received relatively little attention except that the Nixon administration attempted to work out a more comprehensive test of vouchers in the state of New Hampshire. However, this plan was aborted by the president's resignation, and vouchers were seldom discussed until a movement arose in the early 1980s to introduce vouchers in California. Led by Professors John Coons and Stephen Sugarman, the California movement attempted to collect sufficient voter signatures and approval to introduce vouchers on a statewide basis.

Education by Choice: The Case for Family Control, by Coons and Sugarman (1978), analyzed many of the issues and possibilities regarding the delivery of vouchers to parents for their children's education and resulted in the preparation of a specific plan that would have established two new types of schools in California: "New Private Schools," which would be eligible for government vouchers, and "New Public Schools," which school districts, higher education institutions, or other public agencies could establish or designate to receive vouchers. As long as the New Schools met state requirements for hiring, employment, admissions policies, curriculum, and facilities and reserved at least 25 percent of their places for enrollment of low-income students on a nondiscriminatory basis, they would be eligible to redeem government vouchers.

Although California efforts to introduce vouchers failed in 1981 and 1982, the topic is likely to arise again in California and elsewhere in the future. The arguments put forth by Coons and Sugarman and their supporters address several fundamental issues involving the relationships between families, schools, and other government and nongovernmental agencies, and the issues involved cannot be expected simply to disappear from public debate (Nathan 1985). Coons and Sugarman called attention to some of these issues:

> *Family choice for the nonrich could lead to an end to the American double standard. Among those who can afford private school, society leaves the goals and means of education to the family; for the rest of society, the informing principles are politically determined and implemented through compulsory assignments to a particular public school. . . . [If society moves] in a variety of ways toward freedom and responsibility for the family, the present world of schools will increasingly appear an anachronism. . . . The significance of the current political favor for the family is that it provides a respite—a breathing space in history—during which arguments about the family as a responsible political unit can expect a serious hearing for the first time in a century. (1978, 2–3, 200–203)*

Voucher possibilities were raised again in 1985 when U.S. Secretary of Education William Bennett helped prepare legislation that would have provided parents of children served by Chapter 1 with vouchers equal to the amount spent on disadvantaged Chapter 1 students in their local public-school district. The vouchers, varying in value from $280 in some locations to $1,133 in others and averaging $656 for 1986, would have enabled Chapter 1 students to choose among a variety of nonpublic and public schools. In addition to expanding choice, according to Bennett and other supporters, the voucher legislation would encourage constructive competition in education and increase parental involvement (Lewis 1986).

The proposed 1985 legislation for Chapter 1 vouchers generated some support but also widespread and vocal opposition and criticism. The Council of Chief State School Officers, for example, voted unanimously to oppose it, and the president of the American Association of School Administrators stated, "this proposal is just another way to give public money to private schools" (Stimson 1986, 26). Other major reasons for opposition included complaints that the legislation would reduce Chapter 1 funding for public schools, would not ensure that private schools receiving vouchers used these funds to provide special help for disadvantaged students, would constitute an administrative burden for public schools, and would tend to drain relatively well motivated students from the public schools (Stimson 1986; Bastian et al. 1986). Secretary Bennett subsequently abandoned the proposed legislation in November 1986, stating that the administration would seek to pursue expanded choice in education through other means.

Perspectives on the Role of Public and Nonpublic Schools

As noted in the preceding sections, advocates of financial assistance and other forms of support for nonpublic schools argue that such encouragement is desirable in order to enhance diversity in the educational system and expand choice for parents and students, to provide improved opportunities for economically disadvantaged students and minority students who attend ineffective public schools, and to enable nonpublic schools to continue offering an alternative for parents who believe that public schools do not place sufficient stress on religious or moral values.

Among the concerns most frequently expressed by opponents of assistance to nonpublic schools are the worries that such assistance would reduce enrollment and support for public schools and that social goals they believe have been historically well served by the public schools thereby would suffer serious erosion (Raywid 1987). Many opponents also believe that growth of the nonpublic system will magnify negative trends toward increasingly greater concentration of disadvantaged students in the public schools. This latter point of view has been articulated by federal Judge Thomas Wiseman:

> *Why should we be concerned about erosion of support for the public schools? Why should it bother us if there appears to be a trend toward a sharp division of society, in which the children of the affluent attend private schools and the public school system exists for the poor and black? . . . The answer to these questions lies in the recognition—the realization that public education has been the leavening agent by which our multi-ethnic, multi-racial society has been able to rise and become a whole loaf.*
>
> *It is* because *we had public schools, which most children attended, that we were able to assimilate so rapidly the great influx of immigrants. . . .*
>
> *It is largely* because *we had public schools, in which children from the most diverse of backgrounds learned to live and work together at an early age, that we have been able to maintain social harmony in such a heterogeneous conglomerate of people. (quoted in Price and Woodard 1985, 251)*

The conclusions one reaches concerning government assistance to nonpublic schools in the United States should be informed at least in part by analysis of the potential and probable positive and negative impacts on the public as well as the nonpublic system. The functions performed historically and currently by the public schools and possibilities for attaining them through nonpublic schools also should be considered. One useful example of an attempt to initiate this type of analysis has been provided by Charles Kniker (1985). He maintains that the public or "common" system of education traditionally was "expected" to serve five major goals:

1. Training in common citizenship.
2. Transmitting of a common set of values.
3. Promoting unity through common experiences for students of diverse background.
4. Providing common opportunities for students with differing social and economic backgrounds.
5. Developing widely accepted views of reforms to solve social problems.

After extensive discussion of changes that have occurred in schools and society, Kniker concluded that nonpublic schools now serve or can serve the functions involving common citizenship, values, and viewpoints regarding reform as well as the public schools do, but that the public schools are better situated to provide common experiences for building "unity from diversity" and for providing "common opportunities" to the disadvantaged. He concludes his essay with these comments:

> *The term "common school" has a proud history and . . . intent which is still valid. . . . We are more than individuals. Each of us is a member of many publics. Sooner or later, we must learn how to communicate with those publics as we face intimate personal problems and urgent social concerns. Self-contained educational systems, whether they are religious, economic, racial, geographical, forfeit that necessary function of the "common" school.*
>
> *A special word needs to be said to readers who are professional educators in the public sector. . . . The openness of the public schools is one test of whether it is truly a "common" school. If your needs must be met at the expense of the students, if you ignore valid criticisms from patrons, if you blame others for all your problems, then society can legitimately ask others to become our next common school. (Kniker 1985, 198)*

As regards the extent to which nonpublic schools are in a position to help provide common educational experiences for a diverse student body, data cited earlier in this chapter indicate that Catholic schools frequently have enrollment that is diverse racially and even socioeconomically, but that most other nonpublic schools do not appear to be nearly as diverse as the Catholic system. Of course it also is true that tax credits, vouchers, and other forms of assistance might help nonpublic schools attract many more minority students and severely disadvantaged students, provided they are not excluded by admissions criteria and other obstacles to enrollment. Many advocates of assistance to nonpublic schools would like to encourage such diversity through legislative guidelines for participation in an aid program.

Catholic and other nonpublic schools also might play a larger role than they do now in providing improved education for disadvantaged students if they received substantial financial assistance to facilitate such an effort. Our summary of research on achievement in public and nonpublic schools indicated that many nonpublic schools already are providing excellent opportunities for disadvantaged students, even though their capacity for doing so may be linked to or dependent on selection of students relatively high in motivation and home environment. On the other hand, governmental or other enhancement of the nonpublic system might harm the public schools by facilitating further withdrawal of middle-class and upward-mobile students, thus also reinforcing and increasing the problems associated with concentrated poverty in urban school districts.

It also should be noted that one's conclusions regarding the important issues involved in public policy toward nonpublic schools might be determined largely in accordance with interpretations regarding research on their differential characteristics and effectiveness. For example, if it is true that nonpublic schools are more successful and that the reasons for this success primarily involve more effective policies and practices (as argued by Coleman, Hoffer, and Kilgore 1981) and/or greater autonomy and independence (Chubb and Moe 1986), then the responses that seem desirable might include financial assistance for nonpublic schools and efforts to reduce unproductive organizational arrangements in public schools. If, on the other hand, nonpublic schools either are not more effective or are more effective primarily due to advantages in selecting students, then an analyst would be relatively more inclined to oppose public aid for nonpublic schools and to view such aid as potentially harmful to the public system.

EXERCISES

1. Are minority students significantly enrolled in nonpublic schools in your community? What is their social class background? Is there reason to believe they are learning more than they might in the public schools?
2. Visit a church-affiliated elementary or secondary school in your community and prepare a class report describing how its approach to education reflects its religious orientation.
3. To what extent do proposals for education vouchers and tuition tax credits reflect political and economic philosophies and positions? What political goals may influence the arguments of supporters and opponents?
4. After reading Wayne Fuller's book on *The Old Country School*, outline the advantages and disadvantages of the movement that consolidated rural school districts.
5. Discuss computer use in schools with teachers or administrators from a local school district. Do they believe it is helping to improve student achievement? How much are computers used in educating disadvantaged students?

SUGGESTIONS FOR FURTHER READING

1. The voucher concept and its educational applications are described and analyzed in a book by Mecklenburger and Hostrup entitled *Education Vouchers: From Theory to Alum Rock*. A useful history and analysis of the voucher movement is available in a 1977 article by David K. Cohen and Eleanor Farrar in *The Public Interest*.
2. The fascinating history of the Chicago Catholic schools is told in James W. Sander's *The Education of an Urban Minority: Catholics in Chicago, 1833–1965*.
3. *Religious Schooling in America*, edited by James C. Carper and Thomas C. Hunt, includes chapters on Catholic, Lutheran, Calvinist, Seventh-Day Adventist, and Christian as well as Jewish Day Schools.

4. As indicated in its subtitle, *The Old Country School* by Wayne Fuller tells "The Story of Rural Education in the Middle West." Traditional rural education also is described in several sections of *Main Street on the Middle Border* by Lewis Atherton.
5. *God's Choice*, by Alan Peshkin, is a case study of a fundamentalist Christian school.

13

School Reform and Effectiveness

At the conclusion of Chapter 2 we pointed out that education in our postindustrial, metropolitan society is in a state of crisis related to the deepening problems posed by international economic competition, introduction of high technology as a fundamental consideration in social, political, and economic development, and inadequate functioning of the educational system for a large proportion of students, particularly minority students in concentrated poverty neighborhoods in big cities.

The emergence of this crisis has not gone unnoticed or unremarked. As we describe in the first section of this final chapter, the general challenge to improve the effectiveness of education has had center-stage recognition since 1983, when a series of national reports focused public attention on indicators of low academic achievement, substantial adult illiteracy, significant high school dropout rates, and other problems involving education. Subsequent developments, also described in the next section, have continued to reflect and generate both serious concern at all levels of government and a variety of efforts to bring about reform of the educational system, particularly through action at the state level.

By the latter part of the 1980s, the sense of urgency being expressed about the crisis in U.S. schools and society had reached an unprecedented level. Early in 1987, for example, Arkansas Governor William Clinton told members of the American Association of Colleges of Teacher Education, "We don't have as much time as people think" to reform the schools. Without fundamental reform, he proceeded to point out, there will be a constantly widening gulf between the highly educated, well-paid segment of the work force and those who have not received an adequate education (Education Daily 1987b, 4).

Participation of business and civic leaders in calling for and supporting educational reform also has reached an unprecedented level, particularly as regards the challenge of improving the performance of students disadvantaged by economic status and/or minority background. Thus, in 1987 business leaders appeared for the first time before congressional committees considering reauthorization and expansion of Chapter 1 and other federal programs to assist low-achieving students. Also, a group of corporate leaders representing the American Can Company, the Aluminum Company of America, the State Street Bank and Trust Company, A.T.&T., and the Pacific Telesis Group provided this testimony:

> *Our collective appearance here today is intended to underscore the importance we attach to national efforts to provide educational opportunities for disadvantaged and low-income children and our specific support for the renewal of the Chapter 1 program of federal education aid for disadvantaged and low-income children.*

One of the best examples of growing national recognition of the need for massive efforts to improve education for students at-risk due to their disadvantaged background and status in postindustrial, metropolitan society has been provided by the Forum of Educational Organization Leaders (FEOL). Bringing together the leaders of eleven major national organizations dealing with various aspects of education, the FEOL on June 1, 1987, issued a statement on "Meeting the Needs of Children and Youth at Risk of School Failure," which included the following observations:

> *As we have carried forward our grand experiment in universal free public education, we have largely fashioned a system that has served well those who are white, middle to upper income, well motivated, and from relatively stable families. As students have deviated more and more from that norm, the system has served them less and less well. We sometimes seem to say to them, "We've provided the system. It's not our fault if you don't succeed." Whether that attitude is right or wrong, the critical mass of at-risk children and youth has grown so large proportionately that we are in some danger of being toppled by our sense of rightness and righteousness. Instead of blaming the students for not fitting the system, we must design and implement a structure that provides appropriate educational services to those most at risk. . . .*
>
> *To accomplish those objectives will require: changes in federal, state, and local educational policies; curriculum modifications; alterations in the time and place where education occurs; different relationships between the schools and a host of other institutions and agencies in the community; strengthening of parent/school relationships; more extensive and different pupil services; more measureable accountability for student learning; greater fiscal resources; and changes in the expectations of education throughout the schooling hierarchy. . . .*
>
> *. . . . The appropriate level of government (state and/or federal) must legislatively guarantee to each at-risk youngster the array of necessary educational services which are reasonably calculated to result in his or her graduation from high school. Never before has such a broad guarantee of educational services been made to individual children as an investment in the nation's future. (Forum of Educational Leaders 1987)*

National Reports and Developments, 1983–1988

National concern for improvement of the educational system in the United States was greatly stimulated in 1983 when the National Commission on Excellence in Education, appointed by U.S. Secretary of Education Terrel Bell, released its report and recommendation under the title *A Nation at Risk*. The United States is threatened, the National Commission concluded, by a "rising tide of mediocrity" in education. Stating that the United States has been moving toward "unthinkable, unilateral educational disarmament," the National Commission also concluded that "if an unfriendly foreign government had attempted to impose on America the mediocre educational performance that exists today, we might well have viewed it as an act of war" (National Commission 1983, 14).

A Nation at Risk documented many aspects of what its members perceived to be decline or inadequacy in the educational system, including weakening of high-school graduation requirements, high rates of illiteracy, declining achievement scores, and unsatisfactory graduation rates. The commission proceeded to recommend more stringent requirements and higher expectations for students in the "Five New Basics" (English, mathematics, science, social studies, computer science). Recommendations for improving achievement in the New Basics included assignment of more homework, emphasis on study skills, a longer school day and a longer school year, and improvements in management and organization of schools. Regarding teachers and teaching, the Commission recommended that:

1. Teacher preparation programs should have higher standards.
2. Salaries for teachers should be professionally competitive and performance-based.* School districts should establish career ladders for teaching personnel.
3. Teacher contracts should be for eleven months a year.
4. Grants and loans should be available to attract students into teaching.
5. New teachers should be supervised by master teachers.
6. Alternative routes to teacher certification should be established.

A number of other national reports on the status of education and recommendations for improving it also were published in 1983 and 1984. For example, the College Board published *Academic Preparation for College* (1983), the Education Commission of the States published the report of its Task Force on Education for Economic Growth, and the Twentieth Century Fund published the report of its National Task Force on Federal Elementary and Secondary Education Policy. (The latter two reports are summarized in Table 13.1). These reports, together with numerous other national, state, and local studies, called for action to improve the performance of students and teachers at all levels of the educational system.

The various national, state, and local reports on the status of education received considerable and continuing attention throughout the United States and undoubtedly played an important part in stimulating and reinforcing efforts

* Performance-based remuneration usually refers to arrangements for paying teachers in accordance with extra contributions beyond regular classroom teaching, assumption of additional responsibilities involving classroom instruction, and/or highly rated performance in carrying out instruction or other tasks. Among the most common arrangements for performance-based remuneration are career ladders, which facilitate and reward teachers for undertaking more responsibilities and for improving their preparation; master teacher programs, which differentiate teachers' roles and responsibilities; and mentor programs, in which outstanding senior teachers provide leadership for other teachers. Most performance-based remuneration programs provide additional salary as an incentive for stimulating high levels of performance. One particularly controversial and seldom-used approach to performance-based remuneration is merit pay, in which teachers' basic salary is dependent on their evaluation rating.

Table 13.1 *Summary of Themes and Recommendations in Two 1983 National Reports on Improving Education*

Report: Task Force on Education for Economic Growth, *Action for Excellence.* Denver: Education Commission of the States.

Theme: Technological change and global competition make it imperative to equip students with skills that go beyond the basics. For productive participation in a society that depends even more heavily on technology, students will need more than minimum competence in reading, writing, mathematics, science, reasoning, the use of computers, and other areas.

Major Recommendations

1. Develop and implement state plans for improving education.
2. Improve the financial status of teachers. This should include salary increases and establishment of career ladders.
3. Improve academic performance by strengthening standards, discipline, and curriculum and increasing the school day or school year.
4. Provide quality assurance in education. This would include evaluation of teachers, revised teacher certification requirements, and student achievement testing.
5. Improve leadership and managment in the schools, including establishing higher standards for the recruitment, training, and monitoring of principals.
6. Provide additional services for unserved or underserved students.

Report: Task Force on Federal Elementary and Secondary Education Policy, *Making the Grade.* New York: Twentieth Century Fund.

Theme: Schools should provide the same core components for all students. These include basic skills of reading, writing, and calculating; technical capability in computers; training in science and foreign language; and knowledge of civics. The federal government should provide for the national security by ensuring a strong education system.

Major Recommendations

1. Establish a master teacher program to reward teaching excellence.
2. Provide an opportunity for all students to acquire proficiency in a second language.
3. Go beyond basic scientific literacy and provide advanced training in science and mathematics.
4. Enhance programs to assist handicapped and disadvantaged children.

to improve the schools, particularly at the level of state government. Many states had introduced minimum competency tests for students in the 1970s, and some had established or were moving to establish other new policies, such as career ladders for teachers, state supervision of deficient schools or school districts, and competency testing of new teachers and administrators. Many governors and state legislators used the national reports as support for their efforts to establish accountability mechanisms through which they hoped to assure the public that maintaining or increasing taxes for education actually resulted in effective or improved educational programming. Additional or accelerated movement toward increased state testing, stronger graduation requirements, improvement in teacher salaries, introduction of performance-based teacher evaluation, and other actions recommended in the national reports thus occurred in most if not all states. By 1987, school initiatives at the state level included the following reforms (Pipho 1986a):

1. Thirteen states had initiated various performance-based remuneration programs involving career ladders, mentor teacher arrangements, or other incentives for teachers, and sixteen more were either sponsoring pilot programs or developing plans for future programs.
2. Thirty-two states had introduced or continued tests for initial certification of teachers.
3. Forty-five states had altered requirements for graduation, almost always in the direction of increased rigor.
4. Fifteen states either lowered the school entrance age or increased the age for compulsory attendance, or took both steps.
5. Seven states had provided for intervention in operating and governing academically deficient districts.
6. Twenty-seven states had introduced some approach to alternative certification of new teachers.

However, not all observers were positive about the direction or adequacy of the reforms highlighted in the national reports and the concomitant actions states were taking to carry them out. Few observers quarreled with the reports' emphasis on improving the schools to reverse a rising tide of mediocrity, but many viewed what was happening as more a rising tide of national reports and state regulation than as a coherent and promising attempt to bring about meaningful improvements needed in the educational system. Several of the most common and trenchant criticisms and doubts are summarized below.

1. Many of the reports largely ignored the problems involved in improving the performance of low-achieving students—particularly disadvantaged students in urban areas (Bastian et al. 1986; Shanker 1988). This criticism has been expressed by A. Harry Passow (1984):

> *The reports of the eighties . . . fail to attend to the particular problems and needs of schools with large populations of poor and minority children. . . . If there is a real crisis in education, it is in the urban schools. . . . The implicit assumption in many of these reports is that disadvantaged youngsters are really no different from other students and to believe otherwise is both anti-intellectual and anti-democratic. . . . Simply recommending that school personnel set tougher, stiffer academic demands, and crack down on discipline problems without effecting necessary changes in pedagogy, curriculum, and personnel is an inadequate solution. (Passow 1984, 680)*

2. The reports are not likely to have much positive impact because they mostly ignored important school governance issues that will determine whether

reform efforts succeed or fail (Chubb 1988). Myron Lieberman (1986) has expressed and summarized this point of view:

> *Competent media treatment of* A Nation at Risk *when it was released would probably have consigned it to oblivion. Its failure to deal with such critical issues as the inefficient governance structure, collective bargaining, and teacher-tenure law are only part of the explanation of its futilitarian nature. Significantly, the national commission that sponsored the report deliberately avoided several issues in order to have a unamimous report. There would be nothing necessarily wrong with this if the commission had informed the American people of this important fact. Minimally, its failure to do so reflects a lack of candor. (Lieberman 1986, 20)*

3. In concentrating on actions that lend themselves to legislative mandates (e.g., increased graduation requirements, a longer school day), the reports thereby not only minimized the need for fundamental changes in teaching and learning but also generally neglected and even obscured the kinds of change efforts required to bring about major reform in the functioning of schools. (A later section in this chapter discusses research and analysis on the change process and requirements for fundamental reform.) Many observers thus concluded that *A Nation at Risk* and other reports were unlikely to accomplish any more real improvement in the schools than had previous calls for improvement in education (Spady 1983). This point of view was expressed by Glen Harvey:

> *A number of policy-related changes designed to respond to recent recommendations are particularly likely to result in only illusory school improvement. Raising the graduation requirements from three to four years of English, for example, without improving the content of instruction . . . only gives the impression of improving the level of educational attainment. . . . A substantial number of schools, districts, and states were in the midst of their own school improvement efforts at the time the National Commission on Excellence set into motion the national call . . . [but] energies were redirected . . . [and well-planned] efforts were weakened or even lost in the redirection. (Harvey 1984, 9)*

A somewhat similar viewpoint was articulated by National Education Association President Mary Futrell (1986; Rodman 1988), with special reference to recommendations for improving the quality and output of the teaching force:

> *Policymakers are giving new meaning to the term myopia. Policymakers, by and large, do not want to hear that reform efforts, to be effective, must target a complex constellation of problems . . . [or that] real reform must address the everyday realities of the learning workplace. Above all, policymakers do not want to hear that educational reform is hard work. . . .*
>
> *Our schools today are structurally decrepit, still shaped by an organizational model appropriate to nineteenth century industry. This model does little to en-*

liven the imagination . . . [or to] encourage collegial cooperation. It does much to intensify isolation.

. . . We must reform the reform movement. And the reform of reform must begin with releasing all educators from the structural straightjackets in which they are now strapped. Without this change, all the reform documents that have been written will become no more than faded reminders of what might have been. (Futrell 1986, 6)

4. The reports both built on and extended actions in many states to define and test students' minimum competency skills, and in so doing they reinforced rather than countered tendencies to emphasize mechanical, low-order skills that are easiest to teach and test. The effects of minimum competency testing sometimes are destructive, particularly in concentrated poverty schools in which students can spend years memorizing and regurgitating factual material to pass competency tests, whereas students in middle-class schools quickly pass the tests and proceed to instruction placing more emphasis on higher-order skills (Levine and Eubanks 1986–87). This type of concern and criticism has been expressed in a report published by the Ford Foundation (1984):

The current emphasis on minimum basic skills, with mandated curricula and methods of teaching and testing, has narrowed the scope of education for some students. Often, too, these mandated programs underuse teachers' abilities and, worse, neglect the development of students' ability to think, analyze, and inquire. In some schools, the basic skills "floor" has become the "ceiling" of achievement. (Ford Foundation 1984, 68)

5. Related to its dependence on bureaucratic and legislative mandates and its emphasis on minimum competency testing, the reform movement has functioned in conjunction with other developments to deprofessionalize or "de-skill" the teaching force. Deprofessionalization of teachers refers to administrative control policies and practices that stimulate or force teachers to simplify curriculum and instruction for the purpose of ensuring that students demonstrate a specified level of mastery on easy-to-grade tests.

Linda McNeil (1986; 1988) has characterized the behavior of many teachers subject to such policies and practices in terms of "defensive teaching," "fragmentation" of the curriculum to fit the tests, "omission" of important material and topics not tested, "mystification" of topics in the sense that regurgitation takes precedence over understanding, and "defensive simplification," through which teachers back off from in-depth instruction in order to gain minimal compliance from students. (These kinds of dynamics are discussed in more detail in a later section of this chapter.) Many observers believe that administrative control associated with the reform movement has exacerbated the tendencies described by McNeil, which appear to be clearly antithetical to the task of improving student performance in critical thinking and other higher-order skills.

6. The national reports did not spell out or communicate the costs of making reform a reality, much less provide for financing the heavy costs required to

carry out effectively their own recommendations. In this regard, the American Association of School Administrators (1984) estimated that implementing just two proposals from *A Nation at Risk*—raising beginning teachers' salaries to a market sensitive level and lengthening the school term to 200 days a year, 7 hours a day—would require a 27 percent increase in existing school budgets.

Subsequent Developments

Three years after the publication of *A Nation at Risk*, the Carnegie Task Force on Teaching As a Profession (1986) released *A Nation Prepared: Teachers in the 21st Century*. Following and building on widespread discussion and on a variety of state government initiatives associated with and frequently stimulated by the earlier national reports, sponsors and authors of *A Nation Prepared* clearly had tried to identify some of the most important and urgent steps toward fundamental reform and to take account of criticisms as well as subsequent developments and experience. Among the first reactions to *A Nation Prepared* were predictions that it would replace *A Nation at Risk* as the keystone for further debate and a statement by New Jersey Governor Thomas Kean that "all state policymakers are going to have to respond to this report" (Olson 1986b).

Representing the views and recommendations of a fourteen-member task force of business, civic, and educational leaders, *A Nation Prepared* portrayed a world economy in the middle of a "profound transformation" that requires the United States to replace mass-production techniques relying on low-skilled labor with highly skilled workers using advanced technology. Accomplishing this transformation, according to the report, requires that U.S. society place much more stress on learning as contrasted with schooling through an educational system sufficiently challenging and rigorous to ensure that students acquire "complex, non-routine intellectual" skills. The report also stressed that a "massive effort" is needed to improve education for the nation's growing proportion of low-income and minority students. Major recommendations in *A Nation Prepared* included the following seven suggestions:

1. Provide teachers with salaries and career opportunities comparable to those in other professions. Salaries should be based on teachers' responsibilities, productivity, competence, and seniority.
2. Create a hierarchical teaching profession to include a corps of lead teachers who will have leadership responsibilities in the schools.
3. Give teachers more control over what happens in schools, and in turn hold them more accountable for student performance.
4. Establish a national board, as in law and medicine, to set higher standards for teachers and to certify those who meet them.
5. Award schoolwide bonuses to teachers, based on such measures as achievement, attendance, and dropout rates.

6. Require that future teachers obtain a bachelor's degree *before* participating in professional training; replace undergraduate education majors with a new professional curriculum at the graduate level.
7. Increase the pool of minority teachers by providing incentives and better general education for minority students.

Authors of *A Nation Prepared* also argued that the costs of implementing its agenda for upgrading the teaching profession and the schools would be substantial but not as large as otherwise might be the case because high rates of replacement and turnover in the teaching force will make it possible to introduce better-prepared teachers relatively quickly and easily. Even though some estimates placed the cost of implementation at 40 billion dollars or more during the 1987–1997 period, several task force members as well as other observers stated that the public would support additional investment in education if taxpayers believed there really would be significant improvements in teaching and learning (Olson 1986b).

A first major and potentially momentous step toward implementation of recommendations in *A Nation Prepared* was taken in May 1987, when the Carnegie Forum on Education and the Economy announced the establishment of the National Board for Professional Teaching Standards, a nonprofit organization to issue certificates to teachers who demonstrate mastery of prescribed standards of professional knowledge and ability. The sixty-three-member board that will design governing structures and operating policies includes more than forty teachers. The board is to work in cooperation with research-and-development personnel at Stanford University and other institutions at which efforts are underway to improve assessment of teachers' skills and knowledge (Payzant 1988). An associate director of the Carnegie forum estimated that the board might require as much as 50 million dollars over five years to support development of improved assessment instruments.

It should be noted that somewhat parallel and analogous efforts to improve or reform the teaching profession also are being pursued by the Holmes Group, a consortium of deans of many of the best-known schools and colleges of education throughout the United States. Its first major report, *Tomorrow's Teachers* (1986), highlighted the goals of making the education of teachers intellectually sound; recognizing differences in knowledge, skill, and commitment among teachers; creating relevant, defensible standards of entry into the teaching profession; connecting education schools more closely with elementary and secondary schools; and making schools better places for teachers to work and learn.

With representation from major research universities in all fifty states, the Holmes Group operated for several years with fluid membership and preliminary position papers and then met in January 1987 formally to establish its structure and practices (Lanier 1987). The group is still in the process of formulating its operating agenda and priorities, but it already has retreated from its initial position (echoing *A Nation Prepared*) that undergraduate teacher education should be entirely abolished at institutions that participate in preparing teachers for prestigious and well-paid leadership roles in the public schools.

Shortly after the Carnegie Task Force on Teaching As a Profession released *A Nation Prepared,* the National Governors' Association (1986) published an important report, *Time for Results: The Governors' 1991 Report on Education,* which incorporated the findings of seven gubernatorial task forces organized to draw up five-year plans and action agendas dealing respectively with teaching, leadership and management, parent involvement and choice, readiness for school, technology, facilities, and college quality. The recommendations of each task force are shown in Table 13.2. Tennessee Governor Lamar Alexander's introduction to *Time for Results* included the following comments and explanations:

> *The governors are ready for some old-fashioned horse trading. We'll regulate less, if schools and school districts will produce better results. . . . Have all the governors agreed on this report? No.* Time for Results *has as its sole purpose helping governors be better governors. It is our best advice to each other. . . . Why are the governors getting involved? Because without their leadership, most of what needs to be done won't get done. American public education has fallen into some deep ruts. . . . Governors want a new compact with professional educators in America, so that we can lead a coalition of everyone interested in schools and take the next steps together. That is why we are joining with the Education Commission of the States and the Council of Chief State School Officers to devise a system to keep up with the results of this report on a yearly basis. (Alexander 1986, 202–204)*

As is apparent in Table 13.2, *Time for Results* incorporated and sometimes elaborated on earlier reform reports and initiatives, but it also was responsive in some ways to a number of criticisms and objectives that had been widespread in earlier stages of the reform movement. Regarding teaching, for example, the gubernatorial task force chaired by Thomas Kean of New Jersey recommended that there be "recognition for outstanding teaching." Rather than explicitly supporting continued reliance on performance-based incentives for this purpose, however, the text of the task force's report emphasized that "the public must offer teachers a professional work environment and all that goes with it . . . [including] a real voice in decisions . . . [and] the chance to design the standards that define professional performance and ways to assess that performance (Kean 1986, 205). The Task Force on Readiness for school placed very strong emphasis on the problems of disadvantaged students, and its recommendations, like those of the Task Force on Leadership and Management, were much more precise and detailed than comparable recommendations in most earlier reports. Thus, *Time for Results* occasionally did succeed in identifying specific steps and goals that governors and other supporters of reform can examine in 1991 to determine whether substantial progress actually has taken place.

In addition to reports such as *A Nation Prepared* and *Time for Results,* which dealt with reform of schools for all students, several recent reports have been particularly concerned with disadvantaged students. Probably the most impressive and influential of these reports is *Children in Need,* prepared by the Committee for Economic Development (1987). A nonprofit organization rep-

Table 13.2 *Recommendations of Seven Gubernatorial Task Forces That Prepared Sections of* **Time for Results: The Governors' 1991 Report on Education**

Teaching

1. Convene a statewide panel to review the national teacher-policy reports.
2. Support the creation of a national board of professional teacher standards.
3. Develop state initiatives to encourage professional school environments.
4. Challenge the higher-education community on teacher education.
5. Build the case for sustained real-dollar increases in education spending.
6. Define and put in place a comprehensive teacher-recruitment strategy.
7. Announce the end of emergency teaching licenses.
8. Listen to teachers, principals, board members, and others.
9. Recognize outstanding teaching.
10. Establish a state-intervention procedure for cases of education bankruptcy.

School Facilities

1. States should focus existing "community-education" initiatives on the shared use of facilities. Particular attention should be given to community groups providing day-care and latch-key services.
2. States should encourage school districts to make more efficient use of school buildings, including the adoption of year-round school calendars.
3. States should act to restore school buildings in which maintenance needs or safety improvements have been deferred.
4. States should establish policies regarding the disposition of obsolete and excess buildings, based upon long-term goals and demographics as well as the needs of adjacent districts for building space.
5. To provide continuing, in-depth information and technical assistance, states should encourage established educational organizations to develop greater expertise in this field.

Leadership and Management

1. Begin a dialogue to determine the state's broad goals for education and identify ways for schools to achieve these goals.
2. Revise state selection and certification requirements to reflect the skills and knowledge needed by effective principals.
3. Match the content of state-approved educational-administration programs to the training needed by effective school principals.
4. Develop a system to evaluate principals effectively and accurately.
5. Provide in-service training to school administrators through, for example, state-sponsored training centers or higher-education institutions.
6. Provide incentives and technical assistance to districts to promote school-site management and improvement.
7. Collect statewide information on the process and the outcomes of schooling.
8. Reward principals and schools for performance and effectiveness.
9. Highlight success by documenting and disseminating effective strategies and models.
10. Be patient and remain committed.

Parent Involvement and Choice

1. Provide technical assistance to school districts and universities by encouraging instruction in effective parent-involvement techniques to be included in preservice and recertification training programs of all teachers and administrators.
2. Create the climate for greater parent involvement.

Table 13.2 (*continued*)

3. Provide incentives to school districts.
4. Expand opportunities for students by adopting legislation permitting families to select from among kindergarten to 12th-grade public schools in the state. High-school students should be able to attend accredited public postsecondary degree-granting institutions during their junior and senior years.

Readiness of At-Risk Students

State Initiatives to Assure That At-Risk Children and Youth Meet the New Educational Standards:

1. Provide extra help in the basic skills for students who have major deficiencies.
2. Develop incentives, technical assistance, and training for teachers and principals to employ effective school and classroom procedures and practices.
3. Provide a challenging curriculum for all children.
4. Provide valid and reliable assessment of student performance so students, parents, and teachers can work to correct deficiencies.
5. Reward schools for making progress in educating all children, including at-risk children.
6. Establish cooperative programs involving schools and homes so parents can learn *how* to support their children's teachers.
7. Develop incentive programs or direct state aid to reduce class sizes of kindergarten and the lower grades.
8. Establish alternative programs to work with high-school students who have dropped out of school.
9. Establish a mechanism for state interventions into school districts when progress is not being made with low-achieving students.

State Initiatives to Help At-Risk Young Children Become Ready for School:

1. Provide in-house assistance for first-time, low-income parents of high-risk infants.
2. Develop outreach initiatives using all community and religious organizations to assist young children who have only an absentee parent(s) or guardian(s) as his or her source of nurturance.
3. Provide kindergarten for all 5-year-old children.
4. Provide quality early-childhood-development programs for at-risk 4-year olds, and, where feasible, 3-year-olds.
5. Provide all interested parents of preschool children with information on successful parenting practices.
6. Stress continued improvement of developmental and educational programs in day-care centers for preschool children. This includes improving staff development and inservice training and providing for accreditation or similar standards for day-care centers.
7. Develop state and local structures through which all agencies work together to provide appropriate programs for children and their parents.

Technology

Provide Technical Assistance to:

1. Help school districts and schools write informed, appropriate plans on the use of technology. Such assistance could come from the state department of education, intermediate units, universities, and outstanding school- or district-based educators.
2. Help school districts, schools, and universities develop and establish continuous training programs on the appropriate uses of technology and ways to incorporate it into their curriculum.

Table 13.2 *(continued)*

3. Share data on costs and achievement from experiments being conducted within their respective states.
4. Aggregate purchases and establish wider markets.

Provide Financial Assistance to:

1. Encourage appropriate local-district planning for the use of technology by providing financial support to help districts purchase equipment to implement the plan.
2. Establish and improve training programs for educators about cost-effective ways to use educational technology.
3. Encourage and assist school districts that are willing to experiment with ways to restructure school environments to increase educator productivity by using various forms of educational technology.
4. Encourage greater cooperation among the states through the creation of consortiums and other technical-assistance arrangements.
5. Establish independent institutes for research and demonstration of technology in education, modeled on the National Science Foundation.
6. Recognize each state's most creative technology-using educators.
7. Make technology more available for students from low-income families.

College Quality

1. Governors, state legislatures, state coordinating boards, and institutional governing boards should clearly define the role and mission of each public higher-education institution in their states.

   Governors also should encourage the governing boards of each independent college to clearly define its mission.
2. Governors, state legislatures, coordination boards, governing boards, administrators, and faculties should re-emphasize—especially in universities that give high priority to research and graduate instruction—the fundamental importance of undergraduate instruction.
3. Each college and university should implement systematic programs that use multiple measures to assess undergraduate student learning. The information gained from assessment should be used to evaluate institutional and program quality. Information about institutional and program quality also should be made available to the public.
4. Governors, state legislatures, and state coordinating boards should adjust funding formulas for public colleges and universities to provide incentives for improving undergraduate student learning, based upon the results of comprehensive assessment programs. Independent colleges and universities should be encouraged to do likewise.
5. Governors, state legislatures, coordinating boards, and governing boards should reaffirm their strong commitment to access to public higher education for students from all socio-economic backgrounds.
6. The higher-education accrediting community should require colleges and universities to collect and utilize information about undergraduate student outcomes. Demonstrated levels of student learning and performance should be a consideration in granting institutional accreditation.

Source: National Governors' Association 1986.

resenting many large corporations and higher-education institutions, the Committee noted low achievement and high dropout rates among economically and socially disadvantaged students and concluded that the United States "can ill afford such an egregious waste of human resources. . . . Allowing this to continue will not only impoverish these children, it will impoverish our nation—culturally, politically, and economically."

After concluding that education reforms are "doomed" without much more effective early childhood education for disadvantaged students, *Children in Need* proceeded to recommend massive improvements in educational programs to help preschool students, increase cooperation between schools and families, provide assistance for pregnant teenagers and other "high-risk" mothers, create more alternative school settings, reduce the size of schools and classes, and introduce "radical" redefinitions in school purposes and structures. Former Proctor and Gamble Chairman Owen Butler spoke for many of his committee colleagues in further concluding that business should respond by leading a "third wave of reform" to improve education for the disadvantaged (Olson 1987c).

Another potentially important document that may help shape reform of education in positive directions is the 1987 report on improving assessment of student achievement prepared by the Study Group, a twenty-two-member committee chaired by Tennessee Governor Lamar Alexander and supported by funds from several private foundations. The report, *The Nation's Report Card*, assessed the "accomplishments and shortcomings" of the National Assessment of Educational Progress (NAEP) and endeavored to determine whether and how a national assessment of achievement in elementary and secondary schools should be carried out in the future. After pointing out that some data previously disseminated by the U.S. Department of Education have been "wretchedly inadequate," the Study Group recommended that work should proceed on developing better national assessments for the future. Seven specific recommendations (Study Group 1987, 7–10) were to:

1. Maintain continuity with the NAEP data base.
2. Include regular assessment of reading, writing, literacy, mathematics, science, technology, history, geography, and civics.
3. Focus on the "transition" grades (four, eight, and twelve) as well as on seventeen-year-olds and older students.
4. Create an Educational Assessment Council.
5. Provide for "add-on" assessments so that states, districts, and even buildings can be assessed on a voluntary basis.
6. Continue to include private school students.
7. Increase federal funding so that annual spending on national assessment rises from the 4 to 6 million dollar level of the NAEP to the range of 20 to 30 million dollars.

The Study Group's recommendations dealing with "Content and Coverage" placed special emphasis on avoiding the pitfalls and negative consequences of much previous minimum competency testing that has focused on mechanical skills and factual knowledge, thereby encouraging districts and schools to concentrate on low-level instruction. Before recommending that the NAEP should "make the assessment of higher-order thinking a central concern of future assessments," *The Nation's Report Card* stated:

> *One theme that will continually reappear in this report is a concern for the measurement of more complex levels of thinking and reasoning. We are convinced that it is time for the national assessment to devote closer attention to the measurement of more complex skills. . . . Until recently . . . careful definition and measurement of these skills has taken second place to a more limited measurement of factual knowledge based largely upon memory or very simple reasoning tasks. . . .*
>
> *We recognize of course that the effort to define, assess, and teach this level of skill is a well-established one in education. Education at its best has always stressed the value of learning how to think, and not merely knowing what to think. What is new, however, is the emergence of a commitment in recent years to develop and assess these skills among all members of the national community. Such a challenging objective had to await the development of new insights into the exact nature of these skills, and the best ways to measure and evaluate them.*
>
> *Recent developments in the many allied disciplines that study thinking and learning have now placed the accomplishment of this goal within our reach. The past two decades have witnessed an explosion of new ideas about how human beings learn and what happens in higher-order thinking. At the same time powerful new computer technologies now make available a range of measurement tools sophisticated and sensitive enough to measure complex thinking with some accuracy. These new ideas and methods suggest fresh approaches to familiar old problems that have hampered the definition and measurement of higher-level thinking in the past. (Study Group 1987, 15–16)*

Like the National Governors' Association, the Council of Chief State School Officers (CCSSO) has indicated vigorous support for massive efforts to improve the education of disadvantaged students. In a policy paper entitled "Assuring Educational Success for Students at Risk" that its members endorsed unanimously, the CCSSO stated that "state law should provide the supporting health, social welfare, employment, housing, safety, transportation, and other human services which, together with the educational programs, are reasonably calculated to enable all persons to graduate from high school."

As regards education, the CCSSO said that every student should be *guaranteed* "enrollment in a school with systematically designed and delivered instruction of demonstrable effectiveness, and with adequate and up-to-date learning technologies and materials of proven value" (Council of Chief State School Officers 1987, 7). Other reports issued by the CCSSO indicated that implementation of its policy regarding guarantees may require support for students to transfer from low-achieving schools or districts to "successful" locations elsewhere, "state takeovers" of school districts that are financially or educationally "distressed," reduction in the concentration of low achievers at low achieving schools, and introduction of a system of school-site planning and decision making (Burch 1988).

Conclusions Regarding National Reform

Although little systematic research is available and it obviously is extremely difficult if not impossible to determine what has been taking place in fifty states and more than fifteen thousand school districts, educators must try to identify and delineate the major developments that are likely to or should be pursued in the future, as well as the directions and problems that have emerged in the past. Tentative and preliminary though one must be in drawing conclusions, some sense of the status of the reform movement and the critical issues with which it is grappling is a necessary prerequisite in trying to determine what should be done to solve the central problems facing the educational system in the United States. Our assessment of some of the most important developments and issues currently confronting the reform movement is provided below.

1. The reform movement to date has largely neglected the necessity of bringing about fundamental reform of organizational structures and governance as well as of instructional arrangements and practices in the schools. While it is true that a few states such as Colorado and Maryland have encouraged and helped some districts plan for fundamental reform, most states have avoided the difficult and expensive issues involved in moving beyond mandated bureaucratic initiatives.

At the building and district levels, the situation is very uneven. Many schools and districts are exploring or even implementing fundamental changes in organizational and instructional arrangements and structures. However, most schools apparently are not yet doing so, and directions for the future are not clear. (Possibilities for fundamental reform, particularly at the high school level, are discussed later in this chapter.)

2. Dilemmas involving perceived needs for testing and accountability on the one hand and emphasis on higher-order skills and independent learning on the other are still far from being resolved. Although there is increased recognition of the dangers of low-level testing that drives instruction toward further stress on memorization and regurgitation of factual material, minimum competency testing that may be having this effect also has continued to increase (Madaus 1988). Efforts to introduce and improve testing of higher-order skills probably will accelerate in the future, but this trend is likely to require years of development, and financial as well as other forms of support may not be adequate.

3. Efforts to change preparation and remuneration arrangements for teachers have been proceeding through the work of the Carnegie Task Force on Teaching as a Profession, the Holmes Group, and other organizations, but there is a disgreement on key issues, such as whether a teaching certificate should

require postbachelor's degree preparation and whether teaching careers, responsibilities, and pay should be differentiated for master teachers, regular teachers, teacher aides, and other teaching positions. For example, the National Education Association has consistently opposed proposals to create lead teachers, as proposed by the Carnegie Task Force. Also, active opposition from teachers' groups along with very high costs and other problems encountered in conceptualizing and implementing career ladders and other performance-based approaches in Florida, Tennessee, Texas, and elsewhere have blocked development and further implementation in many states (Jacobson 1986; Olson 1987b). Regarding establishment in 1987 of the National Board for Professional Teaching Standards, the president of the American Association of School Administrators expressed concern that teachers' groups were trying to take over the schools, and the president of the National School Boards Association expressed dissatisfaction with the limited role given to school board members (Olson 1987a).

4. Dilemmas and tensions involving the general promotion of excellence on the one hand and of educational equity on the other have not been systematically confronted and resolved. Many analysts believe that the two types of goals can be harmonized provided that adequate attention and resources are devoted to each one, and that the schools can and should improve the performance of all student groups at the same time that massive efforts are under way to help the disadvantaged. Contradictions are likely to arise in practice, however, particularly when reform programs are sporadic and superficial and do not satisfactorily address the most serious underlying problems in the educational system.

With regard to expansion of graduation requirements and to competency testing of students, for example, introduction of rigorous requirements and standards of performance may help improve instruction for the average student, but implemented in isolation these reforms may increase failure and dropout rates for disadvantaged students (McDill, Natriello, and Pallas 1986). Officials of the Children's Defense Fund summarized this pitfall: "Competency testing without appropriate remediation for those failing (as in at least nineteen state reform packages) simply stigmatizes and frustrates those students, increasing the likelihood that those students will drop out" (Education Forum 1984, 10).

Regarding testing of teachers, similarly, data in Chapter 10 indicate that failure rates among minority candidates are disproportionately high, thus helping generate an incipient crisis in the availability of minority teachers. Testing of teachers as advocated in *A Nation Prepared* and numerous other reform reports may lead to improvements in the overall quality of the teaching force, but grave, negative consequences may follow if this goal is attained without ensuring an adequate supply of minority teachers. Thus, a representative of the American Association for the Advancement of Science was quick to point out that creators of the National Board for Professional Teaching Standards had given little meaningful attention to the problems of recruiting and preparing minority teachers, and that they thus had "saved the toughest questions in this reform movement for last" (*Education Daily* 1987a, 6).

5. Rather than continuing to reinforce historical trends toward further deskilling of teachers, the reform movement must be basically transformed to em-

phasize empowerment of teachers to encourage and assist them in making productive decisions concerning effective delivery of instruction in their classrooms (Maeroff 1988). Empowerment of teachers has been receiving increasing recognition as a key factor in research and analysis dealing with effective classroom instruction. For example, Gerald Duffy and his colleagues (1987) at Michigan State University have studied the implementation of reading instruction. They found that school improvement efforts that specify in detail the materials, methods, and skills to be emphasized in the classroom have had dysfunctional results in terms of regimenting teachers and hampering effective instruction:

> *When district school administrators establish procedures to ensure coverage of . . . [specific] materials, teachers are left with little time for anything else . . . and they stop making decisions about what to teach and how to teach it. . . . This happens because the expectations set for teachers lead them to . . . see themselves as technicians who follow directions rather than as professionals who adapt curricular materials to the particular needs of individual students or groups. . . . [Such approaches] may be effective in teaching students certain automatized skills but are less effective in developing cognitive processing. . . .*
>
> *Educational leaders . . . must communicate that the centrally imposed directives are flexible conceptual guidelines, not scripts to be followed by rote. . . . Only by committing ourselves to a model that encourages teachers to be in cognitive control of their instruction can we make significant progress toward educational reform. (Duffy, Roehler, and Putnam 1987, 358–359, 364)*

6. Related to the need for reform to emphasize empowerment among teachers, the reform movement must recognize that instructional goals involving the development of students' higher-order thinking and comprehension skills are not likely to be attained through continued dependence on narrow prescriptions for teacher-centered delivery of instruction. Many school districts and even entire states have established lesson-delivery guidelines in an effort to ensure that teachers can be held accountable for implementing instruction more effectively. However, the teaching approaches that lend themselves to such mandates frequently are not productive in substantially enhancing the development of higher-order skills (Shulman 1987). This problem has been summarized by Harriet Tyson-Bernstein in her examination of the Texas Teacher Appraisal System (TTAS), which was implemented statewide in 1985:

> *The TTAS manual says, "no single model of teaching is mandated by the statewide teacher appraisal system," but it is clear that Texas has taken the position that "direct teaching" is the one best model. It rewards teachers who lecture and question a relatively passive class but not teachers who help students struggle through difficult tasks—such as science experiments, English composition, or computer programming—on their own. Even though the system might lead to the removal of some incompetent teachers, the price of that achievement would be high. The kind of teaching rewarded by TTAS tends to improve elementary basic*

skills test scores in the short run but to inhibit the development of curiosity and higher realms of thinking. (Tyson-Bernstein 1987, 29)

However, calling attention to the traps that states and school districts have encountered in mandating teaching behaviors that are relatively easy for an assessor to observe does not necessarily mean one should reject all possibilities for systematically assessing the delivery of classroom instruction. Provided that school reform efforts are built on and reflect knowledge about the change process in schools and that the prerequisites for successful change are in place when improvements are mandated in schools and classrooms, teacher appraisal arrangements that consider the problems created by narrow prescription may contribute positively to national reform goals. Possibilities and considerations involved in undertaking successful reform are explored in some detail in the remainder of this chapter.

Business Participation in School Improvement and Reform

In addition to the contributions some business leaders have made in helping to initiate and support demands for reform of the educational system, business and industry appear to be playing a growing role in working directly with the schools to bring about improvement (Mann 1988). Carol Shakeshaft and Roberta Trachtman (1986–87) have surveyed the largest corporations in the United States in order to determine whether and how they participate in public-school improvement efforts. Shakeshaft and Trachtman reported that 73 percent were participating in various joint ventures, most commonly (45 percent) in one or another type of Adopt-a-School program in which they provide specific assistance to a particular school or group of schools. Types of assistance most often provided include speakers and resource people for instruction, sponsorship of achievement awards, career days and conferences, tutoring, and donation of equipment. Shakeshaft and Trachtman also reported that business leaders were not attempting to "vocationalize" the schools but instead "overwhelmingly" supported an emphasis on academic rather than vocational goals in the schools (1986–87, 30).

Manuel Justiz and Marilyn Kameen (1987) also have examined some of the partnerships through which business and the schools are endeavoring to improve the effectiveness of public education, particularly for disadvantaged students in big cities. Justiz and Kameen report that several promising approaches are being replicated in a number of locations. For example, the Cooperative Federation for Educational Experiences (COFFEE) Project, initiated by the Digital Equipment Corporation to provide computer-related education in Oxford, Massachusetts, is being implemented at fourteen sites nationwide. Also, the Cities in Schools Project supported by Atlantic Richfield and other corporations is working to help improve educational opportunities for inner-city students in fourteen cities.

The best-known approach for joining business and the public schools in a substantial effort to improve and reform education is the Boston Compact initiated by business, civic, governmental, and civic leaders in 1982 (Levine and Trachtman 1988). In forming the compact, business and public-school officials committed themselves to the attainment of annual measurable goals. For the first year, business leaders agreed to recruit at least 200 companies to participate in programs for hiring public-school graduates and for providing employment for students. School officials agreed to reduce absenteeism and the dropout rate by 5 percent, to introduce competency requirements for graduation, and to increase the placement rate of graduates into higher education or full-time employment by 5 percent. "The message the Compact now sends to Boston's young people," according to Robert Schwartz and Jeannette Hargroves, is that "if you stay in school, work hard, and master the basics, you will be helped to find a job" (1986–87, 15).

As of 1987, approximately 350 companies were participating in the Boston Compact, and the project had expanded to involve a number of agencies, activities, and components that include the following (Lawlor 1987):

1. Establishment of an Action Center for Educational Services and Scholarships (ACCESS), which provides eligible Boston graduates with financial assistance to attend college.
2. Participation of the Private Industry Council in providing staff to coordinate the contributions of Compact companies and in providing job counseling and career education in Boston high schools.
3. Inclusion of more than twenty local colleges and universities in efforts to expand higher-education opportunities for graduates and to provide various forms of assistance to elementary and secondary schools in Boston. These institutions pledged to help place at least 75 percent of Boston's 1989 high-school graduates in higher education.
4. Establishment of Support for Early Education Development (SEED) to improve education for Boston's preschool and primary children.
5. Creation of Compact Ventures to work with potential dropouts and other at-risk adolescents in Boston high schools.

Early results associated with the partnerships forged among the Boston Compact, the public schools, and other institutions have been mostly encouraging. As shown in Table 13.3, the number of high-school graduates hired for full-time employment through the Private Industry Council increased from 415 in 1983 to 967 in 1986. Large increases were also registered in part-time and summer employment of students. Data for the graduating class of 1985 showed that 93 percent were either in college or working full-time in 1986 (Lawlor 1987) and that the unemployment rate among recent graduates has fallen to 4.5 percent—far below the national figure of 17 percent (Lacayo 1986). However, low unemployment rates among Boston graduates may be attributable primarily to the fact that unemployment in the Boston area generally has been low. Moreover, the dropout rate at Boston high schools is still only slightly below the 1982

Table 13.3 *Number of High School Students Employed through the Boston Compact, 1982–1986*

	1982	1983	1984	1985	1986
Graduates hired full time in cooperation with the Private Industry Council	na	415	607	823	967
Students in summer jobs program	852	1,181	1,766	2,320	2,591
Students in after-school jobs programs	274	504	1,046	1,106	na

Source: Adapted from Schwartz and Hargroves, 1986–1987.

rate of 44 percent, and leaders of the Boston Compact are developing and implementing multimillion dollar plans to help young people stay in school and improve their performance (Schwartz and Hargroves 1986–87). Meanwhile, the National Alliance of Business has announced that it will work to initiate projects similar to the Boston Compact in seven other big cities (Rothman 1987b).

Effective Schools Research

As we note in Chapters 7 and 8, schools with high proportions of poverty students usually have had low achievement. Many educators, following research reported by James Coleman et al. (1966) and Christopher Jencks et al. (1972), believed that schools could not become much more effective than they already are in working with large numbers of disadvantaged low achievers. However, research and experience in the 1980s have been much more encouraging about the possibilities for making inner-city schools and, indeed, most or all schools substantially more successful than they have been. Examples of research and analysis that support such a conclusion are described and discussed in this and the following sections.

Elementary Level

A Phi Delta Kappa-sponsored study (1980) of successful urban (i.e., big-city) elementary schools concluded that these schools shared the following characteristics in addition to outstanding leadership: (1) clearly stated goals and objectives; (2) reductions in adult/child ratios; (3) structured learning environments; and (4) high levels of parental contact with the school and parental involvement with school activities. Similarly, Ronald Edmonds (1979) and his colleagues studied elementary schools in New York and Michigan in which low-income students were achieving at a level comparable to more advantaged students and concluded that the "most tangible and indispensable characteristics" of these schools were (1) strong administrative leadership; (2) a climate of expectation in which no children are permitted to fall below minimum levels of achievement; (3) an orderly and quiet rather than rigid and oppressive atmosphere; (4) a strong emphasis on acquisition of basic skills; (5) concentration of school resources and energy on attainment of fundamental objectives; and (6) frequent monitoring of student progress.

At the same time, researchers have been trying to identify the characteristics of unusually effective schools in general, not just those in big cities or in concentrated poverty neighborhoods. As one might expect, the results of their studies are similar to those concerned more specifically with inner-city schools. The characteristics of effective schools as portrayed in this already large and growing literature have been summarized by staff of the Connecticut School Effectiveness Project (Shoemaker 1982):

1. A *safe and orderly environment* that is not oppressive and is conducive to teaching and learning.
2. A *clear school mission* through which the staff shares a commitment to instructional goals, priorities, assessment procedures, and accountability.
3. *Instructional leadership* by a principal who understands and applies the characteristics of instructional effectiveness.
4. A climate of *high expectations* in which the staff demonstrates that all students can attain mastery of basic skills.
5. High *time on task* brought about when a high percentage of students' time is spent engaged in planned activities to master basic skills.
6. Frequent *monitoring of student progress* using the results to improve individual performance and also to improve the instructional program.
7. Positive *home-school relations* in which parents support the schools' basic mission and play an important part in helping to achieve it.

More detail regarding the characteristics of unusually effective elementary schools—in this case, inner-city elementary schools—is provided in an exploratory study (Levine and Stark, 1982) of instructional and organizational arrangements at high-achieving inner-city elementary schools in Chicago, Los Angeles, and Community District 19 in Brooklyn, New York. District 19 schools had introduced a comprehensive reading approach that placed emphasis on the Chicago Mastery Learning Reading Program (CMLRP), which is explicitly designed to teach reading comprehension and other higher-order cognitive skills to urban students in kindergarten through eighth grade. Several of the Los Angeles schools included in the study had participated in the Curriculum Alignment Project (Niedermeyer and Yelon 1981), in which school faculties attend workshops that help them coordinate instructional materials and methods with frequent tests on specific skills selected for emphasis at each grade and classroom. When the training is successful, teachers are less likely to rely on basal texts regardless of whether they are too advanced for some students or too simple for others; instead, their goal is to select sections from texts and other available materials or to create new materials that are most appropriate for teaching a specific skill to a particular group of students. Drawing on the CMLRP, Curriculum Alignment training, and/or other approaches, the unusually effective inner-city schools in this study exemplified the following characteristics:

Instructional Processes and Arrangements

1. Curriculum objectives, teaching materials, and testing were being painstakingly aligned with each other, whether through the Curriculum Alignment Project in Los Angeles, the introduction of the CMLRP in District 19, or some other less formal approach. Particular attention was being given to appropriate pacing of instruction.
2. Arrangements more effective than the customary Title I "pullout" approach had been introduced for dealing with the learning problems of low-achieving students. In general, this means that rather than removing students for additional instruction uncoordinated with the regular classroom, arrangements were made to coordinate fully compensatory and regular instruction. In some cases, achievement improvements were produced through grouping of the lowest achieving students in very small classes taught by highly skilled teachers.
3. Relatively great emphasis was placed on teaching higher-order cognitive skills.
4. Steps had been taken to make sure that appropriate instructional materials were easily and immediately available to teachers.
5. Explicit efforts had been made to minimize teachers' record-keeping chores.
6. Emphasis was placed on improving the quality of students' homework and on parent involvement in student learning.

Organizational Processes and Arrangements

1. Instructional planning emphasized grade-level decision-making by teachers.
2. Supervision had become much more outcome-based, in part because teachers at each grade level had devised a schedule for introducing specific skills, because data on students' skill acquisition were collected as part of instruction, and because appropriate materials were available for teaching and testing.
3. Comparative monitoring of classroom progress (i.e., charting and comparing student performance across classrooms) was carried out, partly for the purpose of setting minimum goals for introduction and pacing of lessons and materials.

Leadership Characteristics and Emphases

1. Administrators were both supportive of teachers and skilled in providing a structured institutional pattern in which teachers could function effectively.
2. Administrators were willing and able to interpret and, frequently, to bend rules and regulations in a manner that enhanced rather than reduced the effectiveness of their institutions.

Conclusions from the research on successful schools are being used in working to improve the effectiveness of instruction in the public schools, both in the inner city and elsewhere. In addition, state officials in Connecticut, Florida, New Jersey, and several other states are providing a variety of support services to help low-performing schools establish more effective practices. Among eighteen Milwaukee elementary schools that have been participating in a project to raise achievement in the inner city, the percentage of fifth-grade students reading in the lowest performance category decreased from 55 percent in 1979 to 30 percent in 1985. Maureen McCormack-Larkin (1985; Levine and Eubanks 1986–87) has studied developments in this group of Milwaukee schools and has identified five important practices in schools with the greatest achievement gains:

1. Continuous faculty planning for full content coverage of the most important learning skills and objectives.
2. Development of a schoolwide homework policy requiring daily completion of assignments. Teachers enforced the policy by monitoring exits at dismissal and sending empty-handed students back to their rooms.
3. Introduction of daily and weekly schedules and other mechanisms to accelerate the pacing of instruction.
4. Flexible practices to avoid rigid homogeneous grouping.
5. Departure from social promotions.

Thus, it appears that while in the past infrequently encountered successful inner-city elementary schools were mavericks attributable mainly to the efforts of an atypical principal, it now is possible to create such schools through careful planning and implementation of improved arrangements for curriculum and instruction (Eubanks and Levine 1983; Levine and Leibert 1987). Success in this effort in turn could mean that disadvantaged students, particularly those at big-city poverty schools, will have a much better chance to succeed in schools and society.

A number of analysts have gone much further in trying to identify characteristics of unusually effective schools. For example, David Squires, William Huitt, and John Segars (1983) prepared a list of fifty characteristics they used to construct a school-diagnosis questionnaire. Stuart Purkey and Marshall Smith (1983) have provided a list of nine organizational-structure variables and four process variables that their review of research indicated are characteristics of unusually effective schools.

Intermediate Level

Relatively few studies have succeeded in identifying the distinctive characteristics of effective secondary schools. One reason for the shortage of research is the small number of secondary schools that stand out as having high achievement compared to other schools similar in socioeconomic composition. Difficult as it has been to find unusually successful elementary schools (in terms of academic achievement), finding successful secondary schools has been even more difficult.

A few intermediate schools, however, have demonstrated that their students' achievement can be raised to relatively high levels. Following a search for high-achieving inner-city intermediate schools (defined as junior high schools including grades 7, 8, and 9 or middle schools including grades 7 and 8), Levine and his colleagues (1984) identified five such schools in four big cities. In addition to concluding that these schools had the same general characteristics that researchers had identified for effective elementary schools, the investigators found that effective inner-city intermediate schools in their sample exemplified these four common characteristics:

1. Organizational arrangements facilitated improved reading performance among low-achieving students.
2. Teachers emphasized achievement of higher-order cognitive skills.
3. Guidance and personal development of students were emphasized.
4. Expectations and requirements for student performance were high throughout the school.

Each successful intermediate school described in this study had a different approach and mixture of approaches for attaining the goals implicit in these four characteristics. Some approaches used by these schools included:

1. Effective arrangements for low achievers
   a. Small classes of low achievers taught by highly skilled teachers
   b. More time devoted to reading, language, and math
   c. Individual and small-group tutoring
   d. School-within-a-school units for low achievers
2. Emphasis on higher-order skills
   a. Availability of elective courses emphasizing these skills
   b. Instructional materials designed to teach higher-order skills
   c. Improved coordination between electives and regular courses
   d. Instructional strategies designed to develop thinking and comprehension skills
3. Emphasis on guidance and personal development
   a. Large numbers of counselors and guidance personnel
   b. Elective courses emphasizing personal development
   c. Use of community agencies
   d. Group counseling
4. High institutional expectations
   a. Contracts with students and parents
   b. Required summer school for failure in any subject
   c. Schoolwide point systems for students
   d. Weekly or biweekly report cards

Each of the five schools described in the study had made structural changes to improve the performance of their students, particularly their low achievers. By structural change, we mean major modifications in the school schedule as well as in how students and teachers are assigned to classes. For example, one school had changed the typical pattern so that classes of low achievers were much smaller than average classes; another had assigned seventh and eighth graders to only two teachers each for English, social studies, science and math; and several schools had reduced the time devoted to science and social studies in order to increase the allocation for reading and math. Such changes appear to be prerequisite to school effectiveness at the secondary level (Firestone and Herriott 1982).

The characteristics of effective inner-city intermediate schools probably are important in intermediate schools elsewhere, although a given characteristic may be more important in one type of school than in another. Emphasis on students' higher-order thinking skills and on personal development is a general component of middle-school philosophy; from this point of view the successful inner-city schools identified by Levine and his colleagues had not accomplished much more than introduction of basic structural changes to implement ideas commonly advocated by specialists on the education of secondary students.

Senior High Level

Because there are far fewer successful inner-city schools at the senior high level than at the elementary and intermediate levels and because high schools usually are much more complex than are the lower schools, relatively little is known about the characteristics of unusually successful senior high schools. Among the few inner-city high schools for which there are data indicating that substantial gains have been made in improving student performance is South Boston High School. Following desegregation of the Boston Public Schools in December 1975, South Boston became a desegregated high school attended by predominantly low-income and low-achieving white and black students. Reform of South Boston took several years to accomplish during a time of continuing turmoil related to desegregation, financial problems, and political upheaval in the Boston school system, but by 1980 data on improvement in the performance of students were encouraging and impressive.

Between 1979 and 1980, for example, average reading scores improved from the 16th percentile to the 40th percentile in the ninth grade and from the 18th to the 32nd percentile in the tenth grade. In addition, the percentage of graduates attending postsecondary education institutions increased from less than 8 percent in 1976 to 40 percent in 1980. Considerations that appear to have been most important in accounting for these and other improvements at South Boston included the following (Kozberg and Winegar 1981; personal observations of the authors):

— A new principal and administrative team made major changes in traditional organizational patterns and practices and insisted that staff members re-examine their instructional methods in order to develop more effective approaches for educating disadvantaged adolescents and youth.

— Associated with these changes, more than two-thirds of the previous faculty were replaced by teachers willing to discard traditional methods and practices that were largely ineffective.

— A number of in-school and out-of-school alternatives were initiated to address the learning problems and preferences of students. These alternatives include a self-contained school-within-a-school emphasizing academic learning, a minischool emphasizing experiential learning and individualized instruction, and a Transportation Learning Center. The academic learning alternative provides a relatively structured and traditional curriculum, but the teachers are specially selected and constitute an interdisciplinary team that provides an exciting learning environment.

— Nearly all ninth and tenth graders were placed in reading and writing courses rather than in traditional English classes, and methods used to teach reading and writing were drawn from sound theory and research regarding learning among disadvantaged adolescents.

— Students were placed in mathematics courses rather than in business mathematics, which primarily repeated beginning arithmetic.

— Work-study programs based on learning opportunities in the community were made available to many students after the ninth grade. In particular, paid work-study assignments were focused at selected sites such as Boston City Hospital, and participating students received coordinated instruction in subjects jointly planned by the academic staff and the work-study staff. Providing work-study experience beginning in the tenth grade and coordinating academic and vocational instruction proved highly motivating for students who previously had been alienated from school.

— Discipline throughout the school was very firm but also fair. Stricter attendance and tardiness policies were introduced with the assistance of parents, the Student Council, and community representatives.

— Strong security measures were imposed as needed to ensure the safety of students. Measures of this kind included the appointment of a youth-oriented security patrol and the partitioning of dangerous locations.

— School spirit and pride were systematically emphasized.

— Systematic guidance in learning and personal development was emphasized for students in the ninth and tenth grades. In part, this approach is carried out through a required Career Exploration course in the ninth grade. In addition, emphasis is placed on providing structured assistance for ninth graders through the selection of youth-oriented personnel to serve as homeroom teachers and the establishment of Ninth Grade Support groups. In addition, the fact that South Boston is a small school allowed all administrators and counselors to know every student by name.

— An effective in-school suspension program was introduced. The South Boston approach differs from those at most other inner-city schools in that participating students are fully isolated from the remainder of the school in order to emphasize the severity of their rules violations.

— The level of staffing for administration, program and teacher supervision, counseling, and related services was adequate to bring about and monitor extensive change throughout the school. In the case of South Boston, this meant more than one administrative staff member for every 100 students, but other inner-city high schools in less turbulent and difficult environments probably require less than half this amount of staffing.

— A conscious and explicit effort has been made to draw on resources in the local neighborhood and the larger community in order to provide better educational opportunities and to overcome the many educational and personal problems that hinder learning among inner-city adolescents and youth. For example, arrangements with Tufts University psychologists and psychiatrists have provided important help to emotionally disturbed students and special education students, and local social work agencies have provided a range of individual and family counseling services.

Because no two schools have exactly the same problems and situations, one cannot conclude that other senior high schools would be successful if they introduced the same programs and changes as did South Boston. However, some of the South Boston characteristics, such as systematic emphasis on school spirit, firm but fair discipline, small schools and classes, and emphasis on development of reading and math skills, have received considerable support in research on effective high-school approaches for improving student performance, particularly among low achievers (National Institute of Education 1978; Featherstone 1987).

In addition, South Boston illustrates structural changes that can be used to improve the delivery of education in senior high schools. After studying the literature on high schools that are trying to improve the performance of low achievers in reading and other subjects, Levine and Sherk (1983) identified three promising structural changes:

1. *School-within-a-school for low achievers.* Students who can read but are more than two or three years below grade level are assigned to a school-within-a-school serving from 80 to 120 students and staffed by 4 or 5 teachers (English, reading, math, science, and social studies) and a coordinator. If teachers in this type of program are specially selected for their ability and willingness to work with low achievers, participating students can make very large gains in reading and other basic skills.
2. *Achievement centers.* The achievement center is a promising approach developed at Cleveland Heights (Ohio) High School. After specific learning objectives are identified for a given grade and subject area (for example, tenth-grade English), an achievement center is established for both remedial and developmental purposes. Students who do not have skills prerequisite for a particular unit or who need special assistance in developing their full potential will attend the achievement center instead of or in addition to the regular

class. Achievement center placement generally replaces the regular class for no more than two or three weeks.

3. *A longer and different school day.* Possibilities for changing the school day to facilitate student achievement in various subjects are exemplified by the John Dewey High School in Brooklyn, New York. Dewey appears to have successfully provided effective educational opportunities for its diverse student body through such interrelated changes as a lengthened school day, provision of smaller classes and extra assistance for low-achieving students, and establishment of independent learning centers in every major subject.

Considerations Affecting Interpretation of Effective Schools Research

Readers of effective schools research and analysis should be aware of a number of considerations that may affect interpretation and conclusions. First, various definitions of school effectiveness are widely divergent. Some persons refer to a school with unusually high academic achievement, usually after taking account of social class; others may be referring to a self-renewing school that continuously identifies and solves internal problems, or to a school that promotes students' personal growth, or to a school that has had increases in academic performance, or to a school that concentrates on developing independent study skills and appreciation of learning.

Second, most research on effective schools is correlational. Researchers have identified characteristics (correlates) of unusually effective schools, but only a few have manipulated a particular variable, such as expectations for students or leadership of the principal, to assess effects on achievement. Dependence on correlational research makes it difficult to be certain that efforts to improve a given characteristic will make any real difference in students' performance.

Third, other methodological problems have left much of the research vulnerable to criticism (Good and Brophy 1986). For example, schools identified as effective in a given subject (e.g., reading) during a given year may not be effective on other measures or on the same measure in subsequent years. In addition, statistical controls for students' social class and family background frequently have not been adequate to attribute high achievement to school characteristics (Stephenson and Levine 1987).

Fourth, the identification of general characteristics cited in the effective schools research does not provide teachers and principals with much specific guidance about what they should do in the schools. For example, saying that a school requires a productive climate and good leadership does not provide much direct help in determining how to accomplish these goals.

Fifth, it should be noted that several writers (e.g., Sowell 1974) who have tried to identify unusually effective inner-city high schools have cited schools that either constituted high-dropout environments in which only a relatively small and selective group of students advanced beyond the ninth or tenth grade or used extremely rigorous discipline policies that led many students to leave and thus provided a better learning environment for those who remained. The latter strategy may be defensible on several grounds, particularly if a school district establishes small alternative schools for students eliminated from regular high schools. However, schools using this strategy offer little guidance for identifying the characteristics of senior high schools that successfully serve a population consisting of mostly disadvantaged low achievers.

Finally, most research has been concerned entirely or largely with inner-city schools. Schools identified as unusually effective in such studies generally have been poverty schools in which academic achievement is higher than that at most other schools with similarly disadvantaged students. It is more difficult to identify unusually effective schools outside the inner city, where high achievement is more common. In addition, the key components of effectiveness outside the inner city probably differ in some respects from those at poverty schools. Research conducted by Phillip Hallinger and Joseph Murphy (1986), for example, indicated that principals of unusually effective elementary schools enrolling students high in socioeconomic status focused more on technical than on climate goals and were relatively more indirect in providing leadership as compared with principals of unusually effective schools enrolling low-status students. A similar study by Stringfield and Teddlie (1987) found that principals of unusually effective middle-class schools were less active in the teacher-hiring process than were principals of effective poverty schools.

Research on the Delivery of Effective Instruction

Much research has been conducted during the 1970s and 1980s, and much has been learned about delivery of effective instruction. Although there naturally is considerable overlap between research on effective schools and research dealing with effective instruction or effective teaching, the two areas of study can be thought of as conceptually distinct: studies of effective instruction are concerned with classroom-level implementation, whereas effective schools research as most frequently defined deals with schoolwide characteristics. Of course, it is apparent that a school cannot be unusually successful unless its teachers deliver instruction effectively, but schools that are not particularly successful compared to other schools with similar students can and frequently do have some outstanding teachers.

Classroom Management

Studies of classroom instruction indicate that effective teachers tend to be particularly successful with respect to classroom management and that teachers who merit this description exemplify a variety of behaviors, such as the following (Brophy 1982; Doyle 1986), to establish and enhance discipline and motivation. These teachers

1. Arrange the physical environment to avoid disruption or misbehavior.
2. Establish clear routines and rules at the beginning of the academic term and thereafter.
3. Make sure students understand what will be tolerated and know what to do if they need help.
4. Provide smooth and efficient transitions between activities.
5. Provide a variety of assignments and learning experiences to maintain interest.
6. Constantly monitor the class for indications of inattention or confusion.
7. Use a variety of approaches, such as eye contact and verbal directions, to focus attention during lessons.
8. Avoid responding emotionally to problems.

Effective Teaching

Thousands of studies have been conducted on various aspects of instructional delivery, and hundreds of formulations have been offered to describe the major aspects of effective teaching based on this large research literature. Although it is not possible to summarize this body of knowledge fully or to take account of all important findings in a brief capsulization, Jere Brophy and Thomas Good (1986) have provided a representative summary in their chapter on "Teacher Behavior and Student Achievement in the *Handbook of Research on Teaching* edited by Merlin Wittrock (1986). Highlights of their summary indicate that student learning is related to such instructional variables as these five:

1. High opportunity to learn and time for learning; pacing of instruction to ensure high content coverage.
2. Academic instruction emphasis with high expectations for students and high allocation of available time for instruction.
3. High student engagement rates and effective classroom management.
4. Appropriate levels of difficulty in activities suited to students' current level of needs and interests.
5. High or at least moderate rates of success for students as they progress through the curriculum.

In providing this summary and integration of research, Brophy and Good also note that there is a tension between the goal of maximizing content coverage by pacing students as rapidly as possible and the goal involving

> *the needs to (a) move in small steps so that each new objective can be learned readily and without frustration; (b) see that the students practice the new learning until they achieve consolidated mastery . . . and (c) where necessary, see that the students learn to integrate the new learning with other concepts and skills and to apply it efficiently in problem-solving situations. The pace at which the class can move will depend on the students' abilities and developmental levels, the*

nature of the subject matter, the student-teacher ratio, and the teacher's managerial and instructional skills. (Brophy and Good 1986, 361)

Brophy and Good also found that research indicates that students achieve more when there is "active teaching" through which the teacher "presents information and develops concepts through lecture and demonstration, elaborates this information in the feedback given following responses, . . . prepares the students for follow-up seatwork activities by giving instructions and going through practice examples, monitors progress on assignments after releasing the students to work independently and follows up with appropriate feedback and reteaching when necessary" (p. 361). Brophy and Good also proceed to discuss the findings of research with regard to such teaching variables as giving information, questioning the students, reacting to student responses, and handling seatwork and homework assignments.

Another representative formulation of some effective-instruction research has been provided by Barak Rosenshine and Robert Stevens (1986). They identified six "fundamental instructional functions" that constitute a structured teaching approach "particularly useful when teaching younger students, slower students, and students of all ages and abilities during the first stage of instruction with unfamiliar material" (p. 378). The six functions Rosenshine and Stevens identify and then analyze in much more detail are (1) daily review and checking homework, (2) presentation, (3) guided practice, (4) corrective and feedback, (5) independent practice (seatwork), and (6) weekly and monthly reviews. This type of approach also has been referred to frequently as "direct instruction" or "explicit teaching" (Rosenshine 1986).

Teaching for Comprehension and Problem Solving

Even the strongest proponents of active teaching, direct instruction, and similar research-based effective teaching formulations recognize that teacher-centered instruction that provides structured learning activities to teach discrete skills is an incomplete and sometimes unsuitable approach for developing comprehension and reasoning, problem-solving, critical thinking, and other higher-order skills and competencies (Anderson, Hiebert, Scott, and Wilkinson 1985). Rosenshine (1986), for example, has observed that effective teaching research is more pertinent to the teaching of discrete skills, such as decoding of words and computation in math, than to the understanding of complex material. Marzano and his colleagues (1987) have reviewed research dealing with development of students' cognitive functioning and concluded that direct-instruction formulations are too restrictive to accommodate the variety of teaching and learning activities and strategies required to develop dynamic knowledge focusing on higher-order mental processes. They summarize some of this research:

Prescriptive teaching of skills can actually inhibit the learning process because it does not allow students to progress through the important "shaping" and "per-

> *sonalizing" stage of learning dynamic information. . . . [The direct instruction model] can foster an inaccurate and unhealthy tone which suggests that the teacher should be monitoring students to make sure they are "doing it right." . . . When knowledge is static in nature, the instructional goal is for students to be able to assimilate the information into their existing knowledge base. . . . [But when the goal shifts to dynamic use of static knowledge the teacher should] act as guide to insure that all students had a common core of understanding but . . . also would encourage and foster personal and quite divergent connections made by individual students . . . [and would] provide situations in which students encountered the static knowledge in a variety of contexts. . . . The above discussion argues against the use of a single model of instruction and emphasizes the need for a repertoire of instructional models and strategies. (Marzano et al. 1987, 240–244)*

During the past decade, much progress has been made in identifying a range of skills and cognitive functions that should or could be addressed and in devising instructional methods and materials to provide effective instruction focusing on thinking and other higher-order mental processes. By the mid-1980s, more than thirty instructional programs with sets of materials had been developed that focus on improving students' thinking capabilities (Costa 1985; Chance 1986).

To systematize the work being done in this important field, Robert Marzano and his colleagues (1987) prepared a typology of thinking dimensions for use in the planning of curriculum and instruction to improve students' cognitive functioning. Published for the Association Collaborative for Teaching Thinking (an umbrella group representing twenty-eight national organizations) by the Association for Supervision and Curriculum Development, the typology describes five major dimensions of thinking, three of which are subdivided into subdimensions of cognitive skills and processes (Table 13.4) that in turn include many additional more discrete aspects of cognitive functioning. The five major dimensions of thinking specified in this project are:

1. Metacognition (involving self-regulation of one's own learning).
2. Creative thinking.
3. Critical thinking.
4. Thinking processes.
5. Thinking skills.

Emphasis throughout this and other similar typologies is on learning-to-learn strategies and skills and on development of capacity for self-directed and independent learning.

Within the wide range of cognitive processes and skills subsumed under such headings as "Teaching of Thinking," the subdimension (see Table 13.4) that has received most attention in educational research and development has been comprehension in reading. Many instructional methods and approaches for improving students' ability to read with understanding have been either

Table 13.4 *Three Major Dimensions of Thinking in a Typology for Planning Curriculum and Instruction*

Metacognition*	Thinking Processes	Thinking Skills
Knowledge and control of self	Concept formation	Focusing
Commitment	Principle formation	Information gathering
Attitudes	Comprehending	Remembering
Attention	Problem solving	Organizing
Knowledge and control of process	Decision making	Analyzing
Declarative, procedural, and conditional knowledge	Research	Generating
Maintaining executive control	Composing	Integrating
	Oral discourse	Evaluating

* Metacognition refers to a person's ability to monitor and control his or her progress toward a goal.
Note: Two other dimensions—creative thinking and critical thinking—also are identified and discussed as part of this typology.
Source: Marzano et al., 1987 (draft).

devised or refined during the past two decades (Harris and Cooper 1985). Surveying these developments, David Pearson (1985) of the University of Illinois Center for the Study of Reading has referred to the increase in our knowledge of teaching for comprehension as a "revolution" in pedagogy. Ten of the many comprehension-enhancement methods developed or further refined and demonstrating positive results in terms of student achievement are the following:

1. Concept mapping, story mapping, advanced organizers, and other approaches for providing schema to help students comprehend what they read (Harris and Cooper 1985; Jones and Idol 1988; Joyce and Showers 1988).
2. Reciprocal teaching and other forms of cooperative learning through which students are helped to take active responsibility for understanding material and for helping each other carry out comprehension tasks (Palincsar 1987).
3. Questioning techniques to develop higher-order learning through prereading, reading process, and postreading strategies and activities (Anthony and Raphael 1987).
4. Directed reading-thinking activities that guide students in developing an understanding of the presentation and content of written and oral discourse (Harris and Cooper 1985; Sirois and Davis 1985).
5. Prediction techniques, which systematically ask students to predict what they will encounter in reading based on previous knowledge and on activation of their previous knowledge (Presseisen 1987).
6. Scaffolding approaches through which teachers model thought processes and then help students gradually accept responsibility for formulating questions and hypotheses (Jones 1986; Jones and Idol 1988).

7. Metacognitive strategies for helping students learn to understand and regulate their own reading and learning. (Duffy et al. 1986; Duffy, Roehler, and Putnam 1987; Harris and Cooper 1985; Palincsar 1987).
8. Learning-to-learn strategies (Jones 1986) such as are incorporated in Chicago Mastery Learning Reading (Jones, Friedman, Tinzman, and Cox 1985) and other sets of materials (Presseisen 1985).
9. Mediation activities to stimulate growth in understanding, as in the Instrumental Enrichment program developed by Reuven Feuerstein (1980; Link 1985).
10. Concept development methods that help students understand and apply concepts and related vocabulary (Klausmeier 1985; Sirois and Davis 1985; Marzano et al. 1987).

The many strategies, materials, and programs now available to help deliver more effective instruction dealing with comprehension in reading and other subjects, problem-solving in math, and thinking processes in general provide a stark contrast to the patterns of instruction historically and currently still typical of many or most elementary and secondary classrooms. Research has amply documented that very little classroom time in the United States (or elsewhere) is devoted to instruction focusing on or supportive of enhanced comprehension, problem-solving, or thinking and higher-order mental processing (Boyer 1983; Cuban 1983; Goodlad 1984; MacGinitie and MacGinitie 1986).

For example, Dolores Durkin (1978–79) observed reading instruction in elementary classrooms and reported that virtually no time was spent in actually instructing students to move beyond literal comprehension. Similarly, Thomas Good and Douglas Grouws (1987) and other researchers (e.g., Porter et al. 1986) have reported that only a small proportion of time in math classes is spent introducing and explaining concepts or teaching higher-order skills and understandings; most math instruction is devoted to drill, practice, and procedural detail. Good and Grouws also point out that much is known about how to teach problem-solving and other higher-order math skills more effectively and that staff development can be successful in helping teachers improve math instruction for this purpose. Thus, it appears that opportunities are plentiful and technical means are available for revamping and reforming instruction to meet the challenge of substantially improving students' performance with respect to higher-order mental processes, particularly among disadvantaged students.

Issues in Improving Comprehension, Problem Solving, and Cognitive Development

Possessing the technical knowledge to provide much more effective instruction focusing on higher-order mental processes does not ensure that meaningful change to accomplish this objective will actually occur. Educators also must recognize and take action to overcome the major impediments to successful change and must devise and implement workable and realistic plans that can overcome these obstacles. Central issues in developing such plans are discussed in the following sections.

Considerations and Obstacles in Delivery of Instruction Emphasizing Cognitive Development

Many obstacles encountered in attempting to provide effective instruction with respect to higher-order mental processes and cognitive development involve the regularities of schooling (Goodlad 1984) and the tendencies for instruction to become fixated on low-level learning, particularly in classes or schools with many disadvantaged, low achievers. Several of the most important of these tendencies are described in this section.

Institutional Realities and Classroom Management Requirements. Philip Jackson (1968), John Goodlad (1984), Linda McNeil (1986), John Mergendoller (1988), and many others have pointed out that the realities perceived by teachers and administrators responsible for the welfare and behavior of many students result in an emphasis on obedience to rules and regulations designed to ensure orderly conduct. Walter Doyle (1985a) has documented how emphasis on order in turn works against a focus on higher-order learning because tasks involving "recall or predictable algorithms, such as those found in vocabulary or grammar assignments," tend to proceed most "smoothly and efficiently" (Doyle 1985, 12). Doyle also has pointed out that "higher level tasks are often difficult to carry out" because

> *the flow of activity slows down in the class when students find the work difficult or risky to accomplish . . . and student error rates go up. . . . When this happens, problems of student attention and motivation to work can occur. These conditions create tensions in a classroom between the academic task system and the demands for pace and momentum inherent in the management of classroom groups. (Doyle 1985, 60)*

Student Preference for Lower-Order Skills. Many students prefer low-level learning activities that they can complete easily and quickly rather than more challenging work that requires much more physical and mental exertion and that also exposes them to more risk of failure (Holt 1964; Herndon 1968). This pattern has been described in the work of Walter Doyle and other researchers. Doyle also has pointed out that tasks emphasizing understanding and reasoning are "high in inherent ambiguity and risk for students" so that the probability of failure also is high (Doyle 1985, 12). Many students respond to the challenge of higher-order assignments by attempting to

> *increase the explicitness of a teacher's instructions. . . . [For example, two researchers] met with strong resistance . . . when they attempted to shift informa-*

> *tion-processing demands in a mathematics class from routine or procedural tasks to understanding tasks. The students refused to cooperate and argued that they had a right to be told what to do. . . . [After their experience, the researchers] commented that "it is no longer a mystery why so many teachers and so many textbooks present ninth-grade algebra as a rote algorithmic subject." (Doyle 1983, 184–185)*

Bargains, Accommodations, and Compromises. As described by Walter Doyle, the realities of classroom interaction generate a tendency for many students to resist challenging, intellectual tasks. A long series of studies conducted in the 1970s and 1980s has described how this tendency helps generate bargains and treaties through which teachers and students agree to the establishment of minimal standards and passive, mechanical learning. Although an agreement of this kind is apparent in many elementary schools, it is particularly characteristic of intermediate and senior high schools. In addition to Doyle, Ernest Boyer (1983), Philip Cusick (1983), John Goodlad (1984), Theodore Sizer (1984), Arthur Powell (1985), Robert Hampel (1986), and many others have studied and described the genesis and effects of arrangements that lead to or involve a focus on minimal standards and low-level learning. Michael Sedlak and his colleagues (Sedlak, Wheeler, Pullin, and Cusick 1986) have described some major aspects of the situation in secondary schools:

> *For a variety of reasons . . . [many students] invest their time and energy outside the school in activities that reward them financially, offer them some semblance of adult responsibility, or treat them as valued consumers. . . .*
>
> *In most high schools, there exists a complex, tacit conspiracy to avoid rigorous, demanding, academic inquiry. A "bargain" of sorts is struck that demands little academically of either teachers or students. . . .*
>
> *[Several studies have shown how] students sought to minimize requirements, delay or postpone assignments, and receive the highest grades they could for the least amount of effort. . . . The negotiation process often invalidated efforts to evaluate achievement. (Sedlak, Wheeler, Pullin, and Cusick 1986, 13, 5, 101–102)*

Another important aspect of the bargain struck by teachers involves their reactions to efforts made to establish systematic standards for teaching and learning in the schools. Reacting to sometimes nonexistent standards in many secondary schools, school board members, administrators, legislators, and other decision makers have introduced specific prescriptions and schedules for teaching and testing specific skills, particularly during the recent era of reform in education (Madaus 1988). As mentioned earlier in this chapter, however, many observers believe that the effects of such mandates will be harmful for many students in the absence of prerequisites for successful change (e.g., much greater resources, extensive staff development, and modified organizational arrangements) at the school building level. Thus, Sedlak and his colleagues considered the recent national wave of "content-oriented initiatives" and concluded that this movement "risks driving resistant and even many indifferent students into disruption and rebellion" (p. 57). In addition, Theodore Sizer (1984), Linda McNeil (1986; 1988), and others have described how prescriptions for teaching and testing a wide range of skills and objectives have forced many teachers to compromise between their desire to provide challenging, in-depth learning and the constant pressure they perceive to cover defined curriculum.

The problems and dilemmas posed by educators' attempts to maintain some degree of cooperation from students on the one hand and to raise expectations and standards on the other appear to be particularly acute in schools enrolling a relatively high proportion of low achieving, disadvantaged students. In this regard, Miller, Leinhardt, and Zigmond (1987) studied a blue-collar secondary school and found that much of the education offered there involved an accommodation designed to "adjust the mechanisms of school life to bring them into correspondence with the realities of adolescent life" (p. 12). After 206 observations and many interviews, the authors reported that "administrators and teachers consciously tried to limit the demands made on students" and that "students were aware of the accommodating aspects of their environment and even came to anticipate accommodation" (pp. 25–26). While accommodation helps reduce failure and dropping out, however, it has "unintended negative side effects" that

> *limit levels of academic engagement and limit the ultimate usefulness of the school experience. . . . Believing that there will always be a second chance, learning that you can get through school without challenge and hard work, and being bored may teach students to look for second chances, to not seek challenges or hard work, and to not be persistent. (Miller, Leinhardt, and Zigmond 1987, p. 26)*

Low Expectations and Low-Level Learning Scripts for Low Achievers. As we pointed out in Chapters 7 and 8, low expectations and requirements appear to play an important part in generating and reinforcing low performance levels among many disadvantaged students (Payne 1984). We also concluded that high standards are particularly difficult to establish and maintain in concentrated poverty schools with high proportions of low achievers. Thus, raising of standards and expectations has been a key component in the effective schools movement.

Tendencies for instruction to concentrate on low-level learning skills in both elementary and secondary schools appear to be magnified in the case of low-achieving students, in part because some teachers do not believe many of their poorly functioning students can perform much better. In line with those beliefs and perceptions, some teachers apparently develop a script that confines low achievers to passive, mechanical learning assignments and experiences. Thus, Richard Shavelson (1985) found indications of low-level scripts for low achievers in a case study of an elementary teacher who was asked to use her "high-ability student script" with her low-ability group. According to Shavelson, the high-ability script involved changing to a more difficult textbook, emphasizing discussion of the meaning of the stories, asking questions for which more than one answer might be acceptable, and switching from highly constrained formats to unconstrained papers. Shavelson reported that the behavior and performance of students in the low-ability group greatly improved.

As we suggested in the preceding sections, low-level scripts for low achievers also originate in part from the behavior and attitudes of the students themselves, who may wish to avoid intellectual risks and respond as if they were incapable of improving their performance in the classroom. Jere Brophy (1986) and other researchers have reported, for example, that low achievers typically are more concerned with completing assignments than with understanding their content.

In addition, there are indications that disadvantaged black students (and perhaps other minority students as well) sometimes internalize low-level learning scripts that significantly impede their school progress. Thus, Ray Hammond of a private organization that works with high-school students and Jeffrey Howard of the African Methodist Episcopal Church have observed a tendency among black youth in the inner city to "avoid engagement in intellectual competition." Hammond and Howard believe that this avoidance behavior represents a self-fulfilling prophecy that "arises when the larger society projects an image of black intellectual inferiority *and* when that image is internalized at a less-than-conscious level by black people over a number of generations" (Hammond and Howard 1986, 61). They also point to frequent derogatory nicknaming (e.g., nerd, egghead) of school-oriented students as evidence of widespread avoidance behavior among black students.

Teachers' Preferences and Handicaps. Emphasis on passive, lower-order learning and mechanical skills also arises in part from factors involving teachers' preferences and characteristics. Low-level material and skills are easier to teach and test than are higher mental processes. Tendencies to stress lower-order learning understandably are particularly prevalent among teachers who have large classes, are overloaded with paperwork or other organizational burdens, and/or work in difficult schools with a high proportion of low-achieving students. Preparing lessons to help students acquire higher-order skills and understandings, assigning and grading more complex written assignments and independent research, and/or working in other ways to provide active learning experiences are difficult undertakings that require time and energy on the part of the teacher. In addition, some teachers are not intellectually or personally capable or prepared to function effectively in a classroom that stresses cognitive development and movement toward independent learning.

Mediated Development to Assist Low Achievers

As described above, research and development personnel have devised and refined many instructional approaches and programs for helping students progress with respect to cognitive functioning and higher-order mental processes. We also have emphasized that the provision of explicit assistance to enhance cognitive growth in a step-by-step framework is particularly important for disadvantaged low achievers, whose previous experience has provided limited preparation for functioning at a high level in processing abstract knowledge in the classroom. Thus, recent research has emphasized the importance of providing systematic, mediated assistance in helping students—particularly low-achieving students—acquire metacognitive controls, learning-to-learn strategies, and other skills and understandings required to improve cognitive functioning.

Sema Brainin (1985) has reviewed the research on Feuerstein's Instrumental Enrichment program and other mediated learning approaches to improve the cognitive development of low-achieving preadolescents and adolescents and reported that such mediation appears to have some positive results when it has attended adequately to such "essential conditions" as sharing with the learner "an intentional and analytic approach to the learning process itself," developing an "awareness of the meaning of stimuli and their relevance in ever-larger contexts increasingly remote from direct experience," and enabling learners to "experience and express cognitive growth in productive ways." She also cautions, however, that there has been little investigation to determine what approaches work best and how they can be implemented most effectively in specific situations and that a particularly "critical facet" of meaningful efforts to help achievers involves recognizing the "importance of taking realistic account of the professional growth required for teachers to become effective cognitive educators" (Brainin 1985, 139, 144).

Failure to Move beyond Order and Structure

Despite the particular importance of providing continuing mediated support to help low-achieving students develop higher-order skills and improve in cognitive functioning, teachers working with disadvantaged lower-achievers frequently tend to become fixated on the structured learning aspects of this challenge and to ignore the imperative to move toward more active, independent learning. This mistake is particularly easy to make because highly structured learning combined with effective classroom management tends to produce a more orderly environment, which teachers, administrators, parents, and students rightly perceive to be a prerequisite for successful instruction. Sedlak and his colleagues have described this tendency as a "social trap" in which success in classroom management can "delude" teachers into thinking they are meeting their responsibilities "at the expense of the formal objective of maximizing academic learning" (Sedlak, Wheeler, Pullin, and Cusick 1986, 102). And as we noted in Chapter 3, attempts to move rapidly toward independent learning in schools enrolling many disadvantaged students frequently have involved misguided efforts that produced little more than chaos in the classroom.

It is difficult to find a proper and productive balance between low achievers' needs for mastering initial basic skills and the challenge to help them proceed beyond low-level mechanical learning. Because students functioning far below grade level do have severe deficiencies in such beginning skills as word identification and computation, it generally is important to correct these deficiencies in the primary grades if possible and in later grades if necessary (Sizemore 1985). On the other hand, research also indicates that movement toward higher-order learning can help students master and retain mechanical skills because it provides them with schema for organizing and remembering information and that effective instruction emphasizing higher-mental processes results in as much or more growth in lower-level learning as does instruction limited primarily to lower-mental processes (Soled 1987, 1988; Bloom 1988).

High Costs of Effective Instruction to Improve Cognitive Development

Amid much uncertainty concerning the selection and implementation of instructional approaches for improving students' cognitive development and functioning, one conclusion seems apparent: The financial costs of moving in this direction successfully on a widespread basis will be large. In part, this is because providing mediated instruction requires considerable personal contact and individualized attention from teachers and other faculty, particularly in the case of low achievers who have not yet learned to work well independently.

In addition, the costs of training and retraining teachers to be what Brainin called "cognitive educators" will be much higher than generally have been expended or even contemplated in teacher training. This conclusion was one lesson reported by Ruth Kurth and Linda Stromberg (1984), who worked with a small group of teachers in an effort to provide more teaching of comprehension and to "promote independent reading" in a suburban elementary school. Kurth and Stromberg concluded that although these goals can be attained and have a positive impact on achievement, success depended on "continuous, almost Herculean efforts" (p. 22). Similarly, Putnam, Roehler, and Duffy (1987) have been working to help elementary teachers implement more effective comprehension instruction and have concluded that "the development of cognitive skills and independent decision making" demands "elaborate staff development . . . [during which time there must be] sensitive, individual assistance that is responsive to each teacher's particular background, current context, and emerging understandings of what is being learned" (p. 24).

Expenditures on public education have risen a great deal since 1983. By far the largest proportion of increasing expenditures is allocated to higher teacher salaries, frequently leaving little if any additional funding for other important goals, such as reduced class size, staff development, provision of technical assistance for teachers, and instructional materials to help up-date curriculum and instruction. It is not certain that expenditures will rise fast enough in the future and/or will be adequately focused to support a massive effort to improve students' cognitive functioning and higher-order mental processing.

Exemplary Approaches for Improving Instruction

A number of approaches have been developed that appear to be successful in improving cognitive functioning and other aspects of achievement when they are implemented well. To illustrate the possibilities being tried in school districts throughout the United States, this section describes four approaches that have helped improve the achievement of disadvantaged students.

Teacher Expectations and Student Achievement Training

Developed by personnel at the office of the Los Angeles County Superintendent of Schools, Teacher Expectations and Student Achievement (TESA) training is being widely used and has had considerable success in raising expectations for low-achieving students and in improving teacher-student interactions (Kerman 1979). The TESA approach was developed because research had indicated that teachers' interactions with low achievers tend to be less supportive of achievement than is true with respect to higher-achieving students. In addition to having more opportunity to respond to questions, high achievers also receive more cues from teachers than do low achievers (Brophy and Good 1986). Training in TESA is intended to help teachers change this type of pattern.

Consisting initially of five workshops scheduled about one month apart, TESA training emphasizes fifteen important teaching behaviors, including higher-order questioning, provision of individual support for students, and equitable distribution of opportunity. Participants observe each other four times following each workshop, and data from these observations are provided to help them examine their interactions with students. Implementation of TESA thus is based on research indicating that staff development tends to be most effective when teachers observe and assist one another in actual classrooms.

Mastery Learning

Chapter 8 provides a brief description of the mastery learning approach developed by Benjamin Bloom and his colleagues and cites several sources indicating that it appears to have been successful in raising the achievement of disadvantaged students in some locations. The five major steps in the mastery-learning sequence defined by Bloom and his colleagues (e.g., Block and Anderson 1975; Guskey 1985) are to:

1. Define a specific learning objective.
2. Teach the understanding or skills embodied in the objective.
3. Use a criterion-referenced test to assess mastery.

4. Provide corrective instruction for nonmasters and enrichment or acceleration for students who did master the objective.
5. Retest the students who received corrective instruction.

Bloom and his colleagues advocate whole-group instruction during the initial teaching phase, whereas some other mastery-learning developers (e.g., Hyman and Cohen 1979) emphasize small-group and individual instruction throughout the mastery sequence. Many approaches other than mastery learning concentrate on student mastery of specific learning skills. Such approaches can be viewed as mastery-type learning, but more often are referred to as outcomes-based instruction (Rubin and Spady 1984).

Data on the implementation of mastery learning as defined by Bloom indicate that it can bring about very large gains in student achievement, particularly among low achievers. When well implemented, mastery learning can raise the student now at the fiftieth percentile to the ninetieth percentile or above, and the low achiever now at the fifteenth percentile can improve to the fiftieth percentile or above. Gains of this magnitude are possible when mastery learning is combined with enhancement of students' initial skills on concepts prerequisite to the instruction, provision of appropriate cues and feedback, emphasis on students' active participation, and/or work with parents to improve the home learning environment. Bloom (1984) concludes, moreover, that these gains can be attained for higher-order learning not just for mechanical learning of factual information.

The research by Bloom and his colleagues has been conducted mostly with individual classes using teacher-made tests, but recent research indicates that comparable results can be attained on a schoolwide basis using standardized tests. Jones and Spady (1985) have examined mastery learning in Johnson City, New York; Red Bank, New Jersey; and in several other school districts. They conclude that very large gains in academic achievement have been registered when mastery learning has been implemented effectively.

However, as also is true with respect to other approaches that emphasize teacher-centered delivery of instruction on specific skills, mastery learning is particularly susceptible to misimplementation caused in part by overemphasis on narrow, mechanical skills that are easiest to teach and test. In addition, teachers frequently have been overloaded with record-keeping chores, and many educators implementing mastery learning have ignored the findings of research (described later in this chapter) regarding successful implementation of change in the schools. In general, effective implementation of mastery learning requires systematic attention to prerequisites for success, such as manageable class size, large amounts of planning time for teachers, and provision of adequate time for corrective instruction (Levine 1985).

Student Team Learning

Chapter 9 refers to research indicating that cooperative learning arrangements have contributed to achievement gains in desegregated classrooms, in part because such arrangements appear to fit the learning styles of many minority students. Probably the best known example of a cooperative learning approach is Student Team Learning (STL) developed by Robert Slavin and his colleagues at The Johns Hopkins University. Student Team Learning is being widely used because it has demonstrated impressive success in helping improve classroom participation and achievement of many groups of students in various settings, not just minority students in desegregated classes (Slavin 1980; 1983).

The STL approach uses a number of techniques in which students work in four- or five-member learning teams and receive recognition based on the extent to which all team members complete and master a common set of skills. Students' scores are based on their performance in comparison with other students who start at the same level or on improvement over their own previous performance, thus making it possible for all students to score well if they work diligently. Studies of STL have shown positive outcomes in reading, math, social studies, science, and other subjects. When implemented well, STL also has produced significant gains in students' attitudes toward school and self-concept.

The developers of Student Team Learning also have been testing several modified versions called Team Accelerated Individualization (TAI) and Cooperative Integrated Reading and Composition (CIRC). Research on TAI, which combines team learning, individualization, and mastery learning in teaching math in the middle grades, indicates that it can produce large improvements in student attitudes as well as in achievement (Slavin, Madden, and Leavey 1984). Research on CIRC, which combines team learning with specially prepared materials to coordinate instruction in reading, language arts, and writing, has produced significant achievement gains among regular students and mainstreamed special-education students in the middle grades (Madden, Stevens, and Slavin 1986).

Degrees of Reading Power Comprehension Development Approach

Another promising approach is the comprehension development framework built in part on the Degrees of Reading Power (DRP) test developed by the College Board. Unlike mastery learning and Student Team Learning, which generally have been accepted most readily and implemented most effectively on a schoolwide basis in elementary and intermediate schools, the DRP comprehension development approach is frequently being introduced most successfully at the senior-high level.

The first step in this approach is to obtain comprehension scores for all students by administering the DRP test. Unlike other standardized tests of reading comprehension, the DRP provides an assessment that indicates how well a student actually can comprehend prose he or she encounters inside and outside of school. It also is criterion-referenced in the sense that it assesses students' actual level of comprehension, not just whether a high or low achiever is above or below some abstract grade level as designated by other standardized reading tests.

After determining students' comprehension levels, the second step is to align instructional materials with the comprehension level of one's students. The aim at this point and subsequently is to provide materials that do not frustrate students in completing homework and other independent learning activities, while using materials slightly beyond students' current functional level during instruction designed to help students gain in comprehension. Because this approach aims at improving comprehension in social studies, science, and other subjects, which presumably is a central goal of education in all subject areas, the DRP comprehension development framework is intended to enhance comprehension throughout the curriculum.

The third and most extensive step in the DRP approach is to help faculty introduce comprehension-development teaching and learning strategies in line with students' current functional levels and problems (Harris and Cooper 1985). At this stage, teachers are assisted in selecting and using appropriate strategies from among the many available possibilities, such as higher-order questioning, directed thinking activities, concept mapping, cooperative team learning, and others mentioned elsewhere in this chapter. Successful results in terms of improving student achievement have been reported in Levittown, New York (Sirois and Davis 1985), and in several other school districts.

Combinations of Approaches

Promising instructional approaches such as those described are not mutually exclusive. Drawing on a larger research base concerned with the characteristics of effective schools and effective instruction, they can be and frequently are combined with each other and with other promising approaches involving change in testing, instructional and organizational arrangements and policies, staff development, and other interventions to improve education. Thus, as in the examples noted above, STL is being combined with mastery learning as part of TAI, the DRP approach can draw on STL, TESA can be an important component in introducing mastery learning or STL, and DRP testing can be used to help keep mastery learning focused on higher-order skill development.

In addition, these approaches can help educators become more successful in developing higher-order learning, particularly among low achievers, because they emphasize or allow for emphasis on providing instructional support to enhance students' cognitive develpment. Indeed, much of the problem educators face in working to improve instruction substantially is to find the right mixtures and adaptations of promising approaches and then to implement them according to a systematic plan that reflects awareness of school-reform research cited in the following section.

Accomplishing School Improvement and Reform

Identifying instructional and organizational changes that may improve schools substantially is not the same as actually bringing about successful change. Analysis of efforts to improve schools during the past few decades has provided information and understanding concerning the issues that should be addressed and the steps that should be taken to enhance the likelihood of successful reform. Among the themes that research indicates should be emphasized are the nine described below.

Problem-Solving Orientation and Critical Inquiry

The introduction of an innovation frequently has little or no effect on student achievement because a variety of problems arise to hinder practical implementation. For example, specialists may prepare an outstanding math curriculum for sixth graders and school districts may purchase the new curriculum materials, but teachers may choose not to use the materials, may use them improperly because they do not fit the testing schedule, or may not know how to use them. Innovations are not likely to be implemented successfully unless the organization introducing them focuses continually on identifying and solving day-to-day implementation problems (Hawley 1978; Goodlad 1987). In addition, the attitude exemplified by faculty in a school participating in a successful reform effort is of critical inquiry or critical reflection aimed at re-examining current goals and practices and of search for improved ways of organizing and delivering instruction more effectively (Henshaw, Wilson, and Morefield 1987).

School-Level Emphasis

Because the innovating organization must identify and solve day-to-day problems, the focus in bringing about change must be at the level of the individual school building, where many of the problems occur (Goodlad 1987; Rankin 1983).

Staff Development

Schoolwide staff development focusing on improved delivery of instruction is a core activity in the school improvement process (Joyce and Showers 1988). In the case of an elementary school, the entire staff should participate; in secondary schools, departments may be the appropriate unit for some activities. Kenneth Sirotnik (1987) reports that the amount of time required for productive change through staff development possibly will amount to the equivalent of one full day per week and two paid months during the summer. Staff development usually is most successful when it takes place during the regular school day.

Collection of Data

One particularly important activity in implementing major change involves collection of data to identify problems in a school's instructional arrangements and outcomes. Other things being equal, faculty will be more likely to change their behavior and practices if data clearly indicate a need for such change. For this reason, many successful change efforts have emphasized the collection of appropriate data to help set directions for instructional improvements. Questionnaires, interviews, and documents can be analyzed to identify problems and issues that impede implementation of more effective instruction (Fullan 1982; Schmuck and Runkel 1985).

Faculty Involvement and Collegial Collaboration

Many studies support the conclusion that teacher involvement in decisions about how to implement an innovation can be important in determining whether it is successful (Rankin 1983; Lieberman and Rosenholtz 1987). This is not surprising inasmuch as people who are expected to alter their working patterns will be more likely to accept change if they have a part in selecting and shaping it than if it is imposed by others. In addition, teachers as grass-roots workers are in the best position to identify the practical obstacles that will hinder successful implementation.

Furthermore, research supports the conclusion that collegial collaboration and planning for improvement are two of the most important and productive aspects of faculty involvement in school reform efforts (Little 1981; Zahorik 1987). Collegial collaboration, including staff development activities in which teachers observe and critique each other's work and address obstacles to effective delivery of instruction, may be indispensable in improving instructional and organizational arrangements and school culture (Lieberman and Rosenholtz 1987).

Combined Bottom-Up and Top-Down Approach

Because research had emphasized the importance of faculty participation in decisions, analysts in the 1960s and 1970s tended to emphasize a bottom-up approach in order to develop a sense of ownership among teachers. However, research in the 1980s has supported the importance of top-down components in initiating change successfully. Insistence on and support for change by administrators, school board members, and others at the district and state levels frequently are required if successful implementation is to occur at the classroom level. Thus, two comprehensive, independent studies of innovation (Huberman and Miles 1982; Marsh and Berman 1984) have concluded that top-down initiation and support frequently are required to effectuate and institutionalize long-term improvements. Matthew Miles has described the stance of top-level administrators who communicate to principals and teachers an understanding that "we are going to try a new approach, you are going to implement it, and we are going to help you." Miles believes that administrative pressure and support frequently lead teachers to develop mastery of an innovation. Mastery then helps them develop the commitment to implement the change effectively (Miles 1983).

Implementability

The success of school improvement and reform efforts also depends on whether the changes introduced are implementable in the sense that they have high potential for being adopted and used effectively by teachers. David Crandall, Jeffrey Eiseman, and Karen Louis (1986) have summarized five of the key dimensions that affect implementability:

1. *Compatibility* with the social context of prospective users.
2. *Accessibility* to prospective users who do not already share the conceptual framework of the designers.
3. *Observability* that enables prospective users to assess the innovation in terms of their own reality.
4. *Craft legitimization* that indicates the innovation has been workable in field testing or actual school situations.
5. *Adaptability* that allows users to engage in local adaptation.

Regarding adaptability, Crandall, Eiseman, and Louis have examined the research on implementation of educational innovations and further concluded that a difficult-to-attain balance must be achieved between making necessary changes to fit particular schools or classrooms on the one hand and ensuring implementation of the most central core components of the innovation on the other hand (1986, 32–33).

Development of Shared Agreements

Successful implementation of a major innovation requires change in many institutional arrangements, including scheduling of staff and student time, development of new behaviors and attitudes on the part of teachers and students, and selection and use of instructional methods and materials. The building principal, who is responsible for arrangements throughout the institution, usually is the key person in successfully implementing change. In addition, the faculty must have a shared culture, or shared vision of the kinds of changes that are possible and necessary to improve their instructional practice; otherwise, the staff is unlikely seriously to consider proposals that require significant changes in existing arrangements and behaviors (Blendinger and Jones 1988).

Some schools require much more time and effort to develop shared agreements than do others (Goodlad 1987). At some schools there is considerable agreement that achievement must be improved and that this requires change in many current arrangements; here, the problems of change management are largely technical. At many other schools, however, verbal recognition of the need for improvement does not denote any real willingness to change current practices. In these schools, the initial emphasis must be on the very difficult task involved in developing and shaping a new set of agreements and understandings concerning the school's purpose and everyday practices. Ann Lieberman and Susan Rosenholtz (1987) have summarized the difficulty and importance of attaining this fundamental change in school culture:

> *There is evidence that the building of a more professional culture is what makes effective schools. Tying effectiveness to raising achievement scores oversimplifies the complexity of building such a culture and puts the emphasis in the wrong place. The reality of schools, as we have come to understand them, is far more complicated. The web of social relations, the pressure for standardization in the face of diversity, the discomfort at the creation of new roles for teachers, the constant stream of society's problems that come to school with students, the impatience with how long it takes for organizations to change, the lure of technical answers to social problems, and the lack of understanding of the processes of changing organizations and their accompanying people problems, all point to how much we are learning but how far we still need to go. (Lieberman and Rosenholtz 1987, 87)*

Nonbureaucratic Implementation

Successful implementation of fundamental reforms in the delivery of instruction cannot be accomplished primarily through bureaucratic approaches that overemphasize filling out of forms and collection of data—even computerized data—to determine whether teachers and schools are responding to central directives. As we discuss earlier in this chapter, much of the national reform effort has taken the form of mandated change involving course requirements, instructional schedules, teacher presentation of specified subject matter following prescribed steps for delivering instruction, and other aspects of school operation, together with accountability and appraisal systems to ensure that the directives are being carried out. However, decades of research and experience indicate that substantial improvement depends on technical assistance from support personnel working closely with teachers on a personal basis, not on piles of forms, detailed deadlines, and other bureaucratic control mechanisms (Levine and Leibert 1987). Kenneth Sirotnik (1987) has summarized this imperative in the school reform process:

> *One forum that I am convinced is wholly inappropriate is the current wave of computerized management information systems for districts and schools, and the related attempts to construct . . . [quantity indicators] by which to judge school effectiveness. . . . Having worked on the idea of school-based, comprehensive information systems for a number of years, I have come to see more clearly how people can make good use of these systems. But I cannot emphasize enough the importance of being aware of how such systems can use people. . . . Certainly information is useful, but mainly in context and mainly by people willing to work in the trenches of school improvement. Otherwise, my guess is that information systems (and indexes constructed therefrom) will be mostly devices to lend scien-*

tific credibility to accountability systems concerned more with symbols than substance. (Sirotnik 1987, 44–45)

At-Risk or Marginal Students and Dropouts

Attention to the problems of students who are low achieving or have been encountering other problems in school has been coalescing under such designations as at-risk students, marginal students, and potential dropouts. In general, such designations refer to the significant proportion of students whose educational performance and opportunities probably will not be improved significantly simply by adding more rigorous course requirements or otherwise imposing external standards such as are present in minimal competency tests.

The term *at-risk student* can denote a general category that sometimes has been applied broadly to students whose disadvantaged economic or social background is associated with lack of success in the public schools. (This seems to be the usage favored in the statement by the Forum of Educational Leaders cited earlier in this chapter.) Other definitions, such as the following one by Gary Wehlage, Robert Rutter, and Anne Turnbaugh (1987), specifically cite low achievement and alienation from the school as elements in the underlying formulation:

> *The at-risk student is . . . a young person who comes from a low socioeconomic background which may include various forms of family stress or instability. If the young person is consistently discouraged by the school because he or she receives signals about academic inadequacies and failures, perceives little interest or caring from teachers, and sees the institution's discipline as both ineffective and unfair, then it is not unreasonable to expect that the student will become alienated and uncommitted to getting a high school diploma. (Wehlage, Rutter, and Turnbaugh 1987, 71)*

Gary Wehlage and his colleagues have been developing and assessing educational programs for at-risk students as defined here. As a result of these activities, they have described a general model for delivering improved education for at-risk students either in school-within-a-school units or in alternative schools. The four parts of this model (Wehlage, Rutter, and Turnbaugh 1987) include the following aspects:

1. *Administration and organization.* A learning unit ideally should include 25 to 100 students with 2 to 6 faculty, small enough to provide "face-to-face relationships on a continuing basis" and to enable teachers to express a caring relationship as well as to "personalize and individualize their instructional efforts." Teachers should control admissions and dismissals and also should have autonomy in scheduling and in dealing with difficult students.

2. *Teacher culture.* Teachers must believe that at-risk students "deserve a renewed opportunity" to learn, must develop a strong sense of joint cooperation focused on making learning more stimulating, and must be willing to deal with "certain problems in the home, community, or peer groups" that affect their students' behavior in school.
3. *Curriculum.* Curriculum and teaching must incorporate individualization, clear objectives, provision of prompt feedback and concrete evidence of progress, and an active role for students. Initial emphasis should be on remediation of serious basic skills deficits, but learning activities emphasizing such topics as sex education, parenting instruction, health care and nutrition, and community social-service also should be included.
4. *Experiential learning.* Planned, experiential learning activities in roles such as volunteer at a day-care center or nursing home or intern in a hospital, newspaper office, or law enforcement agency should be included, in part to place students in contact with adults who exemplify "characteristics of responsibility, the work ethic, and the ability to build positive human relationships (Wehlage, Rutter, and Turnbaugh 1987, 71–73).

Wehlage and his colleagues have reported positive results in implementing their model. Other approaches, such as some that use vocational education more systematically, also have been successful, but in general it appears that special programs and alternatives to help at-risk students at the intermediate or high-school level either have included or probably would benefit from incorporation of some version of the components just enumerated. Even though the model developed by Wehlage and his colleagues has proven particularly useful in working with at-risk students who have become severely alienated from the school, programs aimed at helping less alienated low achievers can be successful when they enroll 100 or more students and also depart in some other respects from the full model.

Marginal Students

A formulation somewhat similar to the at-risk category has been provided by Robert Sinclair and Ward Ghory (1987), who have analyzed problems and possibilities for improvement in educational programs for marginal students. Sinclair and Ghory define *marginality* with reference to such behaviors as low achievement, truancy, class cutting, tardiness, disciplinary infractions, and dissatisfaction with school among a "shadow population . . . of young people who are not being well served by the American public schools" (p. 41). Although there is no way to estimate precisely the percentage of students who are marginal according to these or related criteria, Sinclair and Ghory point to such indicators as the widespread reading problems experienced by junior high students and conclude that educational institutions and their environments must be "reshaped" to promote more constructive behavior among the high proportions of marginal students enrolled in many schools (p. 36).

After noting that "becoming marginal" generally proceeds through four "levels of seriousness" from "testing" to "coasting," "retreating," and finally, "rebelling," Sinclair and Ghory identify eight "counterproductive regularities" that contribute to the difficulties of marginal learners:

1. Large-group instruction that results in uncorrected errors in learning.
2. Narrowness of traditional instruction favoring advanced students.
3. Inflexibility in school schedules.
4. Differential treatment by ability group or track.
5. "Misuses of evaluation that reinforce a student's status" as successful or marginal.
6. Exclusion of teachers and parents from curriculum development and reform.
7. Teacher organizations that limit reform efforts.
8. "Insufficient and inequitable funding that restricts the scope of improvement" (Sinclair and Ghory, pp. 53, 62).

In addition to supporting movement away from these "counterproductive regularities," Sinclair and Ghory emphasize providing marginal students with skills in "learning to learn," "content thinking," "basic reasoning," and "communication" (pp. 100–106). Like Wehlage and his colleagues, Sinclair and Ghory also emphasize the importance of providing marginal or at-risk students with opportunities for experiential learning in nonschool settings.

Although the problems of many marginal or at-risk students certainly are apparent at the elementary level, difficulties experienced by this population become most obvious and pronounced at the secondary level, when students move into the relatively impersonal environment of intermediate and senior high schools. Earlier in this chapter we cite the importance of fundamental reform in instructional and organizational arrangements of secondary schools, and we also emphasize both the importance and the difficulties of moving toward a greater emphasis on active learning and higher-order skills, as proposed by Sinclair and Ghory and by Wehlage and his colleagues. These goals are interrelated inasmuch as substantial movement toward more meaningful education for marginal and other students probably is dependent on fundamental reform of secondary schools. We return to the topic of high school reform in a concluding section of this chapter.

Dropouts

Growing national dissatisfaction with the quality of education in general has both generated and reflected concern for the high school dropout rate and the career limitations that will be encountered by many young people who do not complete high school. As we point out in Chapter 2, most non-Hispanic white students complete high school and the dropout rate for black students has declined, but the dropout rate for minority students still is disproportionately high and half or more of the students in inner-city neighborhoods in big cities are not completing high school. The unsurprising results of research on characterstics of high-school dropouts indicate that on the average they are lower than high-school graduates in socioeconomic status, previous achievement, and attendance, and higher in hostility toward school, disruptiveness, delinquency, drug usage, truancy, and other measures of alienation (Pallas 1986; Mensch and Kandel 1988).

Some of the concern with recent dropout rates may be unjustified inasmuch as many dropouts return to school and obtain diplomas or pass graduation-equivalency exams (Finn 1987). However, the high correlation between dropping out and socioeconomic status as well as the high rates among disadvantaged students in the inner city indicate that failure to complete high school is a serious national problem (Rumberger 1987; Burch 1988). Gary Wehlage and Robert Rutter (1986) have studied the reasons for dropping out among urban adolescents and concluded that the five major types of dropouts in this population include students who:

1. Reject traditional pedagogy,
2. Perceive little or no relation between schooling and future income,
3. Leave school because of family, economic, and social obligations,
4. Are unable to cope with poverty environments and lack of success in school, or
5. Are fundamentally rejected by the schools.

Other observers (e.g., Kyle, Lane, Sween, and Triana 1986) also have pointed out that some inner-city students in particularly disorganized communities leave school primarily because of physical dangers that exist in and around their schools.

Many interventions have been proposed, and many programs have been or are being implemented to reduce the dropout rate. Among the possible (and not mutally exclusive) steps most often advocated and emphasized are the following eight:

1. *Early intervention* to help potential dropouts experience more success in school and develop more positive attitudes in elementary and intermediate schools (Pallas 1986).
2. *Alternative* opportunities such as schools-within-a-school, magnet schools, career academies, in-school suspension programs, street academies, high-school outposts, and storefront schools (Fortenberry and White 1987; Wehlage, Rutter, and Turnbaugh 1987).
4. *Smaller schools and classes* that can facilitate more personal contact between students and teachers (Reinhard 1987).
5. *Vocational education* opportunities that might enhance motivation and provide more experience of success for potential dropouts (Hamilton 1986).
6. *Employment linkages* to provide part-time employment and skill training (Fortenberry and White 1987; Hamilton 1988) along with other possibilities (dis-

cussed at the conclusion of Chapter 6) to improve the transition to work and adulthood.
7. *Counseling* and *special services and programs* such as those for delinquents or pregnant girls (Mann 1986; National Governors' Association 1987).
8. *Revisions in curriculum and instruction* to make education more relevant, motivating, and successful for disinterested and/or alienated students (Ekstrom, Goertz, Pollack, and Rock 1986; Firestone and Rosenblum 1987).

Each general approach for reducing the dropout rate and making schools more effective for potential dropouts has some support in research. For example, Stephen Hamilton (1986) surveyed the research on antidropout programs emphasizing vocational education and other aspects of learning outside of regular academic classes and concluded that experiential learning along these lines can increase holding power when it is implemented well and coordinated with regular instruction. Nevertheless, others who have surveyed the research on antidropout programs have concluded that we do not now clearly understand what interventions and mixtures of interventions work best in differing circumstances and how they should be implemented optimally in the schools (Mann 1986).

Crucial Issues in Moving Further toward School Reform

Throughout this book, and particularly throughout this chapter, we identify important issues and problems in considering possibilities for improving education in elementary and secondary schools. We do not attempt to review or summarize all of the relevant themes introduced and discussed; instead, we highlight three issues that deserve more explicit attention if the school reform movement is to be successful in radically improving the effectiveness of instruction. These three issues involve grouping and tracking in elementary and secondary schools, the growing imperative to undertake substantial reorganization of secondary schools, and the need to increase students' engagement in learning.

Grouping and Tracking

Our initial discussions of grouping and tracking in Chapters 2 and 8 conclude that assigning students to classes or tracks according to previous achievement or ability scores generally has had detrimental effects for low achievers but that the issues involved in devising effective organizational arrangements for instruction are complex and difficult (Passow 1988). Earlier in this chapter and in Chapter 8, we also cite unusually effective inner-city schools, indicating that some grouping by previous achievement can be productive if it results in improved arrangements for teaching low achievers.

Part of the problem in reaching conclusions about grouping and tracking involves the fact that heterogeneous assignment of students to very diverse classes usually has not been successful unless it has used effective individualized and small-group methods that allow students to proceed at their own pace (continuous-progress instruction). Unfortunately, individualized, continuous-progress instruction requires an enormous amount of planning, effort, and instructional resources (Scriven 1975; Cohen 1986; Bennett and Desforges 1988). When teachers do not receive sufficient resources for individualized, continuous guidance, students often spend much of their time in unproductive seatwork. Large classes with very diverse composition are difficult to work with effectively even when teachers use Student Team Learning and other techniques that can help them deal with diversity.

For reasons described in Chapters 2 and 8, however, alternatives to heterogeneous assignment, such as ability grouping and tracking, usually have been unsuccessful, at least for low achievers. In cases in which some degree of homogeneous grouping of low-achieving students has been relatively successful, emphasis has been on maintaining full content coverage and a rapid pace of instruction, on bolstering students' self-concept, and on otherwise working to overcome problems inherent in homogeneous assignment (Leinhardt and Pallay 1982; Sizemore 1985). One potential advantage of homogeneous grouping of the lowest-achieving students is that it can make the job of teachers throughout the school much more manageable (Eubanks and Levine 1987a).

In general, we believe it is best to avoid or minimize homogeneous grouping to the extent possible, particularly in racially and socioeconomically mixed settings where such grouping may generate segregation within or across classrooms. In many schools, however, strictly heterogeneous organization may not be feasible, and some amount of homogeneous grouping may be more workable, provided that appropriate special assistance is available to the lowest achievers. In the latter situation, we agree with recent reviews of research in which Robert Slavin (1986, 1987) identified the following "general principles for making ability grouping an effective practice" at the elementary level:

> *Students should remain in heterogeneous classes at most times, and be regrouped by ability only in subjects in which reducing heterogeneity is particularly important (for example, math and reading). . . . Grouping plans must reassess student placements frequently and allow for easy reassignments based on student progress. (Slavin 1986, 4)*

Beyond these principles, we believe that some new terminology is desirable for partially circumventing the frequently emotional controversy between those who support and those who oppose homogeneous grouping. The best language we have identified for this purpose involves the concept of leveling, which advocates making a broad distinction between readers and nonreaders, or, sometimes, between good readers, poor readers, and nonreaders (Sizemore 1985). Once this distinction is made, special assistance can be provided for poor readers and nonreaders. A similar distinction probably should be made between students who are above and below some level of minimally adequate functioning in mathematics.

As regards tracking of students into separate programs for the college-bound, business education, vocational studies, general education, or other categories, research we cite in Chapter 7 indicates that such differentiation plays an important part in limiting or hampering the achievement and aspirations of students in nonacademic tracks. In addition, many researchers who have examined the data on differences between public and nonpublic schools (see Chapter 12) have concluded that the relatively widespread tracking in the public system functions to depress the horizons and performance of many students. After studying tracking and its effects in U.S. secondary schools, Mortimer Adler (1979), Ernest Boyer (1983), Theodore Sizer (1984), and other educators have strongly recommended that schools should minimize or reduce their tracking systems and initiate improvements to allow for effective instruction in an expanded common curriculum.

Reorganization of Secondary Schools

Previous sections of this chapter cite secondary-school studies in which observers such as Ernest Boyer and Theodore Sizer have concluded that intermediate and senior high schools in the United States generally are not providing adequate education for many of their students. Martin Lazerson (1986) reviewed a number of these studies and was struck by the "awesome mindlessness" they found present at the high-school level, and Michael Sedlak and his colleagues (1986) have pointed out that the reform movement's typical concentration on raising standards and requirements without seriously addressing underlying problems threatens the secondary school's historic mission to provide equal and effective opportunities for all groups of students in the United States. If we do not find a way to deliver meaningful "academic learning for everyone," these authors concluded, the new standards either will become a "crueler form of screening and pushing" students out of the schools or "they will be rescinded and watered down in the name of practicality" (Sedlak, Wheeler, Pullin, and Cusick 1986, 23).

The underlying problems in secondary schools are much deeper and more pervasive than is recognized in a relatively simple and inexpensive solution stressing imposition of more credits to graduate, increase in minimal competency testing, stricter supervision and evaluation of teachers, or other external requirements for change. As we point out in preceding sections, intermediate and senior high schools are not functioning effectively for many students due to a host of interrelated reasons involving problems of classroom management, stress on passive, low-level learning, and adolescents' disinterest in the curriculum, among other causes.

Some indication of the pervasiveness of the problems has been provided in a study of ninth graders that the National Association of Secondary School Principals conducted in a representative sample of 141 secondary schools in 48 states and the District of Columbia. Based partly on data collected by observers who followed a randomly selected ninth grader in each school on March 7, 1984, the

Table 13.5 *Observers' Ratings of Ninth Graders' Experience in School*

Statement	Average Rating by Observers*
Did the student receive direct instruction in skill areas such as reading or writing?	1.70
Was the student recognized individually by at least one teacher during the day?	1.25
Was the student involved in situations calling for value discrimination, critical thinking, or analysis of options?	1.65
Did the student have opportunity to elect or select anything in his or her learning activities?	1.67
Did the student initiate conversation with a teacher during class or outside of class?	1.39

* 1 = little or no evidence of the phenomenon
2 = some evidence
3 = a great deal of evidence.
(See the text of this chapter for additional information.)

Source: Adapted from Lounsbury and Johnston 1985.

authors of the study (Lounsbury and Johnston 1985) concluded that there is a "clear lack of meaningful intellectual interaction between students and teachers," that the curriculum is highly fragmented into separate subjects, that there is little provision for student diversity, and that most students sit passively for long periods of time (p. 73). As shown in Table 13.5, students generally received little direct instruction in reading or writing, were seldom recognized individually by teachers, did not initiate much conversation with teachers inside or outside of class, and had relatively little involvement in critical thinking or in selecting learning activities.

As suggested by the authors and studies cited as well as by other sources, problems in U.S. secondary schools are so pervasive and entrenched that they probably will not be successfully addressed without major reform in how schools are organized and operated. Earlier in this chapter we note the example of South Boston and also describe three kinds of major organizational changes (i.e., schools-within-a-school, achievement centers, and a longer and different school day) that can help enhance the performance of low achievers and improve the functioning of urban high schools. As is apparent from other material in this chapter, however, reorganization probably will be required to improve secondary education not only in the cities but also throughout the United States. National and societal requirements to make secondary education more meaningful and to orient instruction more toward higher mental processes should receive priority attention in the future.

Among the suggestions to guide reorganization and reform of secondary schools are those offered by Ernest Boyer, Arthur Powell, Theodore Sizer, and other educators who have participated with them in studying high schools.

Related to their proposals about reduced tracking and greater emphasis on thinking and cognitive development, these authors and studies have offered a variety of recommendations for major reorganization. Boyer (1983), for example, called for breaking up large high schools into smaller units, for flexibility to permit larger blocks of instructional time, and for a class size limit of twenty in basic English/writing courses taught by teachers with no more than two such classes per term. Sizer (1984) recommended that high-school teachers should work in teams of 7 or 8 with about 100 students each.

Arthur Powell (1985), in a comparable analysis, compared the typical high school to a "shopping mall" in which students do their "own thing," learning is "just another consumer choice," and "unspecial" students easily become lost. He concluded this portrayal by saying:

> *Changes [to engage teenagers seriously in school studies] will require major structural reform. . . . Teachers need a more flexible day . . . to get away from the exhausting routine of large-group instruction . . . [and to] spend time with students in different formats. . . . Students need to have their class time reduced because so many classes are wholly boring and without educational purpose, because students need other kinds of contact with teachers, and because they need more time to work on their own.*
>
> *Only when the structure of the school day is significantly different from its present form will we be sure that school arrangements characterized by variety, choice, and neutrality have been supplanted by arrangements emphasizing purpose, push, and personalization. (Powell 1985, 261)*

Engagement in Learning

Another overriding imperative in many U.S. schools is to increase students' engagement in learning. For a variety of reasons including difficulties of maintaining order in impersonal institutions enrolling many students, mandated requirements for covering large amounts of material in limited periods of time, and competition with the mass media, much of what takes place in school—particularly at the secondary level—neither engages students' interest in learning nor motivates them to undertake challenging assignments. Thus, Linda McNeil (1986, 1988) has found that the low-level agreements between teachers and students generate boring instruction that further alienates many students. Also, the national Study of Schooling by John Goodlad (1984) and his colleagues indicated that much of the time in our schools is devoted to teacher presentation of material to students, who seldom participate actively or overtly express joy, anger, or other feelings (also see Table 13.5).

Many educators and other observers have recognized the need to increase engagement in learning among working-class as well as other students. Among the suggestions most frequently emphasized are to provide these students' with more successful and challenging learning environments in the early grades so they will not bring a history of failure to secondary schools, to build in opportunities for more active learning focused on themes that engage students' interests, to provide a better match between classroom instruction and students' conceptual levels and learning styles (see Chapters 8 and 10), to take better account of peer and community influences in delivering instruction (see Chapter 5), to introduce more experiential learning opportunities for adolescents (Chapter 6), to support the establishment of magnet and alternative schools (Chapters 10 and 12), and to modify school arrangements in order to establish school-within-a-school units or other approaches to reorganization as described in the preceding section. It is doubtful whether the school reform movement ultimately will be successful unless suggestions of these kinds are addressed systematically and comprehensively throughout the educational system.

Although very widespread, disengagement from classroom learning appears to be most prevalent among low-achieving working-class students. Evidence for this conclusion is found, among other sources, in the analysis of Jeannie Oakes (see Chaper 2 in this book), Arsene Boykin (see Chapter 8), and Peter McLaren (1986). McLaren studied working-class Portuguese students in a Canadian school and found that their instruction contributed to disengagement because it was incongruent with cultural patterns emphasizing tactile and sensual experience, informality, and other aspects of working-class experience and street culture. One result was that the school's curriculum was perceived and rejected as being school knowledge detached from the social knowledge that working-class students acquire in daily life.

Conclusion: School Reform and the Educational Crisis in Metropolitan Society

In Chapter 2, we describe how the developing educational crisis in postindustrial metropolitan society centers on the emergence of an underclass in socioeconomically and frequently racially isolated inner-city neighborhoods. Other sections of this book also describe related developments involving low school achievement, crime and delinquency, teenage pregnancy, unemployment, and other problems particularly acute among children and youth in concentrated poverty neighborhoods in big cities.

Recent data indicate that real improvements in students' performance are being registered in schools enrolling disadvantaged students in some big cities. In some cases, as we point out in Chapter 7 and earlier in this chapter, such gains seem to have been produced in part through the implementation of unusually successful effective schools projects, along with other instructional improvement activities. As shown in Table 13.6, for example, the average reading scores of elementary students in the Kansas City (Missouri) Public Schools improved markedly between 1980 and 1987, at which time they had reached or were only a little below national norms. (Gains in the mechanics of language and in math computation in the three districts shown in Table 13.6 have been even larger than the reading gains.) Data not shown in Table 13.6 also dem-

Table 13.6 ***Improvements in Average Reading Scores in Three Big-City School Districts***

Kansas City, Mo. (median grade equivalent)

Grade	*1978*	*1982*	*1987*	*National Norm**
3	3.1	3.3	3.8	3.9
6	5.5	6.0	6.4	6.8
8	6.7	7.6	8.0	8.7

San Diego minority isolated schools (percentage of students above national median)

Grade	*1980*	*1986*	*National Norm**
3	34	64	50
6	27	48	50
9	19	41	50
11	36	47	50

Washington, D.C. (median grade equivalent)

Grade	*1978*	*1982*	*1987*	*National Norm**
3	3.0	3.8	4.1	3.8
6	5.1	6.2	6.8	6.8
9	6.8	7.9	9.4	9.8

* National norms cited are for the beginning of the time periods dealt with and have since increased slightly.

Source: Anderson 1987; Behnke et al., 1986; Kansas City, Missouri, Public Schools; Nagel 1986.

onstrate comparable gains in achievement at the district's predominantly black elementary schools. In San Diego, data for that district's minority-isolated schools show very large achievement gains in reading through the eleventh grade, and Washington, D.C.—which has long been more than 90 percent minority—also has had very large gains through at least the ninth grade.

Although a significant part of the achievement gains registered in Kansas City, Washington, D.C., and some other cities (e.g., Atlanta) probably are spurious effects of more rigorous promotions policies,* it appears that these gains partly reflect improved delivery of instruction in the classroom (Levine and Eubanks 1986/87). Kansas City, for example, has implemented a number of important changes, including provision of an assistant to the principal for instruction, reduction of Chapter 1 pullout arrangements, sponsorship of TESA training in many schools, and introduction of Chicago Mastery Learning Reading. As part of a court-ordered desegregation plan, San Diego's minority-isolated

* Retaining students in grade generally increases longitudinal scores such as those shown in Table 13.6, even when there is no improvement in students' annual rate of growth.

schools have participated in an effective schools project (the Achievement Goals Program) that stresses mastery learning, improved classroom management, direct instruction, increased time on task, greater emphasis on higher-order skills and language learning, and staff development (Courter and Ward 1983). The San Diego schools also have introduced a radical curriculum alignment that inhibits teachers from proceeding page-by-page through texts at the pace of the slowest students.

Despite improvements that appear to have taken place in some cities, many measures and considerations involving the performance of disadvantaged urban students nationally are primarily negative. Six such indicators include the following:

1. NAEP and other data (see Chapter 2) continue to show inadequate achievement levels among disadvantaged urban students.
2. Dropout rates at many inner-city schools and in some big cities exceed 40 or 50 percent.
3. Even urban districts that have registered large achievement gains at the elementary level generally continue to report very low achievement at the secondary level. As shown in Table 13.6, for example, eighth- and ninth-grade reading scores in Kansas City and Washington, D.C., are still far below the national average. Nationwide, achievement in big-city high schools can only be viewed as abysmally low. (For an example, see Figure 2.6.)
4. As indicated in this chapter and elsewhere in this book, elementary and secondary schools in the United States place relatively little stress on the development of thinking skills and higher mental processes, particularly in schools with many disadvantaged low achievers. The ideal of a high-level, academically oriented common curriculum for all students (see the concluding sections of Chapter 2) is far from realization.
5. Most national and state school reform reports and efforts have not systematically addressed or generated the massive changes needed in U.S. secondary schools in general and in inner-city secondary schools in particular.
6. Innovations such as mastery learning and effective schools projects are not being implemented effectively in many urban school districts and elsewhere (Levine 1986; 1987).

Thus, the situation with respect to the academic performance of poverty students in big cities continues to be generally dismal with respect to such key learning skills as comprehension in reading even though some big-city districts appear to have made genuine progress. Comparable generalizations can be offered about the goal of reducing racial isolation for urban minority students. As we show in Chapter 9, much desegregation has been achieved in small towns and cities and rural areas, as well as in a few larger cities that have had some success in implementing plans on a regional basis. Overall, however, large numbers and proportions of minority students still attend socioeconomically and racially isolated schools that reinforce the disadvantages these students experience growing up in segregated poverty environments.

Nevertheless, recognition of the need for comprehensive improvements in education combined with coordinated efforts in other areas to address the plight of young people and families in the inner city may be growing. One example of a comprehensive framework for action has been provided in a 1987 report of the Joint Center for Political Studies. After discussing the "ferocious" network of economic and social problems that has emerged in "badly deteriorated inner cities," the report called for radical improvements in education at all levels, along with concomitant efforts in employment training, antidiscrimination legislation, social welfare programs, and other areas (Committee on Policy for Racial Justice 1987).

The problems involved in improving education for disadvantaged children and youth intersect with the larger national challenge to improve the functioning of our educational system with respect to students' cognitive development and mastery of higher-order learning skills and objectives.

As we point out in the first two chapters and elsewhere in this book, many observers believe that international competitiveness depends on nationwide improvements in students' acquisition of the higher-order skills and understandings required in an advanced, postindustrial society. Solutions to both sets of challenges in turn depend on the educational system's success in implementing the findings of research concerning how teaching and schooling can be made more effective in providing students with these skills and understandings. The impressive attainments of a relatively small proportion of unusually successful schools and projects cited in this chapter illustrate what could be accomplished in the future on a widespread basis.

EXERCISES

1. Interview teachers in a nearby school district concerning the school reform movement of the 1980s. Do they believe that national and state reform reports and efforts have had a positive impact? Which actions or changes do they perceive have been useful? Which do they think have been nonproductive or damaging?
2. Observe instruction in a high school class for college-bound students and then in a class for students who probably will not attend college. What differences appear to be present in teacher and school expectations for students? What do you think might be done to raise expectations successfully in either or both classes?
3. What are school districts in your community doing to prevent or reduce dropouts? Are these efforts succeeding? Are evaluation reports available? What do district officials believe are the major obstacles to success?
4. Why is there tension between the aims of educational excellence and educational equity? What efforts that contribute to one goal might detract from the other? What might be done to enhance the attainment of both goals?

5. Compare and contrast the recommendations of *A Nation at Risk*, prepared by the National Commission on Excellence in Education, with *Time for Results*, prepared by the National Governors' Association.
6. If you live in or near a big city, examine data on student performance to determine whether or how much academic achievement has improved during the past five or ten years. If gains have been registered, what changes in instruction and educational programming do school officials believe have been most responsible?
7. What do faculty in your school or college think about the Holmes Report? Do they believe its recommendations are likely to be implemented?

SUGGESTIONS FOR FURTHER READING

1. The Spring 1985 issue of *Teachers College Record* and the Fall 1986 issue of *Metropolitan Education* are devoted largely to discussion and analysis of the dropout problem.
2. *The Great School Debate*, edited by Beatrice and Ronald Gross, presents a wide variety of perspectives and viewpoints on school reform reports and proposals.
3. *Creating Effective Schools*, by Wilbur Brookover and his colleagues, describes an intensive in-service training program to improve achievement and learning climate in elementary and secondary schools.
4. The February 1971 issue of the *Phi Delta Kappan* describes several successful inner-city elementary schools in which academic achievement was higher than usual for such schools. Material in this issue includes an analysis of actions that might help accomplish this goal in other inner-city schools.
5. The Summer 1985 issue of *The Journal of Negro Education* is a theme issue describing successful policies, practices, and programs at inner-city schools.
6. Much of the material in the May 1986 issue of *Educational Leadership* deals with the teaching of thinking.
7. The March 1987 issue of *Educational Leadership* is devoted largely to the education of at-risk students.
8. *Reading, Thinking, and Concept Development*, edited by Theodore Harris and Eric Cooper, describes a variety of instructional strategies for improving students' thinking skills and comprehension.
9. *Improving Student Achievement through Mastery Learning Programs* (D. U. Levine, ed., 1985) provides analysis and illustrations regarding successful implementation of mastery learning.
10. Analysis of and reactions to the Holmes Group report and recommendations are provided in *Reforming Teacher Education*, edited by Jonas F. Soltis.
11. Many of the forces leading to low standards and emphasis on low-level learning in U.S. schools are described, illustrated, and analyzed by Linda McNeil in *Contraditions of Control*.

12. The developments and detours, twists and turns, claims and counterclaims, and pronouncements and renunciations of the school reform movement can be followed week by week and month by month in *Education Week*, the *Phi Delta Kappan*, and other periodicals.
13. The U.S. Department of Education (1987) has prepared an excellent summary of much of the effective schools and related research. Titled *Schools That Work. Educating Disadvantaged Children*, single copies were available free of charge as of 1988 by writing to *Schools That Work*, Pueblo, Colorado 81009.
14. A report entitled *Saving Urban Schools* (Carnegie Foundation for the Advancement of Teaching 1988) proposes radical improvement and reform in the financing, organization, and operation of urban schools.

Bibliography

Aaron, H. J. 1977. *Healthy, wealthy, and wise: Backdoor approaches to education.* Cambridge, MA: Aspen Institute for Humanistic Studies. (p. 253)

Abrahams, R. D. 1970. *Deep down in the jungle . . . Negro narrative folklore from the streets of Philadelphia.* Chicago: Aldine. (p. 112)

Abrams, C. 1965. *The city is the frontier.* New York: Harper and Row. (p. 90)

Abrams, J. D. 1988. Outcomes and basics reinforce each other. *The School Administrator* 45 (2): 47–49. (p. 273)

Abravanel, M. D., and Mancini, P. K. 1980. Attitudinal and demographic constraints. In *Urban revitalization,* edited by Donald B. Rosenthal. Beverly Hills, CA: Sage. (p. 321)

Academy for Educational Development. 1982. A new direction for bilingual education in the 1980's. *Focus of the National Clearinghouse for Bilingual Education.* No. 10: 1–4. (p. 412)

Addams, J. 1938. *Twenty years at Hull House.* New York: Macmillan. (p. 433)

Adler, M. 1979. *Poverty children and their language.* New York: Grune and Stratton. (pp. 379, 549)

Adler, M. J. 1982. *The Paideia proposal.* New York: Macmillan. (p. 92)

Advisory Committee on Child Development. 1976. *Toward a national policy for children and families.* Washington, DC: National Academy of Sciences. (p. 128)

Ahlstrom, W. M., and Havighurst, R. J. 1971. *400 losers: Delinquent boys in high school.* San Francisco: Jossey-Bass. (p. 214)

Alexander, K. L.; Cook, M.; and McDill, E. L. 1977. *Curriculum tracking and educational stratification: Some further evidence.* Baltimore: The Johns Hopkins University Center for Social Organization of Schools, Report no. 237. (p. 164)

Alexander, K. L., and McDill, E. L. 1976. Selection and allocation within schools: Some causes and consequences of curriculum placement. *American Sociological Review* 41: 963–981. (pp. 164–165, 241)

Alexander, L. 1986. Time for results: An overview. *Phi Delta Kappan* 68 (3): 202–204. (p. 503)

Almeida, P. M. 1977. Children's television and the modeling of proreading behaviors. *Education and Urban Society* 10 (November): 55–60. (p. 142)

Alter, J. 1988. Why we can't wait any longer. *Newsweek* 111 (10): 42–43. (pp. 17, 371, 385)

American Association of School Administrators. 1984. *The cost of reform.* Arlington, VA: American Association of School Administrators. (p. 501)

Ames, C., and Felker, D. W. 1977. Children's achievement attributions and reinforcing behaviors in relation to self-concept and reward structure. Paper presented at the annual meeting of the American Education Research Association, April. (p. 270)

Amir, Y. 1969. Contact hypothesis in ethnic relations. *Psychological Bulletin* 71: 319–342. (p. 329)

Anderson, N. 1959. *The urban community: A world perspective.* New York: Holt, Rinehart & Winston. (p. 91)

Anderson, R. B. 1977. The effectiveness of follow-through: What have we learned? Paper presented at the annual meeting of the American Education Research Association, April 5. (p. 291)

Anderson, R. C.; Hiebert, E. H.; Scott, J. A.; and Wilkinson, J. A. G. 1985. *Becoming a nation of readers: Report of the Commission on Reading.* Washington, DC: National Institute of Education. (p. 525)

Anderson, S. 1987. Personal communication with compilation of unpublished data. (p. 553)

Andersson, B-E. 1973. Project YG—A study of a group of Swedish urban adolescents. In *Topics in human development*, edited by H. Thomae. Basel/New York: Karger. (p. 159)

Anthony, H. M., and Raphael, T. E. 1987. Using questioning strategies to promote students' active comprehension of content area material. Michigan State University Institute for Research on Teaching, Occasional Paper No. 109. (p. 527)

Anyon, J. 1980. Social class and the hidden curriculum of work. *Journal of Education* 162: 67–92. (pp. 242–243)

———. 1983. Social class and the hidden curriculum of work. In *The hidden curriculum and moral education*, edited by Henry Giroux and David Purpel. Berkeley, CA: McCutchan. (p. 242)

Apple, M. W. 1981. Reproduction, contestation, and curriculum. In *New directions in education: Critical perspectives.* Buffalo, NY: Department of Social Foundations and Comparative Education Center, State University of New York. (p. 258)

———, ed. 1982a. *Cultural and economic reproduction in education.* Boston: Routledge and Kegan Paul. (p. 258)

———, ed. 1982b. *Culture, class, and the state: Reproduction and contradiction in education.* Boston: Routledge and Kegan Paul. (p. 258)

———. 1985. *Education and power.* Boston: Ark. (p. 258)

Apple, M. W., and Weis, L., eds. 1983. Ideology and practice in schooling. Philadelphia: Temple University. (p. 259)

Applebaum, E. 1985. New jobs in insurance. *IFG Policy Notes* Summer: 3–4. (p. 28)

Appleton, N. 1983. *Cultural pluralism in education.* New York: Longman. (pp. 430, 434)

Arce, C. H. 1982. Maintaining a growing culture. *ISR Newsletter* 10 (4): 7–8. (p. 370)

Arias, B. 1978. Report to the Superior Court of the State of California for the County of Los Angeles. November 14. (p. 393)

Arias, M. B. 1986. The context of education for Hispanic students: An overview. *American Journal of Education* 95 (1): 26–57. (p. 392)

Ariès, P. 1965. *Centuries of childhood: A social history of family life.* New York: Random House. (p. 95)

Armor, D. J. 1980. White flight and the future of school desegregation. In *School desegregation: Past, present, and future*, edited by W. G. Stephan and J. R. Feagin. New York: Plenum. (p. 315)

Armstrong, J. M. 1985. A national assessment of participation and achievement of women in mathematics. In *Women and mathematics: Balancing the equation*, edited by Susan F. Chipman, Lorelei R. Brush, and Donna M. Wilson. Hillsdale, NJ: Erlbaum. (p. 441)

Associated Press, 1987. Students at black colleges hit hard by grant cuts. *The New York Times* April 1. (p. 66)

Astin, A. W. 1969. Folklore of selectivity. *Saturday Review* December 20: 57–59 (p. 297)

———. 1985. *Achieving educational excellence.* San Francisco: Jossey-Bass. (p. 60)

Atherton, L. 1984. *Main street on the middle border.* Bloomington: Indiana University Press. (p. 492)

Au, K. H. 1985. Development and implementation of the KEEP reading program. In *Reading comprehension: From research to practice*, edited by J. Orasanu. Hillsdale, NJ: Erlbaum. (p. 427)

Au, K. H., and Kawakami, A. J. 1985. Research currents: Talk story and learning to read. *Language Arts* 62 (4): 406–411. (p. 427)

Auletta, K. 1982. *The underclass.* New York: Random House. (pp. 23, 374)

Austin, J. 1984. "Prepared statement" in Youth and the justice system. Can we intervene earlier? Hearing before the U.S. House of Representatives Select Committee on Children, Youth, and Families. Washington, DC: U.S. Government Printing Office, May 18. (6) (pp. 196–197)

Austin, R. L. 1980. Adolescent subcultures of violence. *The Sociological Quarterly* 21: 545–561. (p. 192)

Bachen, C. M.; Hornby, M. C.; Roberts, D. F.; and Hernandez-Ramos, P. F. 1982. Television viewing behavior and the development of reading skills: Survey evidence. Paper presented at the annual meeting of the American Educational Research Association, March 19. (p. 144)

Bachman, J. G.; O'Malley, P. M.; and Johnson, J. 1978. Adolescence to adulthood: Change and stability in the lives of young men. Ann Arbor: Survey Research Center, University of Michigan. (p. 214)

Bahr, H. M.; Chadwick, B. A.; and Strauss, J. H. 1979. *American ethnicity.* Lexington, MA: D.C. Heath. (pp. 259, 434)

Bailyn, B. 1986. *Voyagers to the West.* New York: Knopf. (p. 112)

Baker, K. A. 1985. Research evidence of a school discipline problem. *Phi Delta Kappan.* 66 (7): 482–487. (p. 282)

Baker, K. A., and de Kanter, A. A. 1981. Effectiveness of bilingual education: A review of the literature. Paper prepared for the U.S. Office of Education, Office of Planning, Budget, and Evaluation, September. (p. 406)

Baltzell, E. G. 1958. *Philadelphia gentleman: The making of a national upper class.* Glencoe, IL: Free Press. (p. 40)

Bane, M. J. 1976. *Here to stay: American families in the twentieth century.* New York: Basic Books. (pp. 130, 149)

Banks, J. A. 1984. *Teaching strategies for ethnic studies,* 3rd ed. Boston: Allyn and Bacon. (p. 433)

———. 1988. *Multiethnic education: Theory and practice,* 2nd ed. Boston: Allyn and Bacon. (pp. 429, 433)

Barth, R. 1979. Home-based reinforcement of school behavior: A review and analysis. *Review of Educational Research* 49 (3): 436–458 (p. 124)

Bastian, A., et al. 1986. *Choosing equality.* Philadelphia: Temple University Press. (pp. 488, 498)

Batey, A., and Cowell, R. N. 1987. *Distance education: An overview.* Portland, OR: The Northwest Regional Educational Laboratory. (p. 474)

Becker, H. J. 1979. Personal networks of opportunity in obtaining jobs: Racial differences and effects of segregation. Paper presented at the annual meeting of the American Educational Research Association, San Francisco, March. (p. 332)

———. 1986a. Reports from the 1985 national survey. *Instructional Uses of School Computers* No. 1 (June): 1–10. (p. 469)

———. 1986b. Reports from the 1985 national survey. *Instructional Uses of School Computers* No. 2 (August): 1–12. (pp. 469–470)

Becker, W. C. 1977. Teaching reading and language to the disadvantaged: What we have learned from field research. *Harvard Educational Review* 47: 518–543. (p. 306)

Behnke, G., et al. 1986. Testing results for minority isolated schools, Spring 1986. San Diego: San Diego City Schools. (p. 553)

Behr, G. E., and Hanson, R. A. 1977. Differential access to instruction: A source of educational inequality. Paper presented at the annual meeting of the American Educational Research Association, April. (p. 267)

Bejar, I. I. 1981. Does nutrition cause intelligence? A reanalysis of the Cali Experiment. *Intelligence* 5: 49–68. (p. 139)

Belenky, M. F.; Clinchy, B. M.; Goldberger, N. R.; and Tarule, J. M. 1986. *Women's ways of knowing.* New York: Basic Books. (p. 465)

Bell, D. 1973. *The coming of post-industrial society.* New York: Basic Books. (pp. 25, 185, 248)

———. 1976. *The cultural contradictions of capitalism.* New York: Basic Books. (p. 185)

Bem, S. 1974. The measurement of psychological androgyny. *Journal of Consulting and Clinical Psychology* 42: 155–162. (p. 460)

Benbow, C. P., and Stanley, J. C. 1980. Sex differences in mathematical ability: Fact

or artifact? *Science* 210 (12): 1262–1264. (p. 446)

Bendix, R., and Lipset, S. 1953. *Class status and power: A reader in social stratification.* New York: The Free Press. (p. 40)

Beniger, J. R. 1986. *The control revolution.* Cambridge, MA: Harvard University Press. (p. 26)

Bennett, D. A. 1979. The impact of court ordered desegregation: A defendant's view. Paper presented at an ERIC conference on Impact of Courts on Schools. (p. 349)

Bennett, N., and Desforges, C. 1988. Matching classroom tasks to students' attainments. *The Elementary School Journal* 88 (2): 221–234 (pp. 267, 548)

Benson, C. S. 1979. Household production of human capital: Time uses of parents and children as inputs. Paper presented at the annual meeting of the American Educational Research Association, March 3. (p. 138)

Berger, B., and Berger, P. L. 1983. *The war over the family: Capturing the middle ground.* New York: Doubleday. (p. 150)

Berger, B. M. 1960. *Working class suburb.* Berkeley: University of California Press. (p. 40)

Berger, P. L. 1979. The worldview of the new class: Secularity and its discontents. In *The New Class?*, edited by B. Bruce-Briggs. New Brunswick, NJ: Transaction. (p. 6)

Bergmann, B. 1986. *The economic emergence of women.* New York: Basic Books. (pp. 442, 465)

Bernstein, B. 1961. Social class and linguistic development: A theory of social learning. In *Education, economy and society*, edited by A. H. Halsey, J. Floud, and C. A. Anderson. New York: The Free Press. (p. 237)

———. 1975. *Class, codes and control.* London and Boston: Routledge and Kegan Paul. (pp. 110, 237, 243)

———. 1986. On pedagogic discourse. In *Handbook of theory and research for the sociology of education*, edited by John G. Richardson. New York: Greenwood. (p. 237)

Best, R. 1983. *We've all got scars: What boys and girls learn in elementary school.* Bloomington: Indiana University Press. (pp. 456–457)

Bianchi, S. M., and Spain, D. 1986. *American women in transition.* New York: Russell Sage. (pp. 125, 440)

Biddle, B. J.; Bank, B. J.; and Marlin, M. M. 1980. Parental and peer influence on adolescents. *Social Forces* 58: 1057–1079. (p. 158)

Binzen, P. 1970. *Whitetown.* New York: Random House. (pp. 40, 108, 265)

Blank, R. 1984. Magnet schools offer diversity and quality. *Educational Leadership* 42 (7): 72. (p. 341)

Blechman, E. A. 1982. Are children with one parent at psychological risk? A methodogical review. *Journal of Marriage and the Family* 44: 179–195. (p. 134)

Blendinger, J., and Jones, L. T. 1988. Create a healthy school culture. *The School Administrator* 45 (4): 22–26. (p. 541)

Block, J. H., and Anderson, L. W. 1975. *Mastery learning in classroom instruction.* New York: Macmillan. (p. 535)

Bloom, B. S. 1964. *Stability and change in human characteristics.* New York: John Wiley. (p. 116)

———. 1976. *Human characteristics and school learning.* New York: McGraw-Hill. (p. 272)

———. 1984. The search for methods of group instruction as effective as one-to-one tutoring. *Educational Researcher* 13 (6): 4–16. (p. 536)

———. 1988. All our children learning well in elementary school and beyond. *Principal* 67 (4): 12–17. (pp. 272, 534)

Bluestone, B., and Harrison, B. 1987. The grim truth about the job 'miracle.' *The New York Times.* February 1: 5.3, 3. (p. 29)

Bock, D. F., and Moore, E. G. J. 1986. *Advantage and disadvantage: A profile of American youth.* Hillsdale, NJ: Erlbaum. (p. 446)

Bollens, J. C., and Schmandt, H. J. *The metropolis.* New York: Harper & Row. (p. 90)

Bond, L. 1982. Testing the testers: The Nader-Nairn report on the ETS. *Change* 14 (1): 56–61. (p. 70)

Boocock, S. S. 1976. *Students, schools, and educational policy: A sociological view.* Cambridge, MA: Aspen Institute for Humanistic Studies. (pp. 127, 158)

Bottoms, G., and Copa, P. 1983. A perspective on vocational education today. *Phi Delta Kappan* 64 (5): 348–354. (p. 62)

Boudon, R. 1973. *Education, opportunity, and social inequality: Changing prospects in western society.* New York: John Wiley. (p. 231)

Boulding, E. 1979. *Children's rights in the wheel of life.* New Brunswick, NJ: Transaction. (p. 461)

———. 1987. Changing gender roles in familial, occupational, and civic settings. In *Society as educator in an age of transition,* edited by Kenneth D. Benne and Steven Tozer. Eighty-sixth yearbook of the National Society for the Study of Education, Part II. Chicago: University of Chicago Press. (p. 461)

Bouvier, L. F., and Agresta, A. J. 1985. The fastest-growing minority. *American Demographics* 7 (5): 31–33, 46. (p. 414)

Bowles, S. 1975. Unequal education and the reproduction of the social division of labor. In *Schooling in a corporate society,* edited by Martin Carnoy. New York: David McKay. (p. 249)

Bowles, S., and Gintis, H. 1976. *Schooling in capitalist America.* New York: Basic Books. (p. 248)

———. 1981. Education as a site of contradictions in the reproduction of the capital-labor relationship: Second thoughts on the "correspondence principle." *Economic and Industrial Democracy* 2: 223–242. (p. 249)

Boyer, E. 1983. *High school.* New York: Harper and Row. (pp. 528, 530, 549–551)

Boyer, E. L. 1987. *Student service: The new Carnegie Unit.* Lawrenceville, NJ: Princeton University Press. (p. 210)

Boykin, A. W. 1978. Psychological/behavioral verve in academic/task performance: Pretheoretical considerations. *The Journal of Negro Education* 47: 343–354. (pp. 263, 427)

Braddock, J. H. II. 1981. Race, athletics, and educational attainment: Dispelling the myths. *Youth and Society* 12 (March): 335–350. (p. 166)

———. 1987. Social and academic consequences of school desegregation. Paper prepared for the Conference on Future Designs for Educational Equity, St. Louis, April. (p. 332)

Bradley, L. A., and Bradley, G. W. 1977. The academic achievement of black students in desegregated schools: A critical review. *Review of Educational Research* 47:399–449. (p. 324)

Brainin, S. S. 1985. Mediated learning: Pedagogic issues in the improvement of cognitive functioning. In *Review of Research in Education 12,* edited by Edmund W. Gordon. Washington, DC: American Educational Research Association. (p. 533)

Brake, M. 1980. *The sociology of youth culture and subcultures.* Boston: Routledge and Kegan Paul. (p. 103)

Bridgman, A. 1984. Schools urged to seek solutions to troubles of latch-key children. *Education Week* 3 (36): 10, 15. (p. 145)

———. 1986. Workplace remains sex-segregated, panel concludes. *Education Week* 5 (17): 10. (p. 442)

Brittain, C. V. 1963. Adolescent choices and parent-peer cross pressures. *American Sociological Review* 28: 385–391. (p. 156)

Broderick, P. C., and Sewell, T. E. 1983. Learned helplessness and attributions for success and failure in children of different social class. Paper presented at the annual meeting of the American Educational Research Association, Montreal, April. (p. 264)

Bronfenbrenner, U. 1970. *Two worlds of childhood: U.S. and U.S.S.R.* New York: Russell Sage. (p. 159)

———. 1974. Is early intervention effective? A report on longitudinal evaluations of preschool programs. DHEW No. (OHD) 74–25. Washington, DC: U.S. Department of Health, Education and Welfare. (pp. 273, 286, 305)

———. 1977. The calamitous decline of the American family. Congressional Record—Extension of Remarks, January 4, E40–E43. (p. 13)

Brookover, W. B., et al. 1982. *Creating effective schools.* Holmer Beach, FL: Learning Publications. (p. 556)

Brophy, B. 1986. Middle-class squeeze. *U.S. News and World Report*. 101 (7): 36–41. (p. 30)

Brophy, J. E. 1982. Classroom organization and management. *The Elementary School Journal* 82: 265–285. (p. 523)

———. 1985. Interactions of male and female students with male and female teachers. In *Gender influences in classroom interaction*, edited by Louise Cherry Wilkinson and Cora B. Marrett. Orlando, FL: Academic Press. (p. 454)

———. 1986. On motivating students. Michigan State University Institute for Research on Teaching Occasional Paper No. 101. (p. 532)

Brophy, J. E., and Good, T. L. 1986. Teacher behavior and student achievement. In *Handbook of research on teaching*, 3rd ed., edited by Merlin C. Wittrock. New York: Macmillan. (pp. 265, 524–525, 535)

Brotman, B. 1982. Facing up to the underclass in America. *Chicago Tribune* September 26: 1. (p. 22)

Brown, B. F. 1980. A study of the school needs of children from one-parent families. *Phi Delta Kappan* 61 (April): 537–540. (p. 135)

Brown, C. 1969. *Manchild in the promised land*. New York: Macmillan. (p. 112)

Bruce-Briggs, B. 1979. An introduction to the idea of the new class. In *The new class?*, edited by B. Bruce-Briggs. New Brunswick, NJ: Transaction. (pp. 5–6, 39)

Bryk, A. S.; Holland, P. B.; Lee, V. E.; and Carriedo, R. A. 1984. *Effective Catholic schools: An exploration*. Washington, DC: National Catholic Education Association. (p. 481)

Buie, J. 1987. Pregnant teen-agers: New view of old solution. *Education Week* 6 (28): 32. (p. 208)

Burbridge, L. C. 1983. *Employment and training programs for youth: An interpretation and synthesis of measured outcomes*. Washington, DC: The Urban Institute. (p. 301)

Burch, S. 1988. Commission reports on children at risk. *Black Issues in Higher Education* 4 (20): 15 (pp. 509, 546)

Burke, G., and Rumberger, R. W. 1987. *The future impact of technology on work and education*. Philadelphia: Falmer. (p. 28)

Burr, W. R., et al. 1979. *Contemporary theories about the family*. New York: Free Press. (p. 150)

Burrill, L. E. 1987. How well should a high school graduate read? *NASSP Bulletin* 71 (497): 61–72. (p. 54)

Burt, M., and Dulay, H. 1980. A misdiagnosed population. *Educational Researcher* 9 (7): 29. (p. 399)

Buscemi, M. 1985. What schools are doing to prevent alcohol and drug abuse. *The School Administrator* 42 (9): 11–14. (pp. 204–205)

Butts, R. F. 1974. Public education and political community. *History of Education Quarterly* 14: 165–184. (p. 253)

California Assessment Program. 1982. *Survey of sixth grade school achievement and television viewing habits*. Sacramento: California State Department of Education. (p. 144)

Campbell, P. B.; Gardner, J. A.; and Seitz, P. 1982. *High school vocational graduates: Which doors are open?* Columbus: The Ohio State University National Center for Research in Vocational Education. (p. 63)

Caplan, N. 1985. Working toward self-sufficiency. *ISR Newsletter* 13 (1): 4–5, 7. (p. 416)

Caplan, P. J.; MacPherson, G. M.; and Tobin, P. 1985. Do sex differences in spatial abilities exist? *American Psychologist* 40 (7): 786–799. (p. 448)

Cárdenas, J. A. 1977. Bilingual education, segregation, and a third alternative. *Inequality in Education* 19 (February): 19–22. (p. 404)

Carelli, A. O., ed. 1988. *Sex equity in education*. Springfield, IL: Thomas. (p. 458)

Carew, J. V. 1976. Environmental stimulation: A longitudinal observation study of how people influence the young child's intellectual development in his everyday environment. Paper presented at the Annual Meeting of the American Educational Research Association, San Francisco, April 22. (pp. 122–123)

Carlson, A. C. 1987. Children in poverty and other legacies of the redistributive state. *Persuasion at Work* 19 (1): 1–5. (p. 36)

Carnegie Commission on Higher Education. 1983. Opportunities for women in higher education. New York: McGraw-Hill. (p. 438)

Carnegie Corporation. 1977. Postscript from an interview with Kenneth Keniston. *Carnegie Quarterly* 25 (4): 10–12. (p. 133)

Carnegie Council on Policy Studies in Higher Education. 1979. *The federal role in post-secondary education: Unfinished business, 1975–1980*. San Francisco: Jossey-Bass. (p. 211)

Carnegie Foundation for the Advancement of Teaching. 1988. *Saving urban schools*. Lawrenceville, NJ: Princeton University Press. (p. 557)

Carnegie Task Force on Teaching as a Profession, 1986. *A nation prepared: Teachers in the 21st century*. New York: Carnegie Corporation. (pp. 501, 503)

Carnoy, M. 1974. *Education as cultural imperialism*. New York: David McKay. (p. 249)

———. 1982. Education, economy, and the state. In *Cultural and economic reproduction in education*, edited by Michael Apple. Boston: Routledge and Kegan Paul. (p. 249)

———. 1987. High technology and education: An economist's view. In *Society as educator in an age of transition*, edited by Kenneth D. Benne and Stephen Tozer. Eighty-sixth yearbook of the National Society of Education, Part I: Chicago: Univeristy of Chicago Press. (p. 29)

Carnoy, M., and Levin, H. M. 1985. *Schooling and work in the democratic state*. Stanford, CA: Stanford University Press. (p. 250)

Carper, J. C., and Hunt, T. C., eds. 1984. *Religious schooling in America*. Birmingham, AL: Religious Education Press. (p. 491)

Carter, C. S., and Greenough, W. T. 1979. Sending the right sex messages. *Psychology Today* 13 (4): 112. (p. 447)

Carter, L. F. 1984. The sustaining effects study of compensatory and elementary education. *Educational Researcher* 13 (7): 4–13. (p. 293)

Carter, M. C., and Levine, D. U. 1977. Ethnicity, home environment and reading achievement. Kansas City, Missouri: University of Missouri at Kansas City Center for the Study of Metropolitan Problems in Education, mimeographed. (pp. 137, 148–149)

Carter, T. P., and Chatfield, M. L. 1986. Effective bilingual schools: Implications for policy and practice. *American Journal of Education* 95 (1): 200–232. (p. 410)

Caruso, D. R., and Detterman, K. K. 1981. Intelligence research and social policy. *Phi Delta Kappan* 63 (3): 183–187. (p. 286)

Castellanos, C. 1980. Bilingual education versus school desegregation: Resolving the conflict. *NJEA Review* 53 (6): 7–16 (p. 410)

Castells, M. 1985. High technology, economic restructuring, and the urban-regional process in the United States. In *High technology, space, and society*, edited by Manuel Castells. Beverly Hills, CA: Sage. (pp. 28–29, 88)

Cavallo, D. 1981. *Muscles and morals*. Philadelphia: University of Pennsylvania Press. (p. 257)

Cazden, C. B. 1985. Effectiveness of instructional features in bilingual education classrooms. Paper presented at the annual meeting of the American Educational Research Association, Chicago, April. (p. 410)

Chafe, W. H. 1972. *The American woman: Her changing social, economic, and political roles, 1920–1970*. New York: Oxford University Press. (p. 464)

Chaikind, S. 1986. *College enrollment patterns of black and white students*. Washington, DC: Decision Resources Corporation. (p. 59)

Chall, J., and Mirsky, A., eds. 1978. *Education and the brain*. Seventy-Seventh Yearbook of the National Society for the Study of Education. Chicago: University of Chicago Press. (p. 150)

Chance, P. 1986. *Thinking in the classroom: A survey of programs*. New York: Teachers College Press. (p. 526)

Charters, W. W., Jr., and Gage, N. L., eds. 1963. *Readings in the social psychology of education*. Boston: Allyn and Bacon. (p. 91)

Chase-Lansdale, P. L., and Vinovskis, M. A. 1987. Should we discourage teenage marriage? *The Public Interest* No. 87: 38–48. (p. 206)

Cherlin, A., and Walters, P. B. 1981. Trends in United States' men's and women's sex-role attitudes: 1972 to 1978. *American Sociological Review* 46: 453–460. (p. 440)

Children's Defense Fund. 1985. *Black and white children in America.* Washington, DC: Children's Defense Fund. (pp. 36, 126)

Chinoy, E. 1955. *Automobile workers and the American dream.* New York: Doubleday. (p. 40)

Chipman, S. F.; Brush, L. R.; and Wilson, D. M., eds. 1985. *Women and mathematics: Balancing the equation.* Hillsdale, NJ: Erlbaum. (pp. 445, 465)

Chipman, S. F., and Wilson, D. M. 1985. Understanding mathematics course enrollment and mathematics achievement: A synthesis of the research. In *Women and mathematics: Balancing the equation,* edited by Susan F. Chipman, Lorelei R. Brush, and Donna M. Wilson. Hillsdale, NJ: Erlbaum. (p. 445)

Chiswick, B. R. 1982. Differences in educational attainment among racial and ethnic groups. Patterns and preliminary hypotheses. Paper presented for a conference of the National Academy of Education, Chicago, May. (p. 387)

Christensen, B. J. 1987. "The white woman's burden": The cultural clash between American feminists and ethnic minorities. *The Family in America* 1 (2): 1–10. (pp. 375, 463)

———. 1988. America's retreat from marriage. *The Family in America* 1 (12): 1–8 (p. 124)

Chubb, J. E. 1988. Why the current wave of school reform will fail. *The Public Interest* No. 90: 28–49. (p. 499)

Chubb, J. E., and Moe, T. M. 1985. Politics, markets, and the organization of schools. Paper presented at the annual meeting of the American Political Science Association, New Orleans, August. (p. 481)

———. 1986. *Politics, markets, and the organization of schools.* Washington, DC: The Brookings Institution. (p. 481)

Cibulka, J. G.; O'Brien, T. J.; and Zewe, D. 1982. *Inner-city private elementary schools: A study.* Milwaukee: Marquette University Press. (p. 478)

Clark, R. 1983. *Family life and school environment.* Chicago: University of Chicago Press. (pp. 121, 150)

Clarke-Stewart, A. 1977. *Child care in the family: A review of research and some propositions for policy.* New York: Academic Press. (pp. 134, 150)

Clasen, D. R., and Brown, B. B. 1986. The relationship between adolescent peer groups and school performance. Paper presented at the annual meeting of the American Educational Research Association, San Francisco, April. (pp. 162–163)

Clausen, J. A. 1966. Family structure, socialization and personality. In *Review of child development research,* Vol. 2, edited by M. L. Hoffman and L. W. Hoffman. New York: Russell Sage Foundation, pp. 1–54. (pp. 149–150)

Clausen, J. A., and Williams, J. R. 1963. Sociological correlates of child behavior. In *Child Psychology,* edited by Harold W. Stevenson. Sixty-Second Yearbook of the National Society for the Study of Education, Part 1. Chicago: University of Chicago Press. (p. 150)

Clay, P. L. 1981. *Single parents and the public schools. How does the partnership work?* Columbia, MD: National Committee for Citizens in Education. (p. 135)

Cloward, R. A., and Ohlin, L. E. 1960. *Delinquency and opportunity: A theory of delinquent gangs.* New York: The Free Press. (p. 197)

Coale, A. J., and Zelnik, M. 1963. *New estimates of fertility and population in the United States.* Princeton, NJ: Princeton University Press. (p. 126)

Cocaine use rising. 1985–86. *ISR Newsletter* Winter: 578. (p. 202)

Cohany, S. 1986. What happened to the high school class of 1985? *Monthly Labor Review* 109 (10): 28–30. (pp. 45, 58)

Cohen, A. M. 1977. The social equalization fantasy. *Community College Review* 5 (Fall): 74–82. (p. 258)

Cohen, D. K., and Farrar, E. 1977. Power to the parents? The story of educational vouchers. *The Public Interest* 48 (Summer): 72–97. (pp. 487, 491)

Cohen, E. G. 1980. Design and redesign of the desegregated school. In *School desegregation: Past, present and future*, edited by W. G. Stephan and J. Feagin. New York: Plenum. (p. 330)

———. 1986. On the sociology of the classroom. In *The contributions of the social sciences to educational policy and practice*, edited by J. Hannaway and M. E. Lockheed. Berkeley, CA: McCutchan. (p. 548)

Cohen, G. 1981. Culture and educational attainment. *Harvard Educational Review* 51: 270–285. (pp. 98, 236)

Cohen, S. 1976. The history of American education, 1900–1976: The uses of the past. *Harvard Educational Review* 46: 298–330. (p. 253)

Coie, J. D., and Kupersmidt, J. 1983. A behavioral analysis of emerging social status in boy's groups. *Child Development* 54: 1400–1416. (p. 154)

Coie, J. D., and Whidby, J. 1986. Gender differences in the basis for social rejection in childhood. Paper presented at the annual meeting of the American Educational Research Association, San Francisco, April. (p. 154)

Cole, M. 1985. Mind as a cultural achievement: Implications for IQ testing. In *Learning and teaching the ways of knowing*, edited by Elliot Eisner. Eighty-Fourth Yearbook of the National Society for the Study of Education, Part II. Chicago: University of Chicago Press. (p. 428)

Coleman, J. S. 1959. Academic achievement and the structure of competition. *Harvard Educational Review* 29: 331–351. (p. 162)

———. 1961. *The adolescent society*. New York: The Free Press. (pp. 162, 178)

———. 1982. *Public schools, private schools, and the public interest*. American Education 18 (1): 17–22. (p. 479)

Coleman, J. S., and Hoffer, T. 1987. *Public and private high schools: The impact of communities*. New York: Basic Books. (pp. 101, 481)

Coleman, J. S.; Hoffer, T.; and Kilgore, S. 1981. *Public and private schools*. Washington, DC: National Center for Education Statistics. (pp. 478–480)

Coleman, J. S., and Husen, T. 1985. *Becoming adult in a changing society*. Paris: Organization for Economic Co-operation and Development. (p. 212)

Coleman, J. S., et al. 1966. Equality of educational opportunity. Washington, DC: U.S. Government Printing Office. (pp. 241, 279, 387, 514)

———. 1974. Youth: *Transition to adulthood. Report of the panel on youth of the president's science advisory committee*. Chicago and London: University of Chicago Press. (pp. 180, 198, 214)

Coleman, R. P., and Neugarten, B. L. 1971. *Social status in the city*. San Francisco: Jossey-Bass. (pp. 9, 40, 259)

College Board. 1983. *Academic preparation for college*. New York: The College Board. (p. 496)

Colman, W. G. 1977. Schools, housing, jobs, transportation: Interlocking metropolitan problems. In *School desegregation in metropolitan areas: Choices and prospects*, edited by Ronald D. Henderson and Mary von Euler. Washington, DC: National Institute of Education, pp. 27–41. (p. 87)

Committee on Ability Testing. 1982. *Ability testing: uses, consequences, and controversies*. Washington, DC: National Academy Press. (p. 70)

Committee for Economic Development. 1985. *Investing in our children*. Washington, DC: Committee on Economic Development. (p. 71)

———. 1987. *Children in need: Investment strategies for the disadvantaged*. Washington, DC: Committee for Economic Development. (p. 503)

Committee on Policy for Racial Justice. 1987. *Black initiative and governmental responsibility*. Washington, DC: Joint Center for Political Studies. (p. 555)

Compton, N.; Duncan, M.; and Hruska, J. 1986. *Student pregnancy*. Washington, DC: National Education Association. (pp. 208, 214)

Comptroller General of the United States. 1977. *Preventing mental retardation—more can be done*. Washington, DC: Comptroller

General of the United States. (pp. 139, 199)

Comstock, G. 1977. Types of portrayal and aggressive behavior. *Journal of Communication* 27 (Summer): 189–198. (p. 142)

Conant, J. B. 1959. *The American high school today*. New York: McGraw-Hill. (p. 92)

Condry, J. C., and Siman, M. A. 1974. Characteristics of adult- and peer-oriented children. *Journal of Marriage and the Family* 36: 543–554. (p. 159)

Congressional Budget Office, 1986. *Trends in educational achievement*. Washington, DC: Congress of the United States. (p. 54)

———. 1988. *Trends in family income: 1970–1986*. Washington, DC: U.S. Government Printing Office. (pp. 34, 36)

Connell, R. W.; Ashenden, D. J.; Kessler, S.; and Dowsett, G. W. 1982. *Making the difference*. Boston: George Allen & Unwin. (p. 254)

Coons, J. E., and Sugarman, S. D. 1978. *Education by choice. The case for family control*. Berkeley: University of California Press. (pp. 487–488)

Cooper, E. J. 1986. Excerpts from testimony. *Outcomes* 6 (1): 10–12. (p. 54)

Corcoran, M., and Courant, P. 1985. Sex-role socialization and occupational segregation: An exploratory investigation. University of Wisconsin–Madison IRP Discussion Paper DP #797–85. (p. 443)

Cordasco, F., and Bucchioni, E. 1972. Introduction. In *The Puerto Rican community and its children on the mainland: A sourcebook for teachers, social workers and other professionals*, edited by F. Cordasco and E. Bucchioni. Metuchen, NJ: Scarecrow, pp. 14–18. (p. 392)

Corsaro, W. A. 1988. Routines in the peer culture of American and Italian school children. *Sociology of Education* 61: 1–14. (p. 152)

Costa, A., ed. 1985. *Developing minds: A resource book for teaching thinking*. Alexandria, VA: Association for Supervision and Curriculum Development. (p. 526)

Coughlin, E. K. 1988. Working plight of the "underclass" catches attention of researchers. *The Chronicle of Higher Education* 34 (29): A4–A8. (pp. 17, 373, 385)

Coulson, J. E. 1976. *National evaluation of the Emergency School Aid Act (ESAA): Survey of the second-year studies*. Santa Monica, CA: System Development Corporation. (p. 326)

Council of Chief State School Officers. 1987. *Assuring educational success for students at risk*. Policy statement approved by the members of the Council, Asheville, NC. (p. 508)

Council of Great City Schools. 1987. *Challenges to urban education: Results in the making*. Washington, DC: Council of Great City Schools. (pp. 83–84)

Courter, R. L., and Ward, B. A. 1983. Staff development for school improvement. In *Staff development*, edited by Gary A. Griffin and Kenneth J. Rehage. Eighty-Second Yearbook of the National Society for the Study of Education, Part II. Chicago: University of Chicago Press. (p. 554)

Crain, R. L. 1970. School integration and occupational achievement of Negroes. *American Journal of Sociology* 75: 593–606. (p. 331)

Crain, R. L., and Mahard, R. E. 1982. *Desegregation plans that raise black achievement: A review of the research*. Santa Monica, CA: Rand. (pp. 315, 325)

Crain, R. L.; Mahard, R. E.; and Narot, R. E. 1982. *Making desegregation work*. Cambridge, MA: Ballinger. (p. 315)

Crandall, D. P.; Eiseman, J. W.; and Louis, K. E. 1986. Strategic planning issues that bear on the success of school improvement efforts. *Educational Administration Quarterly* 22 (3): 21–53. (p. 541)

Crawford, J. 1986a. Lawmakers, lobbyists challenge E.D.'s bilingual-education data. *Education Week* 5 (32): 13. (p. 405)

———. 1986b. One-third of Navajos drop out annually, new study finds. *Education Week* 6 (13): 1, 14. (p. 418)

———. 1987. Bilingual education: Language, learning, and politics. *Education Week*. 6 (27): 19–50. (pp. 401, 407)

Cremin, L. A. 1977. *Traditions of American education*. New York: Basic Books. (pp. 168–169)

Crisis. 1986. Interview. Dr. Nathan Hare. *The Crisis* 93 (3): 30–35, 45–46. (p. 375)

Cross, T. 1984. *The black power imperative.* New York: Faulkner. (pp. 376, 434)

Crosswhite, F. J., et al. 1985. *Second international mathematics study summary report for the United States.* Champaign, IL: Stipes. (p. 54)

Crouse, J. 1985. Does the SAT help colleges make better selection decisions? *Harvard Educational Review* 55: 198–219. (p. 70)

C.S.R. 1985. *The impact of Head Start on children, families, and communities.* Washington, DC: United States Department of Health and Human Services. (p. 286)

Cuban, L. 1983. *How teachers taught.* New York: Longman. (p. 528)

Currie, E. 1985. *Confronting crime: An American challenge.* New York: Pantheon. (p. 200)

Curtis, R. Q., Jr. 1975. Adolescent orientations toward parents and peers: Variations by sex, age, and socioeconomic status. *Adolescence* 10: 483–494. (p. 157)

Cusick, P. A. 1983. *The egalitarian ideal and the American high school.* New York: Longman. (pp. 162, 530)

Danzig, R., and Szanton, P. 1986. *National service: What would it mean?* New York: The Ford Foundation. (p. 209)

Danziger, S., and Gottschalk, P. 1986. How have families with children been faring? University of Wisconsin–Madison Institute for Research on Poverty Discussion Paper No. 801–86. (pp. 373–374)

Dar, Y., and Resh, N. 1986. Classroom intellectual composition and academic achievement. *American Educational Research Journal* 23 (3): 357–374. (p. 49)

Darity, W. A., and Myers, S. L. 1984. Does welfare dependency cause female headship? The case of the black family. *Journal of Marriage and the Family* 46: 765–779. (p. 376)

Darlington, R. B., et al. 1980. Preschool programs and later school competence of children from low-income families. *Science* 208 (April): 202–204. (p. 288)

Dave, R. H. 1963. *The identification and measurement of environmental process variables that are related to educational achievement.* Ph.D. dissertation, University of Chicago. (p. 118)

Davidson, H. H., and Greenberg, J. W. 1969. *School achievers from a deprived background.* New York: City College of the City University of New York. (p. 115)

Davis, A. 1948. *Social-class influences upon learning.* Cambridge, MA: Harvard University Press. (p. 40)

Davis, A., and Havighurst, R. J. 1947. *Father of the man.* Boston: Houghton Mifflin. (p. 149)

Davis, K. 1980. A theory of teenage pregnancy in the United States. In *Adolescent pregnancy and child-bearing: Findings from research,* edited by Catherine S. Chilman. Washington, DC: U.S. Government Printing Office. (pp. 206–207)

Day, R. D. 1988. The mother-state-child "family": Cul-de-sac or path to the future? *The Family in America* 2 (3): 1–8. (p. 129)

De Avila, E. A., and Ulibarri, D. M. 1980. Theoretical perspectives on the selection of instructional techniques for Hispanic students. In *Educating English-speaking Hispanics,* edited by Leonard A. Valverde, Rose Castro Feinberg, and Esther M. Marquez. Washington, DC: Association for Supervision and Curriculum Development. (pp. 405, 413)

Delaney, P. 1975. System is blamed for delinquency. *The New York Times* May 5. (p. 283)

Demos, J. 1983. *Past, present, and personal.* New York: Oxford University Press. (p. 112)

Derber, C. 1979. *The pursuit of attention.* New York: Schenkman. (p. 464)

Dervarics, C. 1985. Panel report lauds success of job corps, seeks continued funding. *Higher Education Daily* 13 (158): 5. (p. 301)

Desmond, E. W. 1987. Out in the open. *Time* 130 (22): 80–90. (p. 203)

Deutsch, M., et al. 1964. *Communication of information in the elementary classroom.* New York: Institute for Developmental Studies. (p. 267)

DeVos, G. 1982. Adaptive strategies in U.S. minorities. In *Minority mental health,* edited by Enrico E. Jones and Sheldon J. Korchin. New York: Praeger. (p. 223)

DeYoung, A. J. 1987. The status of American rural education research: An integrated review and commentary. *Review of Educational Research* 57: 123–148. (p. 471)

Diamond, E. E., and Tittle, C. K. 1985. Sex equity in testing. In *Handbook for achieving sex equity through education*, edited by Susan S. Klein. Baltimore: The Johns Hopkins University Press. (p. 454)

Dillard, J. L. 1972. *Black English*. New York: Random House. (p. 379)

Division of Vocational and Technical Education. 1979. *Status of vocational education in 1979*. Washington, DC: United States Department of Health, Education and Welfare. (p. 450)

Dobriner, W. M. 1963. *Class in suburbia*. Englewood Cliffs, NJ: Prentice-Hall. (p. 40)

Dobson, D. P. 1985. *The application of immersion education in the United States*. Rosslyn, VA: National Clearinghouse for Bilingual Education. (p. 405)

Doeringer, P. B., and Piore, M. J. 1971. *Internal labor markets and manpower analysis*. Lexington, MA: Heath-Lexington. (p. 41)

Doll, R. C., and Levine, D. U. 1972. Toward a definition of "structure" in the education of disadvantaged students. In *Opening opportunities for disadvantaged learners*, edited by A. Harry Passow. New York: Teachers College Press. (pp. 104–105)

Dorr, A. 1986. *Television and children*. Beverly Hills, CA: Sage. (pp. 142, 144, 150)

Dougherty, K. 1987. The effects of community colleges: Aid or hindrance to socioeconomic attainment? *Sociology of Education* 60: 86–103. (p. 61)

Doyle, D. P. 1982. A den of inequity: Private schools reconsidered. *American Education* 18 (8): 11–17. (p. 482)

Doyle, W. 1983. Academic work. *Review of Educational Research* 53: 159–199. (p. 530)

———. 1985. Effective secondary classroom practices. In *Reaching for excellence*, edited by Regina M. J. Kyle. Washington, DC: The National Institute of Education. (p. 529)

———. 1986. Classroom organization and management. In *Handbook of research on teaching*, edited by Merlin C. Wittrock. New York: Macmillan. (p. 523)

Duffy, G. G., et al. 1986. The relationship between explicit verbal explanation during reading skill instruction and student awareness and achievement. *Reading Research Quarterly* 21: 237–282. (p. 528)

Duffy, G. G.; Roehler, L. R.; and Putnam, J. 1987. Putting the teacher in control: Basal reading textbooks and instructional decision making. *The Elementary School Journal* 87 (3): 357–366. (pp. 511, 528)

Dulay, H., and Burt, M. 1982. Bilingual education: A close look at its effects. *Focus of the National Clearinghouse for Bilingual Education* 1: 1–4. (p. 406)

Dunivant, N. 1982. The relationship between learning disabilities and juvenile delinquency: Brief summary of research findings. Paper published by the National Center for State Courts, Williamsburg, VA. (p. 199)

Durkheim, E. 1956. *Education and Sociology*. Glencoe, IL: Free Press. (p. 187)

Durkin, D. 1978–79. What classroom observation reveals about reading comprehension instruction. *Reading Research Quarterly* 14: 481–533. (p. 528)

Easterlin, R. A. 1980. *Birth and fortune: The impact of numbers on personal welfare*. New York: Basic Books. (p. 127)

Eccles, J. S. 1986. Gender-roles and women's achievement. *Educational Researcher* 15 (6): 15–19. (pp. 458–459)

Eccles, J. S., and Blumenfeld. 1985. Classroom experiences and student gender: Are there differences and do they matter? In *Gender influences in classroom interaction*, edited by Louise Cherry Wilkinson and Cora B. Marrett. Orlando, FL: Academic Press. (p. 454)

Eckland, B. E.; Henderson, L. B.; and Kolstad, A. J. 1981. *College attainment four years after high school*. Washington, DC: National Center for Education Statistics. (p. 47)

Eddy, P. 1978. Does foreign language study aid native language development? *ERIC/CLL News Bulletin* No. 1: 1–2. (p. 405)

Eder, D., and Parker, S. 1987. The cultural production and reproduction of gender. *Sociology of Education* 60: 200–213. (p. 155)

Edmonds, R. 1979. Effective schools for the urban poor. *Educational Leadership* 38: 15–24. (p. 514)

Education Advocates Coalition. 1980. Misclassification of minorities in "educable mentally retarded classes." *Integrateducation* 18 (1–4): 113–115. (p. 141)

Educational Testing Service. 1980. *Test use and validity: A response to charges in the Nader/Nairn report on ETS.* Princeton, NJ: Educational Testing Service. (p. 70)

Education Daily. 1987a. Hard work lies ahead in attempt to transform schools. *Education Daily* 20 (92): 5–6. (p. 510)

———. 1987b. Governor warns of polarization of society without education reforms. *Education Daily* 20 (29): 4. (p. 494)

Education Forum. 1984. Education reports prompt state reform. *CDF Reports* December: 10. (p. 510)

Eells, K., et al. 1951. *Intelligence and cultural differences.* Chicago: University of Chicago Press. (p. 67)

Egan, T. 1988. Proposal to curb busing in Seattle seeks to attract whites to schools. *The New York Times* March 28: A17. (p. 342)

Ekstrom, R. B.; Goertz, M. E.; Pollack, J. M.; and Rock, D. A. 1986. Who drops out of high school and why? Findings from a national study. *Teachers College Record* 87: 356–373. (p. 547)

Elardo, R.; Bradley, R.; and Caldwell, B. M. 1975. The relation of infants' home environments to mental test performance from six to thirty-six months: A longitudinal analysis. *Child Development* 46: 71–76. (p. 121)

Elliott, D. S.; Huizinga, D.; and Ageton, S. S. 1985. *Explaining delinquency and drug use.* Beverly Hills, CA: Sage, 1985. (6) (pp. 157, 197, 199–200)

Ellis, J. E. 1988. The black middle class. *Business Week* 3042: 62–70 (p. 371)

Epps, E. G. 1974. Schools and cultural pluralism. In *Cultural pluralism,* edited by Edgar G. Epps. Berkeley, CA: McCutchan. (p. 433)

Epstein, E. H. 1972. Social class, ethnicity, and academic achievement: A cross-cultural approach. *The Journal of Negro Education* 14: 202–215. (p. 137)

Epstein, N. 1977. *Language, ethnicity, and the schools: Policy alternatives for bilingual-bicultural education.* Washington, DC: The George Washington University Institute for Educational Leadership. (pp. 403–404, 411)

Erickson, F. 1985. *Qualitative methods in teaching.* Lansing: Michigan State University Institute for Research on Teaching. (p. 428)

Erickson, F., and Mohatt, G. 1982. The cultural organization of participation structures in two classrooms of Indian students. In *Doing the ethnography of schooling,* edited by George Spindler. New York: Holt, Rinehart and Winston. (p. 428)

Ethington, C. A., and Wolfle, L. M. 1986. A structural model of mathematics achievement for men and women. *American Educational Research Journal* 23 (1): 65–75. (p. 445)

Eubanks, E. E., and Levine, D. U. 1977. The PUSH program for excellence in big-city schools. *Phi Delta Kappan* 58: 383–388. (pp. 106, 171)

———. 1983. A first look at effective schools projects in New York and Milwaukee. Phi Delta Kappan 64: 697–702. (p. 517)

———. 1987a. Administrative and organizational arrangements and considerations. In *Educating the black child,* edited by Dorothy S. Strickland and Eric J. Cooper. Washington, DC: Howard University Press. (p. 548)

———. 1987b. Ancillary relief components in urban school desegregation. The University of Chicago National School Desegregation Project Working Paper No. 8. (p. 323)

Evangelauf, J. 1987. Students' borrowing quintuples in decade, raising the specter of a 'debtor generation.' *The Chronicle of Higher Education* January 7: 1, 18. (p. 65)

Everhart, R. B. 1983. *Reading, writing, and resistance.* Boston: Routledge and Kegan Paul. (p. 254)

Exter, T. 1987. How many Hispanics? *American Demographics* 9 (5): 36–39, 67. (p. 391)

Farley, R. 1984. *Blacks and whites.* Cambridge, MA: Harvard University Press. (p. 374)

Farnsworth, M.; Schweinhart, L. J.; and Berrueta-Clement. 1985. Preschool intervention, school success and delinquency in a high-risk sample of youth. *American Educational Research Journal* 22: 445–464. (p. 287)

Feagans, L. 1982. The development and importance of narratives for school adaptation. In *The language of children reared in poverty,* edited by Lynne Feagans and Dale Clark Farran. New York: Academic Press. (p. 238)

Feagans, L., and Farran, D. C., eds. 1982. *The language of children reared in poverty.* New York: Academic Press. (p. 258)

Featherman, D. L., and Hauser, R. M. 1976. Changes in the socioeconomic stratification of the races, 1962–1973. *American Journal of Sociology* 82: 621–651. (pp. 229, 245)

———. 1978. *Opportunity and change.* New York: Academic Press. (pp. 224–225, 227, 229–230, 245–246, 387–388, 393–394)

Featherstone, H. 1987. Orderly classrooms and corridors: Why some have them and others don't. *The Harvard Educational Letter* 3 (5): 1–5. (p. 521)

Feingold, A. 1988. Cognitive gender differences are disappearing. *American Psychologist* 43 (2): 95–103. (pp. 445–446)

Fennema, E. 1982. Overview of sex-related differences in mathematics. Paper presented at the Annual Meeting of the American Educational Research Association, New York. March. (p. 445)

Ferguson, A. 1977. Androgyny as an ideal for human development. In *Feminism and philosophy.* Totewa, NJ: Littlefield, Adams. (p. 460)

Ferndandez, R., and Vellez. 1985. Race, color, and language in the changing public schools. In *Urban ethnicity in the United States,* edited by Lionel Maldonado and Joan Moore. Beverly Hills, CA: Sage. (p. 57)

Feuerstein, R. 1980. *Instrumental enrichment.* Baltimore: University Park Press. (p. 528)

Fiddmont, Norman. 1976. *Achievement in inner city schools.* School of Education, University of Missouri, Kansas City. (p. 279)

Finn, C. E., Jr. 1987. The high school dropout puzzle. *The Public Interest* No. 87: 3–22. (p. 546)

Finn, J. D.; Dulberg, L.; and Reis, J. 1979. Sex differences in educational attainment: A cross-national perspective. *Harvard Educational Review* 49: 477–503. (p. 444)

Firestone, S. 1970. *The dialect of sex: The case for feminist revolution.* New York: William Morrow and Co. (p. 464)

Firestone, W. A., and Herriott, R. E. 1982. Prescriptions for effective elementary schools don't fit secondary schools. *Educational Leadership* 40: 51–53. (p. 519)

Firestone, W. A., and Rosenblum, S. 1987. First year project: A study of alienation and commitment in five urban districts. Paper presented at the annual meeting of the American Educational Research Association. Washington, DC, April. (p. 547)

Fishman, J. A. 1977. Bilingual education—A perspective. *IRCD Bulletin* 12 (Spring): 1–12. (pp. 408, 412)

Fiske, E. B. 1987. Enrollment of minorities in colleges stagnating. *The New York Times* April 4: 1, 24. (pp. 65, 385)

Fitzpatrick, J. P. 1972. Transition to the mainland. In *The Puerto Rican community and its children on the mainland: A sourcebook for teachers, social workers and other professionals,* edited by Francesco Cordasco and Eugene Bucchioni. Metuchen, NJ: Scarecrow, pp. 114–120. (p. 398)

Flynn, J. R. 1980. *Race, IQ, and Jensen.* London: Routledge and Kegan Paul. (p. 69)

———. 1987. Massive IQ gains in 14 nations: What IQ tests really measure. *Psychological Bulletin* 101: 171–191. (p. 69)

Foley, J.; Manaker, M.; and Schwartz, J. L. 1986. *National service and America's future.* Washington, DC: Youth Policy Institute. (p. 209)

Ford Foundation, 1984. *City high schools: A recognition of progress.* New York: Ford Foundation. (p. 500)

Fordham, S. 1988. Racelessness as a factor in black students' school success: Pragmatic strategy or Pyrrhic victory? *Harvard Educational Review* 58 (1): 54–84. (p. 378)

Forehand, G.; Ragosta, M.; and Rock, D. A. 1977. *School conditions and race relations.* Princeton, NJ: Educational Testing Service. (p. 328)

Fortenberry, R. N., and White, B. L. 1987. Districts grapple with dropout problem. *The School Administrator* 44 (3): 11–13. (p. 546)

Forum of Educational Organization Leaders. 1987. Statement on meeting the needs of children and youth at risk of school failure. Washington, DC: Forum of Educational Organization Leaders. (p. 493)

Foster, S. G. 1982. Success of minority engineering programs may have promise for secondary schools. *Education Week* 2 (9): 1, 17. (p. 298)

Frechtling, J. A., and Nyitray, M. S. 1977. The structure and content of compensatory education programs: A research strategy for evaluating Title I's effects on services and effects on students. Paper presented at the annual meeting of the American Educational Research Association, April. (p. 285)

Freeman, R. B., and Holzer, H. T. 1985. Young blacks and jobs—what we now know. The Public Interest. No. 78: 18–31. (p. 192)

———. 1986. *The black youth unemployment crisis.* Chicago: University of Chicago Press. (p. 192)

Friedan, B. 1963. *The feminine mystique.* New York: Dell. (pp. 436, 464)

———. 1981. *The second stage.* New York: Random House. (pp. 461–462, 464)

Friedenberg, E. Z. 1959. *The vanishing adolescent.* Boston: Beacon Press. (p. 178)

Friedrich, O. 1985. The changing face of America. *Time* July 8: 26–33. (p. 361)

Fuchs, E., and Havighurst, R. J. 1972. *To live on this earth: American Indian education.* Garden City, NY: Doubleday Anchor Books. (pp. 421–422, 433)

Fuerst, J. S. 1976. Report from Chicago: A program that works. *The Public Interest* 43 (Spring): 59–69. (p. 289)

———. 1977. Child-parent centers: An evaluation. *Integrated Education* 15 (May–June): 17–20. (p. 289)

Fullan, M. 1982. *The meaning of educational change.* New York: Columbia University Teachers College Press. (p. 540)

Fuller, W. E. 1985. *The old country school.* Chicago: The University of Chicago Press. (pp. 470–473, 491)

Furstenberg, F. F., Jr. 1988. Bringing back the shotgun wedding. *The Public Interest* No. 90: pp. 121–127. (p. 207)

Furstenberg, F. F., Jr.; Brooks-Gunn, J.; and Morgan, S. Philip. 1987. *Adolescent mothers in later life.* New York: Cambridge University Press. (p. 207)

Futrell, M. H. 1986. Restructuring teaching: A call for research. *Educational Researcher* 15 (10): 5–8. (pp. 499–500)

Gabarino, J., and Plantz, M. C. 1980. *Urban environments and urban children.* New York: Institute for Urban and Minority Education, Teachers College, Columbia University. (p. 98)

Galbraith, J. K. 1958. *The affluent society.* Boston: Houghton Mifflin. (p. 79)

———. 1982. *Emergency interim survey: Fiscal condition of 48 large cities.* Washington, DC: U.S. Government Printing Office. (p. 79)

Gallagher, W. 1988. Sex and hormones. *The Atlantic Monthly* 261 (4): 77–82. (p. 447)

Gallaher, A. 1961. *Plainville fifteen years later.* New York: Columbia University Press. (p. 39)

Gamoran, A. 1986a. Instructional and institutional effects of ability grouping. *Sociology of Education* 59: 185–198. (p. 49)

———. 1986b. The stratification of high school learning opportunities. Paper delivered at the annual meeting of the American Education Research Association, San Francisco, April. (p. 165)

Gans, H. J. 1962. *The urban villagers.* New York: The Free Press. (p. 99)

———. 1967. *The Levittowners.* New York: Pantheon Books, Random House. (p. 40)

———. 1976. The role of education in the escape from poverty. In *Education, inequality, and national policy,* edited by N. F.

Ashline, T. R. Pazzullo, and C. I. Norris. Lexington, MA: D.C. Heath. (p. 24)

Gappert, G., and Knight, R. V., eds. 1982. *Cities in the 21st century*. Beverly Hills, CA: Sage. (p. 91)

Garreau, J. 1982. *The nine nations of North America*. New York: Avon. (p. 370)

Garrison, M., and Hammil, D. 1971. Who are the retarded? *Exceptional Children* 38: 13–20. (p. 140)

Gelb, S. A., and Mizokawa, D. T. 1986. Special education and social structure: The commonality of 'exceptionality.' *American Educational Research Journal* 23 (4): 543–557. (p. 140)

Genesee, F. 1985. Second language learning through immersion: A review of U.S. programs. *Review of Educational Research* 55 (4): 541–561. (p. 406)

Genova, W. J., and Walberg, H. J. 1981. *A practitioner's guide for achieving student integration in city high schools*. Washington, DC: U.S. Government Printing Office. (p. 315)

Gerson, R. P., and Damon, W. 1978. Moral understanding and children's conduct. *New Directions for Child Development* 2: 41–59. (p. 155)

Gersten, R., and Woodward, J. 1985. A case for structured immersion. *Educational Leadership* 43 (1): 75–79. (p. 406)

Getzels, J. W. 1978. The school and the acquisition of values. In *From youth to constructive adult life: The role of the public school*, edited by Ralph W. Tyler. Berkeley, CA: McCutchan, pp. 43–66. (p. 183)

Gifford, B. R. 1986. Excellence and equity in teacher competency testing: A policy perspective. *The Journal of Negro Education* 55 (3): 251–271. (p. 426)

Gilbert, S. II., and Gay, G. 1985. Improving the success in school of poor black children. *Phi Delta Kappan* 67 (2): 133–137. (pp. 263, 427)

Gilligan, C. 1982. *In a different voice: Psychological theory and women's development*. Cambridge, MA: Harvard University Press. (p. 462)

Giroux, H. A. 1983. Theories of reproduction and resistance in the new sociology of education: A critical analysis. *Harvard Educational Review* 53: 253–297. (pp. 255, 259)

———. 1988. *Teachers as intellectuals*. South Hadley, MA: Bergin and Garvey. (pp. 255, 259)

Giroux, H. A., and McLaren, P. 1986. Teacher education and the politics of engagement: The case for democratic schooling. *Harvard Educational Review* 56: 213–238. (pp. 255, 259)

Giroux, H. A., and Purpel, D. 1983. *The hidden curriculum and moral education*. Berkeley, CA: McCutchan. (p. 258)

Gisi, L. G., and Forbes, R. H. 1982. *The information society: Are high school graduates ready?* Denver: Education Commission of the States. (p. 27)

Glaser, D. 1979. Economic and sociocultural variables affecting rates of youth unemployment, delinquency, and crime. *Youth and Society* 11 (1): 53–82. (pp. 197–198)

Glaser, E. M., and Ross, H. L. 1970. *A study of successful persons from seriously disadvantaged backgrounds*. U.S. Dept. of Labor Office of Special Manpower Programs. (p. 23)

Glasgow, D. G. 1980. *The black underclass. Poverty, unemployment, and entrapment of ghetto youth*. San Francisco: Jossey–Bass. (p. 22)

Glass, D. V., ed. 1954. *Social mobility in Britain*. London: Routledge and Kegan Paul. (p. 227)

Glazer, N., ed. 1985. *Clamor at the gates*. San Francisco: ICS Press. (p. 434)

Glidewell, J. C.; Kantor, M. B.; Smith, L. M.; and Stringer, L. H. 1966. Socialization and social structure in the classroom. In *Review of research in child development 2*, edited by Martin and Lois Hoffman. New York: Russell Sage Foundation. (p. 178)

Glueck, S., and Glueck, E. T. 1950. *Unraveling juvenile delinquency*. New York: Commonwealth Fund. (p. 198)

———. 1968. *Delinquents and nondelinquents in perspective*. Cambridge, MA: Harvard University Press. (p. 198)

Goldberg, K. 1986. Blacks push strategies to improve their education. *Education Week* 6 (13): 1–15. (pp. 477–478)

———. 1987. Many homeless children reported out of school. *Education Week* 6 (26): 6. (p. 147)

Goldberger, A., and Cain, G. 1982. The causal analysis of cognitive outcomes in the Coleman, Hoffer, and Kilgore report. *Sociology of Education* 55 (2): 103–122. (p. 480)

Goldin, C. 1985. Understanding the gender gap. *New Perspectives* 17 (4): 9–13. (p. 442)

Goldsmith, W. W. 1982. Poverty and profit in urban growth and decline. In *Race, poverty and the urban underclass*, edited by Clement Cottingham. Lexington, MA: D.C. Heath. (p. 18)

Goldthorpe, J. H. 1980. *Social mobility and class structure in modern Britain.* Oxford: Clarendon Press. (p. 228)

Gonzalez, G. A. 1980. The non-Spanish speaking Hispanic child: Curriculum concerns/supervisory initiatives. In *Educating English-speaking Hispanics*, edited by Leonard A. Valverde, Rosa Castro Feinberg, and Esther M. Marquez. Washington, DC: Association for Supervision and Curriculum Development. (pp. 399–400)

González, J. 1975. Coming of age in bilingual/bicultural education: An historical perspective. *Inequality in Education* 19: 5–17. (pp. 402, 404, 412)

Good, T., and Brophy, J. E. 1986. School effects. In *Handbook of research on teaching*, edited by Merlin C. Wittrock. New York: Macmillan. (p. 522)

Good, T. L. 1981. Teacher expectations and student perceptions: A decade of research. *Educational Leadership* 38: 415–422. (p. 265)

Good, T. L., and Grouws, D. A. 1987. Increasing teachers' understanding of mathematical ideas through inservice training. *Phi Delta Kappan* 68: 778–783. (p. 528)

Good, T. L., and Marshall, S. 1984. Do students learn more in heterogeneous or homogeneous groups? In *The social context of instruction*, edited by Margaret T. Hallinan and Aage B. Sørensen. New York: Academic Press. (p. 49)

Goodlad, J. I. 1984. *A place called school.* New York: McGraw-Hill. (pp. 89, 152–153, 528–530)

———. 1987. Structure, process, and an agenda. In *The ecology of school renewal*, edited by John I. Goodlad. Eighty-Sixth Yearbook of the National Society for the Study of Education, Part I. Chicago: University of Chicago Press. (pp. 539, 541)

Goodman, G. 1979. *Choosing sides.* New York: Schocken Books. (p. 257)

Gordon, C. W. 1957. *The social system of the high school.* New York: The Free Press. (p. 178)

Gordon, E. W. 1976. Equal opportunity in education. *IRCD Bulletin* 11 (Winter): 1–15. (p. 298)

Gordon, M. W. 1964. *Assimilation in American life: The role of race, religion and origins.* New York: Oxford University Press. (pp. 40, 362, 367, 433)

Gottfredson, L. S. 1979. Racial differences in the evolution of educational and occupational aspirations. Paper presented at the annual meeting of the American Educational Research Association, San Francisco, March. (p. 387)

———. 1984. *The role of intelligence and education in the division of labor.* Baltimore: Center for Social Organization of Schools. (p. 71)

Gottmann, J. 1961. *Megalopolis: The urbanized northeastern seaboard of the United States.* New York: Twentieth Century Fund. (p. 91)

Gould, S. J. 1980. Jensen's last stand. *The New York Review of Books* 27 (7): 38–44. (p. 69)

———. 1981. *The mismeasure of man.* New York: Norton. (p. 69)

Graham, P. A. 1987. Black teachers: A drastically scarce resource. *Phi Delta Kappan* 68 (8): 598–605. (p. 426)

Grant, G. 1988. *The world we created at Hamilton High 1953–1987.* Cambridge, MA: Harvard University Press. (p. 378)

Graue, M. E.; Weinstein, T.; and Walberg, H. J. 1982. The effects of family-intervention programs on learning in early childhood: A meta-evaluation. Unpublished manuscript. University of Illinois–Chicago Circle Office of Evaluation Research. (p. 124)

Grayson, D. A., and Martin, M. D. 1986. Gender expectations and student achievement. Paper presented at the annual meeting of the American Educational Research Association, San Francisco, April. (p. 458)

Greeley, A. M. 1963. *Religion and career.* New York: Sheed and Ward. (p. 40)

———. 1980. School desegregation and ethnicity. In *School desegregation: Past, present, and future,* edited by Walter G. Stephan and Joseph R. Feagin. New York: Plenum. (pp. 366, 433)

Green, J. 1982. Applying the lessons of research. The need for mandated training in federal youth employment programs. *Education and Urban Society* 14 (Nov.): 55–66. (p. 193)

Green, J. L. 1983. Research on teaching as a linguistic process. A state of the art. In *Review of research in education 10,* edited by Edmund W. Gordon. Washington, DC: American Educational Research Association, chapter 6. (p. 262)

Greenberg, H., and Davidson, H. 1972. Home background and school achievement of black urban ghetto children. *American Journal of Orthopsychiatry* 42: 803–810. (p. 263)

Greene, E. 1986. Shifts in students' attitudes seen threat to liberal arts. *The Chronicle of Higher Education* November 5: 1, 5. (p. 184)

Greider, W. 1988. The Rolling Stone survey. *Rolling Stone* No. 523: 34–54. (p. 184)

Gross, B., and Gross, R., eds. 1985. *The great school debate.* New York: Simon and Schuster Touchstone. (p. 556)

Grubb, N. W. 1984. The bandwagon once more: Vocational preparation for high-tech occupations. *Harvard Educational Review* 54: 429–451. (p. 29)

Gudat, S. 1988. Satellite network helps keep rural schools open. *Phi Delta Kappan* 69 (7): 533–534. (p. 474)

Guidubaldi, J. 1984. Adjusting to divorce. Paper presented at the annual meeting of the American Educational Research Association, New Orleans, April 22. (p. 133)

Guinagh, B. J., and Gordon, I. J. 1976. *School performance as a function of early stimulation.* Gainesville, FL: University of Florida Institute for Development of Human Resources. (p. 288)

Guskey, T. R. 1985. *Implementing mastery learning.* Belmont, CA: Wadsworth. (pp. 306, 535)

Guttentag, M., and Ross, M. 1972. Movement responses in simple concept learning. *American Journal of Orthopsychiatry* 42: 657–665. (p. 263)

Guttentag, M., and Secord, P. F. 1983. *Too many women? The sex ratio question.* Beverly Hills, CA: Sage. (pp. 375, 465)

Hacker, A. H. 1979. Two "new classes" or none? In *The new class?,* edited by B. Bruce-Briggs. New Brunswick, NJ: Transaction. (p. 6)

———. 1988. Black crime, white racism. *The New Yorker review of books* 35 (3): 36–42. (pp. 18, 25, 223, 247, 388–389)

Haertel, E. 1985. *Comparing achievement in public and private schools.* Palo Alto, CA: Stanford University Institute for Research on Educational Finance and Governance. (p. 481)

Hafner, A. L. 1985. Gender differences in college students' educational and occupational aspirations: 1971–1983. Paper presented at the annual meeting of the American Educational Research Association, Chicago, April. (p. 442)

Hafner, A. L., and White, D. M. 1981. Bias in mental research. *Harvard Educational Review* 51 (4): 577–586. (p. 70)

Hahn, A., and Lerman, R. 1985. *What works in youth employment policy?* Washington, DC: National Planning Association. (pp. 191–192)

Hakuta, K. 1986. *Mirror of language.* New York: Basic Books. (pp. 405, 412)

Hakuta, K., and Gould, L. J. 1987. Synthesis of research on bilingual education. *Educational Leadership* 44 (6): 38–45. (p. 406)

Hallinan, M. T., and Teixeira, R.A. 1987. Students' interracial friendships: Individual characteristics, structural effects, and racial differences. *American Journal of Education* 95: 563–583. (p. 329)

Hallinger, P., and Murphy, J. F. 1986. The social context of effective schools. *American Journal of Education* 94 (3): 328–355. (p. 523)

Halpern, D. F. 1986. *Sex differences in cognitive abilities.* Hillsdale, NJ: Erlbaum. (pp. 448, 465)

Halsey, A. H. 1976. Towards meritocracy? The case of Britain. In *Power and ideology in education,* edited by Jerome Karabel and A. H. Halesy. New York: Oxford University Press, pp. 173–186. (p. 233)

Halsey, A. H.; Heath, A. F.; and Ridge, J. M. 1980. *Origins and destinations: Family class and education in modern Britain.* New York: Oxford University Press. (pp. 231–232)

Hamilton, S. F. 1986. Raising standards and reducing dropout rates. *Teachers College Record* 87: 410–429. (pp. 546–547)

———. 1988. *The interaction of family, community, and work in the socialization of youth.* Washington, DC: William T. Grant Foundation Commission on Youth and America's Future. (pp. 209, 546)

Hammond, R., and Howard, J. P. 1986. Doing what's expected of you: The roots and the rise of the dropout culture. *Metropolitan Education* No. 2: 53–71. (p. 532)

Hampel, R. L. 1986. *The last little citadel: American high schools since 1940.* Boston: Houghton Mifflin. (p. 530)

Handlin, O. 1951. *The uprooted.* Boston: Little Brown. (p. 112)

———. 1959. *The newcomers.* Cambridge, MA: Harvard University Press. (pp. 112, 433)

Hanks, M. 1979. Race, sexual status and athletics in the process of educational achievement. *Social Science Quarterly* 60 (3): 482–496. (p. 167)

Hannay, H. J., and Levin, H. S. 1987. *Cerebration. About the human brain.* National Forum 67 (2): 1–3. (pp. 446, 448)

Hansen, D. A. 1986. Family-school articulations: The effects of interaction rule mismatch. *American Educational Research Journal* 23: 643–659. (p. 65)

Hansen, J. S. 1986. Student loans: Are they overburdening a generation? Paper prepared for the Joint Economic Committee of the U.S. Congress. (p. 110)

Hanson, D. J. 1980. Drug education: Does it work? In *Drugs and the youth culture,* edited by Frank R. Scarpitti and Susan K. Datesman. Beverly Hills, CA: Sage. (p. 205)

Harber, J. R., and Bryan, D. N. 1976. Black English and the teaching of reading. *Review of Educational Research* 46: 387–405. (p. 379)

Harrington, M. 1983. Americans in limbo. *Harper's* 266 (1595): 48–53. (p. 228)

Harris, B. 1978. *Beyond her sphere: Women and the professions in American history.* Westport, CT: Greenwood. (p. 465)

Harris, E. W. 1988. An "up" experience with minority achievement. *The School Administrator* 45 (4): 34–35 (p. 379)

Harris, N., et al. 1975. *The integration of American schools: Problems, experiences, solutions.* Boston: Allyn and Bacon. (p. 357)

Harris, T. L., and Cooper, E. J. 1985. *Reading, thinking, and concept development.* New York: College Entrance Examination Board. (pp. 527–528, 538, 556)

Harrison, B. 1972a. Education and underemployment in the urban ghetto. *American Economic Review* 62: 796–812. (pp. 245–247)

———. 1972b. Education, training, and the urban ghetto. Baltimore: The Johns Hopkins University Press. (pp. 21–22)

Harrison, B.; Tilley, C.; and Bluestone, B. 1986. *The great U-turn.* Washington, DC: Congressional Joint Economic Committee. (p. 29)

Harrison, C. H. 1987. *Student service.* Princeton, NJ: The Carnegie Foundation for the Advancement of Teaching. (p. 214)

Hart, G. 1987. Education: The key to America's third century." *Congressional Record-Senate* February 3: S1527–S1530. (p. 71)

Harvey, G. 1984. Recent reports concerning education or the road to Nirvana: You can't get there from here. Paper presented at the annual meeting of the American Educational Research Association, New Orleans, April. (p. 499)

Hatchett, D. 1986. A conflict of reasons and remedies. *The Crisis* 93 (3): 36–41, 46–47. (pp. 375–376)

Havighurst, R. J. 1964. *The public schools of Chicago.* Chicago: Chicago Public Schools. (p. 243)

———. 1966. Overcoming value differences. In *The inner city classroom: Teacher behaviors,* edited by Robert D. Strom. Columbus, OH: Merrill. (p. 106)

———. 1968. *Metropolitanism: Its challenge to education.* Chicago: University of Chicago Press. (p. 91)

———. 1971a. Minority subcultures and the law of effect. In *Educating the disadvantaged,* edited by Allan C. Ornstein et al. New York: AMS Press. (p. 428)

———. 1971b. Nurturing the cognitive skills in health. *Journal of School Health* 42 (2): 73–76. (p. 138)

———. 1976. The relative importance of social class and ethnicity in human development. *Human Development* 19: 56–64. (p. 138)

Havighurst, R. J.; Bowman, P. H.; Liddle, G. F.; Mathews, C. V.; and Pierce, J. V. 1962. *Growing up in River City.* New York: John Wiley. (pp. 8, 40, 217)

Havighurst, R. J., and Morgan, H. G. 1951. *The social history of a war-boom community.* New York: Longmans, Green. (p. 8)

Havighurst, R. J.; Neugarten, B. L.; and Falk, J., eds. 1971. *Society and education: A book of readings,* 2nd ed. Boston: Allyn and Bacon. (p. 250)

Hawkins, R. B., Jr. 1982. Tuition tax credits: Another voice. *American Education* 18 (8): 9–10. (p. 485)

Hawley, W. D. 1978. Horses before carts: Developing adaptive schools and the limits of innovation. In *Making change happen?,* edited by Dale Mann. New York: Columbia University Teachers College Press. (p. 539)

———. 1983. Achieving quality integrated education—with or without federal help. *Phi Delta Kappan* 64 (5): 334–338. (p. 314)

Hawley, W. D., et al. 1982. *Strategies for effective desegregation: Lessons from research.* Lexington, MA: Lexington Books. (p. 314)

Heath, S. B. 1983. *Ways with words: Language, life, and work in communities and classrooms.* New York: Cambridge University Press. (p. 237)

Heath, S. B., and McLaughlin, M. W. 1987. A child resource policy: Moving beyond dependence on school and family. *Phi Delta Kappan* 68 (8): 576–580. (pp. 120, 237)

Helge, D., and Marrs, L. 1981. *Personal recruitment and retention in rural America.* Bellingham: Western Washington University. (p. 472)

Henderson, R. D., and von Euler, M., eds. 1977. *School desegregation in metropolitan areas: Choices and prospects.* Washington, DC: U.S. Government Printing Office. (p. 357)

Hendrickson, G. L. 1977. Review of Title 1 evaluation studies. Paper presented at the annual meeting of the American Educational Research Association, April. (p. 293)

Henshaw, J.; Wilson, C.; and Morefield, J. 1987. Seeing clearly: The school as the unit of change. In *The ecology of school renewal,* edited by John I. Goodlad. Eighty-Sixth Yearbook of the National Society for the Study of Education, Part I. Chicago: University of Chicago Press. (p. 539)

Hentoff, N. 1977. *Does anybody give a damn?* New York: Knopf. (p. 306)

Herbers, J. 1986. *The new heartland.* New York: New York Times Books. (p. 92)

———. 1987. Poverty of blacks spreads in cities. *The New York Times* January 26: A1, A27. (p. 76)

Herndon, J. 1968. *The way it spozed to be.* New York: Bantam. (pp. 104, 111, 305–306, 529)

Herrnstein, R. J. 1982. IQ testing and the media. *The Atlantic* 250 (2): 68–74. (p. 69)

Hess, A. G., Jr., and Laubec, D. 1985. *Dropouts from the Chicago Public Schools.* Chicago: Chicago Panel on Public School Policy and Finance. (p. 82)

Hess, R. D., and McDevitt, T. M. 1984. Some cognitive consequences of material intervention techniques: A longitudinal study. *Child Development* 55: 2017–2030. (p. 121)

Hess, R. D., and Shipman, V. C. 1965. Early experience and the socialization of cognitive modes in children. *Child Development* 36: 869–886. (pp. 114, 238)

Hess, R. D., and Torney, J. 1967. *The development of political attitudes in children.* Chicago: Aldine. (p. 150)

Hill, S., and Owings, M. 1986. Completion time for bachelor's degrees. *OERI Bulletin* November. (p. 59)

Hindelang, M. J. 1981. Variations in sex–race–age-specific incidence rates of offending. *American Sociological Review* 46: 461–474. (p. 128)

Hobbs, D. J. 1982. *Reinventing the wheel: The school and community as partners in rural development.* Denver: Mid-Continent Regional Educational Laboratory. (p. 472)

Hobinger, P. C., and Offer, D. 1982. Prediction of adolescent suicide: A population model. *American Journal of Psychiatry* 139: 302–307. (p. 188)

Hodges, H. M., Jr. 1968. Peninsula people: Social stratification in a metropolitan complex. In *Permanence and change in social class,* edited by Clayton Lane. Cambridge, MA: Schenkman Publishing. (pp. 9, 13–14, 39)

Hodgkinson, H. L. 1986. Reform? Higher education? Don't be absurd. *Phi Delta Kappan* 68: 271–274. (p. 37)

Hoffman, M. L., and Hoffman, L. W., eds. 1964. *Review of child development research.* New York: Russell Sage Foundation. (p. 150)

Hogan, D. 1982. Education and class formation: The peculiarities of the Americans. In *Cultural and economic reproduction in education,* edited by Michael Apple. Boston: Routledge and Kegan Paul. (p. 258)

Holland, A., and Andre, T. 1988. Participation in extracurricular activities in secondary school: What is known, what needs to be known? *Review of Educational Research* 57 (4): 437–466. (pp. 166–167)

Holland, C. 1988. Doctor of sexology. *Psychology Today* 22 (5): 45–48. (p. 448)

Holland, J. 1980. *Women's occupational choice. The impact of sexual diversions in society.* Stockholm, Sweden: Stockholm Institute of Education. (p. 463)

———. 1981. Social class and changes in orientation to meaning. *Sociology* 15 (February): 1–18. (p. 237)

Hollingshead, A. B. 1949. *Elmtown's youth.* New York: John Wiley. (pp. 8, 40)

———. 1957. *Two factor index of social position.* New Haven, CT: Yale Station. (p. 3)

Holmes, M. 1988. A pessimistic conclusion—general education and the public school. In *Cultural literacy and the idea of general education,* edited by Ian Westbury and Alan Purves. Chicago: University of Chicago Press. (pp. 114, 121, 233, 244, 259)

Holmes Group. 1986. *Tomorrow's teachers.* East Lansing, MI: Holmes Group. (p. 502)

Holt, J. 1964. *How children fail.* New York: Pitman. (p. 529)

Holt, S. L. 1985. Wiring rural school into educational reform. *Education Week* 4 (42): 36. (p. 474)

Hoover, E. M., and Vernon, R. 1959. *Anatomy of a metropolis.* Cambridge, MA: Harvard University Press. (p. 90)

Hope, K. 1982. A liberal theory of prestige. *American Journal of Sociology* 87: 1011–1031. (p. 4)

Hormik, R. 1981. Out-of-school television and schooling: Hypotheses and methods. *Review of Educational Research* 51: 193–214. (p. 144)

Horner, M. A. 1969. Fail: Bright women. *Psychology Today* 3 (6): 36–38. (p. 452)

Howe, F. 1982. Feminist scholarship. *Change* 14 (3): 12–20 (p. 458)

Howe, W. J. 1988. Education and demographics. *Monthly Labor Review* 111 (1): 3–9. (pp. 19, 27–28)

Howell, F. M., and McBroom, L. W. 1982. Social relations at home and at school: An analysis of the correspondence principle. *Sociology of Education* 55 (1): 40–52. (p. 243)

Huba, G. J., and Bentler, P. M. 1980. The role of peer and adult models for drug taking at different stages in adolescence. *Journal of Youth and Adolescence* 9: 449–465. (p. 203)

Huberman, A. M., and Miles, M. B. 1982. *Motivation up close: A field study in 12 school settings.* Andover, MA: The Network. (p. 540)

Hulbert, A. 1984. Children as parents. *The New Republic* 191 (11): 15–22. (p. 208)

Hume, M. 1988. Presidential commission reviews education voucher proposals. *Education Daily* 21 (54): 1–2. (p. 486)

Hunt, D. E. 1965. *Indicators of developmental change in lower class children.* Cooperative Research Project S–166. Syracuse, NY: Syracuse University. (p. 264)

———. 1975. Person-environment interaction: A challenge found wanting before it was tried. *Review of Educational Research* 45: 209–230. (pp. 274, 427)

Hunt, D. E.; Joyce, B. R.; Greenwood, J. A.; Noy, J. E.; Reid, R.; and Weil, M. 1974. Student conceptual level and models of teaching: Theoretical and empirical coordination of two models. *Interchange* 5 (3): 19–30. (p. 274)

Hunt, M. 1979. Psychological development: Early experience. *Annual Review of Psychology* 30: 103–143. (pp. 116, 139)

Hurn, C. J. 1978. *The limits and possibilities of schooling*. Boston: Allyn and Bacon. (p. 258)

Hyman, J. S., and Cohen, S. A. 1979. Learning for mastery: Ten conclusions after 15 years and 3,000 schools. *Educational Leadership* 37: 104–109. (p. 536)

Ianni, F. A. J. 1980. A positive note on schools and discipline. *Educational Leadership* (March): 452–458. (p. 283)

Iiams, T. M. 1977. The gathering storm over bilingual education. *Phi Delta Kappan* 59: 226–230. (pp. 408, 412)

Images of fear. 1985. *Harper's* 270 (No. 2620): 41. (p. 128)

Inciardi, J. A. 1980. Youth, drugs, and street crime. In *Drugs and the youth culture*, edited by Frank R. Scarpitti and Susan K. Datesman. Beverly Hills, CA: Sage. (p. 204)

Inkeles, A. 1975. The emerging social structure of the world. *World Politics* 27: 467–495. (p. 248)

Inkeles, A., and Smith, D. H. 1974. *Becoming modern: Individual change in countries.* Cambridge, MA: Harvard University Press. (pp. 239–240)

Inkeles, A., et al. 1983. *Exploring individual modernity*. New York: Columbia University Press. (p. 240)

Irvine, J. J. 1986. Teacher-student interactions: Effects of student race, sex, and grade level. *Journal of Educational Psychology* 78 (1): 14–21. (pp. 454–455)

Jackson, P. W. 1968. *Life in classrooms.* New York: Holt. (p. 529)

Jacobson, R. L. 1986. Teacher unions give qualified backing to Carnegie proposals on school reform. *The Chronicle of Higher Education* 32 (20): 1, 22. (p. 510)

Jaeger, S., and Sandhu, H. 1985. Southeast Asian refugees: English language development and acculturation. *Focus* No. 21: 1–4. (p. 416)

Jaffe, F. S., and Dryfoos, J. G. 1980. Fertility control services for adolescents: Access and utilization. In *Adolescent pregnancy and childbearing: Findings from research.* Washington, DC: U.S. Government Printing Office. (p. 208)

Jencks, C. 1987. Genes and crimes. *The New York review of books* 34 (2): 33–41. (pp. 69, 200)

Jencks, C., et al. 1972. *Inequality: A reassessment of the effects of family and schooling in America.* New York: Basic Books. (pp. 230, 514)

———. 1979. *Who gets ahead? The determinants of economic success in America.* New York: Basic Books. (pp. 230–231, 258, 387)

Jencks, C., and Crouse, J. 1982. Should we relabel the SAT . . . or replace it? *Phi Delta Kappan* 63: 659–663. (p. 70)

Jensen, A. R. 1968. Social class, race, and genetics: Implications for education. *American Educational Research Journal* 5: 1–42. (p. 68)

———. 1969. How much can we boost IQ and scholastic achievement? *Harvard Educational Review* 39: 1–123. (p. 68)

———. 1980. *Bias in mental testing.* New York: The Free Press. (pp. 69–70)

———. 1981. *Straight talk about mental tests.* New York: The Free Press. (p. 70)

Jessor, R.; Chase, J. A.; and Donovan, J. E. 1980. Psychosocial correlates of marijuana use and problem drinking in a national sample of adolescents. *American Journal of Public Health* 70: 604–613. (pp. 157, 203)

Jessor, R., and Jessor, S. L. 1977. *Problem behavior and psychosocial development: A longitudinal study of youth.* New York: Academic Press. (pp. 157, 214)

Johnson, D. W., and Johnson, R. T. 1981. The key to healthy development and socialization. *Character* 2 (11): 1–8. (pp. 160, 331)

Johnson, L. B. 1965. Message from the President of the United States relative to the problems and future of the central city and its suburbs, March 2. (p. 356)

Johnson, N. J., and Sanday, P. R. 1971. Subcultural variations in an urban population. *American Anthropologist* 73: 128–143. (p. 377)

Johnston, L. D., et al. 1985. *Use of licit and illicit drugs by America's high school students 1975–84*. Ann Arbor: University of Michigan Institute for Survey Research. (6) (pp. 201–202)

Jones, B. F. 1986. Quality and equality through cognitive instruction. *Educational Leadership* 43 (7): 5–11. (p. 527)

Jones, B. F.; Friedman, L. B.; Tinzmann, M.; and Cox, B. F. 1985. Enriched mastery learning: A model of enriched comprehension instruction. In *Improving student achievement through mastery learning programs*, edited by Daniel U. Levine. San Francisco: Jossey-Bass. (p. 528)

Jones, B. F., and Idol, L., eds. 1988. *Dimensions of thinking and cognitive instruction*. Hillsdale, NJ: Erlbaum. (p. 527)

Jones, B. F., and Spady, W. G. 1985. Enhanced mastery learning as a solution to the two sigma problem. In *Improving student achievement through mastery learning programs*, edited by Daniel U. Levine. San Francisco: Jossey-Bass. (p. 536)

Jones, E. F., et al. 1986. *Teenage pregnancy in industrialized countries*. New Haven, CT: Yale University Press. (p. 206)

Jones, K. M. 1986. The black male in jeopardy. *The Crisis*. 93 (3): 16–21, 44–47. (p. 375)

Jordan, C. 1984. Cultural compatibility and the education of Hawaiian children: Implications for mainland educators. *Education Research Quarterly* 8 (4): 59–69. (p. 427)

Joyce, B., and Showers, B. 1987. The power of school. *Phi Delta Kappan* 68: 352–355. (p. 101)

———. 1988. *Student achievement through staff development*. New York: Longman. (pp. 527, 539)

Justiz, M. J., and Kameen, M. C. 1987. Business offers a hand to education. *Phi Delta Kappan* 68 (5): 379–383. (p. 512)

Kagan, J. 1984. *The nature of the child*. New York: Basic Books. (p. 139)

Kagan, J., and Klein, R. E. 1973. Cross-cultural perspectives on early development. *American Psychologist* 28: 947–961. (p. 139)

Kahl, J. A. 1957. *The American class structure*. New York: Holt, Rinehart & Winston. (p. 40)

Kallen, H. M. 1924. *Culture and democracy in the United States*. New York: Boni and Liveright. (p. 364)

Karabel, J., and Halsey, A. H. 1977. Educational research: A review and interpretation. In *Power, ideology and education*, edited by J. Karabel and A. H. Halsey. New York: Oxford University Press, chapter 1. (p. 257)

Karoniaktatie. 1986. Indian unemployment commentary. *Awkesasne Notes* 18 (5): 11–13. (p. 418)

Kasarda, J. D. 1985. Urban change and minority opportunities. In *The new urban reality*, edited by Paul E. Peterson. Washington, DC: The Brookings Institution. (p. 376)

Kasarda, D. J., and Billy, J. O. G. 1985. Social mobility and fertility. In *Annual review of sociology*, edited by Ralph H. Turner and James F. Short, Jr. Palo Alto, CA: Annual Reviews. (pp. 222, 376)

Katz, I. 1964. Review of evidence relating to effects of desegregation on the intellectual performance of Negroes. *American Psychologist* 19: 381–399. (p. 309)

Kean, T. H. 1986. Who will teach? *Phi Delta Kappan* 68 (3): 205–207. (p. 503)

Keefe, S. E.; Reck, U. M. L.; and Reck, G. 1983. Ethnicity and education in Southern Appalachia: A review, *Ethnic Groups* 5: 199–226. (pp. 424, 426, 470)

Keith, T. Z., and Page, E. B. 1985. Do Catholic high schools improve minority students achievement? *American Educational Research Journal* 22 (3): 337–349. (p. 480)

Keniston, K. 1972. *Youth and dissent*. New York: Harcourt Brace Jovanovich. (pp. 181, 214)

Keniston, K., and the Carnegie Council on Children. 1977. *All our children: The American family under pressure.* New York: Harcourt Brace Jovanovich. (p. 131)

Kennedy, M. M. 1987. *The effectiveness of Chapter 1 services.* Washington, DC: U.S. Government Printing Office. (pp. 293, 306)

Kennedy, M. M.; Jung, R. K.; and Orland, M. E. 1986. *Poverty, achievement and the distribution of compensatory education services.* Washington, DC: U.S. Government Printing Office. (pp. 284, 293)

Kerewsky, W., and Lefstein, L. 1982. Young adolescents and their communities: A shared responsibility. In *3:00 to 6:00* P.M.*: Young adolescents at home and in the community,* edited by Leah M. Lefstein, et al. Carrboro, NC: Center for Early Adolescence, University of North Carolina at Chapel Hill. (p. 176)

Kerman, S. 1979. Teacher expectations and student achievement. *Phi Delta Kappan* 60: 716–718. (p. 535)

Kessler, C., and Quinn, M. E. 1977. Child-language development in two socio-economic environments. Paper presented at the annual meeting of the American Educational Research Association, April. (p. 273)

Kett, J. F. 1977. *Rites of passage: Adolescence in America 1970 to the present.* New York: Basic Books. (p. 178)

Kiesler, S., Sproull, L., and Eccles, J. S. 1983. Second-class citizens? *Psychology Today* 17 (3): 42–48. (p. 468)

Killian, J. E., and Byrd, D. M. 1988. Teachers' perspectives on what promotes instructional improvement in rural schools. Paper presented at the annual meeting of the American Educational Research Association, April. (p. 471)

Kim, H. 1977. Education of the Korean immigrant child. *Integrateducation* 15 (Jan.–Feb.): 15–18. (p. 428)

Kimball, S. T., and McClellan, J. E. 1962. *Education and the new America.* New York: Random House. (p. 40)

Kimmel, M. 1988. Ms. Scoutmaster. *Psychology Today* 22 (5): 64–65. (p. 175)

Kimmich, M. H. 1985. *America's children. Who cares?* Washington, DC: The Urban Institute. (p. 374)

Kimura, D. 1985. Male brain, female brain: The hidden difference. *Psychology Today* 19 (11): 50–58. (p. 448)

Kirsch, I. S., and Jungeblut, A. 1986. *Literacy: Profiles of America's young adults.* Princeton, NJ: Educational Testing Service. (pp. 54, 71)

Klapp, O. E. 1969. *Collective search for identity.* New York: Holt, Rinehart & Winston. (p. 102)

Klausmeier, H. J. 1985. *Educational psychology.* Harper and Row. (p. 528)

Klein, N. D. 1977. *Special education: Definition, law and policy.* Cleveland: Cleveland State University, mimeographed. (p. 141)

Klein, S. F., ed. 1985. *Handbook for achieving sex equity through education.* Baltimore: The Johns Hopkins University Press. (pp. 458, 465)

Klein, Z., and Eshel, Y. 1980. *Integrating Jerusalem's schools.* New York: Academic Press. (p. 326)

Klingelhofer, E. L., and Longacre, B. J. 1972. A case in point. *The Research Reporter* 7 (3): 5–7. (p. 298)

Knight, R. V. 1982. City development in advanced industrial societies. In *Cities in the 21st century,* edited by Gary Goppert and Richard V. Knight. Beverly Hills, CA: Sage. (pp. 87–88)

Kniker, C. R. 1985. Reflections on the continuing crusade for common schools: Glorious failures, shameful harvests, or . . . ? In *Religious schooling in America,* edited by James C. Carper and Thomas C. Hunt. Birmingham, AL: Religious Education Press. (pp. 489–490)

Kohlberg, L. 1966. Moral education in the schools: A developmental view. *School Review* 74: 1–29. (p. 178)

Kohn, M. L. 1969. *Class and conformity: A study in values.* Homewood, IL: Dorsey. (p. 234)

———. 1987. Cross-national research as an analytic strategy. *American Sociological Review* 52: 713–731. (p. 234)

Kohn, M. L., and Schooler, C. 1973. Occupational experience and psychological functioning: An assessment of reciprocal effects. *American Sociological Review* 38: 97–118. (p. 235)

Kolata, G. B. 1980. Math and sex: Are girls born with less ability? *Science* 210 (12): 1234–1235. (p. 446)

Kolstad, A. J., and Owings, J. A. 1986. *High school dropouts who change their minds about school.* Washington, DC: U.S. Department of Education. (p. 55)

Komisar, L. 1972. *The new feminism.* New York: Warner Books. (p. 464)

Konopka, G. 1977. *Young girls: A portrait of adolescence.* Englewood Cliffs, NJ: Prentice-Hall. (p. 174)

Koretz, D., and Vantresca, M. 1984. *Poverty among children.* Washington, DC: U.S. Congressional Budget Office. (pp. 35, 76, 125)

Korsters, M. H., and Ross, M. N. 1988. A shrinking middle class? *The Public Interest* 90: 3–27. (p. 30)

Kozberg, G., and Winegar, J. 1981. The South Boston story: Implications for secondary schools. *Phi Delta Kappan* 62 (April): 565–569. (p. 519)

Kozol, J. 1967. *Death at an early age.* Boston: Houghton Mifflin. (p. 305)

Kramer, R. 1986. The third wave. *Wilson Quarterly* 10 (4): 110–129. (p. 461)

Krashen, S. 1981. *Second language acquisition and second language learning.* Oxford: Pergamon. (p. 405)

Krol, R. A. 1980. A meta analysis of the effects of desegregation on academic achievement. *The Urban Review* 12: 211–224. (p. 325)

Krug, M. M. 1972. White ethnic studies: Prospects and pitfalls. *Phi Delta Kappan* 53: 322–324. (p. 366)

Kulieke, M. J.; Rosenbaum, J. E.; Rubinowitz, L. S.; and McCareins, A. C. 1985. The effects of residential integration on mother's educational and occupational expectations for their children. Paper presented at the annual meeting of the American Educational Research Association, Chicago, April (p. 355)

Kulik, C., and Kulik, J. A. 1982. Effects of ability grouping on secondary school students. *American Educational Research Journal* 19 (3): 415–428. (p. 49)

Kulik, C.; Kulik, J. A.; and Schwalb, B. J. 1982. College programs for high-risk and disadvantaged students: A meta-analysis of findings. Paper presented at the annual meeting of the American Educational Research Association, New York, March. (p. 298)

Kulik, J. A. 1983. Synthesis of research on computer-based instruction. *Educational Leadership* 41 (1): 19–21. (p. 467)

Kulik, J. A., and Kulik, C. C. 1987. Effects of ability groupings on student achievement. *Equity and Excellence* 23 (1–2): 22–30. (p. 49)

Kurth, R. J., and Stromberg, L. J. 1984. Improving the teaching of comprehension in elementary schools: A second year report. Paper presented at the annual meeting of the American Educational Research Association, New Orleans, April. (p. 534)

Kuttner, R. 1987. The patrimony society. *The New Republic* 196 (19): 18–21. (pp. 30, 38)

Kvaraceus, W. D., and Miller, W. B. 1959. Delinquent behavior: Culture and the individual. Washington, DC: National Education Association. (p. 198)

Kyle, D. L., Lane, J., Sween, J. A., and Triana, A. 1986. *We have a choice. Students at risk of leaving Chicago Public Schools.* Chicago: De Paul University Center for Research on Hispanics. (p. 546)

Lacayo, R. 1986. Spreading the wings of an idea. *Time* 128 (12): 61. (p. 513)

Lake, R. W. 1981. *The new suburbanites. Race and housing in the suburbs.* New Brunswick, NJ: Rutgers University. (pp. 77, 91)

Landers, L. A. Nontraditional vocational education leads women toward economic gain, PEER says. *Educational Daily* 27 (64): 4. (p. 450)

Landry, B. 1987. *The new black middle class.* Berkeley: University of California Press. (pp. 245, 373, 434)

Lang, D. 1987. Equality, prestige, and controlled mobility in the academic hierarchy. *American Journal of Education* 95 (3): 441–466. (p. 61)

Lanier, A. S. 1982. Let us now praise Catholic schools. *Chicago* 31 (10): 147–153. (p. 477)

Lanier, J. E. 1987. Letter from the president. *The Holmes Group Forum* No. 1: 1. (pp. 477, 502)

Laosa, L. M. 1977. Maternal teaching strategies in Mexican-American families: Socioeconomic factors affecting intra-group variability in how mothers teach their children. Paper presented at the annual meeting of the American Educational Research Association, April 8. (p. 137)

Lapointe, A. 1987. Test results provide data useful to educators planning to improve schools. *NASSP Bulletin* 71 (497): 73–78. (p. 53)

Lareau, A. 1987. Social class differences in family-school relationships: The importance of cultural capital. *Sociology of Education* 60: 73–85. (p. 234)

Larson, M. A., and Dittmann, F. E. 1975. *Compensatory education and early adolescence: Reviewing our national strategy.* EPRC 2158–7. Menlo Park, CA: Stanford Research Institute. (p. 294)

Lasch, C. 1977. *Haven in a heartless world: The family besieged.* New York: Basic Books. (pp. 149, 186)

———. 1978. *The culture of narcissism: American life in an age of diminishing expectations.* New York: Warner Books. (p. 186)

Lavin, D.; Alba, R. D.; and Silberstein, R. A. 1981. *Right vs. privilege.* New York: The Free Press. (p. 296)

Lavin, D.; Murtha, J.; Kaufman, B.; and Hyllegard, D. 1986. Long-term educational attainment in an open-access university system: Effects of ethnicity, economic status, and college type. Paper presented at the annual meeting of the American Educational Research Association, San Francisco, April. (p. 296)

Lawlor, J. 1987. Boston learns the business of education. *USA Today.* February 12: 1–2. (p. 513)

Lazar, I., et al. 1977. Preliminary findings of the developmental continuity longitudinal study. Paper presented at the Office of Child Development Conference on "Parents, Children, and Continuity," May. (p. 288)

Lazerson, M. 1986. Review of "A study of high schools." *Harvard Educational Review.* 56: 37–48. (p. 549)

Lee, H. 1960. *To kill a mockingbird.* Philadelphia: Lippincott. (p. 112)

Lee, R. H. 1955. *The city.* Philadelphia: Lippincott. (p. 91)

Lee, V. E., and Bryk, A. S. 1988. Curriculum tracking as mediating the social distribution of high school achievement. *Sociology of Education* 61: 78–94. (p. 481)

Leff, L. 1980. In inner-city schools, getting an education is often a difficult job. *The Wall Street Journal* February 5: 1, 18. (p. 281)

Leifer, A. D.; Gordon, N. J.; and Graves, S. B. 1975. Children's television: More than mere entertainment. *Harvard Educational Review* 44: 213–245. (p. 142)

Leinhardt, G., and Pallay, A. 1982. Restrictive educational settings: Exile or haven? *Review of Educational Research* 54 (4): 557–578. (pp. 267, 548)

Leming, J., and Hollifield, J. 1985. Cooperative learning: A research success story. *Educational Researcher* 14 (4): 28–29. (p. 331)

Lemlech, J. K. 1977. *Handbook for successful urban teaching.* New York: Harper & Row. (p. 306)

Lenski, G. 1961. *The religious factor.* New York: Doubleday. (p. 40)

Leontief, W. 1985. The choice of technology. *Scientific American* 252 (6): 37–45. (p. 28)

Lepper, M. R., and Chabay, R. W. 1985. Intrinsic motivation and instruction: Conflicting views on the role of motivational processes in computer-based education. *Educational Psychologist* 20 (4): 217–230. (p. 467)

Lerner, R. M., and Shea, J. A. 1982. Social behavior in adolescence. In *Handbook of developmental psychology,* edited by Benjamin Wolman. Englewood Cliffs, NJ: Prentice-Hall. (p. 155)

Levin, H. M. 1976. Educational opportunity and social inequality in western Europe. *Social Problems* 24: 148–172. (p. 248)

Levin, H. M.; Guthrie, J. W.; Kleindorfer, G. B.; and Stout, R. T. 1971. School achievement and postschool success: A review. *Review of Educational Research* 41: 1–16. (pp. 45, 299)

Levin, H. M., and Rumberger, R. W. 1985. Choosing a proactive role for education. *IFG Policy Perspectives* Summer: 1–4. (p. 28)

Levine, D. U. 1966. *Raising standards in inner city schools.* Washington, DC: Council for Basic Education. (p. 271)

———. 1968. Cultural diffraction in the social system of the low-income school. *School and Society* 96 (2306): 206–210. (p. 105)

———. 1972. The unfinished identity of metropolitan man. In *Teaching about life in the city.* The Forty-Second Yearbook of the National Council for the Social Studies, edited by Richard Wisniewski. Washington, DC: National Council for the Social Studies. (p. 109)

———. 1985. Key considerations for achieving success in mastery learning programs. In *Improving student achievement through master learning programs,* edited by Daniel U. Levine. San Francisco: Jossey-Bass. (pp. 273, 306, 536)

———. 1986. Update on the effective schools movement: Research and results. *Educator's Forum.* Fall: 2–3. (p. 554)

———. 1987. Mastery learning. *Educator's Forum* Fall: 12, 15. (p. 554)

Levine, D. U., ed. 1985. *Improving student achievement through mastery learning programs.* San Francisco: Jossey-Bass. (p. 556)

Levine, D. U., et al., 1972. The home environments of students in a high achieving inner-city parochial school and a nearly public school. *Sociology of Education* 45: 435–445. (pp. 109, 483)

———. 1979. Concentrated poverty and reading achievement in seven big cities. *The Urban Review* 11 (2): 63–80. (p. 275)

Levine, D. U., and Campbell, C. 1978. Magnet schools. In *Citizens guide to quality education: A report of the citizens' council for Ohio schools,* edited by Rachel B. Tompkins. Cleveland: Citizens' Council for Ohio Schools. (p. 334)

Levine, D. U., and Eubanks, E. E. 1986. The promise and limits of regional desegregation plans for central city school districts. *Metropolitan Education* 1 (1): 36–51. (pp. 350–351)

———. 1986–1987. Achievement improvement and non-improvement at concentrated schools in big cities. *Metropolitan Education* 1 (3): 92–107. (pp. 273, 500, 517, 553)

Levine, D. U.; Eubanks, E. E.; and Roskoski, L. S. 1980. *Social class and home background of magnet and non-magnet students.* Kansas City: University of Missouri–Kansas City School of Education. (p. 483)

Levine, D. U., and Havighurst, R. J., eds. 1977. *The future of big city schools: Desegregation policies and magnet alternatives.* Berkeley, CA: McCutchan. (p. 357)

Levine, D. U., and Leibert, R. E. 1987. Improving school improvement plans. *The Elementary School Journal* 87 (4): 397–412. (pp. 517, 542)

Levine, D. U., and Levine, R. F. 1977. The social and instructional setting for metropolitan integration. In *School desegregation in metropolitan areas: Choices and prospects,* edited by Ronald D. Henderson and Mary von Euler. Washington, DC: The National Institute of Education. (p. 346)

Levine, D. U.; Levine, R. F.; and Eubanks, E. E. 1984. Characteristics of effective inner city intermediate schools. *Phi Delta Kappan* (65): 707–711. (p. 518)

———. 1985. Successful implementation of instruction at inner-city schools. *Journal of Negro Education* 54: 313–331. (p. 267)

Levine, D. U., and Meyer, J. K. 1977. Level and rate of desegregation and white enrollment decline in a big city school district. *Social Problems* 24: 451–462. (p. 321)

Levine, D. U.; Mitchell, E. S.; and Havighurst, R. J. 1970. Family status, type of high school and college attendance. Kansas City: Center for the Study of Metropolitan Problems in Education. (pp. 164, 251–252, 275)

Levine, D. U., and Sherk, J. K. 1983. Organizational arrangements to increase productive time for reading in high schools.

Statement prepared for International Reading Association response to *A nation at risk.* (p. 521)

Levine, D. U., and Stark, J. 1982. Instructional and organizational arrangements that improve achievement in inner-city schools. *Educational Leadership* 40 (3): 41–48. (pp. 267, 515)

Levine, M., and Trachtman, R. 1988. *American business and the public school.* New York: Teachers College Press. (p. 513)

Levitan, S. A., and Mangum, G. L. 1969. *Federal training and work programs in the sixties.* Ann Arbor, MI: Institute of Labor and Industrial Relations. (p. 301)

Levy, F., and Michel, R. C. 1985. Are baby boomers selfish? *American Demographics* (4): 38–41. (p. 30)

———. 1986. *The economic future of the baby boom.* Washington, DC: The Urban Institute. (p. 29)

Lewis, A. C. 1986. ED's 'pro-choice' plan: If at first you don't succeed. *Phi Delta Kappan* 67 (5): 331–332. (pp. 401, 488)

———. 1987. Their hearts are as important as their heads. *Phi Delta Kappan* 68 (8): 572–573. (pp. 209–210)

———. 1988. We've been down this road before. *Phi Delta Kappan* (69)8: 548–549. (p. 28)

Lewis, H.; Kobak, S.; and Johnson, L. 1978. Family, religion, and colonialism in central Appalachia. In *Colonialism in modern America,* edited by L. L. Johnson and D. Askins. Boone, NC: Appalachian Consortium Press. (p. 425)

Lewis, O. 1961. *Children of Sanchez.* New York: Random House. (pp. 111, 263)

———. 1966. *La vida.* New York: Random House. (p. 111)

Lieberman, A., and Rosenholtz, S. 1987. The road to school improvement: Barriers and bridges. In *The ecology of school renewal,* edited by John I. Goodlad. Eighty-Sixth Yearbook of the National Society for the Study of Education, Part I. Chicago: University of Chicago Press. (pp. 540–542)

Lieberman, M. 1986. Why reform was 'dead on arrival.' *Education Week.* 5 (20): 20. (p. 499)

Liebow, E. 1967. *Tally's corner.* Boston: Little, Brown. (p. 21)

Ligon, G.; Hester, J.; Baenen, N.; and Matuszek, P. 1977. A study of the relationship between affective and achievement measures. Paper presented at the annual meeting of the American Educational Research Association, April. (p. 269)

Lindsay, B., ed. 1983. *Comparative perspectives of third world women,* 2nd ed. New York: Praeger. (p. 465)

Lines, P. M. 1986. The new private schools and their historic purpose. *Phi Delta Kappan* 67 (5): 373–379. (p. 476)

Link, F. R., ed. 1985. *Essays on the intellect.* Alexandria, VA: Association for Curriculum Development. (p. 528)

Lipkin, J. 1982. The troubling equity issue in computer education: Is computer literacy the answer or the problem? *Education Times* 3 (38): 7. (pp. 467–468)

Lipsitz, J. 1977. *Growing up forgotten: A review of research and programs concerning early adolescence.* Lexington, MA: Lexington Books. (pp. 174–175, 178)

Little, J. W. 1981. *School success and staff development: The role of staff development in urban desegregated schools.* Boulder, CO: Center for Action Research. (p. 540)

Lloyd, C. B., and Niemi, B. T. 1971. *The economics of sex differentials.* New York: Columbia University Press. (pp. 442, 465)

Lockheed, M. E. 1986. Determinants of student computer use: An analysis of data from the 1984 National Assessment of Educational Progress. Paper prepared for the Educational Testing Service Education Policy Research and Services Division, September. (p. 469)

Lockheed, M. E., et al. 1985. *Sex and ethnic differences in middle school mathematics, science and computer science: What do we know?* Princeton, NJ: Educational Testing Service. (p. 444)

Longanecker, D. 1982. What will it cost? *IFG Policy Perspectives.* Winter: 1–2. (p. 485)

Longman, P. 1985. Justice between generations. *The Atlantic* 255 (6): 73–81. (pp. 36–37)

Lotto, L. S. 1985. The unfinished agenda: Report from the National Commission on Secondary Vocational Education. *Phi Delta Kappan* 66: 568–573. (p. 64)

Lounsbury, J. H., and Johnston, J. H. 1985. *How fares the ninth grade? A day in the life of a ninth grader.* Washington, DC: National Association of Secondary School Principals. (p. 550)

Lucker, D. W.; Rosenfield, R.; Sikes, J.; and Aronson, R. 1976. Performance in the interdependent classroom: A field study. *American Education Research Journal* 13: 115–123. (p. 330)

Lynn, L. E., Jr. 1973. *The effectiveness of compensatory education: Summary and review of the evidence.* Report of the Assistant Secretary for Planning and Evaluation, U.S. Department of Health, Education and Welfare, Washington, DC. (p. 292)

———. 1977. A decade of policy developments in income maintenance systems. In *A decade of federal anti-poverty programs*, edited by Robert H. Haveman. New York: Academic Press. (p. 20)

Lyons, N. P. 1983. Two perspectives: On self, relationships, and morality. *Harvard Educational Review* 53 (2): 125–145. (p. 462)

Lyson, T. A. 1981. The changing sex composition of college curricula: A shift-share approach. *American Educational Research Journal* 18 (4): 503–511. (p. 442)

Lytle, J. 1988. Is special education serving minority students? *Harvard Educational Review* 58 (1): 116–120. (p. 140)

McAdoo, H. P., ed. 1981. *Black families.* Beverly Hills, CA: Sage. (p. 374)

Maccoby, E. E. 1958. *Readings in social psychology.* New York: Holt, Rinehart & Winston. (pp. 149, 235)

Maccoby, E. E., and Jacklin, C. N. 1974. *Psychology of sex differences.* Palo Alto, CA: Stanford University Press. (p. 446)

McCormack-Larkin, M. 1985. Ingredients of a successful school effectiveness project. *Educational Leadership* 42: 31–37. (pp. 350, 517)

McDill, E. L.; Natriello, G.; and Pallas, A. M. 1986. A population at risk: Consequences of tougher school standards for student dropouts. *American Journal of Education* 94: 135–181. (p. 510)

McGarry, D. D. 1982. The advantages and constitutionality of tuition tax credits. *Educational Freedom* 15 (2): 1–52. (p. 483)

MacGinitie, W. H., and MacGinitie, R. K. 1986. Teaching students not to read. In *Literacy, society, and schooling*, edited by Suzanne de Castell, Allan Luke, and Kieran Egan. Cambridge: Cambridge University Press. (p. 528)

McGuiness, D. 1979. How schools discriminate against boys. *Human Nature* February: 87–88. (p. 455)

McIntire, R. G.; Hughes, L. W.; and Say, M. W. 1982. Houston's successful desegregation plan. *Phi Delta Kappan* 63 (8): 536–538. (p. 338)

McKelvey, T. V., ed. 1973. *Metropolitan school organization.* Vol. 1, Basic problems and patterns. Vol. 2, Proposals for reform. Berkeley, CA: McCutchan. (p. 91)

McKinney, S., and Schnare, A. B. 1987. Trends in residential segregation by race: 1960–1980. Washington, DC: The Urban Institute. (p. 78)

McKnight, C. C., et al. 1987. *The underachieving curriculum.* Champaign, IL: Stipes. (p. 54)

McLaren, P. 1986. *Schooling as a ritual performance.* London: Routledge and Kegan Paul. (p. 552)

Macleod, D. I. 1983. *Building character in the American boy.* Madison: The University of Wisconsin Press. (5) (pp. 173–174, 178)

Mclure, W. P., and Pence, A. M. 1971. Early childhood and basic elementary and secondary education. In *Planning to finance education*, edited by Roe Johns et al. Gainsville, FL: National Education Finance Project. (p. 300)

McMahon, P. J., and Tschetter, J. H. 1986. The declining middle-class: A further analysis. *Monthly Labor Review* 109 (9): 21–24. (p. 30)

McMurrin, L. R. 1985. Magnet schools achieve excellence and racial balance. *The School Administrator* 42, No. 9: 28, 32. (p. 350)

McNeil, L. M. 1986. *Contradictions of control: School structure and school knowledge.* New

York: Routledge and Kegan Paul. (pp. 500, 529, 531, 551, 556)

———. 1988. Contradictions of control. *Phi Delta Kappan* 69 (6): 432–438. (pp. 500, 531, 551)

McPherson, M. 1986. Who should pay for college and when? *Change* May/June: 9. (p. 65)

Madaus, G. F. 1988. The influence of testing on the curriculum. In *Critical issues in curriculum*, edited by Laurel N. Tanner and Kenneth J. Rehage. Chicago: University of Chicago Press. (pp. 89, 509, 530)

Madden, N. A.; Stevens, R. J.; and Slavin, R. E. 1986. *Reading instruction in the mainstream: A cooperative learning approach.* Baltimore: The Johns Hopkins University Center for Research on Elementary and Middle Schools. (p. 537)

Maehr, M. L. 1983. *Motivational factors in school-achievement.* Washington, DC: U.S. Department of Education. (p. 270)

Maeroff, G. I. 1988. The empowerment of teachers: Overcoming the crisis of confidence. New York: Teachers College Press. (p. 511)

Magnet, M. 1987. America's underclass: What to do? *Fortune.* 115 (10): 130–150. (p. 22, 374, 376)

Mahoney, M. A. 1976. The American family: Centuries and decades of change. *National Elementary School Principal* 55 (May–June): 6–11. (pp. 130–131)

Mallar, C. D. 1979. A comprehensive evaluation of the Job Corps program. *The MPR Policy Newsletter* Spring: 4–6. (p. 301)

———. 1980. The economic impact of the Job Corps program. *The MPR Policy Newsletter* Fall: 9–12. (p. 301)

Mancini, J. K. 1981. *Strategic styles. Coping in the inner city.* Hanover, NH: University Press of New England. (p. 41)

Mann, D. M. 1986. Can we help dropouts: Thinking about the undoable. *Teachers College Record* 87: 307–324. (p. 547)

———. 1988. The honeymoon is over. *Phi Delta Kappan* (69) 8: 573–575. (p. 512)

Marino, C. D., and McCowan, R. J. 1976. The effects of parent absence on children. *Child Study Journal* 6 (March): 165–182. (p. 134)

Marjoribanks, K. 1972. Ethnic and environmental influences on mental abilities. *Journal of American Sociology* 78:323–336. (p. 137)

Marks, J. L. 1985. *The enrollment of black students in higher education: Can declines be prevented?* Atlanta: Southern Regional Education Board. (p. 384)

Marsh, D. D., and Berman, P. 1984. Conceptualizing the problem of increasing the capacity of schools to implement reform efforts. Paper presented at the annual meeting of the American Educational Research Association, New Orleans, April. (p. 540)

Marshak, R. E. 1981. Open access, open admissions, open warfare. Part one. *Change* 13 (8): 12–19, 51–53. (pp. 295–296)

———. 1982. Open access, open admissions, open warfare. Part two. *Change* 14 (1): 30–42. (p. 295)

Martin, J. 1986. Redefining the educated person: Rethinking the significance of gender. *Educational Researcher* 15 (6): 6–10. (pp. 463)

Martin, O. L. 1987. A comparative analysis of the educational plight of urban black and rural white high school students: Are their needs similar? Paper presented at the annual meeting of the American Educational Research Association, Washington, DC, April. (p. 471)

Marvin, M., et al. 1976. *Planning assistance programs to reduce school violence and disruption.* Washington, DC: U.S. Department of Justice, National Institute for Juvenile Justice and Delinquency Prevention. (pp. 282–283)

Marzano, R. J., et al. 1987. *Dimensions of thinking.* Alexandria, VA: Association for Supervision and Curriculum Development (draft). (pp. 525–528)

Massey, C. G.; Scott, M. V.; and Dornbusch, A. 1975. Racism without racists: Institutional reform in urban schools. *The Black Scholar* 7 (March): 3–11. (p. 269)

Mathes, W. A., and Carlson, R. V. 1986. Conditions for practice: The reasons teachers selected rural schools. Paper presented at the annual meeting of the American Educational Research Association, April. (p. 472)

Mathews, A., Jr. 1978. Perceived barriers. In *Desegregation and education concerns of the Hispanic community.* National Institute of Education Conference Report, June 26–28. Washington, DC: U.S. Government Printing Office. (p. 411)

Mayer, K. 1963. The changing shape of the American class structure. *Social Research* 30: 458–468. (p. 11)

Mayeske, G. W., et al. 1971. *A study of our nation's schools.* Washington, DC: U.S. Government Printing Office. (p. 241)

Mead, M., and Wolfenstein, M. 1955. *Childhood in contemporary cultures.* Chicago: University of Chicago Press. (p. 149)

Mecklenburger, J. A., and Hostrup, R. W., eds. 1972. *Education vouchers: From theory to Alum Rock.* Homewood, IL: ETC Publications. (p. 491)

Medrich, E. A. 1982. Time use outside school: Community services and facilities in the lives of young adolescents. In *3:00 to 6:00 P.M.: Young adolescents at home and in the community,* edited by Leah M. Lefstein, et al. Carrboro: Center for Early Adolescence, University of North Carolina at Chapel Hill. (p. 176)

Mensch, B. S., and Kandel, D. B. 1988. Dropping out of high school and drug involvement. *Sociology of Education* 61: 95–113. (p. 546)

Mercer, J. R. 1973. *Labelling the mentally retarded.* Berkeley, CA: University of California Press. (pp. 68, 137)

Mergendoller, J., et al. 1988. Task demands and accountability in middle-grade science classes. *The Elementary School Journal* 88 (2): 251–265. (p. 529)

Metz, M. H. 1986. *Different by design.* New York: Routledge and Kegan Paul. (pp. 306, 357)

Mielke, D. 1978. *Teaching mountain children.* Boone, NC: Appalachian Consortium Press. (p. 425)

Miles, M. B. 1983. Unraveling the mystery of institutionalization. *Educational Leadership* 41 (3): 14–19. (p. 540)

Miller, D. R., and Swanson, G. E. 1958. *The changing American parent.* New York: Wiley. (p. 149)

Miller, H. P. 1964. *Rich man, poor man: The distribution of income in America.* New York: Thomas Y. Crowell Company. (p. 16)

Miller, J. A. 1988. G.A.O. analysis says anti-drug efforts poorly evaluated. *Education Week* 7 (22): 16. (p. 204)

Miller, J. M., and Sidebottom, D. 1985. *Teachers. Finding and keeping the best in small and rural districts.* Washington, DC: The American Association of School Administrators. (pp. 471–472)

Miller, L. S. 1986. Nation-building and education. *Education Week.* 5 (34): 52. (p. 88)

Miller, S. E.; Leinhardt, G.; and Zigmond, N. 1987. Experiential features of secondary schooling for high risk LD students. Paper presented at the annual meeting of the American Educational Research Association, Washington, DC, April. (p. 531)

Miller, W. 1973. *Violence by youth group and youth groups as a crime problem in major American cities.* Washington, DC: U.S. Government Printing Office. (p. 282)

Millett, K. 1971. *Sexual politics.* New York: Avon. (p. 464)

Mills, C. J., and Noyes, H. L. 1984. Patterns and correlates of initial and subsequent drug use among adolescents. *Journal of Consulting and Clinical Psychology* 52: 231–243. (p. 203)

Mills, C. W. 1951. *White collar.* New York: Oxford University Press. (p. 40)

Milne, A.; Myers, D.; Rosenthal, A.; and Ginsburg, A. 1986. Single parents, working mothers, and the educational achievement of school children. *Sociology of Education* 59: 125–139. (p. 133)

Mirga, T. 1983. Busing will not help to desegregate Chicago schools, federal judge rules. *Education Week* 2 (17): 9, 19. (p. 345)

Mizokawa, D. T., and Moroshima, J. K. 1979. The education for, by, and of Asian/Pacific Americans, I and II. *Research Review of Equal Education* 3 (3 & 4): 1–33, 1–39. (p. 417)

Monaghan, P. 1987. A model project combats Indians' educational crisis. *The Chronicle of Higher Education* 38 (31): 3. (p. 423)

Montague, B. 1986a. Battles waged over in-school clinics. *Education Week* 5 (38): 4, 15. (p. 209)

———. 1986b. Rural educators say "networking" key. *Education Week* 6 (6): 5, 17. (p. 471)

Monti, D. J. 1985. *A semblance of justice.* Columbia: University of Missouri Press. (p. 357)

Moore, K. A.; Simms, M. C.; and Betsey, C. L. 1986. *Choice and circumstance.* New Brunswick, NJ: Transaction. (p. 207)

Morgan, H. 1980. How schools fail black children. *Social Policy* 10 (4): 49–54. (p. 263)

Morgan, R., ed. 1970. *Sisterhood is powerful: An anthology of writings from the women's liberation movement.* New York: Random House. (p. 464)

Morris, V. C., and Pai, Y. 1976. *Philosophy and the American school.* Boston: Houghton Mifflin. (p. 434)

Moss, H. A. 1967. Sex, age, and state as determinants of mother-infant interaction. *Merrill-Palmer Quarterly* 13 (1): 19–36. (p. 449)

Mosteller, F., and Moynihan, D. P., eds. 1972. *On equality of educational opportunity.* New York: Random House. (p. 241)

Mullin, S. P., and Summers, A. A. 1983. Is more better? The effectiveness of spending on compensatory education. *Phi Delta Kappan* 64 (5): 330–343. (p. 293)

Mumford, L. 1961. *The city in history.* New York: Harcourt Brace Jovanovich. (p. 91)

Musgrove, F. 1966. *The family, education, and society.* London: Routledge and Kegan Paul. (p. 97)

Muuss, R., ed. 1971. *Adolescent behavior and society: A book of readings.* New York: Random House. (p. 178)

Myers, D. E.; Milne, A. M.; Baker, K.; and Ginsburg, A. 1987. Student discipline and high school performance. *Sociology of Education* 60: 18–33. (p. 133)

Nachtigal, P. M. 1982. *Rural education.* Boulder, CO: Westview. (p. 475)

Nagel, T. 1986. A longitudinal study of systematic efforts to raise standardized test scores using factors from school effectiveness research. Paper presented at the annual meeting of the American Educational Research Association, April. (p. 553)

Nairn, A., et al. 1980. *The reign of ETS: The corporation that makes up minds.* Washington, DC: Nader and Associates. (p. 70)

Naisbitt, J. 1982. *Megatrends. Ten new directions transforming our lives.* New York: Warner Books. (p. 26)

Nasaw, D. 1985. *Children of the city.* New York: Oxford University. (p. 112)

Nathan, J. 1985. The rhetoric and the reality of expanding educational choices. *Phi Delta Kappan.* 66 (7): 476–481. (p. 488)

National Academy of Sciences. 1982a. *Families that work: Children in a changing world.* Washington, DC: National Academy Press. (p. 145)

———. 1982b. *Placing children in special education: A struggle for equity.* Washington, DC: National Academy Press. (p. 141)

National Advisory Commission on Civil Disorders. 1968. *Report of the National Advisory Commission on Civil Disorders.* Washington, DC: U.S. Government Printing Office. (p. 369)

National Advisory Council on Women's Educational Programs. 1982. *Educational equity: A continuing quest.* Washington, DC: U.S. Department of Education. (p. 457)

National Assessment of Educational Progress. 1981a. Three national assessments of reading: Changes in peformance, 1970–80. Washington, DC: U.S. Government Printing Office. (p. 444)

———. 1981b. Has Title I improved education for disadvantaged students? Evidence from three national assessments of reading. Report No. SY–DS–50. Denver: National Assessment of Educational Progress. (pp. 293, 444)

———. 1981c. Private students read better, but . . . . *NAEP Newsletter* 14 (1): 3. (p. 480)

———. 1985. *The reading report card.* Princeton, NJ: Educational Testing Service. (pp. 50, 52–53, 119–120, 143, 382, 444)

———. 1987. *Learning to be literate.* Princeton, NJ: Educational Testing Service. (pp. 383–384)

National Black Child Development Institute. 1985. *Child care in the public schools: Incubator of inequality?* Washington, DC: National Black Child Development Institute. (p. 126)

National Catholic Education Association. 1987. *United States Catholic elementary and secondary schools, 1986–87.* Washington, DC: National Catholic Education Association. (pp. 475–477)

National Center for Education Statistics. 1981. *The condition of education.* Washington, DC: U.S. Government Printing Office. (pp. 444, 476)

———. 1982. *Projections of non-English background and limited English proficient persons in the United States to the year 2000.* Washington, DC: U.S. Government Printing Office. (p. 392)

———. 1984. *Two years after high school.* Washington, DC: U.S. Government Printing Office. (pp. 58, 381)

———. 1985. *The condition of education.* Washington, DC: U.S. Government Printing Office. (pp. 47, 56, 444)

National Commission on Excellence in Education. 1983. *A nation at risk: The imperative for educational reform.* Washington, DC: U.S. Government Printing Office. (pp. 496, 555)

National Commission on Secondary Vocational Education. 1984. *The unfinished agenda.* Columbus, OH: National Center for Research in Vocational Education. (p. 63)

National Commission on Youth. 1980. *The transition from youth to adulthood: A bridge too long.* Boulder, CO: Westview Press. (p. 184)

National Governors' Association. 1986. *Time for Results: The governors' 1991 report on education.* Washington, DC: National Governors' Association. (pp. 506, 555)

———. 1987. *Bringing down the barriers.* Washington, DC: National Governors' Association Center for Research. (pp. 547, 555)

National Institute on Drug Abuse. 1977. *Marijuana and health.* Sixth annual report to the U.S. Congress. Washington, DC: U.S. Government Printing Office. (p. 203)

National Institute of Education. 1978. *Violent schools—safe schools.* Washington, DC: U.S. Government Printing Office. (p. 521)

National School Boards Association. 1988. *A national imperative: Educating for the 21st century.* Washington, DC: National School Boards Association. (p. 302)

National Science Foundation. 1982. *Teletext and videotext in the United States.* New York: McGraw-Hill. (p. 127)

National Society for the Study of Education. 1975. *Youth,* edited by Robert J. Havighurst and Philip H. Dreyer. Seventy-Fourth Yearbook, Part 1. Chicago: University of Chicago Press. (p. 214)

National Task Force on Educational Technology. 1986. *Transforming American education: Reducing the risk to the nation.* Washington, DC: U.S. Office of Education Office of Educational Research and Improvement. (p. 470)

Neinhuis, M. 1986. Early-intervention plan's effects mixed. *Education Week* 6 (13): 9. (p. 287)

Neugarten, B. L. 1949. The democracy of childhood. In *Democracy in Jonesville,* edited by W. Lloyd Warner and Associates. New York: Harper and Row. (pp. 156–157)

Neugarten, B. L., and Neugarten, D. A. 1987. The changing meanings of age. *Psychology Today* 21 (5): 29–33. (pp. 173, 439)

Nevi, C. 1987. In defense of tracking. *Educational Leadership* 44 (6): 24–26. (p. 50)

Newcomb, T. H. 1970. Open admissions: Before the deluge. Paper prepared for distribution at the Closing General Session of the National Conference on Higher Education sponsored by the American Association for Higher Education, March 4. (p. 297)

Newcomer, M. 1959. *A century of higher education for American women.* New York: Harper & Row. (p. 464)

Newitt, J., et al. 1984. *School-to-work transition programs: A policy analysis.* Croton-on-Hudson, NY: Hudson Institute. (p. 190)

Newson, J., and Newson, E. 1976. *Seven years old in the home environment.* London: George Allen Unwin, Ltd. (pp. 238–239)

Niedermeyer, F., and Yelon, S. 1981. Los Angeles aligns instruction with essential skills. *Educational Leadership* 38 (8): 618–620. (p. 515)

Nottelmann, E. D. 1982. Children's adjustment in school: The interaction of physical maturity and school transition. Paper presented at the annual meeting of the American Educational Research Association, March 20. (p. 161)

Novak, M. 1971. *The rise of the unmeltable ethnics.* New York: Macmillan. (pp. 365–366, 433)

Nuttall, E. V., et al. 1976. The effects of family size, birth order, sibling separation and crowding on the academic achievement of boys and girls. *American Educational Research Journal* 13: 217–223. (p. 136)

NWREL. 1987. Principals praise the effective practices in Indian education training. *The Northwest Report* February: 5. (p. 428)

Oakes, J. 1985. *Keeping track.* New Haven, CT: Yale University Press. (p. 49)

Odden, A., and Vincent, P. E. 1976. *The fiscal impact of declining enrollments in four states—Michigan, Missouri, South Dakota, and Washington.* Denver: Education Commission of the States. (p. 302)

Office of Educational Research and Improvement. 1988. *Trends in minority enrollment in higher education.* Washington, DC: U.S. Department of Education. (pp. 58, 375, 426)

Ogbu, J. U. 1978. *Minority education and caste: The American system in cross-cultural perspective.* New York: Academic Press. (pp. 223, 377)

———. 1982. Social forces as a context of ghetto children's school failure. In *The language of children reared in poverty,* edited by Lynne Feagans and Dale Clark Farran. New York: Academic Press. (pp. 140, 223, 377–378, 434)

———. 1988. A commentary. In Stephen F. Hamilton, *The interaction of family, community, and work in the socialization of youth.* Washington, DC: William T. Grant Foundation Commission on Youth and America's Future. (p. 377)

O'Keefe, M. 1986. College costs. *Change* May/June: 6–8. (pp. 64, 66)

Olneck, M. R., and Bills, D. B. 1980. What makes Sammy run? An empirical assessment of the Bowles-Gintis correspondence theory. *American Journal of Education* 89 (1): 27–61. (p. 252)

Olson, D. H., and Miller, B. C., eds. 1983. *Family studies review yearbook.* Beverly Hills, CA: Sage. (p. 150)

Olson, L. 1986a. Many bilingual pupils unaided, study finds. *Education Week* 5 (17): 1, 17. (p. 405)

———. 1986b. Carnegie report: A 'powerful synthesis' that raises both hopes and questions. *Education Week* 5 (31): 1, 18. (pp. 501–502)

———. 1987a. Certification panel gets cool reception from some administrators. *Education Week* 6 (35): 1, 16. (p. 510)

———. 1987b. Performance-based pay systems for teachers are being re-examined. *Education Week* 6 (29): 1, 16–17. (p. 510)

———. 1987c. Reforms 'Doomed,' says panel, without early family aid. *Education Week* 7 (1): 1, 43. (p. 507)

O'Reilly, R. P. 1969. *Racial and social class isolation in the schools.* New York: New York State Department Division of Research Office of Research and Evaluation. (p. 279)

Orfield, G. 1977. Response II. In *Language ethnicity, and the schools: Policy alternatives for bilingual-bicultural education.* Washington, DC: The George Washington University Institute for Educational Leadership. (p. 412)

———. 1981. *Toward a strategy for urban integration. Lessons in school and housing policy from twelve cities.* New York: Ford Foundation. (pp. 353–354)

———. 1982. Desegregation of black and Hispanic students from 1968 to 1980. Paper prepared for the Joint Center for Political Studies. (pp. 312, 392)

———. 1987. Racial change in U.S. enrollments, 1968–1984. The University of Chicago National School Desegregation

Project Working Papers, No. 1. (pp. 34, 313, 411)

Orfield, G., and Monfort, F. 1987. Are American schools resegregating in the Reagan era? The University of Chicago National School Desegregation Project Working Papers, No. 14. (pp. 313–314, 392)

Ornstein, A. C.; Levine, D. U.; and Wilkerson, D. A. 1975. *Reforming metropolitan schools.* Pacific Palisades, CA: Goodyear. (p. 306)

Orr, J. B., and Nichelson, P. F. 1970. *The radical suburb.* Philadelphia: Westminster Press. (pp. 101–102)

Ortega Gassett, J. 1958. *Man and crisis.* New York: Norton. (p. 102)

Otto, L. B. 1982. Extracurricular activities. In *Improving educational standards and productivity,* edited by Herbert J. Walberg. Berkeley, CA: McCutchan. (p. 167)

Owen, S. A., and Ranick, D. L. 1977. The Greenville program: A commonsense approach to basics. *Phi Delta Kappan* 58: 531–533. (p. 271)

Pacheco, L. C. 1977. Educational renewal: A bilingual-bicultural imperative. *Educational Horizons* 55: 168–176. (p. 403)

Page, E. B., and Grandon, G. M. 1979. Family configurations and mental ability: Two theories contrasted with U.S. data. *American Educational Research Journal* 16: 257–272. (p. 136)

Page, E. B., and Keith, T. Z. 1981. Effects of U.S. private schools: A technical analysis of two recent claims. *Harvard Educational Review* 51 (4): 497–509. (p. 480)

Palincsar, A. S. 1987. Reciprocal teaching: Field evaluations in remedial and content-area reading. Paper presented at the annual meeting of the American Educational Research Association, Washington, DC, April. (pp. 527–528)

Pallas, A. M. 1986. *The determinants of high school dropout.* Baltimore: The Johns Hopkins University Center for Social Organization of Schools Report No. 364. (p. 546)

Pallas, A. M., and Alexander, K. L. 1983. Sex differences in quantitative SAT performance. New evidence on the differential coursework hypothesis. *American Educational Research Journal* 20 (2): 165–182. (p. 446)

Palmer, F. H., n.d. *The effects of minimal early intervention on subsequent IQ scores and reading achievement.* Stony Brook, NY: State University of New York. (p. 287)

Panel on Adolescent Pregnancy and Childbearing. 1986. *Risking the future: Adolescent sexuality, pregnancy, and childbearing.* Washington, DC: National Research Council. (p. 209)

Panel on Policies and Prospects for Metropolitan and Nonmetropolitan America. 1980. *Urban America in the eighties: Perspectives and prospects.* Washington, DC: U.S. Government Printing Office. (p. 79)

Panel on Secondary School Education for the Changing Workplace. 1984. *High schools and the changing workplace.* Washington, DC: National Academy Press. (p. 29)

Papagiannis, G. J.; Klees, S. J.; and Bickel, R. N. 1982. Toward a political economy of educational innovation. *Review of Educational Research* 52: 245–290. (p. 250)

Parker, J. G., and Asher, S. R. 1986. Predicting long term outcomes from peer rejection: Studies of dropping out, delinquency, and adult psychopathology. Paper presented at the annual meeting of the American Educational Research Association, San Francisco, April 1986. (pp. 153–154)

Pascal, A. 1977. *What do we know about school desegregation?* Santa Monica, CA: The Rand Corporation, P–5777. (pp. 326–327)

Passow, A. H. 1970. *Reaching the disadvantaged learner.* New York: Teachers College, Columbia University. (p. 306)

———. 1984. Tackling the reform reports of the 1980s. *Phi Delta Kappan* 65 (10): 674–683. (p. 498)

———. 1988. Issues of access to knowledge. In *Critical issues in curriculum,* edited by Laurel N. Tanner and Kenneth J. Rehage. Chicago: University of Chicago Press. (pp. 48, 547)

Patchen, M. 1982. *Black-white contact in schools: Its social and academic effects.* West Lafayette, IN: Purdue University Press. (p. 324)

Patterson, O. 1979. The black community: Is there a future? In *The third century: America as a post-industrial society*, edited by Seymour Martin Lipset. Stanford, CA: Hoover Institution. (pp. 78–79)

Pavuk, A. 1987. Families with children constitute third of the homeless, mayors say. *Education Week* 6 (34): 12. (pp. 147, 475)

Payne, C. M. 1984. *Getting what we ask for.* Westport, CT: Greenwood. (pp. 242, 306, 531)

Payzant, T. W. 1988. Standards board makes significant gains. *The School Administrator* 45 (2): 29–31. (p. 502)

Pearce, D. 1980. Breaking down barriers: New evidence on the impact of metropolitan school desegregation on housing patterns. Washington, DC: National Center for Desegregation Policy. (p. 352)

Pearson, D. P. 1985. *The comprehension revolution: A twenty-year history of process and practice related to reading comprehension.* University of Illinois at Urbana—Champaign Center for the Study of Reading Report No. 57. (p. 527)

Pebley, A. R., and Bloom, D. E. 1982. Childless Americans. *American Demographics* 4 (1): 18–21. (p. 126)

Peng, S. S. 1982. *Effective high schools: What are their attributes?* Washington, DC: National Center for Education Statistics. (p. 480)

———. 1985. Enrollment patterns of Asian American students in post-secondary education. Paper presented at the annual meeting of the American Educational Research Association. Chicago, April. (p. 417)

Peng, S. S.; Fetters, W. B.; and Kolstad, A. J. 1981. *High school and beyond: A national longitudinal study for the 1980s.* National Center for Educational Statistics. Washington, DC: U.S. Government Printing Office. (pp. 444–445)

Personik, V. A. 1985. A second look at industry output and employment trends to 1985. *Monthly Labor Review* 198 (11): 26–41. (pp. 26–27)

Peshkin, A. 1986. *God's choice.* Chicago: The University of Chicago Press. (p. 492)

Petersen, A. C. 1980. Biopyschosocial processes in the development of sex-related differences. In *The psychobiology of sex differences and sex roles*, edited by J. E. Parson. New York: Hemispheric Publishing Corporation. (p. 447)

Peterson, P. E. 1985. *The politics of school reform 1870–1940.* Chicago: University of Chicago Press. (p. 259)

Peterson, R. A., and DeBord, L. 1966. *Supportiveness of the home and academic performance of disadvantaged boys.* Nashville: George Peabody College for Teachers Institute of Mental Retardation and Intellectual Development. (p. 137)

Pettigrew, T. F. 1971. *Racially separate or together?* New York: McGraw-Hill. (p. 369)

———. 1973. Busing: A review of the evidence. *The Public Interest* (Winter): 81–118. (p. 327)

———. 1978. Report to the Superior Court of the State of California for the County of Los Angeles, November 14. (pp. 331, 393)

———. 1985. New black-white patterns: How best to conceptualize them? In *Annual review of sociology*, edited by Ralph H. Turner and James F. Short, Jr. Palo Alto, CA: Annual Reviews. (p. 388)

Pfeifer, J. K. 1986. *Teenage suicide: What can the schools do?* Bloomington, IN: Phi Delta Kappa. (p. 188)

Phelps, E. B. 1980. Youth groups and agencies. In *Toward adolescence: The middle school years*, edited by Mauritz Johnson. Seventy-Ninth Yearbook of the National Society for the Study of Education, Part I. Chicago: University of Chicago Press. (p. 175)

Phi Delta Kappa. 1980. *Why do some urban schools succeed?* Bloomington, IN: Phi Delta Kappa. (p. 514)

Philadelphia Public Schools. 1977. Test scores continue to rise. *Perspective: An In-Depth Look at the Philadelphia Public Schools* June. (p. 289)

Piaget, J. 1932. *The moral judgment of the child.* New York: Harcourt Brace Jovanovich. (p. 178)

Pierce, C. M.; Carew, J. V.; and Willis, D. 1977. An experiment in racism: TV commercials. *Education and Urban Society* 10 (November): 61–87. (p. 143)

Pileggi, N. 1977. How fifteen-year-olds get away with murder. *New York* 10 (June 13): 36–44. (p. 128)

Pincus, F. L. 1980. The false promises of community colleges: Class conflict and vocational education. *Harvard Educational Review* 50 (August): 332–361. (p. 91)

Pipho, C. 1986a. States move reform closer to reality. *Phi Delta Kappan.* 68 (4): K1–K8. (p. 498)

———. 1986b. Technology erases boundaries. *Education Week* 5 (32): 23. (p. 474)

Plisko, V., and Stern, J. D. 1985. *The condition of education.* Washington, DC: National Center for Education Statistics. (p. 55)

Pollock, L. A. 1983. *Forgotten children.* Cambridge: Cambridge University Press. (p. 96)

Porat, M. 1977. *Information economy: Definition and measurement.* Washington, DC: U.S. Department of Commerce. (p. 26)

Porter, A. G., et al. 1986. Content determinants. Michigan State University Institute for Research on Teaching Research Series Paper No. 179. (p. 528)

Porter, P. R. 1976. *The recovery of American cities.* New York: Two Continents. (pp. 86–87, 90)

Portes, A., and Wilson, K. L. 1976. Black-white differences in educational attainment. *American Sociological Review* 41: 414–431. (pp. 246, 384)

Poulos, R. W.; Rubenstein, E. A.; and Liebert, R. M. 1975. Positive social learning. *Journal of Communications* 25 (Autumn): 90–97. (p. 142)

Powell, A. G. 1985. Being unspecial in the shopping mall high school. *Phi Delta Kappan* 67: 255–261. (pp. 530, 551)

Prager, J.; Longshore, D.; and Seeman, M. 1986. *School desegregation research.* New York: Plenum. (p. 358)

Presseisen, B. Z. 1987. *Thinking skills throughout the curriculum.* Bloomington, IN: Pi Lambda Theta. (pp. 527–528)

Preston, S. H. 1984. Children and the elderly in the U.S. *Scientific American* 251 (6): 44–49. (pp. 34, 37)

Pride, C. A., and Woodard, D. 1985. *The burden of busing.* Knoxville: The University of Tennessee Press. (p. 489)

Purkey, S., and Smith, M. S. 1983. Effective schools: A review. *The Elementary School Journal* 83 (4): 427–452. (p. 517)

Purpel, D. 1988. *The moral and spiritual crisis in education.* South Hadley, MA: Bergin and Garvey. (p. 259)

Putnam, J.; Roehler, L. R.; and Duffy, G. R. 1987. *The staff development model of the teacher explanation project.* Michigan State University Institute for Research on Teaching Occasional Research Paper No. 108. (p. 534)

Quantz, R. A. 1981–82. Mild mental retardation and race. *Educational Studies* 12 (Winter): 387–393. (p. 140)

Rainwater, L. 1970. *Behind ghetto walls: Black families in a federal slum.* Chicago: Aldine. (pp. 100, 111)

Rainwater, L.; Coleman, R. P.; and Handel, G. 1959. *Workingman's wife.* New York: Oceana Publications. (p. 40)

Ramirez, M. III. 1976. Cultural democracy through bilingual education. *Consortium Currents* 3 (Spring–Summer): 11–15. (p. 413)

Ramirez, M. III and Castaneda. 1974. *Cultural democracy, bicognitive development, and education.* New York: Academic Press. (p. 413)

Ramos, M. 1980. The hippies: Where are they now? In *Drugs and the youth culture*, edited by Frank R. Scarpitti and Susan K. Datesman. Beverly Hills, CA: Sage. (p. 204)

Ranbow, S., and Sirkin, J. R. 1985. Minorities and college: 'A time bomb.' *Education Week* 4 (30): 1, 13–14. (p. 385)

Randour, M. L.; Strasburg, G. L.; and Lipman-Blumen, J. 1982. Women in higher education: Trends in enrollments and degrees earned. *Harvard Educational Review* 52 (2): 189–202. (p. 451)

Rankin, S. C. 1983. A view from the schools. In *Staff development*, edited by Gary A. Griffin. Eighty-Second Yearbook of the National Society for the Study of Education, Part II. Chicago: University of Chicago Press. (pp. 539–540)

Raspberry, W. 1976. The discipline revival. *Washington Post* February 2. (p. 171)

Raudenbush, S., and Bryk, A. S. 1986. A hierarchical model for studying school effects. *Sociology of Education* 59 (1): 1–17. (p. 480)

Ravitch, D. 1977. *The revisionists revised: Studies in the historiography of American education.* Proceedings of the National Academy of Education 4. Palo Alto, CA, pp. 1–84. (p. 253)

Raywid, M. A. 1987. Public choice, yes; Vouchers, no! *Phi Delta Kappan* 68 (10): 762–769. (pp. 338, 486, 489)

———. 1984. Synthesis of research on schools of choice. *Educational Leadership* 45 (7): 70–78. (p. 338)

———. 1988. The accomplishments of schools of choice. Paper prepared for the U.S. Department of Education. (p. 338)

Read, M. S. 1976. *Malnutrition, learning, and behavior.* Washington, DC: National Institute for Child Health and Human Development, Center for Research for Mothers and Children. DHEW Publication No. 76–1036. (p. 139)

Rehberg, R. A., and Rosenthal, E. 1975. *Class and merit in the American high school: A multistudy analysis.* Binghamton: State University of New York at Binghamton Center for Comparative Political Research, Paper no. 27. (pp. 165, 257)

Reinhard, B. 1987. Sex, drugs, and dropping out: Governors come face to face with real world. *Education Daily* 20 (132): 3–4. (p. 546)

Reiss, A. J., Jr. 1961. *Occupations and social status.* New York: The Free Press. (p. 3)

Resnick, D. P., and Resnick, L. B. 1985. Standards, curriculum, and performance. *Educational Researcher* 14 (4): 5–20. (pp. 88–90, 299)

Restak, R. M. 1979. The other differences between girls and boys. *Educational Leadership* 37: 232–235. (p. 455)

Rhine, R. W. 1981. *Making schools more effective: New directions from follow through.* New York: Academic Press. (p. 306)

Rice, E. E. 1981. Should the family protection act be passed? Yes. *Update on Law-Related Education* 5 (2): 19–20, 65. (p. 131)

Richardson, R. C. 1985. How are students learning? *Change* 17 (3): 43–49. (p. 244)

Riesman, D., et al. 1950. *The lonely crowd.* New Haven: Yale University Press. (pp. 13, 25)

Riessman, F. 1962. *The culturally deprived child.* New York: Harper & Row. (pp. 112, 306)

Rist, R. C. 1973. *The urban school: A factory for failure.* Cambridge, MA: MIT Press. (p. 266)

———. 1981. Walking through a house of mirrors: Youth education and employment training. *Education and Urban Society* (November): 3–14. (p. 189)

———. 1986. *Finding work.* New York: Falmer. (p. 214)

Roberts, J. L. 1982. Boston schools worry about costs and crime as much as education. *The Wall Street Journal* May 13: 1, 22. (p. 303)

Robey, B. 1983. Speaking of Hispanics. *American Demographics* 5 (6): 2–4. (p. 392)

Robinson, V. 1981. Community colleges: Education's biggest growth industry has an uncertain mission. *Education Times* November 23. (p. 91)

Rodman, B. 1988. Push for reform 'dying,' says Futrell. *Education Week* 7 (27): 4. (p. 499)

Rodriguez, A. 1975. Introduction. *Inequality in Education* 3 (February). (p. 402)

Rodriguez, R. 1982. *The hunger of memory.* Boston: Godine. (pp. 112, 432)

Rollings, E. M., and Nye, F. I. 1979. Wife-mother employment, family, and society. In *Contemporary theories about the family,* edited by Wesley R. Burr, Reuben Hill, F. Ivan Nye, and Ira L. Reiss, Vol. 1. New York: The Free Press. (p. 145)

Rollins, B. C., and Thomas, D. L. 1979. Parental support, power, and control techniques in the socialization of children. In *Contemporary theories about the family,* edited by W. R. Burr, et al. New York: Free Press. (pp. 120–121)

Rölvaag, O. E. 1927. *Giants in the earth.* New York: Harper. (p. 433)

Ropers, R. H. 1985. The rise of the urban homeless. *Public Affairs Report* 26 (5–6): 1–14. (pp. 146–147)

Rose, E. 1986. Drug-education programs widespread, but vary greatly in content. *Education Week* 5 (26): 7. (p. 205)

Rose, H. 1982. The future of black ghettos. In *Cities in the 21st century*, edited by Gary Goppert and Richard V. Knight. Beverly Hills, CA: Sage. (p. 77)

Rosen, B. C. 1959. Race, ethnicity, and the achievement syndrome. *American Sociological Review* 24: 47–60. (p. 222)

Rosenbaum, J.; Rubinowitz, L.; and Kulieke, M. 1985. *Low-income black children in white suburban schools.* Evanston, IL: Northwestern University. (pp. 354–355)

Rosenbaum, J. E. 1976. *Making inequality*. New York: John Wiley. (p. 91)

Rosenbaum, J. E.; Kulieke, M. J.; and Rubinowitz, L. S. 1987. Low-income black children in white suburban schools. *The Journal of Negro Education.* 56 (1): 35–43. (p. 354)

Rosenberger, L. 1985. Letting in 'latchkey' children. *New York Times* August 18: 5.12, 17–18. (p. 145)

Rosenholtz, S. 1977. The multiple abilities curriculum: An intervention against the self-fulfilling prophecy. Ph.D. dissertation, Stanford University. (p. 330)

Rosenshine, B. V. 1976. Classroom instruction. In *The psychology of teaching methods*, edited by N. L. Gage. Chicago: University of Chicago Press.

———. 1986. Synthesis of research on explicit teaching. *Educational Leadership.* 43 (7): 60–69. (p. 525)

Rosenshine, B. V., and Stevens, R. 1986. Teaching functions. In *Handbook of research on teaching*, edited by Merlin C. Wittrock. New York: Macmillan. (p. 525)

Rossell, C. 1987. *The carrot or the stick in school-desegregation policy*. Washington, DC: U.S. Department of Education. (p. 315)

Rossi, P. H., and Rossi, A. S. 1961. Some effects of parochial school education in America. *Daedalus* 90 (Spring): 300–328. (p. 40)

Rotberg, I. C. 1982. Some legal and research considerations in establishing federal policy in bilingual education. *Harvard Educational Review* 52 (2): 149–168. (pp. 404, 407)

Rothchild, J., and Wolf, S. B. 1976. *The children of the counterculture*. Garden City, NY: Doubleday. (p. 112)

Rothman, R. 1986. Raise status of teaching, colleges told. *Education Week* 6 (9): 7. (p. 59)

———. 1987a. Mathematics scores show U.S. is a "nation of underachievers." *Education Week* 6 (17): 1, 20–21. (p. 54)

———. 1987b. Schools, businesses form partnerships in 7 cities. *Education Week* 6 (22): 4. (p. 514)

———. 1988. 'Computer competence' still rare among students, assessment finds. *Education Week* 7 (29): 1, 20. (p. 468)

Rubel, R. J. 1980. Extent, perspectives, and consequences of violence and vandalism in public schools. In *Violence and crime in the schools*, edited by Keith Baker and Robert J. Rubel. Lexington, MA: D.C. Heath. (p. 281)

Rubin, L. G. 1976. *Worlds of pain: Life in the working-class family*. New York: Basic Books. (pp. 99,112)

Rubin, S. E., and Spady, W. G. 1984. Achieving excellence through outcome-based instructional delivery. *Educational Leadership* 41 (8): 37–44. (p. 536)

Rumberger, R. W. 1987. High school dropouts: A review of issues and evidence. *Review of Educational Research* 57: 101–121. (p. 546)

Russell, C. 1983. The news about Hispanics. *American Demographics* 5 (3): 15–25. (p. 391)

———. 1985. The new homemakers. *American Demographics* 7 (10): 23–27. (p. 440)

Rustin, B. 1987. The King to come. *The New Republic* 196 (10): 19–21. (p. 389)

Ryan, F. A. 1982. The federal role in American Indian education. *Harvard Educational Review* 52 (4): 423–430. (p. 422)

Ryan, J. A. 1973. *White ethnics: Their life in working-class America.* Englewood Cliffs, NJ: Prentice-Hall. (p. 112)

Ryder, N. B. 1974. The family in developed countries. *Scientific American* 231 (3): 123–132. (pp. 129–130)

Sadker, M., and Sadker, D. 1985. Sexism in the classroom: From grade school to graduate school. *Phi Delta Kappan* 67 (7): 512–515. (p. 454)

Safilios-Rothschild, C. 1979. *Sex role socialization and sex discrimination: A synthesis and critique of the literature.* Washington, DC: National Institute of Education. (pp. 449, 453)

St. John, N. H. 1975. *School desegregation: Outcomes for children.* New York: Wiley. (p. 324)

Salzman, S. A. 1988. Father absence, socioeconomic status, and race: Relations to children's cognitive performance. Paper presented at the annual meeting of the American Educational Research Association, April. (p. 133)

Sanday, P. R. 1972. *On the causes of IQ differences between groups and the implications for social policy considerations.* Pittsburgh: School of Urban and Public Affairs, Carnegie-Mellon University. (p. 68)

Sanders, J. W. 1977. *The education of an urban minority: Catholics in Chicago, 1833–1965.* New York: Oxford University Press. (pp. 475, 491)

Scarr, S. 1981a. Implicit messages. *American Journal of Education* 89: 330–338. (p. 69)

———. 1981b. *IQ: Race, social class and individual differences. New studies of old problems.* Hillsdale, NJ: Lawrence Erlbaum Associates. (p. 69)

Schacter, F. F. 1979. *Everyday mother talk to toddlers: Early intervention.* New York: Academic Press. (pp. 379, 408)

Schmuck, R. A., and Runkel, P. J. 1985. *The Handbook of Organizational Development in Schools,* 3rd ed. Palo Alto, CA: Mayfield. (p. 540)

Schneir, M., ed. 1972. *Feminism: The essential historical writings.* New York: Vintage Books. (p. 464)

Schnore, A. B. 1977. *Residential segregation by race in U.S. metropolitan areas: An analysis across cities and over time.* Washington, DC: The Urban Institute.

Schramm, W.; Lyle, J.; and Parker, E. E. 1960. *Television in the lives of our children.* Palo Alto, CA: Stanford University Press. (p. 127)

Schreiner, T. 1986. California's minority majority. *American Demographics* 8 (4): 39. (p. 391)

Schunk, D. H. 1987. Peer models and children's behavioral change. *Review of Educational Research* 57: 149–174. (p. 154)

Schwartz, J. 1988. Closing the gap. *American Demographics* 10 (1): 29, 41. (p. 442)

Schwartz, R., and Hargroves, J. 1986–87. The Boston compact. *Metropolitan Education* No. 3: 14–24. (pp. 513–514)

Schwartz, T. 1988. Daisy Tsui. *New York* 21 (17): 115, 117. (p. 414)

Schweinhart, L. J. 1987. What is and is not implied in the study of three preschool curriculum models. Paper presented at the annual meeting of the American Education Research Association. Washington, DC, April. (p. 288)

Schweinhart, L. J., and Weikart, D. P. 1977. Research report—can preschool education make a lasting difference? *Bulletin of the High/Scope Foundation* 4 (Fall): 1–4. (p. 287)

———. 1980. *Young children grow up: The effects of the Perry Preschool Program on youths through age 15.* Ypsilanti, MI: High/Scope Educational Research Foundation. (p. 287)

———. 1985. Evidence that good early childhood programs work. *Phi Delta Kappan* 66 (8): 545–553. (p. 300)

Scott, K. P., and Schau, C. G. 1985. Sex equity and sex bias in instructional materials. In *Handbook for achieving sex equity through education,* edited by Susan S. Klein. Baltimore: Johns Hopkins University Press. (pp. 453–454)

Scott, R. R., and McPartland, J. M. 1982. Desegregation as national policy. Correlates of racial attitudes. *American Educational Research Journal* 19 (3): 397–414. (p. 329)

Scriven, M. 1975. Problems and prospects for individualization. In *Systems of individualized education,* edited by Harriet Talmadge. Berkeley, CA: McCutchan. (p. 548)

Sears, R. R.; Maccoby, E. E.; and Levin, H. 1957. *Patterns of child rearing.* Evanston, IL: Row, Peterson. (p. 149)

Sederberg, C. H. 1986. Economic role of school districts in rural communities. Paper presented at the annual meeting of the American Education Research Association, San Francisco, April. (p. 472)

Sedlak, M. W.; Wheeler, C. W.; Pullin, D. C.; and Cusick, P. A. 1986. *Selling students short.* New York: Teachers College Press. (pp. 530, 533, 549)

Select Committee. 1986. *Safety net programs: Are they reaching poor children?* Washington, DC: U.S. House of Representatives Select Committee on Children, Youth, and Families. (pp. 28, 208)

Select Committee on Children, Youth, and Families. 1986. *Teen pregnancy: What is being done?* Washington, DC: U.S. Government Printing Office. (p. 205)

———. n.d. *Teen pregnancy in the U.S. A fact sheet.* Washington, DC: U.S. House of Representatives. (p. 206)

Sennett, R. 1973. Middle-class families and urban violence. The experience of a Chicago community in the nineteenth century. In *The American family in social-historical perspective,* edited by Michael Gordon. New York: St. Martin's Press. (p. 103)

Shade, B. J. 1982. Afro-American cognitive style: A variable in school success? *Review of Educational Research* 52 (2): 219–244. (p. 265)

Shakeshaft, C., and Trachtman, R. 1986–87. Business as usual: Exploring private sector participation in American public schools. *Metropolitan Education* No. 3: 25–31. (p. 512)

Shanker, A. 1988. Opting out of the old stuff. *The New York Times* April 3: E–9. (p. 498)

Shavelson, R. T. 1985. Schemata and teaching routines: A historic perspective. Paper presented at the annual meeting of the American Educational Research Association. Chicago, April. (p. 531)

Shea, B. M. 1976. Schooling and its antecedents: Substantive and methodological issues in the status attainment process. *Review of Educational Research* 46: 463–526. (pp. 229, 241, 246)

Sheff, D. 1988. Portrait of a generation. *Rolling Stone* No. 525: 46–65. (p. 187)

Shepherd-Look, D. L. 1982. Sex differentiation and the development of sex roles. In *Handbook of developmental psychology,* edited by B. Wolman. Englewood Cliffs, NJ: Prentice-Hall. (pp. 134, 448)

Sher, J. P. 1983. Education's ugly duckling: Rural schools in urban nations. *Phi Delta Kappan* 65 (4): 257–262. (p. 471)

Sherman, J. 1977. Effects of biological factors on sex-related differences in mathematics achievement. In *Women and mathematics: Research perspectives for change,* edited by L. H. Fox and E. Fennema. Washington, DC: National Institute of Education. (pp. 446–447)

Shipman, V. C., et al. 1976. *Disadvantaged children and their first school experiences.* Princeton, NJ: Educational Testing Service. (p. 122)

Shoemaker, J. 1982. Effective schools: Putting the research to the ultimate test. *Pre Post Press* 2: 1–2. (p. 515)

Shorter, E. 1975. *The making of the modern family.* New York: Basic Books. (pp. 95–97, 129, 168)

Shostak, A. B., and Gomberg, W., eds. 1964. *Blue-collar world.* Englewood Cliffs, NJ: Prentice-Hall. (p. 40)

Shulman, L. S. 1987. Knowledge and teaching: Foundations of the new reform. *Harvard Educational Review.* 57 (1): 1–22. (p. 511)

Siegal, A. E. 1975. Communicating with the next generation. *Journal of Communication* 25 (Autumn): 14–24. (p. 127)

Sinclair, R. L., and Ghory, W. J. 1987. *Reaching marginal students.* Berkeley, CA: McCutchan. (pp. 544–545)

Singer, R. N. 1977. To err or not to err: A question for the instruction of psychomotor skills. *Review of Educational Research* 47: 479–498. (p. 299)

Sirois, H. A., and Davis, R. L. 1985. *School improvement through instructional design: Matching teaching strategies and instruc-*

tional materials to students. New York: The College Board. (pp. 527–528, 538)

Sirotnik, K. A. 1987. Evaluation in the ecology of schooling: The process of school renewal. In *The ecology of school renewal,* edited by John I. Goodlad. Eighty-Sixth Yearbook of the National Society for the Study of Education, Part I. Chicago: University of Chicago Press. (pp. 539, 542–543)

Sizemore, B. A. 1985. Pitfalls and promises of effective schools research. *Journal of Negro Education* 54: 269–288. (pp. 534, 548)

Sizer, T. R. 1984. *Horace's compromise.* Boston: Houghton Mifflin. (pp. 530–531, 551)

Skeels, H. M. 1966. *Adult status of children with contrasting early life experiences.* Monograph of the Society for Research in Child Development, 31, no. 6, Serial 105. Chicago: University of Chicago Press. (pp. 117, 139)

Skeels, H. M., and Dye, H. B. 1939. *A study of the effect of differential stimulation on mentally retarded children.* Proceedings and addresses of the American Association of Mental Deficiency. 44 (1): 114–136. (pp. 116–117)

Sklonick, A., and Skolnick, J. H., eds. 1971. *Family in transition.* Boston: Little, Brown. (p. 150)

Skovholt, J. 1978. Feminism and men's lives. *Counseling Psychologist* April: 3–10. (p. 455)

Slavin, R. E. 1977a. *Student team learning techniques: Narrowing the achievement gap between the races.* Baltimore: The Johns Hopkins University Center for Social Organization of Schools, Report No. 228. (p. 330)

———. 1977b. *Student learning team and scores adjusted for past achievement: A summary of field experiments.* Baltimore: The Johns Hopkins University Center for Social Organization of Schools, Report No. 227. (p. 330)

———. 1980. Cooperative learning. *Review of Educational Research* 50: 315–342. (pp. 331, 358, 537)

———. 1983. *Cooperative learning.* New York: Longman. (pp. 331, 537)

———. 1986. How ability grouping affects student achievement in elementary schools. *CREMS* June: 2–4 (p. 548)

———. 1987. Grouping for instruction in the elementary school. *Educational Psychologist* 22 (2): 109–127. (p. 267)

Slavin, R. E.; Madden, N. A.; and Leavey, M. 1984. Combining cooperative learning and individualized instruction: Effects on mathematics, attitudes, and behavior. *Elementary School Journal* 84: 409–422. (p. 537)

Smith, B. 1965. *They closed their schools: Prince Edward County, Virginia, 1951–64.* Chapel Hill: University of North Carolina Press. (p. 357)

Smith, G. P. 1986. Unresolved issues and new developments in teacher competency testing. *Urban Educator* 8 (1): 1–16. (p. 426)

Smith, J. K., and Wick, J. W. 1976. Practical problems of attempting to implement a mastery learning program in a large city school system. Paper presented at the annual meeting of the American Educational Research Association, April 19–23. (p. 273)

Smith, J. P. 1982. Race and human capital. Paper prepared for a conference of the National Academy of Education, Chicago, May. (p. 247)

Smith, J. P., and Welch, F. R. 1986. *Closing the gap.* Santa Monica, CA: Rand. (pp. 384, 385–386)

Snider, W. 1987a. Massachusetts district backs plan to integrate its students on basis of language, not race. *Education Week* 6 (20): 1, 15. (p. 341)

———. 1987b. New York's dropout data reanalyzed. *Education Week* 6 (24): 17. (p. 82)

———. 1987c. Study finds rise in cocaine smoking. *Education Week* 6 (24): 9. (pp. 203–204)

Snow, C. E.; Dubber, C.; and De Blauw, A. 1982. Routines in mother-child interaction. In *The language of children reared in poverty,* edited by Lynne Feagans and Dale Clark Farran. New York: Academic Press. (p. 238)

Soled, S. W. 1987. Teaching processes to improve both higher as well as lower mental process achievement. Paper presented at the annual meeting of the American Educational Research Association, Washington, DC: April. (p. 534)

———. 1988. Does mastery learning improve higher order thinking as well as rote learning? Paper presented at the annual meeting of the American Educational Research Association, New Orleans, April. (p. 534)

Soltis, J. F. 1987. *Reforming teacher education: The impact of the Holmes Group Report.* New York: Teachers College Press. (p. 556)

Sonenstein, F. 1985. *Risking paternity: Sex and contraception among adolescent males.* Washington, DC: Urban Institute. (pp. 207–208)

Sørensen, A. B., and Hallinan, M. T. 1986. Effects of ability grouping on growth in academic achievement. *American Educational Research Journal* 23: 529–542. (p. 49)

Sowell, T. 1974. Black excellence: The case of Dunbar high school. *The Public Interest* Spring: 5–12. (p. 522)

———. 1978a. Ethnicity in changing America. *Daedalus* (Winter) 107: 213–237. (pp. 69, 222, 364)

———, ed. 1978b. *American ethnic groups.* Washington, DC: Urban Institute. (p. 222)

———. 1981. *Ethnic America.* New York: Basic Books. (pp. 220–222, 225, 259)

Spady, W. G. 1983. The illusion of reform. *Educational Leadership* 41 (1): 31–32. (p. 499)

Spectorsky, A. C. 1955. *The exurbanites.* Philadelphia: J. B. Lippincott. (p. 40)

Spenner, K. I. 1985. The upgrading and downgrading of occupations: Issues, evidence, and implications for education. *Review of Educational Research* 55: 125–154. (p. 27)

Spitz, H. R. 1986. *The raising of intelligence: A selected history of attempts to raise retarded intelligence.* Hillsdale, NJ: Erlbaum. (pp. 118, 288)

"The split-level economy." 1986. *The New Republic* No. 3712 (March 10): 5–6. (p. 30)

Squires, D. A.; Huitt, W. G.; and Segars, J. K. 1983. *Effective schools and classrooms: A research-based perspective.* Washington, DC: Association for Supervision and Curriculum Development. (p. 517)

Stafford, F. P. 1987. Women's work, sibling competition, and children's school performance. *The American Economic Review* 77 (5): 972–980. (pp. 130, 136)

Stalford, C. B. 1977. Historical perspectives on disruption and violence in schools. Paper presented at the annual meeting of the American Educational Research Association. New York, April 5. (p. 282)

Staples, R., and Mirandé, A. 1980. Racial and cultural variations among American families: A decennial review of the literature on minority families. *Journal of Marriage and the Family* 42 (4): 887–902. (pp. 374–375, 414–415)

Steel, L., and Schubert, J. G. 1983. The effectiveness of Upward Bound in preparing disadvantaged youth for postsecondary education. Paper presented at the annual meeting of the American Educational Research Association, Montreal, April. (p. 294)

Steelman, L. C. 1985. A tale of two variables: A review of the intellectual consequences of sibship size and birth order. *Review of Educational Research* 55: 353–386. (p. 136)

Steelman, L. C., and Doby, J. T. 1983. Family size and birth order as factors on the IQ performance of black and white children. *Sociology of Education* 56: 101–109. (p. 136)

Steen, L. A. 1987. Mathematics education: A predictor of scientific competitiveness. *Science* 237 (July 17): 251–252, 303. (p. 55)

Stein, J. A.; Newcomb, M. D.; and Bentler, P. M. 1987. An 8-year study of multiple influences on drug use and drug use consequences. *Journal of Personality and Social Psychology* 53 (6): 1094–1105. (p. 203)

Steinberg, A. 1988. Cultural differences in the classroom. *The Harvard Education Letter* 4 (2): 1–4. (p. 427)

Steinberg, S. 1981. *The ethnic myth: Race, ethnicity, and class in America.* New York: Atheneum. (pp. 223–224)

Stendler, C. B. 1949. *Children of Brasstown.* Urbana: Bureau of Research and Service of the College of Education, University of Illinois. (p. 40)

Stephan, W. G., and Feagin, J. R., eds. 1980. *School desegregation: Past, present, and future.* New York: Plenum. (p. 357)

Stephenson, R. S., and Levine, D. U. 1987. Are effective or meritorious schools meretricious? *The Urban Review* 19 (1): 25–34. (p. 522)

Sternberg, R. J. 1984. What should intelligence tests test? *Educational Researcher* 13 (1): 5–15. (p. 70)

Sternlieb, G. 1974. The city as sandbox. In *Suburban dynamics and the future of the city*, edited by James W. Hughes. New Brunswick, NJ: Rutgers University Center for Urban Policy Research. (p. 75)

Sternlieb, G., and Burchell, R. W. 1973. *Residential abandonment.* New Brunswick, NJ: Rutgers University. (p. 74)

Sternlieb, G., and Hughes, J. W. 1988. Black households. *American Demographics* 10 (4): 35–37. (pp. 28, 373)

Stimson, J. 1986. Battlelines on vouchers are drawn clearly. *The School Administrator* 43 (2): 25–26. (p. 488)

Stinchcombe, A. L. 1964. *Rebellion in a high school.* Chicago: Quadrangle. (p. 197)

Stinchcombe, A. L.; Medill, M. J.; and Walker, D. 1969. Is there a racial tipping point in changing schools? *Journal of Social Issues* 25: 127–136. (p. 321)

Stockard, J. 1980. Sex inequities in the experiences of students. In *Sex equity in education*, edited by J. Stockard et al. New York: Academic Press. (p. 445)

Stone, L. 1974. The massacre of the innocents. *The New York Review of Books* 21 (November 14): 25–31. (pp. 97–98, 129)

Stonehill, R. M., and Anderson, J. I. 1982. *An evaluation of ESEA Title I—program operations and education effects.* Washington, DC: U.S. Government Printing Office. (p. 293)

Strasburg, P. A. 1978. *Violent delinquents: A report to the Ford Foundation from the Vera Institute of Justice.* New York: Monarch. (pp. 197, 200)

Strauss, A. L. *Images of the city.* New York: The Free Press. (p. 91)

Stringfield, S., and Teddlie, C. 1987. A time to summarize: Six years and three phases of the Louisiana school effectiveness study. Paper presented at the annual meeting of the American Educational Research Association. Washington, DC, April. (p. 523)

Strodtbeck, F. L. 1958. Family interaction, values and achievement. In *Talent and society*, by David C. McClelland, Alfred L. Baldwin, Urie Bronfenbrenner, and Fred L. Strodtbeck. Princeton, NJ: D. Van Nostrand, chapter 4. (p. 222)

Strother, D. B. 1984. Latchkey children: The fastest-growing special interest group in the schools. *Phi Delta Kappan* 66 (4): 290–293. (p. 146)

Study Group. 1987. *The nation's report card.* Cambridge, MA: National Academy of Education. (pp. 507–508)

Subcommittee on Civil and Constitutional Rights of the U.S. House of Representatives Committee on the Judiciary. 1982. *School desegregation.* Washington, DC: U.S. Government Printing Office. (p. 314)

Suttles, G. D. 1968. *The social order of the slum: Ethnicity and territory in the inner city.* Chicago: University of Chicago Press. (pp. 40, 259)

Svanum, S.; Ringle, R. G.; and McLaughlin, J. E. 1982. Father absence and cognitive performance in a large sample of six- to eleven-year-old children. *Child Development* 53: 136–143. (pp. 133–134)

Sweet, D. A. 1986. Extracurricular activity participants outperform other students. *OERI Bulletin* September. (p. 166)

Taggart, R. 1982. Lessons from experience with employment and training programs for youth. In *Education and work*, edited by Harry F. Silberman. Eighty-First Yearbook of the National Society for the Study of Education, Part II. Chicago: University of Chicago Press. (pp. 192–193)

Takei, Y. 1981. Asian-Pacific education after Brown and Lau. Paper presented at the annual meeting of the American Educational Research Association, Los Angeles, April. (p. 414)

Tallman, I., and Morgner, R. 1970. Life-style differences among urban and suburban blue-collar families. *Social Forces* 48: 334–348. (p. 99)

Teske, S. 1987. Governor warns of polarization of society without education reforms. *Education Daily* 20 (29): 4. (p. 78)

———. 1988. Students lack knowledge and training to use computers, NAEP says. *Education Daily* 21 (65): 1–2. (p. 468)

Thomas, G. E.; Alexander, K. L.; and Eckland, B. K. 1977. *Access to higher education: How important are race, sex, social class, and academic credentials for college access?* Baltimore: The Johns Hopkins University Center for Social Organization of Schools, Report No. 226. (p. 384)

Thomas, P. 1967. *Down these mean streets.* New York: New American Library. (pp. 40, 263)

Thomas, T. C., and Pelavin, S. H. 1976. Patterns in ESEA Title I reading achievement. Project 4537. Menlo Park, CA: Stanford Research Institute. (p. 292)

Thornberry, T. 1987. Toward an interactional theory of delinquency. *Criminology* 25 (4): 863–891. (p. 200)

Thornburg, H. D. 1979. Can the middle school adapt to the needs of its students? *Colorado Journal of Educational Research* 19 (1): 26–29. (p. 161)

———. 1980. Developmental characteristics of middle schoolers and middle school organization. Paper presented at the annual meeting of the American Educational Research Association, Boston, April 8. (pp. 156, 161)

Tikinoff, W. J. 1985. *Applying significant bilingual instructional features in the classroom.* Rosslyn, VA: InterAmerica Research Associates. (p. 409)

Tinto, V. 1978. Does schooling matter? A retrospective assessment. In *Review of research in education 5*, edited by Lee S. Shulman. Itasca, IL: Peacock. (p. 258)

———. 1981. Higher education and occupational attainment in segmented labor markets: Recent evidence from the United States. *Higher Education* 10: 499–516. (p. 233)

Tittle, C. R.; Villenez, W. J.; and Smith, D. A. 1978. The myth of social class and criminality: An empirical assessment of the empirical evidence. *American Sociological Review* 43: 643–656. (p. 196)

Tobias, S., and Weissbrod, G. 1980. Anxiety and mathematics: An update. *Harvard Educational Review* 50 (1): 63–70. (pp. 445, 452)

Treiman, D. J. 1977. *Occupational prestige in comparative perspective.* New York: Academic Press. (p. 4)

Troike, R. C. 1981. Synthesis of research on bilingual education. *Educational Leadership* 38 (6): 498–504. (pp. 401, 405)

Tsang, S-L., and Wing, L. C. 1985. *Beyond Angel Island: The education of Asian Americans.* Oakland, CA: ARC Associates. (pp. 415–416)

Tucker, E. 1977. The follow through planned variation experiment: What is the payoff? Paper presented at the annual meeting of the American Educational Research Association, April 5. (p. 290)

Tugend, A. 1984. Suicide: Unsettling worry for schools. *Education Week* 4 (9): 1, 12–13. (p. 188)

———. 1986. Suicide's "unanswerable logic." *Education Week* 5 (39): 15–19. (p. 188)

Turow, J. 1981. *Entertainment, education, and the hard sell. Three decades of network children's television.* New York: Praeger. (p. 145)

Tussing, A. D. 1975. Emergence of the new unemployment. *Intellect* 103: 303–311. (p. 41)

Tye, K. A. 1985. *The junior high school. School in search of a mission.* Lanham, MD: University Press of America. (p. 163)

Tyler, R. W., ed. 1978. *From youth to constructive adult life: The role of the public school.* Berkeley, CA: McCutchan. (p. 214)

Tyson-Bernstein, H. 1987. The Texas Teacher Appraisal System: What does it really appraise? *American Educator* 11 (1): 26–31. (p. 512)

United States Bureau of the Census. 1960. *U.S. Census of population: 1960 final report PC–1B.* Washington, DC: U.S. Government Printing Office. (pp. 75, 182)

———. 1967. *Social and economic conditions of Negroes in the United States.* Current Population Reports, Series P–23, No. 24, October. (p. 19)

———. 1970. *U.S. Census of population: 1970 final report, PC (1A)*. Washington, DC: U.S. Government Printing Office. (pp. 73, 75)

———. 1975. *Current Population Reports*. Series P–25, No. 601. Washington, DC: U.S. Government Printing Office. (p. 182)

———. 1977. *Social indicators. 1976*. Washington, DC: U.S. Government Printing Office. (p. 126)

———. 1980. *Current population reports*. Series P–20, No. 354. Washington, DC: U.S. Government Printing Office. (pp. 75, 361)

———. 1981. *Current population reports*. Series P–20, No. 347; Series P–60, No. 124. Washington, DC: U.S. Government Printing Office. (p. 372)

———. 1984. *Projections of the population of the United States, by age, sex, and race: 1983 to 2080*. Washington, DC: U.S. Government Printing Office. (pp. 31–33)

———. 1985. *Current Population Reports*. Series P–20, No. 403. Washington, DC: U.S. Government Printing Office. (p. 395)

———. 1986. *Current population reports*. Series P–25, No. 998. Washington, DC: U.S. Government Printing Office. (p. 32)

———. 1987. *After-school care of schoolage children: December 1984*. Series P–23, No. 149. Washington, DC: U.S. Government Printing Office. (p. 145)

United States Bureau of Labor Statistics. 1977. *Working women: A data book*. Washington, DC: U.S. Government Printing Office. (p. 441)

———. 1982. *Labor force statistics*. Washington, DC: U.S. Department of Labor. (p. 441)

United States Commission on Civil Rights. 1972. *The excluded student: Educational practices affecting Mexican Americans in the Southwest*. Mexican-American Educational Series, Report III. Washington, DC: U.S. Government Printing Office. (p. 397)

———. 1974. *Toward quality education for Mexican-Americans*. Washington, DC: U.S. Government Printing Office. (p. 397)

———. 1982a. *Unemployment and underemployment among blacks, Hispanics, and women*. Washington, DC: U.S. Government Printing Office. (p. 442)

———. 1982b. *Youth unemployment*. Washington, DC: U.S. Government Printing Office. (p. 194)

———. 1985. *Recent activities against citizens and residents of Asian descent*. Washington, DC: U.S. Government Printing Office. (p. 415)

United States Department of Education. 1982. *Digest of education statistics*. Washington, DC: U.S. Government Printing Office. (p. 46)

———. 1987. *Schools that work. Educating disadvantaged children*. Washington, DC: U.S. Government Printing Office. (p. 556)

United States Department of Education and United States Department of Labor. 1988. *The bottom line: Basic skills in the workplace*. Washington, DC: U.S. Department of Labor. (p. 27)

United States Department of Health, Education and Welfare. 1975. *Sex stereotyping in children's readers*. Washington, DC: U.S. Government Printing Office, p. 35. (p. 453)

United States Department of Health and Human Services. 1982. *Television and behavior: Ten years of scientific progress and implications for the eighties*. Vol. 1. Summary report. Washington, DC: U.S. Government Printing Office. (p. 142)

United States Department of Labor. 1977. *Employment and training report of the president*. Washington, DC: U.S. Government Printing Office. (p. 373)

———. 1981. Employment and earnings. Washington, DC: U.S. Department of Labor. (p. 373)

United States General Accounting Office. 1980. *CETA demonstration provides lessons on implementing youth programs*. Washington, DC: U.S. Government Printing Office. (p. 193)

———. 1986. *School dropouts*. Washington, DC: U.S. Government Accounting Office. (pp. 55, 57)

United States Office of Education. 1975. *Digest of education statistics*. Washington, DC: U.S. Government Printing Office. (p. 265)

———. 1977. *Instructional strategies in schools with high concentrations of low-income pupils.* Washington, DC: U.S. Office of Education. (pp. 265–266)

United States Public Health Service, Panel of Scientists. 1972. *Report to the Surgeon-General on television violence.* Washington, DC: U.S. Government Printing Office. (p. 142)

United States Senate Subcommittee to Investigate Juvenile Delinquency. 1977. *Our nation's schools—a report card: "A" in school violence and vandalism.* Washington, DC: U.S. Government Printing Office. (pp. 282–283)

Useem, E. L. 1986. *Low tech education in a high tech world.* New York: Free Press. (p. 64)

Valverde, L.; Feinberg, R. C.; and Marquez, E. 1980. *Educating English-speaking Hispanics.* Washington, DC: Association for Supervision and Curriculum Development. (p. 433)

Vanfossen, B. E.; Jones, J. D.; and Spade, J. Z. 1987. Curriculum tracking and status maintenance. *Sociology of Education* 60: 104–122. (pp. 47, 50, 165)

Vargas, J. S. 1986. Instructional design flaws in computer-assisted instruction. *Phi Delta Kappan* 67 (10): 738–744. (p. 467)

Venezky, R. L.; Kaestle, C. F.; and Sum, A. M. 1987. *The subtle danger.* Princeton, NJ: Educational Testing Service. (p. 54)

Vernon, R. 1961. *Metropolis, 1985.* Cambridge, MA: Harvard University Press. (p. 90)

Veroff, J.; Douvan, E.; and Kulka, R. A. 1981. *The inner American: A self-portrait.* New York: Basic Books. (pp. 184, 187)

Viadero, D. 1986a. Drug education: Search for success continues. *Education Week* 6 (5): 1, 11. (p. 205)

———. 1986b. Studies link media coverage to increase in teen-age suicide rate. *Education Week* 6 (3): 5. (p. 188)

———. 1987a. Apparent link between media coverage and 'copycat' suicides worries experts. *Education Week* 6 (28): 1, 20. (p. 188)

———. 1987b. Detroit student's murder provokes angry outcry. *Education Week* 6 (32): 1, 17. (pp. 76, 195, 282)

———. 1987c. More and more students are juggling conflicting demands of school, work. *Education Week* 6 (34): 1, 17. (p. 195)

Vinovskis, M. A. 1986. *The origins of public high schools.* Madison: University of Wisconsin Press. (p. 259)

Violas, P. C. 1978. *The training of the urban working class: A history of twentieth-century American education.* Chicago: Rand McNally. (p. 257)

Wachs, T. D., Uzgiris, I. C., and Hunt, J. McV. 1971. Cognitive development in infants of different age levels and from different environmental backgrounds. *Merrill-Palmer Quarterly* 17: 282–317. (p. 121)

Wagenaar, T. C. 1981. High school seniors' views of themselves and their schools: A trend analysis. *Phi Delta Kappan* 63 (1): 29–32. (pp. 184, 187)

Waggoner, D. 1978. Geographic distribution, nativity, and age distribution of language minorities in the United States: Spring 1976. *National Center for Education Statistics Bulletin* August 22. (p. 392)

Waite, L. J. 1981. U.S. women at work. *Population Bulletin* 36 (2): 3–43. (p. 442)

Walberg, J. J., and Marjoribanks, K. 1976. Family environment and cognitive development: Twelve analytic models. *Review of Educational Research* 46: 527–551. (pp. 135–136)

Walker, C. R., and Guest, R. H. 1952. *The man on the assembly line.* Cambridge, MA: Harvard University Press. (p. 40)

Wall, M. 1986. Technological options for rural schools. *Educational Leadership* 43 (6): 50–52. (p. 474)

Walsh, D. I. 1986. What women want. *American Demographics* 8 (6): 60. (p. 437)

Warner, W. L. 1953. *American life: Dream and reality.* Chicago: University of Chicago Press. (p. 39)

Warner, W. L., and associates. 1949. *Democracy in Jonesville.* New York: Harper & Row. (pp. 7–8, 39)

Warner, W. L., and Lunt, P. S. 1941. *The social life of a modern community.* New Haven, CT: Yale University Press. (pp. 8, 39)

Warner, W. L.; Meeker, M.; and Eells, K. 1960. *Social class in America.* New York: Harper Torchbooks. (pp. 2–3, 8, 40)

Washington, B. T. 1963. *Up from slavery.* Garden City, NY: Doubleday. (p. 433)

Wasserman, H. L. 1972. A comparative study of school performance among boys from broken and intact black families. *The Journal of Negro Education* 41: 137–141. (p. 135)

Weaver, R. C. 1964. The city and its suburbs. *New City* 2 (March): 4–6. (p. 85)

Webb, M. 1987. Peer helping relationships in urban schools. *Clearinghouse on Urban Education Digest* 37: 1–2. (p. 160)

Weber, C. U.; Foster, P. W.; and Weikart, D. P. 1978. *An economic analysis of the Ypsilanti Perry Preschool Project.* Monographs of the High/Scope Educational Research Foundation, No. 5. (p. 300)

Weed, J. A. 1982. Divorce: Americans' style. *American Demographics* 4 (3): 13–17. (p. 124)

Wehlage, G., and Rutter, R. 1986. Dropping out: How much do schools contribute to the problem? *Teachers College Record* 87 (3): 374–392. (p. 546)

Wehlage, G. G.; Rutter, R. A.; and Turnbaugh, A. 1987. A program model for at-risk high school students. *Educational Leadership* 44: 70–73. (pp. 543–544, 546)

Weinberg, M. 1977. *Minority students: A research appraisal.* Washington, DC: U.S. Government Printing Office. (p. 324)

Weiner, B. 1976. An attributional approach for educational psychology. In *Review of research in education 4,* edited by Lee S. Shulman. Itasca, IL: Peacock. (p. 270)

Weintraub, P. 1981. The brain: His and hers. *Discover* 2 (4): 15–20. (p. 448)

Weis, L. 1987. The 1980s: De-industrialization and change in white working class male and female use cultural forms. *Metropolitan Education* no. 5: 82–117. (p. 255)

Weisberg, A. 1983. What research has to say about vocational education and the high schools. *Phi Delta Kappan* 64 (5): 355–359. (pp. 62–63)

Wells, E., and Prindle, C. 1986. *'Where's room 185?' How schools can reduce their dropout problem.* Chicago: Chicago Panel on Public School Policy and Finance. (p. 283)

West, J. 1945. *Plainville, U.S.A.* New York: Columbia University Press. (pp. 8, 39)

Westoff, C. F. 1981. Some speculations on the future of marriage and fertility. In *Teenage sexuality, pregnancy, and childbearing,* edited by Frank F. Furstenberg, Jr., Richard Lincoln, and Jane Menken. Philadelphia: University of Pennsylvania. (p. 127)

Whyte, W. F. 1943. *Street-corner society.* Chicago: University of Chicago Press. (p. 40)

Wichess, S. F. 1984. Jobs for America's graduates: A youth employment program that means business. *The Clearing House* 57: 197–200. (p. 190)

Wigfield, A., and Meece, J. L. 1988. Mass anxiety in elementary and secondary school students. Paper delivered at the annual meeting of the American Educational Research Association, New Orleans, April. (p. 445)

Wiggington, E. 1986. *Foxfire 7-9.* Garden City, NJ: Anchor. (p. 425)

Wilcox, K. A. 1978. Schooling and socialization for work roles: A structural inquiry into cultural transmission in an urban American community. Unpublished Ph.D. dissertation, Harvard University. (p. 242)

Wilkerson, R. M., and White, K. P. 1988. Effects of the 4MAT system of instruction on students' achievement, retention, and attitudes. *The Elementary School Journal* 88 (4): 357–368.

Williams, S. S. 1987. The politics of the black child's language. In *Ethnicity and language,* edited by Winston A. Van Horne and Thomas V. Tonnesen. Madison: The University of Wisconsin System Institute on Race and Ethnicity. (pp. 379, 434)

Williams, T. M., and Kornblum, W. 1985. *Growing up poor.* Lexington, MA: Lexington. (pp. 170, 192, 197)

Willie, C. V., ed. 1979. *The caste and class controversy.* New York: General Hall. (pp. 386–387)

Willie, C. V., and Uchitelle, S. 1987. Country and city transfers: Central city black students and suburban white students. The University of Chicago National School Desegregation Project Working Paper No. 9. (p. 357)

Willig, A. C. 1985. A meta-analysis of selected studies on the effectiveness of bilingual education. *Review of Educational Research* 55 (3): 269–317. (p. 406)

Willis, B. H.; Thomas, S. N.; and Hoppe, M. H. 1985. *Changing minds in a changing world*. Research Triangle Park, NC: Southeastern Regional Council for Educational Improvement. (p. 143)

Willis, P. 1979. *Learning to labour: How working class kids get working class jobs*. Westmead, England: Saxon House. (pp. 178, 258–259, 378)

Willms, D. 1982. Is there any private school advantage? *IFG Policy Perspectives* Winter: 1–2. (p. 480)

Wilms, W. W. 1987. Proprietary schools. *Change* January/February: 10–22. (p. 66)

Wilson, A. B. 1959. Residential segregation of social classes and aspirations of high school boys. *American Sociological Review* 24: 836–845. (pp. 164, 320)

———. 1967. Educational consequences of segregation in a California community. *Racial isolation in the public schools*. Vol. 2. U.S. Commission on Civil Rights. Washington, DC: U.S. Government Printing Office, Appendix C3, pp. 165–206. (p. 241)

Wilson, J. Q. 1983. *Thinking about crime*, 2nd ed. New York: Basic Books. (p. 214)

Wilson, J. Q., and Herrnstein, R. J. 1985. *Crime and human nature*. New York: Simon and Schuster. (pp. 198, 200)

Wilson, R. W., and Melendez, S. E. 1986. *Minorities in higher education*. Washington, DC: American Council on Education. (p. 385)

Wilson, W. J. 1978. *The declining significance of race: Blacks and changing institutions*. Chicago: University of Chicago Press. (p. 386)

———. 1979. The declining significance of race: Revisited but not revised. In *The caste and class controversy*, edited by Charles V. Willie. New York: General Hall. (p. 387)

———. 1987. *The truly disadvantaged: The inner-city, the underclass and public policy*. Chicago: University of Chicago Press. (pp. 17–18, 375, 385)

Wilson, W. J., and Aponte, R. 1985. Urban poverty. In *Annual review of sociology*, edited by Ralph H. Turner and James F. Short, Jr. Palo Alto, CA: Annual Reviews. (pp. 18, 376)

Wilson, W. J., and Neckerman, K. M. 1984. *Poverty and policy: Retrospect and prospects*. University of Wisconsin–Madison Institute for Research on Poverty Conference Paper. (p. 376)

Winard, A. I. 1970. Delineation of current poverty areas in big cities. Paper delivered at the annual meeting of the Population Association, of America, Atlanta, Georgia, April 16–18. (p. 18)

Winn, M. 1977. *The plug-in drug: Television, children, and the family*. New York: Viking. (p. 143)

Wise, A. E. 1988. Legislative learning revisited. *Phi Delta Kappan* 69 (5): 328–333 (p. 89)

Witelson, S. F., and Swallow, J. A. 1987. Individual differences in human brain function. *National Forum* 67 (2): 17–24. (p. 448)

Wittrock, M. C., ed. 1986. *Handbook of research on teaching*. New York: Macmillan. (p. 524)

Wolf, R. M. 1964. The identification and measurement of environmental process variables related to intelligence. Ph.D. dissertation, University of Chicago. (p. 118)

Wolman, J. 1976. Black flight adds to cities' problems. *Kansas City Star* (December 28). (pp. 77, 320)

Wolters, R. 1984. *The burden of Brown*. Knoxville: The University of Tennessee Press. (p. 357)

Wong, S. C. 1987. The language needs of school-age Asian immigrants and refugees in the United States. In *Ethnicity and language*, edited by Winston A. Van Horne and T. V. Tonnesen. Madison: The University of Wisconsin System Institute on Race and Ethnicity. (pp. 406, 434)

Woodson, R. L. 1981a. *A summons to life: Mediating structures and the prevention of youth crime*. Cambridge, MA: Ballinger. (p. 200)

———. 1981b. *Youth crime and urban policy*. Washington, DC: American Enterprise Institute for Public Policy Research. (p. 201)

Wright, J. D., and Wright, S. R. 1976. Social class and parental values for children: A partial replication and extension of the Kohn thesis. *American Sociological Review* 41: 527–537. (p. 235)

Wrigley, J. 1982. A message of marginality: Black youth, alienation, and unemployment. Chapter 10 in *Education and work*, edited by Harry F. Silberman. Eighty-First Yearbook of the National Society for the Study of Education, Part II. Chicago: University of Chicago Press. (pp. 194, 268)

Wynne, E. A., and Hess, M. 1986. Long-term trends in youth conduct and revival of traditional value patterns. *Educational Evaluation and Policy Analysis.* 8: 294–308. (pp. 187–188, 196, 213)

Yankelovich, D. 1968. *Is scouting in tune with the times?* New Brunswick, NJ: Boy Scouts of America. (p. 174)

———. 1972. *Changing values on the campus.* New York: Simon and Schuster. (pp. 183, 214)

———. 1981. Searching for self-fulfillment in a world turned upside down. *American Demographics* 4 (3): 27–32, 43–44. (p. 186)

Young, M., ed. 1973. *The American family in social-historical perspective.* New York: St. Martin's Press. (p. 149)

Young, M., and Willmott, P. 1973. *The symmetrical family.* New York: Random House. (pp. 97, 99)

Zabin, L. S.; Hirsch, M. B.; Smith, E. A.; Street, R.; and Hardy, J. B. 1986. Evaluation of a pregnancy prevention program for urban teenagers. *Family Planning Perspectives* 18: 119–126. (p. 208)

Zahorik, J. A. 1987. Teachers' collegial interaction: An exploratory study. *Elementary School Journal* 87: 385–396. (p. 540)

Zajonc, R. B. 1976. Family configuration and intelligence. *Science* 192: 227–336. (p. 136)

———. 1986. Family factors and intellectual test performance: a reply to Steelman. *Review of Educational Research* 56: 365–371. (p. 136)

Zangwill, I. 1909. *The melting pot.* New York Macmillan. (p. 363)

Zigler, E. 1970. Social class and the socialization process. *Review of Educational Research* 40: 87–110. (pp. 150, 237)

Zigler, E. F. 1973. Project Head Start: Success or failure? *Children Today* 2 (Nov.–Dec.): 2–71. (p. 286)

Zill, N. 1982. The condition of American children and youth: The need for a balanced appraisal. Paper presented at the annual meeting of the Association for the Advancement of Science, July 27. (p. 130)

Index